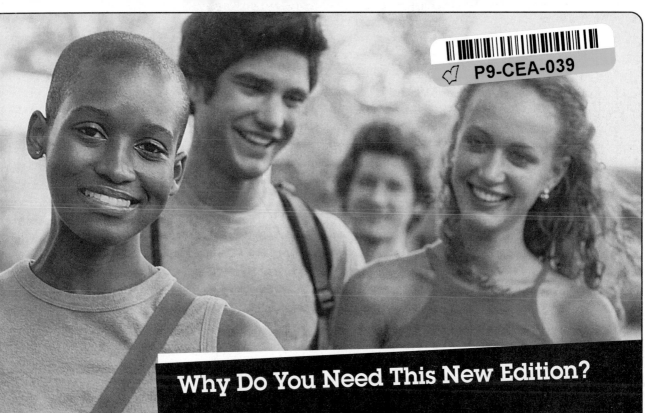

Why Do You Need This New Edition?

Here are seven great reasons . . .

1. NEW! Section summarizing the most important and lasting theoretical contributions to clinical practice (Chapter 4).

2. Revised presentation of concepts of Bowenian theory for greater clarity and clinical focus (Chapter 5).

3. Clearer explication of basic concepts of structural family theory, as well as updated section on techniques, emphasizing recent greater emphasis on cognition (Chapter 7).

4. NEW! Additional case studies and clinical emphasis throughout Guidelines for production problem solving conversations (Chapter 10).

5. NEW! Section on Sex and the Internet (Chapter 11).

6. NEW! Section on Neuroscience and Relationships (Chapter 11).

7. NEW! Chapter on the role of research in understanding what works best in family therapy.

Fifth Edition

The Essentials of Family Therapy

Michael P. Nichols

College of William and Mary

Allyn & Bacon

Boston   Columbus   Indianapolis   New York   San Francisco   Upper Saddle River
Amsterdam   Cape Town   Dubai   London   Madrid   Milan   Munich   Paris   Montreal   Toronto
Delhi   Mexico City   Sao Paulo   Sydney   Hong Kong   Seoul   Singapore   Taipei   Tokyo

Executive Editor: *Ashley Dodge*
Editorial Assistant: *Carly Czech*
Senior Marketing Manager: *Wendy Albert*
Marketing Assistant: *Kyle VanNatter*
Production Editor: *Karen Mason*

Manufacturing Buyer: *Debbie Rossi*
Cover Administrator: *Joel Gendron*
Editorial Production and Composition Service:
  TextTech International
Photo Researcher: *PoYee Oster*

Credits appear on page 368, which constitutes an extension of the copyright page.

Library of Congress Cataloging-in-Publication Data

Nichols, Michael P.
  The essentials of family therapy / Michael P. Nichols. — 5th ed.
    p.   ; cm.
  Includes bibliographical references and indexes.
  ISBN-13: 978-0-205-78723-4
  ISBN-10: 0-205-78723-1
  1. Family psychotherapy. I. Title.
  [DNLM: 1. Family Therapy. WM 430.5.F2 N621e 2011]
  RC488.5.N528 2011
  616.89'156—dc22   2009045258

10 9 8 7 6 5 4   [HP] 14 13 12

Allyn & Bacon
is an imprint of

www.pearsonhighered.com

ISBN 10: 0-205-78723-1
ISBN 13: 978-0-205-78723-4

Contents

PART II *The Classic Schools of Family Therapy*

8 EXPERIENTIAL FAMILY THERAPY   143

9 PSYCHOANALYTIC FAMILY THERAPY   163

PART III *Recent Developments
in Family Therapy*

12 SOLUTION-FOCUSED THERAPY   247

13 NARRATIVE THERAPY   266

Foreword

It was a great honor to be asked to write the foreword for the fifth edition of *The Essentials of Family Therapy*. Throughout this book, Mike Nichols has given students, as well as teachers of family therapy, a tremendous gift. I have assigned earlier editions to my students so that they might experience a journey through the evolution of this tremendous field. I have relied on this book to convey the excitement of the discovery and elaboration of the new worldview each model of family therapy introduced, as well as the important concepts and unique contributions it offered. My students have been very appreciative of the book's clear presentation of the history of family therapy and its essential principles.

I came of age in the field during what Mike Nichols describes as "The Golden Age of Family Therapy." As a graduate student in the early 1970s, my heroes and heroines were the pioneers of family therapy, such as Nathan Ackerman, John Elderkin Bell, Ivan Boszormenyi-Nagy, Salvador Minuchin, Murray Bowen, Jay Haley, Don Jackson, Cloe Madanes, Mara Selvini Palazzoli, Virginia Satir, Carl Whitaker, and others. So many of these giants are no longer with us, but Mike Nichols has a unique talent for bringing them to life and, at the same time, placing them in historical context so that they can continue to influence new generations of family therapists.

Reading this edition has given me the rare opportunity to revisit my own personal journey as a family therapist, which has profoundly influenced the direction of my life and career. I was initially drawn to the work of Salvador Minuchin and his colleagues, who were among the first family therapists to work with poor, ethnic minority families. As an intern at the Philadelphia Child Guidance Clinic from 1974 to 1975, I was privileged to learn structural family therapy from Salvador Minuchin, as well as from Harry Aponte, Braulio Montalvo, Bernice Rosman, and Charles Fishman. I was also trained to incorporate strategic family therapy techniques by Jay Haley. In reading the chapters in this book, I felt again the sensation that I "stand on the shoulders of these giants."

After obtaining my doctorate in psychology over thirty years ago, my first job was at what Nichols describes as another early center of family therapy: The Family Studies Section at Albert Einstein College of Medicine in the Bronx, New York, started by Israel Zwerling and Marilyn Mendelsohn. It was there that I first encountered the work of Murray Bowen, as Phil Guerin, a later director, was strongly influenced by Bowen's work and had incorporated it into the center. The chapter on "Bowen Family Systems Therapy" in this book captures the excitement of this model and Bowen's seminal ideas, including differentiation of self, emotional triangles, multigenerational emotional processes, and emotional cutoff. Chapter 5 also shows the model evolved and was elaborated upon by others trained by Bowen, such as Betty Carter and Monica McGoldrick, who developed the concept of the family life cycle. Each has influenced my own work, particularly with multigenerational extended families in ethnic minority groups.

As Nichols has shown, the family therapy movement has really been many movements. It was very interesting for me to revisit the revolutionary role of the feminist critique of family therapy and the transformative power of the postmodern narrative therapy approach. This book addresses the integrative models that have moved away from the orthodoxy of the original theories and the growing movement toward evidence-based practice in the family therapy field.

It was fascinating for me as an author to read the summary of my own work in this book. Nichols does an excellent job of describing my work as well as the seminal contributions of Monica McGoldrick and Ken Hardy and our emphasis on the importance of understanding the culture, race, and socioeconomic level of the families we treat. Just as it is hard to imagine a time prior to the 1950s when the worldview in the mental health field did not include family therapy, it is also difficult now to imagine the time prior to the 1970s when culture and race were largely ignored in books on psychotherapy. It was the family therapy movement that first opened the door and embraced these concepts.

Consistent with the tradition established in other editions of Mike Nichols's books, this fifth edition includes new material related to important developments in the field, such as an informative section on advances in neuroscience. He also explores one of the most significant developments of the twenty-first century, that is, the role of the Internet and the benefits and challenges that technology has introduced. His discussion of the critical issue of the role of cybersex in couple relationships will be especially helpful for practitioners of marriage and family therapy. Similarly, he addresses the concern felt by many parents in protecting their adolescents from sexual predators and inappropriate sexual activities that the availability of the Internet has made widespread.

Throughout this book, Mike Nichols has been able to strike a unique balance between giving the leaders of the field the respect they deserve while remaining objective and honest about the challenges they faced. He captures not only the breakthroughs in family therapy but also the controversies and major critiques of the times. He deserves our highest praise for this powerful book and for the major contribution that it has made, and will continue to make through this new edition, to the field of family therapy.

Nancy Boyd-Franklin, Ph.D.

Preface

One thing that tends to get lost in academic discussions of family therapy is the feeling of accomplishment that comes from sitting down with an unhappy family and being able to help them. Beginning therapists are understandably anxious and not sure they'll know how to proceed. ("How do you get *all of them* to come in?") Veterans often speak in abstractions. They have opinions and discuss big issues—postmodernism, narrative reconstructionism, second-order cybernetics. While it's tempting to use this space to say Important Things, I prefer to be a little more personal. Treating troubled families has given me the greatest satisfaction imaginable, and I hope that the same is or will be true for you.

Changes in This Edition

In this fifth edition of *The Essentials of Family Therapy,* I describe the full scope of family therapy—its rich history, classic schools, latest developments—but with increasing emphasis on practical issues. Changes in this edition include:

- A new section on Sex and the Internet
- A new section on the Neuroscience of family relationships
- A new chapter on the role of research in understanding what works best in family therapy
- Revised and clarified presentation of basic theoretical concepts that students have had trouble grasping
- An updated section on techniques of structural family therapy
- Guidelines for productive problem-solving conversations
- A new summary of theoretical concepts
- Quite a few more case studies
- A more consistent emphasis on clinical technique throughout

Albert Einstein once said, "If you want to learn about physics, pay attention to what physicists do, not what they say they do." When you read about therapy, it can be hard to see past the jargon and political packaging to the essential ideas and practices. So in preparing this edition, I've traveled widely to visit and observe actual sessions of the leading practitioners. I've also invited leaders in the field to share some of their best case studies with you. The result is a more pragmatic, clinical focus. I hope you like it.

Acknowledgments

So many people have contributed to my development as a family therapist and to the writing of this book that it would be impossible to thank them all. But I would like to single out a few. To the people who taught me family therapy—Lyman Wynne, Murray Bowen, and Salvador Minuchin—thank you.

I'd also like to thank some of the people who went out of their way to help me prepare this fifth edition: Yvonne Dolan, Jerome Price, Deborah Luepnitz, William Madsen, Frank Dattilio, Vicki Dickerson, Randy Walton, and Salvador Minuchin. To paraphrase John, Paul, George, and Ringo, I get by with *a lot* of help from my friends—and I thank them one and all. I am especially grateful to Carly Czech at Allyn & Bacon for making a difficult job easier.

Finally, I would like to thank my postgraduate instructors in family life: my wife, Melody, and my children, Sandy and Paul. In the brief span of forty years, Melody has seen me grow from a shy young man, totally ignorant of how to be a husband and father, to a shy middle-aged man, still bewildered and still trying. My children never cease to amaze me. If in my wildest dreams I had imagined children to love and be proud of, I wouldn't even have come close to anyone as fine as Sandy and Paul.

1

The Foundations of Family Therapy

Case Study

There wasn't much information on the intake sheet. Just a name, Holly Roberts, the fact that she was a senior in college, and her presenting complaint: "trouble making decisions."

The first thing Holly said when she sat down was, "I'm not sure I need to be here. You probably have a lot of people who need help more than I do." Then she started to cry.

It was springtime. The tulips were up; the trees were turning light, leafy green; and purple clumps of lilacs perfumed the air. Life and all its possibilities stretched out before her, but Holly was naggingly, unaccountably depressed.

The decision Holly was having trouble making was what to do after graduation. The more she tried to figure it out, the less able she was to concentrate. She started sleeping late, missing classes. Finally, her roommate talked her into going to the Health Service. "I wouldn't have come," Holly said. "I can handle my own problems."

I was into cathartic therapy back then. Most people have stories to tell and tears to shed. Some of the stories, I suspected, were dramatized to elicit sympathy. Most people seem to give themselves permission to cry only with some very acceptable excuse. Of all the human emotions we're ashamed of, feeling sorry for ourselves tops the list.

I didn't know what was behind Holly's depression, but I was sure I could help. I felt comfortable with depressed people. Ever since my senior year in high school when my friend Alex died, I'd been a little depressed myself.

After Alex died, the rest of the summer was a dark blur. I cried a lot. And I got mad whenever anyone suggested that life goes on. Alex's minister said that his death wasn't really a tragedy, because now "Alex was with God in heaven." I wanted to scream, but I numbed myself instead. In the fall I went off to college, and even though it seemed disloyal to Alex, life did go on. I still cried from time to time, but with the tears came a painful discovery. Not all of my grief was for Alex. Yes, I loved him. Yes, I missed him. But his death also provided me with the justification to cry about the everyday sorrows in my own life. Maybe grief is always like that. At the time, though, it struck me as a betrayal. I was using Alex's death to feel sorry for myself.

What, I wondered was making Holly so sad? In fact, Holly didn't have a dramatic story. Her feelings weren't focused. After those first few minutes in my office, she rarely cried. When she did, it was more of an involuntary tearing up than a sobbing release. She talked about not knowing what she wanted to do with her life. She talked about not having a boyfriend, but she didn't say much about her family. If the truth be told, I wasn't terribly interested. Back then I thought home was the place you left in order to grow up.

Holly was hurting and needed someone to lean on, but something made her hold back, as though she didn't feel safe, didn't quite trust me. It was frustrating. I wanted to help.

A month went by and Holly's depression got worse. I started seeing her three times a week, but we weren't really getting anywhere. One Friday afternoon, Holly was feeling so despondent that I didn't think she should go back to her dorm alone. I asked her instead to lie down on the couch in my office, and with her permission, I called her parents.

Mrs. Roberts answered the phone. I told her that I thought she and her husband should come to Rochester and meet with me to discuss the advisability of Holly taking a medical leave of absence and going home. Unsure as I was of my authority back then, I steeled myself for an argument. Mrs. Roberts surprised me by agreeing to come at once.

The first thing that struck me about Holly's parents was the disparity in their ages. Mrs. Roberts looked like a slightly older version of Holly; she couldn't have been much over thirty-five. Her husband looked sixty. It turned out that he was Holly's stepfather. They had married when Holly was sixteen.

Looking back, I don't remember much that was said in that first meeting. Both parents were worried about Holly. "We'll do whatever you think best," Mrs. Roberts said. Mr. Morgan (Holly's stepfather) said they could arrange for a good psychiatrist "to help Holly over this crisis." But Holly said she didn't want to go home, and she said this with more energy than I'd heard from her in a long time. That was on Saturday. I said there was no need to rush into a decision, so we arranged to meet again on Monday.

When Holly and her parents sat down in my office on Monday morning, it was obvious that something had happened. Mrs. Roberts's eyes were red

from crying. Holly glowered at her and looked away. Mr. Morgan turned to me. "We've been fighting all weekend. Holly heaps abuse on me, and when I try to respond, Lena takes her side. That's the way it's been since day one of this marriage."

The story that came out was one of those sad tales of jealousy and resentment that turns ordinary love into bitter, injured feelings and, all too often, tears families apart. Lena Roberts was thirty-four when she met Tom Morgan. He was a robust fifty-six. The second obvious difference between them was money. He was a successful stockbroker who'd retired to run a horse farm. She was waitressing to support herself and her daughter. It was a second marriage for both of them.

Lena thought Tom could be the missing father figure in Holly's life. Unfortunately, she couldn't accept all the rules Tom felt invited to enforce. And so he became the wicked stepfather. He made the mistake of trying to take over, and when the predictable arguments ensued, Lena sided with her daughter. There were tears and midnight shouting matches. Twice Holly ran away to a friend's house for a few days. The triangle nearly proved the marriage's undoing, but things calmed down when Holly went off to college.

Holly expected to leave home and not look back. She would make new friends. She would study hard and choose a career. She would never depend on a man to support her. Unfortunately, she left home with unfinished business. She hated Tom for the way he picked on her and for the way he treated her mother. He was always demanding to know where her mother was going, who she was going with, and when she would be back. If she was the least bit late, there would be a scene. Why did her mother put up with it?

Blaming her stepfather was simple and satisfying. But another set of feelings, harder to face, was eating at Holly. She hated her mother for marrying Tom and letting him be so mean to her. What had her mother seen in him? Had she sold out for a big house and a fancy car? Holly didn't have answers to these questions; she didn't even allow them into full awareness. Unfortunately, repression doesn't work like locking something in a closet and forgetting about it. It takes a lot of energy to keep unwelcome emotions at bay.

Holly found excuses not to go home much during college. It didn't even feel like home anymore. She buried herself in her studies. But rage and bitterness gnawed at her until, in her senior year, facing an uncertain future, knowing only that she couldn't go home again, she gave in to hopelessness. No wonder she was depressed.

I found the whole story sad. Not knowing much about family dynamics and never having lived in a stepfamily, I wondered why they couldn't just try to get along. Why did they have so little sympathy for each other? Why couldn't Holly accept her mother's right to find love a second time around? Why couldn't Tom respect the priority of his wife's relationship with her daughter? Why couldn't Lena listen to her daughter's adolescent anger without getting so defensive?

That session with Holly and her parents was my first lesson in family therapy. Family members in therapy talk not about actual experiences but about reconstructed memories that resemble the original experiences only in certain ways. Holly's memories resembled her mother's memories very little and her stepfather's not at all. In the gaps between their truths was little room for reason and no desire to pursue it.

Although that meeting may not have been terribly productive, it did put Holly's unhappiness in perspective. No longer did I see her as a tragic young woman, all alone in the world. She was that, of course, but she was also a daughter torn between running away from a home she no longer felt part of and being afraid to leave her mother alone with a man she didn't trust. I think that's when I became a family therapist.

To say that I didn't know much about families, much less about techniques for helping them, would be an understatement. But family therapy isn't just a new set of techniques. It's a whole new approach to understanding human behavior—as fundamentally shaped by its social context.

$\mathcal{T}$HE MYTH OF THE HERO

Ours is a culture that celebrates the uniqueness of the individual and the search for an autonomous self. Holly's story could be told as a coming-of-age drama: a young person's struggle to break away from childhood and provincialism, to take hold of adulthood and promise and the future. If she fails, we're tempted to look inside the young adult, the failed hero.

Although the unbounded individualism of the hero may be encouraged more for men than for women, as a cultural ideal it casts its shadow on us all. Even if Holly cared about connection as much as autonomy, she may be judged by the prevailing image of accomplishment.

We were raised on the myth of the hero: the Lone Ranger, Robin Hood, Wonder Woman. When we got older we searched out real-life heroes: Eleanor Roosevelt, Martin Luther King, Nelson Mandela. These were men and women who stood for something. If only we could be a little more like these larger-than-life individuals who seemed to rise above their circumstances.

Only later did we begin to realize that the circumstances we wanted to rise above were part of the human condition—our inescapable connection to our families. The romantic image of the hero is based on the illusion that authentic selfhood can be achieved as an autonomous individual. We do many things alone, including some of our most heroic acts, but we are defined and sustained by a network of human relationships. Our need to worship heroes is partly a need to rise above inadequacy and self-doubt; it is also perhaps equally a product of imagining a life unfettered by all those pesky relationships that somehow never quite go the way we want them to.

When we do think about families, it's often in negative terms—as burdens holding us back or as destructive forces in the lives of our patients. What catches our attention are differences and discord. The harmonies of family life—loyalty, tolerance, mutual aid, and assistance—often slide by unnoticed, part of the taken-for-granted background of life. If we would be heroes, then we must have villains.

There's a lot of talk these days about *dysfunctional families*. Unfortunately, much of this amounts to little more than parent bashing. People suffer because of what *their parents* did: their mother's criticism, their father's distance—these are the causes of individuals' unhappiness. Perhaps this is an advance on stewing in guilt and shame, but it's a long way from understanding what really goes on in families.

One reason for blaming family sorrows on the personal failings of parents is that it's hard for the average person to see past individual personalities to the structural patterns that make them a family—a system of interconnected lives governed by strict but unspoken rules.

People feel controlled and helpless not because they are victims of parental folly and deceit but because they don't understand the forces that tie husbands and wives and parents and children together. Plagued by anxiety and depression, or merely troubled and uncertain, some people turn to psychotherapy for consolation. In the process, they turn away from the irritants that propel them into therapy. Chief among these are unhappy relationships—with friends and lovers, and with our families. Our disorders are private ailments. When we retreat to the safety of a synthetic relationship, the last thing we want is to take our families with us. Is it any wonder, then, that when Freud ventured to explore the dark forces of the mind, he locked the family outside the consulting room?

$\mathcal{P}$SYCHOTHERAPEUTIC SANCTUARY

It's tempting to look back on the days before family therapy and see those who insisted on segregating patients from their families as exponents of a fossilized view of mental disorder, according to which psychiatric maladies were firmly embedded in the heads of individuals. Considering that clinicians didn't begin treating families together until the mid-1950s, it's tempting to ask, What took them so long?

Freud excluded the family from psychoanalysis to help patients feel safe to explore the full range of their thoughts and feelings.

In fact, there are good reasons for conducting therapy in private.

The two most influential approaches to psychotherapy in the twentieth century, Freud's psychoanalysis and Rogers's client-centered therapy, were both predicated on the assumption that psychological problems arise from unhealthy interactions with others and can best be alleviated in a private relationship between therapist and patient. Freud wasn't interested in the living family; he was interested in the family-as-remembered. By conducting treatment in private, Freud safeguarded patients' trust in the sanctity of the therapeutic relationship and thus maximized the likelihood that they would repeat, in relation to the analyst, the understandings and misunderstandings of childhood.

The therapy Carl Rogers developed was designed to help patients uncover their real feelings. Unhappily, said Rogers, our innate tendency toward *self-actualization* gets subverted by our craving for approval. We learn to do what we think others want, even though it may not be what's best for us.

Gradually, this conflict between self-fulfillment and need for approval leads to denial and distortion of our authentic selves—and even the feelings that signal them. We swallow our anger, stifle our exuberance, and bury our lives under a mountain of expectations.

The Rogerian therapist listens sympathetically, offering understanding, warmth, and respect. In the presence of such an accepting listener, patients gradually get in touch with their own inner promptings.

Like the psychoanalyst, the client-centered therapist maintains absolute privacy in the therapeutic relationship to avoid any possibility that patients' feelings might be subverted to win approval. Only an objective outsider could be counted on to provide the unconditional acceptance to help patients rediscover their real selves. That's why family members had no place in the process of client-centered therapy.

*F*AMILY VERSUS INDIVIDUAL THERAPY

As you can see, there are valid reasons for conducting psychotherapy in private. But although there is a strong claim to be made for individual psychotherapy, there are equally strong claims to be made for family therapy.

Keep in mind that individual therapy and family therapy each offer an approach to treatment—and a way of understanding human behavior. Both have their virtues. Individual therapy provides the concentrated focus to help people face their fears and learn to become more fully themselves. Individual therapists recognize the importance of family life in shaping personality, but they assume that these influences are internalized and that intrapsychic dynamics become the dominant forces controlling behavior. Treatment can and should therefore be directed at the person and his or her personal makeup. Family therapists, on the other hand, believe that the dominant forces in our lives are located externally, in the family. Therapy based on this framework is directed at changing the structure of the family. When a family's organization is transformed, the life of every family member is altered accordingly.

This last point—that changing a family changes the life of each of its members—is important enough to elaborate. Family therapy influences the entire family; therefore, improvement can be lasting because each and every family member is changed *and* continues to exert synchronous change on each other.

Almost any sort of human difficulty can be treated with either individual or family therapy. But certain problems are especially suited to a family approach, among them problems with children (who must, regardless of what happens in therapy, return home to their parents), complaints about a marriage or other intimate relationship, family feuds, and symptoms that develop at the time of a major family transition.

If problems that arise around family transitions make a therapist think first about the role of the family, individual therapy may be especially useful when people identify something about themselves that they've tried in vain to change while their social environment remains stable. Thus, if a woman gets depressed during her first year at college, a therapist might wonder if her sadness is related to leaving home and leaving her parents alone with each other. But if the same woman were to get depressed in her thirties, say, during a long period of stability in her life, we might wonder if there's something about her approach to life that hasn't worked for her. Examining her life in private—away from troubled relationships—doesn't mean, however, that she should believe that she can fulfill herself in isolation from the other people in her life.

The view of persons as separate entities, with families acting on them, is consistent with the way we experience ourselves. We recognize the influence of other people—especially as obligation and constraint—but it's hard to see that we are embedded in a network of relationships, that we are part of something larger than ourselves.

*T*HE POWER OF FAMILY THERAPY

The power of family therapy derives from bringing parents and children together to transform their interactions. Instead of isolating individuals from the emotional origins of their conflict, problems are addressed at their source.

mobile

What keeps people stuck is their inability to see their own participation in the problems that plague them. With eyes fixed firmly on what those recalcitrant others are doing, it's hard for most people to see the patterns that bind them together. The family therapist's job is to give them a wake-up call. When a husband complains that his wife nags and the therapist asks him how he contributes to her doing that, the therapist is challenging the husband to see the hyphenated him-and-her of their interactions.

Case Study

When Bob and Shirley came for help with marital problems, her complaint was that he never shared his feelings; his was that she always criticized him. This, of course, is a classic trading of complaints that keeps couples stuck as long as they fail to see the reciprocal pattern in which each partner provokes in the other precisely the behavior he or she can't stand. So the therapist said to Bob, "If you were a frog, what would you be like if Shirley changed you into a prince?" When Bob countered that he doesn't talk with her because she's so critical, it seemed to the couple like the same old argument. But the therapist saw this as the beginning of change—Bob speaking up more. One way to create an opening for change in rigid families is to

support the blamed person and help bring him back into the fray.

When Shirley criticized Bob for complaining, he tried to retreat, but the therapist said, "No, continue. You are still a frog."

Bob tried to shift responsibility back to Shirley. "Doesn't she have to kiss me first?" But the therapist said, "No, in real life that comes afterward. You have to earn it."

In the opening of *Anna Karenina*, Tolstoy wrote: "All happy families resemble one another; each unhappy family is unhappy in its own way." Every family may be unhappy in its own way, but we all stumble over the same familiar challenges of family life. It's no secret what these challenges are—learning to live together, dealing with difficult relatives, chasing after children, coping with adolescence, and so on. What not everyone realizes, however, is that a relatively small number of systems dynamics, once understood, illuminate these challenges and enable families to move successfully through the predictable dilemmas of life. Like all healers, family therapists sometimes deal with bizarre and baffling cases, but much of their work is with ordinary human beings learning life's painful lessons. Their stories, and the stories of the men and women of family therapy who have undertaken to help them, are the inspiration for this book.

Questions to Consider

1. What would be some good reasons for recommending individual therapy rather than family therapy in certain cases?
2. While it's possible to address both the psychology of individuals and their interactions, what are some of the trade-offs of focusing on

the system or focusing on individuals in a family therapy case?
3. How could you teach a course on psychopathology that recognized the influence of the family on various mental illnesses?

Recommended Readings

Lasch, C. 1977. *The culture of narcissism.* New York: Norton.

Nichols, M. P. 1987. *The self in the system.* New York: Brunner/Mazel.

Nichols, M. P. 2008. *Inside family therapy,* 2nd ed. Boston: Allyn & Bacon.

2

The Evolution of Family Therapy

In this chapter, we explore the antecedents and early years of family therapy. There are two fascinating stories here: one of personalities, one of ideas. The first story revolves around the pioneers, visionary iconoclasts who broke the mold of seeing life and its problems as a function of individuals and their psychology. Make no mistake: The shift from an individual to a systemic perspective was a revolutionary one, providing those who grasped it with a powerful tool for understanding and resolving human problems.

The second story in the evolution of family therapy is one of ideas. The restless curiosity of the first family therapists led them to ingenious new ways of conceptualizing the joys and sorrows of family life.

As you read this history, stay open to surprises. Be ready to reexamine easy assumptions—including the assumption that family therapy began as a benevolent effort to support the institution of the family. The truth is, therapists first encountered the family system as an adversary.

THE UNDECLARED WAR

Although we came to think of asylums as places of cruelty and detention, they were originally built to rescue the insane from being locked away in the family attic. Accordingly, except for purposes of footing the bill, hospital psychiatrists have kept families at arm's length. In the 1950s, however, two puzzling developments forced therapists to recognize the family's power to alter the course of treatment.

Therapists began to notice that often when a patient got better, someone else in the family got worse, almost as though the family *needed* a symptomatic member. As in the game of hide-and-seek, it didn't seem to matter who was "it" as long as someone played the part. In one case, Don Jackson (1954) was treating a woman for depression. When she began to improve, her husband complained that she was getting worse. When she continued to improve, her husband lost his job. Eventually, when the woman was completely well, her husband killed himself. Was this man's stability predicated on having a sick wife?

Another strange story of shifting disturbance was that patients frequently improved in the hospital only to get worse when they went home.

Case Study

In a bizarre case of Oedipus revisited, Salvador Minuchin treated a young man hospitalized several times for trying to scratch out his own eyes. The man functioned normally in Bellevue but returned to self-mutilation each time he went home. He could be sane, it seemed, only in an insane world.

It turned out that the young man was extremely close to his mother, a bond that grew even tighter during the seven years of his father's mysterious absence. The father was a compulsive gambler who disappeared shortly after being declared legally incompetent. The rumor was that the Mafia had kidnapped him. When, just as mysteriously, the father returned, his son began his bizarre attempts at self-mutilation. Perhaps he wanted to blind himself so as not to see his obsession with his mother and hatred of his father.

But this family was neither ancient nor Greek, and Minuchin was more pragmatist than poet. So he challenged the father to protect his son by beginning to deal directly with his wife and then challenged the man's demeaning attitude toward her, which had made her seek her son's proximity and protection. The therapy was a challenge to the family's structure and, in Bellevue, working with the psychiatric staff toward easing the young man back into the family, into the lion's den.

Minuchin confronted the father, saying, "As a father of a child in danger, what you're doing isn't enough."

"What *should* I do?" asked the man.

"I don't know," Minuchin replied. "Ask your son." Then, for the first time in years, father and son began talking to each other. Just as they were about to run out of things to say, Dr. Minuchin commented to the parents: "In a strange way, he's telling you that he prefers to be treated like a young child. When he was in the hospital he was twenty-three. Now that he's returned home, he's six."

What this case dramatizes is how parents use their children as a buffer to protect them from intimacy. To the would-be Oedipus, Minuchin said, "You're scratching your eyes for your mother, so that she'll have something to worry about. You're a good boy. Good children sacrifice themselves for their parents."

Families are made of strange glue—they stretch but never let go. Few blamed the family for outright

malevolence, yet there was an invidious undercurrent to these observations. The official story of family therapy is one of respect for the family, but maybe none of us ever quite gets over the adolescent idea that families are the enemy of freedom.

The impact of a patient's improvement on the family isn't always negative. Fisher and Mendell (1958) reported a spread of positive changes from patients to other family members. Whether the influence patients and their families have on each other is malignant or benign isn't the point. The point is that change in one person changes the system.

SMALL GROUP DYNAMICS

Those who first sought to understand and treat families found a ready parallel in small groups. **Group dynamics** are relevant to family therapy because group life is a complex blend of individual personalities and superordinate properties of the group.

In 1920, the pioneering social psychologist William McDougall published *The Group Mind,* in which he described how a group's continuity depends on the group being an important idea in the minds of its members; on the need for boundaries and structures in which differentiation of function could occur; and on the importance of customs and habits, so that relationships could be fixed and defined.

A more scientific approach to group dynamics was ushered in during the 1940s by Kurt Lewin, whose *field theory* (Lewin, 1951) guided a generation of researchers, industrial psychologists, group therapists, and agents of social change. Drawing on the Gestalt school of perceptual psychology, Lewin developed the notion that a group is more than the sum of its parts. This transcendent property of groups has obvious relevance to family therapists, who must work not only with individuals but also with family systems—and their famous resistance to change.

Analyzing what he called *quasi-stationary social equilibrium,* Lewin pointed out that changing group behavior first requires "unfreezing." Only after something shakes up a group's beliefs are its members likely to accept change. In individual therapy this process is initiated by the disquieting experiences that lead people to seek help. Once an individual accepts the status of patient, that person has already begun to unfreeze old habits. When families come for treatment, it's a different story.

Many family members aren't sufficiently unsettled by the symptomatic member's predicament to think about changing their own ways. Furthermore, family members bring their primary reference group with them, with all its traditions and habits. Consequently, more effort is required to unfreeze, or shake up, families before real change can take place. The need for unfreezing foreshadowed early family therapists' concerns about disrupting family **homeostasis,** a notion that dominated family therapy for decades.

Wilfred Bion was another student of group dynamics who emphasized the group as a whole, with its own dynamics and structure. According to Bion (1948), most groups become distracted from their primary tasks by engaging in patterns of *fight–flight, dependency,* or *pairing.* Bion's "basic assumptions" are easily extrapolated to family therapy: Some families skirt around hot issues like a cat circling a snake. Others use therapy to bicker endlessly, never really contemplating compromise, much less change. Dependency masquerades as therapy when families allow therapists to subvert their autonomy in the name of problem solving. Pairing is seen in families when a parent colludes with the children to undermine the other parent.

The **process/content** distinction in group dynamics likewise had a major impact on family treatment. Experienced therapists learn to attend as much to *how* families talk as to the content of their discussions. For example, a mother might tell her daughter that she shouldn't play with Barbie dolls because she shouldn't aspire to an image of bubble-headed beauty. The *content* of the mother's message is "Respect yourself as a person, not an ornament." But if the mother expresses her point of view by disparaging the daughter's wishes, then the *process* of her message would be "Your feelings don't count."

Unfortunately, the content of some discussions is so compelling that therapists get sidetracked from the process. Suppose, for example, that a therapist invites a teenage boy to talk with his mother about wanting to drop out of school. Say the boy mumbles something about school being stupid, and his mother responds with a lecture about the need for an education. A therapist who gets drawn in to support the mother's position may be making a mistake. In terms of content, the mother might be right: A high school diploma can come in handy. But maybe it's more important at that moment to help the boy learn to speak up for himself—and for his mother to learn to listen.

Role theory, explored in the literature of psychoanalysis and group dynamics, had important applications to the study of families. The expectations that roles carry bring regularity to complex social situations.

Roles tend to be stereotyped in most groups. Virginia Satir (1972) described family roles such as "the placator" and "the disagreeable one" in her book *Peoplemaking.* If you think about it, you may have played a fairly predictable role in your family. Perhaps you were "the good child," "the moody one," "the rebel," or "the successful child." The trouble is, such roles can be hard to put aside.

One thing that makes role theory so useful in understanding families is that roles tend to be reciprocal and complementary. Say, for example, that a woman is slightly more anxious to spend time together with her boyfriend than he is. Maybe, left to his own devices, he'd call twice a week. But if she calls three times a week, he may never get around to picking up the phone. If their relationship progresses and this pattern is played out, she may always play the role of the pursuer and he the distancer. Or take the case of two parents, both of whom want their children to behave at the dinner table. But let's say that the father has a slightly shorter fuse—he tells them to quiet down five seconds after they start getting rowdy, whereas his wife would wait half a minute. If he always speaks up first, she'll never get a chance. Eventually, these parents may become polarized into complementary roles of strictness and leniency. What makes such reciprocity resistant to change is that the roles reinforce each other.

It was a short step from observing a patient's reactions to other members of a group—some of whom might be similar to siblings or parents—to observing interactions in real families. Given the multitude of techniques for exploring interpersonal relationships developed by group therapists, it was natural that some family therapists would apply a group treatment model to working with families. After all, what is a family but a collective group of individuals?

From a technical viewpoint, group and family therapies are similar: Both are complex and dynamic, more like everyday social reality than individual therapy. In groups and families, patients must react to a number of people, not just a therapist, and therapeutic use of this interaction is the definitive mechanism of change in both settings. Consequently, many group and family therapists endeavor to remain relatively decentralized so that patients in the room will relate to each other.

On closer examination, however, we can see that the differences between families and groups are so significant that group therapy has only limited applicability to family treatment. Family members have a long history and, more importantly, a future together. Revealing yourself to strangers is safer than exposing yourself to members of your own family. In fact, serious harm can be done by therapists who are so naive as to push family members to always "be completely honest and open" with each other. There's no taking back rash disclosures that might better have remained private—the affair, long since over, or the admission that a woman *does* care more about her career than her children. Continuity, commitment, and shared distortions all make family therapy different from group therapy.

Therapy groups are designed to provide an atmosphere of warmth and support. This feeling of safety among sympathetic strangers cannot be part of family therapy, because instead of separating treatment from a stressful environment, the stressful environment is brought into treatment. Furthermore, in group therapy, patients can have equal power and status, whereas democratic equality isn't appropriate in families. Someone has to be in charge. Furthermore, the official patient in the family is likely to feel isolated and stigmatized. After all, he or she is "the problem." The sense of protection in being part of a compassionate group of strangers, who won't have to be faced across the dinner table, doesn't exist in family therapy.

THE CHILD GUIDANCE MOVEMENT

It was Freud who introduced the idea that psychological disorders were the consequence of unsolved problems of childhood. Alfred Adler was the first of Freud's followers to pursue the implication that treating the growing child might be the most effective way to prevent adult neuroses. To that end, Adler organized child guidance clinics in Vienna, where not only children but also families and teachers were counseled. Adler's approach was to offer encouragement and support to help alleviate children's feelings of inferiority, so they could work out a healthy life style, achieving confidence and success through social usefulness.

Although child guidance clinics remained few in number until after World War II, they now exist in every city in the United States, providing for the study and treatment of childhood problems and the complex social and family forces contributing to them. Gradually, child guidance workers concluded that the real problem wasn't the obvious one—the child's symptoms—but rather the tensions in the family that were the source of those symptoms. At first, the tendency was to blame the parents, especially the mother.

The chief cause of childhood psychological problems, according to David Levy (1943), was *maternal overprotectiveness*. Mothers who had themselves been deprived of love growing up became overprotective of their children. Some were domineering, others overindulgent. Children of domineering mothers were submissive at home but had difficulty making friends; children with indulgent mothers were disobedient at home but well behaved at school.

During this period, Frieda Fromm-Reichmann (1948) coined one of the most damning terms in the history of psychiatry: the **schizophrenogenic mother.** These domineering, aggressive, and rejecting women, especially when married to passive men, were thought to provide the pathologic parenting that produced schizophrenia.

The tendency to blame parents, especially mothers, for problems in the family was an evolutionary misdirection that continues to haunt the field. Nevertheless, by paying attention to what went on between parents and children, Levy and Fromm-Reichmann helped pave the way for family therapy.

Although the importance of the family was recognized, mothers and children were still treated separately, and discussion between therapists was discouraged on the grounds that it might compromise the individual therapeutic relationships. The usual arrangement was for a psychiatrist to treat the child while a social worker saw the mother. Counseling the mother was an adjunct to treating the child. In this model, the family was viewed as an extension of the child rather than the other way around.

The emphasis in the child guidance movement eventually changed from seeing parents as the problem to seeing problems in the relationships among patients, parents, and significant others. This shift had profound consequences. No longer was psychopathology located within individuals; no longer were parents villains and patients victims. Now their interaction was the problem.

John Bowlby's work at the Tavistock Clinic exemplified the transition to a family approach. Bowlby (1949) was treating a teenager and making slow progress. Feeling frustrated, he decided to see the boy and his parents together. During the first half of a two-hour session, the child and parents took turns complaining, each blaming the other. During the second half of the session, Bowlby interpreted to each of them what he thought each contributed to the problem. Eventually, by working together, all three members of the family developed some sympathy for each other's point of view.

Although he was impressed with the usefulness of this conjoint interview, Bowlby remained wedded to the one-to-one format. Family meetings might be a useful catalyst but only as an adjunct to the *real* treatment, individual psychoanalytic therapy.

What Bowlby tried as an experiment, Nathan Ackerman saw to fruition—family therapy as the primary form of treatment. Once he saw the need to understand the family in order to diagnose problems, Ackerman soon took the next step—family treatment. Before we get to that, however, let us examine parallel developments in social work and research on schizophrenia that led to the birth of family therapy.

$\mathcal{R}$ESEARCH ON FAMILY DYNAMICS AND THE ETIOLOGY OF SCHIZOPHRENIA

Gregory Bateson—Palo Alto

One of the groups with the strongest claim to originating family therapy was Gregory Bateson's schizophrenia project in Palo Alto, California. The Palo Alto project began in the fall of 1952 when Bateson received a grant from the Rockefeller Foundation to study the nature of communication. All communications, Bateson contended (Bateson, 1951), have two different levels or functions—*report* and *command*. Every message has a stated content, as, for instance, "Wash your hands, it's time for dinner," but in addition, the message carries how it is to be taken. In this case, the second message is that the speaker is in charge. This second message—**metacommunication**—is covert and often unnoticed. If a wife scolds her husband for running the dishwasher when it's only half full and he says OK but turns around and does exactly the same thing two days later, she may be annoyed that he doesn't listen to her. She means the message. But maybe he didn't like the metamessage. Maybe he doesn't like her telling him what to do as though she were his mother.

Bateson was joined in 1953 by Jay Haley and John Weakland. In 1954, Bateson received a two-year grant from the Macy Foundation to study schizophrenic communication. Shortly thereafter, the group was joined by Don Jackson, a brilliant psychiatrist who served as clinical consultant.

The group's interests turned to developing a **communications theory** that might explain the origin and nature of schizophrenia, particularly in the context of families. Worth noting, however, is that in the early days of the project, none of them thought of actually observing schizophrenics and their families. Once they agreed that schizophrenic communication might be a product of what was learned inside the family, the group looked for circumstances that could lead to such confused and confusing patterns of speech.

In 1956 Bateson and his colleagues published their famous report "Toward a Theory of Schizophrenia," in which they introduced the concept of the **double bind.** They assumed that psychotic behavior might make sense in the context of pathologic family communication. Patients weren't crazy in some meaningless way; they were an extension of a crazy family environment. Consider someone in an important relationship where escape isn't feasible and response is necessary. When he or she receives two contradictory messages on different levels but finds it difficult to detect or comment on the inconsistency (Bateson, Jackson, Haley, & Weakland, 1956), that person is in a double bind.

Because this difficult concept is often misused as a synonym for paradox or simply contradiction, it's worth reviewing all the features of the double bind as the authors listed them:

1. Two or more persons in an important relationship.
2. Repeated experience.
3. A primary negative injunction, such as "Don't do X or I will punish you."
4. A second injunction at a more abstract level conflicting with the first, also enforced by punishment or perceived threat.
5. A tertiary negative injunction prohibiting escape and demanding a response. Without this restriction the victim won't feel bound.
6. Finally, the complete set of ingredients is no longer necessary once the victim is conditioned to perceive the world in terms of double binds; any part of the sequence becomes sufficient to trigger panic or rage.

Most examples of double binds in the literature are inadequate because they don't include all of the critical features. Robin Skynner, for instance, cited

(1976): "Boys must stand up for themselves and not be sissies"—but "Don't be rough . . . don't be rude to your mother." Confusing? Yes. Conflict? Maybe. But these two messages don't constitute a double bind; they're merely a contradiction. Faced with two such statements, a child is free to obey either one, alternate, or even complain about the contradiction. This and many similar examples neglect the specification that the two messages are conveyed on different levels.

A better example is one given in the original article by Bateson, Jackson, Haley, and Weakland (1956). A young man recovering in the hospital from a schizophrenic episode was visited by his mother. When he put his arm around her, she stiffened. But when he withdrew, she asked, "Don't you love me anymore?" He blushed, and she said, "Dear, you must not be so easily embarrassed and afraid of your feelings." Following this exchange, the patient assaulted an aide and had to be put in seclusion.

Another example of a double bind is a teacher who urges his students to participate in class but gets impatient if one of them actually interrupts with a question or comment. Then a baffling thing happens. For some strange reason that scientists have yet to decipher, students tend not to speak up in classes in which their comments are disparaged. When the professor finally does get around to asking for questions and no one responds, he gets angry. ("Students are so passive!") If any of the students has the temerity to comment on the professor's lack of receptivity, he'll probably get even angrier. Thus the students will be punished for accurately perceiving that the teacher really wants only his own ideas to be heard and admired. (This example is, of course, purely hypothetical.)

We're all caught in occasional double binds, but the schizophrenic has to deal with them continually—and the effect is maddening. Unable to comment on the dilemma, the schizophrenic responds defensively, perhaps by being concrete and literal, perhaps by speaking in metaphors. Eventually, the schizophrenic may come to assume that behind every statement lies a concealed meaning.

The discovery that schizophrenic symptoms made sense in the context of some families may have been a scientific advance, but it had moral and political overtones. Not only did these investigators see themselves as avenging knights bent on rescuing **identified patients** by slaying family dragons, but they were also crusaders in a holy war against the psychiatric establishment. Outnumbered and surrounded by hostile critics, the champions of family therapy challenged the orthodox assumption that schizophrenia was a biological disease. Psychological healers everywhere cheered. Unfortunately, they were wrong.

The observation that schizophrenic behavior seems to *fit* in some families doesn't mean that families *cause* schizophrenia. In logic, this kind of inference is called "Jumping to Conclusions." Sadly, as we will see, families of schizophrenic members suffered for years under the implication that they were to blame for the tragedy of their children's psychoses.

Theodore Lidz—Yale

Theodore Lidz challenged the notion that maternal rejection was the major distinguishing feature of schizophrenic families. Frequently the more destructive influence was that of fathers (Lidz, Cornelison, Fleck, & Terry, 1957). After describing some of the pathologic characteristics of fathers in schizophrenic families, Lidz turned his attention to deficits in the marital relationship. The theme underlying his findings was an absence of *role reciprocity*. In a successful relationship, it's not enough to fulfill your own role, that is, to be an effective person; it's also necessary to balance your role with your partner's, that is, to be an effective pair.

In focusing on the failure to arrive at cooperative roles, Lidz identified two general types of marital discord. In the first, **marital schism,** husbands and wives chronically undercut each other's worth and compete openly for their children's affection. Their marriages are combat zones. The second pattern, **marital skew,** involves serious psychopathology in one partner who dominates the other. Thus, one parent becomes passive and dependent while the other appears to be a strong parent figure but is, in fact, a pathologic bully. In all these families,

unhappy children are torn by conflicting loyalties and weighed down with the pressure to balance their parents' precarious marriages.

Lyman Wynne—National Institute of Mental Health

Lyman Wynne's studies of schizophrenic families began in 1954 when he started seeing the parents of his hospitalized patients in twice-weekly therapy sessions. What struck Wynne about these disturbed families was the strangely unreal qualities of both positive and negative emotions, which he labeled *pseudomutuality* and *pseudohostility,* and the nature of the boundaries around them—*rubber fences*—apparently flexible but actually impervious to outside influence (especially from therapists).

Pseudomutuality is a façade of togetherness that masks conflict and blocks intimacy (Wynne, Ryckoff, Day, & Hirsch, 1958). Such families are so preoccupied with fitting together that there's no room for separate identities. The surface togetherness of pseudomutual families obscures the fact that they can't tolerate either deeper, more honest relationships or independence.

Pseudohostility is a different guise for a similar collusion to obscure *alignments* and *splits* (Wynne,

Lyman Wynne's studies linked *communication deviance* in families to thought disorder in schizophrenic patients.

1961). Although noisy and intense, it signals only a superficial split. Pseudohostility is more like the bickering of a situation-comedy family than real animosity. Like pseudomutuality, it blurs intimacy and affection as well as deeper conflicts, and like pseudomutuality, pseudohostility distorts communication and impairs rational thinking about relationships.

The **rubber fence** is an invisible barrier that stretches to permit obligatory extrafamilial involvement, such as going to school, but springs back if that involvement goes too far. The family's rigid role structure is thus protected by social isolation. The most damaging feature of the rubber fence is that those who most need outside contact to correct family distortions are the ones allowed it least. Instead of being a subsystem of society (Parsons & Bales, 1955), the schizophrenic family becomes a sick little society unto itself.

Wynne linked the new concept of *communication deviance* with the older notion of *thought disorder.* He saw communication as the vehicle for transmitting thought disorder, the defining characteristic of schizophrenia. Communication deviance is a more interactional concept than thought disorder and more readily observable than double binds. By 1978 Wynne had studied more than 600 families and gathered incontrovertible evidence that disordered styles of communication are a distinguishing feature of families with young adult schizophrenics. Similar disorders also appear in families of borderlines, neurotics, and normals but are progressively less severe (Singer, Wynne, & Toohey, 1978). This observation—that communication deviance isn't confined solely to schizophrenic families but exists on a continuum (greater deviance with more severe pathology)—is consistent with other studies that describe a spectrum of schizophrenic disorders.

Role Theorists

The founders of family therapy gained momentum for their fledgling discipline by concentrating on verbal communication. Doing so may have been adaptive at the time, but focusing exclusively on this one aspect of family life neglected both individual intersubjectivity and broader social influences.

Role theorists, like John Spiegel, described how individuals were differentiated into social roles within family systems. This important fact was obscured by oversimplified versions of systems theory, according to which individuals were treated like cogs in a machine. As early as 1954, Spiegel pointed out that the system in therapy includes the therapist as well as the family (an idea reintroduced later as **second-order cybernetics**). He also made a valuable distinction between *interactions* and *transactions.* Billiard balls *interact*—they collide with each other but remain fundamentally unchanged. People *transact*—they come together in ways that not only alter each other's course but also bring about internal changes.

R. D. Laing's analysis of family dynamics was more polemical than scholarly, but his observations helped popularize the family's role in psychopathology. Laing (1965) borrowed Karl Marx's concept of **mystification** (class exploitation) and applied it to the "politics of families." Mystification refers to the distorting of children's experience by denying or relabeling it. One example of this is a parent telling a child who's feeling sad, "You must be tired" (*Go to bed and leave me alone*). Similarly, the idea that good children are always quiet breeds compliant but spiritless children.

The prime function of mystification is to maintain the status quo. Mystification contradicts perceptions and feelings and, more ominously, reality. When parents mystify a child's experience, the child's existence becomes inauthentic. Because their feelings aren't accepted, these children project a *false self* and keep the *real self* private. In mild instances, this produces a lack of authenticity, but if the real self/false self split is carried to extremes, the result is madness (Laing, 1960).

𝓜ARRIAGE COUNSELING

For many years, there was no apparent need for a separate profession of marriage counselors. People with marital problems were more likely to discuss them with their doctors, clergy, lawyers, and teachers than to seek out mental health professionals. The first professional centers for marriage counseling were established in about 1930. Paul Popenoe opened the American Institute of Family Relations in Los Angeles, and Abraham and Hannah Stone opened a similar clinic in New York. A third center was the Marriage Council of Philadelphia, begun in 1932 by Emily Hartshorne Mudd (Broderick & Schrader, 1991).

At the same time these developments were taking place, a parallel trend among some psychoanalysts led to conjoint marital therapy. Although the majority of analysts have always followed Freud's prohibition against contact with a patient's family, a few broke the rules and experimented with therapy for married partners.

In 1948, Bela Mittleman of the New York Psychoanalytic Institute became the first to publish an account of concurrent marital therapy in the United States. Mittleman suggested that husbands and wives could be treated by the same analyst and that by seeing both it was possible to reexamine their irrational perceptions of each other (Mittleman, 1948). This was a revolutionary point of view from an analyst: that the reality of object relationships may be at least as important as their intrapsychic representations.

Meanwhile, in Great Britain, where object relations were the central concern of psychoanalysts, Henry Dicks and his associates at the Tavistock Clinic established a Family Psychiatric Unit. Here couples referred by the divorce courts were helped to reconcile their differences (Dicks, 1964). Subsequently, Michael and Enid Balint affiliated their Family Discussion Bureau with the Tavistock Clinic, adding the clinic's prestige to their marital casework agency and indirectly to the field of marriage counseling.

In 1956, Mittleman wrote a more extensive description of his views on marital disorders and their treatment. He described a number of complementary marital patterns, including aggressive/submissive and detached/demanding. These odd matches are made, according to Mittleman, because courting couples distort each other's personalities through the eyes of their illusions: She sees his independence as strength; he sees her dependency as admiration.

At about this time Don Jackson and Jay Haley were also writing about marital therapy within the framework of communications analysis. As their ideas gained prominence among marital therapists, the field of marital therapy was absorbed into the larger family therapy movement.

Many writers don't distinguish between marital and family therapy. Therapy for couples, according to this way of thinking, is just family therapy applied to a particular subsystem. We tend to agree with this perspective, and therefore you will find our description of various approaches to couples and their problems embedded in the discussions of the models considered in this book. There is, however, a case to be made for considering couples therapy a distinct enterprise (Gurman, 2008).

Historically, many of the influential approaches to couples therapy came before their family therapy counterparts. Among these are cognitive-behavioral marital therapy, object relations marital therapy, emotionally focused couples therapy, and many of the integrative approaches considered in Chapter 14.

Beyond the question of which came first, couples therapy differs in practice from family therapy in allowing for more in-depth focus on the experience of individuals. Sessions with the whole family tend to be noisy affairs. While it's possible in this context to spend time talking with family members about their wishes and fears, it isn't possible to spend much time exploring the psychology of any one individual— much less two. Doing therapy with couples, on the other hand, permits greater focus on both dyadic exchanges and the underlying experience of intimate relationships.

$\mathcal{F}$ROM RESEARCH TO TREATMENT: THE PIONEERS OF FAMILY THERAPY

We have seen how family therapy was anticipated by developments in hospital psychiatry, group dynamics, interpersonal psychiatry, the child guidance movement, and research on schizophrenia. But who actually started family therapy?

Although there are rival claims to this honor, the distinction should probably be shared by John Elderkin Bell, Don Jackson, Nathan Ackerman, and Murray Bowen. In addition to these founders of family therapy,

Jay Haley, Virginia Satir, Carl Whitaker, Lyman Wynne, Ivan Boszormenyi-Nagy, and Salvador Minuchin were also significant pioneers.

John Bell

John Elderkin Bell, a psychologist at Clark University in Worcester, Massachusetts, who began treating families in 1951, occupies a unique position in the history of family therapy. Although he may have been the first family therapist, he is mentioned only tangentially in two of the most important historical accounts of the movement (Guerin, 1976; Kaslow, 1980). The reason for this is that although he began seeing families in the 1950s, he didn't publish his ideas until a decade later. Moreover, unlike the other parents of family therapy, he had few offspring. He didn't establish a clinic, develop a training program, or train well-known students.

Bell's approach (Bell, 1961, 1962) was taken directly from group therapy. *Family group therapy* relied primarily on stimulating open discussion to help families solve their problems. Like a group therapist, Bell intervened to encourage silent participants to speak up, and he interpreted the reasons for their defensiveness.

Bell believed that family group therapy goes through predictable phases, as do groups of strangers. In his early work (Bell, 1961), he structured treatment in a series of stages, each of which concentrated on a particular segment of the family. Later, he became

less directive and allowed families to evolve through a naturally unfolding sequence.

Palo Alto   *Strategic*

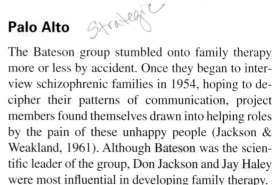

The Bateson group stumbled onto family therapy more or less by accident. Once they began to interview schizophrenic families in 1954, hoping to decipher their patterns of communication, project members found themselves drawn into helping roles by the pain of these unhappy people (Jackson & Weakland, 1961). Although Bateson was the scientific leader of the group, Don Jackson and Jay Haley were most influential in developing family therapy.

Jackson rejected the psychodynamic concepts he learned in training and focused instead on the dynamics of interchange between persons. Analysis of communication was his primary instrument. By 1954 Jackson had developed a rudimentary family therapy, which he reported in a paper, "The Question of Family Homeostasis," delivered to the American Psychiatric Association convention in St. Louis. Borrowing from biology and systems theory, Jackson described families as homeostatic units.

Jackson's concept of **family homeostasis**—families as units that resist change—was to become the defining metaphor of family therapy's early years. In hindsight, we can say that the focus on homeostasis overemphasized the conservative properties of families. At the time, however, the recognition that families resist change was enormously productive for understanding what keeps people stuck.

In "Schizophrenic Symptoms and Family Interaction" (Jackson & Weakland, 1959), Jackson illustrated how patients' symptoms preserve stability in their families. In one case a young woman diagnosed as a catatonic schizophrenic had as her most prominent symptom a profound indecisiveness. When she did behave decisively, her parents fell apart. Her mother became helpless and dependent; her father became literally impotent. In one family meeting, her parents failed to notice when the patient made a simple

John Elderkin Bell

One of the first family therapists was John Elderkin Bell, who began treating families in the early 1950s. His approach to family therapy involved a step-by-step plan of attack to treat family problems in stages. His model was an outgrowth of group therapy and was aptly named *family group therapy*. Bell believed that the treatment of families should follow a series of stages designed to encourage communication among family members and to solve family problems.

decision. Only after listening to a taped replay of the session *three times* did the parents finally hear their daughter's statement. The patient's indecision was neither crazy nor senseless; rather it protected her parents from facing their own difficulties. This is one of the earliest published examples of how even psychotic symptoms can be meaningful in the family context. This paper also contains the shrewd observation that children's symptoms are often an exaggerated version of their parents' problems.

Another construct important to Jackson's thinking was the dichotomy between *symmetrical* and *complementary* relationships. (Like so many of the seminal ideas of family therapy, this one was first articulated by Bateson.) **Complementary relationships** are those in which partners are different in ways that fit together, like interlocking pieces of a jigsaw puzzle: If one is logical, the other is emotional; if one is weak, the other is strong. **Symmetrical relationships** are based on equality and similarity. Marriages between two partners who both have careers and share housekeeping chores are symmetrical. (Incidentally, if you actually find a couple who share housekeeping equally, you'll know you're not in Kansas, Dorothy!)

Jackson's **family rules** hypothesis was simply a means of summarizing the observation that within any committed unit (dyad, triad, or larger group), there were redundant behavior patterns. Rules (as any student of philosophy learns when studying determinism) can describe regularity rather than regulation. A second part of the rules hypothesis was that family members use only some of the full range of behavior available to them. This seemingly innocent fact is what makes family therapy so useful.

Jackson's therapeutic strategies were based on the premise that psychiatric problems resulted from the way people behave with each other in a given context. Human problems were interactional *and* situational. To resolve problems, Jackson sought first to distinguish interactions (*redundant behavior patterns*)

Don Jackson

The vibrant and creative talent of Don Jackson led to his prominent place among the founders of family therapy. A graduate of Stanford University School of Medicine, Jackson rejected the psychoanalytic concepts of his training in favor of cybernetics and communication theory, which he used to develop a pragmatic, problem-solving model of therapy.

Jackson's particular genius was in describing how patterns of communication reflect unspoken rules that govern relationships. According to Jackson, the early stage of a relationship is a kind of bargaining game in which the partners work out the rules that will subsequently govern the nature of their relationship. These "marital quid pro quos" are the bases on which the marriage contract will be written. Jackson died in 1968.

that were functional from those that were dysfunctional (*problem maintaining*). To do so, he observed when problems occurred and in what context, who was present, and how people responded to the problem. Given the assumption that symptoms are homeostatic mechanisms, Jackson would wonder out loud how a family might be worse off if the problem got solved. An individual might want to get better, but the family may need someone to play the sick role. Even positive change can be a threat to the defensive order of things.

A father's drinking, for example, might keep him from making demands on his wife or enforcing discipline over his children. Unfortunately, some family therapists jumped from the observation that symptoms *may* serve a purpose to the assumption that some families *need* a sick member, which, in turn, led to a view of parents victimizing **scapegoated** children. Despite the fancy language, this approach was in the time-honored tradition of blaming parents for the failings of their children. If a six-year-old misbehaves around the house, perhaps we should look to his parents. But a husband's drinking isn't necessarily his wife's fault, and certainly it wasn't fair to imply that families were responsible for the psychotic symptoms of their schizophrenic members.

Looking back, we can see how the **cybernetic** metaphor of the family as a machine led to a view of the therapist as more mechanic than healer. In their zeal to rescue family "scapegoats" from the clutches of their "pathological families," early family therapists may have provoked some of the resistance they complained of.

The great discovery of the Bateson group was that there is no such thing as a simple communication: Every message is qualified by another message on another level. In *Strategies of Psychotherapy,* Jay Haley (1963) explored how covert messages are used in the struggle for control that characterizes many relationships. Symptoms, he argued, represent an incongruence between levels of communication. The symptomatic person does something, such as touching a doorknob six times before turning it, while at the same time denying that he's *really* doing it. He can't help it; it's his condition. Meanwhile, the person's symptoms—over which he has no control—have consequences. A person with a compulsion of such proportions can hardly be expected to get himself out of the house in the morning, can he?

Since symptomatic behavior wasn't reasonable, Haley didn't rely on reasoning with patients to help them. Instead, therapy became a strategic game of cat and mouse.

Haley (1963) defined therapy as a directive form of treatment and acknowledged his debt to Milton Erickson, with whom he studied hypnosis. In what he called *brief therapy,* Haley zeroed in on the context and possible function of the patient's symptoms. His first moves were designed to gain control of the therapeutic relationship. Haley cited Erickson's device of advising patients that in the first interview they may be willing to say some things and they'll want to withhold others and that the latter, of course, should be withheld. Here the therapist is directing patients to do what they would do anyway and thus subtly gaining the upper hand.

The decisive techniques in brief therapy were *directives.* As Haley put it, it isn't enough to explain problems to patients; what counts is getting them to *do* something about them.

One of Haley's patients was a freelance photographer who compulsively made silly blunders that ruined every picture. Eventually, he became so preoccupied with avoiding mistakes that he was too nervous to take pictures at all. Haley instructed the man to go out and take three pictures, making one deliberate error in each. The paradox here is that you can't accidentally make a mistake if you are doing so deliberately.

In another case, Haley told an insomniac that if he woke up in the middle of the night he should get out of bed and wax the kitchen floor. Instant cure! The cybernetic principle here is: People will do anything to get out of housework.

Another member of the Palo Alto group who played a leading role in family therapy's first decade was Virginia Satir, one of the great charismatic healers. Known more for her clinical artistry than for theoretical contributions, Satir's impact was most vivid to those lucky enough to see her in action. Like her confreres, Satir was interested in communication, but she added an emotional dimension that helped counterbalance what was otherwise a relatively cool and calculated approach.

Satir saw troubled family members as trapped in narrow roles, like *victim, placator, defiant one,* and *rescuer,* that constrained relationships and sapped self-esteem. Her concern with freeing family members from the grip of such life-constricting roles was consistent with her major focus, which was always on the individual. Thus, Satir was a humanizing force in the early days of family therapy, when many were so enamored of the systems metaphor that they neglected the emotional lives of families. One thing Satir was justly famous for was her ability to turn negatives into positives.

In one case, cited by Lynn Hoffman (1981), Satir interviewed the family of an adolescent boy, son of the local minister, who had gotten two of his classmates pregnant. On one side of the room sat the boy's parents and siblings. The boy sat in the opposite corner with his head down. Satir introduced herself and said to the boy, "Well, your father has told me a lot about the situation on the phone, and I just want to say before we begin that we know one thing for sure: We know you have good seed." The boy looked up in amazement as Satir turned to the boy's mother and asked brightly, "Could you start by telling us your perception?"

The 1964 publication of Satir's book *Conjoint Family Therapy* did much to popularize family therapy. This book, along with *Pragmatics of Human Communication* (Watzlawick, Beavin, & Jackson, 1967), helped make the Palo Alto group's brand of systemic thinking the leading model of the 1960s.

Murray Bowen

Like many of the founders of family therapy, Murray Bowen was a psychiatrist who specialized in schizophrenia. Unlike others, however, he emphasized theory in his work, and to this day Bowen's theory is the most fertile system of ideas that family therapy has produced.

Bowen began his clinical work at the Menninger Clinic in 1946, where he studied mothers and their schizophrenic children. His major interest at the time was mother–child symbiosis, which led to his concept of **differentiation of self** (autonomy from others and separation of thought from feeling). From Menninger, Bowen moved to the National Institute of Mental Health (NIMH), where he developed a project to hospitalize whole families with schizophrenic members. It was this project that expanded the concept of mother–child symbiosis to include the role of fathers and led to the concept of **triangles** (diverting conflict between two people by involving a third). In 1959 Bowen left NIMH for Georgetown Medical School, where he was a professor of psychiatry and director of his own training program until his death in the fall of 1990.

Beginning in 1955, when Bowen started bringing family members together to discuss their problems, he was struck by their **emotional reactivity.** Feelings overwhelmed thinking and drowned out individuality. Bowen felt the family's tendency to pull him into the center of this **undifferentiated family ego mass,** and he had to make a concerted effort to remain objective (Bowen, 1961). The ability to remain neutral and attentive to the process, rather than the content, of family discussions is what distinguishes a therapist from a participant in a family's drama.

To control the level of emotion, Bowen encouraged family members to talk to him, not to each other. He found that it was easier for people to listen without becoming reactive when family members spoke to the therapist instead of to each other.

Bowen discovered that therapists weren't immune from being sucked into family conflicts. This awareness led to his greatest insight. Whenever two people are struggling with conflict they can't resolve, there is an automatic tendency to involve a third party. In fact, as Bowen came to believe, the triangle is the smallest stable unit of relationship.

A husband who can't stand his wife's habitual lateness, but who also can't stand up and tell her so, may start complaining to his children. His complaining may release tension, but the very process of complaining to a third party makes him less likely to address the problem at its source. We all complain about other people from time to time, but what Bowen realized was that this triangling process is destructive when it becomes a regular feature of a relationship.

Another thing Bowen discovered about triangles is that they spread out. In the following case, a family became entangled in a whole labyrinth of triangles.

Case Study

One Sunday morning, "Mrs. McNeil," who was anxious to get the family to church on time, yelled at her nine-year-old son to hurry up. When he told her to "quit bitching," she slapped him. At that point her fourteen-year-old daughter, Megan, grabbed her, and the two of them started wrestling. Then Megan ran next door to her friend's house. When the friend's parents noticed that she had a cut lip and Megan told them what had happened, they called the police.

One thing led to another, and by the time the family came to therapy, the following triangles were in place: Mrs. McNeil, who'd been ordered out of the house by a family court judge, was allied with her lawyer against the judge; she also had an individual therapist who joined her in thinking she was being hounded unfairly by the child protective workers. The nine-year-old was still mad at his mother, and his father supported him in blaming her for flying off the handle. Mr. McNeil, who was a recovering alcoholic, formed an alliance with his sponsor, who felt that Mr. McNeil was on his way to a breakdown unless his wife started being more supportive. Meanwhile, Megan had formed a triangle with the neighbors, who thought her parents shouldn't be allowed to have children. In short, everyone had an advocate—everyone, that is, except the family unit.

In 1966 an emotional crisis occurred in Bowen's family that led him to initiate a personal voyage of discovery that turned out to be as significant for Bowen's theory as Freud's self-analysis was for psychoanalysis.

As an adult, Bowen, the oldest of five children from a tightly knit rural family, kept his distance from his parents and the rest of his extended family. Like many of us, he mistook avoidance for emancipation. But as he later realized, unfinished emotional business stays with us, making us vulnerable to repeat conflicts we never got around to working out with our families.

Bowen's most important achievement was detriangling himself from his parents, who'd been accustomed to complaining to him about each other. Most of us are flattered to receive such confidences. But Bowen came to recognize this triangulation for what it was. When his mother complained about his father, he told his father: "Your wife told me a story about you; I wonder why she told me instead of you." Naturally, his father discussed this with his mother, and naturally, she was annoyed.

Although his efforts generated the kind of emotional upheaval that comes of breaking family rules,

Bowen's maneuver was effective in keeping his parents from trying to get him to take sides—and made it harder for them to avoid discussing things between themselves. Repeating what someone says to you about someone else is one way to stop triangling in its tracks.

Through his efforts in his own family, Bowen discovered that differentiation of self is best accomplished by developing person-to-person relationships with as many members of the family as possible. If visiting is difficult, letters and phone calls can help reestablish relationships, particularly if they're personal and intimate. Differentiating one's self from one's family is completed when these relationships are maintained without becoming emotionally reactive or taking part in triangles.

Nathan Ackerman

Nathan Ackerman was a child psychiatrist whose pioneering work with families remained faithful to his psychoanalytic roots. Although his interest in intrapsychic conflict may have seemed less innovative than the Palo Alto group's focus on communication as feedback, he had a keen sense of the overall organization of families. Families, Ackerman said, may give the appearance of unity, but underneath they are split into competing factions. This you may recognize as similar to the psychoanalytic model of individuals who, despite apparent unity of personality, are actually minds in conflict, driven by warring drives and defenses.

Ackerman joined the staff of the Menninger Clinic and in 1937 became chief psychiatrist of the Child Guidance Clinic. At first he followed the child guidance model, having a psychiatrist treat the child and a social worker see the mother. By the mid-1940s, he began to experiment with the same therapist seeing both. Unlike Bowlby, Ackerman did more than use these conjoint sessions as a temporary expedient; instead, he began to see the family as the basic unit of treatment.

In 1955 Ackerman organized the first session on family diagnosis at a meeting of the American Orthopsychiatric Association. At that meeting, Jackson,

Nathan Ackerman

Nathan Ackerman's ability to understand families enabled him to look beyond behavioral interactions and into the hearts and minds of each family member. He used his forceful personality to uncover the family's defenses and allow their feelings, hopes, and desires to surface. Ackerman's psychoanalytic training is evident in his contributions and theoretical approach to family therapy. Ackerman proposed that underneath the apparent unity of families there existed a layer of intrapsychic conflict that divided family members into factions.

Together with Don Jackson, Ackerman founded the first family therapy journal, *Family Process,* which is still the leading journal of ideas in the field.

Bowen, Wynne, and Ackerman learned about each other's work and joined in a sense of common purpose. Two years later Ackerman opened the Family Mental Health Clinic of Jewish Family Services in New York City and began teaching at Columbia University. In 1960 he founded the Family Institute, which was renamed the Ackerman Institute following his death in 1971.

Although other family therapists downplayed the psychology of individuals, Ackerman was as concerned with what goes on inside people as with what goes on between them. He never lost sight of feelings, hopes, and desires. In fact, Ackerman's model of the family was like the psychoanalytic model of individuals writ large; instead of conscious and unconscious issues, Ackerman talked about how families confront some issues while avoiding others, particularly those involving sex and aggression. He saw his job as a therapist as one of stirring things up, bringing family secrets out into the open. He was an *agent provocateur,* prompting revelations and confrontations with his wit and willingness to stick his nose into personal family issues.

To encourage families to relax their emotional restraint, Ackerman himself was unrestrained. He freely sided first with one member of a family and then with another. He didn't think it was necessary—or possible—always to be neutral; instead, he believed

that balance was achieved in the long run by moving back and forth, giving support now to one, later to another family member. At times he was unabashedly blunt. If he thought someone was lying, he said so. To critics who suggested this directness might generate too much anxiety, Ackerman replied that people get more reassurance from honesty than from false politeness.

Ackerman urged therapists to become emotionally engaged with families and to bring dormant conflicts into the open. How does a therapist encourage candid disclosures? Ackerman did it by challenging avoidance and emotional dishonesty ("tickling the defenses"). Perhaps his most enduring contribution was his consistent respect for individual persons *and* whole families; he never lost sight of the self in the system.

Carl Whitaker

Even among the iconoclastic founders of family therapy, Carl Whitaker stood out as the most irreverent. His view of psychologically troubled people was that they were alienated from feeling and frozen into devitalized routines (Whitaker & Malone, 1953). Whitaker turned up the emotional temperature. His "Psychotherapy of the Absurd" (Whitaker, 1975) was a blend of warm support and emotional goading, designed to loosen people up and help them get in touch with their experience in a deeper, more personal way.

Given his bold and inventive approach to therapy, it isn't surprising that Whitaker became one of the first to experiment with family treatment. In 1943 he and John Warkentin, working in Oakridge, Tennessee, began including spouses and eventually children in treatment. Whitaker also pioneered the use of cotherapy in the belief that a supportive partner helped free therapists to react without fear of countertransference.

Whitaker never seemed to have an obvious strategy, nor did he use predictable techniques, preferring, as he said, to let his unconscious run the therapy

(Whitaker, 1976). Although his work seemed totally spontaneous, even outrageous at times, it had a consistent theme. All of his interventions had the effect of promoting flexibility. He didn't so much push families to change in a particular direction as he challenged them to open up—to become more fully themselves and more fully together.

In 1946 Whitaker became chairman of the department of psychiatry at Emory University, where he continued to experiment with family treatment with a special interest in schizophrenics and their families. During this period Whitaker organized a series of forums that led to the first major convention of the family therapy movement. Beginning in 1946 Whitaker and his colleagues began twice-yearly conferences during which they observed and discussed each other's work with families. The group found these sessions enormously helpful, and mutual observation, using one-way vision screens, has since become one of the hallmarks of family therapy.

Whitaker resigned from Emory in 1955 and entered private practice, where he and his partners at the Atlanta Psychiatric Clinic developed an *experiential* form of psychotherapy, using a number of highly provocative techniques in the treatment of families, individuals, groups, and couples (Whitaker, 1958).

During the late 1970s, Whitaker seemed to mellow and also to add a greater understanding of family dynamics to his shoot-from-the-hip interventions. In the process, the former wild man of family therapy became one of its elder statesmen. Whitaker's death in April 1995 left the field with a piece of its heart missing.

Ivan Boszormenyi-Nagy

Ivan Boszormenyi-Nagy, who came to family therapy from psychoanalysis, was one of the seminal thinkers in the movement. In 1957 he founded the Eastern Pennsylvania Psychiatric Institute in Philadelphia, where he attracted a host of highly talented colleagues. Among these were James Framo, one of the few psychologists in the early family therapy movement, and Geraldine Spark, a social worker who worked with Boszormenyi-Nagy as cotherapist and coauthor of *Invisible Loyalties* (Boszormenyi-Nagy & Spark, 1973).

This group was joined by Ross Speck, who did his psychiatric residency in the early 1960s and developed, along with Carolyn Attneave, **network therapy,** which broadened the context of treatment beyond the nuclear family. In this approach, as many people as possible who are connected to the patient are invited to attend therapy sessions. Often as many as fifty people, including extended family, friends, neighbors, and teachers, are brought together to discuss ways to support and help the patient change (Speck & Attneave, 1973).

Boszormenyi-Nagy went from being an analyst, prizing secrecy and confidentiality, to a family therapist, fighting the forces of pathology on an open battlefield. One of his most important contributions was to add ethical accountability to the usual therapeutic goals and techniques. According to Boszormenyi-Nagy, neither pleasure nor expediency is a sufficient guide to human behavior. Instead, he believed that family members have to base their relationships on trust and loyalty and that they must balance the ledger of entitlement and indebtedness. He died in 2008.

Salvador Minuchin

When Minuchin first burst onto the scene, it was the drama of his clinical interviews that people found captivating. This compelling man with an elegant Latin accent would seduce, provoke, bully, or bewilder families into changing—as the situation required. But even Minuchin's legendary flair didn't have the same galvanizing impact as the practical simplicity of his structural model.

Minuchin began his career as a family therapist in the early 1960s when he discovered two patterns common to troubled families: Some are *enmeshed*—chaotic and tightly interconnected; others are *disengaged*—isolated and seemingly unrelated. Both types lack clear lines of authority. Enmeshed parents are too entangled with their children to exercise leadership; disengaged parents are too distant to provide effective support.

Family problems are tenacious and resistant to change because they're embedded in powerful but unseen structures. Take, for example, a mother futilely remonstrating with a willful child. The mother can scold, punish, or reward, but as long as she's enmeshed (overly involved) with the child, her efforts lack force because she lacks authority. Moreover, because the behavior of one family member is always related to that of others, the mother will have trouble stepping back as long as her husband remains disengaged.

Once a social system such as a family becomes structured, attempts to change the rules constitute what family therapists call **first-order change**— change within a system that itself remains invariant. For the mother in the previous example to start practicing stricter discipline would be an example of first-order change. The enmeshed mother is caught in an illusion of alternatives. She can be strict or lenient; the result is the same because she remains trapped in a triangle. What's needed is **second-order change**—a change in the system itself.

Minuchin worked out his ideas while struggling with the problems of juvenile delinquency at the Wiltwyck School for Boys in New York. Family therapy with urban slum families was a new development, and publication of his discoveries (Minuchin, Montalvo, Guerney, Rosman, & Schumer, 1967) led to his being invited to become the director of the Philadelphia Child Guidance Clinic in 1965. Minuchin brought Braulio Montalvo and Bernice Rosman with him, and they were joined in 1967 by Jay Haley. Together they transformed a traditional child guidance clinic into one of the great centers of the family therapy movement.

The techniques of *structural family therapy* fall into two general strategies. First the therapist must accommodate to the family in order to "join" them. To begin by challenging a family's preferred mode of relating is almost guaranteed to provoke resistance. If, instead, the therapist starts by trying to understand and accept the family, they'll be more likely to accept treatment. (No one is eager to accept advice from someone who doesn't understand them.) Once this initial joining is accomplished, the structural family therapist begins to use *restructuring* techniques. These are active maneuvers designed to disrupt dysfunctional structures by strengthening diffuse boundaries and loosening rigid ones (Minuchin & Fishman, 1981).

In 1981 Minuchin moved to New York and established what is now known as the Minuchin Center for the Family, where he pursued his dedication to teaching family therapists from all over the world and his commitment to social justice by working with the foster care system. He also continued to turn out a steady stream of the most influential books in the field. His 1974 *Families and Family Therapy* is deservedly the most popular book in the history of family therapy, and his 1993 *Family Healing* contains some of the most moving descriptions of family therapy ever written.

Other Early Centers of Family Therapy

In New York, Israel Zwerling and Marilyn Mendelsohn organized the Family Studies Section at Albert Einstein College of Medicine. Andrew Ferber was named director in 1964, and later Philip Guerin, a protégé of Murray Bowen, joined the section. Nathan Ackerman served as a consultant, and the group assembled an impressive array of family therapists with diverse orientations. These included Chris Beels, Betty Carter, Monica McGoldrick, Peggy Papp, and Thomas Fogarty. Philip Guerin became director of training in 1970, and shortly thereafter, in 1973, he founded the Center for Family Learning in Westchester, where he and Thomas Fogarty developed one of the finest family therapy training programs in the nation.

In Galveston, Texas, Robert MacGregor and his colleagues developed *multiple impact therapy* (MacGregor, 1967). It was a case of necessity being the mother of invention. MacGregor's clinic served a population scattered widely over southeastern Texas, and many of his clients had to travel hundreds of miles. Because they had to come such distances, most of these people were unable to return for weekly sessions. Therefore, to have maximum impact in a short time, MacGregor assembled a team of professionals who worked intensively with the families for two full days. Although few family therapists have used such marathon sessions, the team approach continues to be one of the hallmarks of the field.

In Boston, the two most significant early contributions to family therapy were both in the experiential wing of the movement. Norman Paul developed an *operational mourning* approach designed to resolve impacted grief, and Fred and Bunny Duhl set up the Boston Family Institute, where they developed *integrative family therapy.*

In Chicago, the Family Institute of Chicago and the Institute for Juvenile Research were important centers of the early scene in family therapy. At the Family Institute, Charles and Jan Kramer developed a clinical training program that was later affiliated with Northwestern University Medical School. The Institute for Juvenile Research also mounted a training program under the leadership of Irv Borstein, with the consultation of Carl Whitaker.

The work of Nathan Epstein and his colleagues, first formulated in the department of psychiatry at McMaster University in Hamilton, Ontario, was a problem-centered approach (Epstein, Bishop, & Baldarin, 1981). The McMaster model goes step by step—elucidating the problem, gathering data, considering alternative resolutions, and assessing the learning process—to help families understand their interactions and build on their newly acquired coping skills. Epstein later relocated to Brown University in Providence, Rhode Island.

Important developments in family therapy also occurred outside the United States. Robin Skynner (1976) introduced psychodynamic family therapy at the Institute of Family Therapy in London. British psychiatrist John Howells (1971) developed a system of family diagnosis as a necessary step for planning therapeutic intervention. West German Helm Stierlin (1972) integrated psychodynamic and systemic ideas for treating troubled adolescents. In Rome, Maurizio Andolfi worked with families early in the 1970s and founded, in 1974, the Italian Society for Family Therapy; Mara Selvini Palazzoli and her colleagues founded the Institute for Family Studies in Milan in 1967.

Now that you've seen how family therapy emerged in several different places at once, we hope you haven't lost sight of one thing: There is a tremendous satisfaction in seeing how people's behavior makes sense in the context of their families. Meeting with a family for the first time is like turning on a light in a dark room.

THE GOLDEN AGE OF FAMILY THERAPY

In their first decade, family therapists had all the bravado of new kids on the block. "Look at this!" Haley and Jackson and Bowen seemed to say when they discovered how the whole family was implicated in the symptoms of individual patients. While they were struggling for legitimacy, family clinicians emphasized their common beliefs and downplayed their differences. Troubles, they agreed, came in families. But if the watchword of the 1960s was "Look at this!"—emphasizing the leap of understanding made possible by seeing whole families together—the rallying cry of the 1970s was "Look what I can do!" as the new kids flexed their muscles and carved out their own turf.

The period from 1970 to 1985 saw the flowering of the famous schools of family therapy when the pioneers established training centers and worked out the implications of their models. The leading approach in the 1960s was the *communications model* developed in Palo Alto. The book of the decade was Watzlawick, Beavin, and Jackson's *Pragmatics of Human Communication,* the text that introduced the systemic version of family therapy. The model of the 1980s was *strategic therapy,* and the books of the decade described its three most vital approaches: *Change,* by Watzlawick, Weakland, and Fisch;[1] *Problem-Solving Therapy,* by Jay Haley; and *Paradox and Counterparadox,* by Mara Selvini Palazzoli and her Milan associates. The 1970s belonged to Salvador

---

[1]Although actually published in 1974, this book and its sequel, *The Tactics of Change*, were most widely read and taught in the 1980s.

Minuchin. His *Families and Family Therapy* and the simple yet compelling model of *structural family therapy* it described dominated the decade.

Structural theory seemed to offer just what family therapists were looking for: a simple way of describing family organization and a set of easy-to-follow steps to treatment. In hindsight, we might ask whether the impressive power of Minuchin's approach was a product of the method or the man. (The answer is, probably a little of both.) In the 1970s, however, the widely shared belief that structural family therapy could be easily learned drew people from all over the world to what was for a decade the epicenter of the family therapy movement: the Philadelphia Child Guidance Clinic.

The strategic therapy that flourished in the 1980s was centered in three unique and creative groups: the Palo Alto Mental Research Institute's brief therapy group, including John Weakland, Paul Watzlawick, and Richard Fisch; Jay Haley and Cloe Madanes, codirectors of the Family Therapy Institute of Washington, D.C.; and Mara Selvini Palazzoli and her colleagues in Milan. But the leading influence in the decade of strategic therapy was exerted by Milton Erickson, albeit from beyond the grave.

Erickson's genius was much admired and much imitated. Family therapists came to idolize Erickson the way we as children idolized Captain Marvel. We'd come home from Saturday matinees all pumped up, get out our toy swords, put on our magic capes—and presto! *We* were superheroes. We were just kids and so we didn't bother translating our heroes' mythic powers into our own terms. Unfortunately, many of those who were starstruck by Erickson's legendary therapeutic tales did the same thing. Instead of grasping the principles on which they were predicated, many therapists just tried to imitate his "uncommon techniques." To be any kind of competent therapist, you must keep your psychological distance from the supreme artists—the Minuchins, the Milton Ericksons, the Michael Whites. Otherwise you end up aping the magic of their styles rather than grasping the substance of their ideas.

Part of what made Jay Haley's strategic directives so attractive was that they were a wonderful way to gain control over people—for their own good—without the usual frustration of trying to convince them to do the right thing. (Most people already know what's good for them. The hard part is getting them to *do* it.) So, for example, in the case of a person who is bulimic, a strategic directive might be for the patient's family to set out a mess of fried chicken, french fries, cookies, and ice cream. Then, with the family watching, the patient would mash up all the food with her hands, symbolizing what goes on in her stomach. After the food was reduced to a soggy mess, she would stuff it into the toilet. Then when the toilet clogged, she would have to ask the family member she resented most to unclog it. This task would symbolize not only what the person with bulimia does to herself but also what she puts the family through (Madanes, 1981).

What the strategic camp added to Erickson's creative problem solving was a simple framework for understanding how families got stuck in their problems. According to the Mental Research Institute (MRI) model, problems develop and persist from mismanagement of ordinary life difficulties. The original difficulty becomes a problem when mishandling leads people to get stuck in more-of-the-same solutions. It was a perverse twist on the old adage, "If at first you don't succeed, try, try again."

The Milan group built on the ideas pioneered at MRI, especially the use of the therapeutic double bind, or what they referred to as *counterparadox*. Here's an example from *Paradox and Counterparadox* (Selvini Palazzoli, Boscolo, Cecchin, & Prata, 1978). The authors describe counterparadoxical approach to a six-year-old boy and his family. At the end of the session, young Bruno was praised for acting crazy to protect his father. By occupying his mother's time with fights and tantrums, the boy generously allowed his father more time for work and relaxation. Bruno was encouraged to continue doing what he was already doing, lest this comfortable arrangement be disrupted.

The appeal of the strategic approach was pragmatism. Making use of the cybernetic metaphor, strategic therapists zeroed in on how family systems were regulated by negative feedback. They achieved results simply by disrupting the interactions that maintained symptoms. What eventually turned therapists off to these approaches was their gamesmanship. Their interventions were transparently manipulative. The result was like watching a clumsy magician—you could see him stacking the deck.

Meanwhile, as structural and strategic approaches rose and fell in popularity, four other models of family therapy flourished quietly. Though they never took center stage, *experiential, psychoanalytic, behavioral,* and *Bowenian* models grew and prospered. Although these schools never achieved the cachet of family therapy's latest fads, each of them produced solid clinical approaches, which will be examined at length in subsequent chapters.

Looking back from soberer times, it's difficult to convey the excitement and optimism that energized family therapy in its golden age. Training centers sprouted up all over the country, workshops were packed, and the leaders of the movement were celebrated like rock stars. Active and forceful interveners, their self-assurance was infectious. Minuchin, Whitaker, Haley, Madanes, and Selvini Palazzoli seemed to rise above the limitations of ordinary talk therapy. Young therapists needed inspiration, and

they found it. They learned from the masters, and they idolized them.

Sometime in the mid-1980s, a reaction set in. Despite optimistic assumptions, these activist approaches didn't always work. So the field took revenge on those they'd idealized by cutting them down to size. Maybe it was Haley's manipulativeness that turned them off or the fact that Minuchin sometimes seemed more bossy than brilliant. Family therapists had marveled at their creativity and tried to copy it, but creativity can't be copied.

By the end of the 1980s, the leaders of the major schools were growing older and their influence was waning. What once seemed heroic now seemed aggressive and overbearing. A series of challenges—feminist and postmodern critiques, the reemergence of analytic and biological models, the magic bullet Prozac, the success of recovery programs like Alcoholics Anonymous, the ugly facts of wife beating and child abuse that challenged the notion that domestic problems were always a product of relationships—shook our confidence in the models we knew to be true, knew would work. We'll take a closer look at these challenges in subsequent chapters.

Summary

1. Family therapy has a short history but a long past. For many years therapists resisted the idea of seeing a patient's relatives in order to safeguard the privacy of the patient–therapist relationship. Freudians excluded the real family to uncover the unconscious, introjected family; Rogerians kept relatives away to provide unconditional positive regard; and hospital psychiatrists discouraged family visits because they might disrupt the benign milieu of the hospital.

2. Several converging developments in the 1950s led to a new view—namely, that the family was a living system, an organic whole. Hospital psychiatrists noticed that often when patients improved, someone else in the family got worse. Thus it became clear that change in any one person changes the whole

system. Eventually, it became apparent that changing the family might be the most effective way to change the individual.

3. Although practicing clinicians in hospitals and child guidance clinics prepared the way for family therapy, the most important breakthroughs were achieved in the 1950s by workers who were scientists first, healers second. In Palo Alto, Gregory Bateson, Jay Haley, Don Jackson, and John Weakland discovered that schizophrenia made sense in the context of *pathologic family communication*. Schizophrenics weren't crazy in some meaningless way; their behavior was understandable in the context of their families. At Yale, Theodore Lidz found a striking pattern of instability and conflict in the families of schizophrenics. *Marital schism* (open conflict) and *marital skew* (pathologic balance) had profound effects on the development of children. Murray Bowen's observation of how mothers and their schizophrenic offspring go through cycles of closeness and distance was the forerunner of the *pursuer–distancer* dynamic. By hospitalizing whole families for observation and treatment, Bowen implicitly located the problem of schizophrenia in an *undifferentiated family ego mass* and even extended it beyond the nuclear family to three generations. Lyman Wynne linked schizophrenia to the family by demonstrating how *communication deviance* contributes to thought disorder.

4. These observations launched the family therapy movement, but the excitement they generated blurred the distinction between what researchers observed and what they concluded. What they observed was that the behavior of schizophrenics *fit* with their families; what they concluded was that the family must be the *cause* of schizophrenia. A second conclusion was even more influential. Family dynamics—double binds, pseudomutuality, undifferentiated family ego mass—began to be seen as products of a system rather than as features of persons who share certain qualities because they live together. Thus was born a new creature, the *family system.*

5. Who was the first to practice family therapy? This turns out to be a difficult question. As in every field, there were visionaries who anticipated the development of family therapy. Freud, for example, treated "Little Hans" by working with his father as early as 1908. Such experiments, however, weren't sufficient to challenge the hegemony of individual therapy until the climate of the times was receptive. In the early 1950s, family therapy was begun independently in four different places: by John Bell at Clark University, Murray Bowen at NIMH, Nathan Ackerman in New York, and Don Jackson and Jay Haley in Palo Alto.

6. These pioneers had distinctly different backgrounds. Not surprisingly, the approaches they developed were also quite different. This diversity still characterizes the field today. Had family therapy been started by a single person, as was psychoanalysis, it's

unlikely that there would have been so much creative competition so soon.

7. In addition to those just mentioned, others who made significant contributions to the founding of family therapy were Lyman Wynne, Theodore Lidz, Virginia Satir, Carl Whitaker, Ivan Boszormenyi-Nagy, Robert MacGregor, and Salvador Minuchin.

8. What we've called family therapy's golden age—the flowering of the schools in the 1970s and 1980s—was the high-water mark of our self-confidence. Armed with Haley's or Minuchin's latest text, therapists pledged allegiance to one school or another and set off with a sense of mission. What drew them to activist approaches was certainty and charisma. What soured them was hubris. To some, structural family therapy—at least as they had seen it demonstrated at workshops—began to seem like bullying. Others saw the shrewdness of the strategic approach as manipulative. The tactics were clever but cold. Families were described as stubborn; they couldn't be reasoned with. You don't tell a cybernetic machine what you really believe. Therapists got tired of that way of thinking.

9. In the early years, family therapists were animated by a tremendous sense of enthusiasm and conviction. Today, in the wake of postmodern critiques, managed care, and a resurgence of biological psychiatry, we're less sure of ourselves. In subsequent chapters we'll see how today's family therapists have managed to synthesize creative new ideas with some of the best of the earlier models. But as we explore each of the famous models in depth, we'll also see how some good ideas have been unwisely neglected.

10. All the complexity of the family therapy field should not, however, obscure its basic premise: The family is the context of human problems. Like all human groups, the family has emergent properties—the whole is greater than the sum of its parts. Moreover, no matter how many and varied the explanations of these emergent properties, they all fall into two categories: *structure* and *process.* The structure of families includes *triangles, subsystems,* and *boundaries.* Among the processes that describe family interaction—*emotional reactivity, dysfunctional communication,* and so on—the central concept is circularity. Rather than worrying about who started what, family therapists understand and treat human problems as a series of moves and counter-moves, in repeating cycles.

Questions to Consider

1. Which of the early concepts of family therapy—complementarity, differentiation of self, homeostasis, resistance—are inherently sexist? Which could be used to support sexist assumptions?

2. Which of Bion's three basic assumptions (fight–flight, pairing, dependency) best describes how you and your classmates behave in your least favorite classes?

3. Which of family therapy's early concepts and methods might tend to foster an adversarial relationship with families? What in your own background might predispose you to approach certain family members as adversaries (e.g., controlling mothers, distant fathers)?

Key Concepts

coalition An alliance between two persons or social units against a third.

communications theory The study of relationships in terms of the exchange of verbal and nonverbal messages.

complementary relationship Relationship based on differences that fit together in which qualities of one make up for lacks in the other.

cybernetics The study of self-controlling processes in systems, especially the analysis of positive and negative feedback loops.

differentiation of self Psychological separation of intellect and emotions and independence of self from others; opposite of *fusion*.

double bind A conflict created when a person receives contradictory messages on different levels of abstraction in an important relationship and cannot leave or comment.

emotional reactivity The tendency to respond in a knee-jerk emotional fashion, rather than calmly and objectively.

family homeostasis The tendency of families to resist change in order to maintain a steady state.

family rules A descriptive term for redundant behavioral patterns.

family system The family conceived as a collective, whole entity made up of individual parts plus the way they function together.

first-order change Superficial change in a system that itself stays invariant.

group dynamics The interactions among group members that emerge as a result of properties of the group rather than merely of their individual personalities.

homeostasis A balanced steady state of equilibrium.

identified patient The symptom-bearer or official patient as identified by the family.

marital schism Lidz's term for pathologic overt marital conflict.

marital skew Lidz's term for a pathologic marriage in which one spouse dominates the other.

metacommunication Every message has two levels, report and command; metacommunication is the implied command or qualifying message.

mystification Laing's concept that many families distort their children's experience by denying or relabeling it.

network therapy A treatment devised by Ross Speck in which a large number of family and friends are assembled to help resolve a patient's problems.

process/content Distinction between how members of a family or group relate (process) and what they talk about (content).

pseudohostility Lyman Wynne's term for superficial bickering that masks pathologic alignments in schizophrenic families.

pseudomutuality Wynne's term for the façade of family harmony that characterizes many schizophrenic families.

rubber fence Wynne's term for the rigid boundary surrounding many schizophrenic families, which allows only minimal contact with the surrounding community.

scapegoat A member of the family, usually the identified patient, who is the object of displaced conflict or criticism.

schizophrenogenic mother Fromm-Reichmann's term for aggressive, domineering mothers thought to precipitate schizophrenia in their offspring.

second-order change Basic change in the structure and functioning of a system.

second-order cybernetics The idea that anyone attempting to observe and change a system is therefore part of that system.

symmetrical relationship In relationships, equality or parallel form.

triangle A three-person system; according to Bowen, the smallest stable unit of human relations.

undifferentiated family ego mass Bowen's early term for emotional "stuck-togetherness" or fusion in the family, especially prominent in schizophrenic families.

Recommended Readings

Ackerman, N. W. 1958. *The psychodynamics of family life.* New York: Basic Books.

Bowen, M. 1960. A family concept of schizophrenia. In *The etiology of schizophrenia,* D. D. Jackson, ed. New York: Basic Books.

Greenberg, G. S. 1977. The family interactional perspective: A study and examination of the work of Don D. Jackson. *Family Process. 16:* 385–412.

Haley, J., and Hoffman, L., eds. 1968. *Techniques of family therapy.* New York: Basic Books.

Jackson, D. D. 1957. The question of family homeostasis. *The Psychiatric Quarterly Supplement. 31:* 79–90.

Jackson, D. D. 1965. Family rules: Marital quid pro quo. *Archives of General Psychiatry. 12:* 589–594.

Weakland, J. H. 1960. The "double-bind" hypothesis of schizophrenia and three-party interaction. In *The etiology of schizophrenia,* D. D. Jackson, ed. New York: Basic Books.

References

Bateson, G. 1951. Information and codification: A philosophical approach. In *Communication: The social matrix of psychiatry,* J. Ruesch and G. Bateson, eds. New York: Norton.

Bateson, G., Jackson, D. D., Haley, J., and Weakland, J. 1956. Toward a theory of schizophrenia. *Behavioral Sciences. 1:* 251–264.

Bell, J. E. 1961. *Family group therapy.* Public Health Monograph #64. Washington, DC: U.S. Government Printing Office.

Bell, J. E. 1962. Recent advances in family group therapy. *Journal of Child Psychology and Psychiatry. 3:* 1–15.

Bion, W. R. 1948. Experience in groups. *Human Relations. 1:* 314–329.

Boszormenyi-Nagy, I., and Spark, G. L. 1973. *Invisible loyalties: Reciprocity in intergenerational family therapy.* New York: Harper & Row.

Bowen, M. 1961. Family psychotherapy. *American Journal of Orthopsychiatry. 31:* 40–60.

Bowlby, J. P. 1949. The study and reduction of group tensions in the family. *Human Relations. 2:* 123–138.

Broderick, C. B., and Schrader, S. S. 1991. The history of professional marriage and family therapy. In *Handbook of family therapy,* Vol. II, A. S. Gurman and D. P. Kniskern, eds. New York: Brunner/Mazel.

Dicks, H. V. 1964. Concepts of marital diagnosis and therapy as developed at the Tavistock Family Psychiatric Clinic, London, England. In *Marriage counseling in medical practice,* E. M. Nash, L. Jessner, and D. W. Abse, eds. Chapel Hill: University of North Carolina Press.

Epstein, N. B., Bishop, D. S., and Baldarin, L. M. 1981. McMaster model of family functioning. In *Normal family problems,* F. Walsh, ed. New York: Guilford Press.

Fisher, S., and Mendell, D. 1958. The spread of psychotherapeutic effects from the patient to his family group. *Psychiatry. 21:* 133–140.

Fromm-Reichmann, F. 1948. Notes on the development of treatment of schizophrenics by psychoanalytic psychotherapy. *Psychiatry. 11:* 263–274.

Guerin, P. J. 1976. Family therapy: The first twenty-five years. In *Family therapy: Theory and practice,* P. J. Guerin, ed. New York: Gardner Press.

Gurman, A. S. 2008. *Clinical handbook of couple therapy,* 4th ed. New York: Guilford Press.

Haley, J. 1963. *Strategies of psychotherapy.* New York: Grune & Stratton.

Hoffman, L. 1981. *Foundations of family therapy.* New York: Basic Books.

Howells, J. G. 1971. *Theory and practice of family psychiatry.* New York: Brunner/Mazel.

Jackson, D. D. 1954. Suicide. *Scientific American. 191:* 88–96.

Jackson, D. D., and Weakland, J. H. 1959. Schizophrenic symptoms and family interaction. *Archives of General Psychiatry. 1:* 618–621.

Jackson, D. D., and Weakland, J. H. 1961. Conjoint family therapy, some considerations on theory, technique, and results. *Psychiatry. 24:* 30–45.

Kaslow, F. W. 1980. History of family therapy in the United States: A kaleidoscopic overview. *Marriage and Family Review. 3:* 77–111.

Laing, R. D. 1960. *The divided self.* London: Tavistock Publications.

Laing, R. D. 1965. Mystification, confusion and conflict. In *Intensive family therapy,* I. Boszormenyi-Nagy and J. L. Framo, eds. New York: Harper & Row.

Levy, D. 1943. *Maternal overprotection.* New York: Columbia University Press.

Lewin, K. 1951. *Field theory in social science.* New York: Harper.

Lidz, T., Cornelison, A., Fleck, S., and Terry, D. 1957. Intrafamilial environment of the schizophrenic patient. I: The father. *Psychiatry. 20:* 329–342.

MacGregor, R. 1967. Progress in multiple impact theory. In *Expanding theory and practice in family therapy,* N. W. Ackerman, F. L. Bateman, and S. N. Sherman, eds. New York: Family Services Association.

Madanes, C. 1981. *Strategic family therapy.* San Francisco: Jossey-Bass.

Minuchin, S. 1974. *Families and family therapy.* Cambridge, MA: Harvard University Press.

Minuchin, S., and Fishman, H. C. 1981. *Family therapy techniques.* Cambridge, MA: Harvard University Press.

Minuchin, S., Montalvo, B., Guerney, B. G., Rosman, B. L., and Schumer, F. 1967. *Families of the slums.* New York: Basic Books.

Mittleman, B. 1948. The concurrent analysis of married couples. *Psychoanalytic Quarterly. 17:* 182–197.

Mittleman, B. 1956. Analysis of reciprocal neurotic patterns in family relationships. In *Neurotic interaction in marriage,* V. W. Eisenstein, ed. New York: Basic Books.

Parsons, T., and Bales, R. F. 1955. *Family, socialization and interaction process:* Glencoe, IL: Free Press.

Satir, V. 1964. *Conjoint family therapy.* Palo Alto, CA: Science and Behavior Books.

Satir, V. 1972. *Peoplemaking.* Palo Alto, CA: Science and Behavior Books.

Selvini Palazzoli, M., Boscolo, L., Cecchin, G., and Prata, G. 1978. *Paradox and counterparadox.* New York: Jason Aronson.

Singer, M. T., Wynne, L. C., and Toohey, M. L. 1978. Communication disorders and the families of schizophrenics. In *The nature of schizophrenia,* L. C. Wynne, R. L. Cromwell, and S. Matthysse, eds. New York: Wiley.

Skynner, R. 1976. *Systems of family and marital psychotherapy.* New York: Brunner/Mazel.

Speck, R., and Attneave, C. 1973. *Family networks: Rehabilitation and healing.* New York: Pantheon.

Stierlin, H. 1972. *Separating parents and adolescents.* New York: Quadrangle/New York Times Books.

Watzlawick, P. A., Beavin, J. H., and Jackson, D. D. 1967. *Pragmatics of human communication.* New York: Norton.

Whitaker, C. A. 1958. Psychotherapy with couples. *American Journal of Psychotherapy. 12:* 18–23.

Whitaker, C. A. 1975. Psychotherapy of the absurd: With a special emphasis on the psychotherapy of aggression. *Family Process. 14:* 1–16.

Whitaker, C. A. 1976. A family is a four-dimensional relationship. In *Family therapy: Theory and practice,* P. J. Guerin, ed. New York: Gardner Press.

Whitaker, C. A., and Malone, T. P. 1953. *The roots of psychotherapy.* New York: Balkiston.

Wynne, L. C. 1961. The study of intrafamilial alignments and splits in exploratory family therapy. In *Exploring the base for family therapy,* N. W. Ackerman, F. L. Beatman, and S. N. Sherman, eds. New York: Family Services Association.

Wynne, L. C., Ryckoff, I., Day, J., and Hirsch, S. I. 1958. Pseudomutuality in the family relationships of schizophrenics. *Psychiatry. 21:* 205–220.

3

Basic Techniques of Family Therapy

The challenge of describing the basic techniques of family therapy is that there are many ways of doing things. In fact, there are alternative approaches to almost every aspect of treatment, from whom to invite to when and how to terminate. Nevertheless, there are widely shared principles of family therapy, and we offer the following guidelines as a beginning framework for clinical practice.

THE STAGES OF FAMILY THERAPY

The Initial Telephone Call

The goals of the initial contact are to get an overview of the presenting problem and to arrange for the family to come for a consultation. Listen to the caller's description of the problem and identify all members of the household as well as others who might be involved (including the referral source and other agencies). Although the initial phone call should be brief, it's important to establish a connection with the caller as a basis for engagement. Then schedule the first interview, specifying who should attend (usually everyone in the household) and the time and place.

While there are things you can learn to say to encourage the whole family to attend, the most important consideration is attitudinal. First, understand and respect that the worried mother who wants her child to be treated individually or the unhappy husband who wants to talk to you alone has a perfectly legitimate point of view, even if it doesn't happen to coincide with your own. But if you expect to meet with the whole family, at least for an initial assessment, a matter-of-fact statement that that's how you work will get most families to agree to a consultation.

When the caller presents the problem as limited to one person, a useful way to broaden the focus is to ask how the problem is affecting other members of the family. If the caller balks at the idea of bringing in the family or says that a particular member won't attend, say that you'll need to hear from everyone, at least initially, in order to get as much information as possible. Most people accept the need to give their points of view; what they resist is the implication that they're to blame.[1]

---

[1]Not all therapists routinely meet with the entire family. Some find they have more room to maneuver by meeting first with individuals or subgroups and then gradually involving others. Others attempt to work with the *problem-determined system*, only those people directly involved. If a therapist suspects violence or abuse, individual sessions may enable family members to reveal what they might not discuss in front of the whole family. The point to remember is that family therapy is more a way of looking at things than a technique based on always seeing the whole family together.

Finally, because most families are reluctant to sit down and face their conflicts, a reminder call before the first session will help cut down on the no-show rate.

The First Interview

The goal of the first interview is to build an alliance with the family and develop a hypothesis about what's maintaining the presenting problem. It's a good idea to come up with a tentative hypothesis (in technical terms, a "hunch") after the initial phone call and then test it in the first interview. The point isn't to jump to conclusions but to start actively thinking. In addition to developing a hypothesis about what may be constraining a family from solving their problems, it's also important to think about what things family members are already doing, or have done in the past, that support them in moving forward in their lives.

The primary objectives of a consultation are to establish rapport and to gather information. Introduce yourself to the contact person and then to the other adults. Ask parents to introduce their children. Shake hands with everyone. Orient the family to the room (observation mirrors, videotaping, toys for children) and to the format of the session (length and purpose). Repeat briefly what the caller told you over the phone (so as not to leave others wondering) and then ask for elaboration. Once you've acknowledged that person's point of view ("So what you're saying is . . . ?"), ask the other members of the family for their viewpoints.

One of the things beginning therapists worry about is that bringing in the whole family may lead to a shouting match that will escalate out of control. The antidote to arguing is insisting that family members speak one at a time. Giving everyone a chance to talk and be heard is a good idea in every case; with emotionally reactive families, it's imperative.

Most families are anxious and uncertain about therapy. They're not sure what to expect, and they may be uncomfortable discussing their concerns with the entire family present. Above all, most people are afraid that someone is going to blame them or expect them to change in ways they aren't

prepared to. For these reasons, it's important to establish a bond of sympathy and understanding with every member of the family.

A useful question to ask each person is, "How did *you* feel about coming in?" This helps establish the therapist as someone willing to listen. If, for example, a child says "I didn't want to come" or "I think it's stupid," you can say "Thanks for being honest."

In gathering information, some therapists find it useful to take a family history and many use a **genogram** to diagram the extended family network (see Chapter 5). Others believe that whatever history is essential will emerge in the natural course of events; they prefer to concentrate on the family's presenting complaint and the circumstances surrounding it.

Family therapists develop hypotheses about how family members might be involved in the presenting problem by asking what they've done to try to solve it and by watching how they interact. Ideas are as important as actions, so it's useful to notice unhelpful explanations as well as unproductive interactions.

Two kinds of information that are particularly important are solutions that don't work and transitions in the life cycle. If whatever the family has been doing to resolve their difficulties hasn't worked, it may be that those attempts are part of the problem. A typical example is overinvolved parents trying to help a shy child make friends by coaxing and criticizing. Sometimes family members will say they've "tried everything." Their mistake is inconsistency. They give up too quickly.

Despite the natural tendency to focus on problems and what causes them, it is a family's strengths, not their weaknesses, that are most important in successful therapy. Therefore, a therapist should search for resilience (Walsh, 1998). What have these people done well? How have they successfully handled problems in the past? Even the most disheartened families have had times when they were successful, although those positive episodes may be obscured by the frustration they feel over their current difficulties.

Although it isn't always apparent (especially to them), most families seek treatment because they have failed to adjust to changing circumstances. If a couple develops problems within a few months after a baby's birth, it may be because they haven't shifted effectively from being a unit of two to a unit of three. A young mother may be depressed because she doesn't have enough support. A young father may be jealous of the attention his wife lavishes on the new baby.

Although the strain of having a new baby may seem obvious, it's amazing how often depressed young mothers are treated as though there were something wrong with them—"unresolved dependency needs," "inability to cope," perhaps, or maybe a Prozac deficiency. The same is true when families develop problems around the time a child enters school or reaches adolescence or any other developmental shift. The transitional demands on the family are obvious, *if* you think about them.

Young therapists may have no experience with some of the challenges their clients are struggling with. This underscores the need for therapists to remain curious and respectful of families' predicaments rather than jumping to conclusions. For example, a young, married therapist couldn't understand why so many clients with young children rarely went out together as a couple. He assumed that they were avoiding being alone together. Once he had small children of his own, he began to wonder how those couples got out at all!

Family therapists explore the **process** of family interaction by asking questions about how family members relate to each other and by inviting them to discuss their problems with one another in the session. The first strategy, asking *process* or *circular* questions, is favored by Bowenians, and the second, inviting them to discuss their problems, by structural therapists. In either case, the question is, What's keeping the family stuck?

Once a therapist has met with a family, learned about the problem that brings them to treatment, made an effort to understand the family's context, and formulated a hypothesis about what needs to be done to resolve the problem, he or she should make a recommendation to the family. This might include consulting another professional (a learning disability expert, a physician, a lawyer) or even suggesting that the family doesn't need—or doesn't seem ready

for—treatment. Most often, however, the recommendation will be for further meetings. Although many therapists try to make recommendations at the end of the first interview, doing so may be hasty. If it takes two or three sessions to form a bond with the family, understand their situation, and determine the feasibility of working with them, then take two or three sessions.

If you think you can help the family with their problems, offer them a **treatment contract.** Acknowledge why they came in, say that it was a good idea, and say that you think you can help. Then establish a meeting time, the frequency and length of sessions, who will attend, the presence of observers or use of videotape, the fee, and how insurance will be handled. Remember that resistance doesn't magically disappear after the first (or fourteenth) session, so stress the importance of keeping appointments, the need for everyone to attend, and your willingness to hear about dissatisfactions with the therapy. Finally, don't forget to emphasize the family's goals and the strengths they have demonstrated to meet them.

First-Session Checklist

1. Make contact with each member of the family, and acknowledge his or her point of view about the problem and feelings about coming to therapy.
2. Establish leadership by controlling the structure and pace of the interview.
3. Develop a working alliance with the family by balancing warmth and professionalism.
4. Compliment clients on positive actions and family strengths.
5. Maintain empathy with individuals and respect for the family's way of doing things.
6. Focus on specific problems and attempted solutions.
7. Develop hypotheses about unhelpful interactions around the presenting problem. Be curious about why these have persisted. Also notice helpful interactions that can support the family in moving forward.

8. Don't overlook the possible involvement of family members, friends, or helpers who aren't present.
9. Negotiate a treatment contract that acknowledges the family's goals and specifies the therapist's framework for structuring treatment.
10. Invite questions.

The Early Phase of Treatment

The early phase of treatment is devoted to refining the initial hypothesis about what's maintaining the problem and beginning to work on resolving it. Now the strategy shifts from building an alliance to challenging actions and assumptions. Most therapists are able to figure out what needs to change; what sets good therapists apart is their willingness to push for those changes.

"Pushing for change" may suggest a confrontational style. But what's required to help people risk change isn't any one particular way of working; rather, it's a relentless commitment to helping make things better. This commitment is evident in Michael White's dogged questioning of problem-saturated stories, Phil Guerin's calm insistence that family members stop blaming each other and start looking at themselves, and Virginia Goldner's determined insistence that violent men take responsibility for their behavior.

No matter what techniques a therapist uses to push for change, it's important to maintain a therapeutic alliance. Although the term *therapeutic alliance* may sound like jargon, there's nothing abstract about it: It means listening to and acknowledging the client's point of view. It is this empathic understanding that makes family members feel respected—and makes them open to accepting challenges.

Regardless of what model they follow, effective therapists are persistent in their pursuit of change. This doesn't just mean perseverance. It means being willing to intervene, at times energetically. Some therapists prefer to avoid confrontation and find it more effective to use gentle questions or persistent encouragement. But regardless of whether they work directly (and at times use confrontation) or indirectly (and avoid it), good therapists are finishers. Strategies vary, but what sets the best therapists apart is their commitment to doing what it takes to see families through to successful resolution of their problems.

Effective family therapy addresses interpersonal conflict, and the first step is to bring it into the consulting room and locate it between family members. Often this isn't a problem. Couples in conflict or parents arguing with their children will usually speak right up about their disagreements. If a family only came because someone sent them (the court, the school, the Department of Protective Services), begin by addressing the family's problem with these agencies. How must the family change so as to resolve their conflict with these authorities?

When one person is presented as the problem, a therapist challenges **linearity** by asking how others are involved (or affected). What was their role in creating (or managing) the problem? How have they responded to it?

For example, a parent might say, "The problem is Malik. He's disobedient." The therapist might ask, "How does he get away with that?" or "How do you respond when he's disobedient?" A less confrontive therapist might ask, "When do you notice this?" or "What does he do that seems disobedient?" or "How does this disobedience affect you?"

Or perhaps the client says, "It's me. I'm depressed." The therapist might ask, "Who in the family is contributing to your depression?" The response "No one" would bring a follow-up question like, "Then who's helping you with it?"

Challenges can be blunt or gentle, depending on the therapist's style and assessment of the family. The point isn't to switch from blaming one person (a disobedient child, say) to another (a parent who doesn't discipline effectively) but to broaden the problem to an interactional one—to see the problem as shared and comaintained. Maybe Mother is too lenient with Malik because she finds Father too strict. Moreover, she may be overinvested in the boy because of emotional distance in the marriage.

The best way to challenge unhelpful interactions is to point out patterns that seem to be keeping people stuck. A useful formula is "The more you do *X*, the more he does *Y*, and the more you do *Y*, the more she does *X*." (For *X* and *Y*, try substituting *nag* and *withdraw* or *control* and *rebel*.) Incidentally, when you point out what people are doing that isn't working, it's a mistake to tell them what they *should* be doing. Once you shift from pointing out something to giving advice, the clients' attention shifts from their behavior to your advice. Consider this exchange:

> *Therapist:* When you ignore your wife's complaints, she feels hurt and angry. You may have trouble accepting the anger, but she doesn't feel supported.
> *Client:* What should I do?
> *Therapist:* I don't know. Ask your wife.

Even though family therapists sometimes challenge assumptions or actions, they continue to listen to people's feelings. Listening is a silent activity, rare at times, even among therapists. Family members seldom listen to each other for long without becoming defensive. Unfortunately, therapists don't always listen, either—especially when they're eager to jump in with advice. But remember that people aren't likely to reconsider their assumptions until they've been heard and understood.

Homework can be used to test flexibility (simply seeing if it's carried out measures willingness to change), to make family members more aware of their roles in problems (telling people just to notice something, without trying to change it, is often instructive), and to suggest new ways of relating. Typical homework assignments include suggesting that overinvolved parents hire a babysitter and go out together, having argumentative partners take turns talking about their feelings and listening without saying anything (but noticing tendencies to become reactive), and having dependent family members practice spending time alone (or with someone outside the family) and doing more things for themselves. Homework assignments that are likely to generate conflict, such as negotiating house rules with teenagers, should be avoided. Difficult discussions should be saved for when the therapist can act as referee.

Early-Phase Checklist

1. Identify major conflicts and bring them into the consulting room.
2. Develop a hypothesis and refine it into a **formulation** about what the family is doing to perpetuate (or fail to resolve) the presenting problem. Formulations should consider process and structure, family rules, triangles, and boundaries.
3. Keep the focus on primary problems and the interpersonal conditions supporting them. But do not neglect to support constructive interactions.
4. Assign homework that addresses problems and the underlying structure and dynamics perpetuating them.
5. Challenge family members to see their own roles in the problems that trouble them.
6. Push for change, both during the session and between sessions at home.
7. Make use of supervision to test the validity of formulations and effectiveness of interventions.

The Middle Phase of Treatment

When therapy is anything other than brief and problem focused, much of the middle phase is devoted to helping family members deal more constructively with each other in sessions. If a therapist is too active in this process—filtering all conversation through himself or herself—family members won't learn to deal with each other and will continue to manage only as long as they remain in therapy.

For this reason, in the middle phase the therapist should take a less active role and encourage family members to interact more with each other. As they do so, the therapist can step back and observe. When dialogue bogs down, the therapist can either point out what went wrong or simply encourage family members to keep talking—but with less interruption and criticism.

When family members address their conflicts directly, they tend to become reactive. Anxiety is the enemy of listening. Some therapists (Bowenians, for example) attempt to control anxiety by having family members talk only to them. Others prefer to let family members deal with their own anxiety by helping them learn to talk with each other less defensively (by saying how they feel and acknowledging what others say). However, even therapists who work primarily with family dialogue need to interrupt when anxiety escalates and conversations become destructive.

Thus in the middle phase of treatment, the therapist encourages family members to begin to rely on their own resources. The level of anxiety is regulated by alternating between having family members talk with each other and with the therapist. In either case the therapist encourages family members to get beyond blaming to talking directly about what they feel and what they want—and to learn to see their own part in unproductive interactions.

What enables therapists to push for change without provoking resistance is an empathic bond with clients. We mentioned the working alliance in our discussion of the opening session, but it's such an important subject that we would like to reemphasize it. Although there is no formula for developing good relationships with clients, four attitudes are important in maintaining an effective therapeutic alliance: calmness, curiosity, empathy, and respect.

Calmness on the part of the therapist is an essential antidote to the anxiety that keeps families from seeing their dilemmas in a broader perspective. Calmness conveys confidence that problems, however difficult, can be resolved. Curiosity implies that the therapist doesn't know all the answers. The curious therapist says in effect, "I don't fully understand, but I'd like to."

Empathy and respect have been reduced to the status of clichés, but since we think both are essential, let us be clear about what we mean. People resist efforts to change them by therapists they feel don't understand them. That means that a therapist who can't step into his or her clients' shoes and get a sense of what the world looks like to them will find it difficult to make progress. Some therapists are all too ready to say "I understand" when they don't. You can't fake empathy.

Instead of telling an overprotective mother that you understand her worrying about her children, be honest enough to ask, "How did you learn to be a worrier?" or say, "I've never been a single mom. Tell me what it is that scares you."

Finally, respect. What passes for respect in therapists isn't always sincere. Being respectful doesn't mean treating people with kid gloves, nor does it mean accepting their version of events as the only possible way to look at the situation. Respecting clients means treating them as equals, not patronizing them or deferring to them out of the fear of making them angry. Respecting people means believing in their capacity for change.

Middle-Phase Checklist

1. Use intensity to challenge family members, ingenuity to get around resistance, and empathy to get underneath defensiveness.
2. Avoid being so directive that the family members don't learn to improve their own ways of relating to each other.
3. Foster individual responsibility and mutual understanding.
4. Make certain that efforts to improve relationships are having a positive effect on the presenting complaint.
5. When meeting with subgroups, don't lose sight of the whole family picture, and don't neglect any individuals or relationships—especially those contentious ones that are so tempting to avoid.
6. Does the therapist take too active a role in choosing what to talk about? Have the therapist and family developed a social relationship that has become more important than addressing conflicts? Has the therapist assumed a regular role in the family (an empathic listener to the spouses or a firm parent figure to the children), substituting for a missing function in the family? When therapists find themselves drawn to taking an active response to family members' needs, they should ask themselves who in the family should be taking that role, and then encourage that person to do so.

Termination

Termination comes for brief therapists as soon as the presenting problem is resolved. For psychoanalytic therapists, therapy is a long-term learning process and may continue for years. For most therapists, termination comes somewhere between these two extremes and has to do with the family feeling they have achieved what they came for and the therapist's sense that treatment has reached a point of diminishing returns.

In individual therapy, where the relationship to the therapist is often the primary vehicle of change, termination focuses on reviewing the relationship and saying good-bye. In family therapy, the focus is more on what the family has been doing. Termination is therefore a good time to review what they've accomplished.

It can be helpful to ask clients to anticipate upcoming challenges: "How will you know when things are heading backward, and what will you do?" Families can be reminded that their present harmony can't be maintained indefinitely and that people have a tendency to overreact to the first sign of relapse, which can trigger a vicious cycle. To paraphrase Zorba the Greek, life *is* trouble. To be alive is to confront difficulties. The test is how you handle them.

Finally, although in the business of therapy no news is usually good news, it might be a good idea to check in with clients a few weeks after termination to see how they're doing. This can be done with a letter, phone call, or brief follow-up session. A therapeutic relationship is, of necessity, somewhat artificial or at least constrained. But there's no reason to make it less than human—or to forget about families once you've terminated with them.

Termination Checklist

1. Has the presenting problem improved?
2. Is the family satisfied that they have achieved what they came for, or are they interested in continuing to learn about themselves and improve their relationships?
3. Does the family have an understanding of what they were doing that wasn't working and how to avoid the recurrence of similar problems in the future?
4. Do minor recurrences of problems reflect lack of resolution of some underlying dynamic or merely that the family has to readjust to function without the therapist?
5. Have family members developed and improved relationships outside the immediate family context as well as within it?

*F*AMILY ASSESSMENT

The reason we decided to consider assessment after the general guidelines for treatment is that assessment is a complex subject, deserving of more consideration than it usually gets.

The Presenting Problem

Every first session presents the fundamental challenge of being a therapist: A group of unhappy strangers walks in and hands you their most urgent problem—and expects you to solve it.

> "My fifteen-year-old is failing tenth grade. *What should I do?*"
> "We never talk anymore. *What's happened to our marriage?*"
> "It's me. I'm depressed. *Can you help me?*"

There are land mines in these opening presentations: "What should we do?" "What's wrong with Johnny?" These people have been asking themselves these questions for some time, maybe years. And they usually have fixed ideas about the answers, even if they don't always agree. Furthermore, they have typically evolved strategies to deal with their problems, which, even if they haven't worked, they insist on repeating. In this, they are like a car stuck in the mud, with wheels spinning, sinking deeper and deeper into the mire.

The stress of life's troubles makes for anxiety, and anxiety makes for rigid thinking. Thus, families who come for therapy tend to hold tenaciously to their assumptions: "He (or she) is hyperactive, depressed, bipolar, insensitive, selfish, rebellious," or some other negative attribute that resides inside the complicated machinery of the stubborn human psyche. Even when the complaint is phrased in the form of "*We* don't communicate," there's usually an assumption of where the responsibility lies—and that somewhere is usually elsewhere.

Exploring the presenting symptom is the first step in helping families move from a sense of helplessness to an awareness of how, by working together, they can overcome their problems. It may seem obvious that the first consideration should be the presenting complaint. Nevertheless, it's worth emphasizing that inquiry into the presenting problem should be detailed and empathic. The minute some therapists hear that a family's problem is, say, misbehavior or poor communication, they're ready to jump into action. Their training has prepared them to deal with misbehaving children and communication problems, and they know what needs to be done. But before therapists get started, they should realize that they're *not* dealing with misbehaving children or communication problems; rather, they're dealing with a unique instance of one of these difficulties.

In exploring the presenting complaint, the goal for a systemic therapist is to question the family's settled certainty about who has the problem and why. Therefore, the first challenge for a family therapist is to move families from *linear* ("It's Johnny") and *medical model* thinking ("He's hyperactive") to an *interactional* perspective. To initiate this shift, a therapist begins by asking about the presenting problem. But these inquiries are aimed not merely at getting details about the condition-as-described but to open up the family's entrenched beliefs about what is the problem and who has it.

Helpful questions convey respect for family members' feelings but skepticism about accepting the identified patient as the only problem in the family. Helpful questions continue to explore and open things up. Helpful questions invite new ways of seeing the problem, or the family generally. Unhelpful questions accept things as they are described and concentrate only on the identified patient. To be effective in this first stage, a therapist's attitude should be "I don't quite understand, but I'm interested. I'm curious about the particular way you organize your life." A therapist who is too ready to ingratiate himself or herself by saying, "Oh, yes, I understand," will close off exploration.

The next thing to explore is the family's attempts to deal with the problem: What have they tried? What's been helpful? What hasn't been helpful? Has anyone other than those present been involved in trying to help (or hinder) with these difficulties? This exploration opens the door to discovering how family members may be responding in ways that perpetuate the presenting problem. This isn't a matter of shifting blame—say, from a misbehaving child to an indulgent parent.[2] Nor do we mean to suggest that family problems are typically caused by how people treat the identified patient.

In fact, what family therapists call *circular causality* is a misnomer. The shift from linear to circular thinking not only expands the focus from individuals to patterns of interaction but also moves away from cause-and-effect explanations. Instead of joining families in a logical but unproductive search for who started what, circular thinking suggests that problems are sustained by an ongoing series of actions and reactions. Who started it? It rarely matters.

Understanding the Referral Route

It's important for therapists to understand who referred their clients and why. What are their expectations? What expectations have they communicated to the family? It's important to know whether a family's participation is voluntary or coerced, whether all or only some of them recognize the need for treatment, and whether other agencies will have continuing involvement with the case.

---

[2]It's always worth remembering that even actions that perpetuate problems usually have benign intentions. Most of us are doing the best we can.

When therapists make a family referral, they often have a particular agenda in mind.

A college student's counselor once referred him and his family for treatment. The young man had uncovered a repressed memory of sexual abuse and assumed that it must have been committed by his father. The family therapist was somehow supposed to mediate between the young man, who couldn't imagine who else might have been responsible for this vaguely remembered incident, and his parents, who vehemently denied that any such thing had ever happened.

Did the counselor expect confrontation, confession, atonement? Some sort of negotiated agreement? What about the boy himself? It's best to find out.

It's also important to find out if clients have been in treatment elsewhere. If so, what happened? What did they learn about themselves or their family? What expectations or concerns did previous therapy generate? It's even more important to find out if anyone in the family is currently in treatment. Few things are more likely to stall progress than two therapists pulling in different directions.

Identifying the Systemic Context

Regardless of who a therapist elects to work with, it's imperative to have a clear understanding of the interpersonal context of the problem. Who all is in the family? Are there important figures in the life of the problem who aren't present? Perhaps a live-in boyfriend? A grandmother who lives next door? Are other agencies involved? What's the nature of their input? Does the family see them as helpful?

Remember that family therapy is an approach to people in context. The most relevant context may be the immediate family, but families don't exist in a vacuum. It may be important to meet with the teachers and counselors of a child who's having trouble at school. There are even times when the family isn't the most important context. Sometimes, for example, a college student's depression has more to do with what's going on in the classroom or dormitory than with what's happening back home.

Stage of the Life Cycle

Most families come to treatment not because there's something inherently wrong with them but because they've gotten stuck in a life-cycle transition (see Chapter 4). Sometimes this will be apparent. Parents may complain, for example, that they don't know what's gotten into Janey. She used to be such a good girl, but now that she's fourteen, she's become sullen and argumentative. (One reason parenting remains an amateur sport is that just when you think you've got the hang of it, the kids get older and throw you a whole new set of curves.) Adolescence is that stage in the **family life cycle** when young parents have to grow up and relax their grip on their children.

Sometimes it isn't obvious that a family is having trouble adjusting to a new stage in the life cycle. Couples who marry after living together for years may not anticipate how matrimony stirs up unconscious expectations about what it means to be a family. More than one couple has been surprised to discover a sharp falling off in their sex life after tying the knot. At other times significant life-cycle changes occur in the grandparents' generation, and you won't always learn of these influences unless you ask.

Always consider life-cycle issues in formulating a case. One of the best questions a therapist can ask is, Why now?

Family Structure

The simplest systemic context for a problem is an interaction between two parties. She nags and he withdraws. Parental control provokes adolescent rebellion, and vice versa. But sometimes a dyadic perspective doesn't take in the whole picture.

Family problems become entrenched because they're embedded in powerful but unseen structures.

Regardless of what approach a therapist takes, it's wise to understand the family's **structure.** What are the **subsystems** and the nature of the **boundaries** between them? What is the status of the boundary around the couple or the family? What **triangles** are present? Are individuals and subsystems protected by boundaries that allow them to operate without undue interference—but with access to support?

In enmeshed families, parents may intrude into sibling conflicts so regularly that brothers and sisters never learn to settle their own differences. In disengaged families, parents may not only refrain from interrupting sibling quarrels but also fail to offer sympathy and support for children who feel bad about a sibling's treatment.

Here, too, there is a temporal dimension. If a wife goes back to work after years of staying home with the children, the parental subsystem is challenged to shift from a complementary to a symmetrical form. Whether or not family members complain directly about these strains, they're likely to be relevant.

Communication

Although some couples come to therapy saying they have "communication problems" (usually meaning that one person won't do what the other one wants), working on communication has become a cliché in family therapy. But because communication is the vehicle of relationship, all therapists deal with it.

Although conflict doesn't magically disappear when family members start to listen to each other, it's unlikely that conflict will get solved *before* they start to listen to each other (Nichols, 2009). If, after a session or two (and the therapist's encouragement), family members still seem unable to listen to each other, talk therapy will likely be an uphill battle.

Family members who learn to listen to each other with understanding often discover that they don't need to change each other (Jacobson & Christensen, 1996). Many problems can be solved, but the problem of living with other people who don't always see things the way you do isn't one of them.

Drug and Alcohol Abuse

The most common mistake novice therapists make regarding substance abuse is to overlook it. Substance abuse is especially common with people who are depressed or anxious. It's also associated with violence, abuse, and accidents. Although it may not be necessary to ask every client about drug and alcohol consumption, it's critical to inquire carefully if there is any suspicion that this may be a problem. Don't be too polite. Ask straightforward and specific questions. Questions that may help to uncover problem drinking (Kitchens, 1994) include the following:

- Do you feel you are a normal drinker?
- How many drinks a day do you have?
- How often do you have six or more drinks?
- Have you ever awakened after a bout of drinking and been unable to remember part of the evening before?
- Does anyone in your family worry or complain about your drinking?
- Can you stop easily after one or two drinks? Do you?
- Has drinking ever created problems between you and your partner?
- Have you ever been in trouble at work because of your drinking?
- Do you ever drink before noon?

These same questions can be asked about substances other than alcohol. If a member of a family who's seeking couples or family therapy is abusing drugs or alcohol, talk therapy will not likely be the answer to the family's problems.

Domestic Violence and Sexual Abuse

If there is any hint of domestic violence or sexual abuse, the therapist should look into it. The process of questioning can start with the family present, but when there is a suspicion of abuse or neglect, it may be wise to meet with family members individually to allow them to talk more openly.

Most states require professionals to report any suspicion of child abuse. Reporting suspected abuse can jeopardize a therapeutic alliance, but sometimes therapy needs to take second place to the interests of safety. Any clinician who considers not reporting suspected child abuse should consider the possible consequences of making a mistake.

Perpetrators and victims of childhood sexual maltreatment don't usually volunteer this information. Detection is up to the therapist, who may have to rely on indirect clues. Further exploration may be indicated if a child shows any of the following symptoms: sleep disturbance, encopresis or enuresis, abdominal pain, an exaggerated startle response, appetite disturbance, sudden unexplained changes in behavior, overly sexualized behavior, regressive behavior, suicidal thoughts, or running away (Edwards & Gil, 1986).

Extramarital Involvements

The discovery of an extramarital affair is a crisis that will strike many couples sometime in their relationship. Infidelity is common, but it's still a crisis and can destroy a marriage.

Extramarital involvements that don't involve sexual intimacy, although less obvious, can sabotage treatment if one or both partners regularly turn to third parties to deal with issues that should be worked out together. (One clue that an outside relationship is part of a triangle is that it isn't talked about.) Would-be helpful third parties may include family members, friends, and therapists.

A couple once came to therapy complaining that the intimacy had gone out of their relationship. It wasn't so much a matter of conflict; they just never seemed to spend any time together. After a few weeks of slow progress, the wife revealed that she'd been seeing an individual therapist. When the couples therapist asked why, she replied that she needed someone to talk to. When he asked why she hadn't told him, she said, "You didn't ask."

Gender Issues

Gender inequalities contribute to family problems in a variety of ways. A wife's dissatisfaction may have deeper roots than the family's current problems. A husband's reluctance to become more involved in the family may be as much a product of cultural expectations as a flaw in his personality.

Every therapist must work out individually how to avoid the extremes of naively ignoring gender inequality or imposing his or her personal point of view on clients. One way to strike a balance is to raise questions but allow clients to find their own answers. You can raise moral questions without being moralistic. It is, however, not reasonable to assume that both partners enter marriage with equal power or that complementarity between spouses is the only dynamic operating in their relationship.

Conflict over gender expectations, whether discussed openly or not, is especially common given the enormous shifts in cultural expectations over recent decades. Is it still considered a woman's duty to follow her husband's career, moving whenever necessary for his advancement? Is it still true that women should be strong, self-supporting, and the primary (which often turns out to be a euphemism for *only*) caregivers for infants and young children?

Regardless of the therapist's values, do the gender roles established in a couple seem to work for them? Or do unresolved differences, conflict, or confusion appear to be sources of stress? Perhaps the single most useful question to ask about gender equality is, How does each of the partners experience the fairness of give-and-take in their relationship?

It's not uncommon for differences in gender socialization to contribute to conflict in couples (Patterson, Williams, Grauf-Grounds, & Chamow, 1998), as the following example illustrates.

Case Study

Kevin complained that Courtney was always checking up on him, which made him feel that she didn't trust him. Courtney insisted that she asked about what Kevin was doing only in order to be part of his life. She expected the same interest in her life from him. She wasn't checking up on him; she just wanted them to share things.

When Courtney asked Kevin too many questions, he got angry and withdrew, which made her feel shut out. Happy not to be interrogated any further, Kevin didn't notice how hurt and angry Courtney was until finally she exploded in tearful recrimination. Kevin felt helpless in the face of Courtney's crying, and so he did his best to placate her. When he reassured her that he loved her and promised to tell her more about what was going on in his life, she calmed down and peace was restored. Until the next time.

For couples like Courtney and Kevin, gender socialization contributes to the pursuer–distancer dynamic. Men are typically socialized to value independence and to resist anything they see as an effort to control them. Thus, Kevin interpreted Courtney's questions about his activities as attempts to restrict his freedom. Courtney, on the other hand, was socialized to value caring and connection. Naturally, she wanted to know what was going on in Kevin's life. She couldn't understand why he got so defensive about her wanting them to check in with each other.

While it's a mistake to ignore gender socialization in favor of family dynamics, it's also a mistake to assume that gender socialization isn't influenced by family dynamics. In the preceding example, the enmeshed family that Courtney grew up in reinforced the notion that family members should share everything and that having independent activities was disloyal. Kevin's reluctance to tell his wife everything he was doing resulted partly from his coming from a family with two bossy and controlling parents.

Cultural Factors

In assessing families for treatment, therapists should consider the unique subculture of a family (McGoldrick, Pearce, & Giordano, 2005) as well as how unquestioned assumptions from the larger culture may affect a family's problems (Doherty, 1991). In working with minority families, it may be more important for therapists to develop *cultural sensitivity* than to actually share the same background as their clients. Families may come to trust a therapist who has taken the time to learn about their particular culture as much as one who happens to be of the same race or nationality.

One way to develop cultural sensitivity is to make connections after working hours. For example, a white therapist could attend an African American church service in the community where his or her clients live, go to a Latino dance, or visit an Asian community center. Doing these things won't make you an expert, but it may demonstrate to client families that you care enough to respect their ways. It's also important to take a *one-down position* in regard to cultural and ethnic diversity—that is, to ask your clients to teach you about their experience and traditions, rather than play the role of expert.

The challenge for the practitioner is twofold: learning to respect diversity and developing sensitivity to some of the issues faced by members of other cultures. Numerous books are available that describe the characteristics and values of various racial and ethnic groups, many of which are listed in the section on multiculturalism in Chapter 11. In addition to these academic books, novels such as *Love in the Time of Cholera, Beloved, The Scent of Green Papaya, The Mambo Kings Play Songs of Love, The Joy Luck Club*, and so on often bring other cultures vividly to life.

In working with clients from other cultures, it's more important to be respectful of differences and curious about other ways of doing things than to attempt to become an expert on ethnicity. However, while it's important to respect other people's differences, it can be a problem to accept uncritically statements to the effect that "We do these (counterproductive) things because of our culture." Unfortunately, it's difficult for a therapist from another culture to assess the validity of such claims. Perhaps the best advice is to be curious. Stay open minded, but ask questions.

7HE ETHICAL DIMENSION

Most therapists are aware of the ethical responsibilities of their profession:

- Therapy should be for the client's benefit, not to work out unresolved issues for the therapist.
- Clients are entitled to confidentiality, and so limits on privacy imposed by requirements to report to probation officers, parents, and managed care companies should be made clear from the outset.
- Therapists should avoid exploiting the trust of their clients (and students) and therefore must make every effort to avoid dual relationships.
- Professionals are obligated to provide the best possible treatment; if they aren't qualified by training or experience to meet the needs of a particular client, they should refer the case to someone who is.

Whenever there is any question or doubt regarding ethical issues, it's a good idea to consult with a colleague or supervisor.

A good place to start understanding the ethical responsibilities of clinical practice is by studying the guidelines of your profession. The *Ethics Code of the American Psychological Association* (APA), for example, outlines these principles:

- Psychologists offer services only within the areas of their competence, based on education, training, supervision, or professional experience.
- Where there is evidence that an understanding of age, gender, race, ethnicity, culture, national origin, religion, sexual orientation, disability, language, or socioeconomic status is essential for effective implementation of services, psychologists have or seek out training and supervision in these areas—or they make appropriate referrals.
- When psychologists become aware of personal problems that might interfere with their professional duties, they take appropriate

measures, such as obtaining professional assistance and determining whether they should limit, suspend, or terminate their work-related duties.

The *Code of Ethics for the National Association of Social Workers* (NASW) mandates the following:

- Social workers should not engage in dual relationships with clients or former clients.
- Social workers should not solicit private information from clients unless it is essential to providing services.
- Social workers should not disclose confidential information to third-party payers unless clients have authorized such disclosure.
- Social workers should terminate services to clients when such services are no longer required.

While some of these principles may seem obvious, they provide fairly strict guidelines within which practitioners should operate. When it comes to working with couples and families, however, complications arise that create a host of unique ethical dilemmas. When, for example, should a family therapist share with parents information learned in sessions with a child? If a twelve-year-old starts drinking, should the therapist tell the parents?

Recently, professional codes of conduct have added guidelines to address issues involved in treating couples and families. For example, the APA specifies that when a psychologist provides services to several people in a relationship (such as spouses or parents and children), he or she must clarify at the start which individuals are clients and what relationship he or she will have with each one. Moreover, if the psychologist may be called on to perform potentially conflicting roles (such as family therapist and then witness for one party in divorce proceedings), he or she must attempt to clarify and change or withdraw from the roles as appropriate.

The NASW states that when a social worker provides services to a couple or family members, he or she should clarify with all parties what professional obligations he or she has to the various individuals receiving services. Also, when a social worker provides counseling to families, he or she should ask all parties to agree to each individual's right to confidentiality.

The American Association for Marriage and Family Therapy (AAMFT, 1991) publishes its own code of ethics, which covers many of the same issues as the codes of the APA and NASW. The AAMFT, however, directly addresses complications with respect to confidentiality when a therapist sees more than one person in a family. Without a written waiver, a family therapist should not disclose information received from any family member, even to other family members, presumably. As with many things, however, it may be easier to expound ethical principles in the classroom than to apply them in the crucible of clinical practice.

It's clear that therapists must protect their clients' right to confidentiality. But what if a woman reveals that she's having an extramarital affair and isn't sure whether to end it? When she goes on to say that her marriage has been stale for years, the therapist recommends a course of couples therapy to see if the marriage can be improved. The woman agrees. But when the therapist then suggests that she either break off the affair or tell husband about it, the woman adamantly refuses. What should the therapist do?

One way to resolve ambiguous ethical dilemmas is to use your own best judgment. In the case of the woman who wanted to work on her marriage but wasn't willing to end her affair or inform her husband, a therapist might decline to offer therapy under circumstances that would make it unlikely to be effective. In that case, the therapist would be obligated to refer the client to another therapist.

Subprinciple 1.6 of the *AAMFT Code of Ethical Principles* states the following:

Marriage and family therapists assist persons in obtaining other therapeutic services if a marriage and

family therapist is unable or unwilling, for appropriate reasons, to see a person who has requested professional help.

And Subprinciple 1.7 makes this statement:

Marriage and family therapists do not abandon or neglect clients in treatment without making reasonable arrangements for the continuation of such treatment.

Given the same set of circumstances, another therapist might decide that treating the couple even though the woman refused to end her affair might make it possible for the woman to break off the affair later or to talk to her husband about it. In this scenario the therapist would be bound by the principle of confidentiality not to reveal what the woman discussed in private.

While the outlines of ethical professional conduct are clear, the pressures on practitioners are often powerful and subtle. When dealing with clients who are having an affair or considering divorce (or marriage, for that matter), therapists may be influenced by their own unconscious attitudes as well as the clients' projections. What would you assume, for example, about a therapist whose depressed, married clients all tended to get divorced after their individual therapy? What might you speculate about the level of satisfaction in that therapist's own marriage?

Trusting your own judgment in an ambiguous ethical situation risks imposing your own values on what should be a professional decision. The principles of sound ethical practice are wider, and may be stricter, than most people's private morality and good intentions. When in doubt, clinicians should ask themselves two questions. First, What would happen if the client or important others found out about my actions? Thus, for example, strategically telling two siblings, each in a separate conversation, that only he or she is mature enough to end the fighting between them violates the "what if?" principle, because it's entirely possible that one or both siblings might brag to the other about what the therapist said. (Trust me!)

The second question is, Can you talk to someone you respect about what you're doing (or considering)? If you're afraid to discuss with a supervisor or colleague that you are treating two married couples in which the wife of one is having an affair with the husband of the other or that you're considering lending a client money, you may be guilty of the arrogance of assuming that you are above the rules that govern your profession. Feeling compelled to keep something secret suggests that it may be wrong. The road to hell is paved with the assumption that this situation is special, this client is special, or that you are special.

The following red flags should signal potential unethical practices:

Specialness—believing that something about the situation is special and that the ordinary rules don't apply

Attraction—feeling intense attraction of any kind, not only romantic but also being impressed with the status of the client

Alterations in the therapeutic frame—having longer or more frequent sessions, engaging in excessive self-disclosure, being unable to say no to the client, and other things that signal a potential violation of professional boundaries

Violating clinical norms—not referring someone in a troubled marriage for couples therapy, accepting personal counseling from a supervisor, and so on

Professional isolation—not being willing to discuss your decisions with professional colleagues

$\mathcal{F}$AMILY THERAPY WITH SPECIFIC PRESENTING PROBLEMS

Once, most family therapists assumed their approach could be applied to almost any problem. Today, it has become increasingly common to develop specific techniques for particular populations and problems.

The following sections address special treatment approaches for two frequently encountered clinical problems: marital violence and sexual abuse of children. While we hope these suggestions will provide some ideas for dealing with these difficult situations, remember that responsible therapists recognize the limits of their expertise and refer cases they aren't equipped to handle to more experienced practitioners.

Marital Violence

The question of how to treat marital violence polarizes the field like no other. The prevailing paradigm is to separate couples, assigning the offender to an anger management program and treating his partner in a battered women's group (Edleson & Tolman, 1992; Gondolf, 1995). Traditional couples therapy is seen as dangerous because placing a violent man and his abused partner in close quarters and inviting them to address contentious issues puts the woman in danger and provides the offender with a platform for self-justification (Bograd, 1992; Hansen, 1993). Treating the partners together also implies that they share responsibility for the violence and confers a sense of legitimacy on a relationship that may be malignant.

The argument for seeing violent couples together is that violence is the outcome of mutual provocation—an escalation, albeit unacceptable, of the emotionally destructive behavior that characterizes many relationships (Goldner, 1992; Minuchin & Nichols, 1993). When couples are treated together, violent men can learn to recognize the emotional triggers that set them off and to take responsibility for controlling their actions. Their partners can learn to recognize the same danger signals and to take responsibility for ensuring their own safety.

Because few systemic therapists advocate treating couples together when the violence has gone beyond pushing and shoving, some of the debate between advocates of a systemic versus an offender-and-victim model is between apples and oranges. Michael Johnson (1995) argues that there are two types of partner violence in families. The first is *patriarchal terrorism,* which is part of a pattern in which violence is used to exercise control over the partner. Patriarchal terrorism is frequent and severe and tends to escalate over time. The second type is *common couple violence,* which doesn't involve a pattern of power and control. This violence erupts as a response to a particular conflict, is more likely to be mutual, tends to occur infrequently, and tends not to escalate. Nevertheless, many feminist thinkers remain opposed to couples therapy when any form of violence is present (Avis, 1992; Bograd, 1984).

In the absence of empirical evidence showing gender-specific group treatment to be safer or more effective than couples therapy (Brown & O'Leary, 1995; Feldman & Ridley, 1995), clinicians remain split into two camps when it comes to the treatment of marital violence. Rather than choose between attempting to resolve the relationship issues that lead to violence or concentrating on providing safety and protection for the victims, it's possible to combine elements of both approaches—not, however, by doing traditional couples therapy.[3]

In working with violent couples, there must be no compromise on the issue of safety. However, this doesn't have to mean choosing between therapeutic neutrality (and focusing on relationship issues) or advocating on behalf of the victim (and focusing on safety). It's possible to pursue both agendas. Relationship issues can be construed as mutual, but the perpetrator must be held responsible for the crime of violence. As Pamela Anderson said when her husband Tommy Lee was arrested for domestic battery, "It takes two people to start an argument; but it only takes one to break the other one's nose."

In the initial consultation with couples in which there is a suspicion of violence, it's useful to meet with the partners together and then separately. Seeing the couple together permits you to see them in action, while speaking with the woman privately allows you to inquire whether she has left out information about the level of violence or other forms of intimidation to which she has been subjected.

Violent men and battered women trigger strong reactions in anyone who tries to help them. When such couples seek therapy, they are often polarized between love and hate, blaming and feeling ashamed, wanting to escape and remaining obsessed with each other. Thus, it's not surprising that professional helpers tend to react in extremes: siding with one against the other, refusing ever to take sides, exaggerating or minimizing danger, treating the partners like children or like monsters—in other words, splitting into good and bad, just like the dynamics of the couples themselves. In order to form an alliance with both partners, it's important to convey respect for them as persons, even if you can't condone all of their actions.

To assess the level of violence, it's important to ask direct questions: How often do conflicts between the two of you end in some kind of violence? When did this happen most recently? What's the worst thing that's ever happened? It's important to find out if any incidents have resulted in injuries, if weapons have been used, and if the woman is currently afraid.

In addition to assessing the level of violence, a therapist must also evaluate the partners' ability to work constructively in therapy. Is the man willing to accept responsibility for his behavior? Is he argumentative or defensive toward his partner? Toward the therapist? Is the woman willing to take responsibility for her own protection, making her physical safety the first priority? Is the couple able to talk together and take turns, or are they so emotionally reactive that the therapist must constantly interrupt to control them?

If a therapist decides to treat the couple together, it's essential to establish zero tolerance for violence. One way of doing this is to make therapy contingent on no further episodes of physical aggression. Virginia Goldner and Gillian Walker (Goldner, 1998) define the first couple of sessions as a consultation to determine whether it's possible to create a "therapeutic safety zone," where issues can be confronted without putting the woman in harm's way. They use these initial sessions to focus on the risk of violence and the question of safety, reserving the right to terminate the consultation and propose other treatment alternatives if they feel the case is too dangerous for couples therapy.

---

[3]The following guidelines draw on the work of Virginia Goldner and Gillian Walker, codirectors of the Gender and Violence Project at the Ackerman Institute.

With most couples it's useful to encourage dialogue as a way of exploring how the partners communicate. But violent couples tend to be emotionally reactive, and when that's the case, it's better to have them take turns talking to the therapist.

One of the best antidotes to emotionality is to ask for specific, concrete details. A good place to start is with the most recent violent incident. Ask each partner for a detailed, moment-to-moment description of exactly what happened. Be alert for linguistic evasions. A violent man may describe his actions as the result of his partner's "provocation" or of "built-up pressures." Thus, it's not he who hits his wife; it's the pressures that are the culprit. A more subtle form of evasion is for the violent partner to describe the problem as his impulsivity. When arguments escalate, he starts to "lose it." In this formulation, the man's impulsive actions are not a choice he makes but an unavoidable consequence of emotions welling up inside him.

To this kind of evasion, a therapist might respond, "When you say you start to 'lose it,' let's think about what you mean. What happened inside of you at that moment that you felt justified in breaking your promise never to hit her again?" The therapeutic task is to hold the man accountable for his violence, while also trying to understand him in complex and sympathetic terms. This double agenda is in contrast to either a shaming approach, which only exacerbates the man's rage, or trying to understand the couple's dynamics, without also holding the man responsible for his actions.

Once both partners have begun to own responsibility for their actions—he for choosing to control his violent impulses, she for taking steps to ensure her safety—it becomes possible to explore the relationship issues that lead to escalating emotional reactivity (Holtzworth-Munroe, Meehan, Rehman, & Marshall, 2002). This does *not* mean, however, that at a certain point violent couples can be treated just like any other couple. Exploring the interactional processes that both partners participate in should never be allowed to imply that both are equally *responsible* for acts of violence.

When the couple is ready to explore relationship issues, it should be possible to encourage dialogue, so that the therapist and couple can understand what transpires when they try to talk with each other. This brings the relationship into the consulting room. It's one thing to tell a man that he should leave before he gets too angry. It's another thing to actually observe the beginnings of emotional escalation and ask him if he's aware that he's started to get upset and interrupt his partner. It then becomes possible to say, "*This* is the moment when you should leave." At this same point, his partner can be asked if she has begun to feel the first signs of tension and fear.

Taking time-out is an almost universally employed strategy in marital violence programs. Recognizing the cues of escalating anger (racing heart, growing agitation, standing up, pacing) and removing oneself from the situation before violence occurs is encouraged as a way to head off destructive actions that the partners will later regret. Saying "I'm feeling angry (or scared), and I'm going to take a time-out" helps distinguish this safety device from simply refusing to talk. Each person must be responsible for his or her own time-outs. Telling the other person to take a time-out is not allowed, nor is trying to stop the other from leaving.

Although eliminating escalating aggressive interactions must be the first priority, couples should also learn more constructive methods of addressing their differences. Here, there is a paradox: Violent men must learn to control their behavior, but it is counterproductive to stifle their complaints. In fact, it is precisely this kind of suppression that leads to the emotional buildups that result in violent explosions. Moreover, a man who resorts to violence with his partner is usually a weak man—weak in the sense of not knowing how to articulate his feelings in a way that his partner can hear. Thus, in helping couples learn to negotiate their differences, it is essential to ensure that both partners learn to speak up and to listen to each other.

Sexual Abuse of Children

When treating a family in which a child has been sexually abused, the primary goals are (1) ensuring that the abuse doesn't recur and (2) reducing the long-term effects of the trauma (Trepper & Barrett, 1989). As with marital violence, treatment of sexual abuse tends to involve one of two approaches: a *child protective approach,* which can undermine the integrity of the family, or a *family systems approach,* which can fail to protect the child. We recommend supporting the family while at the same time protecting the child. When these goals seem incompatible—for example, when a father has raped his daughter—protecting the child should take precedence.

Assessment of sexual abuse is often complicated by divergent stories about what happened (Herman, 1992). A father may say that touching his daughter's labia was accidental, whereas the daughter may report that this has happened repeatedly. A grandfather may claim that his caressing of his grandson is perfectly innocent, while the child experiences it as abusive. A child protective worker may believe that a mother is tacitly supporting her husband's abuse of her child, while a family therapist may see a woman who is doing her best to save her marriage. Such discrepancies must be resolved by social and legal agencies.

The first priority is restricting unsupervised access to children for the offender. Next a careful assessment should be made to uncover other possible incidents of abuse or patterns of inappropriate sexual expression (Furniss, 1991). The offender must take responsibility for his behavior and receive appropriate treatment for his actions (which may include legal punishment). Often these measures will have already been taken by a child protective agency before the family is referred for therapy.

One of the goals of therapy should be to establish a support system to break through the isolation that facilitates abuse and inhibits disclosure. For this reason, many programs favor a multimodal approach that includes individual, group, and family sessions (Bentovim, Elton, Hildebrand, Tranter, & Vizard, 1988; Trepper & Barrett, 1989). Family sessions should be geared toward increasing support for the victimized child, which may entail strengthening the parental unit.

When a child is the victim of sexual abuse, social control agents may have to step in to protect the child, which can involve taking over what might be considered parental responsibilities. In the long run, however, it is the family who will be responsible for the child. Therefore, supporting the parents in developing appropriate ways of carrying out their responsibilities, rather than taking over for them, is usually in the best interests of the child.

In cases where a father or stepfather is sent to jail for sexual crimes against his children, part of a therapist's job is to help the family draw a boundary that excludes the offender. The same is true if the children are taken out of the home and sent to live with relatives or foster parents. Subsequently, however, if reunion is planned, therapy will involve gradually reopening this boundary through visits and phone calls, which gives the family and therapist the opportunity to work together to improve the family's functioning.

One of the keys to helping resolve the trauma of abuse is to give the child a safe forum to explore his or her complex and often ambivalent feelings about what happened. In addition to feeling violated and angry, the child may feel guilty about having gotten an adult in trouble. Often a child will secretly blame the other parent, usually the mother, for not preventing the abuse. And finally, the child may fear that his or her mother's dependence on the abuser might result in his return, leaving the child again vulnerable to abuse.

A combination of individual and conjoint sessions helps make it safe to talk about feelings. Meeting first with the nonoffending parent (or parents) allows the mother (or parents) to describe what happened and to express feelings about the abuse without having to edit what she says because the child is present.[4] Among the mother's complex feelings will

---

[4]For the sake of simplicity, the following discussion will assume the common instance of a stepfather as abuser and a mother and her abused daughter as clients.

surely be rage and a sense of betrayal. But a part of her may still love the abuser and miss him if he's been incarcerated. She may also feel guilty for not having protected her child. It's important to make it safe for her to share all of these feelings.

When first meeting with the mother and abused daughter, it's reassuring to say that although they will probably eventually want to talk about the abuse, it's up to them to choose where to start. It's also helpful to give parents and children the choice of how much to talk about the abuse and whether to do so first in an individual session or conjointly. If children opt to discuss their feelings privately, they should be reassured that it's up to them to decide what they subsequently want to share with their parents.

When meeting with abused children, it's helpful to explain that the more they talk about what happened, the less troubling their feelings are likely to be. However, it's essential to let them decide when and how much to open up. Abused children need to recover a sense of control over their lives (Sheinberg, True, & Fraenkel, 1994).

When family members talk about their feelings, it's wise to keep in mind that feelings don't come in either/or categories. One way to help make it safe for them to talk about complex or even contradictory emotions is to use the metaphor of parts of the self (Schwartz, 1995). Thus, an abused child might be asked, "Does part of you think your mother should have figured out what was happening?" Likewise, the mother might be asked, "Does part of you miss him?"

One problem with meeting privately with a child is that doing so creates secrets. At the end of such sessions, it's helpful to ask the child what she wants to share with her family and how she wants to do it. Some children ask the therapist to take the lead in opening up some of what they want their mothers to understand but find it hard to talk about. Finally, although it's important to help children voice any thoughts they may have about feeling guilty for what happened, after exploring these feelings, abused children need to hear over and over that what happened was not their fault.

Questions to Consider

1. What are the pros and cons of meeting with less than the whole family for an initial consultation?

2. Which of the suggestions in this chapter for practicing family therapy do you disagree with? Why?

3. In clinics where you have worked or observed, what practices seem to unnecessarily violate clients' confidentiality?

4. Should a therapist keep the confidences of a thirteen-year-old child from his or her parents? Why or why not?

Key Concepts

boundaries   Emotional barriers that protect and enhance the integrity of individuals, subsystems, and families.

family life cycle   Stages in a family's life—from separating from parents through getting married, having children, retiring, and so on—that generally require modifications in the family's structure.

formulation   A therapeutic hypothesis about what is responsible for creating and maintaining a client's presenting problem.

genogram   A schematic diagram of a family system that uses squares for representing males, circles for females, horizontal lines for marriages, and vertical lines for children.

linearity   The notion that one event is a cause and the other is its effect; in behavior, the idea that one behavior is a stimulus and the other a response. Linear thinking is the opposite of circular thinking, in which events are thought to be related in a series of interacting loops.

process How members of a family or group relate; in contrast to content, which is what they talk about.

structure Recurrent patterns of interaction that define and stabilize the shape of a relationship.

subsystems Smaller units in families, determined by generation, gender, or function.

treatment contract An explicit agreement between the client(s) and therapist that specifies the terms of therapy, including things such as frequency and length of sessions, who is to attend, and fees.

triangle A three-person system; according to Bowen, the smallest stable unit of human relations.

Recommended Readings

Anderson, C., and Stewart, S. 1983. *Mastering resistance: A practical guide to family therapy.* New York: Guilford Press.

Madsen, W. C. 2007. *Collaborative therapy with multistressed families,* 2nd ed. New York: Guilford Press.

Minuchin, S., and Fishman, H. C. 1981. *Family therapy techniques.* Cambridge, MA: Harvard University Press.

Minuchin, S., Nichols, M. P., and Lee, W-Y. 2006. *Assessing families and couples: From symptom to system.* Boston: Allyn & Bacon.

Nichols, M. P. 2009. *The lost art of listening,* 2nd ed. New York: Guilford Press.

Patterson, J. E., Williams, L., Grauf-Grounds, C., and Chamow, L. 1998. *Essential skills in family therapy.* New York: Guilford Press.

Taibbi, R. 1996. *Doing family therapy: Craft and creativity in clinical practice.* New York: Guilford Press.

References

American Association for Marriage and Family Therapy. *1991 AAMFT code of ethics.* Washington, DC: Author.

Avis, J. M. 1992. Where are all the family therapists? Abuse and violence within families and family therapy's response. *Journal of Marital and Family Therapy. 18:* 223–233.

Bentovim, A., Elton, A., Hildebrand, J., Tranter, M., and Vizard, E., eds. 1988. *Child sexual abuse within the family.* London: Wright.

Bograd, M. 1984. Family systems approaches to wife battering: A feminist critique. *American Journal of Orthopsychiatry. 54:* 558–568.

Bograd, M. 1992. Values in conflict: Challenges to family therapists' thinking. *Journal of Marital and Family Therapy. 18:* 243–257.

Brown, P. D., and O'Leary, K. D. 1995. *Marital treatment for wife abuse: A review and evaluation.* Paper presented at the Fourth International Family Violence Research Conference, Durham, NC.

Doherty, W. 1991. Family therapy goes postmodern. *Family Therapy Networker. 15*(5): 36–42.

Edelson, E., and Tolman, R. 1992. *Intervention for men who batter.* Newbury Park, CA: Sage Publications.

Edwards, D. L., and Gil, E. 1986. *Breaking the cycle: Assessment and treatment of child abuse and neglect.* Los Angeles: Association for Advanced Training in Behavioral Science.

Feldman, C. M., and Ridley, C. A. 1995. The etiology and treatment of domestic violence between adult partners. *Clinical Psychology: Science and Practice. 2:* 317–348.

Furniss, T. 1991. *The multiprofessional handbook of child sexual abuse: Integrated management, therapy, and legal intervention.* London: Routledge.

Goldner, V. 1992. Making room for both/and. *Family Therapy Networker. 16*(2): 55–61.

Goldner, V. 1998. The treatment of violence and victimization in intimate relationships. *Family Process. 37:* 263–286.

Gondolf, E. W. 1995. Gains and process in state batterer programs and standards. *Family Violence and Sexual Assault Bulletin. 11:* 27–28.

Hansen, M. 1993. Feminism and family therapy: A review of feminist critiques of approaches to family violence (pp. 69–82). In *Battering and family therapy: A feminist perspective,* M. Hansen and M. Harway, eds. Newbury Park, CA: Sage Publications.

Herman, J. L. 1992. *Trauma and recovery.* New York: Basic Books.

Holtzworth-Munroe, A., Meehan, J. C., Rehman, U., and Marshall, A. D. 2002. Intimate partner violence: An introduction for couple therapists. In *Clinical handbook of couple therapy,* 3rd ed., A. Gurman and N. Jacobson, eds. New York: Guilford Press.

Jacobson, N. S., and Christensen, A. 1996. *Integrative couple therapy.* New York: Guilford Press.

Johnson, M. P. 1995. Patriarchal terrorism and common couple violence: Two forms of violence against women. *Journal of Marriage and the Family. 57:* 283–294.

Kitchens, J. M. 1994. Does this patient have an alcohol problem? *Journal of the American Medical Association. 272:* 1782–1787.

McGoldrick, M., Pearce, J., and Giordano, J. 2005. *Ethnicity and family therapy,* 3rd ed. New York: Guilford Press.

Minuchin, S., and Nichols, M. P. 1993. *Family healing: Tales of hope and renewal from family therapy.* New York: Free Press.

Nichols, M. P. 2009. *The lost art of listening,* 2nd ed. New York: Guilford Press.

Patterson, J. E., Williams, L., Grauf-Grounds, C., and Chamow, L. 1998. *Essential skills in family therapy.* New York: Guilford Press.

Schwartz, R. C. 1995. *Internal family systems therapy.* New York: Guilford Press.

Sheinberg, M., True, F., and Fraenkel, P. 1994. Treating the sexually abused child: A recursive, multimodal program. *Family Process. 33:* 263–276.

Trepper, T. S., and Barrett, M. J. 1989. *Systemic treatment of incest: A therapeutic handbook.* New York: Bruner/Mazel.

Walsh, F. 1998. *Strengthening family resilience.* New York: Guilford Press.

4

The Fundamental Concepts of Family Therapy

Prior to the advent of family therapy, the individual was regarded as the locus of psychological problems and the target for treatment. If a mother called to complain that her fifteen-year-old son was depressed, a clinician would meet with the boy to find out what was wrong. A Rogerian might look for low self-esteem, a Freudian for repressed anger, a behaviorist for a lack of reinforcing activities. But all would assume that the forces shaping the boy's mood were located within him and that therapy, therefore, required only the presence of the patient and a therapist.

Family therapy changed all that. Today, if a mother were to seek help for a depressed teenager, most therapists would meet with the boy and his parents together. If a fifteen-year-old is depressed, it's not unreasonable to assume that something might be going on in his family. Perhaps the boy's parents don't get along and he's worried that they might get divorced. Maybe he's having a hard time living up to the expectations created by a successful older sister.

Suppose you are the therapist. You meet with the boy and his family and discover that he's not worried about his parents or jealous of his sister. In fact, everything "is fine" at home. He's just depressed. Now what?

That "now what?" feeling is a common experience when you start seeing families. Even when there is something obviously wrong—the boy is worried about his parents or everybody is shouting and no one is listening—it's often hard to know where to begin. You could start by trying to solve the family's problems for them. But then you wouldn't be helping them deal with *why* they're having problems.

To address what's making it hard for a family to cope with their problems, you have to know where to look. For that, you need some way of understanding what makes families tick. You need a theory.

When they first began to observe families discussing their problems, therapists could see immediately that everyone was involved. In the clamor of noisy quarrels, however, it's hard to get beyond the impact of personalities—the sullen adolescent, the controlling mother, the distant father—to see the patterns that connect them. Instead of concentrating on individuals and their personalities, family therapists consider how problems may be, at least in part, a product of the relationships surrounding them. How to understand those relationships is the subject of this chapter.

CYBERNETICS

The first and perhaps most influential model of how families operate was **cybernetics**, the study of feedback mechanisms in self-regulating systems. What the family shares with other cybernetic systems is a tendency to maintain stability by using information about its performance as feedback.

At the core of cybernetics is the **feedback** loop, the process by which a system gets the information necessary to maintain a steady course. This feedback includes information about the system's performance relative to its external environment as well as the relationship among the system's parts. Feedback loops can be negative or positive. This distinction refers to the effect they have on deviations from a homeostatic state, not whether they are beneficial. **Negative feedback** indicates how far off the mark a system is straying and the corrections needed to get it back on course. It signals the system to restore the status quo. Thus, negative feedback is not such a negative thing. Its vital, error-correcting information gives order and self-control to automatic machines, to the body and the brain, and to people in their daily lives. **Positive feedback** is information that confirms and reinforces the direction a system is taking.

A familiar example of negative feedback occurs in the home heating system. When the temperature drops below a certain point, the thermostat triggers the furnace to heat the house back to the pre-established range. It is this self-correcting feedback loop that makes the system cybernetic, and it is the system's response to change as a signal to restore its previous state that illustrates negative feedback.

Figure 4.1 shows the basic circularity involved in a feedback loop. Each element has an effect on the next, until the last element "feeds back" the cumulative effect into the first part of the cycle. Thus A affects B, which in turn affects C, which feeds back to A, and so on.

In the example of a home heating system, A might be the room temperature; B, the thermostat; and C, the furnace. Figure 4.2 shows a similar cybernetic feedback loop in a couple. In this case, Jan's housecleaning efforts (output) affect how much housework gets done, which subsequently affects how much housecleaning Billie has to do, which then feeds back (input) to how much housecleaning Jan thinks still needs to be done, and so on.

The cybernetic system turned out to be an apt metaphor for describing how families maintain stability (Jackson, 1959). Sometimes stability is a good thing, as, for example, when a family continues to function as a cohesive unit despite being threatened by conflict or stress. Sometimes, however, resisting change isn't such a good thing, as when a family fails to accommodate to the growth of one of its members. More about this later.

Like negative feedback, positive feedback can have desirable or undesirable consequences. If left unchecked, the reinforcing effects of positive feedback tend to compound a system's errors, leading to **runaway** processes. The hapless driver on an icy road who sends positive feedback to his automobile

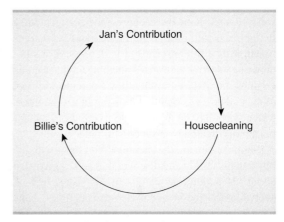

Figure 4.2 Feedback loop in a couple's housecleaning efforts

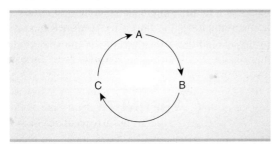

Figure 4.1 Circular causality of a feedback loop

engine by stepping on the accelerator can spiral out of control because his brakes are useless to provide the negative feedback to stop the car. Similarly, malignant worry, phobic avoidance, and other forms of neurotic behavior may start out with a relatively trivial concern and build into an out-of-control process.

Consider, for example, that a panic attack may begin as a relatively harmless instance of being out of breath, but a panicky response to breathlessness may spiral into a terrifying experience. For a more complex example, take the workings of the federal government. Presidents generally surround themselves with advisers who share their viewpoints and who, because they're eager to maintain access, tend to support whatever position the president takes. Their positive feedback can result in a president's taking a bad policy and running with it—like Lyndon Johnson's escalation of the Vietnam War. Fortunately, however, the checks and balances provided by the legislative and judicial branches usually provide the negative feedback to keep administrations from going too far in one direction. To survive and adapt to the world around them, all communication systems—including families—need a healthy balance of positive and negative feedback. As we will see, however, early family therapists tended to overemphasize negative feedback and resistance to change.

Cybernetics was the brainchild of MIT mathematician Norbert Wiener (1948), who developed what was to become the first model of family dynamics in an unlikely setting. During World War II, Wiener was asked to design a better way to control the targeting of antiaircraft artillery (Conway & Siegelman, 2005). The German bombers blackening the skies over Europe flew at speeds exceeding 300 miles per hour and at altitudes as high as 30,000 feet. The flight of an artillery shell to that height could take as long as twenty seconds, and firing that shot accurately—nearly two miles downrange—was no simple task. Wiener's solution was to incorporate a system of internal feedback that enabled antiaircraft guns to automatically regulate their own operations. The signal used to control the artillery was a self-regulating *servomechanism*—the technical term for the first automated machines.

To capture the essence of the new science of communication and control by feedback, Wiener chose the name *cybernetics,* from the Greek for "steersman." He distinguished two major modes of information, discrete or continuous—digital or analog—and their diverse applications in communication, electronic computing, and automatic control systems. Moreover, he pointed out that the new technical methods of control by information feedback were, in essence, the same universal processes that nature long ago selected as its basic operating system for all living things (Wiener, 1948). He even suggested that cybernetic theory could be used to explain mental illnesses as self-reinforcing patterns of behavior—as the brain gets stuck in a biochemical rut.

Because cybernetics emerged from the study of machines, where positive feedback loops led to destructive runaways, causing the machinery to break down, the emphasis was on negative feedback and the maintenance of **homeostasis,** a balanced steady state of equilibrium. The system's environment would change—the temperature would go up or down—and this change would trigger negative feedback mechanisms to bring the system back to homeostasis—the heat would go on or off. Negative feedback loops control everything from endocrine systems to ecosystems. Animal species are balanced by starvation and predators when they overpopulate and by increases in birth rates when their numbers are depleted. Blood sugar levels are balanced by increases in insulin output when they get too high and increases in appetite when they get too low.

As applied to families, cybernetics focused attention on: (1) **family rules,** which govern the range of behavior a family system can tolerate (the family's homeostatic range); (2) **negative feedback** mechanisms that families use to enforce those rules (guilt, punishment, symptoms); (3) **sequences of family interaction** around a problem that characterize a system's reaction to it (feedback loops); and (4) what happens when a system's accustomed negative feedback is ineffective, triggering **positive feedback loops.**

Examples of positive feedback loops are those pesky vicious cycles in which the actions taken only make things worse. The well-known *self-fulfilling prophecy* is one such positive feedback loop: One's apprehensions lead to actions that precipitate the feared situation, which in turn justifies one's fears, and so on. Another example of positive feedback is the *bandwagon effect*—the tendency of a cause to gain support simply because of its growing number of adherents. You can probably think of some fads and more than a few pop music groups that owe much of their popularity to the bandwagon effect.

As an example of a self-fulfilling prophecy, consider a young therapist who expects men to be uninvolved in family life. She believes that fathers *should* play an active role in the lives of their children, but her own experience has taught her not to expect much. Suppose she's trying to arrange for a family consultation, and the mother says that her husband won't be able to attend. How is our hypothetical therapist likely to respond? She might accept the mother's statement at face value and thus collude to ensure what she expected. Alternatively, she might challenge the mother's statement aggressively, thereby displacing her attitude toward men into her relationship with the mother—or push the mother into an oppositional stance with her husband.

To shift to a family example: In a family with a low threshold for the expression of anger, Marcus, the adolescent son, blows up at his parents over their insistence that he not stay out past midnight. Mother is shocked by his outburst and begins to cry. Father responds by grounding Marcus for a month. Rather than reducing Marcus's deviation—bringing his anger back within homeostatic limits—this feedback produces the opposite effect: Marcus explodes and challenges their authority. The parents respond with more crying and punishing, which further increases Marcus's anger, and so on. In this way, the intended negative feedback (crying and punishing) becomes positive feedback. It amplifies rather than diminishes

Marcus's deviation. The family is caught in a positive feedback runaway, otherwise known as a vicious cycle, which escalates until Marcus runs away from home.

Later, cyberneticians like Walter Buckley and Ross Ashby recognized that positive feedback loops aren't always bad; if they don't get out of hand, they can help systems adjust to changed circumstances. Marcus's family might need to recalibrate their rules to accommodate an adolescent's increased assertiveness. The crisis that this positive feedback loop produced could lead to a reexamination of the family's rules—if the family could step out of the loop long enough to get some perspective. In so doing they would be using **metacommunication,** communicating about their ways of communicating, a process that can lead to a change in a system's rules (Bateson, 1956).

Family cyberneticians focused on the feedback loops within families, otherwise known as patterns of communication, as the fundamental source of family dysfunction. Hence, the family theorists most influenced by cybernetics came to be known as the *communications school* (see Chapter 6). Faulty communication results in inaccurate feedback, so the system cannot self-correct (change its rules) and consequently overreacts or underreacts to change.

$\mathcal{S}$YSTEMS THEORY

Experience teaches that what shows up as one person's behavior may be a product of relationship. The same individual may be submissive in one relationship, dominant in another. Like so many qualities we attribute to individuals, submissiveness is only half of a two-part equation. In fact, family therapists use a host of concepts to describe how two people in a relationship contribute to what goes on between them, including *pursuer–distancer, overfunctioning–underfunctioning, control-and-rebel cycles,* and so on. The advantage of such concepts is that either party can change his or her part in the pattern. But while it's relatively easy to discover themes in two-person relationships, it's more difficult to see patterns of interaction in larger groups like families. That's why family therapists found systems theory so useful.

Systems theory had its origins in the 1940s, when theoreticians began to construct models of the structure and functioning of mechanical and biological units. What these theorists discovered was that things as diverse as jet engines, amoebas, and the human brain all share the attributes of a system—that is, an organized assemblage of parts forming a complex whole.

According to systems theory, the essential properties of living systems arise from the relationships among their parts. These properties are lost when the system is reduced to isolated elements. The whole is always greater than the sum of its parts. Thus, from a systems perspective, it would make little sense to try to understand a child's behavior by interviewing him without the rest of his family.

Although some therapists use terms like *systemic* and *systems theory* to mean little more than considering families as units, systems actually have a number of specific and interesting properties. To begin with, the shift from looking at individuals to considering the family as a system means shifting the focus to patterns of relationship.

Let's take a simple example. If a father scolds his son, his wife tells him not to be so harsh, and the boy continues to misbehave, a systemic analysis would concentrate on this sequence, for it is this *sequence of interaction* that reveals how the system functions. To focus on inputs and outputs, a systems analysis deliberately avoids speculating about individuals or asking *why* they do what they do. The most radical expression of this systemic perspective was the **black box** metaphor:

> The impossibility of seeing the mind "at work" has in recent years led to the adoption of the Black Box concept . . . applied to the fact that electronic hardware is by now so complex that it is sometimes more expedient to disregard the internal structure of a device and concentrate on the study

of its specific input–output relations. . . . This concept, if applied to psychological and psychiatric problems, has the heuristic advantage that no ultimately unverifiable intrapsychic hypotheses need be invoked and that one can limit oneself to observable input–output relations, that is, to communication (Watzlawick, Beavin, & Jackson, 1967, pp. 43–44).

Viewing people as black boxes may seem like the ultimate expression of mechanistic thinking, but this metaphor had the advantage of simplifying the field of study by eliminating speculation about the mind in order to concentrate on people's input and output (communication, behavior).

Among the features of systems seized on by early family therapists, few were more influential than *homeostasis,* the self-regulation that allows systems to maintain themselves in a state of dynamic balance. Don Jackson's notion of family homeostasis emphasized that dysfunctional families' tendency to resist change went a long way toward explaining why, despite heroic efforts to improve, so many patients remain stuck (Jackson, 1959). Today we look back on this emphasis on homeostasis as exaggerating the conservative properties of families and underestimating their resourcefulness.

Thus, although many of the cybernetic concepts used to describe machines could be extended by analogy to human systems like the family, living systems, it turns out, cannot be adequately described by the same principles as mechanical systems.

General Systems Theory

In the 1940s, an Austrian biologist, Ludwig von Bertalanffy, attempted to combine concepts from systems thinking and biology into a universal theory of living systems—from the human mind to the global ecosphere. Starting with investigations of the endocrine system, he began extrapolating to more complex social systems and developed a model that came to be called **general systems theory.**

Mark Davidson, in his fascinating biography *Uncommon Sense* (1983), summarized Bertalanffy's definition of a system as any entity maintained by the mutual interaction of its parts, from atom to cosmos, and including such mundane examples as telephone, postal, and rapid transit systems. A Bertalanffian system can be physical like a television set, biological like a cocker spaniel, psychological like a personality, sociological like a labor union, or symbolic like a set of laws. . . . A system can be composed of smaller systems and can also be part of a larger system, just as a state or province is composed of smaller jurisdictions and also is part of a nation (p. 26).

The last point is important. Every system is a sub-system of larger systems. But family therapists tended to forget about this spreading network of influence when they adopted the systems perspective. They treated the family as a system while ignoring the larger systems of community, culture, and politics in which families are embedded.

Bertalanffy used the metaphor of an organism for social groups, but an organism that was an **open system,** continuously interacting with its environment. Open systems, as opposed to **closed systems** (e.g., machines), sustain themselves by exchanging resources with their surroundings—for example, taking in oxygen and expelling carbon dioxide. Another property of living systems that mechanists forgot was that they don't just react to stimuli; they actively initiate efforts to flourish.

Bertalanffy was a life-long crusader against the mechanistic view of living systems, particularly those living systems called people. He believed that, unlike machines, living organisms demonstrate **equifinality,** the ability to reach a final goal in a variety of ways.

With a mechanical system, there is a direct cause-and-effect relationship between the initial conditions and the final state. But in a biological or social system, like a family, final results may be achieved with different initial conditions and in different ways. Thus, there is never only one way to achieve a family's objectives.

Living organisms are active and creative. They work to sustain their organization, but they aren't motivated solely to preserve the status quo. In an open system, feedback mechanisms operate so that the system receives information from the environment, which helps it adjust. For example, the cooling of the blood from a drop in environmental temperature stimulates centers in the brain to activate heat-producing mechanisms so that temperature is maintained at a steady level. Family therapists picked up on the concept of homeostasis, but, according to Bertalanffy, an overemphasis on this conservative aspect of the organism reduced it to the level of a machine: "If [this] principle of homeostatic maintenance is taken as a rule of behavior, the so-called well-adjusted individual will be [defined as] a well-oiled robot" (quoted in Davidson, 1983, p. 104).

Early systems models of the family were based on the concept of a closed system and emphasized the role of negative feedback in maintaining homeostatic equilibrium. Families are more aptly described, in Walter Buckley's (1968) terms, as *complex adaptive systems.* Such systems are open and susceptible to significant changes in the nature of the components themselves with important consequences for the system as a whole. Their feedback control loops make possible not only self-regulation (as in homeostatic systems) but also self-direction, such that a system may modify its structure in order to evolve. Unlike mechanical systems, which strive only to maintain a fixed structure, family systems seek not only to remain stable but also to change when necessary to adapt to new circumstances. Buckley coined the term **morphogenesis** to describe this elastic quality of adaptive systems.

To summarize, Bertalanffy brought up many of the issues that have shaped family therapy:

- A system as more than the sum of its parts
- Emphasis on interaction within and among systems versus reductionism
- Human systems as ecologic organisms versus mechanism
- Concept of equifinality
- Homeostatic reactivity versus spontaneous activity

$\mathcal{S}$OCIAL CONSTRUCTIONISM

Systems theory taught us to see how people's lives are shaped by their interchanges with those around them. In focusing on patterns of interaction, however, systems theory left something out. Actually, two things: how family members' beliefs affect their actions and how cultural forces shape those beliefs.

Constructivism

Constructivism captured the imagination of family therapists when studies of brain function showed that we can never know the world as it exists out there; all we can know is our subjective experience of it. Research on neural nets (Von Foerster, 1981) and experiments on the vision of frogs (Maturana & Varela, 1980) indicated that the brain doesn't process images literally, like a camera, but rather registers experience in patterns organized by the nervous system.[1] Nothing is perceived directly. Everything is filtered through the mind of the observer.

When this new perspective on knowing was reported to the family field by Paul Watzlawick (1984), the effect was a wake-up call—alerting us to the importance of cognition in family life.

Constructivism is the modern expression of a philosophical tradition that goes back as far as the eighteenth century. Immanuel Kant (1724–1804), one of the pillars of Western philosophy, regarded knowledge as a product of the way our imaginations are organized. The outside world doesn't simply impress itself onto the *tabula rasa* (blank slate) of our minds, as British empiricist John Locke (1632–1704) believed. In fact, as Kant argued, our minds are anything but blank. They are active filters through which we process and interpret the world.

Constructivism first found its way into psychotherapy in the *personal construct theory* of George Kelly (1955). According to Kelly, we make sense of the world by creating our own constructs of the environment. We interpret and organize events, and we make predictions that guide our actions on the basis of these constructs. You might compare this interpreting of experience to seeing the world through a pair of eyeglasses. Because we may need to adjust constructs, therapy became a matter of revising old constructs and developing new ones—trying on different lenses to see which ones enable a person to navigate the world in more satisfying ways.

The first application of constructivism in family therapy was the technique of **reframing**—relabeling behavior to shift how family members respond to it. Clients respond very differently to a child seen as "hyperactive" than to one perceived as "misbehaving." Likewise, the parents of a rebellious ten-year-old will feel better about themselves if they become convinced that, rather than being "ineffectual disciplinarians," they have an "oppositional child." The first diagnosis suggests that the parents should get tough but also that they probably won't succeed. The second suggests that coping with a difficult child requires strategizing. The point isn't that one description is more valid than the other but rather that if whatever label a family applies to its problems leads to ineffective coping strategies, then perhaps a new label will alter their viewpoint and lead to a more effective response.

When constructivism took hold of family therapy in the mid-1980s, it triggered a fundamental shift in emphasis. Systems metaphors focused on behavior and interaction; constructivism shifted the focus to the assumptions people have about their problems. Meaning itself became the target. The goal of therapy changed from interrupting problematic patterns of behavior to helping clients find new perspectives in their lives.

Constructivism teaches us to look beyond behavior to the ways we interpret our experience. Moreover, in a world where all truth is relative, the perspective of the therapist has no more claim to objectivity than that of the clients. Thus, constructivism undermined the status of the therapist as an objective authority with privileged knowledge of cause and cure. It's probably

---

[1] The eye of the frog, for example, doesn't register much but lateral movement—which may be all you really need to know if your main interest in life is catching flies with your tongue.

well to remember that even our most cherished metaphors for family life—"system," "enmeshment," "triangles," and so on—are just that: metaphors. They don't exist in some objective reality; they are constructions, some more useful than others.

In emphasizing the idiosyncratic perspective of the individual, constructivists were accused by some (e.g., Minuchin, 1991) of ignoring the social context. Once that solipsistic streak was pointed out, leading constructivists clarified their position: When they said that reality was constructed, they meant *socially* constructed.

The Social Construction of Reality

Social constructionism expands on constructivism much as family therapy expanded individual psychology. Constructivism says that we relate to the world on the basis of our own interpretations. **Social constructionism** points out that those interpretations are shaped by our context.

Suppose a fourteen-year-old consistently disobeys his parents. A constructivist might point out that the boy may think they don't deserve his respect. In other words, the boy's actions are not simply a product of the parents' disciplinary efforts but also of the boy's construction of their authority. A social constructionist would add that an adolescent's attitudes about parental authority are shaped not only by what goes on in the family but also by messages transmitted by the culture at large.

At school or work, at lunch, in phone conversations, at the movies, and from television, we absorb attitudes and opinions that we carry into our families. Television, to pick one extremely potent influence on the average fourteen-year-old, has made today's children more sophisticated and more cynical. As communications scholar Joshua Meyrowitz (1985) argues in *No Sense of Place,* today's children are exposed to the "back stage" of the adult world, to otherwise hidden doubts and conflicts, foolishness and

failures of adult types they see on television. This demystification undermines adolescent confidence in traditional authority structures. It's hard to respect adult wisdom when your image of a parent is Homer Simpson.

Both constructivism and social constructionism focus on interpretation of experience as a mediator of behavior. But while constructivists emphasized the subjective mind of the individual, social constructionists place more emphasis on the intersubjective influence of language and culture. According to constructivism, people have problems not merely because of the objective conditions of their lives but also because of their interpretations of those conditions. What social constructionism adds is a recognition of how such meanings emerge in the process of talking with other people.

Therapy then becomes a process of *deconstruction*—of freeing clients from the tyranny of entrenched beliefs. How this plays out in practice is illustrated in the two most influential recent versions of family therapy: the solution-focused model and narrative therapy.

Inherent in most forms of therapy is the idea that before you can solve a problem, you must figure out what's wrong. This notion seems self-evident, but it is a construction—only one way of looking at things. **Solution-focused therapy** turns this assumption on its head, using a totally different construction—namely, that the best way to solve problems is to discover what people do when they're *not* having the problem.

Suppose, for example, a woman complains that her husband never talks to her. Instead of trying to figure out what's wrong, a solution-focused therapist might ask the woman if she can remember *exceptions* to this complaint. Perhaps she and her husband do have reasonably good conversations when they go for walks or out to dinner. In that case, the therapist might simply suggest that they do more of that. We'll see how solution-focused therapy builds on the insights of constructivism in Chapter 12.

Like their solution-focused colleagues, **narrative** therapists create a shift in their clients' experience by helping them reexamine how they look at things. But whereas solution-focused therapy shifts attention from current failures to past successes in order to mobilize behavioral solutions, narrative therapy's aim is more attitudinal. The decisive technique in this approach—*externalization*—involves the truly radical reconstruction of defining problems not as properties of the persons who suffer them but as alien oppressors. Thus, for example, while the parents of a boy who doesn't keep up with his homework might define him as lazy or a procrastinator, a narrative therapist would talk instead about times when "procrastination" gets the better of him—and times when "it" doesn't.

Notice how the former construction—the boy is a procrastinator—is relatively deterministic, whereas the latter—procrastination sometimes gets the better of him—frees the boy from a negative identity, and turns therapy into a struggle for liberation. We'll talk more about narrative therapy and the process of externalization in Chapter 13.

ATTACHMENT THEORY

As the field matured, family therapists showed a renewed interest in the inner life of the individuals who make up the family. Now, in addition to theories about the broad, systemic influences on family members' behavior, **attachment theory** has emerged as a leading tool for describing the deeper roots of close relationships. By destigmatizing dependency in adults (Bowlby, 1988), attachment theory has elevated connectedness to equal status with autonomy.

Attachment theory has been especially fruitful in couples therapy (e.g., Johnson, 2002), where it helps explain how even healthy adults need to depend on each other. In the early years of family therapy, couples treatment was a therapy without a theory. With few exceptions, therapists treated couples with models designed for families (e.g., Bowen, 1978; Haley, 1976; Minuchin, 1974). The exception was behaviorists, who implied that intimacy was a product of

reinforcement. Nobody talked much about love or longing. Dependency might be okay for children, but in adults, we were told, it was a sign of enmeshment.

In emotionally focused couples therapy, Susan Johnson uses attachment theory to deconstruct the familiar dynamic in which one partner criticizes and complains while the other gets defensive and withdraws. What attachment theory suggests is that the criticism and complaining are protests against disruption of the attachment bond—in other words, the nagging partner may be more insecure than angry.

The notion that how couples deal with each other reflects their attachment history can be traced to the pioneering studies of John Bowlby and Mary Ainsworth. When Bowlby graduated from Cambridge in the 1940s, it was assumed that infants became attached to their mothers as a consequence of being fed. But Konrad Lorenz (1935) showed that baby geese become attached to parents who don't feed them, and Harry Harlow (1958) found that, under stress, infant monkeys prefer the cloth-covered "mothers" that provided contact comfort to the wire-mesh "mothers" that provided food. Human babies, too, become attached to people who do not feed them (Ainsworth, 1967).

In the 1940s and 1950s, a number of studies found that young children who were separated from their mothers go through a series of reactions that can be described as "protest," "despair," and finally "detachment" (e.g., Burlingham & Freud, 1944; Robertson, 1953). In attempting to understand these reactions, Bowlby (1958) concluded that the bond between infants and their parents was based on a biological drive for proximity that evolved through process of natural selection. When danger threatens, infants who stay close to their parents are less likely to be killed by predators.

Attachment means seeking closeness in the face of stress. Attachment can be seen in cuddling up to mother's warm body and being cuddled in return, looking into her eyes and being gazed at fondly, and holding on to her and being held. These experiences are profoundly comforting.

According to Mary Ainsworth (1967), infants use their attachment figures (usually mothers) as a *secure base* for exploration. When an infant feels threatened, he or she will turn to the caregiver for protection and comfort. Variations in this pattern are evident in two insecure strategies of attachment. In the *avoidant* strategy, the infant inhibits attachment seeking; in the *resistant* strategy, the infant clings to mother and avoids exploration.

Security in the relationship with an attachment figure indicates that an infant is able to rely on that person as a source of comfort and protection. When threats arise, infants in secure relationships are able to direct *attachment behavior* (approaching, crying, reaching out) to their caregivers and take comfort in their reassurance. Infants with secure attachments are confident in the availability of their caregivers and, consequently, confident in their interactions in the world.

This confidence is not evident in infants with anxious attachment relationships. Bids for attention may have been met with indifference or rebuff (Bowlby, 1973). As a result, such infants remain insecure about the availability of caregivers. Moreover, Bowlby argued that because attachment relationships are internalized, these early experiences shape expectations for later relationships of friendship, parenting, and romantic love.

Attachment theory is applied to clinical treatment by linking symptomatic expressions of fear and anger to disturbances in attachment relationships. Parents can be helped to understand some of their children's disruptive behavior as stemming from the child's anxiety about the parents' availability and responsiveness. Couples can be helped to understand the attachment fears behind angry and defensive interactions (Gottman, 1994).

Therapists can use attachment theory to illuminate current relationships by showing how a child's misbehavior might reflect an insecure attachment, how a husband's avoidance might be due to ambivalent attachment, or how a wife's animosity may be an expression of anxious attachment. When therapists feel drawn into a family's script, they can avoid taking over a role that's missing in the family by using attachment theory to point out family members' needs for being cared for. Instead of being recruited to comfort a distressed mate or soothe an anxious

child, a therapist can hand back responsibility to the partner or parents and encourage them to become less defensive and more supportive.

• • •

After reading this chronology of how theories in family therapy have evolved, the reader may feel overwhelmed by the number of paradigm shifts in the field. It may help to point out a pattern in this apparent discontinuity. The focus of therapy has expanded toward ever-wider levels of context. This process started when therapists looked beyond individuals to their families. Suddenly, unexplainable behavior began to make sense. Early family therapists concentrated on assessing and altering behavioral interactions surrounding problems. Next it was recognized that those interactions were manifestations of a family's underlying structure, and structure became the target of change. Then a family's structure was seen to be a product of multigenerational processes that were governed by belief systems, and therapists aimed their interventions at those underlying beliefs. More recently, it dawned on therapists that these belief systems didn't arise in a vacuum, hence the current interest in cultural influences.

• • •

Family therapists, naturalists on the human scene, discovered how behavior is shaped by transactions we don't always see. Systems concepts—feedback, circularity, and so on—helped make complex interactions predictable. In keeping with our emphasis on how ideas are actually applied in clinical practice, we now consider the fundamental working concepts of family therapy.

THE WORKING CONCEPTS OF FAMILY THERAPY

Interpersonal Context

The fundamental premise of family therapy is that people are products of their **context.** Because few people are closer to us than our parents and partners, this notion can be translated into saying that a person's behavior is powerfully influenced by interactions with other family members. Thus, the importance of context can be reduced to the importance of family. It can be, but it shouldn't be.

Although the family is often the most relevant context for understanding behavior, it isn't always. A depressed college student, for example, might be more unhappy about what's going on in the dormitory than about what's happening at home.

The clinical significance of context is that attempts to treat individuals by talking to them once a week for fifty minutes may have less influence than their interactions with other people during the remaining 167 hours of the week. Or to put this positively, often the most effective way to help people resolve their problems is to meet with them *and* important others in their lives.

Complementarity

Complementarity refers to the reciprocity that is the defining feature of every relationship. In any relationship, one person's behavior is yoked to the other's. Remember the symbol for yin and yang, the masculine and feminine forces in the universe?

Notice how the two parts are complementary and occupy one space. Relationships are like that. If one person changes, the relationship changes. If Tony starts doing more grocery shopping, Anne likely does less.

Family therapists should think of complementarity whenever they hear one person complaining about another.

Take, for example, John, a husband who says that his wife, Mary, nags. "She's always complaining." From the perspective of complementarity, a family therapist would assume that Mary's complaining is only half of a pattern of mutual influence. Whenever people are perceived as nagging, it probably means that they haven't received a fair hearing for their concerns. Not being listened to by John makes Mary feel angry and unsupported. If, instead of waiting for her to complain, John starts asking her how she feels, Mary will feel more as if he cares about her. Or at least she's likely to feel that way.

Complementarity doesn't mean that people in relationships control each other; it means that they influence each other. A therapist can help family members get past blaming—and the powerlessness that goes with it—by pointing out the complementarity of their actions. "The more you nag, the more he ignores you. *And* the more you ignore her, the more she nags."

Circular Causality

Before the advent of family therapy, explanations of psychopathology were based on linear models: medical, psychodynamic, or behavioral. Etiology was conceived in terms of prior events—disease, emotional conflict, or learning history. With the concept of *circularity,* Bateson helped change the way we think about psychopathology from something caused by events in the past to something that is part of ongoing, circular feedback loops.

The notion of **linear causality** is based on the Newtonian model in which the universe is like a billiard table where the balls act unidirectionally on each other. Bateson believed that although linear causality is useful for describing the world of objects, it's a poor model for the world of living things, because it neglects to account for communication and relationships.

To illustrate this difference, Bateson (1979) used the example of a man kicking a stone. The effect of kicking a stone can be predicted by measuring the force and angle of the kick and the weight of the stone. If the man kicks a dog, on the other hand, the effect will be less predictable. The dog might respond to a kick in any number of ways—cringing, running away, biting, or trying to play—depending on the temperament of the dog and how it interpreted the kick. In response to the dog's reaction, the man might modify his behavior, and so on, so that the number of possible outcomes is unlimited.

The dog's actions (biting, for example) loop back and affect the man's next move (taking the Lord's name in vain, for example), which in turn affects the dog, and so on. The original action prompts a circular sequence in which each subsequent action recursively affects the others. Linear cause and effect is lost in a circle of mutual influence.

This idea of mutual or **circular causality** is enormously useful for therapists because so many families come in looking to find "the cause" of their problems and determine who is responsible. Instead of joining the family in a logical but unproductive search for who started what, circular causality suggests that problems are sustained by an ongoing series of actions and reactions. Who started it? It rarely matters.

Triangles

Most clients express their concerns in linear terms. It might be a four-year-old who is "unmanageable" or perhaps an ex-wife who "refuses to cooperate" about visitation rights. Even though such complaints suggest that the problem resides in a single individual, most therapists would think to look for relationship issues. "Unmanageable" four-year-olds often turn out to have parents who are ineffective disciplinarians; and ex-wives who are "unreasonable" probably have their own sides of those stories. So a therapist, certainly a family therapist, would probably want to see the four-year-old together with her parents and to meet with both the angry father and his ex-wife.

Suppose that the therapist who meets with the four-year-old and her parents sees that indeed the real problem is a lack of discipline. The mother complains that the girl never does what she's told, the father nods in agreement, and the child runs around the room ignoring her mother's requests to sit still. Maybe the parents could use some advice about setting limits. Perhaps. But experience teaches that a child who misbehaves is often standing on one

parent's shoulders. When children are disobedient, it usually means that their parents are in conflict about the rules or how to enforce them.

Perhaps the father is a strict disciplinarian. If so, his wife might feel that she needs to protect her daughter from her husband's harshness, so she becomes more of a friend and ally to her child than a parent-in-charge.

Some parents are so angry with each other that their disagreements are plain to see. But many are less open. Their conflicts are painful, so they keep them private. Maybe they think that their relationship is none of the therapist's business, or perhaps the father has decided that if his wife doesn't like how he does things, "Then she can damn well do them herself!" The point is this: Relationship problems often turn out to be triangular (Bowen, 1978), even though it may not always be apparent.

A less obvious example of triangular complications often occurs in the case of divorced parents who fight over visitation rights. Most divorces generate enough hurt and anger to make a certain amount of animosity inevitable. Add to that a healthy dose of parental guilt (felt and projected), and you have a formula for arguments about who gets the kids for holidays, whose turn it is to buy new sneakers, and who was late picking up or dropping them off last weekend. Meeting with the embattled exes may do little to disconfirm the assumption that the problem is between the two of them. Yet even two people who are very angry at each other will eventually find a way to work things out—unless third parties mix in.

What do you suppose happens when a divorced father complains to his girlfriend about his ex's "unreasonableness"? The same thing that usually happens when one person complains about another. The girlfriend sympathizes with him and, often as not, urges him to get tough with his ex-wife. Meanwhile, the children's mother is equally likely to have a friend encouraging her to become more aggressive. Thus, instead of two people left to work things out between them, one or both of them is egged on to escalate the conflict.

Do *all* relationship problems involve third parties? No, but most do.

Process/Content

Focusing on the **process** of communication (*how* people talk), rather than on its **content** (*what* they talk about), may be the most productive shift a family therapist can make.

Imagine, for example, that a therapist encourages a moody freshman to talk to her parents. Imagine further that the young woman rarely expresses herself in words but rather in passive-aggressive protest and that her parents are, in contrast, all too good at putting their opinions into words. Suppose that the young woman finally begins to express her feeling that college is a waste of time, and her parents counter with an argument about the importance of staying in school. A therapist who is made anxious by the idea that the young woman might actually drop out of college and who intervenes to support the *content* of the parents' position misses an important opportunity to support the *process* whereby the young woman learns to put her feelings into words rather than into self-destructive actions.

Families who come for treatment are usually focused on content issues. A husband wants a divorce, a child refuses to go to school, a wife is depressed. The family therapist talks with the family about the content of their problems but thinks about the process by which they try to resolve them. While the family discusses what to do about the child's refusal to go to school, the therapist notices whether the parents seem to be in charge and whether they support

each other. A therapist who tells the parents how to solve the problem (by making the child go to school) is working with content, not process. The child may start going to school, but the parents won't have improved their decision-making process.

Sometimes, of course, content is important. If a wife is drinking to drown her worries or a husband is molesting his stepdaughter, something needs to be done. But to the extent that therapists focus exclusively on content, they're unlikely to help families become better functioning systems.

Family Structure

Family interactions are predictable—some might say stubborn—because they are embedded in powerful but unseen structures. Dynamic patterns, like pursuer–distancer, describe the *process* of interaction. **Family structure** defines the organization within which those interactions take place. Originally, interactions shape structure, but once established, structure shapes interactions.

Families, like other groups, have many options for relating. Soon, however, interactions that were initially free to vary become regular and predictable. Once these patterns are established, family members use only a small fraction of the full range of alternatives available to them (Minuchin & Nichols, 1993). Families are structured in **subsystems**—determined by generation, gender, common interests, and function—which are demarcated by interpersonal **boundaries**—invisible barriers that regulate the amount of contact with others (Minuchin, 1974).

Like the membranes of living cells, boundaries safeguard the autonomy of the family and its subsystems. By spending time alone together and excluding friends and family from some of their activities, a couple establishes a boundary that protects their relationship from intrusion. Later, if they marry and have children, that boundary is preserved by making time to be alone together without the children. If, on the other hand, the couple includes their children in all of their activities, the boundary separating the generations wears thin and the couple's relationship is sacrificed to parenting. Children won't develop autonomy or initiative if their parents are involved in all of their activities.

Psychoanalytic theory also emphasizes the need for interpersonal boundaries. Beginning with "the psychological birth of the human infant" (Mahler, Pine, & Bergman, 1975), psychoanalysts describe the progressive separation and individuation that culminates in the resolution of oedipal attachments and eventually in leaving home. But this is a one-sided emphasis on poorly defined boundaries. Psychoanalysts pay insufficient attention to the problems of emotional isolation stemming from rigid boundaries. This belief in separation as the model and measure of maturity may be an example of male psychology overgeneralized and unquestioned. The danger of people losing themselves in relationships is no more real than the danger of their isolating themselves from intimacy.

What family therapists discovered is that problems result when boundaries are either too rigid or too diffuse. Rigid boundaries permit little contact with outside systems, resulting in **disengagement.** Disengagement leaves people independent but isolated; it fosters autonomy but limits affection and nurture. **Enmeshed** subsystems have diffuse boundaries: They offer access to support, but at the expense of independence. Enmeshed parents are loving and attentive; however, their children tend to be dependent and may have trouble relating to people outside their family. Enmeshed parents respond too quickly to their children; disengaged parents respond too slowly.

Another important point about boundaries is that they are reciprocal. A mother's enmeshment with her children is related to the emotional distance between her and her husband. The less she gets from her husband, the more she needs from her children—and the more preoccupied she is with her children, the less time she has for her husband.

It should not go unnoticed that these arrangements are gendered. This doesn't make them any more right or wrong. It should, however, make us cautious about blaming mothers for cultural expectations that perpetuate their role as primary caretakers of children (Luepnitz, 1988). A therapist who recognizes the normative nature of the enmeshed-mother/

disengaged-father syndrome but puts the burden on the mother to let go should consider why it doesn't occur to him or her to challenge the father to take hold.

Family Life Cycle

When we think of the life cycle, we tend to think of individuals maturing, mastering the challenges of one age, and then moving on to the next. The cycle of human life may be orderly, but it's not a steady, continuous process. We progress in stages, with plateaus and developmental hurdles that demand change. Periods of growth and change are followed by periods of stability during which changes are consolidated.

The idea of a **family life cycle** adds two things to our understanding of individual development: When a son or daughter heads off to kindergarten or reaches puberty, not only must the child learn to cope with a new set of circumstances, but the whole family must readjust. Moreover, the developmental transitions that affect children aren't merely their own but their parents' as well—in some cases, even their grandparents'. The strain on a fourteen-year-old's relationship with his parents may be due as much to his father's midlife crisis or his mother's worrying about her own father's retirement as anything the boy himself is going through.

Changes in one generation complicate adjustments in another. A middle-aged father may become disenchanted with his career and decide to become more involved with his family just as his children are growing up and pulling away. His wish to get closer may frustrate their need to be on their own.

Or to cite another example becoming more and more familiar, just as a man and woman begin to do more for themselves after launching their children, they may find their children back in the house (after dropping out of school, unable to afford housing, or recovering from an early divorce) and therefore be faced with an awkward version of second parenthood.

One property that families share with other complex systems is that they don't change in a smooth, gradual process but rather in discontinuous leaps. Falling in love and political revolutions are examples of such leaps. Having a baby is like falling in love and undergoing a revolution at the same time.

Sociologists Evelyn Duvall and Reuben Hill applied a developmental framework to families in the 1940s by dividing family life into discrete stages with tasks to be performed at each stage (Duvall, 1957; Hill & Rodgers, 1964). Family therapists Betty Carter and Monica McGoldrick (1980, 1999) enriched this framework by adding a *multigenerational* point of view, recognizing culturally diverse patterns, and considering stages of divorce and remarriage (Table 4.1).

Monica McGoldrick's work reminds therapists that families often have trouble coping with changes in the family life style.

It's important to recognize that there is no universal version of the family life cycle. Not only do families come in a variety of forms—single-parent families, same-sexed couples, stepfamilies—but various religious, cultural, and ethnic groups may have different norms for various stages. The real value of the life-cycle concept isn't so much learning what's normal or expected at particular stages but recognizing that families often develop problems at transitions in the life cycle.

Problems develop when a family encounters a challenge—environmental or developmental—and is unable to accommodate to the changed circumstances. Thus, problems are usually assumed to be a sign not of a dysfunctional family but simply of one that's having trouble adjusting to one of life's turning points.

Family Narratives

The first family therapists looked beyond individuals to their relationships to explain how problems were perpetuated. Actions, it turned out, were embedded in interactions—and, of course, the most obvious interactions are behavioral. Double binds, problem-maintaining sequences, aversive control, triangles—these concepts all focused on behavior. But in addition to being actors in each other's lives, family members are also storytellers.

By reconstructing the events of their lives in coherent narratives, family members are able to make sense of their experience (White & Epston, 1990). Thus, it is not only actions and interactions that shape families' lives but also the stories they construct. The parents of a two-year-old who tell themselves that he's "defiant" will respond very differently from parents who tell themselves that their little one is "spunky."

Family narratives organize and make sense of experience. They emphasize events that reinforce the plot line and filter out events that don't fit. The parents who see their two-year-old as defiant are more likely to notice and remember the times she said no than the times she said yes. A family's interactions and their narrative of events are related in circular fashion: Behavioral events are perceived and organized in narrative form, and this narrative in turn shapes expectations that influence future behavior and so on.

Interest in family narrative has become identified with one particular school, Michael White's *narrative therapy,* which emphasizes the fact that families with problems come to therapy with defeatist narratives that tend to keep them from acting effectively. But a sensitivity to the importance of personal narrative is a useful part of any therapist's work. However much a family therapist may be interested in the process or structure of family relationships, he or she must also learn to respect the influence of how

Stages of the Family Life Cycle

Family Life Cycle Stage	Emotional Process of Transition: Key Principles	Second-Order Changes in Family Status Required to Proceed Developmentally
Leaving home: single young adults	Accepting emotional and financial responsibility for self	a. Differentiation of self in relation to family of origin b. Development of intimate peer relationships c. Establishment of self in respect to work and financial independence
The joining of families through marriage: the new couple	Commitment to new system	a. Formation of marital system b. Realignment of relationships with extended families and friends to include spouse
Families with young children	Accepting new members into the system	a. Adjusting marital system to make space for children b. Joining in childrearing, financial, and household tasks c. Realignment of relationships with extended family to include parenting and grandparenting roles
Families with adolescents	Increasing flexibility of family boundaries to permit children's independence and grandparents' frailties	a. Shifting of parent/child relationships to permit adolescent to move into and out of system b. Refocus on midlife marital and career issues c. Beginning shift toward caring for older generation
Launching children and moving on	Accepting a multitude of exits from and entries into the family system	a. Renegotiation of marital system as a dyad b. Development of adult-to-adult relationships between grown children and their parents c. Realignment of relationships to include in-laws and grandchildren d. Dealing with disabilities and death of parents (grandparents)
Families in later life	Accepting the shifting generational roles	a. Maintaining own and/or couple functioning and interests in face of physiological decline: exploration of new familial and social role options b. Support for more central role of middle generation c. Making room in the system for the wisdom and experience of the elderly, supporting the older generation without overfunctioning for them d. Dealing with loss of spouse, siblings, and other peers and preparation for death

they experience events—including the therapist's input.

Gender

When family therapists first applied the systems metaphor—an organization of parts plus the way they function together—they paid more attention to the organization than to the parts. Families were understood in terms of abstractions like "boundaries," "triangles," and "parental subsystems," while family members were often treated as cogs in a machine. The "parts" of a family system never cease being individual human beings, but the preoccupation with the way families were organized tended to obscure the personhood of the individuals who made up the family, including their psychodynamics, psychopathology, personal responsibility—and gender.

Common sense tells us that gender is a fact of life (though no one should underestimate social scientists' ability to transcend common sense). As long as society expects the primary parenting to be done by mothers, girls will shape their identities in relation to someone they expect to be like, whereas boys will respond to their difference as a motive for separating from their mothers. The result is what Nancy Chodorow (1978) called "the reproduction of mothering."

Traditionally, women have been raised to have more permeable psychological boundaries, to develop their identities in terms of connection, to cultivate their capacity for empathy, and to be at greater risk for losing themselves in relationships. Men, on the other hand, emerge with more rigid psychological boundaries, disown their dependency needs, fear being engulfed, and often have greater difficulty empathizing with others. We all know men who are nurturing and women who are not, but these are exceptions to the rule.

Awareness of gender and gender inequity has long since penetrated not only family therapy but also our entire culture. Translating this awareness into clinical practice, however, is complicated.

There is room for disagreement between those who strive to maintain clinical neutrality and those who believe that failing to raise gender issues in treatment—money, power, child care, fairness, and so on—runs the risk of reinforcing traditional roles and social arrangements (Walters, Carter, Papp, & Silverstein, 1988). It is not possible, however, to be a fair and effective therapist without being sensitive to how gender issues pervade the life of the family. A therapist who ignores gender may inadvertently show less interest in a woman's career, assume that a child's problems are primarily the mother's responsibility, have a double standard for extramarital affairs, and expect—or at least tolerate—a father's nonparticipation in the family's treatment.

If patriarchy begins at home, a gender-sensitive therapist must recognize the enduring influence of early experience and of unconscious fantasies. How children respond to their parents has significance not only for how they get along but also for the men and women they will become. When a girl speaks derisively about her "bitchy" mother, she may inadvertently be disparaging the female in herself. In addition to identification with the same-sex parent, the child's relationship with the other parent is part of what programs future experience with the opposite sex.

A gender-sensitive therapist must also avoid potential inequities in some of the basic assumptions and principles of family therapy. The notion of *circular causality,* for example, which points to mutually reinforcing patterns of behavior, when applied to problems such as battering, incest, or alcoholism, tends to bypass questions of responsibility and makes it hard to consider influences external to the interaction, such as cultural beliefs about appropriate gender behavior. The concept of *neutrality* suggests that all parts of the system contribute equally to its problems and thus renders invisible differences in power and influence. The same is true of *complementarity,* which suggests that in traditional relationships between men and women, the roles are equal though different. Reconciling these contradictions is not always easy, but ignoring them isn't the answer.

Culture

Among the influences shaping family behavior, few are more powerful than the cultural context. A family from Puerto Rico, for example, may have very different expectations of loyalty and obligation from their adult children than, say, a white middle-class family from Minnesota.

One reason for therapists to be sensitive to cultural diversity is to avoid imposing majority values and assumptions on minority groups. There are now a host of excellent books and articles designed to familiarize therapists with families from a variety of backgrounds, including African American (Boyd-Franklin, 1989), Latino (Falicov, 1998), Haitian (Bibb & Casimir, 1996), Asian American (Lee, 1996), and urban poverty (Minuchin, Colapinto, & Minuchin, 2007), to mention just a few. These texts serve as guides for therapists who are about to venture into relatively unknown territory. However, the best way to develop an understanding of people from other cultures is to spend time with them.

Although they are often used interchangeably, there is a difference between culture and ethnicity. **Culture** refers to common patterns of behavior and experience derived from the settings in which people live. **Ethnicity** refers to the common ancestry through which individuals have evolved shared values and customs—especially among groups that are not white Anglo-Saxon Protestants. *Culture* is the more generic term, and we have chosen it here to emphasize that cultural context is always relevant, even with a family who comes from a background similar to the therapist's.

Although cultural influences may be most obvious with families from foreign backgrounds, it is a mistake to assume that members of the same culture necessarily share values and assumptions. A young Jewish therapist might, for example, be surprised at the unsympathetic attitudes of a middle-aged Jewish couple about their children's decision to adopt an African American baby.

Appreciating the cultural context of families is complicated by the fact that most families are influenced by multiple contexts, which makes generalization difficult. For example, as noted by Nancy Boyd-Franklin (1989), middle-class African American families stand astride three cultures. There are cultural elements that may be traced to African roots, those that are part of the dominant American culture, and finally the adaptations that people of color make to racism in the dominant culture. Moreover, the cultural context may vary among family members. In immigrant families, for example, it's not uncommon to see conflicts between parents who retain a strong ethnic identity and children who are eager to assimilate the ways of the host country. First-generation parents may blame their children for abandoning the old ways and dishonoring the family, while the children may accuse their parents of being stuck in the past. Later, the children's children may develop a renewed appreciation for their cultural roots.

The first mistake a therapist can make in working with clients from different backgrounds is to treat cultural differences as deviant. Although a lack of boundaries between a family and their neighbors and kin might seem problematic to a middle-class white therapist, such more inclusive family networks are not atypical for African American families.

The second mistake is to think that a therapist's job is to become an expert on the various cultures he or she works with. While it may be useful for therapists to familiarize themselves with the customs and values of the major groups in their catchment area, an attitude of respect and curiosity about other people's cultures may be more useful than imposing ethnic stereotypes or assuming an understanding of other people. It's important to acknowledge what you don't know.

The third mistake therapists make in working with families from other cultures is to accept everything assumed to be a cultural norm as functional. An effective therapist must be respectful of other people's ways of doing things without giving up the right to question what appears to be counterproductive. Although fluid boundaries may be typical among urban poor families, that doesn't mean it's inevitable for poor families to be dependent on various social services or for agency staff to presume that a family's need entitles workers to enter, unannounced and uninvited, into the family's space, physically and psychologically (Minuchin, Lee, & Simon, 1996).

Summary

We've covered a lot of ground in this chapter—from cybernetics to social constructionism, complementarity to culture. Some of these ideas may be familiar, while others may be new to you. Here's a brief summary.

1. *Cybernetics* is the study of how feedback is used to regulate mechanical systems. Applied to families, cybernetics teaches that when a family functions like a closed system, the response to a problem may actually perpetuate it. To employ this concept clinically, therapists simply identify how family members have been responding to their problems and then get them to try something different.

2. According to *systems theory,* it's impossible to understand the behavior of individual family members without considering how the family system as a whole operates. To do so it may be necessary to look at *process* (how family members interact), and *structure* (how the family is organized).

3. *Constructivism* reintroduced cognition to family therapists. Family systems may be regulated by interpersonal interactions, but those interactions are shaped by how family members interpret each other's behavior. *Social constructionism* reminds us that families are open systems—our interpretations are heavily influenced by assumptions we absorb from the culture.

4. The trajectory of these concepts broadened our focus beyond the individual to relationships, to the family as a whole, and finally to society at large. *Attachment theory* can be seen as part of an effort to restore our grounding in psychology. Attachment theory emphasizes the basic need for security in close relationships, both in childrearing and intimate partnership.

5. In the section on "The Working Concepts of Family Therapy," we tried to show how therapists can apply the insights of these various theories in clinical practice. Beyond the specifics, what we hoped to get across is that families are more than a collection of individuals; they have superordinate properties that may not always be apparent. It may be obvious, for example, that there are always two parties to a relationship—and that problems, as well as solutions, are a function of both parties. But even this reality can get lost in the heat of emotion. This is as true for therapists as for the people involved. Each of the various other working concepts offers its own particular insights into understanding family joys and sorrows.

In the following chapters, we'll see how the various schools of family therapy approach the task of understanding and treating family problems. But even as the models get specific, it's a good idea to keep in mind the general principles of family functioning explained in this chapter.

Questions to Consider

1. What are some common practices in various forms of therapy that violate the principles of general systems theory?
2. What might be some advantages and disadvantages of a family therapist's learning more about psychoanalytic theory?
3. Does attachment theory offer anything to the practicing family therapist other than suggesting that people have deep needs to be connected?
4. How might your own attitudes about gender make it hard for you to be objective in working with certain families or individuals?

Key Concepts

attachment theory   The study of the innate tendency to seek out closeness to caretakers in the face of stress.

black box metaphor   The idea that because the mind is so complex, it is better to study people's input and output (behavior, communication) than to speculate about what goes on in their minds.

boundary   An emotional or physical barrier that protects and enhances the integrity of an individual, subsystem, or family.

circular causality   The idea that actions are related through a series of recursive loops or repeating cycles.

closed system   A system that does not exchange information or material with its environment, as opposed to an open system, which does. Machines are closed systems.

complementarity   The tendency of two parties in a relationship to supply what each one lacks.

complementary   Relationships based on differences that fit together, where qualities of one make up for lacks in the other.

constructivism   A relativistic point of view that emphasizes the subjective construction of reality; implies that what we see in families may be based as much on our preconceptions as on what is actually going on.

content   See **process/content.**

context   The interpersonal milieu that surrounds and influences the behavior of individuals, families, and larger groups.

culture   Common patterns of behavior and experience derived from the settings in which people live.

cybernetics   The study of control processes in systems, especially analysis of the flow of information in closed systems.

disengagement   Psychological isolation that results from overly rigid boundaries around individuals and subsystems in a family.

enmeshment   Loss of autonomy due to a blurring of psychological boundaries.

equifinality   The ability of complex systems to reach a given final goal in a variety of different ways.

ethnicity   The common ancestry through which groups of people evolve shared values and customs.

family life cycle   Stages of family life, from separation from one's parents to marriage, having children, growing older, retirement, and, finally, death.

family rules   A descriptive term for redundant family behavioral patterns, norms, and expectations.

family structure   The functional organization of families that influences how family members interact.

feedback   The return of a portion of the output of a system, especially when used to maintain the output within predetermined limits (negative feedback) or to signal a need to modify the system (positive feedback).

function of the symptom   The idea that symptoms are often ways to distract or otherwise protect family members from threatening conflicts.

general systems theory   A biological model of living systems as whole entities that maintain themselves through continuous input and output from the environment; developed by Ludwig von Bertalanffy.

homeostasis   A balanced steady state of equilibrium.

linear causality   The idea that one event is the cause and another is the effect; in behavior, the idea that one behavior is a stimulus and the other a response.

metacommunication   Every message has two levels, report and command; metacommunication is the implied command or qualifying message.

morphogenesis   The process by which a system changes its structure to adapt to new contexts.

narrative therapy   An approach to treatment that emphasizes the role of the stories people construct about their experience.

negative feedback   See **feedback.**

open system   A system that exchanges information or material with its environment, as opposed to a closed system that does not. Living systems are, by definition, open systems.

positive feedback   See **feedback.**

process/content   Distinction between how members of a family or group relate (process) and what they talk about (content).

reframing   Relabeling a family's description of behavior to make it more amenable to therapeutic change; for example, describing someone as "discouraged" rather than "depressed."

runaway   Unchecked positive feedback that causes a family or system to get out of control.

sequences of family interaction   The recurrent patterns of interpersonal interaction that surround and help explain various problems and behaviors.

social constructionism   Like constructivism, challenges the notion of an objective basis for knowledge. Knowledge and meaning are shaped by culturally shared assumptions.

solution-focused therapy   Steve de Shazer's term for a style of therapy that emphasizes the solutions that families have already developed for their problems.

subsystem   Smaller units in families, determined by generation, gender, or function.

symmetrical   In relationships, equality or parallel form.

systems theory   A generic term for studying a group of related elements that interact as a whole entity; encompasses general systems theory and cybernetics.

triangle   A three-person system; according to Bowen, the smallest stable unit of human relations.

Recommended Readings

Bateson, G. 1971. *Steps to an ecology of mind.* New York: Ballantine.

Bowlby, J. 1988. *A secure base: Clinical application of attachment theory.* London: Routledge.

Carter, E., and McGoldrick, M., eds. 1999. *The expanded family life cycle: A framework for family therapy,* 3rd ed. Boston: Allyn & Bacon.

Haley, J. 1985. Conversations with Erickson. *Family Therapy Networker.* 9(2): 30–43.

Hoffman, L. 1981. *Foundations of family therapy.* New York: Basic Books.

von Bertalanffy, L. 1950. An outline of General System Theory. *British Journal of the Philosophy of Science. 1:* 134–165.

Wiener, N. 1948. *Cybernetics: Or control and communication in the animal and the machine.* Cambridge, MA: Technology Press.

References

Ainsworth, M. D. 1967. *Infancy in Uganda: Infant care and growth of attachment.* Baltimore: Johns Hopkins University Press.

Bateson, G. 1956. *Naven.* Stanford, CA: Stanford University Press.

Bateson, G. 1979. *Mind and nature.* New York: E. P. Dutton.

Bibb, A., and Casimir, G. J. 1996. Haitian families. In *Ethnicity and family therapy.* McGoldrick, M., Giordano, J., and Pearce, J. K., eds. New York: Guilford Press.

Bowen, M. 1978. *Family therapy in clinical practice.* New York: Jason Aronson.

Bowlby, J. 1958. The nature of the child's tie to his mother. *International Journal of Psycho-Analysis. 41:* 350–373.

Bowlby, J. 1973. *Attachment and loss: Vol. 2. Separation.* New York: Basic Books.

Bowlby, J. 1988. *A secure base: Clinical application of attachment theory.* London: Routledge.

Boyd-Franklin, N. 1989. *Black families in therapy: A multisystems approach.* New York: Guilford Press.

Buckley, W. 1968. Society as a complex adaptive system. In *Modern systems research for the behavioral scientist: A sourcebook,* W. Buckley, ed. Chicago: Aldine.

Burlingham, D., and Freud, A. 1944. *Infants without families.* London: Allen & Unwin.

Carter, E., and McGoldrick, M., eds. 1980. *The family life cycle: A framework for family therapy.* New York: Gardner Press.

Carter, E., and McGoldrick, M., eds. 1999. *The expanded family life cycle,* 3rd ed. Boston: Allyn & Bacon.

Chodorow, N. 1978. *The reproduction of mothering.* Berkeley, CA: University of California Press.

Conway, F., and Siegelman, J. 2005. *Dark hero of the information age: In search of Norbert Wiener, the father of cybernetics.* New York: Basic Books.

Davidson, M. 1983. *Uncommon sense.* Los Angeles: J. P. Tarcher.

Duvall, E. 1957. *Family development.* Philadelphia: Lippincott.

Falicov, C. J. 1998. *Latino families in therapy.* New York: Guilford Press.

Gottman, J. 1994. *What predicts divorce.* Hillsdale, NJ: Erlbaum.

Haley, J. 1976. *Problem-solving therapy.* San Francisco: Jossey-Bass.

Harlow, H. 1958. The nature of love. *American Psychologist. 13:* 673–685.

Hill, R., and Rodgers, R. 1964. The developmental approach. In *Handbook of marriage and the family,* H. T. Christiansen, ed. Chicago: Rand McNally.

Jackson, D. D. 1959. Family interaction, family homeostasis, and some implications for conjoint family therapy. In *Individual and family dynamics,* J. Masserman, ed. New York: Grune & Stratton.

Johnson, S. 2002. *Emotionally focused couple therapy with trauma survivors: Strengthening attachment bonds.* New York: Guilford Press.

Kelly, G. A. 1955. *The psychology of personal constructs.* New York: Norton.

Lee, E. 1996. Asian American families: An overview. In *Ethnicity and family therapy,* McGoldrick, M., Giordano, J., and Pearce, J. K., eds. New York: Guilford Press.

Lorenz, K. E. 1935. Der Kumpan in der Umvelt des Vogels. In *Instinctive behavior,* C. H. Schiller, ed. New York: International Universities Press.

Luepnitz, D. A. 1988. *The family interpreted: Feminist theory in clinical practice.* New York: Basic Books.

Mahler, M., Pine F., and Bergman, A. 1975. *The psychological birth of the human infant.* New York: Basic Books.

Maturana, H. R., and Varela, F. J., eds. 1980. *Autopoiesis and cognition: The realization of the living.* Boston: Reidel.

Meyrowitz, J. 1985. *No sense of place.* New York: Oxford University Press.

Minuchin, P., Colapinto, J., and Minuchin, S. 2007. *Working with families of the poor,* 2nd ed. New York: Guilford Press.

Minuchin, S. 1974. *Families and family therapy.* Cambridge, MA: Harvard University Press.

Minuchin, S. 1991. The seductions of constructivism. *Family Therapy Networker. 15*(5): 47–50.

Minuchin, S., Lee, W.-Y., and Simon, G. M. 1996. *Mastering family therapy: Journeys of growth and transformation.* New York: Wiley.

Minuchin, S., and Nichols, M. P. 1993. *Family healing: Tales of hope and renewal from family therapy.* New York: Free Press.

Robertson, J. 1953. *A two-year-old goes to hospital.* [Film]. London: Tavistock Child Development Research Unit.

von Foerster, H. 1981. *Observing systems.* Seaside, CA: Intersystems.

Walters, M., Carter, B., Papp, P., and Silverstein, O. 1988. *The invisible web: Gender patterns in family relationships.* New York: Guilford Press.

Watzlawick, P., ed. 1984. *The invented reality.* New York: Norton.

Watzlawick, P., Beavin, J. H., and Jackson, D. D. 1967. *Pragmatics of human communication.* New York: Norton.

White, M., and Epston, D. 1990. *Narrative means to therapeutic ends.* New York: Norton.

Wiener, N. 1948. *Cybernetics or control and communication in the animal and the machine.* Cambridge, MA: MIT Press.

5

Bowen Family Systems Therapy

*T*he pioneers of family therapy recognized that people are products of their context, but they limited their focus to the nuclear family. Yes, actions are influenced by what goes on in our families. But what are the forces, past and present, that mold those influences? What makes a husband distance himself from family life? What makes a wife neglect her own development to manage her children's lives? Murray Bowen sought answers to such questions in the larger network of extended family relationships.

According to Bowen, human relationships are driven by two counterbalancing life forces: *individuality* and *togetherness*. We need companionship and independence. What makes life interesting—and frustrating—is the tendency for those needs to polarize us. One partner presses for connection, and the other feels crowded and pulls away. As time goes by, this pursuit and withdrawal drive the pair through cycles of closeness and distance.

How successfully people reconcile these two polarities of human nature depends on the extent to which they have learned to manage emotionality, or to use Bowen's term, their *differentiation of self.* More on this later.

Although no one doubts the formative influence of the family, many people imagine that once they leave home they are grown up: independent adults, free at last of their parents' influence. Some people take it as a sign of growth to separate from their parents. Others wish they could be closer to their families but find visits painful, so they stay away to protect themselves from disappointment. Once out of range of the immediate conflict, they forget and deny the discord. But the family remains with us wherever we go. As we will see, unresolved emotional reactivity to our parents is the most important unfinished business of our lives.

*E*VOLUTION OF THE MODEL

Murray Bowen's professional interest in the family began when he was a psychiatrist at the Menninger Clinic in the late 1940s. Turning his attention to the enigma of schizophrenia, Bowen was struck by the exquisite emotional sensitivity between patients and their mothers. Others had called this reactivity *symbiosis,* as though it were some kind of parasitic mutation. Bowen saw it simply as an exaggeration of a natural process, a more intense version of the tendency to react emotionally to one another that exists in all relationships.

In 1954 Bowen moved to the National Institute of Mental Health (NIMH), where he initiated a project of hospitalizing entire families containing a schizophrenic member. What he found was that the volatile

Murray Bowen

Murray Bowen, one of the pioneers of family therapy, emphasized theory as opposed to technique, distinguishing his work from the more behaviorally oriented family therapists. Bowen's therapy was an outgrowth of his psychoanalytic roots and offers the most comprehensive view of human behavior of any approach to family therapy. The goal in the Bowenian model is *differentiation of self*, namely, the ability to remain oneself in the face of external influences, especially the pressures of family life. The Bowenian model considers the thoughts and feelings of each family member as well as the larger network of family relationships that shapes the life of the family.

bond between mothers and their emotionally disturbed offspring inevitably involved the whole family. At the heart of the problem was *anxious attachment*, a pathological form of closeness driven by anxiety. In these troubled families, people were emotional prisoners of the way the others behaved. The hallmark of these emotionally stuck-together, or *fused*, relationships was a lack of personal autonomy.

When the NIMH project ended in 1959 and Bowen moved to Georgetown University, he began working with families whose problems were less severe. What he discovered were many of the same mechanisms he had observed in psychotic families. This convinced him that there is no discontinuity between normal and disturbed families but that all families vary along a continuum from emotional fusion to differentiation.

During his thirty-one years at Georgetown, Bowen developed a comprehensive

theory of family therapy, inspired an entire generation of students, and became an internationally renowned leader of the family therapy movement. He died after a long illness in October 1990.

Among the most prominent of Bowen's students are Philip Guerin and Thomas Fogarty, who joined in 1973 to form the Center for Family Learning in New Rochelle, New York. Under Guerin's leadership, the Center for Family Learning became one of the major centers of family therapy training. Guerin is a laid-back, virtuoso therapist and teacher, and two of his books, *The Evaluation and Treatment of Marital Conflict* and *Working with Relationship Triangles*, are among the most useful in all the family therapy literature.

Betty Carter and Monica McGoldrick are best known for their exposition of the family life cycle (Carter & McGoldrick, 1999) and for championing feminism in family therapy. Michael Kerr was a longtime student and colleague of Bowen's and since 1977 has been

Philip Guerin

The innovative ideas of Philip Guerin (a student of Murray Bowen) led to his development of a sophisticated clinical approach to treating problems of children and adolescents, couples, and individual adults. Guerin's highly articulated model outlines several therapeutic goals, which emphasize the multigenerational context of families, working to calm the emotional level of family members, and defining specific patterns of relationships within families. Guerin's family systems approach is designed to measure the severity of conflict and identify specific areas in need of improvement.

the director of training at the Georgetown Family Center. Kerr is perhaps the most faithful advocate of all Bowen's students, as his brilliant account of Bowen theory in the book *Family Evaluation* (Kerr & Bowen, 1988) richly demonstrates.

*T*HE BASIC MODEL

Family therapy's pioneers were pragmatists, more concerned with action than insight, more interested in technique than theory. Bowen was the exception. He was always more committed to systems theory as a way of thinking than as a set of interventions.

According to Bowen, we have less autonomy in our emotional lives than we like to think. Most of us are more dependent on and more reactive to one another than we realize. Bowen's theory describes how the family, as a multigenerational network of relationships, shapes the interplay of individuality and togetherness using five interlocking concepts (Bowen, 1966, 1976): *differentiation of self, triangles, multigenerational emotional processes, emotional cutoff, and societal emotional process.*

Differentiation of Self

The cornerstone of Bowen's theory is both an intrapsychic and an interpersonal concept. Roughly analogous to *ego strength,* **differentiation of self** is the capacity to think and reflect, to not respond automatically to emotional pressures, internal or external (Kerr & Bowen, 1988). It is the ability to be flexible and act wisely, even in the face of anxiety.

Undifferentiated people are easily moved to emotionality. Their lives are driven by reactivity to those around them. The differentiated person is able to balance thinking and feeling: capable of strong emotion and spontaneity but also possessing the self-restraint that comes with the ability to resist the pull of emotional impulses.

In contrast, undifferentiated people tend to react impetuously—with submissiveness or defiance—toward others. They find it difficult to maintain their own autonomy, especially around anxious issues. Asked what

they think, they say what they feel; asked what they believe, they parrot what they've heard. They agree with whatever you say, or argue with everything. In contrast, differentiated people are able to take stands on issues because they're able to think things through, decide what they believe, and then act on those beliefs.

Emotional Triangles

Take a minute to think about the most troublesome current relationship in your life. That relationship almost certainly involves one or more third persons. Virtually all relationships are shadowed by third parties—relatives, friends, even memories.

What drives **triangles** is anxiety (Guerin, Fogarty, Fay, & Kautto, 1996). As anxiety increases, people experience a greater need for emotional closeness—or in reaction to pressure from others, a greater need for distance. The more people are driven by anxiety, the less tolerant they are of one another and the more they are polarized by differences.

When two people have problems they're unable to resolve, they get to the point where it's hard to talk about certain things. Why go through all that aggravation when it only leads to frustration? Eventually, one or both partners will turn to someone else for sympathy. Or the conflict will draw in a third person to try to fix it. If the third party's involvement is only temporary or pushes the two people to work out their differences, the triangle doesn't become fixed. But if, as often happens, the third person stays involved, the triangle becomes a part of the relationship.

The involvement of a third party decreases anxiety in the twosome by spreading it through three relationships. Thus, for example, a wife upset with her husband's distance may increase her involvement with one of the children. What makes this a triangle is diverting energy that might otherwise go into the marriage. The wife's spending time with her daughter may take pressure off her husband to do things he doesn't care to. However, it also decreases the likelihood that husband and wife will develop interests they can share—and it may undermine the daughter's independence.

A group of three isn't necessarily a triangle. In a viable threesome, each pair can interact independently;

[handwritten margin note: Steward]

[handwritten notes at bottom: it's all about fear / relate to fear of death anxiety / what is our largest fear / we can't conquer? / death → Jesus]

each person has options for his or her behavior; and each can take **I-positions** without trying to change the other two. In a triangle, on the other hand, each pair's interaction is tied to the behavior of the third person; each person is driven by reactive forms of behavior; none of them can take a position without feeling the need to change the other two; and each person is involved in the relationship between the other two. Picture a rubber band around three people who cannot allow it to drop. It constrains their movement such that if two people get closer, the third must move farther away.

Some triangles seem so innocent that we hardly notice their destructiveness. Most parents can't resist complaining to their children once in a while about their mates. "Your mother's always late!" "Your father never lets anyone else drive!" These interchanges seem harmless enough. What makes triangles problematic is that they have a tendency to become habitual.

Triangulation lets off steam but freezes conflict in place. It isn't so much that complaining or seeking solace is wrong, but rather that triangles become chronic diversions that undermine relationships.

Multigenerational Emotional Processes

Emotional forces in families operate over the years in patterns. Bowen originally used the term **undifferentiated family ego mass** to describe an excess of emotional reactivity, or **fusion** in families. If you know someone who overreacts to what you're trying to say because he or she is given to emotional outbursts, then you know how frustrating it can be to deal with emotionally reactive people.

Lack of differentiation in a family produces reactive children, which may be manifest as emotional overinvolvement or *emotional cutoff* from the parents, which in turn leads to fusion in new relationships— because people with limited emotional resources typically project all their needs onto each other. Since this new fusion is unstable, it tends to produce one of the following: (1) emotional distance between the partners; (2) physical or emotional dysfunction

in one partner; (3) overt conflict; or (4) projection of discord onto children. The intensity of these problems is related to the degree of undifferentiation, extent of emotional cutoff from families of origin, and level of stress in the system.

Emotional fusion in a couple creates tension which leads to conflict, emotional distance, or reciprocal over- and underfunctioning.

A common case is when a husband who is emotionally reactive to his family keeps his distance from his wife. This predisposes her to focus on their children. Kept at arm's length by her husband, she becomes anxiously attached to the children, usually with greatest intensity toward one child. This might be the oldest son or daughter, the youngest, or perhaps the child most like one of the parents. This connection is different from caring; it's anxious, enmeshed concern. Since it relieves his own anxiety, the husband accepts his wife's overinvolvement with the children, reinforcing their entanglement and his distance.

The more the mother focuses her anxiety on a child, the more that child's functioning is stunted. This underdevelopment encourages the mother to hover over the child, distracting her from her own anxieties but crippling the child emotionally.

In every generation the child most involved in the family's fusion moves toward a lower level of differentiation (and chronic anxiety), while the least involved child moves toward a higher level of differentiation (and low anxiety).

Parents who anxiously intrude their concerns on their children leave them little choice but to conform or rebel. Instead of learning to think for themselves, such children function in reaction to others. When these children leave home, they expect to become authors of their own lives. They're not going to turn out like their parents! Unfortunately, although we may fight against our inheritance, it usually catches up with us.

me thinks thou dost protest too much

Emotional Cutoff

Emotional cutoff describes the way some people manage anxiety between generations. The greater the emotional fusion between parents and children, the greater the likelihood of cutoff. Some people seek distance by moving away; others do so emotionally by avoiding personal conversations or insulating themselves with the presence of third parties.

Michael Nichols (1986) describes how some people mistake emotional cutoff for maturity:

> We take it as a sign of growth to separate from our parents, and we measure our maturity by independence of family ties. Yet many of us still respond to our families as though they were radioactive. Only one thing robs Superman of his extraordinary power: kryptonite, a piece of his home planet. A surprising number of adult men and women are similarly rendered helpless by even a brief visit from their parents. (p. 190)

Societal Emotional Process

Bowen anticipated the contemporary concern about social influence on how families function. Kerr and Bowen (1988) cite the example of the high crime rate in communities with highly stressful environments. Bowen recognized sexism and class and ethnic prejudice as examples of toxic social emotional processes, but he believed that individuals and families with higher levels of differentiation were better able to resist these destructive social influences.

• • •

To the theoretical concerns of Bowenian therapists, Monica McGoldrick and Betty Carter added gender and ethnicity. These feminist Bowenians believe that ignoring gender inequalities helps perpetuate some of the primary forces that keep men and women trapped in inflexible roles. Moreover, they might point out that the previous sentence is inaccurate in implying that men and women alike are victims of gender bias. Women live with constraining social conditions *and* with men who profit from them—men who may not feel powerful with their wives and mothers but who take for granted social advantages that make it easier for men to get ahead in the world.

McGoldrick has also been a leader in calling attention to ethnic differences among families. Her book *Ethnicity and Family Therapy* (McGoldrick, Pearce, & Giordano, 1982) was a landmark in family therapy's developing awareness of this issue. Without being sensitive to how cultural values differ from one ethnic group to the next, there is a danger of therapists imposing their own ways of looking at things on families whose perspectives aren't dysfunctional but simply different.

Normal Family Development

Optimal development is thought to take place when family members are differentiated, anxiety is low, and partners are in good emotional contact with their own families. Most people leave home in the midst of transforming relationships with their parents from an adolescent to an adult basis. Thus the transformation is usually incomplete, and most of us, even as adults, continue to react with adolescent sensitivity to our parents—or anyone else who pushes the same buttons.

Normally but not optimally, people reduce contact with their parents and siblings to avoid the anxiety of dealing with them. Once out of the house and on their own, people tend to assume that they've put the old difficulties behind them. However, we all carry unfinished business in the form of unresolved sensitivities that flare up in intense relationships wherever we go. Having learned to ignore their role in family conflicts, most people are unable to prevent recurrences in new relationships.

Another heritage from the past is that the emotional attachment between intimate partners comes to resemble that which each had in his or her **family of origin**. People from undifferentiated families continue to be undifferentiated when they form new families. Those who handled anxiety by withdrawal tend to do the same in their marriages. Therefore, Bowen was convinced that differentiation of autonomous personalities, accomplished primarily in the family of origin, was both a description of normal development and a prescription for therapeutic improvement.

Betty Carter and Monica McGoldrick (1999) describe the **family life cycle** as a process of expansion, contraction, and realignment of the relationship system to support the entry, exit, and development of family members.

In the *leaving-home* stage, the primary task for young adults is to separate from their families without cutting off or fleeing to an emotional substitute. This is the time to develop an autonomous self before pairing off to form a new union.

In the *joining of families through marriage* stage, the primary task is commitment to the new couple. This is not simply a joining of two individuals; it is a transformation of two entire systems. Although problems at this stage may seem to be primarily between the partners, they often reflect a failure to separate from families of origin or cutoffs that put too much pressure on a couple. The formation of an intimate partnership requires the partners to shift their primary emotional attachment from their parents and friends to their mates. Making wedding plans, choosing a place to live, buying a car, having a baby, and picking schools are all times when this struggle may become explicit.

Families with young children must adjust to make space for the new additions, cooperate in child rearing, keep the marriage from being submerged in parenting, and realign relationships with the extended family. Young mothers and fathers must meet their children's needs for nurture and control and learn to work together as a team. This is a stressful time, especially for new mothers, and it is the life-cycle stage with the highest divorce rate.

The reward for parents who survive the preceding stages is to have their children turn into adolescents. *Adolescence* is a time when children no longer want to be like Mommy and Daddy; they want to be themselves. They struggle to become autonomous individuals and to open family boundaries—and they struggle however hard they must. Parents with satisfying lives of their own welcome (or at least tolerate) the fresh

Betty Carter

An ardent and articulate feminist, Betty Carter was instrumental in popularizing the concept of the family life cycle and its value in assessing families. Carter emphasized the importance of historical antecedents of family problems and the multigenerational aspects of the life cycle that extended beyond the nuclear family. She expanded the family life-cycle concept by considering the stages of divorce and remarriage. Carter served as codirector of the Women's Project in Family Therapy with Peggy Papp, Olga Silverstein, and Marianne Walters, and she has been an outspoken critic of the gender and ethnic inequalities that serve to keep women in inflexible family roles.

air that blows through the house at this time. Those who insist on controlling their teenagers, as though they were still little ones, may provoke escalations of the rebelliousness that's normal for this period.

In the *launching of children and moving on* stage, parents must let their children go and take hold of their own lives. This can be liberating, or it can be a time of *midlife crisis* (Nichols, 1986). Parents must deal not only with changes in their children's and their own lives but also with changes in their relationship with aging parents, who may need increasing support or at least don't want to act like parents anymore.

Families in later life must adjust to retirement, which not only means a loss of vocation but also an increase in proximity for the couple. With both partners home all day, the house may seem a lot smaller. Later in life families must cope with declining health, illness, and then death, the great equalizer.

One variation in the life cycle that can no longer be considered abnormal is *divorce*. With the divorce rate at 50 percent and the rate of redivorce at 61 percent (Kreider & Fields, 2002), divorce now strikes *how would you counsel a divorcing couple?*

the majority of American families. The primary tasks of a divorcing couple are to end the marriage but maintain cooperation as parents. Some postdivorce families become single-parent families—consisting in the main of mothers and children—and in the majority of those cases, staggering under the weight of financial strain. The alternative is remarriage and the formation of stepfamilies, in which loneliness often is swapped for conflict.   *blended family*
role of step parent

Development of Behavior Disorders

Symptoms result from stress that exceeds a person's ability to manage it. The ability to handle stress is a function of differentiation: The more well-differentiated people are, the more resilient they will be and the more flexible and sustaining their relationships. In less well-differentiated people, it takes less stress to produce symptoms.

If *differentiation* were reduced to *maturity,* this formula wouldn't add much to the familiar diathesis–stress model, which says that disease develops when an individual's vulnerability is overtaxed. The difference is that differentiation isn't just a quality of individuals but also of relationships. A person's basic level of differentiation is largely determined by the degree of autonomy achieved in his or her family, but the *functional level of differentiation* is influenced by the quality of current relationships. Thus, a somewhat immature person who manages to develop healthy relationships is at less risk than an equally immature person who's alone or in unhealthy relationships. Symptoms develop when the level of anxiety exceeds the *system*'s ability to handle it.

According to Bowen, the underlying factor in the genesis of psychological problems is emotional fusion, passed down from one generation to the next. The greater the fusion, the more one is programmed by primitive emotional forces and the more vulnerable to the emotionality of others.   *insecure*

Emotional fusion is based on anxious attachment, which may be manifest either as dependency or isolation. Both the overly dependent and the emotionally isolated person respond to stress with emotional reactivity. What follows is marital conflict, dysfunction

in one of the spouses, overconcern with one of the children, or a combination of all three. Whatever the presenting problem, however, the dynamics are similar: Undifferentiation in families of origin is transmitted to marital problems, which are in turn projected onto a symptomatic spouse or child. Thus are the problems of the past visited on the future.

How Therapy Works

Bowenians don't try to change people, nor are they much interested in solving problems. They see therapy as an opportunity for people to learn about themselves and their relationships so that they can assume responsibility for their own problems. This is not to say, however, that therapists sit back and allow families to sort out their own conflicts. On the contrary, Bowenian therapy is a process of active inquiry in which the therapist, guided by the most comprehensive theory in family therapy, helps family members get past blaming and explore their own roles in family problems.   *goal*

Tracing the pattern of family problems means paying attention to *process* and *structure.* Process refers to patterns of emotional reactivity; structure, to interlocking networks of triangles.

To change a system, modification must take place in the most important triangle in the family—the one involving the marital couple. If a therapist stays in contact with the partners while remaining emotionally neutral, they can begin the process of **detriangulation** and differentiation that will profoundly and permanently change the entire family system.

The clinical methodology tied to this formulation calls for (1) increasing parents' ability to manage their own anxiety, and thereby becoming better able to handle their children's behavior, and (2) fortifying the couple's emotional functioning by increasing their ability to operate with less anxiety in their families of origin.

Understanding, not action, is the vehicle of cure. Therefore, two of the most important elements in Bowenian therapy may not be apparent to anyone who thinks primarily about techniques. The atmosphere of sessions and the therapist's stance are both

* disengaging is an emotional reaction

[handwritten margin note: so clever, can think clearly]

designed to minimize emotionality. Therapists ask questions to foster self-reflection and direct them at individuals one at a time, rather than encourage family dialogues—which have a tendency to get overheated. Because clients aren't the only ones to respond emotionally to family dramas, Bowenian therapists strive to control their own reactivity and avoid triangulation. This is easier said than done. The keys to staying detriangled are to avoid taking sides and to nudge each party toward accepting more responsibility for making things better.

[handwritten margin note: I tend to value more emotional involvement but still keep anxiety under control]

THERAPY

[handwritten margin note: I see emotions as necessary for deep change]

Increasing the ability to distinguish between thinking and feeling, and learning to use that ability to resolve relationship problems, are the guiding principles of Bowenian therapy. Lowering anxiety and increasing *self-focus*—the ability to see one's own role in interpersonal processes—are the primary mechanisms of change.

Assessment

Assessment begins with a history of the presenting problem. Exact dates are noted and later checked for their relationship to events in the extended family. Next comes a history of the nuclear family, including when the parents met, their courtship, their marriage, and childrearing. Particular attention is paid to where the family lived and when they moved, especially in relation to the location of the extended family. The next part of the evaluation is devoted to the history of both spouses' births, sibling positions, significant facts about their childhoods, and the past and current functioning of their parents. All of this information is recorded on a *genogram* covering at least three generations.

Genograms are schematic diagrams listing family members and their relationships. Included are ages, dates of marriage, deaths, and geographic locations. Men are represented by squares and women by circles with their ages inside the figures. Horizontal lines indicate marriages, with the date of the

Figure 5.1   Basic symbols used in genograms

marriage on the line; vertical lines connect parents and children (Figure 5.1).[1]

What makes a genogram more than a static portrait of a family's history is the inclusion of relationship conflicts, cutoffs, and triangles. The fact that Uncle Fred was an alcoholic or that Great Grandmother Sophie migrated from Russia is relatively meaningless without some understanding of the patterns of emotional processes passed down through the generations.

Certain triangles occur most commonly in different developmental stages. In early marriage, in-law triangles are common—raising issues of primacy of attachment and influence. When children are born and when they reach adolescence, parent–child triangles are almost inevitable.

Case Study

Janet and Warren Langdon requested help for their fifteen-year-old son Martin after Mrs. Langdon found marijuana in a plastic bag in his underwear drawer. Mr. and Mrs. Langdon didn't object when the therapist said she'd like to meet with the three of them. It turned out that the discovery of marijuana was just the latest incident in a series of battles between Mrs. Langdon and her son. Lots of fifteen-year-olds experiment with marijuana; not all

---

[1]For more detailed suggestions, see McGoldrick & Gerson, 1985.

of them leave the evidence around for their mothers to find.

After meeting with the family and then talking with the boy and his parents separately, the therapist concluded that Martin didn't appear to have a serious drug problem. Of greater concern, however, were the intensity of his shouting matches with his mother and his poor social adjustment at school. What she told the family was that she was concerned not only about the marijuana but also about these other signs of unhappy adjustment and that she'd like to extend the evaluation by having a couple of additional meetings with Martin and his parents separately. Mr. and Mrs. Langdon agreed, though without much enthusiasm. Martin didn't protest as much as might have been expected.

After his father died, Mr. Langdon and his older sister were raised by their mother. They were all she had left, and she increasingly devoted all her energy to shaping their lives. She was demanding and critical and resentful of anything they wanted to do outside the family. By late adolescence, Warren could no longer tolerate his mother's domineering. His sister was never able to break free; she remained single and lived at home with her mother. Warren, however, was determined to become independent. Finally, in his mid-twenties, he left home and turned his back on his mother.

Janet Langdon came from a close-knit family. She and her four sisters were very attached to each other and remained best friends. After graduating from high school, Janet announced that she wanted to go to college. This violation of the family norm that daughters stay home and prepare to be wives and mothers provoked a major battle between Janet and her parents. They were struggling to hold on, and she was struggling to break free. Janet finally left for college, but she was ever after estranged from her parents.

Janet and Warren were immediately drawn to one another. Both were lonely and cut off from their families. After a brief, passionate courtship, they married. The honeymoon didn't last long.

Never having really differentiated himself from his dictatorial mother, Warren was exquisitely sensitive to any hint of criticism or control. He became furious at Janet's slightest attempt to change his habits. Janet, on the other hand, sought to reestablish in her marriage the closeness she'd had in her family. To be close, though, she and Warren would have to share interests and activities. When she moved toward him, suggesting they do something together, Warren got angry and resentful, feeling his individuality impinged upon. After several months of conflict, the two settled into a period of relative equilibrium. Warren put most of his energy into his work, leaving Janet to adjust to the distance between them. A year later Martin was born.

Both of them were delighted to have a baby, but what was for Warren a pleasant addition to the family was for Janet the answer to a desperate need for closeness. The baby meant everything to her. While he was an infant, she was the perfect mother, loving him extravagantly and caring for his every need. When Warren tried to become involved with his infant son, Janet hovered about making sure he didn't do anything wrong. This infuriated Warren, and after several bitter blowups, he left Martin to his wife's care.

As he learned to walk and talk, Martin got into mischief, as all children do. He grabbed things, refused to stay in his playpen, and fussed when he didn't get his way. His crying was unbearable to Janet, and she found herself unable to set limits on her precious child.

Martin grew up with a doting mother, thinking he was the center of the universe. Whenever he didn't get what he wanted, he threw a tantrum. Bad as things got, at least the family existed in a kind of equilibrium. Warren was cut off from his wife and son, but he had his work. Janet was alienated from her husband, but she had her baby.

Martin's difficulties began when he started school. Used to getting his own way, he found it impossible to get along with other children. His tantrums did nothing to endear him to his schoolmates. Other children avoided him, and he grew up having few friends. With teachers, he acted out his father's battle against any effort to control him. When Janet heard complaints about Martin's behavior, she sided with her son. "Those people don't know how to deal with a creative child!"

Martin grew up with a terrible pattern of adjustment to school and friends but retained his extremely close relationship with his mother. The crisis came with adolescence. Like his father before him, Martin tried to develop independent interests outside the home. However, he was far less capable of separating than his father had been, and his mother was incapable of letting go. The result was the beginning of chronic conflicts between Martin and his mother. Even as they argued and fought, they remained centered on each other. Martin spent more time battling his mother than doing anything else with his life.

Dates of important events, such as deaths, marriages, and divorces, deserve careful study. These events send emotional shock waves through the family, which may open lines of communication, or these issues may get buried and family members progressively more cut off. Another significant piece of information on the genogram is the location of various segments of the family. Dates, relationships, and localities are the framework for exploring emotional boundaries, fusion, cutoffs, critical conflicts, amount of openness, and the number of current and potential relationships in the family.

Figure 5.2 shows symbols that can be used in describing the relationship dynamics among family members. Three parallel lines are used to indicate overly close (or fused) relationships; a zigzag line,

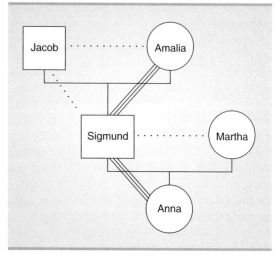

Figure 5.3   Genogram of Sigmund Freud's family.

conflict; a dotted line, emotional distance; and a broken line, estrangement (or cutoff). When these symbols are used, triangular patterns across three generations often become vividly clear—as shown in an abbreviated diagram of Sigmund Freud's family (Figure 5.3).

The history of a nuclear family begins with the courtship of the parents: What attracted them to each other? What was the early period of their relationship like? What were the problems during that period? When were the children born, and how did the parents adapt to the new additions?

If a therapist fails to take a careful history, associations that can help people gain perspective on their problems may be overlooked. Things like moves and important events, such as a husband's cancer surgery two years earlier, may not always be mentioned unless a therapist asks. One woman who had been seeing an individual therapist didn't consider it important enough to mention. "What does my seeing a therapist have to do with my daughter's problems?" she said.

Of particular interest are the stresses a family has endured and how they have adapted. This information helps the therapist to evaluate the intensity of chronic anxiety in a family and whether it is linked

Figure 5.2   Genogram symbols for relationship dynamics

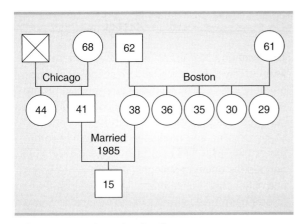

Figure 5.4 Langdon family genogram

more to an overload of difficult life events or to a low level of adaptiveness in the family.

As Figure 5.4 shows, the bare facts of a family genogram provide only a skeleton upon which to flesh out information about the Langdon family.

The decision to extend an assessment beyond the nuclear family depends on the extent of crisis and degree of anxiety the family feels. In the case of the Langdons, both parents seemed eager to discuss their family backgrounds.

Martin's history illustrates Bowen's theory of behavior disorder. Symptoms break out when the "vertical" toxic family issues that come down through the generations intersect with the "horizontal" stresses that come at transition points in the life cycle. Thus, Martin's greatest vulnerability came when the unresolved fusion he inherited from his mother converged with the stress of his adolescent urge for independence.

In gathering information about extended families, a therapist should ascertain which members of the clan are most involved with the family being assessed, for it is the nature of ongoing ties to the extended family that has a great impact on both parents and their role in the nuclear family. Of equal importance, however, is finding out who is *not* involved because people with whom contact has been cut off can be an even greater source of anxiety than the people with whom contact has been maintained.

Therapeutic Techniques

Bowenian therapists believe that understanding how family systems operate is more important than this or that technique. Bowen himself spoke of technique with disdain, and he was distressed to see therapists relying on formulaic interventions.

If there were a magic bullet in Bowenian therapy—one essential technique—it would be the **process question.** Process questions are designed to slow people down, diminish their anxiety, and start them thinking—not just about how others are upsetting them but about how they participate in interpersonal problems.

Process questions are designed to explore what's going on inside people and between them: "When your boyfriend neglects you, how do you deal with it?" "What about your wife's criticism upsets you most?" "When your daughter goes on dates, what goes on inside you?"

Notice how in the following case study, through a series of questions, the therapist attempts to explore the process of the couple's relationship, asking both partners to think about what's going on between them, increase their awareness of their own contributions, and consider what they're planning to do to take responsibility to make things better.

Case Study

In interviewing a couple in which the husband was a recovering alcoholic with a history of abuse, the therapist asked: "Where are you with the thoughts about the damage you've done to your wife and kids with your alcoholism?"

When the man acknowledged responsibility for his abusive behavior and seemed genuinely remorseful, the therapist asked about his progress toward recovery, using process questions to focus on rational planning and personal responsibility. For example:

Therapist: "What makes that step so hard?"
Husband: "Pride."
Therapist: "How does that manifest itself?"
Husband: "I get nasty."

Notice how this line of questioning explores not only the man's personal progress but also how his problems affect others. Relationships take place in a systemic web of connections, but individuals are responsible for their own behavior.

Then the therapist shifted to open a discussion of the wife's role in the couple's difficulties. "So, you're getting better at taking responsibility for the drinking and the behavior connected with it? Do you think your wife appreciates what you're doing and the progress you're making?" And then a few minutes later the therapist asked: "Has your wife ever been able to talk to you about the things she's contributed to the relationship going sour?"

When the therapist asked the wife about her thinking, she reiterated all the annoying things her husband was doing—pressuring her to forgive him and get back together. Although he would eventually like her to consider her own role in the process, the therapist tried to empathize with her upset. "So, he's just bugging you by trying to get you to change your mind?" Then after a few minutes, the therapist tried to shift the wife to thinking more and feeling less. "Can you give me a summary of your thinking— how you came to that conclusion?" When the wife again got angry and blamed her husband, the therapist just listened. A moment later he asked, "What do you do in the face of that abuse?"

Wife: "I get upset."
Therapist: "Do you understand what it is about you that sets him off?"
Wife: "No."
Therapist: "Has he ever been able to tell you?"

The second major technique in Bowenian therapy is the **relationship experiment.** Process questions are designed to help family members realize that it isn't what other people do but how they respond that perpetuates their problems. Relationship experiments are designed to help clients understand what it's like to act counter to their usual emotionally driven responses. Some of these experiments may help clients resolve their problems, but their primary purpose is to help people discover their ability to move against the ways their emotions are driving them.

Case Study

The Kennedys came to therapy because sixteen-year-old David was doing badly in school. David was on the verge of flunking out of an exclusive private school—partly because he was a poor student and partly because his evenings with friends included heavy drinking and marijuana smoking. His father had gotten after him to study harder and had suspended his driving privileges after he came home one school night quite drunk. Unfortunately, these efforts hadn't been very effective because David didn't respect his father, who was an alcoholic and frequently falling-down drunk around the house. David's stepmother, who'd been living with them for only two years, had little ability to control him, and she knew enough not to try.

I told the parents that I wouldn't see them in family therapy because David didn't respect the father who was drunk every night and who, I added, didn't show any signs of being ready to do anything about his drinking. I did agree, however, to see David to try to help him finish the school year with passing grades.

David was able to pass the eleventh grade, and I continued to see him into the following year, not entirely comfortable in my role as substitute father figure. Although I maintained my resolve not to do therapy with a family that included a member who was actively abusing alcohol, I did meet with the family during three or four crises. The first three crises occurred when Mr. Kennedy's drinking (and, it turned out, cocaine abuse) got way out of control and his father and wife insisted that he reenter treatment.

The most prominent triangle in this case was that Mr. Kennedy's wife and father got together to pressure him to quit drinking. He had gone to rehab several times, but even the few times he'd actually finished a program, he had soon returned to drinking. The only reason he ever sought help was as a result of ultimatums from his wife and father. His wife threatened to leave him, and his father threatened to cut him off from the family estate. This case would go nowhere until this triangle could be modified.

I encouraged Mr. Kennedy's wife and father to work on being less reactive while separating from each other around the issue of Mr. Kennedy's drinking. Mr. Kennedy needed to take a stand for himself rather than be compliant to his wife's and his father's wishes. In fact, I wondered aloud with him if taking an honest stance with his family wouldn't mean telling them that he didn't intend to quit drinking. What he decided to tell them was that while he was willing to work on controlling his drinking and use of cocaine, he didn't intend to quit.

I encouraged Mr. Kennedy's father to back off and let the other two battle it out. Reluctantly, he agreed to do so. I then got Mrs. Kennedy to make a clear statement about how she felt about her husband's drinking but to discontinue her fruitless efforts to make him stop. I encouraged her to maintain her connection with her father-in-law but without talking about her husband all the time. Two months later, Mr. Kennedy decided to stop drinking and using cocaine.

This time he successfully completed a twenty-eight-day rehab program and entered Alcoholics Anonymous (AA) and Narcotics Anonymous (NA). Six weeks later he once again relapsed. Over the following eight months, Mr. Kennedy's drinking and cocaine abuse got much, much worse. Finally, after a serious altercation with a Jamaican drug dealer, Mr. Kennedy made a serious decision to get sober. This time, instead of going to the respected local rehabilitation center that his father had recommended, he did some research on his own and decided to enter a famous drug treatment center in California. As of this writing, Mr. Kennedy has been sober for six years.

Bowenian Therapy with Couples.   The essence of couples therapy is to stay connected with both partners without letting them triangle you. In practice, Bowen would connect with each person one at a time, often beginning with the overfunctioning or more motivated partner. He would ask nonconfrontational questions, verify facts, and hear feelings. But he would frame each question to stimulate

thinking rather than encourage expression of feelings. His objective was to explore the perceptions and opinions of each partner without siding emotionally with either one. It's taking sides that keeps people from learning to deal with each other.

When things are calm, feelings can be dealt with more objectively and partners can talk rationally with each other. But when emotion outruns thinking, it's best to ask questions that get couples to think more and feel less—and to talk to the therapist rather than to each other.

Couples who've argued for years about the same old issues are often amazed to discover that the first time they really hear each other is when they listen to their partners talking to a therapist. It's easier to hear when you aren't busy planning your own response. If all else fails to cool things down, Fogarty (1976) recommends seeing spouses in separate sessions.

As partners talk, the therapist concentrates on the *process* of their interaction, not the details under discussion. Focusing on *content* is a sign that the therapist is emotionally entangled. It may be hard to avoid being drawn in by hot topics like money, sex, and discipline of children. But a therapist's job isn't to settle disputes; it's to help couples do so. The aim is to get clients to express thoughts and opinions to the therapist in the presence of their partners. Should one break down in tears, the therapist remains calm and inquires about the thoughts that touched off the tears. If a couple begins arguing, the therapist becomes more active, calmly questioning one, then the other, and focusing on their respective thoughts. Asking for detailed descriptions of events is one of the best ways to cool overheated emotion and make room for reason.

Metaphors of complementarity help to highlight the process of interactions. Fogarty (1976), for example, described the *pursuer–distancer* dynamic. The more one presses for communication and togetherness, the more the other distances—watches television, works late, or goes off with the children. Frequently, partners pursue and distance in different areas. Men commonly distance themselves emotionally but pursue sexually. The trick, according to Fogarty, is "Never pursue a distancer." Instead, help the pursuer explore his or her own inner emptiness: What's in your life besides the other person?

To underscore the need for objectivity, Bowen spoke of the therapist as a "coach" or "consultant." He didn't mean to imply disinterest but rather to emphasize the neutrality required to avoid triangulation. In traditional terms, this is known as *managing countertransference.* Just as analysts are analyzed themselves so they can recognize countertransference, so Bowen considered differentiating a self in one's own family the best way to avoid being emotionally triangled by clients.

To help partners define differentiated identities, it's useful for a therapist to take **I-positions** (Guerin, 1971)—that is, to make nonreactive observations and statements of opinion. The more a therapist takes an autonomous position in relation to the family by refusing to take sides or take over, the easier it is for family members to define themselves to each other. Gradually, family members learn to state their own beliefs and to act on them without attacking others or becoming overly upset by their responses.

After sufficient harmony had been won with progress toward self-differentiation, Bowen taught couples how emotional systems operate and encouraged them to explore those webs of relationship in their own families (Bowen, 1971).

For example, a woman locked into the role of emotional pursuer might be asked to describe her relationship with her father and then compare it with her current relationships. If lessening her preoccupation with her husband and children seemed advisable, the therapist might encourage her to connect with the most emotionally distant member of her family, often her father. The idea wouldn't be to shift her attachment from one set of relationships to another but to help her understand that the intensity of her need is due in part to unfinished business.

Michael Kerr (1971) suggests that when relationships in the nuclear family are being discussed,

therapists should ask occasional questions about the family of origin. If family members see that they are repeating earlier patterns, they're more likely to recognize their own emotional reactivity. Recently, this author saw a couple unable to decide what to do with their mentally ill teenage daughter. Although the daughter was virtually uncontrollable, her mother found it difficult to consider hospitalization. When asked what her own mother would have done, without hesitating she replied that her long-suffering mother would have been too guilt-ridden even to consider placement—"no matter how much she and the rest of the family might suffer." Little more needed to be said.

Bowenian Therapy with Individuals. Bowen's success at differentiation within his own family convinced him that a single highly motivated individual can be the fulcrum for changing an entire family system (Anonymous, 1972). The goal of working with individuals is the same as with larger units: developing person-to-person relationships, seeing family members as people rather than emotionally charged images, learning to recognize triangles, and finally, detriangling oneself (Bowen, 1974).

The actual process of change is begun by learning more about the larger family—who made up the family, where they lived, what they did, and what they were like. Sometimes a "good relationship" turns out to be one in which tension is managed by distancing: infrequent contact, superficial conversation, and gossiping about other family members. Therefore, it's useful to ask for descriptions rather than conclusions—not, "Do you have a good relationship with your parents?" but, "Where do your parents live? How often do you see them? What do you and your mother talk about when you're alone together? Do you ever go out to lunch, just you and your dad?"

Gathering information about the family is an excellent vehicle for the second step toward differentiation, establishing person-to-person relationships with as many family members as possible. This means getting in touch and speaking personally with them, not about other people or impersonal topics. If this sounds easy, try it. Few of us can spend more than a few minutes talking personally with certain family members without getting anxious. When this happens, we're tempted to withdraw, or triangle in another person. Gradually extending the time of personal conversation improves the relationship and helps differentiate a self.

Ultimately, differentiating yourself requires ceasing to participate in interpersonal triangles. The goal is to relate to people without gossiping or taking sides and without counterattacking or defending yourself.

Suppose, for example, that every time you talk to your mother she starts complaining about your father. Maybe it feels good to be confided in. Maybe you have fantasies about rescuing your parents—or at least your mother. In fact, the triangling is destructive to all three relationships: you and Dad, Dad and Mom, and, yes, you and Mom. In triangles, one pair is close and two are distant (Figure 5.5). Sympathizing with Mom alienates Dad. It also makes it less likely that she'll work out her complaints with him.

Once you recognize a triangle for what it is, you can plan to stop participating in it. The idea is to do something to get the other two people to work out their own relationship. The most direct approach is simply to suggest that they do so. In the example just given, you could suggest that your mother discuss her concerns with your father *and* refuse to listen to more complaints. Less direct but more powerful is to tell Dad that his wife has been complaining about him and you don't know why she doesn't tell him about it. She'll be annoyed but not forever. A more

devious ploy is to overagree with Mom's complaints. When she says he's messy, you say he's a complete slob; when she says he's not very thoughtful, you say he's an ogre. Pretty soon she'll begin to defend him. Maybe she'll decide to work out her complaints with him, or maybe she won't. Either way, you'll have removed yourself from the triangle.

Once you look for them, you'll find triangles everywhere. Common examples include griping about the boss, telling someone that your partner doesn't understand you, undercutting your spouse with the children, and watching television to avoid talking to someone. Breaking free of triangles isn't easy, but the rewards are great. The payoff comes not only from enriching those relationships but also from enhancing your ability to relate to anyone—friends, colleagues, clients, and your spouse and children. Furthermore, if you can remain in emotional contact but change the part you play in your family—and maintain the change despite pressures to change back—the family will have to accommodate to your change.

Useful guidelines to resisting the family's attempts to get you to change back to unproductive but familiar patterns of the past have been enumerated by Carter and Orfanidis (1976), Guerin and Fogarty (1972), and Herz (1991). You can also read about how to work on family tensions by resolving your own emotional sensitivities in two marvelous books by Harriet Lerner: *The Dance of Anger* (Lerner, 1985) and *The Dance of Intimacy* (Lerner, 1989).

CURRENT STATUS OF THE MODEL

What makes Bowen's theory so useful is that it describes the emotional forces that regulate how we relate to other people. The single greatest impediment to understanding one another is our tendency to become emotionally reactive. Like all things about relationships, emotionality is a two-way street: Some people express themselves with such emotionalism that others react to that pressure rather than hearing what the person is trying to say. Bowenian theory

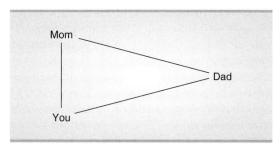

Figure 5.5 Cross-generational triangle

describes this reactivity, traces its origins to the lack of differentiation of self, and explains how to contain emotionalism and move toward self-control—by cultivating relationships widely in the family and learning to listen without becoming defensive or untrue to one's own beliefs.

In Bowenian theory, *anxiety* is the underlying explanation (for why people are dependent or avoidant and why they become emotionally reactive), reminiscent of Freudian conflict theory (which explains all symptoms as the result of conflicts about sex and aggression). The second pivotal concept in the Bowenian system is, of course, *differentiation.* Because differentiation is roughly synonymous with maturity, students might ask to what extent is the proposition that more differentiated people function better a circular argument. In respect to the Bowenian tradition of asking questions rather than imposing opinions, we'll let this stand as an open question for your consideration.

A possible shortcoming of the Bowenian approach is that in concentrating on individuals and their extended family relationships, it may neglect the power of working directly with the nuclear family. In many cases the most direct way to resolve family problems is to bring together everyone in the same household and encourage them to face each other and address their conflicts. These discussions may turn heated and contentious, but a therapist can help family members realize what they're doing and guide them toward understanding.

Families are occasionally so hostile that their dialogues should be interrupted to help individuals get beyond defensiveness to the hurt feelings underneath. At such times, it is useful, perhaps imperative, to block family members from arguing. But an approach such as Bowen's that encourages therapists to always speak to individual family members one at a time may neglect the power of working with families in action.

Phil Guerin and Tom Fogarty have made notable contributions, not only in promulgating Bowenian theory but also in refining techniques of therapy. Both are master therapists. Betty Carter and Monica McGoldrick have made more of a contribution in studying how families work: the normal family life cycle, ethnic diversity, and the destructive impact of gender inequality. Because they are students of the family as well as therapists, some of their interventions have a decidedly educational flavor. In working with stepfamilies, for example, Betty Carter teaches stepparents not to try to assume an equal position with the biological parents. Stepparents have to earn moral authority; meanwhile, what works best is supporting the role of the biological parent. Just as Bowen's approach is influenced by his personal experience, it seems that both Carter and McGoldrick infuse their work as family therapists with their own experience as career women and their convictions about the price of inequality.

Recent reviews of the clinical outcome literature have failed to find any controlled outcome studies that tested the effectiveness of Bowenian therapy (Johnson & Lebow, 2000; Miller, Johnson, Sandberg, Stringer-Seibold, & Gfeller-Strouts, 2000). This isn't surprising, considering that research is usually conducted by academics, most of whom are more interested in behavioral models than in traditional approaches like psychoanalysis and Bowen systems theory. There have, however, been attempts to test the empirical validity of some of the propositions of Bowen's theory.

Three psychometrically sound measures of differentiation of self have been developed. The first is Haber's (1993) Level of Differentiation of Self Scale, which contains twenty-four items that focus on emotional maturity, such as "I make decisions based on my own set of values and beliefs" and "When I have a problem that upsets me, I am still able to consider different options for solving the problem." This scale significantly correlates (negatively) with chronic anxiety and psychological distress, which is consistent with Bowen theory.

Skowron's Differentiation of Self Inventory (DSI; Skowron & Friedlander, 1998) contains four subscales: Emotional Cutoff ("I need to distance myself when people get too close to me," "I would never consider turning to any of my family members for emotional support"); "I"-Position ("I do not change my behavior simply to please another person"); Emotional Reactivity ("At times my feelings get the best of me and I have trouble thinking clearly"); and Fusion with Others ("It has been said of me that I am still very attached to my parents"). As Bowen theory predicts, the DSI correlates significantly with chronic anxiety, psychological distress, and marital satisfaction.

The third scale, Chabot's Emotional Differentiation Scale (CED), was designed to measure Bowen's intrapsychic aspect of differentiation—the ability to think rationally in emotionally charged situations (Licht & Chabot, 2006). The CED asks subjects to respond to seventeen questions that assess integration of thinking and feeling in nonstressful periods and periods of prolonged stress, as well as when relationships are going well and have difficulties.

Research has supported Bowen's notion that differentiation is related to trait anxiety (negatively) (Griffin & Apostal, 1993; Haber, 1993; Skowron & Friedlander, 1998), psychological and physical health problems (negatively) (Bohlander, 1995; Davis & Jones, 1992; Elieson & Rubin, 2001; Haber, 1993; Skowron & Friedlander, 1998), and marital satisfaction (positively) (Haber, 1984; Richards, 1989; Skowron, 2000; Skowron & Friedlander, 1998). Several studies have shown a significant relationship between triangulation and marital distress (Gehring & Marti, 1993; Vuchinich, Emery, & Cassidy, 1988; Wood, Watkins, Boyle, Nogueira, Zimand, & Carroll,

1989) as well as problems in intimate relationships (Protinsky & Gilkey, 1996; West, Zarski, & Harvill, 1986). Finally, consistent with Bowen's belief in the **multigenerational transmission process,** researchers have found that parents' and children's beliefs are highly correlated (e.g., Troll & Bengston, 1979) and that violence (e.g., Alexander, Moore, & Alexander, 1991), divorce (e.g., Amato, 1996), marital quality, (e.g., Feng, Giarrusso, Bengston, & Fry, 1999), eating disorders (e.g., Whitehouse & Harris, 1998), depression (e.g., Whitbeck et al., 1992), and alcoholism (e.g., Sher, Gershuny, Peterson, & Raskin, 1997) are transmitted from one generation to the next.

Ultimately, the status of extended family systems therapy rests not on empirical research but on the elegance of Bowen's theory, clinical experience with this approach, and the personal experience of those who have worked at differentiating themselves in their families of origin. Bowen himself was decidedly cool to empirical research (Bowen, 1976), preferring instead to refine and integrate theory and practice. Like psychoanalysis, Bowen systems theory is probably best judged not as true or false but as useful or not useful. On balance, it seems eminently useful.

Summary

1. Bowen's conceptual lens was wider than most family therapists', although his unit of treatment was often smaller. But even when he met with just individuals or couples, his concern was always with the multigenerational family system. According to Bowen, the major problem in families is *emotional fusion;* the major goal is *differentiation.*

2. Emotional fusion grows out of an instinctual need for others but is an unhealthy distortion of this need based on anxious attachment. Some people manifest fusion directly in an excessive need for togetherness; others mask it with a façade of independence. In either case, contagious anxiety drives automatic responses in close relationships that limit the autonomous functioning of both members of the dyad.

3. In addition to extending his analysis of family problems deeper into the anxieties of individuals, Bowen also extended the focus wider, making the triangle the universal unit of analysis—in principle and in practice. When people can't settle their differences, the automatic tendency to involve third parties stabilizes relationships but freezes conflict in place. Bowen's recognition that the majority of family problems have triangular complications was one of the seminal ideas in family therapy.

4. Bowen discouraged therapists from trying to fix relationships and instead encouraged them to remain neutral while exploring the emotional processes in conflictual relationships with process questions. Bowenian therapists rarely give advice. They just

keep asking questions. The goal isn't to solve people's problems but to help them learn to see their own role in how their family system operates. This self-discovery isn't merely a matter of introspection, because understanding is seen as a tool for repairing relationships and enhancing one's own autonomous functioning.

Six techniques are prominent in the practice of Bowen family systems therapy:

- *Genogram.* In addition to recording biographic data, the genogram is used to trace relationship conflicts, cutoffs, and key triangles. This process of collecting information is sometimes therapeutic in and of itself: Family members often say, "It never occurred to me how all those events fit together." The most comprehensive guide to working with genograms is *Genograms in Family Assessment* (McGoldrick & Gerson, 1985).

- *Neutralizing Triangles.* If a therapist can remain free of the emotional reactivity families bring to therapy, clients will be better able to reduce their own emotionality and begin to think more clearly about their problems. The danger is that the same process of emotional triangulation families use to stabilize their conflicts will engulf the therapist. If so, therapy will be stalemated. On the other hand, if the therapist can remain free of reactive emotional entanglements—in other words, stay detriangled—the family system and its members will calm down to the point where they can begin to work out their dilemmas.

- *Process Questions.* Each family member is asked a series of questions aimed at toning down emotion and fostering objective reflection. Process questions are also used to help manage and neutralize triangles, including the potential triangle(s) that may develop between the therapist and various family members. The process question is aimed at calming anxiety and gaining access to information on how the family perceives the problem and how the mechanisms driving the problem operate. If process questions decrease anxiety, people will be better able to think clearly. This clarity allows them to discover more potential options for managing their problems.

- *Relationship Experiments.* Relationship experiments are carried out around structural alterations in key triangles. The goal is to help family members become aware of systems processes and learn to recognize their own role in them. Perhaps the best illustrations of such experiments are those developed by Fogarty for use with emotional pursuers and distancers. Pursuers are encouraged to restrain their pursuit, stop making demands, decrease pressure for emotional connection, and see what happens in themselves and in the relationship. This exercise isn't designed to be a magic cure (as some people hope) but to help clarify the emotional processes involved. Distancers are encouraged to move toward their partners and communicate personal thoughts and feelings—in other words, to find an alternative to avoiding or capitulating to the other person's demands.

- *Coaching.* Coaching is the Bowenian alternative to the more emotionally involved role common to other forms of therapy. By acting as a coach, the Bowenian therapist hopes to avoid taking over for clients or becoming embroiled in family triangles. Coaching doesn't mean telling people what to do. It means asking questions designed to help people figure out family emotional processes and their role in them.

- *The "I"-Position.* An "I"-position is a calm and clear statement of personal opinion. In situations of increased tension, it often has a stabilizing effect for one person to be able to detach from the emotionality and adopt an "I"-position. Taking a personal stance—saying what you feel instead of what others are doing—is one of the most direct ways to break cycles of emotional reactivity. It's the difference between saying "You're lazy" and "I wish you would help me more," or between "You're always spoiling the children" and "I think we should be stricter with them." It's a big difference.

5. Bowenian therapists not only encourage clients to take I-positions but also do so themselves. For example, after a family session, the mother pulls the therapist aside and confides that her husband has terminal cancer but she doesn't want the children to know. What to do? Take an I-position: Say to the mother, "I believe your children have a right to know about this." What she does, of course, is up to her.

6. Finally, although students of family therapy are likely to evaluate different approaches according to how much sense they make and how useful they

promise to be, Bowen himself considered his most important contribution to be showing the way to make human behavior a science. Far more important than developing methods and techniques of family therapy, Murray Bowen made profound contributions to our understanding of how we function as individuals, how we get along with our families, and how these are related.

Questions to Consider

1. In what kinds of cases might a Bowenian approach be useful in treating individual college students in a counseling center?
2. How is the Bowenian emphasis on self-focus unique in family therapy?
3. To what extent is reducing anxiety—in the therapist and clients—essential to any kind of exploratory therapy? What can a therapist do to reduce his or her own anxiety?
4. What are some advantages and disadvantages of speaking to family members one at a time rather than encouraging them to talk with each other?
5. Are there any members of your extended family from whom you are cut off, and if so, is this situation part of a triangle?

Key Concepts

detriangulation The process by which an individual removes himself or herself from the emotional field of two others.

differentiation of self Psychological separation of intellect and emotions and independence of self from others; opposite of fusion.

emotional cutoff Bowen's term for flight from an unresolved emotional attachment.

family life cycle Stages of family life from separation from one's parents to marriage, having children, growing older, retirement, and, finally, death.

family of origin A person's parents and siblings; usually refers to the original nuclear family of an adult.

fusion A blurring of psychological boundaries between self and others and a contamination of emotional and intellectual functioning; opposite of differentiation.

genogram A schematic diagram of the family system, using squares to represent male family

members, circles to indicate female family members, horizontal lines for marriages, and vertical lines to indicate children.

I-position A statement that acknowledges one's personal opinions rather than blames others ("You never . . .") or moralizes ("Children should always . . .").

multigenerational transmission process Murray Bowen's concept for the projection of varying degrees of immaturity to different children in the same family; the child who is most involved in the family emotional process emerges with the lowest level of differentiation and passes problems on to succeeding generations.

process questions Questions designed to help family members think about their own reactions to what others are doing.

relationship experiments Suggestions for trying new ways of responding to family stresses, designed more to help family members understand how emotional processes work than to solve problems.

triangle   A three-person system; according to Bowen, the smallest stable unit of human relations.

triangulation   Detouring conflict between two people by involving a third person, stabilizing the relationship between the original pair.

undifferentiated family ego mass   Bowen's early term for emotional "stuck-togetherness" or fusion in the family, especially prominent in schizophrenic families.

Recommended Readings

Anonymous. 1972. Differentiation of self in one's family. In *Family interaction,* J. Framo, ed. New York: Springer.

Bowen, M. 1978. *Family therapy in clinical practice.* New York: Jason Aronson.

Carter, E., and Orfanidis, M. M. 1976. Family therapy with one person and the family therapist's own family. In *Family therapy: Theory and practice,* P. J. Guerin, ed. New York: Gardner Press.

Fogarty, T. F. 1976. Systems concepts and the dimensions of self. In *Family therapy: Theory and practice,* P. J. Guerin, ed. New York: Gardner Press.

Guerin, P. J., Fay, L., Burden, S., and Kautto, J. 1987. *The evaluation and treatment of marital conflict: A four-stage approach.* New York: Basic Books.

Guerin, P. J., Fogarty, T. F., Fay, L. F., and Kautto, J. G. 1996. *Working with relationship triangles: The one-two-three of psychotherapy.* New York: Guilford Press.

Kerr, M. E., and Bowen, M. 1988. *Family evaluation.* New York: Norton.

References

Alexander, P. C., Moore, S., and Alexander, E. R. 1991. Intergenerational transmission of violence. *Journal of Marriage and the Family. 53:* 657–667.

Amato, P. R. 1996. Explaining the intergenerational transmission of divorce. *Journal of Marriage and the Family. 58:* 628–640.

Anonymous. 1972. Differentiation of self in one's family. In *Family interaction,* J. Framo, ed. New York: Springer.

Bohlander, J. R. 1995. *Differentiation of self, need-fulfillment, and psychological well-being in married women.* Unpublished doctoral dissertation, New York University.

Bowen, M. 1966. The use of family theory in clinical practice. *Comprehensive Psychiatry. 7:* 345–374.

Bowen, M. 1971. Family therapy and family group therapy. In *Comprehensive group psychotherapy,* H. Kaplan and B. Sadock, eds. Baltimore: Williams & Wilkins.

Bowen, M. 1974. Toward the differentiation of self in one's family. In *Georgetown Family Symposium,*

Vol. 1, F. Andres and J. Lorio, eds. Washington, DC: Department of Psychiatry, Georgetown University Medical Center.

Bowen, M. 1976. Theory in the practice of psychotherapy. In *Family therapy: Theory and practice,* P. J. Guerin, ed. New York: Gardner Press.

Carter, B., and McGoldrick, M., eds. 1999. *The expanded family life cycle,* 3rd ed. Boston: Allyn & Bacon.

Carter, E., and Orfanidis, M. M. 1976. Family therapy with one person and the family therapist's own family. In *Family therapy: Theory and practice,* P. J. Guerin, ed. New York: Gardner Press.

Davis, B., and Jones, L. C. 1992. Differentiation of self and attachment among adult daughters. *Issues in Mental Health Nursing. 13:* 321–331.

Elieson, M. V., and Rubin, L. J. 2001. Differentiation of self and major depressive disorders: A test of Bowen theory among clinical, tradition, and internet groups. *Family Therapy. 29:* 125–142.

Feng, D., Giarrusso, R., Bengston, V. L., and Frye, N. 1999. Intergenerational transmission of marital quality and marital instability. *Journal of Marriage and the Family. 61:* 451–463.

Fogarty, T. F. 1976. Marital crisis. In *Family therapy: Theory and practice,* P. J. Guerin, ed. New York: Gardner Press.

Gehring, T. M., and Marti, D. 1993. The family system test: Differences in perception of family structures between nonclinical and clinical children. *Journal of Child Psychology and Psychiatry. 34:* 363–377.

Griffin, J. M., and Apostal, R. A. 1993. The influence of Relationship Enhancement training on differentiation of self. *Journal of Marital and Family Therapy. 19:* 267–272.

Guerin, P. J. 1971. A family affair. *Georgetown Family Symposium,* Vol. 1, Washington, DC.

Guerin, P. J., and Fogarty, T. F. 1972. Study your own family. In *The book of family therapy,* A. Ferber, M. Mendelsohn, and A. Napier, eds. New York: Science House.

Guerin, P. J., Fogarty, T. F., Fay, L. F., and Kautto, J. G. 1996. *Working with relationship triangles: The one-two-three of psychotherapy.* New York: Guilford Press.

Haber, J. E. 1984. *An investigation of the relationship between differentiation of self, complementary psychological need patterns, and marital conflict.* Unpublished doctoral dissertation, New York University.

Haber, J. E. 1993. A construct validity study of a differentiation of self scale. *Scholarly Inquiry for Nursing Practice. 7:* 165–178.

Herz, F., ed. 1991. *Reweaving the family tapestry.* New York: Norton.

Johnson, S., and Lebow, J. 2000. The "coming of age" of couple therapy: A decade review. *Journal of Marital and Family Therapy. 26:* 23–38.

Kerr, M. 1971. The importance of the extended family. *Georgetown Family Symposium,* Vol. 1, Washington, DC.

Kerr, M., and Bowen, M. 1988. *Family evaluation.* New York: Norton.

Kreider, R. and Fields, J. 2002. *Number, timing, and duration of marriages and divorces.* Washington, DC: Current Population Reports, U.S. Census Bureau.

Lerner, H. G. 1985. *The dance of anger: A woman's guide to changing patterns of intimate relationships.* New York: Harper & Row.

Lerner, H. G. 1989. *The dance of intimacy: A woman's guide to courageous acts of change in key relationships.* New York: Harper & Row.

Licht, C., and Chabot, D. 2006. The Chabot emotional differentiation scale: A theoretically and psychometrically sound instrument for measuring Bowen's intrapsychic aspect of differentiation. *Journal of Marital and Family Therapy. 32:* 167–180.

McGoldrick, M., and Gerson, R. 1985. *Genograms in family assessment.* New York: Norton.

McGoldrick, M., Pearce, J., and Giordano, J. 1982. *Ethnicity in family therapy.* New York: Guilford Press.

Miller, R. B., Johnson, L. N., Sandberg, J. G., Stringer-Seibold, T. A., and Gfeller-Strouts, L. 2000. An addendum to the 1997 outcome research chart. *American Journal of Family Therapy. 28:* 347–354.

Nichols, M. P. 1986. *Turning forty in the eighties.* New York: Norton.

Protinsky, H., and Gilkey, J. K. 1996. An empirical investigation of the construct of personality authority in late adolescent women and their level of college adjustment. *Adolescence. 31:* 291–296.

Richards, E. R. 1989. Self reports of differentiation of self and marital compatibility as related to family functioning in the third and fourth stages of the family life cycle. *Scholarly Inquiry for Nursing Practice. 3:* 163–175.

Sher, K. J., Gershuny, B. S., Peterson, L., and Raskin, G. 1997. The role of childhood stressors in the intergenerational transmission of alcohol use disorders. *Journal of Studies on Alcohol. 58:* 414–427.

Skowron, E. A. 2000. The role of differentiation of self in marital adjustment. *Journal of Counseling Psychology. 47:* 229–237.

Skowron, E. A., and Friedlander, M. L. 1998. The differentiation of self inventory: Development and initial validation. *Journal of Counseling Psychology. 45:* 235–246.

Troll, L., and Bengston, V. L. 1979. Generations in the family. In *Contemporary theories about the family,* Vol. 1. W. R. Burr, R. Hill, F. I. Nye, and I. L. Reiss, eds. New York: Free Press.

Vuchinich, S., Emery, R. E., and Cassidy, J. 1988. Family members as third parties in dyadic family conflict: Strategies, alliances, and outcomes. *Child Development. 59:* 1296–1302.

West, J. D., Zarski, J. J., and Harvill, R. 1986. The influence of the family triangle on intimacy. *American Mental Health Counselors Association Journal. 8:* 166–174.

Whitbeck, L., Hoyt, D., Simons, R., Conger, R., Elder, G., Lorenz, F., and Huck, S. 1992. Intergenerational continuity of parental rejection and depressed affect. *Journal of Personality and Social Psychology. 63:* 1036–1045.

Whitehouse, P. J., and Harris, G. 1998. The intergenerational transmission of eating disorders. *European Eating Disorders Review. 6:* 238–254.

Wood, B., Watkins, J. B., Boyle, J. T., Nogueira, J., Zimand, E., and Carroll, L. 1989. The "psychosomatic family" model: An empirical and theoretical analysis. *Family Process. 28:* 399–417.

6

Strategic Family Therapy

With their compelling application of cybernetics and systems theory, strategic approaches once captivated family therapy. Part of their appeal was a pragmatic, problem-solving focus; but there was also a fascination with strategies to outwit resistance and provoke families into changing, with or without their cooperation. It was this manipulative aspect that eventually turned people against strategic therapy.

The dominant approaches of the twenty-first century have elevated cognition over behavior and encouraged therapists to be collaborative rather than manipulative. Instead of trying to solve problems and provoke change, therapists began to reinforce solutions and inspire change. As a consequence, the once celebrated voices of strategic therapy—Jay Haley, John Weakland, Mara Selvini Palazzoli—have been virtually forgotten. That's too bad, because their strategic approaches introduced two of the most powerful insights in all of family therapy: that families often perpetuate problems by their own actions and that directives tailored to the needs of a particular family can sometimes bring about sudden and decisive change.

EVOLUTION OF THE MODEL

Strategic therapy grew out of the **communications theory** developed in Bateson's schizophrenia project,

which evolved into three distinct models: MRI's brief therapy, Haley and Madanes's strategic therapy, and the Milan systemic model. The birthplace of all three was the Mental Research Institute (MRI), where strategic therapy was inspired by Gregory Bateson and Milton Erickson, the anthropologist and the alienist.

In 1952, funded by a Rockefeller Foundation grant to study paradox in communication, Bateson invited Jay Haley, John Weakland, Don Jackson, and William Fry to join him in Palo Alto. Their seminal project, which can be considered the intellectual birthplace of family therapy, led to the conclusion that the exchange of multilayered messages between people defined their relationships.

Under Bateson's influence, the orientation was anthropological. Their goal was to observe families; they stumbled into family therapy more or less by accident. Given Bateson's disinclination to manipulate people, it's ironic that it was he who introduced project members to Milton Erickson. At a time when therapy was considered a laborious, long-term proposition, Erickson's experience as a hypnotherapist convinced him that people could change suddenly, and he made therapy as brief as possible.

Many of what have been called **paradoxical interventions** came out of Erickson's application of hypnotic principles to turn resistance to advantage

Milton Erickson was the guiding genius behind the strategic approach to therapy.

(Haley, 1981). For example, to induce trance, a hypnotist learns not to point out that a person is fighting going under but instead tells the person to keep his or her eyes open "until they become unbearably heavy."

Don Jackson founded the Mental Research Institute in 1958 and assembled an energetic and creative staff, including Jules Riskin, Virginia Satir, Jay Haley, John Weakland, Paul Watzlawick, Arthur Bodin, and Janet Beavin. After a few years, several of the staff became intrigued by the pragmatic, problem-solving approach of Milton Erickson. This interest led Jackson to establish the Brief Therapy Project under the direction of Richard Fisch. The original group included Arthur Bodin, Jay Haley, Paul Watzlawick, and John Weakland.

What emerged was an elegantly brief approach based on interrupting vicious cycles that occur when attempts to solve problems only make them worse. However, unlike today's therapies, which are brief by default, the Palo Alto approach was brief by design. This approach, known as the MRI model, was described by Watzlawick, Weakland, and Fisch (1974) in *Change: Principles of Problem Formation and Problem Resolution* and in a follow-up volume, *The Tactics of Change: Doing Therapy Briefly* (Fisch, Weakland, & Segal, 1982), which remains the most comprehensive statement of the MRI model.

When Jackson died in 1968 at the age of forty-eight, he left a legacy of seminal papers, the leading journal in the field, *Family Process* (which he co-founded with Nathan Ackerman in 1962), and a great sadness at the passing of such a creative talent. The MRI group and the whole field suffered another painful loss in 1995 when John Weakland died of Lou Gehrig's disease.

Jay Haley was always something of an outsider. He entered the field without clinical credentials and established his reputation as a gadfly and critic. His initial impact came from his writing, in which he infused sarcasm with incisive analysis. In "The Art of Psychoanalysis" (Haley, 1963), Haley redefined psychoanalysis as a game of one-upmanship:

By placing the patient on a couch, the analyst gives the patient the feeling of having his feet up in the air and the knowledge that the analyst has both feet on the ground. Not only is the patient disconcerted by having to lie down while talking, but he finds himself literally below the analyst and so his one-down position is geographically emphasized. In addition, the analyst seats himself behind the couch where he can watch the patient but the patient cannot watch him. This gives the patient the kind of disconcerted feeling a person has when sparring with an opponent while blindfolded. Unable to see what response his ploys provoke, he is unsure when he is one-up and when one-down. Some patients try to solve this problem by saying something like, "I slept with my sister last night," and then whirling around to see how the analyst is responding. These "shocker" ploys usually fail in their effect. The analyst may twitch, but he has time to recover before the patient can whirl fully around and see him. Most analysts have developed ways of handling the whirling patient. As the patient turns, they are gazing off into space, or doodling with a pencil, or braiding belts, or staring at tropical fish. It is essential that the rare patient who gets an opportunity to observe the analyst see only an impassive demeanor. (pp. 193–194)

After the Bateson project disbanded in 1962, Haley moved to MRI until 1967, when he joined Salvador Minuchin at the Philadelphia Child Guidance Clinic. It was there that he became interested in training and supervision, areas in which he made his greatest contribution (Haley, 1996). In 1976 Haley moved to Washington, D.C., where with Cloe Madanes he founded the Family Therapy Institute. Madanes, known as one of the most creative therapists in the field, had previously worked at both MRI and the Philadelphia Child Guidance Clinic. In 1995 Haley left the Family Therapy Institute and moved to San Diego. He died in 2007.

Haley and Madanes are such towering figures that their names often overshadow those who followed in their footsteps. James Keim in California, who developed an innovative way of working with oppositional children, is ably carrying on the Haley–Madanes tradition. Other prominent practitioners of this model include Neill Schiff in Washington, D. C., Scott Sells at the Savannah Family Institute, and Jerome Price in Michigan, who specializes in difficult adolescents.

The MRI model had a major impact on the Milan Associates: Mara Selvini Palazzoli, Luigi Boscolo, Gianfranco Cecchin, and Guiliana Prata. Selvini Palazzoli was a prominent Italian psychoanalyst, specializing in eating disorders, when, out of frustration with the psychoanalytic model (Selvini Palazzoli, 1981), she began to develop her own approach to families. In 1967 she led a group of eight psychiatrists who turned to the ideas of Bateson, Haley, and Watzlawick and formed the Center for the Study of the Family in Milan, where they developed the *Milan systemic model.*

$\mathcal{T}$HE BASIC MODEL

In *Pragmatics of Human Communication*, Watzlawick, Beavin, and Jackson (1967) sought to develop a calculus of human communication, which they stated in a series of axioms. The first of these axioms is that *people are always communicating.* Because all behavior is communicative and because one cannot

---

Jay Haley

A brilliant strategist and incisive critic, Jay Haley was a leading figure in developing the Palo Alto Group's communications model and strategic family therapy, which became popular in the 1970s. He studied with three of the most influential pioneers in the evolution of family therapy—Gregory Bateson, Milton Erickson, and Salvador Minuchin—and combined ideas from each of these innovative thinkers to form his own unique brand of family therapy. Haley developed a brief therapy model that focused on the context and possible function of the patient's symptoms and used directives to instruct patients to act in ways that were contrary to their maladaptive behavior. Haley believed that it was more important to get patients to actively do something about their problems than to help them to understand why they had these problems.

---

not behave, it follows that one cannot *not* communicate. Consider the following example.

Mrs. Rodriguez began by saying, "I don't know what to do with Ramon. He's not doing well in school, and he doesn't help out around the house. All he wants to do is hang with those awful friends of his. But the worst thing is that he refuses to communicate with us."

The therapist turned to Ramon and said, "Well, what do you have to say about all of this?" Ramon said nothing. He just sat slouched in the corner with a sullen look on his face.

Ramon isn't "*not* communicating." He's communicating that he's angry and doesn't want to talk about it. Communication also takes place when it isn't intentional, conscious, or successful—that is, in the absence of mutual understanding.

The second axiom is that *All messages have report and command functions* (Ruesch & Bateson, 1951). The *report* (or content) of a message conveys information, whereas the *command* is a statement about the relationship. For example, the statement, "Mommy, Sandy hit me!" conveys information but also implies a command—*Do something about it.* Notice, however, that the implicit command is ambiguous. The reason for this is that the printed word omits contextual clues. This statement shrieked by a child in tears would have very different implications than if it were uttered by a giggling child.

In families, command messages are patterned as rules (Jackson, 1965) which can be deduced from observed redundancies in interaction. Jackson used the term **family rules** as a description of regularity, not regulation. Nobody lays down the rules. In fact, families are generally unaware of them.

The rules, or regularities, of family interaction operate to preserve **family homeostasis** (Jackson, 1965, 1967). Homeostatic mechanisms bring families back to equilibrium in the face of disruption and thus serve to resist change. Jackson's notion of family homeostasis describes the conservative aspect of family systems and is similar to the cybernetic concept of **negative feedback.** According to communications analysis, families operate as goal-directed, rule-governed systems.

Communications theorists didn't look for underlying motives; instead, they assumed **circular causality** and analyzed patterns of communications linked together in additive chains of stimulus and response as **feedback loops.** When the response to a family member's problematic behavior exacerbates the problem, that chain is seen as a **positive feedback** loop. The advantage of this formulation is that it focuses on interactions that perpetuate problems, which can be changed, rather than inferring underlying causes, which are often not subject to change.

Strategic therapists made the concept of the positive feedback loop the centerpiece of their model. For the MRI group, this translated into a simple yet powerful principle of problem formation: Families encounter many difficulties over the course of their lives; whether a difficulty becomes a *problem* depends on how family members respond to it (Watzlawick, Weakland, & Fisch, 1974). That is, families often make misguided attempts to solve their difficulties and, on finding that the problem persists, apply more of the same attempted solutions. This only escalates the problem, which provokes more of the same and so on—in a vicious cycle.

For example, if Jamal feels threatened by the arrival of a baby sister, he may become temperamental. Then his father might think he's being defiant and try to get him to act his age by punishing him. But his father's harshness only confirms Jamal's belief that his parents love his sister more than him, and so he becomes even more temperamental. Father then becomes more punitive, and Jamal becomes more alienated. This is an escalating positive feedback loop: The family system is reacting to a deviation in the behavior of one of its members with feedback designed to dampen that deviation (negative feedback), but it has the effect of amplifying the deviation (positive feedback).

What's needed is for Father to reverse his solution. If he could comfort rather than criticize Jamal, then Jamal might calm down. The system is governed, however, by unspoken rules that allow only one interpretation of Jamal's behavior—as disrespectful. For Father to alter his solution, this rule would have to be revised.

In most families, unspoken rules govern all sorts of behavior. When a rule promotes the kind of rigid solutions described previously, it isn't just the behavior but the rule that needs to change. When only a specific behavior within a system changes, this is **first-order change,** as opposed to **second-order change,** which occurs when the rules of the system change (Watzlawick, Weakland, & Fisch, 1974). How does one change the rules? One way is by

reframing—that is, changing Father's interpretation of Jamal's behavior from disrespect to fear of displacement, from bad to sad.

Thus, the MRI approach to problems is elegantly simple: (1) identify positive feedback loops that maintain problems; (2) determine the rules that support those interactions; and (3) find a way to change the rules in order to interrupt the problem-maintaining behavior.

Jay Haley added a functionalist emphasis to the cybernetic interpretation with his interest in the interpersonal payoff of behavior. Later, he incorporated structural concepts, developed during the years he spent with Minuchin. For example, Haley might notice that whenever Jamal and his father quarrel, Jamal's mother protects him by criticizing Father for being so harsh. Haley might also see Jamal becoming more agitated when Mother criticizes father, trying to get his parents' attention off their conflicts and onto him.

Haley believed that the rules around the **hierarchical structure** in the family are crucial and found inadequate parental hierarchies lurking behind most problems. Indeed, Haley (1976) suggested that "an individual is more disturbed in direct proportion to the number of malfunctioning hierarchies in which he is embedded" (p. 117).

To counter a problem's payoff, Haley borrowed Erickson's technique of prescribing **ordeals,** so that the price for keeping a symptom outweighed that of giving it up. To illustrate, consider Erickson's famous maneuver of prescribing that an insomniac set his alarm every night to wake up and wax the kitchen floor. Haley tried to explain all therapy as based on ordeals, suggesting that people will often change just to avoid the ordeals inherent in being a client (Haley, 1984).

Cloe Madanes (1981, 1984) also emphasized the functional aspect of problems, particularly the rescuing operations involved when children use their symptoms to engage their parents. For example, when a daughter sees her mother looking depressed, the daughter can provoke a fight that prods the mother into taking charge. Much of Madanes's approach involves finding ways for children to help their parents openly, so that they won't have to resort to symptoms as sacrificial offerings.

Like Haley, Mara Selvini Palazzoli and her associates (1978b) focused on power games in the family and on the protective function symptoms served for the whole family. They explored families' histories over several generations, searching for evidence to confirm their hypotheses about how the children's symptoms came to be necessary. These hypotheses often involved elaborate networks of family alliances and coalitions. They frequently concluded that the patient developed symptoms to protect one or more family members so as to maintain the delicate network of extended family alliances.

Normal Family Development

According to **general systems theory,** normal families, like all living systems, depend on two vital processes (Maruyama, 1968). First, they maintain integrity in the face of environmental challenges through negative feedback. No living system can survive without a coherent structure. On the other hand, too rigid a structure leaves a system ill equipped to adapt to changing circumstances. That's why normal families also have mechanisms of positive feedback. Negative feedback resists disruptions to maintain a steady state; positive feedback amplifies innovations to accommodate to changed circumstances. Recognizing that the channel for positive feedback is communication makes it possible to state the case more plainly: Healthy families are able to change because they communicate clearly and adapt.

The MRI group resolutely opposed standards of normality: "As therapists, we do not regard any particular way of functioning, relating, or living as a problem if the client is not expressing discontent with it" (Fisch, 1978). Thus, by limiting their task to eliminating problems presented to them, the MRI group avoided taking any position regarding how families should behave.

The Milan Associates strove to maintain an attitude of neutrality (Selvini Palazzoli et al., 1980).

They didn't apply preconceived goals or normative models. Instead, by raising questions that helped families examine themselves and that exposed hidden power games, they trusted that families would reorganize on their own.

In contrast to the relativism of these two approaches, Haley's assessments *were* based on assumptions about sound family functioning. His therapy was designed to help families reorganize into more functional structures with clear boundaries and generational hierarchy (Haley, 1976).

Development of Behavior Disorders

According to communications theory, the essential **function of symptoms** is to maintain the homeostatic equilibrium of family systems.[1] Symptomatic families were seen as trapped in dysfunctional, homeostatic patterns of interaction (Jackson & Weakland, 1961). These families cling to their rigid ways and respond to signs of change as negative feedback. That is, change is treated not as an opportunity for growth but as a threat, as the following example illustrates.

Case Study

Laban was a quiet boy, the only child of Orthodox Jewish parents from Eastern Europe. His parents left their small farming community to come to the United States where they both found factory work in a large city. Although they were now safe from religious persecution, the couple felt alien and out of synch with their new neighbors. They kept to themselves and took pleasure in raising Laban.

Laban was a frail child with a number of peculiar mannerisms, but to his parents he was perfect. Then he started school. Laban began to make friends with other children and, eager to be accepted, picked up a number of American habits. He

chewed gum, watched cartoons, and rode his bicycle all over the neighborhood. His parents were annoyed by the gum chewing and by Laban's fondness for television, but they were genuinely distressed by his eagerness to play with gentile children. They may have come to the United States to escape persecution but not to embrace pluralism, much less assimilation. As far as they were concerned, Laban was rejecting their values— "Something must be wrong with him." By the time they called the child guidance clinic, they were convinced that Laban was disturbed, and they asked for help to "make Laban normal again."

In strategic models, there are three explanations of how problems develop. The first is *cybernetic:* Difficulties are turned into chronic problems by misguided solutions, forming positive-feedback escalations. The second is *structural:* Problems are the result of incongruous hierarchies. The third is *functional:* Problems result when people try to protect or control one another covertly, so that their symptoms serve a function for the system. The MRI group limited itself to the first explanation, whereas Haley and the Milan associates embraced all three.

To clarify these differences, consider the following example:

Sixteen-year-old Juwan recently began refusing to leave the house. An MRI therapist might ask his parents how they had tried to get him to venture out. The focus would be on the parents' attempted solution, on the assumption that this was likely to be maintaining Juwan's refusal, and on their explanation or *frame* for Juwan's behavior, believing that their framing of the problem might be driving their false solution.

A Haley-style therapist might be interested in the parents' attempted solutions but would also inquire about their marriage, the ways in which Juwan was involved in struggles between them or other family

---

[1]The notion of symptoms as functional—implying that families *need* their problems—was to become controversial.

members, and the possible protective nature of Juwan's problem. This therapist would be acting on the assumption that Juwan's behavior might be part of a dysfunctional triangle. The therapist might further assume that this triangular pattern was fueled by unresolved conflicts between the parents. Madanes would also be interested in this triangle but in addition would be curious about how Juwan's behavior might be protecting his parents from having to face some threatening issue.

A Milan systemic therapist wouldn't focus so much on attempted solutions but instead would ask about past and present relationships in the family. In so doing, the therapist would be trying to uncover a network of power alliances, often continuing across generations, that constituted the family's "game." Some such game left Juwan in the position of having to use his symptoms to protect other family members. The family might reveal, for example, that if Juwan were to grow up and leave home, his mother would be drawn back into a power struggle between her parents, which she had avoided by having a symptomatic child. Also, by not succeeding in life, Juwan might be protecting his father from the shame of having a child who exceeded him in accomplishment.

How Therapy Works

In the early days of family therapy, the goal was simply to improve communication. Later the goal was refined to altering specific patterns of communication that maintained problems: "We see the resolution of problems as primarily requiring a substitution of behavior patterns so as to interrupt the vicious, positive feedback circles" (Weakland, Fisch, Watzlawick, & Bodin, 1974, p. 149).

A therapist can either point out problematic sequences or simply block them to effect therapeutic change. The first strategy relies on the power of insight and depends on a willingness to change. The second does not; it is an attempt to beat families at their own games.

Jackson and Haley's work was influenced by the hypnotherapy they learned from Milton Erickson. The hypnotist works by giving instructions whose purpose is often obscure. Haley (1961) recommended asking uncooperative patients to do something in order to provoke a rebellious response, which served to make them concede that they were relating to the therapist. He mentions, as an example, directing a schizophrenic patient to hear voices. If the patient hears voices, then he is complying with the therapist's request; if he doesn't hear voices, he can no longer claim to be crazy.

Among the forms of pathologic communication identified were denying that one is communicating, disqualifying the other person's message, confusing levels of communication, discrepant punctuation of communication sequences, symmetrical escalation to competitiveness, rigid complementarity, and paradoxical messages.

A **paradox** is a contradiction that follows correct deduction from logical premises. In family communications, paradoxes usually take the form of *paradoxical injunctions*. A common example is to demand some behavior that by its very nature can only be spontaneous—"You should have more self-confidence." "Tell me you love me." "Be spontaneous!" A person exposed to such paradoxical injunctions is caught in an untenable position. To comply—to act in a spontaneous or self-confident manner—means to be self-consciously deliberate or eager to please. The only way to escape the dilemma is to step outside the context and comment on it, but such **metacommunication** rarely occurs in families. (It's hard to communicate about communication.)

Paradoxical communications are harmless in small doses, but when they take the form of **double binds,** the consequences can be malignant. In a double bind, the two contradictory messages are on different levels of abstraction, and there is an implicit injunction against commenting on the discrepancy. A familiar example is the person who criticizes others for not expressing their feelings but then attacks them when they do.

Continual exposure to paradoxical communication is like the dilemma of a dreamer caught in a nightmare. Nothing the dreamer tries to do in the dream works. The only solution is to step outside the context by waking up. Unfortunately, when you live in a nightmare, it isn't always easy to wake up.

Haley's (1961) direction to hear voices illustrates the technique of **prescribing the symptom.** By instructing a patient to enact symptomatic behavior, the therapist is demanding that something involuntary be done voluntarily. This paradoxical injunction forces one of two outcomes. Either the patient performs the symptom and thus proves it isn't involuntary, or the patient gives up the symptom.

For the MRI school, the way to resolve problems is to change the behavior that's been maintaining them. It's believed that through seeing the results of altering rigid behavioral responses, clients will become more flexible in their problem-solving strategies. When this happens, clients achieve a second-order change—a change in the rules governing their response to problems.

For example, Maria argues with her father about her curfew and her father grounds her. She then runs away and stays with a friend. A first-order intervention at this point might be to help Maria's father find a more effective punishment to tame his out-of-control child. A second-order strategic intervention might be to direct the father to act disappointed and sad around his daughter, implying that he has given up trying to control her. This shifts Maria from feeling trapped by father to feeling concerned about him, and she becomes more reasonable. Her father learns that when attempted solutions aren't working, he needs to try something different. This change is second order in that it alters the rules governing the way father and daughter interact.

Haley (1976) believed that telling people what they're doing wrong only mobilizes resistance. He believed that changes in behavior alter perceptions, rather than the other way around. Madanes (1980) said, "If a problem can be solved without the family's knowing how or why, that is satisfactory" (p. 79).

The Milan group turned this behaviorism on its head. They were more interested in getting families to see things differently (through a reframing technique called *positive connotation* to be discussed later) than in getting them to behave differently. This shift from behavior to cognition set the stage for the constructivist and narrative movements (see Chapters 4 and 13).

$\mathcal{T}$HERAPY

Assessment

The goals of an MRI assessment are to (1) define a resolvable complaint, (2) identify attempted solutions that maintain the complaint, and (3) understand the clients' unique language for describing the problem. The first two goals show where to intervene; the third suggests how.

The first step is to get a very specific behavioral picture of the complaint, who sees it as a problem, and why it's a problem now. When a therapist asks "What is the problem that brings you here today?" many clients reply ambiguously: "We don't communicate," "We think our fourteen-year-old is depressed," or "Clarence seems to be hyperactive." The MRI therapist inquires about exactly what these complaints mean. "We don't communicate" might mean "My son argues with everything I say" or "My husband hides behind the newspaper and never talks to me." "Depressed" might mean sad and withdrawn or sullen and disagreeable; "hyperactive" might mean disobedient or unable to concentrate. A useful device is to ask "If we had a videotape of this, what would it look like?"

Once the problem has been defined, the therapist tries to determine who has tried to solve it and how. Sometimes the attempted solution has obviously made things worse. For example, the wife who nags her husband to spend more time with her is likely to succeed only in driving him further away. Likewise, the parents who punish their son for fighting with his sister might convince him that they do favor her. Or the husband who does everything his wife asks in order to keep the peace may become so resentful that he starts to hate her.

From this inquiry emerges a formulation of the problem-solution loop and the specific behavior that will be the focus of intervention. Typically, the strategic objective will be a 180-degree reversal of what the clients have been doing. Although interventions typically involve prescribing some alternative behavior, the key is to stop the performance of the problem-maintaining solution (Weakland & Fisch, 1992).

Grasping the clients' unique language and ways of seeing their dilemmas is important to framing suggestions in ways they will accept. For example, a devoutly religious wife might be amenable to the suggestion that she pray for her husband to become more involved with the family rather than continue to criticize his failings. In another case, cited by Shoham and Rohrbaugh (2002), a young woman was seen as perpetuating her boyfriend's jealous accusations by trying to reassure him. Unfortunately, these efforts to reason with the boyfriend only ended up in arguments, which were painful enough to threaten the relationship. Because the woman was a devotee of mindfulness meditation, the therapist suggested that the next time the boyfriend asked a jealous question and she felt like defending herself, she should tell him that she was feeling stressed and needed to meditate.

Haley's assessment begins with a careful definition of the problem, expressed from the point of view of every member of the family. Unlike the MRI group, however, Haley also explores the possibility that structural arrangements in the family may be contributing to their problems—especially pathologic triangles and *cross-generational coalitions.*

In addition to structural problems, Haley and Madanes also consider the interpersonal payoff of problem behavior. According to Haley, the apparent helplessness of a patient often turns out to be a source of power in relation to others whose lives are dominated by the demands and fears of the symptomatic

person. A schizophrenic who refuses to take his medication might, for example, avoid having to go to work. Although it's not necessary to decide what is or isn't a real illness, Haley tends to assume that all symptomatic behavior is voluntary. Sometimes this distinction is crucial—as, for example, in cases of drug addiction or losing one's temper.

In the Milan model, assessment begins with a preliminary hypothesis, which is confirmed or disconfirmed in the initial session. These hypotheses are generally based on the assumption that the problems of the **identified patient** serve a protective function for the family. Therefore, assessment of the presenting problem and the family's response to it is based on questions designed to explore the family as a set of interconnected relationships. For example, the reply to a question like "Who has been more worried about this problem, you or your wife?" suggests a hypothesis about the closeness and distance of family members. The ultimate goal of assessment is to achieve a systemic perspective on the problem.

Therapeutic Techniques

Although strategic therapists shared a belief in the need for indirect methods to induce change in families, they developed distinctly different techniques for doing so.

The MRI Approach.   The MRI model follows a six-step treatment procedure:

1. Introducing the treatment setup
2. Inquiring about and defining the problem
3. Estimating the behavior that is maintaining the problem
4. Setting goals for treatment
5. Selecting and making behavioral interventions
6. Terminating therapy

Once the preliminaries are concluded, the therapist asks for a clear definition of the primary problem. If a problem is stated in vague terms, such as "We just don't get along," or in terms of presumptive causes, such as "Dad's job is making him depressed," the therapist helps translate it into a clear and concrete goal, asking questions like "What will be the first small sign that things are getting better?"

After the problem and goal have been defined, MRI therapists inquire about attempted solutions that might be maintaining the problem. In general, solutions that tend to perpetuate problems fall into one of three categories:

1. The solution is to deny that a problem exists; action is necessary but not taken. For instance, parents do nothing despite evidence that their teenage son is using drugs.
2. The solution is an effort to solve something that isn't really a problem; action is taken when it shouldn't be. For example, parents punish a child for masturbating.
3. The solution is an effort to solve a problem within a framework that makes a solution impossible; action is taken but at the wrong level. For instance, a husband buys increasingly expensive gifts for his wife when what she wants is affection.

Once the therapist conceives a strategy for altering the problem-maintaining sequence, clients must be convinced to follow this strategy. To sell their directives, MRI therapists reframe problems to increase the likelihood of compliance. Thus, a therapist might tell an angry teenager that when his father punishes him, it's the only way his father knows how to show his love.

To interrupt problem-maintaining sequences, strategic therapists may try to get family members to do something that runs counter to common sense. Such counterintuitive techniques have been called **paradoxical interventions** (Haley, 1973; Watzlawick, Weakland, & Fisch, 1974).

Case Study

Watzlawick and colleagues (1974) described a young couple who were bothered by their parents' tendency to treat them like children by doing everything for them. Despite the husband's adequate salary, the parents continued to send money and lavish gifts on them, refused to let them pay even part of a restaurant check, and so on. The strategic team helped the couple solve their difficulty with their doting parents by having them become *less* rather than more competent. Instead of trying to show the parents that they didn't need help, the couple was told to act helpless and dependent, so much so that the parents got disgusted and finally backed off.

The techniques most commonly thought of as paradoxical are symptom prescriptions in which a family is told to continue or embellish the behavior they complain about. In some contexts, such a prescription might be made with the hope that the family will try to comply with it and thereby be forced to reverse their attempted solutions. If Jorge, who is sad, is told to try to become depressed several times a day and his family is asked to encourage him to be sad, then they will no longer try ineffectively to cheer him up and he won't feel guilty for not being happy.

At other times, a therapist might prescribe the symptom while secretly hoping that the clients will rebel against this directive. The therapist might encourage Jorge to continue to be depressed because, in doing so, he's helping his brother (with whom Jorge is competitive) feel superior.

Sometimes a therapist might prescribe the symptom with the hope that in doing so the network of relationships that maintain the problem will be exposed. The therapist says that Jorge should remain depressed because that way he can continue to get his mother's attention, which will keep her from looking to his father for affection, since his father is still overinvolved with his own mother, and so on.

To prevent power struggles, MRI therapists avoid assuming an authoritarian position. Their one-down stance implies equality and invites clients to reduce anxiety and resistance. Although some strategists adopt a one-down position disingenuously, this modest stance was consistent with the late John Weakland's own unassuming character. While sitting clouded in the smoke of his pipe, Weakland discouraged families from trying to change too fast, warning them to go slowly and worrying out loud about the possibility of relapse when improvements did occur. This **restraining** technique reinforced the therapist's one-down position.

The Haley and Madanes Approach. Jay Haley's approach is more difficult to describe because it's tailored to address the unique requirements of each case. If *strategic* implies *systematic,* as in the MRI approach, it also implies *artful,* which is especially true of Haley's therapy. As with other strategic approaches, the definitive technique is the use of **directives.** But Haley's directives aren't simply ploys to outwit families or reverse what they're doing. Rather, they are thoughtful suggestions targeted to the specific requirements of each case.

Haley (1976) believes that if therapy is to end well, it must begin properly. Therefore, he devotes a good deal of attention to the opening moves of treatment. Regardless of who is presented as the official patient, Haley begins by interviewing the entire family. His approach to this initial interview follows four stages: a social stage, a problem stage, an interaction stage, and finally a goal-setting stage.

Haley uses the initial minutes of a first session to help everyone relax. He makes a point of greeting each family member and trying to make sure everyone is comfortable. Like a good host, he wants his guests to feel welcome. After the *social stage,* Haley gets down to business in the *problem stage,* asking each person for his or her perspective. Because mothers are usually more central than fathers, Haley recommends speaking first to the father to increase his involvement. This suggestion illustrates Haley's strategic maneuvering, which begins with the first contact and characterizes all subsequent meetings.

Haley listens carefully to the way each family member describes the problem, making sure that no one interrupts until everyone has had a turn. During this phase, Haley looks for clues about triangles and hierarchy, but he avoids sharing these observations because that might make the family defensive.

Once everyone has had a chance to speak, Haley encourages them to discuss their points of view among themselves. In this, the *interactional stage,*

the therapist can observe, rather than just hear about, the interchanges that surround the problem. As they talk, Haley looks for coalitions between family members against others. How functional is the hierarchy? Do the parents work together, or do they undercut each other?

Sometimes Haley ends the first session by giving the family a task. In subsequent sessions, directives play a central role. Effective directives don't usually take the form of simple advice, which is rarely helpful because problems usually persist for a reason.

The following two tasks are taken from Haley's (1976) *Problem-Solving Therapy.*

Case Study

One couple, who were out of the habit of being affectionate with each other, were told to behave affectionately "to teach their child how to show affection." In another case, a mother who was unable to control her twelve-year-old son had decided to send him away to military school. Haley suggested that because the boy had no idea how tough life would be at military school, it would be a good idea for the mother to help prepare him. They both agreed. Haley directed her to teach the boy how to stand at attention, be polite, and wake up early every morning to make his bed. The two of them followed these instructions as if playing a game, with mother as sergeant and son as private. After two weeks the son was behaving so well that his mother no longer felt it necessary to send him away.

One thing unique about Haley's approach was his focus on the interpersonal payoff of psychiatric symptoms. The idea that people get something out of their symptoms has been rejected by most schools of family therapy because they see it as a version of blaming the victim. Haley's point wasn't that people become anxious or depressed in order to manipulate others, but that such problems, once they develop, may come to play a role in interpersonal struggles in the family. It is this covert function of symptoms that Haley explored.

Although MRI therapists speculate about what may be maintaining symptoms, they emphasize other people's misguided solutions and don't consider the interpersonal payoff of the symptoms themselves. The primary goal of hypothesizing in Haley's approach is to understand the heart of the family drama that symptoms revolve around. Haley focused on the meaning behind people's problems and therefore believed problems should have reasonable solutions. The answer is to help families find new ways to solve their problems.

Case Study

In a case treated by Jerome Price (1996), a thirteen-year-old girl was referred to juvenile court because of chronic truancy. She had repeatedly failed to show up at school, and both her parents and school officials had tried a range of threats and punishments, all to no avail. In court, the judge referred the girl to therapy.

Price began by asking questions designed to find out *why* the girl was skipping school. The most obvious question was, "Where do you go when you don't go to school?" To the therapist's surprise, the girl said that she went to the home of her ninety-two-year-old grandmother. The girl's parents assumed that she was taking advantage of her grandmother. However, when Price asked, "Why there?" he learned that the grandmother lived alone and was in constant fear of falling. Her children rarely visited and didn't address her concerns directly, so the granddaughter had taken it upon herself to see that her grandmother was safe.

Price's directives addressed both the purpose of the girl's truancy and the hierarchical imbalance that it reflected in the family. He encouraged the parents to visit the grandmother more often, hire a caregiver to be with her during the day, and arrange activities for her at a local senior center. Knowing that her grandmother was safe—and that her parents were now taking charge—the girl returned to school.

Unlike many contemporary family therapists, practitioners in the Haley/Madanes tradition openly address the issue of interpersonal power in families. Early in his career, Haley (1963) recognized that communication always affects how family members relate to one another in a way that either increases or decreases their influence. This wasn't meant to be a judgment but merely a description of the way things seem to work. Haley devoted much of his effort to observing how power was distributed, misused, and reapportioned, with the idea that a therapist can either naively ignore the presence of power struggles or understand them and use this knowledge to help families relate more equitably and productively.

Case Study

When a man beats a woman, people have no trouble seeing this as an issue of power and its misuse. But when sixteen-year-old Brad (Price, 1996) verbally harassed his mother to get the use of her car, his individual therapist didn't see this as a misuse of power on the young man's part. When Brad proceeded to push his mother to the ground and rip the keys out of her hand, the therapist still insisted on exploring Brad's reasons for being angry at this mother.

When Brad's mother got fed up with this approach and sought treatment from a strategic practitioner, the new therapist focused on how Brad had become so powerful and what it would take to put leadership back in the hands of his mother. Most of the sessions included the mother and Brad's uncle, who cared very much about him and therefore was more than willing to help discuss and carry out decisions. When Brad was faced with a united front of two adults who met with him and a therapist and held meetings with staff at his school, the reformulation of the power balance began calming him down and simplifying his life. He finally reached the point where he could return to acting like a sixteen-year-old son rather than an abusive husband.

As is often the case, the underlying dynamics in this family didn't emerge until after the presenting problem improved. Once Brad started behaving respectfully and performing better in school, his mother's depression became more apparent. In a way, Brad had kept his mother emotionally occupied by reenacting her struggles with his father, which made it unnecessary for her to make new friends, date, and move forward in her life. With Brad improving and no crises to deal with, his mother became conscious of what was missing in her life and, with the therapist's help, was able to address her own future. Haley would see Brad as trying to help his mother by giving her a problem that distracted her from her own. In some cases this "helpfulness" is conscious; it other cases it isn't.

Metaphor is another theme in Haley's approach. In the previous case, Brad's misbehavior, which mimicked that of his parents' previous abusive relationship, could be seen as a metaphor for his mother not having resolved her emotional struggle over past abuse. In this approach, a symptom is often seen as a metaphor for an underlying problem. Thus, a school problem in a child may mirror a work problem of a parent. An underachieving child may be a reflection of an underfunctioning parent. An addicted child may be a clue that someone else in the family is secretly acting in self-destructive ways.

Such was the case in which thirty-seven-year-old Margery asked for help with her three-year-old daughter. Whenever they entered a store, the little girl would steal something such as a pack of gum or candy. Upon further exploration, the therapist learned that Margery was having an affair with her best friend's husband. The metaphor of stealing thus proved apt.

Madanes (1981) describes how one relationship may metaphorically replicate another. As was the case with Brad and his mother, parents can fight with their children about things they should address between themselves. Two children can fight with each other in the same way their parents would be fighting if they weren't distracted by the children. One child can struggle with parents in a way that deflects the heat that otherwise might be directed at a sibling. This is often the case when there is a young adult at home who is not working or going to school, and is generally stuck on the launching pad. A younger sibling may become symptomatic and start failing at school in a way that serves as metaphor to force the parents to deal with the issue of needing to be productive.

Madanes (1984) also addresses power imbalances in couples and how they play a role in a wide range of symptoms. She looks at the areas of couples' lives in which power is regulated, including money, education, control of children, coalitions with in-laws, religion, and sex. It often turns out that the partner with the least power develops the most emotional problems. Symptoms such as depression, headaches, substance abuse, eating disorders, phobias, and so on certainly burden the person who suffers them, but they also burden other family members. Others in the family often try desperately to do something about such symptoms, but the symptomatic person may refuse to seek help, thereby maintaining a perverse sort of power by holding onto troublesome symptoms. Again, this process is typically unconscious, and this way of thinking about it is not offered as some objective truth but rather as one possibly useful clinical hypothesis.

Looking at such struggles in the light of power balancing, a therapist is able to have a more flexible view of the drama a couple is embroiled in. Is the abuser someone who actually needs more of a role in his children's lives? Does a partner need an avocation that can help her feel more successful?

Case Study

This dynamic was the case with Mark and Brianna. After being laid off, Mark became more and more depressed and refused to seek a job. Six months had passed, and he had done little. He spent money as if his income were still coming in while Brianna stayed home with the children despite being in demand as a registered nurse. Brianna berated Mark about his lack of action, shouting at him at times and generally exacerbating his general sense of failure. *She* was the expert on the children. *She* took them to church. *She* had a master's degree, while *he* had only two years of college.

As Mark became more depressed and did increasingly less, Brianna was forced to go back to work and give up staying home with the children. By what he didn't do—"because he was depressed"—Mark dominated the family that had previously dominated him. He now took care of the children (albeit not to Brianna's satisfaction) and stayed home while she worked, and no one went to church because Brianna had to work the graveyard shift on Saturday nights. Mark's depression had equalized the power imbalance that developed when he lost his job and began to feel like a failure. Brianna's emotional control over their lives had previously been offset by the fact that Mark was the breadwinner. When he lost that role, the couple went into imbalance, and Mark had to find another form of power to replace his income. Ironically, the helplessness of depression provided that power.

The artful commonsense component of Haley's strategic therapy can be understood by looking at high-conflict divorce. Rather than think of a high-conflict couple as pathological, Haley would look at them developmentally and in terms of the family life cycle (Haley, 1973). This approach attempts to find benevolent hypotheses that describe clients in the best possible light. Rather than see the ex-spouses as personality disordered, a Haley-style therapist would be more likely to see them as still in need of an emotional divorce (Gaulier, Margerum, Price, & Windell, 2007). Such a conceptualization offers a therapist ideas about what needs to be done to resolve problems.

Case Study

Even after they were divorced, Rob and Melissa continued to argue over every aspect of their seventeen-year-old daughter Marta's existence. When

the therapist asked Marta if these arguments looked like the arguments her parents had when they were married, she sighed and said they "were identical." The therapist asked the parents whether they were really willing to let go of each other once and for all. Both resisted the idea that they were still emotionally married, but the therapist challenged them to prove that they weren't.

The therapist asked both parents to collect memorabilia and write accounts of events from their marriage that they would like to leave behind. The therapist led them through a ritual over about a month in which they brought in the items and accounts, described them individually to each other and said why they no longer wanted these things in their lives, and then ritually burned the items in the therapist's presence. Rob and Melissa were directed to collect the ashes in a jar and sent on a weekend trip to northern Michigan, where they stopped in a virgin pine forest and ritually buried the ashes. At the therapist's suggestion, they took a boat trip and, at a specific time and in a specific way, threw their wedding rings (which they had kept) into the depths of Lake Superior.

James Keim and Jay Lappin (2002) describe a strategic approach to a case with a nagging wife and withdrawing husband. First they reframe the problem as a "breakdown in the negotiation process." A *negotiation,* the couple is told, is a conversation in which one party makes a request and the other names a price. This reframing allows the wife to make requests without thinking of herself as a nag—and the husband to see himself as having something to gain in negotiations, rather than as a brow-beaten husband who is asked to give in to his wife.

Keim and Lappin recommend introducing couples to the negotiation process as experimenting with a "fun exercise" designed to get them back on track with reaching agreements. Then the couple is given a handout with elaborate instructions for negotiating in a constructive fashion and asked to progress from negotiating easy issues in the session to doing so at home and then tackling more difficult issues, first in the session and then at home. Finally, the couple is cautioned that even after negotiating some exchanges, they may choose not to accept the quid pro quo terms. Sometimes it's preferable to endure certain problems than to pay the price of trying to change them.

Madanes used the observation that people will often do something they wouldn't ordinarily do if it's framed as play to develop a whole range of **pretend techniques.** One such strategy is to ask a symptomatic child to pretend to have the symptom and encourage the parents to pretend to help. The child can give up the actual symptom now that pretending to have it is serving the same family function. The following two cases summarized from Madanes (1981) illustrate the pretend technique.

Case Study

A mother sought therapy because her ten-year-old son had night terrors. Madanes suspected that the boy was concerned about his mother, who was poor, spoke little English, and had lost two husbands. Because the boy had night terrors, the therapist asked all the members of the family to describe their dreams. Only the mother and the son had nightmares. In the mother's nightmare, someone was breaking into the house. In the boy's, he was being attacked by a witch. When Madanes asked what the mother did when the boy had nightmares, she said that she took him into her bed and told him to pray to God. She thought his nightmares were the work of the devil.

Madanes's conjecture was that the boy's night terrors were a metaphorical expression of the mother's fears and an attempt to help her. As long as the boy was afraid, his mother had to be strong. Unfortunately, while trying to protect him, she frightened him further by talking about God and the devil. Thus, both mother and child were helping each other in unproductive ways.

The family members were told to pretend that they were home and the mother was afraid that someone might break in. The son was asked to protect his mother. In this way the mother had to pretend

to need the child's help instead of really needing it. At first the family had difficulty playing the scene because the mother would attack the make-believe thief before the son could help. Thus, she communicated that she was capable of taking care of herself and didn't need her son's protection. After the scene was performed correctly, with the boy attacking the thief, they discussed the performance. The mother explained that it was difficult to play her part because she was a competent person who could defend herself.

Madanes sent the family home with the task of repeating this dramatization every evening for a week. If the boy started screaming during his sleep, his mother was to wake him up and replay the scene. They were told that this was important to do no matter how late it was or how tired they were. The son's night terrors soon disappeared.

Cloe Madanes's "pretend techniques" provide a clever way to help break control-and-rebel cycles.

Case Study

A mother sought treatment for her five-year-old because he had uncontrollable temper tantrums. After talking with the family for a few minutes, Madanes asked the boy to show her what his tantrums were like by pretending to have one. "Okay," he said,

"I'm the Incredible Hulk!" He puffed out his chest, flexed his muscles, made a monster face, and started screaming and kicking the furniture. Madanes asked the mother to do what she usually did in such circumstances. The mother responded by telling her son, in a weak and ineffective way, to calm down. She pretended to send him to another room, as she tried to do at home. Next Madanes asked the mother if the boy was doing a good job of pretending. She said he was.

Madanes asked the boy to repeat the scene. This time he was Frankenstein and his tantrum was performed with a rigid posture and a grimacing face. Then Madanes talked with the boy about the Incredible Hulk and Frankenstein and congratulated the mother for raising such an imaginative child.

Following this discussion, the mother and son were told to pretend that he was having a tantrum while she was walking him to his room. The boy was told to act like the Incredible Hulk and to make lots of noise. Then they were told to pretend to close the door and hug and kiss. Next Madanes instructed the mother to pretend *she* was having a tantrum, and the boy was to hug and kiss her. Madanes instructed the mother and son to perform both scenes every morning before school and every afternoon when the boy came home. After every performance, the mother was to give the boy milk and cookies if he did a good job. Thus, the mother was moved from a helpless position to one of authority in which she was in charge of rewarding her son's make-believe performance.

The next week the mother called to say that they didn't need to come for therapy because the boy was behaving very well and his tantrums had ceased.

Haley (1984) returned to his Ericksonian roots in a book called *Ordeal Therapy,* a collection of case studies in which ordeals were prescribed to make symptoms more trouble than they're worth. "If one makes it more difficult for a person to have a symptom than to give it up, the person will give up the symptom" (p. 5). For example, a standard ordeal is for a client to have to get up in the middle of the night and exercise strenuously whenever he or she had symptoms during that day. Another example might be for the client to have to give a present to someone with whom he or she has a poor relationship—for example, a mother-in-law or ex-spouse—each time the symptoms occur.

Haley also used ordeals to restructure families. For example, a sixteen-year-old boy put a variety of items up his behind and then expelled them, leaving his stepmother to clean up the mess. Haley (1984) arranged that after each such episode, the father had to take his son to their backyard and have the boy dig a hole three feet deep and three feet wide, in which he was to bury all the things he was putting up his rear end. After a few weeks of this, Haley reported that the symptom stopped, the father became more involved with his son, and the stepmother became closer to the father.

The current form of Haley/Madanes therapy, called *strategic humanism,* still involves giving directives, but the directives are now more oriented toward increasing family members' abilities to soothe and love than to gain control over one another. This represents a major shift and is in sync with family therapy's movement away from the power elements of hierarchy and toward finding ways to increase harmony.

An excellent example of strategic humanism's blend of compassion and cleverness is James Keim's work with oppositional children (Keim, 1998). He begins by reassuring anxious parents that they aren't to blame for their children's oppositionalism. Next he explains that there are two sides of parental authority—discipline and nurture. To reinforce the parents' authority while avoiding power struggles, Keim encourages them to concentrate on being sympathetic and supportive for a while. The parent who soothes a child with the forgotten language of understanding is every bit as in charge as one who tries to tell the child what to do. After progress has been made in calming the child down—especially in breaking the pattern by which oppositional children control the mood in the family by arguing with everything their parents say—Keim coaches the parents to post rules and enforce consequences. This strategy puts parents back in charge of unruly children without the high-intensity melodrama that usually attends work with this population.

The Milan Model. The original Milan model was highly scripted. Families were treated by male–female cotherapists and observed by other members of the team. The standard format had five parts: presession, session, intersession, intervention, and postsession discussion. As Boscolo, Cecchin, Hoffman, and Penn (1987) describe:

> During the presession the team came up with an initial hypothesis about the family's presenting problem. . . . During the session itself, the team members would validate, modify, or change the hypothesis. After about forty minutes, the entire team would meet alone to discuss the hypothesis and arrive at an intervention. The treating therapists would then go back to deliver the intervention to the family, either by positively connoting the problem situation or by a ritual to be done by the family that commented on the problem situation and was designed to introduce change. . . . Finally, the team would meet for a postsession discussion to analyze the family's reactions and to plan for the next session. (p. 4)

As indicated in this description, the primary intervention was either a *ritual* or a *positive connotation*.

The **positive connotation** was the most distinctive innovation to emerge from the Milan model. Derived from the MRI technique of reframing symptoms as serving a protective function—for example, Carlo needs to continue to be depressed to distract his parents from their marital issues—the positive connotation avoided the implication that family members benefited from the patient's symptoms. This implication made for resistance that the Milan team found could be circumvented if the patient's behavior was construed not as protecting specific people but as preserving the family's overall harmony. Indeed, every family member's behavior was often connoted in this system-serving way.

The treatment team would hypothesize about how the patient's symptoms fit into the family system

and, after a midsession break, the therapists would deliver this hypothesis to the family along with the injunction that they should not try to change. Carlo should continue to sacrifice himself by remaining depressed as a way to reassure the family that he will not become an abusive man like his grandfather. Mother should maintain her overinvolvement with Carlo as a way to make him feel valued while he sacrifices himself. Father should continue to criticize mother and Carlo's relationship so that mother will not be tempted to abandon Carlo and become a wife to her husband.

Family rituals were used to engage members in a series of actions that ran counter to or exaggerated rigid family rules and myths. For example, one family that was enmeshed with their large extended family was told to hold family discussions behind locked doors every other night after dinner, during which each family member was to speak for fifteen minutes about the family. Meanwhile, they were to redouble their courtesy to the other members of the clan. By exaggerating the family's loyalty to the extended family while simultaneously breaking that loyalty's rule by meeting apart from the clan and talking about it, the family could examine and break the rule that perpetuated their dysfunctional system.

Rituals were also used to dramatize positive connotations. For example, each family member might have to express his or her gratitude each night to the patient for having the problem (Boscolo et al., 1987). The Milan group also devised a set of rituals based on an "odd and even days" format (Selvini Palazzoli et al., 1978a). For example, a family in which the parents were deadlocked over parental control might be told that on even days of the week, Father should be in charge of the patient's behavior and Mother should act as if she weren't there. On odd days, Mother is in charge and Father is to stay out of the way. Here, again, the family's rigid sequences are interrupted, and they must react differently to each other.

Positive connotations and rituals were powerful and provocative interventions. To keep families engaged while using such methods, the therapeutic relationship became crucial. Unfortunately, the Milan team originally portrayed therapy as a power struggle with families. Their main advice to therapists was to remain neutral in the sense of avoiding the appearance of taking sides. This **neutrality** was often manifested as distance, so that therapists delivered their dramatic pronouncements while acting aloof. Not surprisingly, families often got angry and didn't return.

In the early 1980s, the original Milan team split around the nature of therapy. Selvini Palazzoli maintained the model's strategic and adversarial bent, although she stopped using paradoxical interventions. Instead she and Guiliana Prata experimented with a ritual called the **invariant prescription,** which they assigned to every family they treated.

Selvini Palazzoli (1986) believed that psychotic and anorexic patients are caught up in a "dirty game," a power struggle originally between their parents into which these patients are pulled. Ultimately, they wind up using their symptoms in an attempt to defeat one parent for the sake of the other. In the invariant prescription, parents were directed to tell their children that they had a secret. They were to go out together for varying periods of time and to do so mysteriously, without warning other family members. Therapy continued this way until the patient's symptoms abated.

In the early 1990s, Selvini Palazzoli reinvented her therapy once more, this time abandoning short-term strategic therapy (invariant prescription included) for long-term therapy with patients and their families (Selvini, 1993). Thus, she came full circle, beginning with a psychodynamic approach, then focusing on family patterns, and finally returning to long-term therapy that emphasizes insight and focuses on the individual. This new therapy revolves around understanding the denial of family secrets and suffering over generations. In this way, it is linked conceptually, if not technically, to her former models.

Boscolo and Cecchin also moved away from strategic intervening but toward a collaborative style of therapy. This approach grew from their conclusion that the value in the Milan model wasn't so much in the directives (positive connotations and rituals), which had been the model's centerpiece, but in the interview process itself. Their therapy came to center around **circular questioning,** a clinical translation of Bateson's notion of double description. Circular questions are designed to decenter clients by orienting them toward seeing themselves in a relational context and seeing that context from the perspectives of other family members. For example, a therapist might ask "How might your father have characterized your mother's relationship with your sister, if he had felt free to speak with you about it?" Such questions are structured so that one has to give a relational description in answer.

By asking about relationship patterns like this, the circular nature of problems becomes apparent. Circular questions have been further refined and cataloged by Peggy Penn (1982, 1985) and Karl Tomm (1987a, 1987b). Boscolo (Boscolo & Bertrando, 1992) remains intrigued with their potential.

Case Study

As an example, let's return to Carlo's family and imagine the following conversation (adapted from Hoffman, 1983):

Q: Who is most upset by Carlo's depression?
A: Mother.
Q: How does Mother try to help Carlo?
A: She talks to him for hours and tries to do things for him.
Q: Who agrees most with Mother's way of trying to help Carlo?
A: The psychiatrist who prescribes his medication.
Q: Who disagrees?
A: Father. He thinks Carlo shouldn't be allowed to do what he wants.
Q: Who agrees with Father?
A: We all think Carlo is babied too much. And Grandma too. Grandpa would probably agree with Mother but he died.
Q: Did Carlo start to get depressed before or after Grandfather's death?
A: Not long after, I guess.

Q: If Grandfather hadn't died, how would the family be different now?

A: Well, Mother and Grandma probably wouldn't fight so much because Grandma wouldn't be living with us. And Mother wouldn't be so sad all the time.

Q: If Mother and Grandma didn't fight so much and Mother wasn't so sad, how do you think Carlo would be?

A: Well, I guess he might be happier too. But then he'd probably be fighting with Father again.

By asking circular questions, the frame for Carlo's problem gradually shifts from a psychiatric one to being symptomatic of changes in the family structure.

Boscolo and Cecchin discovered that the spirit in which these questions were asked determined their usefulness. If a therapist maintains a strategic mind-set—uses the questioning process to strive for a particular outcome—the responses of family members are constrained by their sense that the therapist is after something. If, on the other hand, the therapist asks circular questions out of genuine curiosity (Cecchin, 1987), as if joining the family in a research expedition regarding their problem, an atmosphere can be created in which the family can arrive at new understandings of their predicament.

Other Contributions. Strategic therapists pioneered the *team approach* to therapy. Originally, the MRI group used teams behind one-way mirrors to help brainstorm strategies as did the Milan group. Papp (1980) and her colleagues at the Ackerman Institute brought the team directly into the therapy process by turning the observers into a "Greek chorus" who reacted to events in the session. For example, the team might, for strategic purposes, disagree with the therapist. In witnessing debates between the team and their therapist over what a family should do, family members might feel that both sides of their ambivalence were being represented. Having the team interact openly with the therapist or even with

the family during sessions paved the way for later approaches in which the team might enter the treatment room and discuss the family while the family watched (Andersen, 1987).

Jim Alexander was a behaviorist who, out of frustration with the limits of his behavioral orientation, incorporated strategic ideas. The result was *functional family therapy* (Alexander & Parsons, 1982), which, as the name implies, is concerned with the function that family behavior is designed to achieve (see also Chapter 10). Functional family therapists assume that most family behaviors are attempts to become more or less intimate. Through *relabeling* (another word for *reframing*), they help family members see each other's actions in that benign light. They also help family members set up contingency management programs to help them achieve the kind of intimacy they want. Functional family therapy represents an interesting blend of strategic and behavioral therapies and, unlike other strategic models, retains the behaviorist ethic of basing interventions on sound research.

*C*URRENT STATUS OF THE MODEL

Communications family therapy wasn't just an application of individual psychotherapy to families; it was a radically new conceptualization that altered the very nature of imagination. What was new was the focus on the form and impact of communication, rather than the *content*. Communication was described as feedback, as a tactic in interpersonal power struggles, and as symptoms. In fact, all behavior is communicative.

When communication takes place in a closed system—an individual's fantasies or a family's private conversations—there is little opportunity for adjusting the system. Only when someone outside the system provides input can correction occur. Because the rules of family functioning are largely unknown to the family, the best way to examine them is to consult an expert in communication. Today the concepts of communications theory have been absorbed into the mainstream of family therapy, and its symptom-focused interventions have become the basis of the strategic and solution-focused models.

Strategic therapies reached the height of their popularity in the 1980s. They were clever, prescriptive, and systematic—qualities appreciated by therapists who often felt overwhelmed by the emotionality of families in treatment. Then a backlash set in, and people began criticizing strategic therapy's manipulative aspects. Unfortunately, when communications and strategic therapists were confounded by the anxious inflexibility of some families, they may have exaggerated the irrational power of the family system.

In the 1990s the strategic approaches described in this chapter were replaced on family therapy's center stage by more collaborative models. But even as the field moves away from an overreliance on technique and manipulation, we shouldn't lose sight of valuable aspects of strategic therapy. These include having a clear therapeutic goal, anticipating how families will react to interventions, understanding and tracking sequences of interaction, and the creative use of directives.

Most of the meager research on the effectiveness of strategic therapy isn't rigorous. More than with any other model in this book, information about strategic therapy is exchanged through the case report format. Nearly all of the articles and books on strategic therapy include at least one description of a successful technique or therapy outcome. Thus, strategic therapy appears to have a great deal of anecdotal support for its efficacy (although people tend not to write about their failed cases).

Some early studies of the outcome of family therapies based on strategic therapy helped fuel its popularity. In their classic study, Langsley, Machotka, and Flomenhaft (1971) found that family crisis therapy, with similarities to the MRI and Haley models, drastically reduced the need for hospitalization. Alexander and Parsons found their functional family therapy to be more effective in treating a group of delinquents than a client-centered family approach, an eclectic-dynamic approach, or a no-treatment

control (Parsons & Alexander, 1973). Stanton and Todd (1982) demonstrated the effectiveness of combining structural and strategic therapies for treating heroin addicts. The results were impressive because family therapy resulted in twice as many days of abstinence from heroin as a methadone maintenance program.

In the early 1980s the Milan associates offered anecdotal reports of amazing outcomes with anorexia nervosa, schizophrenia, and delinquency (Selvini Palazzoli, Boscolo, Cecchin, & Prata, 1978b, 1980). Later, however, members of the original team expressed reservations about the model and implied that it wasn't as effective as originally suggested (Boscolo, 1983; Selvini Palazzoli, 1986; Selvini Palazzoli & Viaro, 1988).

Although the original Milan model appears to have gone the way of the dinosaurs, two thriving strategic camps currently exist: the MRI group on the West Coast and the Washington School, started by Haley and Madanes on the East Coast.

• • •

What people came to rebel against was the gimmickry of formulaic techniques. But gimmickry wasn't inherent in the strategic models. For example, the MRI's emphasis on reversing attempted solutions that don't work is a sound idea. People *do* stay stuck in ruts as long as they pursue self-defeating strategies. If, in some hands, blocking more-of-the-same kinds of solutions resulted in a rote application of reverse psychology, that's not the fault of the cybernetic metaphor but of the way it was applied.

Strategic therapists are currently integrating new ideas and keeping up with the postmodern spirit of the twenty-first century. Haley published a book in which the evolution of his thinking is apparent (Haley, 1996), and another book on the influence of the MRI on the field was released (Weakland & Ray, 1995). In addition, some authors have integrated MRI strategic concepts with narrative approaches (Eron & Lund, 1993, 1996). It's good to see that strategic thinking is evolving, because even in this era of the nonexpert therapist, there is still room for thoughtful problem-solving strategies and therapeutic direction.

Summary

1. Communications therapy was one of the first and most influential forms of family treatment. Its theoretical development was based on general systems theory, and the therapy that emerged was a systems approach *par excellence*. Communication was the detectable input and output therapists used to analyze the black box of interpersonal systems.

2. Another of the significant ideas of communications therapy was that families are rule-governed systems, maintained by homeostatic feedback mechanisms. Negative feedback accounts for the stability of healthy families and the inflexibility of dysfunctional ones. Because such families don't have adequate positive feedback mechanisms, they're unable to adjust to changing circumstances.

3. Although there were significant differences among the therapeutic strategies of Haley, Jackson, Satir, and Watzlawick, they were all committed to altering destructive patterns of communication. They pursued this goal by direct and indirect means. The direct approach, favored by Satir (1964), sought to make family rules explicit and teach clear communication. This approach could be described as establishing ground rules, or metacommunication principles, and included such tactics as telling people to speak for themselves and pointing out nonverbal and multilevel channels of communication.

4. The trouble is, as Haley noted, "One of the difficulties involved in telling patients to do something is the fact that psychiatric patients are noted for their hesitation about doing what they are told." For this reason, communications therapists began to rely on more indirect strategies designed to provoke change rather than foster awareness. Telling family members to speak for themselves, for example, may challenge a family rule and therefore meet with resistance. With this realization, communications therapy evolved into a treatment of resistance.

5. Resistance and symptoms were treated with a variety of paradoxical directives, known loosely as *therapeutic double binds*. Milton Erickson's technique of prescribing resistance was used as a lever to gain control, as, for example, when a therapist tells family members not to reveal everything in the first session. The same ploy was used to prescribe symptoms, an action that made covert rules explicit, implied that such behavior was voluntary, and put the therapist in control.

6. Strategic therapy, derived from Ericksonian hypnotherapy and Batesonian cybernetics, developed a body of powerful procedures for treating psychological problems. Strategic approaches vary in the specifics of theory and technique but share a problem-centered, pragmatic focus on changing behavioral sequences in which therapists take responsibility for the outcome of therapy. Insight and understanding are eschewed in favor of directives designed to change the way family members interact.

7. The MRI model tries to remain strictly interactional—observing and intervening into sequences of interaction surrounding a problem rather than speculating about the intentions of the interactants. Haley and Madanes, on the other hand, were interested in motives: Haley mainly in the desire to control others and Madanes in the desire to love and be loved. Unlike the MRI group, Haley and Madanes believed that successful treatment often requires structural change with an emphasis on improving family hierarchy.

8. Like Haley, the Milan Associates originally saw power in the motives of family members. They tried to understand the elaborate multigenerational games that surrounded symptoms. They designed powerful interventions—positive connotation and rituals—to expose these games and change the meaning of the problem. Later, the original group split, with Selvini Palazzoli going through several transformations until her current long-term approach based on family secrets. Cecchin and Boscolo moved away from formulaic interventions, became more interested in the questioning process as a way to help families to new understandings, and in so doing paved the way for family therapy's current interest in conversation and narrative.

Questions to Consider

1. What strategic concepts and techniques could usefully be adopted by practitioners of other approaches?
2. While strategic therapists tend to strategize to manipulate clients, to what extent might it be possible to strategize with clients in a collaborative effort to reverse problem-maintaining solutions? In what kinds of cases might this be more and less feasible?
3. Would an MRI approach be more useful with families who are cooperative or who are resistant?
4. How would you phrase a series of circular questions that would get at the process of communication that occurs in your family therapy class?
5. Are paradoxical interventions necessarily distancing and manipulative?

Key Concepts

circular causality   The idea that events are related through a series of interacting loops or repeating cycles.

circular questioning   A method of interviewing developed by the Milan Associates in which questions are asked that highlight differences among family members.

communications theory   The study of relationships in terms of the exchange of verbal and nonverbal messages.

cybernetics   The study of control processes in systems, especially analysis of the flow of information in closed systems.

directives   Homework assignments designed to help families interrupt homeostatic patterns of problem-maintaining behavior.

double bind   A conflict created when a person receives contradictory messages on different levels of abstraction in an important relationship and cannot leave or comment.

family homeostasis   The tendency of families to resist change to maintain a steady state.

family ritual   A technique used by Selvini Palazzoli and her Milan Associates that prescribes a set of actions designed to change a family system's rules.

family rules   A descriptive term for redundant behavioral patterns.

feedback loops   The return of a portion of the output of a system, especially when used to maintain the output within predetermined limits (negative feedback) or to signal a need to modify the system (positive feedback).

first-order change   Superficial change in a system that stays invariant.

function of symptoms   The idea that symptoms are often ways to distract or protect family members from threatening conflicts.

general systems theory   A biological model of living systems as whole entities that maintain themselves through continuous input and output from the environment; developed by Ludwig von Bertalanffy.

hierarchical structure   Family functioning based on clear generational boundaries in which the parents maintain control and authority.

homeostasis   See **family homeostasis.**

identified patient   The symptom bearer or official patient.

invariant prescription   A technique developed by Mara Selvini Palazzoli in which parents are directed to mysteriously sneak away together.

metacommunication   Every message has two levels, report and command; metacommunication is the implied command or qualifying message.

negative feedback   See **feedback loops.**

neutrality   Selvini Palazzoli's term for balanced acceptance of family members.

ordeal   A paradoxical intervention in which the client is directed to do something that is more of a hardship than the symptom.

paradox   A self-contradictory statement based on a valid deduction from acceptable premises.

paradoxical intervention   A technique used in strategic therapy in which the therapist directs family members to continue their symptomatic behavior. If they conform, they admit control and expose secondary gain; if they rebel, they give up their symptoms.

positive connotation   Selvini Palazzoli's technique of ascribing positive motives to family behavior to promote family cohesion and avoid resistance to therapy.

positive feedback   See **feedback loops.**

prescribing the symptom   A paradoxical technique that forces a patient either to give up a symptom or to admit that it is under voluntary control.

pretend techniques   Madanes's playful paradoxical intervention in which family members are asked to pretend to engage in symptomatic behavior. The paradox is if they are pretending to have a symptom, the symptom cannot be real.

reframing   Relabeling a family's description of behavior to make it more amenable to therapeutic change; for example, describing someone as "lazy" rather than "depressed."

restraining   A strategic technique for overcoming resistance by suggesting that a family not change.

rituals   See **family ritual.**

second-order change   Basic change in the structure of a system.

strategic therapy   Any of several artful approaches that aim to manipulate behavior change to solve family problems.

Recommended Readings

Cecchin, G. 1987. Hypothesizing, circularity and neutrality revisited. *Family Process.* 26: 405–413.

Fisch, R., Weakland, J. H., and Segal, L. 1982. *The tactics of change: Doing therapy briefly.* San Francisco: Jossey-Bass.

Haley, J. 1976. *Problem-solving therapy.* San Francisco: Jossey-Bass.

Haley, J., and Richeport-Haley, M. 2008. *Directive family therapy.* New York: Haworth.

Jackson, D. D. 1961. Interactional psychotherapy. In *Contemporary psychotherapies,* M. T. Stein, ed. New York: Free Press of Glencoe.

Jackson, D. D. 1967. *Therapy, communication and change.* Palo Alto, CA: Science and Behavior Books.

Keim, J. 1998. Strategic therapy. In *Case studies in couple and family therapy,* F. Dattilio, ed. New York: Guilford Press.

Lederer, W., and Jackson, D. D. 1968. *Mirages of marriage.* New York: Norton.

Madanes, C. 1981. *Strategic family therapy.* San Francisco: Jossey-Bass.

Price, J. 1996. *Power and compassion: Working with difficult adolescents and abused parents.* New York: Guilford Press.

Rabkin, R. 1972. *Strategic psychotherapy.* New York: Basic Books.

Selvini Palazzoli, M., Boscolo, L., Cecchin, G., and Prata, G. 1978. *Paradox and counterparadox.* New York: Jason Aronson.

Watzlawick, P., Beavin, J. H., and Jackson, D. D. 1967. *Pragmatics of human communication.* New York: Norton.

Watzlawick, P., Weakland, J., and Fisch, R. 1974. *Change: Principles of problem formation and problem resolution.* New York: Norton.

References

Alexander, J., and Parsons, B. 1982. *Functional family therapy.* Monterey, CA: Brooks/Cole.

Andersen, T. 1987. The reflecting team: Dialogue and meta-dialogue in clinical work. *Family Process. 26:* 415–417.

Boscolo, L. 1983. Final discussion. In *Psychosocial intervention in schizophrenia: An international view,* H. Stierlin, L. Wynne, and M. Wirsching, eds. Berlin: Springer-Verlag.

Boscolo, L., and Bertrando, P. 1992. The reflexive loop of past, present, and future in systemic therapy and consultation. *Family Process. 31:* 119–133.

Boscolo, L., Cecchin, G., Hoffman, L., and Penn, P. 1987. *Milan systemic family therapy.* New York: Basic Books.

Cecchin, G. 1987. Hypothesizing, circularity and neutrality revisited: An invitation to curiosity. *Family Process. 26:* 405–413.

Eron, J., and Lund, T. 1993. An approach to how problems evolve and dissolve: Integrating narrative and strategic concepts. *Family Process. 32:* 291–309.

Eron, J., and Lund, T. 1996. *Narrative solutions in brief therapy.* New York: Guilford Press.

Fisch, R. 1978. Review of problem-solving therapy, by Jay Haley. *Family Process. 17:* 107–110.

Fisch, R., Weakland, J., and Segal, L. 1982. *The tactics of change.* San Francisco: Jossey-Bass.

Gaulier, B., Margerum, J., Price, J., and Windell, J. 2007. *Defusing the high-conflict divorce: A treatment guide for working with angry couples.* Atascadero, CA: Impact Publishers.

Haley, J. 1961. Control in psychotherapy with schizophrenics. *Archives of General Psychiatry. 5:* 340–353.

Haley, J. 1963. *Strategies of psychotherapy.* New York: Grune & Stratton.

Haley, J. 1973. *Uncommon therapy.* New York: Norton.

Haley, J. 1976. *Problem-solving therapy.* San Francisco: Jossey-Bass.

Haley, J. 1981. *Reflections on therapy.* Chevy Chase, MD: Family Therapy Institute of Washington, DC.

Haley, J. 1984. *Ordeal therapy.* San Francisco: Jossey-Bass.

Haley, J. 1996. *Learning and teaching therapy.* New York: Guilford Press.

Hoffman, L. 1983. A co-evolutionary framework for systemic family therapy. In *Diagnosis and assessment in family therapy,* J. Hansen and B. Keeney, eds. Rockville, MD: Aspen Systems.

Jackson, D. D. 1965. Family rules: The marital quid pro quo. *Archives of General Psychiatry. 12:* 589–594.

Jackson, D. D. 1967. Aspects of conjoint family therapy. In *Family therapy and disturbed families,* G. H. Zuk and I. Boszormenyi-Nagy, eds. Palo Alto: Science and Behavior Books.

Jackson, D. D., and Weakland, J. H. 1961. Conjoint family therapy: Some consideration on theory, technique, and results. *Psychiatry. 24:* 30–45.

Keim, J. 1998. Strategic family therapy. In *Case studies in couple and family therapy,* F. Dattilio, ed. New York: Guilford Press.

Keim, J., and Lappin, J. 2002. Structural-strategic marital therapy. In *Clinical handbook of couple therapy,* A. S. Gurman and N. S. Jacobson, eds. New York: Guilford Press.

Langsley, D., Machotka, P., and Flomenhaft, K. 1971. Avoiding mental hospital admission: A follow-up study. *American Journal of Psychiatry. 127:* 1391–1394.

Madanes, C. 1980. Protection, paradox and pretending. *Family Process. 19:* 73–85.

Madanes, C. 1981. *Strategic family therapy.* San Francisco: Jossey-Bass.

Madanes, C. 1984. *Behind the one-way mirror.* San Francisco: Jossey-Bass.

Marayuma, M. 1968. The second cybernetics: Deviation-amplifying mutual causal processes. In *Modern systems research for the behavioral scientist,* W. Buckley, ed. Chicago: Aldine.

Papp, P. 1980. The Greek chorus and other techniques of paradoxical therapy. *Family Process. 19:* 45–57.

Parsons, B., and Alexander, J. 1973. Short term family intervention: A therapy outcome study. *Journal of Consulting and Clinical Psychology. 41:* 95–201.

Penn, P. 1982. Circular questioning. *Family Process. 21:* 267–280.

Penn, P. 1985. Feed-forward: Further questioning, future maps. *Family Process. 24:* 299–310.

Price, J. 1996. *Power and compassion: Working with difficult adolescents and abused parents.* New York: Guilford Press.

Ruesch, J., and Bateson, G. 1951. *Communication: The social matrix of psychiatry.* New York: Norton.

Selvini, M. 1993. Major mental disorders, distorted reality and family secrets. Unpublished manuscript.

Selvini Palazzoli, M. 1981. *Self-starvation: From the intrapsychic to the transpersonal approach to anorexia nervosa.* New York: Jason Aronson.

Selvini Palazzoli, M. 1986. Towards a general model of psychotic games. *Journal of Marital and Family Therapy.* 12: 339–349.

Selvini Palazzoli, M., Boscolo, L., Cecchin, G., and Prata, G. 1978a. A ritualized prescription in family therapy: Odd days and even days. *Journal of Marriage and Family Counseling.* 4: 3–9.

Selvini Palazzoli, M., Boscolo, L., Cecchin, G., and Prata, G. 1978b. *Paradox and counterparadox.* New York: Jason Aronson.

Selvini Palazzoli, M., Boscolo, L., Cecchin, G., and Prata, G. 1980. Hypothesizing—circularity—neutrality: Three guidelines for the conductor of the session. *Family Process.* 19: 3–12.

Selvini Palazzoli, M., and Viaro, M. 1988. The anorectic process in the family: A six-stage model as a guide for individual therapy. *Family Process.* 27: 129–148.

Shoham, V., and Rohrbaugh, M. J. 2002. Brief strategic couple therapy. In *Clinical handbook of couple therapy,* A. S. Gurman and N. S. Jacobson, eds. New York: Guilford Press.

Stanton, D., Todd, T., and Associates. 1982. *The family therapy of drug abuse and addiction.* New York: Guilford Press.

Tomm, K. 1987a. Interventive interviewing: Part I. Strategizing as a fourth guideline for the therapist. *Family Process.* 26: 3–13.

Tomm, K. 1987b. Interventive interviewing: Part II. Reflexive questioning as a means to enable self-healing. *Family Process.* 26: 167–184.

Watzlawick, P., Beavin, J., and Jackson, D. 1967. *Pragmatics of human communication.* New York: Norton.

Watzlawick, P., Weakland, J., and Fisch, R. 1974. *Change: Principles of problem formation and problem resolution.* New York: Norton.

Weakland, J., and Fisch, R. 1992. Brief therapy—MRI Style. In *The first session in brief therapy,* S. H. Budman, N. F. Hoyt, and S. Friedman, eds. New York: Guilford Press.

Weakland, J., Fisch, R., Watzlawick, P., and Bodin, A. 1974. Brief therapy: Focused problem resolution. *Family Process.* 13: 141–168.

Weakland, J., and Ray, W., eds. 1995. *Propagations: Thirty years of influence from the Mental Research Institute.* Binghamton, NY: Haworth Press.

7

Structural Family Therapy

One of the reasons family therapy can be difficult is that families often appear as collections of individuals who affect each other in powerful but unpredictable ways. Structural family therapy provides a framework that brings order and meaning to those transactions. The consistent patterns of family behavior are what allow us to consider that they have **structure,** although of course only in a functional sense. The emotional boundaries and coalitions that make up a family's structure are abstractions; nevertheless, the concept of family structure enables therapists to intervene in a systematic and organized way.

Families usually seek help for a specific problem. It might be a child who misbehaves or a couple who doesn't get along. Family therapists look beyond the specifics of those problems to the family's attempts to solve them. This leads to the dynamics of interaction. The misbehaving child might have parents who scold but never reward him or her. The couple may be caught up in a pursuer–distancer dynamic, or they might be unable to talk without arguing.

What structural family therapy adds to the equation is a recognition of the overall organization that supports those interactions. The "parents who scold" might turn out to be partners who undermine each other because one is wrapped up in the child while the other is an angry outsider. If so, attempts to encourage effective discipline are likely to fail unless the structural problem is addressed and the parents develop a real partnership. Similarly, a couple who don't get along may not be able to improve their relationship until they create a boundary between themselves and intrusive children or in-laws.

The discovery that families are organized into **subsystems** with **boundaries** regulating the contact family members have with each other turned out to be one of the defining insights of family therapy. Perhaps equally important, though, was the introduction of **enactments,** in which family members are encouraged to deal directly with each other in sessions, permitting the therapist to observe and modify their interactions.

EVOLUTION OF THE MODEL

When he first burst onto the scene, Salvador Minuchin's galvanizing impact was as a master of technique. His most lasting contribution, however, was a theory of family structure and set of guidelines to organize therapeutic techniques. This structural approach was so successful that it captivated the field in the 1970s, and Minuchin built the Philadelphia Child Guidance Clinic into a world-famous complex where thousands of family therapists have been trained in structural family therapy.

Salvador Minuchin

Born and raised in Argentina, Salvador Minuchin began his career as a family therapist in the early 1960s when he discovered two patterns common to troubled families: Some are *enmeshed*, chaotic, and tightly interconnected, while others are *disengaged*, isolated, and distant. In his classic text, *Families and Family Therapy*, Minuchin (1974) taught therapists to see family relationships and patterns more clearly. In 1965 Minuchin became the director of the Philadelphia Child Guidance Clinic, which eventually became the world's leading center for family therapy.

In 1969 Minuchin, Haley, Braulio Montalvo, and Bernice Rosman developed a highly successful training program that emphasized hands-on experience, on-line supervision, and the use of videotapes to learn the techniques of structural family therapy. In 1981 Minuchin established a center for the practice and training of structural family therapy in New York, which after his retirement in 1996 was renamed the Minuchin Center for the Family.

Minuchin was born and raised in Argentina. He served as a physician in the Israeli army and then came to the United States, where he studied child psychiatry with Nathan Ackerman. After completing his training, Minuchin returned to Israel in 1952 to work with displaced children. He moved back to the United States in 1954 to begin psychoanalytic training at the William Alanson White Institute, where he studied the interpersonal psychiatry of Harry Stack Sullivan. After the White Institute, Minuchin took a job at the Wiltwyck School for delinquent boys, where he suggested to his staff that they start seeing families.

At Wiltwyck, Minuchin and his colleagues—Dick Auerswald, Charlie King, Braulio Montalvo, and Clara Rabinowitz—taught themselves family therapy, inventing it as they went along. To do so, they built a one-way mirror and took turns observing each other

work. In 1962 Minuchin made a hajj to what was then the mecca of family therapy, Palo Alto. There he met Jay Haley and began a friendship that blossomed into an extraordinarily fertile collaboration.

The success of Minuchin's work with families at Wiltwyck led to a groundbreaking book, *Families of the Slums* (Minuchin, Montalvo, Guerney, Rosman, & Schumer, 1967). Minuchin's reputation as a virtuoso therapist grew, and he was invited to become the director of the Philadelphia Child Guidance Clinic in 1965. The clinic then consisted of fewer than a dozen staff members. From this modest beginning, Minuchin created one of the largest and most prestigious child guidance clinics in the world.

Among Minuchin's colleagues in Philadelphia were Braulio Montalvo, Jay Haley, Bernice Rosman, Harry Aponte, Carter Umbarger, Marianne Walters, Charles Fishman, Cloe Madanes, and Stephen Greenstein—each of whom had a role in shaping structural family therapy. By the 1970s structural family therapy had become the most widely practiced of all systems of family therapy.

After leaving Philadelphia in 1981, Minuchin started his own center in New York, where he continued to practice and teach until 1996, when he retired and moved to Boston. Although he retired (again) and moved to Boca Raton, Florida, in 2005, Dr. Minuchin still travels and teaches throughout the world.

Like players on a team with a superstar, some of Minuchin's colleagues are not as well known as they might be. Foremost among these is Braulio Montalvo, one of the underrated geniuses of family therapy. Born and raised in Puerto Rico, Montalvo, like Minuchin, has always been committed to treating poor and minority families. Like Minuchin, he is also a brilliant therapist, though he favors a gentler, more supportive approach.

Following Minuchin's retirement, the center in New York was renamed the Minuchin Center for the

Family, and the torch was passed to a new generation. Among Minuchin's prominent students are Jorge Colapinto, now at the Ackerman Institute in New York; Jay Lappin, who works with child welfare for the state of Delaware; Michael Nichols, who teaches at the College of William and Mary; and Charles Fishman, in private practice in Philadelphia.

*T*HE BASIC MODEL

Beginners often get bogged down in the content of family problems because they don't have a blueprint to help them see the patterns of family dynamics. Structural family therapy offers such a blueprint. Three constructs are the essential components of structural family theory: *structure, subsystems,* and *boundaries.*

It's easy to understand what's meant by the structure of a house: It's the way the components of the house are organized, how many rooms there are, where the rooms are located, how they are connected, and so on. The family that lives in the house is also organized, but their structure is a little harder to define.

Family structure refers to the way a family is organized into subsystems whose interactions are regulated by boundaries. The *process* of family interactions is like the patterns of conversation at the dinner table. The *structure* of the family is where family members sit in relation to one another. Who sits next to whom makes it easier to interact with some people and less so with others.

To grasp a family's structure, you must look beyond their interactions to the organizational framework within which they occur, and you must keep in mind that what goes on in one part of a family is affected by the organization of the whole system. Now let's see how this organizational structure comes about.

As family transactions are repeated, they foster expectations that establish enduring patterns. Once patterns are established, family members use only a fraction of the full range of behavior available to them. The first time the baby cries or a teenager misses the school bus, it's not clear who will do what. Will the load be shared? Will a quarrel ensue?

Will one person get stuck with most of the work? Soon, however, patterns are set, roles are assigned, and things take on a sameness and predictability. "Who's going to . . .?" becomes "She'll probably . . ." and then "She always. . . ."

Family structure is reinforced by the expectations that establish rules in a family. For example, a rule such as "Family members should always look out for one another" will be manifested in various ways. If a boy gets into a fight with another boy in the neighborhood, his mother will go to the neighbors to complain. If a teenager has to get up early for school, Mother wakes her. If a husband is too hung over to go to work in the morning, his wife calls to say he has the flu. If the parents have an argument, their children interrupt. The parents are so preoccupied with the doings of their children that it keeps them from spending time alone together. These sequences are *isomorphic:* They're structured. Modifying any of them may not change the basic structure, but altering the underlying structure will have ripple effects on all family transactions.

Family structure is shaped partly by universal and partly by idiosyncratic constraints. For example, all families have some kind of **hierarchical structure,** with adults and children having different amounts of authority. Family members also tend to have reciprocal and complementary functions. Often these become so ingrained that their origins are forgotten and they are presumed necessary rather than optional.

If a young mother, overwhelmed by the demands of her infant, gets upset and complains to her husband, he can respond in various ways. Perhaps he'll move closer and share the burdens of child-rearing. This creates a united parental team. If, on the other hand, he decides that his wife is depressed, she may end up in psychotherapy for the emotional support she needs. This creates a structure in which the father remains distant from the mother, and she has to turn outside the family for sympathy.

Whatever the pattern, it tends to be self-perpetuating. Although alternatives are available, families are unlikely to consider them until changing circumstances produce stress in the system.

Families don't walk in and hand you their structural patterns as if they were bringing an apple to the teacher. What they bring is chaos and confusion. You have to uncover the subtext—and you must be careful that it's accurate, not imposed but discovered. Two things are necessary: a theoretical system that explains structure and seeing the family in action. Knowing that a family is a single-parent family or that parents are having trouble with their middle child doesn't tell you what their structure is. Structure becomes evident only when you observe actual interactions among family members.

Consider the following:

A mother calls to complain of misbehavior in her seventeen-year-old son. She is asked to bring her husband, son, and the three younger children to the first session. When they arrive, the mother describes a series of minor ways in which the son is disobedient. He interrupts to say that she's always on his case, he never gets a break from his mother.

This spontaneous bickering between mother and son reveals a preoccupation with each other—a preoccupation no less intense simply because it's conflictual. This sequence doesn't, however, tell the whole story. It doesn't include the father or the other children. They must be engaged to observe their roles in the family structure.

If the father sides with his wife but seems unconcerned, then it may be that the mother's preoccupation with her son is related to her husband's neglect. If the three younger children side with their mother and describe their brother as bad, then it becomes clear that all the children are close to their mother—close and obedient up to a point, then close and disobedient.

Families are differentiated into *subsystems*—based on generation, gender, and function—which are demarcated by interpersonal *boundaries,* invisible barriers that regulate contact with others. A rule forbidding phone calls at dinnertime establishes a boundary that shields the family from intrusion. Subsystems that aren't adequately protected by boundaries limit the development of relationship skills. If children are permitted to interrupt their parents' conversations, the boundary separating the generations is eroded and the couple's relationship is subverted to parenting. If parents always step in to settle arguments between their children, the children won't learn to fight their own battles.

Interpersonal boundaries vary from rigid to diffuse (Figure 7.1). Rigid boundaries are restrictive and permit little contact with outside subsystems, resulting in **disengagement.** Disengaged subsystems are independent but isolated. On the plus side, this fosters autonomy. On the other hand, disengagement limits affection and support. Disengaged families must come under extreme stress before they mobilize assistance. **Enmeshed** subsystems offer closeness and support but at the expense of independent competence. Too much closeness cripples initiative.

Although *structure* suggests a static condition, Minuchin (1974) also described developmental aspects of family organization. Families begin when two people in love decide to share their lives together, but a period of often difficult adjustment is required before they complete the transition from courtship to a functional partnership. They must learn to **accommodate** to each other's needs and styles of interaction. He learns to accommodate to her wish to be kissed hello and good-bye. She learns to leave him alone with his morning paper and coffee. These little arrangements, multiplied a thousand times, may be accomplished easily or only after intense struggle. Whatever the case, this process of accommodation cements the couple into a unit.

The spouse subsystem must also develop a boundary that separates it from parents, children, and other outsiders. All too often, husband and wife give up the space they need for mutual support when children

Rigid Boundary	Clear Boundary	Diffuse Boundary
Disengagement	Normal Range	Enmeshment

Figure 7.1   Interpersonal boundaries

are born. Too rigid a boundary around the couple can deprive the children of care and attention, but in our child-centered culture, the boundary between parents and children is often ambiguous at best.

In *Institutionalizing Madness* (Elizur & Minuchin, 1989), Minuchin makes a compelling case for a structural view of emotional problems that extends beyond the family to encompass the entire community. As Minuchin points out, unless therapists learn to look beyond the limited slice of ecology in which they work to the larger social structures within which their work is embedded, their efforts may amount to little more than spinning wheels.

Normal Family Development

What distinguishes normal families isn't an absence of problems but a functional structure for dealing with them. All couples must learn to adjust to each other, raise their children, deal with their parents, earn a living, and fit into their communities. The nature of these struggles changes with developmental stages and situational crises.

When two people join to form a couple, the structural requirements for the new union are accommodation and boundary making. The first priority is mutual accommodation to manage the myriad details of everyday living. Each partner tries to organize the relationship along familiar lines and pressures the other to comply. They must agree on major issues, such as where to live and if and when to have children. Less obvious but equally important, they must coordinate daily rituals, like what to watch on television, what to eat for supper, when to go to bed, and what to do there.

In accommodating to each other, a couple must negotiate the boundary between them as well as the boundary protecting them from the outside. Each partner tends to be more comfortable with the level of closeness that existed in his or her own family. Because these expectations differ, a struggle ensues that may be the most difficult of the new union. He wants to play poker with the boys; she feels deserted. She wants to talk; he wants to watch ESPN. His focus is on his career; her focus is on the relationship. Each thinks the other unreasonable and terribly hurtful.

Couples must also define a boundary between them and their original families. Rather suddenly, the families they grew up in must take second place to the new marriage. This, too, can be a difficult adjustment, both for newlyweds and for their parents.

The birth of a child transforms the family structure; the pattern of interaction between the parental subsystem and child subsystem must be worked out and later modified to fit changing circumstances. A clear boundary enables the children to interact with their parents but excludes them from the spouse subsystem. Parents and children may eat together, play together, and share much of each other's lives. But there are some things that need not be shared. Husband and wife are sustained as a loving couple and enhanced as parents if they make time to be alone together—to talk, to go out to dinner occasionally, to fight, and to make love. Unhappily, the clamorous demands of children often make parents lose sight of their need to maintain the integrity of their relationship.

In addition to maintaining privacy for the couple, a clear generational boundary establishes a hierarchical structure and allows parents to exercise a position of leadership. All too often this hierarchy is subverted by a child-centered ethos, which affects helping professionals as well as parents. Parents enmeshed with their children tend to argue with them about the rules and to misguidedly share—or shirk—responsibility for making parental decisions. Offering a child a choice in picking out clothes or choosing friends encourages self-reliance. Asking children whether they want to go to school or trying to convince a toddler that it's dangerous to play in the street simply blurs the line of authority.

Minuchin (1974) warns therapists not to mistake growing pains for pathology. Normal families experience anxiety and disruption as their members grow and change. Many families seek help at transitional stages, and therapists should keep in mind that family members may simply be in the process of modifying their structure to adjust to new circumstances.

Development of Behavior Disorders

Modifications in structure are required when a family or one of its members encounters external pressures (a parent is laid off, the family moves) and when developmental transitions are reached (a child reaches adolescence, parents retire). Healthy families accommodate to changed circumstances; less adaptive families increase the rigidity of structures that are no longer functional.

In disengaged families, boundaries are rigid and the family fails to mobilize support when it's needed. Disengaged parents may be unaware that a child is depressed or experiencing difficulties at school until the problem is advanced.

A single mother brought her twelve-year-old son to the clinic after discovering that he had missed two weeks of school. *Two weeks!* thought the therapist; that's a long time not to know your child's been skipping school.

A structural perspective would make two important points. First, the obvious disengagement between this mother and child is no more significant than the disengagement between the mother and school authorities. Second, a structural analysis might help to get past blaming this woman for failing to know what was going on in her son's life. If she's disengaged from her son, what is occupying her elsewhere? Maybe the financial burden of single parenthood is overwhelming. Maybe she's still grief stricken over the death of her husband. The point to remember is that if someone is disengaged in one relationship, she is likely to be preoccupied elsewhere.

In enmeshed families, boundaries are diffuse and family members become dependent on one another. Intrusive parents create difficulties by stunting the development of their children and interfering with their ability to solve their own problems.

Although we may refer to families as *enmeshed* or *disengaged*, it's more accurate to describe particular subsystems as being enmeshed or disengaged. In fact, enmeshment and disengagement tend to be reciprocal, so that, for example, a father who's overly involved with his work is likely to neglect his family. A frequently encountered pattern is an enmeshed mother and a disengaged father—"the signature arrangement of the troubled middle-class family" (Minuchin & Nichols, 1993, p. 121).

Feminists have criticized the notion of an enmeshed-mother/disengaged-father syndrome because they worry about blaming mothers for an arrangement that is culturally sanctioned. This concern is valid. But stereotyping and blame are due to insensitive application of these ideas, not to the ideas themselves. Skewed relationships, whatever their origin, can be problematic, though no one individual should be expected to do all the changing.

Structural therapists use a few simple symbols to diagram structural problems, and these diagrams suggest what changes may be needed. Figure 7.2 shows some of the symbols used to diagram family structure.

One problem often seen by family therapists arises when parents who are unable to resolve conflicts between themselves divert the focus of concern

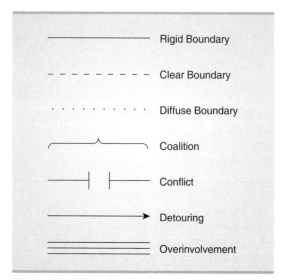

Figure 7.2   Symbols of family structure

Figure 7.4   **Mother-child coalition**

Figure 7.5   Parents enmeshed with children

Figure 7.3   Scapegoating as a means of detouring conflict

onto a child. Instead of worrying about themselves, they worry about the child (see Figure 7.3). Although this reduces the strain on father (F) and mother (M), it victimizes the child (C).

An equally common pattern is when "conflicts between the spouses are played out in the parenting battlefield—and as they pull in different directions, the confused children become casualties" (Minuchin & Nichols, 1993, p. 149). Father says Mother is too permissive; she says he's too strict. He may withdraw, causing her to criticize his lack of involvement, which in turn makes him withdraw further. The enmeshed mother responds to children's needs with excessive concern. The disengaged father

may not respond at all. Both may be critical of the other's way, but they perpetuate each other's behavior with their own. The result is a **cross-generational coalition** between mother and child (Figure 7.4).

Some families function well when the children are young but are unable to adjust to an older child's need for discipline and control. Young children in enmeshed families (Figure 7.5) receive wonderful care: Their parents give them lots of attention. Although such parents may be too tired to have much time for each other, the system may be moderately successful.

If, however, these doting parents don't teach their children to obey rules and respect authority, the children may be unprepared to negotiate their entrance into school. Used to getting their own way, they may be resistant to authority. Several possible consequences may bring the family into treatment. The children may be reluctant to go to school, and their fears may be reinforced by "understanding" parents who permit them to stay home (Figure 7.6). Such a case may be labeled as school phobia and may become entrenched if parents permit their children to remain at home for more than a few days.

Alternatively, the children of such a family may go to school, but because they haven't learned to accommodate to others, they may be rejected by their

Figure 7.6   School phobia

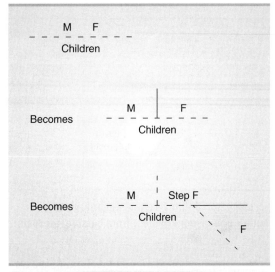

Figure 7.7   Divorce and remarriage

Figure 7.8   Failure to accept a stepparent

schoolmates. Such children often become depressed and withdrawn. In other cases, children enmeshed with their parents become discipline problems, in which case school authorities may initiate counseling.

A major upheaval that requires structural adjustment occurs when divorced partners remarry. Such *blended families* either readjust their boundaries or soon experience transitional conflicts. When a woman divorces, she and her children must learn to readjust to a structure that establishes a clear boundary separating the divorced spouses but still permits contact between father and children; then if she remarries, the family must readjust to functioning with a new husband and stepfather (Figure 7.7).

Sometimes it's hard for a mother and children to allow a stepfather to participate in the parental subsystem. Mother and children have long since established transactional rules and learned to accommodate to each other. The new parent may be treated as an outsider who's supposed to learn the right way of doing things, rather than as a new partner who will give as well as receive ideas about child rearing (Figure 7.8).

The more mother and children insist on maintaining their familiar patterns without including the stepfather, the more frustrated he'll become. The result may lead to child abuse or chronic arguing between the parents. The sooner such families enter treatment, the easier it is to help them adjust to the transition.

An important aspect of structural problems is that symptoms in one family member reflect not only that person's interactions but also other relationships in the family. If Johnny, age sixteen, is depressed, it's helpful to know that he's enmeshed with his mother. Discovering that she demands absolute obedience

and refuses to accept independent thinking or outside relationships helps to explain his depression (Figure 7.9). But that's only one segment of the family system.

Why is the mother enmeshed with her son? Perhaps she's disengaged from her husband. Perhaps she's a widow who hasn't made new friends. Helping Johnny resolve his depression may best be accomplished by helping his mother satisfy her own needs for closeness with other adults in her life.

How Therapy Works

Structural treatment is designed to alter the organization of the family so that its members can better deal with their own problems. The goal of therapy is structural change; problem solving is a byproduct.

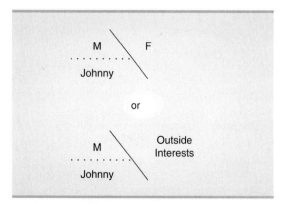

Figure 7.9 Johnny's enmeshment with his mother and disengagement from outside interests

By adjusting boundaries and realigning subsystems, the therapist changes the behavior and experience of each of the family members and thus opens alternative patterns of interaction that can modify family structure. Far from seeing families as inherently flawed, structural therapists see their work as activating latent adaptive patterns that are already in client families' repertoires (Simon, 1995). It's not a matter of creating new structures but of activating dormant ones.

Although every family is unique, families have common structural goals. Most important is the creation of an effective hierarchy. Parents are expected to be in charge, not to relate as equals to their children. With enmeshed families, the goal is to differentiate individuals and subsystems by strengthening the boundaries around them. With disengaged families, the goal is to increase interaction by making boundaries more permeable.

A therapist produces change by joining the family, probing for areas of flexibility, and then activating dormant structural alternatives. **Joining** gets the therapist into the family; *accommodating* to their style gives him or her leverage; and *restructuring* maneuvers transform the family structure.

To join a family, a therapist conveys acceptance of family members and respect for their ways of doing things. If parents come for help with a child's problems, the therapist doesn't begin by asking for the child's opinion. This would convey lack of respect for the parents. Only after successfully joining with a family is it fruitful to attempt restructuring—the often dramatic confrontations that challenge families and encourage them to change.

The first task is to understand the family's view of their problems. This is accomplished by tracking their perspectives in the content they use to explain them and in the process with which they demonstrate them. The family therapist then **reframes** these formulations into one based on an understanding of family structure.

What makes structural family therapy unique is that it uses enactments within therapy sessions to bring about the reframing. This is the sine qua non of structural family therapy: observing and modifying family transactions in the immediate context of the session. Structural therapists work with what they see, not with what family members describe.

THERAPY

Assessment

Because problems are a function of the entire family, it's important to include the whole group for assessment. For example, if a father complains of a child's misbehavior, seeing the child alone won't help the father to state rules clearly or enforce them effectively. Nor will seeing the father and child together stop the stepmother from undercutting the father's authority. Only by seeing the whole family interacting is it possible to get a complete picture of their structure.

Sometimes even the whole family isn't enough, because the family may not always be the complete or even most relevant context. A mother's depression might be due to problems at work. A son's difficulties at school might be due more to the situation at school than to the one in the family. In such instances, structural therapists work with the most relevant context.

Finally, some problems may be treated as problems of the individual. As Minuchin (1974) has written, "Pathology may be inside the patient, in his social context, or in the feedback between them"

(p. 9). Elsewhere Minuchin (Minuchin, Rosman, & Baker, 1978) referred to the danger of "denying the individual while enthroning the system" (p. 91). While interviewing a family to see how the parents deal with their children, a careful observer might notice that one child has a neurological problem or a learning disability. Such problems need to be identified and appropriate referrals made. Usually, when a child has trouble in school, there's a problem in the family or school context—usually, but not always.

Dr. Minuchin and his colleagues recently published a book in which the process of assessment is organized in four steps (Minuchin, Nichols, & Lee, 2007). The first step is to ask questions about the presenting complaint until family members begin to see that the problem goes beyond the symptom bearer to include the entire family. The second step is to help family members see how their interactions may inadvertently be perpetuating the presenting problem. The third step is a brief exploration of the past, focusing on how the adults in the family came to develop the perspectives that now influence their problematic interactions. The fourth step is to explore options that family members can take to interact in more productive ways that will create a shift in the family structure and help resolve the presenting complaint.

Therapeutic Techniques

In *Families and Family Therapy,* Minuchin (1974) listed three overlapping stages in structural family therapy. The therapist (1) joins the family in a position of leadership, (2) maps the family's underlying structure, and (3) intervenes to transform this structure. This program is simple, in the sense that it follows a clear plan, but complicated because of the endless variety of family patterns.

If a therapist's moves are to be effective, they cannot be preplanned or rehearsed. Good therapists are more than technicians. The strategy of therapy, on the other hand, must be organized. In general, structural family therapy follows these steps:

1. Joining and accommodating
2. Enactment
3. Structural mapping
4. Highlighting and modifying interactions
5. Boundary making
6. Unbalancing
7. Challenging unproductive assumptions

Joining and Accommodating. Individual patients generally enter therapy already predisposed to accept the therapist's authority. By seeking treatment, an individual tacitly acknowledges suffering, need for help, and willingness to trust the therapist. Not so with families.

A family therapist is an unwelcome outsider. After all, why did he or she insist on seeing the whole family? Family members expect to be told that they're doing something wrong, and they're prepared to defend themselves.

The therapist must first disarm defenses and ease anxiety. This is done by building an alliance of understanding with each member of the family.

Everyone has a story to tell, and in unhappy families, almost everyone feels misunderstood. The first step in breaking the cycle of misunderstanding is to offer the empathy family members may be temporarily unable to provide each other. Hearing and acknowledging each person's account of the family's sorrows provides information— and begins to release family members from the resentment of unheard feelings. *Joining,* as this empathic connection is called, opens the way for family members to begin listening to each other and establishes a bond with the therapist that enables them to accept the challenges to come.

These initial conversations convey respect, not only for the individuals in the family but also for the family's structural organization. The therapist shows respect for parents by honoring their authority. They, not their children, are asked first to describe the problems. If a family elects one person to speak for the others, the therapist notes this but does not initially challenge it.

Children also have special concerns and capacities. They should be greeted gently and asked simple, concrete questions: "Hi, I'm so-and-so; what's your name? Oh, Laura, that's a nice name. Where do you go to school, Laura?" Avoid the usual grown-up questions ("And what do *you* want to be when you grow up?"). Try something a little fresher ("What do you hate most about school?"). Those who wish to remain silent should be allowed to do so. They will anyway. "And what's your view of the problem?" (Grim silence.) "I see, you don't feel like saying anything right now? That's fine; perhaps you'll have something to say later."

It's particularly important to join with powerful family members as well as angry ones. Special pains must be taken to accept the point of view of the father who thinks therapy is hooey or of the embittered teenager who feels like an accused criminal. It's also important to reconnect with such people at frequent intervals, particularly when things begin to heat up.

Enactment.   Family structure is manifest in the way family members interact. It can't always be inferred from their descriptions. Therefore, asking questions such as "Who's in charge?" or "Do you two agree?" tends to be inconclusive. Families generally describe themselves more as they think they should be than as they are.

Getting family members to talk with each other runs counter to their expectations. They expect to present their case to an expert and then be told what to do. If asked to discuss something in the session, they'll say "We've already talked about this" or "It won't do any good, he (or she) doesn't listen" or "But *you're* supposed to be the expert."

If the therapist begins by giving each person a chance to speak, usually one will say something about another that can be a springboard for an **enactment.** When, for example, one parent says that the other is too strict, the therapist can initiate an enactment by saying "She says you're too strict. Can you answer her?" Picking a specific issue for response is more effective than vague requests, such as "Why don't you talk this over?"

Enactments require three operations. First, the therapist notices a problematic sequence. Perhaps, for example, when the mother talks to her daughter they relate like peers, and the little brother gets left out. Second, the therapist initiates an enactment. For example, the therapist might say to the mother, "Talk this over with your kids." Third, and most important, the therapist must guide the family to modify the enactment. If the mother talks to her children in such a way that she doesn't take responsibility for major decisions, the therapist encourages her to do so as the family continues the enactment.

Once an enactment breaks down, the therapist intervenes in one of two ways: commenting on what went wrong or simply pushing them to keep going. For example, if a father responds to the suggestion to talk with his ten-year-old daughter about how she's feeling by berating her, the therapist could say to the father, "Congratulations." *Father:* "What do you mean?" *Therapist:* "Congratulations; you win, she loses." Or the therapist could simply nudge the transaction by saying to the father, "Good, keep talking, but help her express her feelings more. She's still a little girl; she needs your help."

Once an enactment is begun, the therapist can discover many things about a family's structure. How long can two people talk without being interrupted—that is, how clear is the boundary around their relationship? Does one attack, the other defend? Who is central, and who is peripheral? Do parents bring children into their discussions—that is, are they enmeshed?

Families demonstrate enmeshment by frequently interrupting, speaking for each other, doing things for children that they can do for themselves, or constantly arguing. In disengaged families one may see a husband sitting impassively while his wife cries, a total absence of conflict, a surprising ignorance of important information about the children, or a lack of concern for each other's interests.

If as soon as the first session starts, the children begin running around the room while their parents protest ineffectually, the therapist doesn't need to hear what goes on at home to see the executive incompetence. If a mother and daughter rant and rave at each other while the father sits silently in the corner, it isn't necessary to ask how involved he is at home. In fact, asking may yield a less accurate picture than the one revealed spontaneously.

Structural Mapping.   Preliminary assessments are based on interactions in the first session. In later sessions these formulations are refined and revised.

Although there is some danger of bending families to fit categories when they're applied early, the greater danger is waiting too long. Families quickly *induct* therapists into their culture. A family that initially appears to be chaotic and enmeshed soon comes to be just the familiar Jones family. For this reason, it's critical to develop provisional hypotheses relatively early in the process.

Suppose, for example, that you're about to see a mother, her sixteen-year-old daughter, and the stepfather. The mother called to complain about her daughter's misbehavior. What do you imagine the structure might be? How would you test your hypothesis? A good guess might be that mother and daughter are enmeshed, excluding the stepfather. This can be tested in the session by seeing if mother and daughter talk mostly about each other—whether positively or negatively. The stepfather's disengagement would be confirmed if he and his wife were unable to converse without the daughter's intrusion.

Structural assessments take into account both the problem the family presents and the structural dynamics they display. And they include all family members. In this instance, knowing that the mother and daughter are enmeshed isn't enough; you also have to know what role the stepfather plays. If he's close with his wife but distant from the daughter, finding mutually enjoyable activities for stepfather and stepdaughter will help increase the girl's independence from her mother. On the other hand, if the mother's proximity to her daughter appears to be a function of her distance from her husband, then the marital pair might be the more productive focus.

Highlighting and Modifying Interactions. Once families begin to interact, problematic transactions emerge. Recognizing their structural implications requires focusing on process, not content.

Perhaps a wife complains, "We have a communication problem. My husband won't talk to me; he never expresses his feelings." The therapist then initiates an enactment to see what actually does happen. "Your wife says it's a communication problem; can you respond to that? Talk with her." If, when they talk, the wife becomes domineering and critical while the husband grows increasingly silent, then the therapist sees what's wrong: The problem isn't that he doesn't talk (which is a linear explanation). Nor is the problem simply that she nags (also a linear explanation). The problem is that the more she nags, the more he withdraws, and the more he withdraws, the more she nags.

The trick is to modify this pattern. This may require forceful intervening, or what structural therapists call **intensity.**

Structural therapists achieve intensity by selective regulation of affect, repetition, and duration. Tone, volume, pacing, and choice of words can be used to raise affective intensity. It helps if you know what you want to say. Here's an example of a limp statement: "People are always concerned with themselves, kind of seeing themselves as the center of attention and just looking for whatever they can get. Wouldn't it be nice, for a change, if everybody started thinking about what they could do for others?" Compare that with "Ask not what your country can do for you—ask what you can do for your country." John Kennedy's words had impact because they were brief and to the point. Therapists don't need to make speeches, but they do occasionally have to speak forcefully to get the point across.

Affective intensity isn't simply a matter of clever phrasing. You have to know how and when to be provocative.

Case Study

Mike Nichols recently worked with a family in which a twenty-nine-year-old woman with anorexia nervosa was the identified patient. Although the family maintained a façade of togetherness, it was rigidly structured; the mother and her anorexic daughter were enmeshed while the father was excluded.

In this family, the father was the only one to express anger openly, and this was part of the official rationale for why he was excluded. His daughter was afraid of his anger, which she freely admitted. What was less clear, however, was that the mother had covertly taught the daughter to avoid her father because she herself couldn't deal with him. Consequently, the daughter grew up afraid of her father, and of men in general.

At one point the father, describing how isolated he felt from his daughter, said he thought it was because she feared his anger. The daughter agreed, "It's his fault, all right." The therapist asked the mother what she thought, and she replied, "It isn't *his* fault."

The therapist said, "You're right."

The mother went on, denying her real feelings to avoid conflict, "It's no one's fault."

The therapist answered in a way that got her attention, "That's not true."

Startled, she asked what he meant.

"It's *your* fault," he said.

This level of intensity was necessary to interrupt a rigid pattern of conflict–avoidance that sustained a destructive **coalition** between mother and daughter. The content—who really is afraid of anger—was less important than the structural goal: freeing the daughter from her overinvolvement with her mother.

Intensity can also be achieved by extending the duration of a sequence beyond the point where homeostasis sets back in. A common example is the management of tantrums. Temper tantrums are maintained by parents who give in. They try not to give in; they just don't try long enough.

Case Study

A four-year-old girl began to scream bloody murder when her sister left the room. She wanted to go with her sister. Her screaming was almost unbearable, and the parents were ready to back down. However, the therapist urged that they not allow themselves to be defeated and suggested that they hold her until she calmed down. She screamed for twenty minutes! Everyone in the room was frazzled. But the little girl finally realized that she was not going to get her way, and so she calmed down. Subsequently, the parents were able to use the same intensity of duration to break her of this destructive habit.

Sometimes intensity requires repetition of a theme in a variety of contexts. Infantilizing parents may have to be told not to hang up their child's coat, not to speak for her, not to take her to the bathroom, and not to do many other things that she's capable of doing for herself.

What we're calling *intensity* may strike some as overly aggressive. Although there's no denying that Minuchin and his followers tend to be interventionists, the point of intensity is not to bully people but to push them past the point where they give up on getting through to each other. An alternative strategy is the use of **empathy** to help family members get beneath the surface of their defensive wrangling.

If, for example, the parents of a disobedient child are locked in a cycle of unproductive quarreling in which the mother attacks the father for not being involved and he responds with excuses, a therapist could use intensity to push them to come up with a plan for dealing with their child's behavior. Or the therapist could interrupt their squabbling and, using empathy, talk to them one at a time about what they're feeling. The wife who shows only anger might be covering up the hurt and longing she feels. The husband who neither gets involved nor fights back when he feels attacked might be too annoyed at his wife's anger to see that she needs him. Once these more genuine kinds of emotions are articulated, they can serve as a basis for clients reconnecting with each other in a less defensive manner.

Shaping competence is another method of modifying interactions, and it's a hallmark of structural family therapy. Intensity is used to block the stream of interactions. Shaping competence is like altering the direction of flow. By reinforcing positives, structural therapists help family members use functional alternatives that are already in their repertoire.

Even when people make a lot of mistakes, it's usually possible to pick out something they're doing successfully. A sense of timing helps.

Case Study

For example, in a large chaotic family the parents were extremely ineffective at controlling their children. At one point the therapist turned to the mother and said, "It's too noisy in here. Would you quiet the kids?" Knowing how much difficulty the woman had with discipline, the therapist was poised to comment on any step in the direction of effective management. The mother had to yell "Quiet!" a couple of times before the children momentarily stopped what they were doing.

Quickly—before the children resumed their misbehavior—the therapist complimented her for "loving her kids enough to be firm with them." Thus, the message was "You're a competent person; you know how to be firm." If the therapist had waited until the chaos resumed before telling the mother she should be firmer, the message would be "You're incompetent."

Boundary Making. In enmeshed families, interventions are designed to strengthen boundaries. Family members are urged to speak for themselves, interruptions are blocked, and dyads are helped to finish conversations without intrusion. A therapist who wishes to support the sibling system and protect it from unnecessary parental intrusion might say, "Susie and Sean, talk this over, and everyone else will listen carefully." If children interrupt their parents, a therapist might challenge the parents to strengthen the hierarchical boundary by saying, "Why don't

you get them to butt out so that you two grownups can settle this?"

Although structural therapy is begun with the whole family, subsequent sessions may be held with individuals or subgroups to strengthen their boundaries. An overprotected teenager is supported as an independent person by participating in some individual sessions. Parents so enmeshed with their children that they never have private conversations may begin to learn how if they meet separately with the therapist.

Case Study

When a forty-year-old woman called the clinic for help with depression, she was asked to come in with the rest of her family. It soon became apparent that this woman was overburdened by her four children and received little support from her husband, either as a mate or as a father.

The therapist's strategy was to strengthen the boundary between the mother and children and help the parents move closer together. This was done in stages. First the therapist joined the oldest child, a sixteen-year-old girl, and supported her competence as a potential helper for her mother. Once this was done, the girl was able to assume a good deal of responsibility for her younger siblings, both in sessions and at home.

Freed from their preoccupation with the children, the parents now had the opportunity to talk more with each other. They had little to say, however. This wasn't the result of hidden conflict but instead reflected a marriage of two relatively nonverbal people. After several sessions of trying to get the pair talking, the therapist realized that although talking may be fun for some people, it might not be for others. So to support the bond between the couple, the therapist asked them to plan a special trip together. They chose a boat ride on a nearby lake.

When they returned for the next session, they were beaming. They had a wonderful time. Subsequently, they decided to spend a little time out together each week.

Unbalancing. In boundary making, the therapist aims to realign relationships between subsystems. In *unbalancing,* the goal is to change relationships within a subsystem. What often keeps families stuck in stalemate is that members in conflict are balanced in opposition and, as a result, remain frozen in inaction. In unbalancing, the therapist joins and supports one individual or subsystem.

Taking sides—let's call it what it is—seems like a violation of therapy's sacred canon of neutrality. However, the therapist takes sides to unbalance and realign the system, not because he or she is the arbiter of right and wrong. Ultimately, balance and fairness are achieved because the therapist sides in turn with various members of the family.

Case Study

For example, when the MacLean family sought help for an unmanageable child, a terror who'd been expelled from two schools, Dr. Minuchin uncovered a covert split between the parents, held in balance by not being talked about. The ten-year-old's misbehavior was dramatically visible; his father had to drag him kicking and screaming into the consulting room. Meanwhile, his little brother sat quietly, smiling engagingly—the good boy.

To broaden the focus from an impossible child to issues of parental control and cooperation, Minuchin asked about seven-year-old Kevin, who misbehaved invisibly. He peed on the floor in the bathroom. According to his father, Kevin's peeing on the floor was due to "inattentiveness." The mother laughed when Minuchin said "Nobody could have such poor aim."

Minuchin talked with the boy about how wolves mark their territory and suggested that he expand his territory by peeing in all four corners of the family room.

Minuchin: Do you have a dog?
Kevin: No.
Minuchin: Oh, so you're the family dog?

In the process of discussing the boy who peed—and his parents' response—Minuchin dramatized how the parents polarized and undercut each other.

Minuchin: Why would he do such a thing?
Father: I don't know if he did it on purpose.
Minuchin: Maybe he was in a trance?
Father: No, I think it was carelessness.
Minuchin: His aim must be terrible.

The father described the boy's behavior as accidental; the mother considered it defiant. One reason parents fall under the control of their young children is that they avoid confronting their differences. Differences are normal, but they become detrimental when one parent undercuts the other's handling of the children. (It's cowardly revenge for unaddressed grievances.)

Minuchin's gentle but insistent pressure on the couple to talk about how they respond, without switching to how the children behave, led to their bringing up long-held but seldom-voiced resentments.

Mother: Bob makes excuses for the children's behavior because he doesn't want to get in there and help me find a solution for the problem.
Father: Yes, but when I did try to help, you'd always criticize me. So after a while I gave up.

Like a photographic print in a developing tray, the spouses' conflict had become visible. Minuchin protected the parents from embarrassment (and the children from being burdened) by asking the children to leave the room. Without the preoccupation of parenting, the spouses could face each other, man and woman—and talk about their hurts and grievances. It turned out to be a sad story of lonely disengagement.

Minuchin: Do you two have areas of agreement?

He said yes; she said no. He was a minimizer; she was a critic.

Minuchin: When did you divorce Bob and marry the children?

She turned quiet; he looked off into space. She said softly, "Probably ten years ago."

What followed was a painful but familiar story of how a marriage can drown in parenting. The conflict had never been resolved because it had never surfaced. So the rift had never healed.

With Minuchin's help, the couple took turns talking about their pain—and learning to listen. By unbalancing, Minuchin brought pressure to bear to help this couple break through their differences, open up to each other, fight for what they want, and, finally, begin to come together—as husband and wife and as parents.

Unbalancing is part of a struggle for change that sometimes takes on the appearance of combat. When a therapist says to a father that he's not doing enough or to a mother that she's excluding her husband, it may seem that the combat is between the therapist and the family—that he or she is attacking them. But the real combat is between them and fear—fear of change.

Challenging Unproductive Assumptions. Although structural family therapy is not primarily a cognitive approach, its practitioners sometimes challenge the way clients see things. Changing the way family members relate to each other offers alternative views of their situation. The converse is also true: Changing the way family members view their situation enables them to change the way they relate to each other.

When six-year-old Cassie's parents complain about her behavior, they say she's "hyper," "sensitive," a "nervous child." Such constructions have tremendous power. Is a child's behavior "misbehavior," or is it a symptom of "nervousness?" Is it "naughty," or is it a "cry for help"? Is the child mad or bad, and who is in charge? What's in a name? Plenty.

Sometimes a therapist acts as a teacher, offering information and advice, often about structural matters.

Doing so is likely to be a restructuring maneuver and must be done in a way that minimizes resistance. A therapist does this by delivering a "stroke and kick." If the therapist were dealing with a family in which the mother speaks for her children, he or she might say to her, "You are very helpful" (stroke). But to the child, the therapist might say, "Mommy takes away your voice. Can you speak for yourself?" (kick). Thus mother is defined as helpful but intrusive (a stroke and a kick).

CURRENT STATUS OF THE MODEL

In *Families and Family Therapy,* Minuchin (1974) taught family therapists to see what they were looking at. Through the lens of structural family theory, previously puzzling interactions suddenly swam into focus. Where others saw only chaos and cruelty, Minuchin saw structure: families organized into subsystems with boundaries. This enormously successful book not only taught us to see enmeshment and disengagement but also let us hope that changing them was just a matter of joining, enactment, and unbalancing. Minuchin made changing families look simple.

Anyone who watched Minuchin at work ten or twenty years after the publication of *Families and Family Therapy* would see a creative therapist still evolving. One would still see the patented confrontations ("Who's the sheriff in this family?") but fewer enactments, less stage-directed dialogue. One would also hear bits and pieces borrowed from Carl Whitaker ("When did you divorce your wife and marry your job?") and others. Minuchin combined many things in his work.

To those familiar with his earlier work, all of this raises the question: Is Minuchin still a structural family therapist? The question is of course absurd. We raise it to make a point: Structural family therapy isn't a set of techniques; it's a way of looking at families.

Minuchin recently wrote a book, *Assessing Couples and Families,* that describes his latest thinking about therapeutic techniques (Minuchin, Nichols, & Lee, 2007). In this book, the authors describe a four-stage process of creating a framework for systemic family therapy. The first step ("Is the Customer Always Right?") is to challenge the family certainty that the primary problem is located in the internal machinery of the identified patient in a process of probing but respectful questioning. The second step ("The Supporting Cast") is to explore what family members may be doing to perpetuate the presenting problem. The third step ("The Origin of the Specious") is to explore past experiences that may organize and distort family members' perceptions of the identified patient and thus perpetuate the presenting problem. The fourth step ("New Beginnings") is to explore what family members are willing to do in order to make productive changes. The authors continue to emphasize the need for structural assessment, the use of enactments, and working with experiential intensity ("How to Lose Friends and Influence People"), but as you can see from this description, the structural model has evolved to include a somewhat greater emphasis on cognition and insight.

In *Families of the Slums,* Minuchin and colleagues (1967) described the structural characteristics of low-socioeconomic families and demonstrated the effectiveness of family therapy with this population. Prior to treatment, mothers in client families were found to be either over- or undercontrolling; either way, their children were more disruptive than those in nonclient families. After treatment, mothers used less coercive control yet were clearer and firmer. In this study, seven of eleven families were judged to be improved after six months to a year of family therapy. Although no control group was used, the authors compared their results favorably with the usual 50 percent success rate at Wiltwyck.

Some of the strongest empirical support for structural family therapy comes from a series of studies with psychosomatic children and young adult drug addicts. Studies demonstrating the effectiveness of therapy with psychosomatic children are convincing because of the physiological measures used and dramatic because of the life-threatening nature of the problems.

Minuchin, Rosman, and Baker (1978) reported how family conflict can precipitate ketoacidosis crises in diabetic children. In baseline interviews, parents discussed family problems with their children absent. Normal spouses showed the highest levels of confrontation, whereas psychosomatic spouses exhibited a wide range of conflict-avoidance maneuvers. Next the therapist pressed the parents to increase the level of their conflict while their children observed behind a one-way mirror. As the parents argued, only the psychosomatic children got really upset. Moreover, the distress of these children was accompanied by dramatic increases in free fatty acid levels, a measure related to ketoacidosis. In the third stage of these interviews, the patients joined their parents. Normal and behavior-disorder parents continued as before, but the psychosomatic parents detoured their conflict, either by drawing their children into their discussions or by switching the subject from themselves to the children. When this happened, the free fatty acid levels of the parents fell, whereas the children's levels continued to rise. This study provided strong confirmation of the clinical observation that psychosomatic children are involved in the regulation of stress between their parents.

Minuchin, Rosman, and Baker (1978) summarized the results of treating fifty-three cases of anorexia nervosa with structural family therapy. After a course of treatment that included hospitalization followed by outpatient family therapy, forty-three anorexic children were "greatly improved," two were "improved," three showed "no change," two were "worse," and three had dropped out. Although ethical considerations precluded a control treatment with these seriously ill children, the 90 percent improvement rate is impressive, especially compared with the 30 percent mortality rate for this disorder.

Duke Stanton showed that structural family therapy can be an effective form of treatment for drug addicts and their families. In a well-controlled study, Stanton and Todd (1979) compared family therapy with a family placebo condition and individual therapy. Symptom reduction was significant with structural family therapy. The level of positive change was more than double that achieved in the other conditions, and these positive effects persisted at follow-up of six and twelve months.

More recently, structural family therapy has been successfully applied to establish more adaptive parenting roles in heroin addicts (Grief & Dreschler, 1993) and as a means to reduce the likelihood that African American and Latino youths will initiate drug use (Santiseban et al., 1997). Other studies indicate that structural family therapy is equal in effectiveness to communication training and behavioral management training in reducing negative communication, conflicts, and expressed anger between adolescents diagnosed with ADHD and their parents (Barkley, Guevremont, Anastopoulos, & Fletcher, 1992). Structural family therapy has also been found to be effective for treating adolescent disorders, such as conduct disorders (Chamberlain & Rosicky, 1995; Szapocznik et al., 1989) and anorexia nervosa (Campbell & Patterson, 1995).

Although structural family therapy is so closely identified with Salvador Minuchin that the two were once synonymous, it may be a good idea to differentiate the man from the model. When we think of structural family therapy, we tend to remember the approach as described in *Families and Family Therapy,* published in 1974. That book remains a good introduction to structural theory but emphasizes only the techniques Minuchin favored at the time.

Minuchin himself has evolved considerably in the last thirty-five years, from an often blunt young therapist, always ready to challenge families, to a more seasoned clinician, still challenging but far gentler in his approach. If some of the examples in this chapter strike you as overly aggressive, you may be right. Some of these vignettes were taken from the 1970s when family therapists tended to favor a confrontational style. While the confrontational style may have characterized some practitioners of structural family therapy, it was never an essential feature of this approach.

Minuchin has evolved conceptually as well, from an almost exclusive focus on interpersonal interactions to a consideration of the cognitive perspectives guiding those interactions and the past roots of those perspectives (Minuchin, Nichols, & Lee, 2007). But the structural approach he created also exists independent of his work and is embodied in the definitive literature on this model (e.g., Minuchin, 1974; Minuchin & Fishman, 1981; Minuchin & Nichols, 1993) as well as in the ongoing work of his students and colleagues.

The structural model directs clinicians to look beyond the content of problems, and even beyond the dynamics of interaction, to the underlying family organization that supports and constrains those interactions. Much has changed since 1974, but the structural model still stands, and it continues to be the most widely used way of understanding what goes on in the nuclear family.

Summary

1. Minuchin may be best known for the artistry of his clinical technique, yet his structural theory has become the most widely used conceptual model in the field. The reason structural theory is so popular is that it's simple, inclusive, and practical. The basic concepts—boundaries, subsystems, alignments, and complementarity—are easily applied. They take into account the individual, family, and social context, and they provide a clear organizing framework for understanding and treating families.

2. The most important tenet of this approach is that every family has a structure, and this structure is revealed only when the family is in action. According to this view, therapists who fail to consider the entire family's structure and intervene in only one subsystem are unlikely to effect lasting change. If a mother's overinvolvement with her son is part of a structure that includes distance from her husband, no amount of therapy for the mother and son is likely to bring about basic change in the family.

3. Subsystems are units of the family based on function. If the leadership of a family is taken over by a father and daughter, then they, not the husband and wife, are the executive subsystem. Subsystems are circumscribed and regulated by interpersonal boundaries. In healthy families, boundaries are clear enough to protect independence and permeable enough to allow mutual support. Enmeshed families are characterized by diffuse boundaries, disengaged families by rigid boundaries.

4. Once therapists have gained a family's trust, they promote family interaction while assuming a decentralized role. From this position, they can watch what goes on in the family and make a structural assessment, which includes the problem and the organization that supports it. These assessments are framed in terms of boundaries and subsystems, easily conceptualized as two-dimensional maps used to suggest avenues for change.

5. Once they have successfully joined and assessed a family, structural therapists proceed to activate dormant structures using techniques that alter alignments and shift power within and between subsystems. These restructuring techniques are concrete and sometimes forceful. However, their success depends as much on the joining and assessment as on the power of the techniques themselves.

Questions to Consider

1. What might be lost and what might be gained by exploring past experiences that have shaped how family members currently interact to form a family's structure?
2. How would you diagram the structure of your own family? At what point, if any, did you begin to think of your family's structure as anything other than the natural way families operate?
3. To what extent is the enmeshed-mother/disengaged-father syndrome embedded in social and cultural arrangements that families have little ability to change?
4. If you can, think of clinical situations you've encountered in your training that ignored a family's (or other system's) structure, possibly with unfortunate consequences.

Key Concepts

accommodation   Elements of a system automatically adjust to coordinate their functioning; people may have to work at it.

boundaries   A concept used in structural family therapy to describe emotional barriers that protect and enhance the integrity of individuals, subsystems, and families.

coalition   An alliance between two persons or social units against a third.

cross-generational coalition   An inappropriate alliance between a parent and child who side together against a third member of the family.

disengagement   Minuchin's term for psychological isolation that results from overly rigid boundaries around individuals and subsystems in a family.

empathy   Understanding and acknowledging what someone is really feeling; in structural family therapy, empathy is used to help clients stop bickering and talk about their feelings.

enactment   An interaction stimulated in structural family therapy to observe and then change transactions that make up family structure.

enmeshment   Minuchin's term for loss of autonomy due to a blurring of psychological boundaries.

family structure   The functional organization of a family that determines how family members interact.

hierarchical structure   Family functioning based on clear generational boundaries in which the parents maintain control and authority.

intensity Minuchin's term for changing maladaptive transactions by using strong affect, repeated intervention, or prolonged pressure.

joining A structural family therapy term for accepting and accommodating to families to win their confidence and circumvent resistance.

reframing Relabeling a family's description of behavior to make it more amenable to therapeutic change; for example, describing someone as "discouraged" rather than "depressed."

shaping competence Reinforcing positives rather than confronting deficiences.

structure Recurrent patterns of interaction that define and stabilize the shape of relationships.

subsystem Smaller units in families determined by generation, sex, or function.

Recommended Readings

Minuchin, S. 1974. *Families and family therapy*. Cambridge, MA: Harvard University Press.

Minuchin, S., and Fishman, H. C. 1981. *Family therapy techniques*. Cambridge, MA: Harvard University Press.

Minuchin, S., and Nichols, M. P. 1993. *Family healing: Tales of hope and renewal from family therapy*. New York: Free Press.

Minuchin, S., and Nichols, M. P. 1998. Structural family therapy. In *Case studies in couple and family therapy*, F. M. Dattilio, ed. New York: Guilford Press.

Minuchin, S., Nichols, M. P., and Lee, W.-Y. 2007. *Assessing families and couples: From symptom to system*. Boston: Allyn & Bacon.

Nichols, M. P. 2009. *Inside family therapy*, 2nd ed.. Boston: Allyn & Bacon.

Nichols, M. P., and Minuchin, S. 1999. Short-term structural family therapy with couples. In *Short-term couple therapy*, J. M. Donovan, ed. New York: Guilford Press.

References

Barkely, R., Guevremont, D., Anastopoulos, A., and Fletcher, K. 1992. A comparison of three family therapy programs for treating family conflicts in adolescents with attention-deficit hyperactivity disorder. *Journal of Consulting and Clinical Psychology. 60:* 450–463.

Campbell, T., and Patterson, J. 1995. The effectiveness of family interventions in the treatment of physical illness. *Journal of Marital and Family Therapy. 21:* 545–584.

Chamberlain, P., and Rosicky, J. 1995. The effectiveness of family therapy in the treatment of adolescents with conduct disorders and delinquency. *Journal of Marital and Family Therapy. 21:* 441–459.

Elizur, J., and Minuchin, S. 1989. *Institutionalizing madness: Families, therapy, and society*. New York: Basic Books.

Grief, G., and Dreschler, L. 1993. Common issues for parents in a methadone maintenance group. *Journal of Substance Abuse Treatment. 10:* 335–339.

Minuchin, S. 1974. *Families and family therapy*. Cambridge, MA: Harvard University Press.

Minuchin, S., and Fishman, H. C. 1981. *Family therapy techniques*. Cambridge, MA: Harvard University Press.

Minuchin, S., Montalvo, B., Guerney, B., Rosman, B., and Schumer, F. 1967. *Families of the slums*. New York: Basic Books.

Minuchin, S., and Nichols, M. P. 1993. *Family healing: Tales of hope and renewal from family therapy*. New York: Free Press.

Minuchin, S., Nichols, M. P., and Lee, W.-Y. 2007. *Assessing couples and families: From symptom to system*. Boston: Allyn & Bacon.

Minuchin, S., Rosman, B., and Baker, L. 1978. *Psychosomatic families: Anorexia nervosa in context*. Cambridge, MA: Harvard University Press.

Santiseban, D., Coatsworth, J., Perez-Vidal, A., Mitrani, V., Jean-Gilles, M., and Szapocznik, J. 1997. Brief structural/strategic family therapy with African American and Hispanic high-risk youth. *Journal of Community Psychology. 25:* 453–471.

Simon, G. M. 1995. A revisionist rendering of structural family therapy. *Journal of Marital and Family Therapy. 21:* 17–26.

Stanton, M. D., and Todd, T. C. 1979. Structural family therapy with drug addicts. In *The family therapy of drug and alcohol abuse,* E. Kaufman and P. Kaufmann, eds. New York: Gardner Press.

Szapocznik, J., Rio, A., Murray, E., Cohen, R., Scopetta, M., Rivas-Vasquez, A., Hervis, O., Posada, V., and Kurtines, W. 1989. Structural family therapy versus psychodynamic child therapy for problematic Hispanic boys. *Journal of Consulting and Clinical Psychology. 57:* 571–578.

8

Experiential Family Therapy

An experiential branch of family therapy emerged from the humanistic wing of psychology that, like the expressive therapies that inspired it, emphasized immediate here-and-now experience. Experiential therapy was popular when family therapy was young, when therapists talked about systems but borrowed their techniques from individual and group therapies. From Gestalt therapy and encounter groups came techniques like role-playing and emotional confrontation, while other expressive methods such as sculpting and family drawing bore the influence of the arts and of psychodrama.

In focusing more on emotional experience than on the dynamics of interaction, experiential therapists seemed out of step with the rest of family therapy. Indeed, by emphasizing individuals and their feelings, experiential treatment may never have been as well suited to family therapy as were approaches that dealt with systems and action. With the passing of the inspirational leaders of this tradition, Virginia Satir and Carl Whitaker, the methods they popularized began to seem dated, more a product of the 1960s than of today's world.

Recently, however, experiential approaches have been enjoying a revival. As we will see, two of the newer models, Greenberg and Johnson's (1985) *emotionally focused couples therapy* and Schwartz's

(1995) *internal family systems model,* have combined the emotional impact of an experiential focus on the individual with a more sophisticated understanding of family systems.

As the first great cathartic therapist, Sigmund Freud, discovered, getting in touch with painful feelings is not by itself a complete form of psychotherapy. On the other hand, ignoring or rationalizing unhappy emotions may cheat clients out of the opportunity to get to the heart of their problems. Thus, the experiential emphasis on emotional expression may be a useful counterweight to the reductionistic emphasis on behavior and cognition common to today's problem-solving approaches.

Evolution of the Model

Two giants stand out in the development of experiential family therapy: Carl Whitaker and Virginia Satir. Whitaker was the leading exponent of a free-wheeling, intuitive approach aimed at puncturing pretense and liberating family members to be themselves. He was among the first to do psychotherapy with families, and although he was once considered a maverick, he eventually became one of the most admired therapists in the field. Iconoclastic, even outrageous at times, Whitaker nevertheless retained the respect of the family therapy establishment. He may have been their Puck, but he was one of them.

Whitaker grew up on a dairy farm in upstate New York. Rural isolation bred a certain shyness but also conditioned him to be less bound by social convention. After medical school and a residency in obstetrics and gynecology, Whitaker went into psychiatry, where he became fascinated by the psychotic mind. Unfortunately—or fortunately—back in the 1940s, Whitaker couldn't rely on neuroleptic drugs to blunt the hallucinatory imaginings of his patients. Instead, he listened and learned to understand thoughts—crazy but human—that most of us usually keep buried.

After working at the University of Louisville College of Medicine and the Oakridge Hospital, Whitaker accepted the chair of Emory University's Department of Psychiatry, where he remained from 1946 to 1955. Then, in the face of mounting pressure to make the department more psychoanalytic, Whitaker and his entire faculty, including Thomas Malone, John Warkentin, and Richard Felder, resigned to establish the Atlanta Psychiatric Clinic. Experiential psychotherapy was born of this union, and the group produced a number of provocative and challenging papers (Whitaker & Malone, 1953). In 1965 Whitaker moved to the University of Wisconsin Medical School. After his retirement in the 1980s, he traveled widely to share his wisdom and experience at conventions and workshops. His death in 1995 was a great loss. Among Whitaker's best-known associates are Augustus Napier, now in private practice in Atlanta, and David Keith, at the State University of New York in Syracuse.

The other towering figure among experiential family therapists was Virginia Satir. As an early member of the Mental Research Institute (MRI), Satir emphasized communication (see Chapters 2 and 6) as well as emotional experiencing.

Carl Whitaker

Carl Whitaker's unconventional thinking formed the basis of a bold and inventive approach to family therapy. He believed that active personal involvement was the best way to bring about changes in families and promote flexibility among family members. He relied on his own personality and wisdom rather than on any fixed techniques to stir things up in families and to help family members open up and be more fully themselves.

Satir began seeing families in private practice in Chicago in 1951. In 1955 she was invited to set up a training program for residents at the Illinois State Psychiatric Institute (where one of her students was Ivan Boszormenyi-Nagy). In 1959 Don Jackson invited her to join him at MRI, where Satir became the first director of training. She remained until 1966, when she left to become the director of the Esalen Institute in Big Sur, California.

Satir was the archetypal nurturing therapist in a field enamored with abstract concepts and strategic maneuvers. Her warmth and genuineness gave her tremendous appeal as she traveled the country giving demonstrations and workshops. Her ability to move audiences made her family therapy's most celebrated humanist. Satir died of pancreatic cancer in 1988.

Among the most recent experiential approaches is the **emotionally focused couples therapy** of Leslie Greenberg and Susan Johnson, which draws on Perls, Satir, and the MRI group (Greenberg & Johnson, 1985, 1986, 1988). Another specialized approach to the inner emotional life of families is Richard Schwartz's (1995) **internal family systems therapy,** in which clients' conflicting inner voices are personified as *parts* and then reintegrated using a variety of psychodramatic techniques.

Virginia Satir

Virginia Satir believed that a healthy family life involved open and reciprocal sharing of affection, feelings, and love. What made her unique among family therapy's pioneers was her focus on individual emotional experience and her incorporation of an encounter group style in her work with families. Thus, Satir approached families less as complex systems than as a collection of individuals often stifled by habit and routine. She described family roles, such as "the rescuer" and "the placator," that function to constrain relationships in families. Satir's warmth and caring were evident in her incorporation of feeling and compassion in the therapeutic relationship.

THE BASIC MODEL

Experiential family therapy is founded on the premise that the root cause of family problems is emotional suppression. Although children must learn that they can't always do whatever they feel like doing, many parents have an unfortunate tendency to confuse the *instrumental* and *expressive* functions of emotion. They try to regulate their children's actions by controlling their feelings. As a result, children learn to blunt their emotional experience to avoid criticism. Although this process is more or less universal, dysfunctional families tend to be less tolerant of unruly emotions than most. As a result, children in such families often grow up estranged from themselves and feeling only the residues of repressed affect: boredom, apathy, and anxiety.

While systemic therapists see the roots of symptomatic behavior in the dance of family interactions, experientialists view those interactions as the result of family members shadow dancing with the projections of each other's defenses. From this perspective, attempts to bring about positive change in families are more likely to be successful if family members first get in touch with their real feelings—their hopes and desires as well as their fears and anxieties. Thus, experiential family therapy works from the inside out, helping individuals uncover their honest emotions and then forging more genuine family ties out of this enhanced authenticity.

Theoretical Concepts

Carl Whitaker summed up the experiential position on theory in a paper titled "The Hindrance of Theory in Clinical Work" (Whitaker, 1976a). Theory may be useful for beginners, Whitaker said, but his advice was to give up calculation as soon as possible in favor of just being yourself.

Being antitheoretical is, of course, itself a theoretical position. To say that therapy shouldn't be constrained by theories is to say that it should be spontaneous. Despite Whitaker's disdain for theory, however, experiential family therapy is very much a product of the existential–humanistic tradition.

Much of the theorizing of existential psychologists (e.g., Binswanger, 1967; Boss, 1963) was in reaction to the perceived mechanism of psychoanalysis and behaviorism. In place of *determinism*, existentialists emphasized freedom and the immediacy of experience. Where psychoanalysts posited a structuralized model of the mind, existentialists treated individuals as whole persons and offered a positive model of humanity in place of what they saw as a pessimistic psychoanalytic model. Instead of settling for a reduction of their neuroses, existentialists believed that people should aim for fulfillment.

Despite their disinclination to theorize, certain basic premises define the experiential position. Whitaker emphasized that self-fulfillment depends on family cohesiveness, and Satir stressed the importance of communication among family members, but the basic commitment was to individual self-expression. While there was some talk about family systems (e.g., Satir,

1972), the experiential model of the family was more like a democratic group than a structured organization.

Great emphasis is placed on flexibility and freedom. Treatment is designed to help individual family members find fulfilling roles for themselves, with less concern for the family as a whole. This is not to say that the needs of the family are denigrated but that they are thought to follow on the heels of individual enhancement.[1]

After reading the previous paragraph, David Keith (in a personal letter) helped put into perspective the experiential position on the claims of the individual versus the claims of the family:

> There is a dialectical tension between the individual and the family—between dependence and independence. To overemphasize either individuality or family connectedness is to distort the human condition.

Theories of families as systems are translated into techniques that promote interaction. The emphasis on altering interactions implies an acceptance of whatever level of individual experience is already present. This is where experiential theory differs from systems approaches. Here the emphasis is on expanding experience. The assumption is that opening up individuals to their experience is a prerequisite to breaking new ground for the family group.

The underlying premise of experiential therapy is that the way to promote individual growth and family cohesion is to liberate affects and impulses. Efforts to reduce defensiveness and unlock deeper levels of experiencing rest on an assumption of the basic goodness of human nature.

The exception to the experiential deemphasis on theory is Greenberg and Johnson's emotionally focused couples therapy, which draws on attachment theory (Bowlby, 1969). According to Greenberg and Johnson, emotion organizes attachment responses and serves a communicative function in relationships. When people express their vulnerability directly, they're likely to elicit a compassionate response from their partners. But when an insecurely attached person fears vulnerability and shows anger instead, the

response is more likely to be withdrawal. Thus, the person most in need of attachment may, by being afraid to expose that need, push away the loved ones he or she longs to get close to. The antidote for this dilemma is what experiential therapy is all about: helping people relax their defenses so that deeper and more genuine emotions can emerge.

Normal Family Development

Experiential therapists share the humanistic faith in the natural wisdom of honest emotion. According to this point of view, if people are allowed to follow their own instincts, they tend to flourish. Problems arise because this innate tendency toward **self-actualization** (Rogers, 1951) runs afoul of social pressures. Society enforces repression to tame people's instincts and make them fit for group living. Unhappily, self-control is achieved at the cost of *surplus repression* (Marcuse, 1955). Families add their own controls to achieve peace and quiet, perpetuating **family myths** (Gehrke & Kirschenbaum, 1967) and using **mystification** (Laing, 1967) to alienate children from their experience.

In the ideal situation, parental control isn't excessive, and children grow up in an atmosphere of support for their feelings and creative impulses. Parents pay attention to their children, accept their feelings, and validate their experiences. Children are encouraged to experience life fully and to express the full range of human emotions.

Experiential therapists describe the family as a place of sharing experience (Satir, 1972). Functional families are secure enough to encourage a wide range of experiencing; dysfunctional families are frightened and bloodless. Neither problem-solving skills nor particular family structures are considered as important as nurturing spontaneous experiencing. In short, the healthy family offers its members the freedom to be themselves.

Development of Behavior Disorders

From an experiential perspective, denial of impulses and suppression of feeling are the root of family problems. Dysfunctional families are locked into

---

[1]At one time, however, the family was portrayed as the enemy of freedom and authenticity (Laing & Esterson, 1970).

self-protection and avoidance (Kaplan & Kaplan, 1978). In Harry Stack Sullivan's (1953) terms, they seek *security* rather than *satisfaction.* Their presenting complaints are many, but the basic problem is that they smother emotion and desire.

According to Whitaker (Whitaker & Keith, 1981), there's no such thing as a marriage—only two scapegoats sent out by their families to perpetuate themselves. Together they must work out the inherent conflict in this situation. Couples who remain together eventually reach some kind of accommodation. Whether based on compromise or resignation, reconciling themselves to each other lessens the friction. Dysfunctional families, anxious to avoid conflict, adhere rigidly to the rituals that they establish. Having experienced the anxiety of uncertainty, they now cling to their routines.

In her portrayal of troubled families, Satir (1972) emphasized the atmosphere of emotional deadness. Such families are cold; they stay together out of duty and habit. The adults don't enjoy their children, and the children learn not to respect themselves or care about their parents. In consequence of the lack of warmth in the family, these people avoid each other and preoccupy themselves with work and other distractions.

It's important to notice that the dysfunction Satir described isn't the kind found in diagnostic manuals. Like others in the experiential camp, Satir was as concerned with normal people who lead lives of quiet desperation as with the officially recognized patients families usually focus on. As she (Satir, 1972) put it:

> It is a sad experience for me to be with these families. I see the hopelessness, the helplessness, the loneliness. I see the bravery of people trying to cover up— a bravery that can still bellow or nag or whine at each other. Others no longer care. These people go on year after year, enduring misery themselves or in their desperation, inflicting it on others (p. 12).

Satir stressed the role of destructive communication in smothering feeling and said that there were four dishonest ways people communicate: blaming, placating, being irrelevant, and being super reasonable. What's behind these patterns of inauthentic communication? *Low self-esteem.* If people feel bad about themselves, it's hard to tell the truth about their

feelings, and it's threatening to let others tell them honestly what they feel.

A healthy relationship, according to Susan Johnson, is a secure attachment bond—that is, one characterized by emotional accessibility and responsiveness (Johnson & Denton, 2002). Secure attachment refers both to having grown up with a sense of being lovable and worthwhile and to the confidence that comes from having a secure and rewarding intimate relationship. But when attachment security is threatened, people typically respond with anger—a protest that unfortunately may drive the other person away rather than evoke the desired responsiveness. Recently, Johnson has introduced the notion of *attachment injuries:* traumatic occurrences that damage the bond between partners and, if not resolved, maintain negative cycles and attachment insecurities.

How Therapy Works

In common with others in the humanistic tradition, experiential therapists believe that the way to emotional health is to uncover deeper levels of experiencing. Virginia Satir (1972) put it this way:

> We attempt to make three changes in the family system. First, each member of the family should be able to report congruently, completely, and honestly on what he sees and hears, feels, and thinks, about himself and others, in the presence of others. Second, each person should be addressed and related to in terms of his uniqueness, so that decisions are made in terms of exploration and negotiation rather than in terms of power. Third, differentness must be openly acknowledged and used for growth (p. 120).

Experientialists emphasize the feeling side of human nature—creativity, spontaneity, and the ability to play—and, in therapy, the value of experience for its own sake.

Gus Napier (Napier & Whitaker, 1978) wrote in *The Family Crucible* a nice description of what experiential therapists think causes change. Breakthroughs occur when family members risk being "more separate, divergent, even angrier" as well as "when they risk being closer and more intimate." To help clients dare to take those risks, experiential therapists are alternately provocative and warmly supportive. This permits family members to drop their protective defenses and open up to each other.

Existential encounter is believed to be the essential force in the psychotherapeutic process (Kempler, 1973; Whitaker, 1976a). These encounters must be reciprocal; instead of hiding behind a professional role, the therapist must be a genuine person who catalyzes change using his or her personal impact on families. As Kempler (1968) said:

> In this approach the therapist becomes a family member during the interviews, participating as fully as he is able, hopefully available for appreciation and criticism as well as he is able to dispense it. He laughs, cries and rages. He feels and shares his embarrassments, confusions and helplessness (p. 97).

For Satir, caring and acceptance were the keys to helping people open up to experience, and open up to each other:

> Some therapists think people come into therapy not wanting to be changed; I don't think that's true. They don't think they *can* change. Going into some new, unfamiliar place is a scary thing. When I first begin to work with someone, I am not interested in changing them. I am interested in finding their rhythms, being able to join with them, and helping them go inside to those scary places. Resistance is mainly the fear of going somewhere you have not been (Quoted in Simon, 1989, pp. 38–39).

$\mathcal{T}$HERAPY

Experiential family therapists share the humanistic belief that people are naturally resourceful and if left to their own devices will be energetic, creative, loving, and productive (Rogers, 1951). The task of therapy is therefore seen as unblocking defenses and releasing people's innate vitality.

Assessment

Because experientialists are less interested in solving problems than in enhancing family functioning, they pay limited attention to the specifics of the presenting problem. Moreover, because they focus on individuals and their experience, they have little interest in assessing the structure of family organization.

The following quotation illustrates the experientialist disdain for evaluation: "Diagnoses are the tombstones of the therapist's frustration, and accusations such as defensive, resistant, and secondary gain are the flowers placed on the grave of his buried dissatisfaction" (Kempler, 1973, p. 11). The point seems to be that the objective distance necessary for formal assessment fosters a judgmental attitude and isolates therapists from emotional contact with families.

For most experientialists, assessment takes place informally as the therapist gets to know a family. In the process of developing a relationship, the therapist learns what kind of people he or she is dealing with. Whitaker began by asking each family member to describe the family and how it works. In this way, he got a composite picture of individual family members and their perceptions of the family group. This kind of inquiry is about as formal as most experiential therapists get in sizing up families. The majority of what serves as assessment in this approach is an attempt to decode the defenses that emerge in the ongoing course of trying to help family members open up to each other.

Therapeutic Techniques

In experiential therapy, according to Walter Kempler (1968), there are no techniques, only people. This epigram neatly summarizes the faith in the curative power of the therapist's personality. It isn't so much what therapists do that matters, it's who they are.

However, this point is at least partly rhetorical. Whoever they are, therapists must also do something. Even if what they do isn't planned, it can nevertheless be described. Moreover, experiential therapists tend to do a lot; they're highly active and some (including Kempler) use a number of evocative techniques.

Some use structured devices such as family sculpting and choreography; others like Virginia Satir and Carl Whitaker rely on the spontaneity of just being themselves.

Virginia Satir had a remarkable ability to communicate. Like many great therapists, she was a dynamic personality. But she didn't rely merely on personal warmth. Rather, she worked to clarify communication, turned people away from complaining toward finding solutions, supported the self-esteem of every member of the family, pointed out positive intentions (long before "positive connotation" became a strategic device), and showed by example how to be affectionate (Satir & Baldwin, 1983). She was a loving but forceful healer.

One of Satir's hallmarks was the use of touch. Hers was the language of tenderness. She often began by making physical contact with children, as evidenced in her case "Of Rocks and Flowers."

Case Study

Bob, a recovering alcoholic, was the father of two boys, Aaron (four) and Robbie (two), whose mother had abused them repeatedly—pushing them down stairs, burning them with cigarettes, and tying them up under the sink. At the time of the interview, the mother was under psychiatric care and didn't see the children. Bob's new wife, Betty, had been abused by her previous husband, also an alcoholic. She was pregnant and afraid that the boys would abuse the baby. The boys had already been expressing the violence they'd been exposed to—slapping and choking other children. Bob and Betty, acting out of frustration and fear, responded roughly to the boys, which only increased their aggressiveness.

Throughout the session, Satir showed the parents how to touch the children tenderly and how to hold them firmly to stop them from misbehaving. When Bob started to tell Aaron something from a distance, Satir insisted on proximity and touch. She sat Aaron down in front of his father and asked Bob to take the little boy's hands and speak directly to him.

The following fragments from the session are taken from Andreas (1991).

Those little hands know a lot of things; they need to be reeducated. OK. Now, there is a lot

of energy in both these youngsters, like there is in both of you. And I am going to talk to your therapist about making some room for you to have some respite (from the children). But use every opportunity you can to get this kind of physical contact. And what I would also recommend that you do is that the two of you are clear about what you expect.

And if you (Bob) could learn from Betty how to pay attention (to the kids) more quickly. I would like you to be able to get your message across without a "don't" in it, without a "don't"—and that your strength of your arms when you pick them up—I don't know if I can illustrate it to you, but let me have your arm for a minute (reaching for Bob's forearm). Let me show you the difference. Pick up my arm like you were going to grab me. (Bob grabs her arm.) All right. Now when you do that, my muscles all start to tighten, and I want to hit back. (Bob nods.) Now pick up my arm like you wanted to protect me. (Bob holds her arm.) All right. I feel your strength now, but I don't feel like I want to pull back like this. (Bob says, "yeah.")

And what I'd like you to do is to do *lots* and lots of touching of both of these children. And when things start (to get out of hand), then you go over—don't say anything—go over to them and just take them (demonstrating the protective holding on both of Robbie's forearms) but you have to know in your inside that you're not pulling them (Aaron briefly puts his hands on top of Virginia's and Robbie's arms) like this (demonstrating), but you are taking them in a strong way (stroking Bob's arm with both hands), like you saw the difference. I'll demonstrate it to you (Bob), too. First of all I am going to grab you (demonstrating) like that. (Bob says, "yeah.") You see you want to pull back. All right. Now, at this time what I am going to do is give you some strength (demonstrating holding his arm with both hands. Robbie pats Virginia's hand). But I am not going to ask you to retaliate. Now this is the most important thing for you to start with.

(Virginia turns to Betty and offers her forearm.) OK. Now I'd like to do the same with you. So, take my arm really tight, just (Betty grabs Virginia's arm, and Aaron does, too). Yeah, that's right, like you really wanted to give me "what for." OK. All right. Now give it to me like you want to give me support, but you also want to give me a boundary. (Aaron reaches toward Betty's hand and Virginia takes Aaron's free hand in her free hand.) It's a little bit tight, a little bit tight.

So the next time you see anything coming, what you do is you go and make that contact (Virginia demonstrates by holding Aaron's upper arm) and then let it go soft. (Virginia takes Aaron's hands and begins to draw him out of Betty's lap.) Now, Aaron, I'd like you to come up here so I could demonstrate something to your mother for a minute. (Aaron says, "OK.") Now, let's suppose some moment I'm not thinking and I take you like that (grabbing Betty's arms suddenly with both hands). You see what you want to do? (Betty nods.) All right. Now I am going to do it another way. I am giving you the same message (Virginia holds Betty's arm firmly with both hands, looking directly into her eyes, and starts to stand up), but I am doing it like this. And I am looking at you, and I'm giving you a straight message. OK. Now your body at that point is not going to respond negatively to me. It is going to feel stopped, but not negative. And then I will take you like this. (Virginia puts one arm around Betty's back and the other under her upper arm.) Just like this (Virginia puts both arms around Betty and draws her close) and now I will hold you. I will hold you like that for a little bit.

Following this session, Satir commented on her technique:

There had been so many things happening, and the fear was so strong in relation to these children that if you thought of one image it was like they were monsters. So one of the things that I wanted to do was also to see that they had the capacity to respond with a touch, using myself in that regard by having them put their hands on my face—that was

a kind of mirror for the family itself, the people in the family. And then allowing them, and encouraging them to do that with their own parents. See, touch, that comes out of the kind of ambience which was there at the time, says things no words can say.

To encourage empathy and bring family members closer together, Satir often used the following exercise with parents (adapted from Satir & Baldwin, 1983):

1. Think of a difficult situation with your child. Perhaps your child has been doing something that you haven't known how to handle or that drives you up the wall.

2. Run your movie of this situation from your own point of view. Imagine you are going through this situation with your child again. Notice how you feel, what you see, what you hear.

3. Reexperience this situation, but this time as your child. Visualize the entire situation slowly and in detail, as you would imagine seeing it through the eyes of your child. Let yourself feel what your child must be feeling. Do you notice any feelings that you weren't aware your child might be having? Do you notice something that your child might need or want that you hadn't been aware of?

4. Reexperience the same situation, this time as an observer. Watch and listen to what's happening, and allow yourself to observe both your child and yourself. Do you notice anything about the way you and your child respond to each other? What do you see more clearly about yourself and your child?

Because he favored a personal encounter over a calculated approach, it's not surprising that Whitaker's style was the same with individuals, couples, or groups (Whitaker, 1958). He assiduously avoided directing real-life decisions, preferring instead to open family members up to their feelings and join them in their uncertainty. This may sound trite, but it's an important point. As long as a therapist (or anyone else for that matter) is anxious to change people, it's hard, very hard, to help them feel understood—and even harder to really empathize with them.

A comparison between Whitaker's early work (Whitaker, 1967; Whitaker, Warkentin, & Malone, 1959) and his later work (Napier & Whitaker, 1978) shows how he changed over the years. He started out as deliberately outlandish. He might fall asleep in sessions and then report his dreams; he wrestled with patients; he talked about his own sexual fantasies. In later years he was less provocative. This seems to be what happens to therapists as they mature; they have less need to impose themselves and more willingness to listen.

Because Whitaker's treatment was so intense and personal, he believed it essential that two therapists work together. Having a cotherapist to share the burden keeps therapists from being absorbed in the emotional field of the family. Family therapy tends to activate therapists' own feelings toward certain types of family members. A detached, analytic stance minimizes such feelings; emotional involvement maximizes them.

The trouble with **countertransference** is that it tends to be unconscious. Therapists are more likely to become aware of such feelings after a session is over. Easier still is to observe countertransference in others. Consider the example of Dr. Fox, a married man who specializes in individual therapy, but occasionally sees married couples. In 75 percent of such cases, Dr. Fox encourages the couple to seek a divorce, and his patients have a high rate of following his advice. Perhaps if Dr. Fox were happier in his own marriage or had the courage to change it, he'd be less impelled to guide his patients where he fears to go.

To minimize countertransference, Whitaker recommended sharing feelings openly with the family. If feelings are openly expressed, they're less likely to be acted out.

Whitaker's first sessions (Napier & Whitaker, 1978) were fairly structured, and they included taking a family history. For him, the first contacts with families were opening salvos in "the battle for structure" (Whitaker & Keith, 1981). He wanted the family to know that the therapist was in charge.[2] This

began with the first telephone call. Whitaker (1976b) insisted that the largest possible number of family members attend; he believed that three generations were necessary to ensure that grandparents would support, not oppose, therapy and that their presence would help correct distortions. If significant family members wouldn't attend, Whitaker generally refused to see the family. Why begin with the cards stacked against you?

Along with Virginia Satir, Whitaker was among the foremost exponents of the therapist's use of self as a catalyst for change. But whereas Satir offered a warm, supportive presence, Whitaker was often blunt, even confrontational. Actually, the provocative interventions of someone like Whitaker become acceptable to families only after the therapist has proved to be an understanding and caring person. Before challenging people, it is first necessary to win their trust.

Regardless of whether they are provocative or supportive, experiential therapists are usually extremely active. Instead of leaving family members to work out their own issues with each other, they "Tell him (or her) what you feel!" or ask, "What are you feeling right now?" Just as the best way to get a school teacher's attention is to misbehave, the best way to get an experiential therapist's attention is to show signs of emotion without actually expressing it.

Therapist: I see you looking over at Dad whenever you ask Mom a question. What's that about?

Kendra: Oh, nothing . . .

Therapist: It must mean *something.* Come on, what were you feeling?

Kendra: Nothing!

Therapist: You must have been feeling something. What was it?

Kendra: Well, sometimes when Mom lets me do something, Dad gets mad. But instead of yelling at her, he yells at *me* (crying softly).

Therapist: Tell him.

Kendra: (Angrily, to the therapist) Leave me alone!

---

[2]We might add that there is a big difference between trying to control the structure of sessions and trying to control people's lives.

Therapist: No, it's important. Tell your Dad how you feel.

Kendra: (Sobbing hard) You're always picking on me! You never let me do anything!

Experiential therapists use a number of expressive techniques, including family sculpting (Duhl, Kantor, & Duhl, 1973), family puppet interviews (Irwin & Malloy, 1975), family art therapy (Geddes & Medway, 1977), conjoint family drawings (Bing, 1970), and Gestalt therapy techniques (Kempler, 1973). Among the accoutrements of experiential therapists' offices are toys, doll houses, clay, teddy bears, drawing pens and paper, and batacca bats.

In **family sculpting** the therapist asks one member of a family to arrange the others in a tableau. This is a graphic means of portraying each person's perceptions of the family and his or her place in it. This was a favorite device of Virginia Satir, who frequently used ropes and blindfolds to dramatize the constricting roles family members get trapped into (Satir & Baldwin, 1983).

Case Study

This example of sculpting occurred when a therapist asked Mr. N. to arrange the members of his family into a scene typical of the time when he comes home from work.

Mr. N.: When I come home from work, eh? Okay (to his wife) honey, you'd be by the stove, wouldn't you?

Therapist: No, don't talk. Just move people where you want them to be.

Mr. N.: Okay.

He guided his wife to stand at a spot where the kitchen stove might be and placed his children on the kitchen floor, drawing and playing.

Therapist: Fine, now, still without any dialogue, put them into action.

Mr. N. then instructed his wife to pretend to cook but to turn frequently to see what the kids were up to. He told the children to pretend to play for a while but then to start fighting and complaining to Mommy.

Therapist: And what happens, when you come home?

Mr. N.: Nothing. I try to talk to my wife, but the kids keep pestering her, and she gets mad and says to leave her alone.

Therapist: Okay, act it out.

Mrs. N. acted out trying to cook and referee the children's fights. The children, who thought this a great game, tried to outdo each other getting Mommy's attention. When Mr. N. "came home," he reached out for his wife, but the children came between them until Mrs. N. finally pushed all of them away.

Afterward, Mrs. N. said that she hadn't realized her husband felt ignored. She just thought of him as coming home, saying hello, and then withdrawing into the den with his newspaper and bottle of beer.

Family sculpting is also used to illuminate scenes from the past. A typical instruction is "Remember standing in front of your childhood home. Walk in and describe what typically happened." The idea is to make a tableau portraying one's perceptions of family life. It's a device to focus awareness and heighten sensitivity.

Another expressive exercise is *family art therapy* or *family drawing*. Kwiatkowska (1967) instructs families to produce a series of drawings, including a "joint family scribble," in which each person makes a quick scribble and then the whole family incorporates the scribble into a unified picture. Elizabeth Bing (1970) describes the conjoint **family drawing** as a means to warm families up and free them to express themselves. In this procedure families are told to "Draw a picture as you see yourselves as a family."

The resulting portraits may disclose perceptions that haven't previously been discussed or may stimulate the person drawing the picture to realize something that he or she had never thought of before.

Case Study

A father drew a picture of the family that showed him off to one side, while his wife and children stood holding hands. Although he was portraying a fact well known to his wife and himself, they hadn't spoken openly of it. Once he showed his drawing to the therapist, there was no avoiding discussion.

In another case, when the therapist asked each of the family members to draw the family, the teenage daughter was uncertain what to do. She had never thought much about the family or her role in it. When she started to work, her drawing just seemed to emerge. She was surprised to discover that she'd drawn herself closer to her father and sisters than to her mother.

This provoked a lively discussion between her and her mother about their relationship. Although the two of them spent time together, the daughter didn't feel close because she thought her mother treated her like a child, never talking about her own concerns, and showing only superficial interest in the daughter's life. For her part, the mother was surprised, and not at all displeased, that her daughter felt ready to establish a relationship on a more mutual, caring basis.

In *family puppet interviews,* Irwin and Malloy (1975) ask one of the family members to make up a story using puppets. This technique, originally used in play therapy, is designed to highlight conflicts and alliances. Puppets also provide a safe avenue for symbolic communication. For example, a child who has used a specific puppet to symbolize his anger (e.g., a dinosaur) may simply reach for the dinosaur whenever he feels threatened.

Diana Arad (2004) recently developed the *animal attribution story-telling technique,* which requires family members to choose an animal to represent each member of the family and then tell a story about the animals. The following case summary from Arad illustrates the use of this technique in a family with an aggressive, acting-out nine-year-old.

Case Study

Sara and Jacob Cohen came to therapy with their daughter Dana (age four) and son Roy (nine), who was diagnosed with oppositional defiant disorder. Roy was aggressively rebellious, wet his bed, and alternated between depression and angry outbursts in which he said he wished he were dead. He also showed extreme sibling rivalry with his little sister and frequently punched her during arguments.

Roy entered the office for the first session firmly in his father's grasp. He'd been crying and was determined not to cooperate. The therapist assured him that he wasn't going to be forced to do anything and that he didn't have to participate if he didn't want to.

When the therapist introduced the animal story-telling game, she began by asking Dana, the youngest member of the family, to begin (to prevent her from copying other family members' stories). "If your mother were an animal," the therapist asked, "what animal would she be?"

Dana replied that her mother would be a horse, her father a squirrel, her brother a chicken, and herself a wolf. When asked to make up a story about these animals, Dana related the following:

> Once upon a time, a horse went to visit his friend the chicken. At the same time, a wolf came to eat the chicken, but the horse saved the chicken. Then the squirrel took the chicken and the horse to visit him under his tree and made the chicken laugh.

What this story revealed was that four-year-old Dana, who was seen as the good child and her brother's victim, saw herself (wolf) as an aggressor to her brother (chicken) and as an outsider to the family interaction (not invited to the fun under the squirrel's tree). Her parents were quite surprised by this version of the family. When asked for an example of acting like a wolf, Dana described how when Roy used the computer she would watch from the door and then "attack" his mouse-using hand and then run to her mother. Roy would chase her, "clucking" like a chicken, but he couldn't retaliate because Dana was protected by her mother. Roy usually shouted and raged and then got punished, leaving the computer free for Dana to use.

Here's Roy's story:

Once upon a time, when an elephant (Dad) went for a walk in the jungle, he stepped on a cockroach (Dana). The cockroach got squished, but the elephant did not notice and went on his way. A cat (Roy) came, found the squished cockroach, and thought it was a Frisbee. He took it to his friend the dog (Mom) in order to play with it. They played Frisbee with it until they were fed up and threw it back to where the cat had found it. The elephant came back, took the squished cockroach, and ate it. The cockroach recovered and ran around inside the elephant. This tickled him so that he burst out laughing, expelling the cockroach through his mouth so hard that it landed in the same place where it was stepped on before. Then one day, the elephant went for a walk again and stepped on it again.

Both children's stories portrayed the father as a disengaged figure—a funny squirrel who appears after the danger is gone and a passing elephant who does damage without even noticing. This picture, which did not match the family's official version of the father as loving and involved, was also reflected in the mother's story, in which the father was represented as a mischievous but unapproachable dolphin.

The children's stories helped the parents see Roy in a different light. They agreed that when Roy started raging, cursing, and throwing things, they would consider it "clucking like a chicken," and they would keep their distance. Moreover, the parents took the children's perspectives into account and stopped blaming Roy for all the fights. They decided to enforce equal consequences when the children fought. They were both sent to time-out—"just in case the wolf was at it again." Roy thought this was fair, and sibling rivalry decreased considerably.

Eliana Gil (1994) describes a number of play therapy techniques and explains how they can be used to engage young children in family treatment. In the *typical-day interview,* Gil asks children to pick a day of the week and select dolls (or puppets) to represent the people in their families. Then the therapist asks the child to use the figures to show where people are and what they do throughout the day. Gil recommends asking specifically about television watching, eating habits, sleeping habits, hygiene, anger, and affection. One ten-year-old who had described everything in his house as "fine" responded to a question about what he watched on television after school by listing twelve shows, ending with David Letterman's *Late Show.* When the therapist asked, "What happens after you watch Letterman?" the boy replied, "I go to sleep." When asked, "Who's at home when you go to sleep?" the boy answered, "No one" (from Gil, 1994).

Role-playing is another favorite device. Its use is based on the premise that experience, to be real, must be brought to life in the present. Recollection of past events and consideration of hoped-for or feared future developments can be made more immediate by role-playing them in the session. Kempler (1968) encourages parents to fantasize and role-play scenes from childhood. A mother might be asked to role-play what it was like when she was a little girl, or a father might be asked to imagine himself as a boy caught in the same dilemma as his son.

When someone who isn't present is mentioned, therapists may introduce the Gestalt *empty chair technique* (Kempler, 1973). If a child talks about her grandfather, she might be asked to speak to a chair, which is used to personify Grandfather. Whitaker (1975) used a similar role-playing technique, which he called "psychotherapy of the absurd." This consists of augmenting the unreasonable quality of a patient's response to the point of absurdity. It often amounts to calling a person's bluff, as the following example illustrates:

Patient: I can't stand my husband!
Therapist: Why don't you get rid of him or take up a boyfriend?

At times this takes the form of sarcastic teasing, such as mock fussing in response to a fussy child. The hope is that patients will get objective distance by participating in the therapist's distancing; the danger is that patients will feel hurt at being made fun of.

These techniques have proven useful in individual therapy (Nichols & Zax, 1977) to intensify emotional experiencing by bringing memories into focus and acting out suppressed reactions. Whether such devices are necessary in family therapy is open to question. In individual treatment, patients are isolated from the significant figures in their lives, and role-playing may be useful to approximate being with those people. But because family therapy is conducted with significant people present, it seems doubtful that role-playing and other means of fantasy are necessary. If emotional action is wanted, plenty is available simply by opening dialogue between family members.

Two recent emotive approaches to family therapy that represent a more sophisticated understanding of family dynamics are emotionally focused couples therapy and the internal family systems model.

Emotionally Focused Couples Therapy. Emotionally focused couples therapy works on two levels in succession—uncovering the hurt and longing beneath defensive expressions of anger and withdrawal and then helping couples understand how these feelings are played out in their relationship. Getting in touch with their underlying attachment longings helps partners to express themselves more genuinely and to see each other in a more sympathetic light. This more accurate and sympathetic view helps them have a new experience of each other and to change their interaction.

To begin, the therapist acknowledges each client's immediate feelings—hurt and anger, say—to make them feel understood (Johnson, 1998). Having their feelings validated in this way helps couples deescalate their anxiety and the cycle of their arguing (Greenberg & Johnson, 1988).

"You're getting angrier and angrier. It's upsetting for you to hear Will picture himself as innocent, isn't it?"

By interrupting a couple's quarrel and reflecting what each of them is feeling, the therapist defuses hostility and helps them focus on their experience rather than on each other's crimes. Then, to explore the perceptions that underlie the partners' emotional responses to each other, the therapist asks for a description of what happens at home.

"Oh, so part of you believes him, but part of you is suspicious?

"Part of you is watching and expecting that he'll hurt you?

"Can you tell me about the part that believes him, that he's being honest?"

Next the therapist points out how the couple's emotions are driving them into cycles of escalating polarization. As described in Johnson (1998):

The cycle was formulated in terms of Will's protecting himself by staying distant and avoiding Nancy's anger, and Nancy's being vigilant and fighting to avoid being betrayed again. As she became more insecure and distrustful, Will then felt more helpless and distanced himself further. As he distanced, she felt betrayed and became more enraged. Both were framed as victims of the cycle, which I continually framed as a common problem that the partners need to help each other with (pp. 457–458).

The couple's growing awareness of how their emotional reactivity frustrates their longings sets the stage for uncovering and expressing the emotions that lie beneath their sparring. The resulting expression makes it possible for the couple to deepen their understanding of their destructive pattern with each other, and this circular process continues to be explored in the process of working through.

The value of this more genuine, softer expression of feeling lies not so much in catharsis as in creating a shift in the partners' perceptions of each other. No longer are partners seen as blaming, rejecting, or withdrawn but as lonely, anxious, and afraid. It is seeing the other partner in a new way, not cathartic expression, that leads to change (Greenberg, James, & Conry, 1988).

Attachment theory helps the emotionally focused couples therapist pinpoint the issues that get stirred up when couples talk about their hurts and longings.

"Maybe you feel like no one really loves you?"
"You feel helpless and alone, don't you?"

The impact of this emotional evocation is enhanced by the fact that the partner is present to be addressed in this new and more feelingful way.

"So, can you tell her that?"

The ultimate aim of this work is to enable partners to risk being vulnerable with each other by acknowledging and expressing their attachment needs.

"Only you can face your fear and decide to risk depending on Will. He can't do it, can he? The only one who can drop your defenses and risk trusting him is you, isn't it?"
"What's the worst thing that could happen?"

Again, working together with the couple means that once the partners risk expressing their needs and fears, their mates can be encouraged to respond.

"What happens to you, Will, when you hear this?"

The response to this question will of course be very different once the partners let down their guard and begin to talk about what they're afraid of and what they really want from each other.

The therapist frames couples' experiences in terms of deprivation, isolation, and loss of secure connectedness. This perspective, from attachment theory, helps individuals focus on their own longings rather than on each other's faults and failings.

The process of therapeutic intervention has been described in nine treatment steps (Johnson, Hunsley, Greenberg, & Schindler, 1999):

1. Assessment—creating an alliance and explicating the core issues in the couple's conflict using attachment theory
2. Identifying the problematic interaction cycle that maintains attachment insecurity and relationship distress
3. Uncovering the unacknowledged emotions underlying interactional positions
4. Reframing the problem in terms of a problematic cycle with underlying emotions and attachment needs
5. Encouraging acceptance and expression of disowned needs and aspects of the self
6. Encouraging acceptance of the partner's new openness
7. Encouraging the expression of specific needs and wants and creating an intimate, emotional engagement
8. Facilitating new solutions to unresolved relationship issues
9. Consolidating new positions and more honest expression of attachment needs

In all of these steps the therapist moves between helping partners uncover and express their emotional experience and helping them reorganize the pattern of their interactions. For example:

> The therapist might, then, first help a withdrawn, guarded spouse formulate his sense of paralyzed helplessness that primes his withdrawal. The therapist will validate this sense of helplessness by placing it within the context of the destructive cycle that has taken over the relationship. The therapist will heighten this experience in the session and then help his partner to hear and accept it, even though it is very different from the way she usually experiences her spouse. Finally, the therapist moves to structuring an interaction around this helplessness, as in, "So can you turn to her and can you tell her, 'I feel so helpless and defeated. I just want to run away and hide.'" This kind of statement, in and of itself, represents a move away from passive withdrawal and is the beginning of active emotional engagement (Johnson, Hunsley, Greenberg, & Schindler, 1999, p. 70).

Internal Family Systems Therapy. In the internal family systems model (Schwartz, 1995), conflicting inner voices are personified as subpersonalities or

parts. What makes this device powerful is that even when client family members are at odds with each other, their conflicts are often based on polarizations of part of what they feel. The truth is that people in conflict with each other are often also in conflict within themselves.

The adolescent's defiance and her parents' distrust are only one aspect of the complex feelings they have for each other. Or to choose a different example, the couple caught in a pursuer–distancer pattern may be acting out only those parts of them that are terrified of abandonment and engulfment. By dramatizing the elements of their inner conflicts, internal family systems therapy helps family members sort out their feelings and reconnect with each other in less polarized ways.

To help clients begin to distinguish among their conflicting inner voices, Schwartz begins by introducing the language of parts.

"So there's a part of you that gets upset and angry when your son gets down on himself. Do you think that if that part didn't get so stirred up, it would be easier for you to help him?"

"It sounds like part of you agrees with your husband about getting stricter with the kids, but there's another part that says he's being too harsh. What is that second part? What does it say to you? What is it afraid of?"

By listening carefully to what clients are feeling and then construing their reactions as coming from a part of them, the therapist initiates a shift in family polarizations. It's easier for people to acknowledge that "a part of them" feels—angry, helpless, or whatever—than that "they" (as in all of them) feel that way. A parent who has trouble admitting that he's angry at his son for not doing well in school may find it easier to acknowledge that a part of him gets angry at his son's failures—and moreover that the angry part gets in the way of his sympathetic part.

Once the idea is introduced that various parts of family members are reacting to each other, instead of seeing themselves intrinsically at odds, they can begin to see that parts of one are triggering parts of another. The obvious implication is that if their aggravating emotions are contained in only parts of them, they have other feelings and other possibilities for interaction.

"So that angry part of your father seems to trigger a sad and helpless part of you, is that right?"

And because many such polarizations become triangles, it might be that the father's angry part also triggers a protective part in his wife.

"So when you see your husband's angry part responding to your son, that triggers a protective part in you? A part of you feels that you need to fight your husband to protect your son?"

Instead of having a son who is a failure, a father who is unsympathetic, and parents who can't agree, the family discovers that each of them is having trouble with some of their parts. The father is transformed from a tyrant to a parent struggling with a frustrated and angry part of himself. His wife ceases to be basically at odds with him and instead is seen as having a protective part that gets triggered by his angry part. Instead of being a failure, the son becomes a boy with a part of him that feels helpless in the face of his father's angry part and his parents' conflict.

Like all experiential models, internal family systems therapy is founded on the belief that underneath people's reactive parts lies a healthy self at the core of the personality. When the therapist notices various parts taking over, he or she asks the person first to visualize them and then help them to calm down. If, for example, an angry part were seen as a snarling dog, that person might find that she could calm her anger by approaching the dog and petting it until it felt reassured and settled down. Or to use another example (cited by Schwartz, 1998), if a frightened part were imagined as a rag doll, the client might relax her fears by imagining holding and comforting that doll.

Thus, by personifying people's polarizing emotional reactions as parts and then helping them visualize and reassure these reactive parts, internal family systems therapy releases people from the domination of fear and anger. This in turn allows them to work together more effectively to solve personal and family problems.

CURRENT STATUS OF THE MODEL

Experiential therapy helps family members get beneath the surface of their interactions to explore the feelings that drive them. At its best, this approach helps people drop their defenses and come together with more immediacy and authenticity. Given family therapy's emphasis on behavior and cognition, the effort to help clients uncover the feeling side of their experience is a welcome idea.

Regardless of what approach to family therapy one takes, shifting to individuals and their experience is a good way to break through defensive squabbling. When family members argue, they usually lead with their defenses. Instead of saying, "*I'm* hurt," they say, "*You* make me mad." Instead of admitting they're afraid, they criticize each other. An effective way to interrupt the unproductive escalation of arguments is to explore the feelings of the participants, one at a time. By talking to individuals about what they're feeling—and the roots of such feelings—family members can be helped to get past the defensiveness that keeps them apart and to reconnect on a more genuine level.

But just as approaches that focus entirely on families and their interactions leave something out, so too does an approach that concentrates too narrowly on individuals and their emotional experience. At the peak of experiential therapy's popularity in the 1970s, these therapists approached family therapy as if it were an encounter group for relatives. They put great faith in the value of individual emotional experiencing and had limited appreciation of the role family structure plays in regulating that experience. Not surprisingly, therefore, as family therapy focused more on

organization, interaction, and narrative in the 1980s and 1990s, the experiential model fell out of favor.

As we have already suggested, a therapy designed primarily to elicit feelings may be more suited to encounter groups than to family therapy. However, the prevailing behavioral and cognitive models of family therapy could do with a little more attention to people's feelings. If "more attention to people's feelings" sounds vague, allow us to make it more concrete. Helping family members get in touch with their feelings accomplishes two things: It helps them as individuals to discover what they really think and feel—what they want and what they're afraid of— and it helps them as a family get beyond defensiveness and begin to relate to each other in a more honest and immediate way.

Two particularly creative approaches to helping individuals get in touch with their inner experience are emotionally focused couples therapy and internal family systems therapy. What sets Johnson and Greenberg's therapy apart is its combination of emotional expressiveness and attention to the dynamics of interaction between couples. Emotionally focused couples therapy begins, as all emotive approaches do, by exploring the feelings clients come in with— even or especially if those feelings are defensive. You don't get beneath the surface of what people are feeling by ignoring it.

The combination of uncovering deeper and more vulnerable emotions and teaching couples about the reactive patterns their feelings drive them through creates a meaningful cognitive experience. As Lieberman, Yalom, and Miles (1973) demonstrated with encounter groups, an emotionally intense therapeutic experience brings lasting value only when paired with an intellectual understanding of the significance of those emotions. The only caveat we might offer is that explanations are most useful following an emotionally significant process of uncovering—which is what distinguishes psychotherapy from a conversation with your Aunt Harriet.

Emotionally focused couples therapy maintains that relationship difficulties generally stem from the disowning of attachment needs, creating defensive interactional cycles and ineffective communication patterns. The model identifies these issues and destructive cycles, helps clients acknowledge the feelings underlying these cycles, encourages empathy for the partner's position, and encourages couples to communicate needs and emotions more effectively in the spirit of generating solutions and solidifying new relationship positions to increase intimacy.

Schwartz's internal family systems approach helps family members come together with more understanding by helping individuals sort out their own conflicted experience. Personifying unruly emotions as "parts" is a powerful device for helping people achieve a clarifying distance from their conflicts. Unlike emotionally focused therapy, internal family systems therapy does not lean heavily on didactic explanations. In this approach, emotional experiencing is clarified by learning to differentiate among one's own feelings rather than by explanations offered by the therapist.

In addition to anecdotal reports of successful outcome (Duhl & Duhl, 1981; Napier & Whitaker, 1978) and descriptions of techniques that are effective in catalyzing emotional expression within sessions (Kempler, 1981), emotionally focused couples therapy has received a good deal of empirical support (e.g., Johnson & Greenberg, 1985, 1988; Johnson, Hunsley, Greenberg, & Schindler, 1999; Johnson, Maddeaux, & Blouin, 1998).

Recently, researchers seeking to study the effectiveness of experiential techniques have followed Mahrer's (1982) suggestion to focus on the process, rather than the outcome, of therapy. Because he believed that studies of outcome have little impact on practitioners (who already know that what they do works), Mahrer recommended studying *in-therapy outcomes*—that is, what kinds of interventions produce desired results (emotional expression, more open communication) within sessions. Following Mahrer (1982) and others (Pierce, Nichols, & DuBrin, 1983) who looked at such in-therapy outcomes in individual treatment, Leslie Greenberg and Susan Johnson have found that helping an angry and attacking partner to reveal his or her softer feelings characterizes the best sessions of successful cases (Johnson & Greenberg, 1988) and that intimate self-disclosure leads to more productive sessions (Greenberg, Ford, Alden, & Johnson, 1993).

Once feeling–expression occupied center stage in psychological therapies; today that place is held by *unfortunately* behavior and cognition. Psychotherapists have discovered that people think and act. But that doesn't mean we should ignore the immediate emotional experience that is the main concern of experiential family therapy.

Summary

1. Experiential therapy works from the inside out—strengthening families by encouraging individual self-expression, reversing the usual direction of effect in family therapy. Experiential family therapy is also distinguished by a commitment to emotional well-being as opposed to problem solving. Personal integrity and self-fulfillment are seen as innate human capacities that will emerge spontaneously once defensiveness is overcome. To challenge the familiar and enhance experiencing, therapists use their own lively personalities as well as a host of expressive techniques.

2. Although the experiential model lost popularity in the 1980s, it is now enjoying something of a resurgence, especially in the innovative work of emotionally focused couples therapy and the internal family systems approach. Once the idea that families were systems was both novel and controversial; today it is the new orthodoxy. Now that the pendulum has swung so far in the direction of systems thinking, individuals and their private joys and pains are rarely mentioned. Surely one of the major contributions of experiential family therapy is to remind us not to lose sight of the self in the system.

Questions to Consider

1. Can you imagine how "the value of emotional expression" might be used by someone to justify defensive or abusive onslaughts or other forms of emotional dumping?

2. To what extent do you think the basic premise of experiential therapy—that getting in touch with and expressing one's feelings is therapeutic—is primarily relevant for an educated, middle-class clientele?

3. To what extent is it possible for a family therapist to work with the intrapsychic experience of individual family members without detracting from a focus on their systemic interactions?

4. Can you think of an example where it might be helpful to analyze some conflict or indecision of your own as due to different parts of you having different agendas?

5. What does attachment theory offer a therapist beyond the generalization that people sometimes cover their real feelings with defensive responses?

Key Concepts

countertransference Emotional reactivity on the part of the therapist.

emotionally focused couples therapy A model of therapy based on attachment theory, in which the emotional longings beneath a couple's defensive reactions are uncovered as they are taught to see the reactive nature of their struggles with each other; developed by Leslie Greenberg and Susan Johnson.

existential encounter A relationship based on direct personal contact, rather than artificial professional roles.

family drawing An experiential therapy technique whereby family members are asked to draw their ideas about how the family is organized.

family myths A set of beliefs based on a distortion of historical reality and shared by all family members that help shape the rules governing family functioning.

family sculpting A nonverbal experiential technique in which family members position themselves in a tableau that reveals significant aspects of their perceptions and feelings.

internal family systems therapy A model of family therapy that uses systemic principles and techniques to understand and change intrapsychic processes; developed by Richard Schwartz.

mystification R. D. Laing's concept that many families distort their children's experience by denying or relabeling it.

parts Richard Schwartz's term for the various reactive elements that make up a person's subpersonalities.

role-playing Acting out the parts of important characters to dramatize feelings and practice new ways of relating.

self-actualization Carl Rogers's term for the innate human tendency for each of us to seek what is best for us. A tendency that gets subverted by the need to please but can be released again in the presence of unconditional positive regard.

Recommended Readings

Duhl, F. J., Kantor, D., and Duhl, B. S. 1973. Learning, space and action in family therapy: A primer of sculpture. In *Techniques in family therapy,* D. A. Bloch, ed. New York: Grune & Stratton.

Gil, E. 1994. *Play in family therapy.* New York: Guilford Press.

Greenberg, L. S., and Johnson, S. M. 1988. *Emotionally focused therapy for couples.* New York: Guilford Press.

Keith, D. V., and Whitaker, C. A. 1977. The divorce labyrinth. In *Family therapy: Full length case studies,* P. Papp, ed. New York: Gardner Press.

Laing, R. D., and Esterson, A. 1970. *Sanity, madness and the family.* Baltimore: Penguin Books.

Napier, A. Y., and Whitaker, C. A. 1978. *The family crucible.* New York: Harper & Row.

Neill, J. R., and Kniskern, D. P., eds. 1982. *From psyche to system: The evolving therapy of Carl Whitaker.* New York: Guilford Press.

Satir, V. M., and Baldwin, M. 1983. *Satir step by step: A guide to creating change in families.* Palo Alto, CA: Science and Behavior Books.

Schwartz, R. C. 1995. *Internal family systems therapy.* New York: Guilford Press.

Whitaker, C. A., and Keith, D. V. 1981. Symbolic–experiential family therapy. In *Handbook of family therapy,* A. S. Gurman and D. P. Kniskern, eds. New York: Brunner/Mazel.

References

Andreas, S. 1991. *Virginia Satir: The patterns of her magic.* Palo Alto: Science and Behavior Books.

Arad, D. 2004. If your mother were an animal, what animal would she be? *Family Process. 43:* 249–263.

Bing, E. 1970. The conjoint family drawing. *Family Process. 9:* 173–194.

Binswanger, L. 1967. Being-in-the-world. In *Selected papers of Ludwig Binswanger,* J. Needleman, ed. New York: Harper Torchbooks.

Boss, M. 1963. *Psychoanalysis and daseinanalysts.* New York: Basic Books.

Bowlby, J. 1969. *Attachment and loss:* Vol. 1. *Attachment.* New York: Basic Books.

Duhl, B. S., and Duhl, F. J. 1981. Integrative family therapy. In *Handbook of family therapy,* A. S. Gurman and D. P. Kniskern, eds. New York: Brunner/Mazel.

Duhl, F. J., Kantor D., and Duhl, B. S. 1973. Learning, space and action in family therapy: A primer of sculpture. In *Techniques of family psychotherapy,* D. A. Bloch, ed. New York: Grune & Stratton.

Geddes, M., and Medway, J. 1977. The symbolic drawing of family life space. *Family Process. 16:* 219–228.

Gehrke, S., and Kirschenbaum, M. 1967. Survival patterns in conjoint family therapy. *Family Process. 6:* 67–80.

Gil, E. 1994. *Play in family therapy.* New York: Guilford Press.

Greenberg, L. S., Ford, C. L., Alden, L., and Johnson, S. M. 1993. In-session change in emotionally focused therapy. *Journal of Consulting and Clinical Psychology. 61:* 78–84.

Greenberg, L. S., James, P., and Conry, R. 1988. Perceived change processes in emotionally focused couples therapy. *Journal of Family Psychology. 2:* 1–12.

Greenberg, L. S., and Johnson, S. M. 1985. Emotionally focused couple therapy: An affective systemic approach. In *Handbook of family and marital therapy,* N. S. Jacobson and A. S. Gurman, eds. New York: Guilford Press.

Greenberg, L. S., and Johnson, S. M. 1986. Affect in marital therapy. *Journal of Marital and Family Therapy. 12:* 1–10.

Greenberg, L. S., and Johnson, S. M. 1988. *Emotionally focused therapy for couples.* New York: Guilford Press.

Irwin, E., and Malloy, E. 1975. Family puppet interview. *Family Process. 14:* 179–191.

Johnson, S. M. 1998. Emotionally focused couple therapy. In *Case studies in couple and family therapy,* F. M. Dattilio, ed. New York: Guilford Press.

Johnson, S. M., and Denton, W. 2002. Emotionally focused couple therapy: Creating secure connections. In *Clinical handbook of couple therapy,* 3rd ed., A. S. Gurman and N. S. Jacobson, eds. New York: Guilford Press.

Johnson, S. M., and Greenberg, L. S. 1985. Emotionally focused couples therapy: An outcome study. *Journal of Marital and Family Therapy. 11:* 313–317.

Johnson, S. M., and Greenberg, L. S. 1988. Relating process to outcome in marital therapy. *Journal of Marital and Family Therapy. 14:* 175–183.

Johnson, S. M., Hunsley, J., Greenberg, L., and Schindler, D. 1999. Emotionally focused couples therapy: Status and challenges. *Clinical Psychology: Science and Practice. 6:* 67–79.

Johnson, S. M., Maddeaux, C., and Blouin, J. 1998. Emotionally focused therapy for bulimia: Changing attachment patterns. *Psychotherapy. 35:* 238–247.

Kaplan, M. L., and Kaplan, N. R. 1978. Individual and family growth: A Gestalt approach. *Family Process. 17:* 195–205.

Kempler, W. 1968. Experiential psychotherapy with families. *Family Process. 7:* 88–89.

Kempler, W. 1973. *Principles of Gestalt family therapy.* Oslo, Norway: Nordahls.

Kempler, W. 1981. *Experiential psychotherapy with families.* New York: Brunner/Mazel.

Kwiatkowska, H. Y. 1967. Family art therapy. *Family Process. 6:* 37–55.

Laing, R. D. 1967. *The politics of experience.* New York: Ballantine.

Laing, R. D., and Esterson, A. 1970. *Sanity, madness and the family.* Baltimore: Penguin Books.

Lieberman, M. A., Yalom, I. D., and Miles, M. B. 1973. *Encounter groups: First facts.* New York: Basic Books.

Mahrer, A. R. 1982. *Experiential psychotherapy: Basic practices.* New York: Brunner/Mazel.

Marcuse, H. 1955. *Eros and civilization.* New York: Beacon Press.

Napier, A. Y., and Whitaker, C. A. 1978. *The family crucible.* New York: Harper & Row.

Nichols, M. P., and Zax, M. 1977. *Catharsis in psychotherapy.* New York: Gardner Press.

Pierce, R., Nichols, M. P., and DuBrin, J. 1983. *Emotional expression in psychotherapy.* New York: Gardner Press.

Rogers, C. R. 1951. *Client-centered therapy.* Boston: Houghton Mifflin.

Satir, V. M. 1972. *Peoplemaking.* Palo Alto: Science and Behavior Books.

Satir, V. M., and Baldwin, M. 1983. *Satir step by step: A guide to creating change in families.* Palo Alto: Science and Behavior Books.

Schwartz, R. C. 1995. *Internal family systems therapy.* New York: Guilford Press.

Schwartz, R. C. 1998. Internal family systems therapy. In *Case studies in couple and family therapy,* F. M. Dattilio, ed. New York: Guilford Press.

Simon, R. 1989. Reaching out to life: An interview with Virginia Satir. *The Family Therapy Networker. 13*(1): 36–43.

Sullivan, H. S. 1953. *The interpersonal theory of psychiatry.* New York: Norton.

Whitaker, C. A. 1958. Psychotherapy with couples. *American Journal of Psychotherapy. 12:* 18–23.

Whitaker, C. A. 1967. The growing edge. In *Techniques of family therapy,* J. Haley and L. Hoffman, eds. New York: Basic Books.

Whitaker, C. A. 1975. Psychotherapy of the absurd: With a special emphasis on the psychotherapy of aggression. *Family Process. 14:* 1–16.

Whitaker, C. A. 1976a. The hindrance of theory in clinical work. In *Family therapy: Theory and practice,* P. J. Guerin, ed. New York: Gardner Press.

Whitaker, C. A. 1976b. A family is a four-dimensional relationship. In *Family therapy: Theory and practice,* P. J. Guerin, ed. New York: Gardner Press.

Whitaker, C. A., and Keith, D. V. 1981. Symbolic-experiential family therapy. In *Handbook of family therapy,* A. S. Gurman and D. P. Kniskern, eds. New York: Brunner/Mazel.

Whitaker, C. A., and Malone, T. P. 1953. *The roots of psychotherapy.* New York: Blakiston.

Whitaker, C. A., Warkentin, J., and Malone, T. P. 1959. The involvement of the professional therapist. In *Case studies in counseling and psychotherapy,* A. Burton, ed. Englewood Cliffs, NJ: Prentice Hall.

9

Psychoanalytic Family Therapy

$\mathcal{M}$any of the pioneers of family therapy, including Nathan Ackerman, Murray Bowen, Ivan Boszormenyi-Nagy, Carl Whitaker, Don Jackson, and Salvador Minuchin, were psychoanalytically trained. But with the eager enthusiasm of converts they turned away from the old—psychodynamics—and toward the new—systems dynamics. Some, like Jackson and Minuchin, moved far indeed from their psychoanalytic roots. Others, like Bowen and Boszormenyi-Nagy, retained a distinctly analytic influence in their work.

In the 1960s and 1970s, family therapy followed Jackson and Minuchin in not only ignoring psychoanalytic thinking but denigrating it. Jackson (1967) went so far as to declare the death of the individual, and Minuchin (1989) proclaimed, "We understood that the decontexted individual was a mythical monster, an illusion created by psychodynamic blinders."

Then in the 1980s a surprising shift occurred: Family therapists took a renewed interest in the psychology of the individual. This revival of interest reflected changes in psychoanalysis—from the individualism of Freudian theory to the more relationship-oriented object relations theories and self-psychology, as well as changes in family therapy itself, especially dissatisfaction with the mechanistic elements of the cybernetic model. Among the books calling for a rapprochement with psychoanalysis were *Object*

Relations: A Dynamic Bridge between Individual and Family Treatment (Slipp, 1984), *Object Relations Family Therapy* (Scharff & Scharff, 1987), and *The Self in the System* (Nichols, 1987).

Why did these psychodynamic voices find a receptive audience? Whereas family therapists discovered profound truths about systemic interactions, many believed they were wrong to turn their backs on depth psychology. Anyone who does not flee from self-awareness knows that the inner life is awash in conflict and confusion, most of it never expressed. While systemic therapists focused on the outward expression of this inner life—family interactions—psychoanalytic therapists probed beneath family dialogues to explore individual family members' private fears and longings.

$\mathcal{E}$VOLUTION OF THE MODEL

Freud was interested in the family but saw it as old business—the place where people learned neurotic fears, rather than the current context in which such fears were maintained. Faced with a phobic Little Hans, Freud (1909) was more interested in analyzing the boy's Oedipus complex than in trying to understand what was going on in his family.

Major advances were achieved in the understanding of family dynamics by child psychiatrists who began to analyze mothers and children concurrently (Burlingham, 1951). One example of the fruits of these studies was Adelaide Johnson's (Johnson & Szurek, 1952) explanation of the transmission of *superego lacunae,* gaps in personal morality passed on by parents who do things like tell their children to lie about their age to save a couple of bucks at the movies.

Subsequently, the concurrent analysis of married couples revealed the family as a group of interlocking, intrapsychic systems (Mittlemann, 1948; Oberndorf, 1938). From the 1930s to the 1950s, psychoanalytic researchers became more interested in the contemporary family. Erik Erikson explored the sociologic dimensions of ego psychology. Erich Fromm's observations about the struggle for individuality foreshadowed Bowen's work on differentiation of the self. Harry Stack Sullivan's interpersonal theory emphasized the mother's role in transmitting anxiety to her children.

In the 1950s American psychoanalysis was dominated by ego psychology (which focuses on intrapsychic structures), whereas object relations theory (which lends itself to interpersonal analysis) flourished an ocean away in Britain. In the 1940s Henry Dicks (1963) established the Family Psychiatric Unit at the Tavistock Clinic in England, where teams of social workers attempted to reconcile couples referred by the divorce courts. By the 1960s Dicks (1967) was applying object relations theory to the understanding and treatment of marital conflict.

Meanwhile, the psychoanalysts who helped create family therapy were moving away from psychodynamics, and the analytic influence in their work was deliberately muted. The exception was Nathan Ackerman, the leading family therapist on the East Coast, who of all the pioneers retained the strongest allegiance to psychoanalysis. Students, among them Salvador Minuchin, flocked to New York to observe this master therapist at work. His book *The Psychodynamics of Family Life,* published in 1958, was the first devoted to diagnosis and treatment of families.

Edith Jacobson (1954) and Harry Stack Sullivan (1953) helped bring American psychiatry to an interpersonal point of view. Less well known, but more important to the development of family therapy, was the work carried out at the National Institute of Mental Health (NIMH). When NIMH opened in 1953, Irving Ryckoff moved from Chestnut Lodge, where he'd been working with schizophrenic patients to develop a research project on families of schizophrenics under the leadership of Robert Cohen. He was joined by Juliana Day and Lyman Wynne and later by Roger Shapiro and John Zinner. This group produced a series of thoughtful papers introducing such concepts as *pseudomutuality* (Wynne, Ryckoff, Day, & Hirsch, 1958), *trading of dissociations* (Wynne, 1965), and *delineations* (Shapiro, 1968). But perhaps their most important contribution was the application of the concept of *projective identification* (from Melanie Klein) to family relationships. This group also introduced to psychoanalytic researchers the idea of seeing the family as a unit for study, and to clinicians, the analytic group-interpretive approach to families (Shapiro, 1979).

Jill and David Scharff are leading exponents of object relations family therapy.

In the 1960s Ryckoff and Wynne inaugurated a course in family dynamics at the Washington School of Psychiatry, which led to a family therapy training program. They were joined by Shapiro and Zinner and Robert Winer. In 1975 they recruited Jill Savege (now Scharff) and David Scharff. By the mid-1980s the Washington School of Psychiatry, under the directorship of David Scharff, had become a leading center of psychoanalytic family therapy. The Scharffs left in 1994 to form their own institute.

Among others who have incorporated psychoanalytic theory into family therapy are Helm Stierlin (1977), Robin Skynner (1976), William Meissner (1978), Arnon Bentovim and Warren Kinston (1991), Fred Sander (1979, 1989), Samuel Slipp (1984, 1988), Michael Nichols (1987), Nathan Epstein, Henry Grunebaum, and Clifford Sager.

*T*HE BASIC MODEL

The essence of psychoanalytic treatment is uncovering **unconscious** impulses and defenses against them. It isn't a question of analyzing individuals instead of family interactions; rather, it's knowing where to look to discover some of the basic wants and fears that keep those individuals from interacting in a mature way. Consider the case of Carl and Peggy (Nichols, 1987).

Case Study

Whenever Peggy talked to Carl about their relationship, she got upset and started criticizing. The more upset Peggy got, the quieter Carl became. Only after enduring her tirades for several minutes did Carl get mad and start to shout back at her. As a result, Peggy got exactly the opposite of what she was looking for. Instead of understanding her concerns, Carl felt threatened and withdrew. When that didn't work, he lost his temper. At home, when the same scenario got out of hand, he sometimes slapped her.

The therapist concentrated on interrupting this cycle and then helping the couple see the pattern so that they could prevent its recurrence. Unfortunately, while Carl and Peggy learned to relate more effectively in the therapist's office, at home they forgot. Week after week it was the same story. They would manage to listen to each other in their sessions, but at least once a month they would lose it at home. Eventually, when they got discouraged enough to stop coming, the therapist decided that they just weren't motivated enough to make the necessary changes.

As actors, perhaps we take ourselves too seriously; as observers, we take other selves not seriously enough. As family therapists, we see the actions of our clients as a product of their interactions. Yes, people are connected, but that connectedness should not obscure the fact that the nature of their interactions is partly dictated by psychic organization of unsuspected depth and complexity.

Consider again the case of Carl and Peggy, the combative couple who drifted away from therapy. Their pattern was relatively simple and completely impervious to the therapist's efforts to change it. Why couldn't (wouldn't) Carl stop hitting his wife? The fact that she provoked him doesn't really explain anything. Not every husband who is provoked hits his wife.

Looking back, the therapist remembered how Carl used to say with a concern that seemed somewhat affected, "I *must* control my temper!" She also remembered how dramatically he described his intimidating outbursts and his wife's cowering. And she remembered that when Peggy talked about Carl's brutality, a smile played around the corners of his mouth. These hints of a willful, motivated quality to Carl's abuse could be described in the jargon of psychodynamics, which, because it is alien, might lead some people to dismiss it as a relic of outmoded thinking. Psychodynamic language might imply that Carl's unconscious was responsible for his abusing his wife; he was helpless in the face of inner conflicts.

Psychodynamic theory may be useful to understand the self in the system, but it isn't necessary to be highly technical. If we were to write a dramatic narrative about Carl, we could say that he was misrepresenting, even to himself, his feelings and intentions. He fooled his wife, he fooled himself, and he fooled his therapist (perhaps in part because she kept such a tight rein on her own aggression). Carl, who thinks himself concerned with his temper (his version of nonhuman agency), is actually pleased with his power to intimidate his wife and with the manliness it implies.

This explanation does not replace the interactional one, only complicates it. Carl's attacks were triggered by the couple's interactions, but they were propelled by his own unrecognized insecurities. Knowing the motives behind his behavior enables us to help Carl understand that he hits his wife to make up for feeling weak and to help him find some other way to feel more powerful. As long as therapists stay at the simple behavioral level of interaction, they will make little headway with a certain number of their cases.

Recognizing that people are more complicated than billiard balls means that we sometimes have to delve deeper into their experience. Psychoanalytic theory gets so complex when you get into the specifics that it's easy to get lost. Here are the basics.

Freudian Drive Psychology

At the heart of human nature are the drives—libidinal[1] and aggressive. Mental conflict arises when children learn, and mislearn, that expressing these impulses directly will lead to punishment. The resulting conflict is signaled by unpleasant affect: *Anxiety* is unpleasure associated with the idea (often unconscious) that one will be punished for acting on a particular wish—for example, the anger you're tempted to express might make your partner stop loving you.

---

[1]Libido refers to not just sexual impulses but more broadly to pleasure-seeking in general.

Depression is unpleasure plus the idea (often unconscious) that the feared calamity has already occurred—for example, your anger at your mother long ago made her stop loving you; in fact, nobody loves you.

The balance of conflict can be shifted in one of two ways: by strengthening the defenses against one's impulses or by relaxing defenses to permit some gratification.

Self Psychology

The essence of **self psychology** (Kohut, 1971, 1977) is that every human being longs to be appreciated. If our parents are enthusiastically responsive and appreciative, we internalize this acceptance in the form of a strong, self-confident personality. But to the extent that our parents are unresponsive, flat, or withdrawn, then our craving for appreciation is retained in an archaic manner. As adults we alternately suppress the desire for attention and then allow it to break through whenever we're in the presence of a receptive audience.

The child lucky enough to grow up with appreciative parents will be secure, able to stand alone as a center of initiative, and able to love. The unhappy child, cheated out of loving affirmation, will move through life forever craving the attention he or she was denied.

Object Relations Theory

Psychoanalysis is the study of individuals and their deepest motives. Family therapy is the study of social relationships. The bridge between the two is **object relations theory.** Although the details of object relations theory can be quite complicated, its essence is simple: We relate to others on the basis of expectations formed by early experience. The residue of these early relationships leaves **internal objects**—mental images of self and others built up from experience and expectation. Those internalized objects form the core of the personality—an open system developing and maintaining its identity through social-relatedness, present and past.

In their observations of infants and young children, Rene Spitz and John Bowlby emphasized the child's profound need for *attachment* to a single and constant object. If this need is denied, the result is *anaclitic depression* (Spitz & Wolf, 1946), a turning away from the world and withdrawal into apathy. According to Bowlby (1969), attachment isn't simply a secondary phenomenon, resulting from being fed, but a basic need in all creatures. Those who don't have this experience are vulnerable to even the slightest lack of support and may become chronically dependent or isolated. This, in psychoanalytic terms, explains the genesis of enmeshed and disengaged relationships.

Margaret Mahler observed young children and described a process of **separation–individuation.** After an initial period of total merger, the child begins a gradual process of separation from the mother, progressively renouncing symbiotic fusion with her. The result of successful separation and individuation is a well-differentiated self (Mahler, Pine, & Bergman, 1975). Failure to achieve individuation undermines the development of a cohesive self and a differentiated identity, resulting in overly intense emotional attachments. Depending on the severity of the failure to separate, crises are liable to develop when a child reaches school age, enters adolescence, or prepares to leave home as an adult.

The shift from drives to object relations can also be seen in the interpersonal psychiatry of Harry Stack Sullivan (1953), who emphasized the importance of early mother–child interactions. When a mother is warm and nurturing, her child feels good; when a mother rebuffs or frustrates her child's need for tenderness, the child feels bad; and when the child is exposed to extreme pain or frustration, he or she dissociates to escape anxiety that would otherwise be intolerable. These experiences create the self-dynamisms *good me, bad me,* and *not me,* which then become part of the person's response to future interpersonal situations.

The internal world of **object relations** doesn't correspond to the actual world of real people. It's an approximation, strongly influenced by the earliest object images, **introjections,** and **identifications.** This inner world gradually matures and develops, becoming progressively synthesized and closer to reality. The individual's internal capacity for dealing with conflict and failure is related to the depth and maturity of the internal world of object relations. Trust in one's self and in the goodness of others is based on the confirmation of love from internalized good objects.

Normal Family Development

A child doesn't mature in sublime indifference to the interpersonal world. The infant needs a facilitating environment in order to thrive. This environment doesn't have to be ideal; an *average expectable environment* featuring **good-enough mothering** (Winnicott, 1965a) is sufficient.

The parents' capacity to provide security for the baby's developing ego depends on whether they themselves feel secure. To begin with, the mother must be secure enough to channel her energy into caring for her infant. She withdraws interest from herself and her marriage and focuses it on the baby. As the baby comes to need less, the mother gradually recovers her self-interest, which allows her to permit the child to become independent (Winnicott, 1965b).

To the very young child, parents aren't quite separate individuals; they are, in Kohut's (1971, 1977) term, **selfobjects,** experienced as part of the self. As a selfobject, the mother transmits her love by touch, tone of voice, and gentle words, as though they were the child's own feelings. When she whispers "Mommy loves you," the baby learns that he or she is (a) a person and (b) lovable.

In self psychology, two qualities of parenting are deemed essential for the development of a secure and cohesive self. The first is **mirroring**—understanding plus acceptance. Attentive parents convey a deep appreciation of how their children feel. Their implicit "I see how you feel" validates the child's inner experience. Parents also offer models for **idealization.** The little child who can believe "My mother (or father) is terrific, and I am part of her (or him)" has a firm base of self-esteem. In the best of circumstances, the child, already basically secure in his or her self, draws additional strength from identifying with the power and strength of the parents.

From a psychoanalytic perspective, the fate of the family is largely determined by the early development of individual personalities that make up the family. If the parents are mature and healthy adults, the family will be happy and harmonious.

Some of the most interesting and productive psychoanalytic ideas are contained in descriptions of the psychodynamics of marriage. In the 1950s the marital bond was described as a result of unconscious fantasy (Stein, 1956). We marry a blurry blend of real and hoped-for mates. More recently, and more interestingly, however, psychoanalysts have described the overlapping and interlocking of fantasies and projections (Blum, 1987; Sander, 1989). Some authors have described this as *mutual projective identification* (Dicks, 1967; Zinner, 1976) and others as *neurotic complementarity* (Ackerman, 1966), *marital collusion* (Dicks, 1967), *mutual adaptation* (Giovacchini, 1958), and *conscious and unconscious contracts* (Sager, 1981).

Among psychodynamic family therapists, few made more important contributions than Ivan Boszormenyi-Nagy, whose **contextual therapy,** which emphasizes the ethical dimension of family development. Boszormenyi-Nagy considered relational ethics to be a fundamental force holding families and communities together. In a field that often seeks refuge in the illusion of neutrality, Boszormenyi-Nagy reminded us of the importance of decency and fairness.

For marital partners, Boszormenyi-Nagy's criterion of health is a balance between rights and responsibilities. Depending on their integrity and the complementarity of their needs, partners can develop a trustworthy give and take (Boszormenyi-Nagy, Grunebaum, & Ulrich, 1991). When needs clash, negotiation and compromise are essential.

Development of Behavior Disorders

According to classical psychoanalytic theory, symptoms are attempts to cope with unconscious conflicts and the anxiety that signals the emergence of repressed impulses. As psychoanalytic emphasis shifted from instincts to object relations, infantile dependence and incomplete ego development replaced the oedipal complex and repressed instincts as the core problems in development. Fear-dictated flight from object relations, which begins in early childhood, is now considered the deepest root of psychological problems.

One important reason for relationship problems is that children develop distorted perceptions by attributing qualities belonging to one person to someone else. Freud (1905) called this phenomenon **transference** when his patient Dora displaced feelings for her father onto him and terminated treatment abruptly just as it was on the threshold of success.

Others have observed similar phenomena and called them *scapegoating* (Vogel & Bell, 1960), *trading of dissociations* (Wynne, 1965), *merging* (Boszormenyi-Nagy, 1967), *irrational role assignments* (Framo, 1970), *delineations* (Shapiro, 1968), *symbiosis* (Mahler, 1952), and *family projection process* (Bowen, 1965). Regardless of name, all are variants of Melanie Klein's (1946) concept *projective identification.*

Projective identification is a process whereby the subject perceives an object as if it contained unwelcome elements of the subject's personality and evokes

Ivan Boszormenyi-Nagy

Ivan Boszormenyi-Nagy's emphasis on loyalty, trust, and relational ethics—both within the family and between the family and society—made major contributions to the field of family therapy. An accomplished scholar and clinician, Boszormenyi-Nagy was trained as a psychoanalyst, and his work has encouraged many family therapists to incorporate psychoanalytic ideas into family therapy.

Boszormenyi-Nagy is perhaps best known for developing the contextual approach to family therapy, which emphasizes the ethical dimension of family relationships.

responses from the object that conform to those perceptions. Unlike projection, projective identification is interactional. Not only do parents project anxiety-arousing aspects of themselves onto their children, but the children collude by behaving in a way that confirms their parents' fears. By doing so, they may be stigmatized or scapegoated, but they also gratify aggressive impulses (as, for instance, in delinquent behavior) (Jacobson, 1954), realize their own omnipotent fantasies, receive subtle reinforcement from their families, and avoid the terrible fear of rejection for not conforming (Zinner & Shapiro, 1972). Meanwhile the parents are able to avoid the anxiety associated with certain impulses, experience vicarious gratification, and still punish the children for expressing those impulses. In this way, intrapsychic conflict becomes externalized, with the parent acting as a superego, punishing the child for acting on the dictates of the parental id. That's one reason parents overreact: They're afraid of their own impulses.

Case Study

The J. family sought help controlling fifteen-year-old Paul's delinquent behavior. Arrested several times for vandalism, Paul seemed neither ashamed nor able to understand his compulsion to strike out against authority. As therapy progressed, it became clear that Paul's father harbored a deep but unexpressed resentment of the social conditions that made him work long hours for low wages in a factory, while the "fat cats didn't do shit, but still drove around in Cadillacs." Once the therapist became aware of Mr. J.'s suppressed hatred of authority, she also began to notice that he smiled slightly whenever Mrs. J. described Paul's latest exploits.

Parents' failure to accept that their children are separate beings can take extreme forms, leading to the most severe psychopathology. Lidz (Lidz, Cornelison, & Fleck, 1965) described a mother of identical twins who, when she was constipated, would give her two sons an enema.

Poorly differentiated children face a crisis in adolescence, when developmental pressures for independence conflict with infantile attachments. The outcome may be continued dependence or violent rebellion. But the teenager who rebels as a reaction to unresolved dependency needs is ill-equipped for mature relationships. Behind their façade of proud self-reliance, such individuals harbor deep longings for dependence. When they marry, they may seek constant approval or automatically reject any influence, or both.

Case Study

Mr. and Mrs. B.'s complaints were mirror images. He claimed she was "bossy and demanding"; she said that he "had to have everything his own way." Mr. B. was the youngest in a close-knit family of five. He described his mother as warm and loving but said she tried to smother him and that she discouraged all his efforts to be independent. Subjected to these same pressures, his two older sisters knuckled under and still remain unmarried, living with their parents. Mr. B., however, rebelled against his mother's domination and left home to join the Marines at seventeen. As he related his experience in the Marine Corps and successful business ventures, it was clear that he was fiercely proud of his independence.

Once the story of Mr. B.'s success in breaking away from his domineering mother was brought into the open, both Mr. and Mrs. B. had a clearer understanding of his tendency to overreact to anything he perceived as controlling. Further analysis revealed that while Mr. B. staunchly rejected what he called "bossiness," he nevertheless craved approval. He had learned to fear his deep-seated dependency needs and protect himself with a façade of "not needing anything from anybody." Nevertheless, the needs were still there and had in fact been a powerful determinant of his choice of wife.

When it comes to choosing a romantic partner, psychoanalysts tell us, love is blind. Freud (1921) wrote that the overvaluation of the loved object when we fall in love leads us to make poor judgments based on idealization. The "fall" of falling in love reflects an overflow of narcissistic libido, so that the object of our love is elevated as a substitute for our own unattained ideals. Our own identity glows in the reflected radiance of an idealized companion.

Further complicating romantic relationships is that we hide some of our own needs and feelings in order to win approval. Children learn to suppress feelings they fear may lead to rejection. Winnicott (1965a) dubbed this phenomenon the **false self**—children behave as if they were perfect angels, pretending to be what they are not. In its most extreme form, a false self leads to schizoid behavior (Guntrip, 1969); even in less severe manifestations it affects the choice of a mate. During courtship, both partners are eager to please and therefore present themselves in the best possible light. Powerful dependency needs, **narcissism,** and unruly impulses may be submerged before marriage. Once married, however, spouses relax into themselves, warts and all.

Families as well as individuals experience **fixation** and **regression.** Most families function adequately until they're overtaxed, at which time they become stuck in rigid and dysfunctional patterns (Barnhill & Longo, 1978). When faced with too much stress, families tend to revert to earlier levels of development. The amount of stress a family can tolerate depends on its level of development and the types of fixations its members have.

Psychiatrists, and especially psychoanalysts, have been criticized (Szasz, 1961) for absolving people of responsibility for their actions. To say that someone "acted-out" "repressed" sexual urges through an extramarital affair is to suggest that he or she is not accountable. However, Ivan Boszormenyi-Nagy stressed the idea of ethical accountability in families. Good family relationships include behaving ethically with other family members and considering each member's welfare and interests. Boszormenyi-Nagy believed that family members owe one another loyalty and that they acquire merit by supporting each other. To the degree that parents are fair and responsible, they engender loyalty in their children; however, parents create loyalty conflicts when they ask their children to be loyal to one parent at the expense of the other (Boszormenyi-Nagy & Ulrich, 1981).

Pathologic reactions may develop from **invisible loyalties**—unconscious commitments children take on to help their families to the detriment of their own well-being. For example, a child may get sick to unite parents in concern. Invisible loyalties are problematic because they're not subject to rational scrutiny.

How Therapy Works

Analytic therapists foster insight by looking beyond behavior to the hidden motives below. Naturally, families defend against baring their innermost feelings. After all, it's a great deal to ask of anyone to expose old wounds and deep longings. Psychoanalysts deal with this problem by creating a climate of trust and by proceeding slowly. Once an atmosphere of security has been established, the analytic therapist can begin to identify projective mechanisms and bring them back into the marital relationship. Once they no longer need to rely on projective identification, partners can acknowledge and accept previously split-off parts of their own egos. The therapist helps couples begin to recognize how their present difficulties emerged from unconscious perpetuation of conflicts from their own families.

This work is painful and cannot proceed without the security offered by a supportive therapist. Nichols (1987) emphasizes the need for empathy to create a "holding environment" for the whole family.

Rather than isolate individuals from their families, psychoanalytic therapists convene families to help them learn to be independent as well as related. The case of Barry J. illustrates how the goals of psychoanalytic family therapy were implemented with a particular family.

Case Study

Three months after he went away to college, Barry J. had his first psychotic break. A brief hospital stay made it clear that Barry was unable to withstand separation from his family without decompensating;

therefore, the hospital staff recommended that he should live apart from his parents in order to help him become an independent adult. Accordingly, he was discharged to a group home for young adults and seen twice weekly in individual therapy. Unfortunately, he suffered a second breakdown and within two months was rehospitalized.

As the time for discharge from this second hospitalization approached, the ward psychiatrist decided to convene the entire family in order to discuss plans for Barry's posthospital adjustment. During this meeting it became painfully obvious that powerful forces within the family were impeding any chance for genuine separation. Barry's parents were pleasant people who separately were most engaging and helpful. Toward each other, however, they displayed an icy hatred. During those few moments in the interview when they spoke to each other, their hostility was palpable. Only their concern for Barry prevented their relationship from becoming a battleground—a battleground on which Barry feared one or both of them might be destroyed.

At the staff conference following this interview, two plans for disposition were advanced. One group, recognizing the destructive influence of the family, recommended that Barry be removed as far as possible from his parents and treated in individual psychotherapy. Only by isolating Barry from the family, they argued, was there hope that he could mature into an independent person. Others disagreed, arguing that only by treating them conjointly could the collusive bond between Barry and his parents be resolved. After lengthy discussion, the group decided to try the latter approach.

Most of the early family meetings were dominated by the parents' anxious concern about Barry: about the apartment complex where he lived, his job, his friends, how he was spending his leisure time, his clothes, his grooming—in short, about every detail of his life. Gradually and with the therapist's support, Barry was able to limit how much of his life was open to his parents' scrutiny. As they were less able to preoccupy themselves with him, they began to focus on their own relationship. As Barry became more successful at handling his own affairs, his parents became openly combative.

Following a session during which the parents' marital relationship was the primary focus, the therapist recommended that the parents come for a few couples sessions. Unable to divert their attention to Barry, the Js fought viciously, leaving no doubt that theirs was a seriously destructive relationship.

After two months of internecine warfare—during which time Barry continued to improve—Mr. and Mrs. J. sought a legal separation. Once they were separated, both parents seemed to become happier, more involved with their friends and careers, and less worried about Barry. As they released their stranglehold on their son, both parents began to develop a warmer and more genuine relationship with him. Even after the parents divorced, they continued to attend family sessions with Barry.

In Boszormenyi-Nagy's contextual therapy, the goal is a balance of fairness in the burdens and benefits of adult life. The fulfillment of the individual is seen to include giving as well as taking. Family members are helped to face and overcome irrational, unproductive guilt and to claim their **entitlements.** However, facing realistic guilt—based on actual harm done to others, even inadvertently—is seen as essential to expanding accountability within families. Thus, each person works toward self-fulfillment by asserting his or her rights and by living up to his or her obligations.

$\mathcal{T}$HERAPY

Assessment

Analysts don't postpone treatment until they've made an exhaustive study of their cases; on the contrary, they may not even arrive at a final formulation until the end of treatment. Although analytic clinicians may continue to refine their understanding over the course of treatment, therapy cannot proceed effectively without some dynamic formulation. Beginning therapists—who lack theory as well as experience—sometimes proceed on the assumption that if they merely sit back and listen, understanding will emerge.

This rarely works in family therapy. The following is an abbreviated sketch of an initial psychoanalytic evaluation of a family.

Case Study

After two sessions with the family of Sally G., who was suffering from school phobia, the therapist made a preliminary formulation of the family's dynamics. In addition to the usual descriptions of family members, the presenting problem, and their history, the formulation included assessments of the parents' object relations and the collusive, unconscious interaction of their marital relationship.

Mr. G. had been initially attracted to his wife as a libidinal object who would fulfill his sexual fantasies, including his voyeuristic propensities. Counterbalancing this was a tendency to idealize his wife. Thus, he was deeply conflicted and intensely ambivalent in his sexual relations with her.

At another level, Mr. G. had unconscious expectations that she would be the same long-suffering, self-sacrificing kind of person as his mother. Thus, he longed for motherly consolation. However, these dependent longings were threatening to his sense of masculinity, so he behaved outwardly as though he were self-sufficient and needed no one. That he had a dependent inner object inside himself was shown by his tender solicitude toward his wife and children when they were ill. But they had to be in a position of weakness and vulnerability to enable him to overcome his defenses enough for him to gratify his own dependency needs vicariously.

Mrs. G. expected marriage to provide her with an ideal father. Given this unconscious expectation, the very sexuality that attracted men to her was a threat to her wish to be cherished like a little girl. Like her husband, she was highly conflicted about sexual relations. Raised as an only child, she expected to come first. She was even jealous of her husband's warmth toward Sally and attempted to maintain distance between father and daughter by her own intense attachment to Sally.

At the level of her early selfobject images, she was a greedy, demanding little girl. Her introjection of her mother provided her with a model of how to treat a father figure. Unfortunately, what worked for her mother didn't work for her.

Thus, at an object relations level, both spouses felt themselves to be deprived children, each wanting to be taken care of without having to ask. When these magical wishes weren't granted, both seethed with resentment. Eventually, they reacted to trivial provocations with the underlying rage, and horrible quarrels erupted.

When Sally witnessed her parents' violent altercations, she became terrified that her own murderous fantasies might come true. Although her parents hated their own internalized bad-parent figures, they seemed to act them out with each other. Further enmeshing Sally in their conflict was the fact that the ego boundaries between herself and her mother were blurred—almost as though mother and daughter shared one personality.

Dynamically, Sally's staying home from school could be seen as a desperate attempt to protect her mother herself from her father's attacks and to defend both parents against her own projected murderous fantasies.

An excellent model for developing a psychodynamic focus is the work of Arnon Bentovim and Warren Kinston in Great Britain (Bentovim & Kinston, 1991), who offer a five-step strategy for formulating a focal hypothesis:

1. How does the family interact around the symptom, and how does the family interaction affect the symptom?
2. What is the function of the current symptom?
3. What disaster is feared in the family that keeps them from facing their conflicts more squarely?
4. How is the current situation linked to past trauma?
5. How would the therapist summarize the focal conflict in a short, memorable statement?

Among the metaphors used to describe psycho-analytic treatment, "depth" and "uncovering" feature prominently. All therapies aim to uncover something. Even behaviorists look to uncover unnoticed contingencies of reinforcement before switching to a directive stance. What sets analytic therapy apart is that the process of discovery is protracted and directed not only at conscious thoughts and feelings but also at fantasies and dreams.

Therapeutic Techniques

For all the complexity of psychoanalytic theory, psychoanalytic technique is relatively simple—not easy, but simple. There are four basic techniques: listening, empathy, interpretations, and analytic neutrality. Two of these—listening and analytic neutrality—may not sound terribly different from what other therapists do, but they are.

Listening is a strenuous but silent activity, rare in our culture. Most of the time we're too busy waiting to get a word in edgewise to listen more than perfunctorily. This is especially true in family therapy, where therapists feel a tremendous pressure to *do* something to help troubled families.

This is where the importance of *analytic neutrality* comes in. To establish an analytic atmosphere, it's essential to concentrate on understanding without worrying about solving problems. Change may come about as a by-product of understanding, but the analytic therapist suspends anxious involvement with outcomes. It's impossible to overestimate the importance of this frame of mind in establishing a climate of analytic exploration.

The analytic therapist resists the temptation to reassure, advise, or confront families in favor of a sustained but silent immersion in their experience. When analytic therapists do intervene, they express *empathy* in order to help family members open up, and they make *interpretations* to clarify hidden aspects of experience.

Most psychoanalytic family therapy is done with couples; conflict between partners is taken as the starting point for exploring interpersonal psychodynamics.

Take, for example, a couple who reported having an argument over the breakfast table. A systemic therapist might ask them to talk with each other about what happened, hoping to observe what they do to keep the argument from getting settled. The focus would be on behavior and interaction. A psychoanalytic therapist would be more interested in helping the partners explore their emotional reactions. Why did they get so angry? What do they want from each other? What did they expect? Where did these feelings come from? Rather than try to resolve the argument, the analytic therapist would delve into the fears and longings that lie underneath it.

The signal of intrapsychic conflict is affect. Instead of focusing on who did what to whom, analytic therapists key in on a strong feeling and use it as a starting point for detailed inquiry into its origins: "What were you feeling?" "When have you felt that way before?" "And before that?" "What do you remember?" Rather than stay on the horizontal plane of the couple's behavior, the therapist looks for openings into the vertical dimension of their inner experience.

To summarize, psychoanalytic couples therapists organize their explorations along four channels: (1) internal experience, (2) the history of that experience, (3) how the partner triggers that experience, and, finally, (4) how the context of the session and the therapist's input might contribute to what's going on between the partners. Here's a brief example.

Case Study

Having made great strides over the course of their first few couples sessions, Andrew and Gwen were all the more upset by their inability to settle a heated disagreement about buying a new car. It wasn't the car but how to pay for it that set them so angrily at odds. Andrew wanted to take money out of savings for the down payment to keep the monthly payments low. Gwen was furious. How could he even consider cutting into their savings! Didn't he understand that their mutual fund paid twice as much interest as they'd have to pay on a car loan?

Unfortunately, they were both too bent on changing the other's mind to make any real effort to understand what was going on inside it. The therapist interrupted their arguing to ask each of them what they were feeling and what they were worried about. He wasn't primarily interested in settling the disagreement—although asking about the feelings underlying an altercation is often an effective opening to understanding and compromise. Rather, he felt that the intensity of their reactions indicated that this issue touched key concerns.

Andrew was worried about the burden of monthly expenses. "*Don't you see,*" he implored, "if we don't take out enough to make a substantial down payment, we'll have to worry every month about making the payments?" Gwen was ready to dispute this, but the therapist cut her off. He was more interested in the roots of Andrew's worry than in the couple's trying to convince each other of anything.

It turned out that Andrew had a lifelong fear of not having enough money. Having enough turned out to mean not a big house and a fancy car but enough to spend on things that might be considered indulgent—nice clothes, going out to dinner, flowers, presents. Andrew connected his urge to reward himself with modest material luxuries to memories of growing up in a spartan household. His parents were children of the Depression who thought that things like going out to dinner and buying clothes except when absolutely necessary were frivolous and wasteful.

At a deeper level, Andrew's memories of austerity were a screen for his never having gotten the attention and affection he craved from his rather reserved mother.[2] And so he'd learned to soothe himself with a new shirt or fancy dinner at times when he was feeling low. One of Gwen's chief attractions

was her giving and expressive nature. She was openly affectionate and almost always happy to indulge Andrew's wish to buy something for himself.

Gwen connected her anxiety about having a cushion against the unexpected to memories of her father as an unreliable breadwinner. Unlike Andrew's parents, hers spent freely. They went out to dinner three or four times a week and took expensive vacations, and everyone in the family wore nice clothes. Although her father was a free spender, Gwen remembered him as lacking the foresight to invest wisely or to expand his business beyond its modest success. Although it had never been part of her conscious memories, it seemed that although her father lavished attention and affection on her, he never really took her seriously as a person. He treated her, in the familiar phrase, like "Daddy's little girl," as adorable—and insubstantial—as a kitten. That's why she was so attracted to what she saw as Andrew's serious and self-disciplined nature—and his high regard for her.

How did these two trigger such virulent reactions in each other? Not only did Gwen's anxious need to have money in the bank conflict with Andrew's need to have money to spend, but they each felt betrayed by the other. Part of Gwen's unconscious bargain with Andrew was that she could count on him to be a secure, steady pillar and to build for the future. Part of his unconscious expectations of her were that she would indulge him. No wonder they were so reactive to each other on this issue.

And the therapist's role in all this? On reflection, he realized that he'd been a little too anxious to smooth things over with this couple. Out of his own desire to see marital happiness, he'd controlled the level of conflict in the sessions, intervening actively as a peacemaker. As a result, the couple's progress had come at a price. Deep longings and resentments had been pushed aside rather than explored and resolved. Perhaps, the therapist thought, he'd picked up the couple's fears of facing their own anger.

What use should a therapist make of such countertransferential reactions? Should he disclose his feelings? To say that countertransference may contain useful information isn't to say that it's oracular.

---

[2] In Kohut's terms, Andrew's mother provided an inadequate mirroring selfobject function.

Perhaps the most useful thing to do is look to countertransference for hypotheses that need confirming evidence from the patients' side of the experience. In this case, the therapist acknowledged his sense that he'd been trying too hard to smooth things over, and he asked Gwen and Andrew whether they, too, were a little afraid to open up their anger.

Like many descriptions of clinical work, this one may seem a little pat. How did we get so quickly from arguing about buying a car to hunger for a mirroring selfobject and someone to idealize? Part of the explanation lies in the inevitably condensed account. But it's also important to recognize that one of the things that enables psychoanalysts to see beneath the surface of things is knowing where to look.

Sessions begin with the therapist inviting family members to discuss current concerns, thoughts, and feelings. In subsequent meetings, the therapist might begin by saying nothing or perhaps "Where would you like to begin today?" The therapist then leans back and lets the family talk. Questions are limited to requests for amplification and clarification. "Could you tell me more about that?" "Have the two of you discussed how you feel about this?"

When initial associations and spontaneous interactions dry up, the therapist probes gently, eliciting history, people's thoughts and feelings, and their ideas about family members' perspectives. "What does your father think about your problems? How would he explain them?" This technique underscores the analytic therapist's interest in assumptions and projections. Particular interest is paid to childhood memories. The following vignette shows how transitions are made from the present to the past.

Case Study

Among their major disappointments in each other, Mr. and Mrs. S. both complained that the other one "doesn't take care of me when I'm sick or listen to my complaints at the end of the day." Not only did they share the perception of the other's lack of "mothering," but they both steadfastly maintained that they *were* supportive and understanding.

Mrs. S.'s complaint was typical: "Yesterday was an absolute nightmare. The baby was sick and fussy, and I had a miserable cold. Everything was twice as hard, and I had twice as much to do. All day long I was looking forward to John's coming home. But when he finally did, he didn't seem to care how I felt. He only listened to me for a minute before starting to tell me some dumb story about his office." Mr. S. responded with a similar account but with the roles reversed.

At this point the therapist intervened to ask both spouses to describe their relationships with their mothers. What emerged were two very different but revealing histories.

Mr. S.'s mother was a taciturn woman, for whom self-reliance, personal sacrifice, and unremitting struggle were supreme virtues. Though she loved her children, she withheld indulgence and affection, lest they become "spoiled." Nevertheless, Mr. S. craved his mother's attention and constantly sought it. Naturally, he was often rebuffed. A particularly painful memory was of a time he came home in tears after getting beaten up by a bully at school. Instead of the consoling he hoped for, his mother scolded him for "acting like a baby." Over the years he had learned to protect himself from these rebuffs by developing a façade of independence and strength.

With the second significant woman in his life, his wife, Mr. S. maintained his rigid defensiveness. He never talked about his problems, but because he continued to yearn for compassionate understanding, he resented his wife for not drawing him out. His own failure to risk rejection by asking for support served as a self-fulfilling prophecy, confirming his expectation: *She doesn't care about me.*

Mrs. S.'s background was quite different. Her parents were indulgent and demonstrative. They doted on their only child, communicating their love by expressing constant, anxious concern for her well-being. When she was a little girl, the slightest bump or bruise was an occasion for lavish expressions of concern. She came to marriage used to talking about herself and her problems. At first

Mr. S. was enchanted. *Here is someone who really cares about feelings,* he thought. But when he discovered that she didn't ask him to talk about his own concerns, he became resentful and progressively less sympathetic. This convinced her: *He doesn't care about me.*

After the roots of current family conflicts have been uncovered, interpretations are made about how family members continue to reenact past and often distorted images from childhood. The data for such interpretations come from transference reactions to the therapist or to other family members, as well as from childhood memories. Psychoanalytic therapists deal less with recollections of the past than with reenactments of the past's influence in the present.

Don Catherall (1992) described a very useful process for interpreting projective identification in couples therapy. First, it's important to understand that projective identification isn't some mysterious process in which quantities of one person's experience are passed to the other completely outside of awareness. Rather, the feelings are communicated and provoked by subtle but recognizable signals—though they are usually not focused on. You may have experienced projective identification yourself if you've ever been around someone who was behaving seductively but then acted shocked when you made an advance.

The first step in working with projective identification in couples therapy is to interrupt repetitive squabbling, which is likely to mask any expression of the partners' real feelings. Couples caught up in recurring patterns of conflict and misunderstanding are colluding to avoid feelings of vulnerability. Once a couple's quarreling is blocked, the therapist can explore what the individuals are feeling.

Catherall recommends focusing first on what the *recipient* of the projection is feeling. Once that person's feelings have been clarified, he or she can be helped to communicate those feelings to the partner. To avoid provoking defensiveness, the recipient describing the formerly disavowed feelings is coached to describe only the feelings themselves, not what the projecting partner did to provoke them. Meanwhile,

the *projecting partner* is told just to listen and not comment. When the recipient has finished, the projector is directed to feed back what he or she understood the partner to be saying. This encourages the projecting partner to assume the recipient's point of view and therefore makes it difficult to block identification with those feelings.

The projecting partner is encouraged to empathize with the recipient. Hopefully, at this point, the couple can stop trading accusations and start trying to understand how the other feels. Ideally, this sharing of feelings will help bring the partners closer—to understanding, and to each other.

Case Study

To illustrate, Catherall cites the example of David and Sheila. The more anxious David was to have sex with Sheila, the more sensitive he was to any hint of rejection. He would respond to her disinterest by withdrawing, and they would remain distant until Sheila reached out. Sheila ended up feeling the same unloved feelings that David had felt when his mother shut him out. Meanwhile, David felt powerless with Sheila, just as she had felt with an uncle who had molested her. Each, in other words, was experiencing concordant identifications stimulated through a mutual process of projective identification.

The therapist pursued Sheila's feelings by inquiring what it was like for her when David was so distant. Her initial answer was that it made her angry, but the therapist asked what it made her angry about, and what was she feeling prior to getting angry. Sheila was then able to identify feelings of being unloved, uncared for, and generally lonely. These were the feelings that had been stimulated by David's projective identification, and they were feelings that Sheila would normally disavow by becoming angry and then cold.

Then the therapist asked Sheila to talk with David about what it was like for her to feel lonely and unloved. The therapist was careful to keep Sheila focused on herself and what she was feeling, not on David and what he may have done to cause those feelings. Now that he was not being blamed, David was able to empathize and identify with the feelings of loneliness that Sheila was describing. When the therapist asked him if he knew what it was like to feel that way, David was finally able to talk more directly about the painful feelings that he had been warding off by projecting them onto Sheila.

Psychoanalytic family therapists emphasize that much of what is hidden in family dialogues is not consciously withheld but rather repressed into unconsciousness. The approach to this material is guarded by resistance often manifested in the form of transference. This case study illustrates the interpretation of resistance.

Case Study

Mr. and Mrs. Z. had endured ten years of a loveless relationship in order to preserve the fragile security that marriage offered them. Mrs. Z.'s unexpected and uncharacteristic affair forced the couple to acknowledge the problems in their relationship, and so they consulted a family therapist.

Although they could no longer deny the existence of conflict, both spouses exhibited major resistance to confronting their problems openly. In the first session, both partners said that married life had been "more or less okay"; that Mrs. Z. had some kind of "midlife crisis"; and that it was she who needed therapy.

This request for individual therapy was seen as a resistance to avoid the painful examination of the marriage, and the therapist said so. "It seems, Mr. Z., that you'd rather blame your wife than consider how the two of you might both be contributing to your difficulties. And you, Mrs. Z., seem to prefer accepting all the guilt in order to avoid confronting your husband with your dissatisfaction."

Accepting the therapist's interpretation and agreeing to examine their relationship deprived the couple of one form of resistance, as though an escape hatch had been closed. In the next few sessions both partners attacked each other vituperatively, but they talked only about her affair rather than about problems in the relationship. These arguments weren't productive because whenever Mr. Z. felt anxious he attacked his wife, and whenever she felt angry she became guilty and depressed.

Sensing that their fighting was unproductive, the therapist said, "It's clear that you've put each other through a lot of unhappiness and you're both quite bitter. But unless you get down to talking about specific problems in your marriage, there's little chance that you'll get anywhere."

Thus focused, Mrs. Z. timidly ventured that she'd never enjoyed sex with her husband and wished that he would take more time with foreplay. He snapped back, "Okay, so sex wasn't so great. Is that any reason to throw away ten years of marriage and start whoring around?" At this, Mrs. Z. buried her face in her hands and sobbed uncontrollably. After she regained her composure, the therapist intervened, again confronting the couple with their resistance: "It seems, Mr. Z., that when you get upset, you attack. What makes you so anxious about discussing sex?" Following this the couple was able to talk about their feelings about sex in their marriage until near the end of the session. At this point, Mr. Z. again lashed out at his wife, calling her a whore and a bitch.

Mrs. Z. began the following session by saying that she'd been depressed and upset, crying off and on all week. "I feel so guilty," she sobbed. "You *should* feel guilty!" retorted her husband. Once again, the therapist intervened: "You use your wife's affair as a club. Are you still afraid to discuss problems in your marriage? And you, Mrs. Z., cover your anger with depression. What is it that you're angry about? What was missing in the marriage? What did you want?"

This pattern continued for several more sessions. The spouses who had avoided discussing or even thinking about their problems for ten years used a variety of resistances to veer away from them in therapy. The therapist persisted in pointing out their resistance and urging them to talk about specific complaints.

Psychoanalytic therapists endeavor to foster insight and understanding; they also urge clients to consider what they're going to do about the problems they discuss. This effort—part of the process of *working through*—is more prominent in family therapy than in individual therapy. Boszormenyi-Nagy, for example, believed that family members should not only be made aware of their motivations but also held accountable for their behavior. In contextual therapy, Boszormenyi-Nagy (1987) pointed out that the therapist must help people face the stifling expectations involved in invisible loyalties and then help them find more positive ways of making loyalty payments in the family ledger. What this boils down to is developing a balance of fairness.

CURRENT STATUS OF THE MODEL

Too many family therapists neglect psychology in general and psychoanalytic theory in specific. Regardless of what other approach a therapist uses, the writings of psychoanalytically informed clinicians are a rich resource.

Having said this, we also wish to make a cautionary point. Doctrinaire psychoanalytic family therapies are powerful in the hands of trained psychoanalysts. However, many therapists who get discouraged with the usual contentious family dialogues gravitate to psychoanalytic methods as a way to cut through the defensive wrangling. Interrupting a family's arguments to explore the individuals' feelings is an excellent way to block arguments. If, however, therapists make themselves overly central (by directing all conversation through themselves) or if they overemphasize individuals and neglect family interactions, then the power of family therapy—addressing relationship problems directly—may be lost. Interrupting defensive sparring to get to the hopes and fears that lie beneath is all to the good. But unless these interrogatories are followed by unstructured interchanges among family members themselves, these explorations may produce the illusion of change only as long as the therapist is present to act as detective and referee.

Psychoanalytic therapists have generally resisted empirical attempts to evaluate their work. Because symptom reduction isn't the goal, it can't serve as the measure of success. And since the presence or absence of unconscious conflict isn't apparent to outside observers, whether an analysis is successful depends on subjective judgment. Psychoanalytic clinicians consider the therapist's observations a valid means of evaluating theory and treatment.

The following quotation from the Blancks (1972) illustrates this point. Speaking of Margaret Mahler's ideas, they wrote,

> Clinicians who employ her theories technically question neither the methodology nor the findings, for they can confirm them clinically, a form of validation that meets as closely as possible the experimentalist's insistence upon replication as criterion of the scientific method (p. 675).

Another example of this point of view can be found in the writing of Robert Langs. "The ultimate test of a therapist's formulation," says Langs (1982), "lies in the use of the therapist's impressions as a basis for intervention" (p. 186). What then determines the validity and effectiveness of these interventions? Langs doesn't hesitate: The patient's reactions, conscious and unconscious, constitute the ultimate litmus test. "True validation involves responses from the patient in both the cognitive and interpersonal spheres."

Is the ultimate test of therapy then the patient's reactions? Yes and no. First, patients' reactions are open to interpretation—especially because validation is sought not only in manifest responses but also in unconsciously encoded derivatives. Moreover, this point of view doesn't take into account the changes in patients' lives that occur outside the consulting room. Therapists occasionally report on the outcome of psychoanalytic family therapy but mostly in uncontrolled case studies. One such report is Dicks's (1967) survey of the outcome of psychoanalytic couples therapy at the Tavistock Clinic, in which he rated as having successfully treated 72.8 percent of a random sample of cases.

Summary

1. Psychoanalytically trained clinicians were among the first to practice family therapy, but when they began treating families most of them traded in-depth psychology for systems theory. Since the mid-1980s there's been a resurgence of interest in psychodynamics among family therapists, an interest dominated by object relations theory and self psychology. In this chapter we've sketched the main points of these theories and shown how they're relevant to a psychoanalytic family therapy, integrating depth psychology and systems theory. A few practitioners (e.g., Kirschner & Kirschner, 1986; Nichols, 1987; Slipp, 1984) have combined elements of both; some have developed more frankly psychoanalytic approaches (notably Sander, 1989; Scharff & Scharff, 1987); none has achieved a true synthesis.

2. The essential aim of psychoanalytic therapy is to help people understand their basic motives and resolve conflicts over expressing those yearnings in a healthy fashion. Freudians emphasize libidinal and aggressive impulses, self psychologists focus on the longing for appreciation, and object relations therapists concentrate on the need for secure attachment. But all are united in the belief that couples and families can be helped to get along better if their individual members understand and begin to resolve their own personal conflicts.

3. In practice, psychoanalytic family therapists focus less on the group and their interactions and more on individuals and their feelings. Exploring these feelings is aided by psychoanalytic theory (or theories) that helps clinicians understand the basic underlying issues that all people struggle with.

Questions to Consider

1. To get an idea of how difficult it is to maintain a neutral, analytic attitude, the next time a friend tells you a story or a problem, try to listen with as few questions and as few of your own comments as possible. What distractions from what the other person was saying did you find yourself tempted to pursue?

2. Describe some situations in which resistance might not be just an impediment but a clue to important vulnerabilities and past unhappy experiences.

3. In a sample of clinical material that includes details, analyze the therapist's interventions to find examples of where the therapist might be trying to distract the client(s) from anxiety or pulling for some reassuring response from the client(s). For example, when some therapists make reflections, they seem to be looking for the clients to appreciate that the therapist is being understanding.

4. Can you make sense of the notion that there is such a thing as two-person psychology? Psychoanalytic family therapists claim, for example, that projective identification is an example of two-person psychology. Do you think there is such a thing or just two separate personalities interacting?

5. For a few days, keep track of the extent to which your mood varies with the quality of positive selfobject experiences in your life.

Key Concepts

contextual therapy Boszormenyi-Nagy's model that includes an appreciation of relational ethics.

delineations Parental acts and statements that express the parents' image of their children; may be objective or distorted.

entitlement Boszormenyi-Nagy's term for the amount of merit a person accrues for behaving in an ethical manner toward others.

false self Winnicott's term for a defensive façade that comes to dominate some people's dealings with others.

fixation Partial arrest of attachment or mode of behavior from an early stage of development.

good-enough mothering Winnicott's term for the average-expectable parenting, which is sufficient to nurture a reasonably healthy child.

idealization A tendency to exaggerate the virtues of someone; part of the normal developmental process in children's relationships to their parents and in intimate partnerships.

identification Not merely imitation but appropriation of traits of an admired other.

internal objects Mental images and fantasies of oneself and others; formed by early interactions with caregivers.

introjection A primitive form of identification; taking in aspects of other people, which then become part of the self-image.

invisible loyalties Boszormenyi-Nagy's term for unconscious commitments that children take on to help their families.

mirroring Kohut's term for the expression of understanding and appreciation—not praise but appreciation of what the other is feeling.

narcissism Self-regard. The exaggerated self-regard most people equate with narcissism is pathological narcissism.

object relations Internalized images of self and others based on early parent–child interactions that determine a person's mode of relationship to other people.

object relations theory Psychoanalytic theory derived from Melanie Klein and developed by the British School (Bion, Fairbairn, Guntrip, and Winnicott) that emphasizes relationships and attachment rather than libidinal and aggressive drives as the key issues of human concern.

projective identification A defense mechanism whereby unwanted aspects of the self are attributed to another person and that person is induced to behave in accordance with these projected attributes.

regression Return to a less mature level of functioning in the face of stress.

selfobject Kohut's term for a person related to not as a separate individual but as an extension of the self.

self psychology Kohut's version of psychoanalysis that emphasizes the need for attachment and appreciation rather than sex and aggression.

separation–individuation The process whereby the infant begins, at about two months, to draw apart from the symbiotic bond with mother and develop his or her autonomous functioning.

transference Distorted emotional reactions to present relationships based on unresolved early family relations.

unconscious Memories, feelings, and impulses of which a person is unaware. Often used as a noun, but more appropriately limited to use as an adjective.

Recommended Readings

Ackerman, N. W. 1966. *Treating the troubled family.* New York: Basic Books.

Boszormenyi-Nagy, I. 1987. *Foundations of contextual therapy.* New York: Brunner/Mazel.

Dicks, H. V. 1967. *Marital tensions.* New York: Basic Books.

Donovan, J. M. 2004. *Short-term object relations couples therapy: The five step model.* New York: Brunner-Routledge.

Mitchell, S. A. 1998. *Relational concepts in psychoanalysis.* Cambridge, MA: Harvard University Press.

Nichols, M. P. 1987. *The self in the system.* New York: Brunner/Mazel.

Sander, F. M. 1989. Marital conflict and psychoanalytic theory in the middle years. In *The middle years: New psychoanalytic perspectives,* J. Oldham and R. Liebert, eds. New Haven: Yale University Press.

Scharff, D., and Scharff, J. S. 1987. *Object relations family therapy.* New York: Jason Aronson.

Stern, M. 1985. *The interpersonal world of the infant.* New York: Basic Books.

References

Ackerman, N. W. 1958. *The psychodynamics of family life.* New York: Basic Books.

Ackerman, N. W. 1966. *Treating the troubled family.* New York: Basic Books.

Barnhill, L. R., and Longo, D. 1978. Fixation and regression in the family life cycle. *Family Process. 17:* 469–478.

Bentovim, A., and Kinston, W. 1991. Focal family therapy. In *Handbook of family therapy,* Vol. II, A. S. Gurman and D. P. Kniskern, eds. New York: Brunner/ Mazel.

Blanck, G., and Blanck, R. 1972. Toward a psychoanalytic developmental psychology. *Journal of the American Psychoanalytic Association. 20:* 668–710.

Blum, H. P. 1987. Shared fantasy and reciprocal identification: General considerations and gender–disorder. In *Unconscious fantasy: Myth and reality,* H. P. Blum et al., eds. New York: International Universities Press.

Boszormenyi-Nagy, I. 1967. Relational modes and meaning. In *Family therapy and disturbed families,* G. H. Zuk and I. Boszormenyi-Nagy, eds. Palo Alto: Science and Behavior Books.

Boszormenyi-Nagy, I. 1987. *Foundations of contextual therapy.* New York: Brunner/Mazel.

Boszormenyi-Nagy, I., Grunebaum, J., and Ulrich, D. 1991. Contextual therapy. In *Handbook of family therapy,* Vol. II, A. S. Gurman and D. P. Kniskern, eds. New York: Brunner/Mazel.

Boszormenyi-Nagy, I., and Ulrich, D. N. 1981. Contextual family therapy. In *Handbook of family therapy,* A. S. Gurman and D. P. Kniskern, eds. New York: Brunner/Mazel.

Bowen, M. 1965. Family psychotherapy with schizophrenia in the hospital and in private practice. In *Intensive family therapy,* I. Boszormenyi-Nagy and J. L. Framo, eds. New York: Harper & Row.

Bowlby, J. 1969. *Attachment and loss,* Vol. 1: *Attachment.* New York: Basic Books.

Burlingham, D. T. 1951. Present trends in handling the mother-child relationship during the therapeutic process. *Psychoanalytic study of the child.* New York: International Universities Press.

Catherall, D. R. 1992. Working with projective identification in couples. *Family Process. 31:* 355–367.

Dicks, H. V. 1963. Object relations theory and marital studies. *British Journal of Medical Psychology. 36:* 125–129.

Dicks, H. V. 1967. *Marital tensions.* New York: Basic Books.

Framo, J. L. 1970. Symptoms from a family transactional viewpoint. In *Family therapy in transition,* N. W. Ackerman, ed. Boston: Little, Brown.

Freud, S. 1905. Fragment of an analysis of a case of hysteria. *Collected papers.* New York: Basic Books, 1959.

Freud, S. 1909. Analysis of a phobia in a five-year-old boy. *Collected papers,* Vol. III. New York: Basic Books, 1959.

Freud, S. 1921. Group psychology and the analysis of the ego. *Standard edition. 17:* 1–22. London: Hogarth Press, 1955.

Giovacchini, P. 1958. Mutual adaptation in various object relations. *International Journal of Psychoanalysis. 39:* 547–554.

Guntrip, H. 1969. *Schizoid phenomena, object relations theory and the self.* New York: International Universities Press.

Jackson, D. D. 1967. The individual and the larger context. *Family Process. 6:* 139–147.

Jacobson, E. 1954. *The self and the object world.* New York: International Universities Press.

Johnson, A., and Szurek, S. 1952. The genesis of antisocial acting out in children and adults. *Psycho-analytic Quarterly. 21:* 323–343.

Kirschner, D., and Kirschner, S. 1986. *Comprehensive family therapy: An integration of systemic and psychodynamic treatment models.* New York: Brunner/Mazel.

Klein, M. 1946. Notes on some schizoid mechanisms. *International Journal of Psycho-Analysis. 27:* 99–110.

Kohut, H. 1971. *The analysis of the self.* New York: International Universities Press.

Kohut, H. 1977. *The restoration of the self.* New York: International Universities Press.

Langs, R. 1982. *Psychotherapy: A basic text.* New York: Jason Aronson.

Lidz, T., Cornelison, A., Fleck, S. 1965. *Schizophrenia and the family.* New York: International Universities Press.

Mahler, M. S. 1952. On child psychosis and schizophrenia: Autistic and symbiotic infantile psychoses. *Psychoanalytic Study of the Child, 7:* 286–305.

Mahler, M., Pine, F., and Bergman, A. 1975. *The psychological birth of the human infant.* New York: Basic Books.

Meissner, W. W. 1978. The conceptualization of marriage and family dynamics from a psychoanalytic perspective. In *Marriage and marital therapy,* T. J. Paolino and B. S. McCrady, eds. New York: Brunner/ Mazel.

Minuchin, S. 1989. Personal communication. Quoted from *Institutionalizing madness,* J. Elizur and S. Minuchin, eds. New York: Basic Books.

Mittlemann, B. 1948. The concurrent analysis of married couples. *Psychoanalytic Quarterly. 17:* 182–197.

Nichols, M. P. 1987. *The self in the system.* New York: Brunner/Mazel.

Oberndorf, C. P. 1938. Psychoanalysis of married couples. *Psychoanalytic Review. 25:* 453–475.

Sager, C. J. 1981. Couples therapy and marriage contracts. In *Handbook of family therapy,* A. S. Gurman and D. P. Kniskern, eds. New York: Brunner/Mazel.

Sander, F. M. 1979. *Individual and family therapy: Toward an integration.* New York: Jason Aronson.

Sander, F. M. 1989. Marital conflict and psychoanalytic therapy in the middle years. In *The middle years: New psychoanalytic perspectives,* J. Oldham and R. Liebert, eds. New Haven: Yale University Press.

Scharff, D., and Scharff, J. 1987. *Object relations family therapy.* New York: Jason Aronson.

Shapiro, R. L. 1968. Action and family interaction in adolescence. In *Modern psychoanalysis,* J. Marmor, ed. New York: Basic Books.

Shapiro, R. L. 1979. Family dynamics and object relations theory. In *Adolescent psychiatry,* S. C. Feinstein and P. L. Giovacchini, eds. Chicago: University of Chicago Press.

Skynner, A. C. R. 1976. *Systems of family and marital psychotherapy.* New York: Brunner/Mazel.

Slipp, S. 1984. *Object relations: A dynamic bridge between individual and family treatment.* New York: Jason Aronson.

Slipp, S. 1988. *Technique and practice of object relations family therapy.* New York: Jason Aronson.

Spitz, R., and Wolf, K. 1946. Anaclitic depression: An inquiry into the genesis of psychiatric conditions early in childhood. *Psychoanalytic Study of the Child. 2:* 313–342.

Stein, M. 1956. The marriage bond. *Psychoanalytic Quarterly. 25:* 238–259.

Stierlin, H. 1977. *Psychoanalysis and family therapy.* New York: Jason Aronson.

Sullivan, H. S. 1953. *The interpersonal theory of psychiatry.* New York: Norton.

Szasz, T. S. 1961. *The myth of mental illness.* New York: Hoeber-Harper.

Vogel, E. F., and Bell, N. W. 1960. The emotionally disturbed as the family scapegoat. In *The family,* N. W. Bell and E. F. Vogel, eds. Glencoe, IL: Free Press.

Winnicott, D. W. 1965a. *The maturational process and the facilitating environment.* New York: International Universities Press.

Winnicott, D. W. 1965b. *The maturational process and the facilitating environment: Studies in the theory of emotional development.* New York: International Universities Press.

Wynne, L. C. 1965. Some indications and contradictions for exploratory family therapy. In *Intensive family therapy,* I. Boszormenyi-Nagy and J. L. Framo, eds. New York: Harper & Row.

Wynne, L., Ryckoff, I., Day, J., and Hirsch, S. 1958. Pseudomutuality in the family relations of schizophrenics. *Psychiatry. 21:* 205–220.

Zinner, J. 1976. The implications of projective identification for marital interaction. In *Contemporary marriage: Structure, dynamics, and therapy,* H. Grunebaum and J. Christ, eds. Boston: Little, Brown.

Zinner, J., and Shapiro, R. 1972. Projective identification as a mode of perception and behavior in families of adolescents. *International Journal of Psycho-Analysis. 53:* 523–530.

10

Cognitive-Behavior Family Therapy

When they first began working with families, behavior therapists applied learning theory to train parents in behavior modification and teach couples communication skills. These approaches proved effective with discrete, behavioral problems and well-motivated clients. Anchored as they were in individual psychology, however, behavior therapists had little appreciation of the ways in which misbehavior and poor communication were embedded in family systems.

Behaviorists generally worked in academic settings and, despite developing an armamentarium of useful techniques, remained relatively isolated from mainstream family therapy. The past ten years, however, have seen sweeping changes in behavioral family therapy, with increasing sophistication about family dynamics and the incorporation of cognitive principles.

EVOLUTION OF THE MODEL

Behavior therapy is a descendant of the investigations of Ivan Pavlov, the Russian physiologist whose work on conditioned reflexes led to the development of **classical conditioning.** In classical conditioning, an *unconditioned stimulus (UCS),* such as food, which leads to an *unconditioned response (UCR),* such as salivation, is paired with a *conditioned stimulus (CS),*

such as a bell. The result is that the conditioned stimulus begins to evoke the same response (Pavlov, 1932). Subsequently, John B. Watson used classical conditioning to experimentally induce a phobia in "Little Albert" (Watson & Raynor, 1920), while Mary Cover Jones successfully resolved a similar phobia in the case of "Peter" (Jones, 1924).

In 1948 Joseph Wolpe introduced **systematic desensitization,** with which he achieved great success in the treatment of phobias. According to Wolpe (1948), anxiety is a response of the autonomic nervous system acquired through classical conditioning. Systematic desensitization deconditions anxiety through *reciprocal inhibition* by pairing responses incompatible with anxiety to previously anxiety-arousing stimuli. For example, if Indiana Jones were frightened of snakes, Wolpe would teach Dr. Jones deep muscle relaxation and then have him imagine approaching a snake in gradual steps. Each time Indy became anxious, he would be told to relax. In this way the anxiety evoked by imagining snakes would be systematically extinguished.

Systematic desensitization proved to be even more effective when it included actual practice in approaching the feared situation (*in vivo desensitization*).

Classical conditioning was applied to family problems primarily through the treatment of anxiety-based disorders, including agoraphobia and sexual

flooding is better

183

dysfunction, pioneered by Wolpe (1958) and later elaborated by Masters and Johnson (1970). Effective behavioral treatments for enuresis were also developed using classical conditioning (Lovibond, 1963).

By far the greatest influence on behavioral therapy came from B. F. Skinner's **operant conditioning.** The term *operant* refers to voluntary responses, as opposed to reflexes. The frequency of operant responses is controlled by their consequences. **Reinforcement** is any event, behavior, or object that increases the rate of a particular response. Responses that are *positively reinforced* will repeat more frequently; those that are punished or ignored will be *extinguished.*

The operant conditioner carefully observes target behavior and quantifies its frequency and rate. Then, to complete a **functional analysis of behavior,** the consequences of the behavior are noted to determine the **contingencies of reinforcement.**

For example, someone interested in a child's temper tantrums would begin by observing when they occurred and what the consequences were. A typical finding might be that the child throws a tantrum whenever his parents deny his requests and that the parents give in if the tantrums are prolonged. Thus, the parents would be reinforcing the very behavior they least wanted.

To eliminate the tantrums, they would be taught to ignore them. Moreover, they would be told that giving in, even occasionally, would perpetuate the tantrums because behavior that is *intermittently reinforced* is the most difficult to extinguish. If the child were aware of the contingencies, he might think, "They're not giving in now, but if I keep fussing they eventually will—if not this time, then the next."

Operant conditioning is particularly effective with children because parents have control over reinforcers and punishments. Boardman (1962) trained parents in the effective use of punishment to deal with the aggressive antisocial behavior of their five-year-old.

Wolpe (1958) described how to use parents as cotherapists in anxiety management. Risley and Wolf (1967) trained parents in the operant reinforcement of speech in their autistic children.

In technical terms, these parents were trained to eliminate the contingencies that maintained deviant behavior and to reinforce behavior patterns that were incompatible with the deviant behavior (Falloon, 1991). In plain English, they were taught to ignore bad behavior and reward good behavior.

Although no single figure was responsible for the development of behavioral family therapy, three leaders played dominant roles: a psychologist, Gerald Patterson; a psychiatrist, Robert Liberman; and a social worker, Richard Stuart.

Gerald Patterson, at the University of Oregon, was the most influential figure in developing behavioral parent training. Patterson and his colleagues developed methods for sampling family interactions in the home, trained parents in **social learning theory,** developed programmed workbooks (e.g., Patterson, 1971), and worked out strategies for eliminating undesirable behavior and substituting desirable responses. Among others prominent in this field are Anthony Graziano, Rex Forehand, Daniel and Susan O'Leary, and Roger McAuley.

The second major figure in the development of behavioral family therapy was Robert Liberman. In his 1970 paper "Behavioral Approaches to Family and Couple Therapy," he outlined an operant approach to the family problems of four adult patients with depression, intractable headaches, social inadequacy, and marital discord. In addition to using contingency management of mutual reinforcers, Liberman introduced the use of **role rehearsal** and **modeling** (Bandura & Walters, 1963) to family therapy.

The third major influence on behavioral family therapy was the **contingency contracting** of Richard Stuart (1969). Rather than focus on how the undesired behavior of one family member could be reduced, Stuart focused on how the exchange of positive behavior could be maximized using **reinforcement reciprocity.**

During the 1970s behavioral family therapy evolved into three major packages: parent training, behavioral couples therapy, and sex therapy. At present the leading figures in behavioral couples therapy include Robert Weiss, Richard Stuart, Michael Crowe, Ian Falloon, and Gayola Margolin.

Recently, there has been a rapprochement between stimulus-response models and cognitive theories (e.g., Dattilio, 1998; Epstein, Schlesinger, & Dryden, 1988). **Cognitive-behavior therapy** refers to those approaches inspired by the work of Albert Ellis (1962) and Aaron Beck (1976) that emphasize the need for attitude change to promote and maintain behavioral modification. Among the leaders in cognitive-behavior family therapy are Donald Baucom at the University of North Carolina, Norman Epstein at the University of Maryland, and Frank Dattilio, who is affiliated with Harvard and the University of Pennsylvania.

*T*HE BASIC MODEL

The central premise of behavior therapy is that behavior is maintained by its consequences. Consequences that accelerate behavior are called *reinforcers;* those that decelerate behavior are known as *punishers.*

Some responses may not be recognized as operants—something done to get something—because people aren't aware of the reinforcing payoffs. For example, whining is usually reinforced by attention, although the people doing the reinforcing may not realize it. In fact, a variety of undesired behaviors, including nagging and temper tantrums, are often reinforced by attention. Thus, family problems are frequently maintained under conditions that are counterintuitive.

Extinction occurs when no reinforcement follows a response. Ignoring behavior you don't like is, of course, often the best response. The reason some people fail to credit this is that withholding a response rarely leads to immediate cessation of unwanted behavior, because most behavior problems have been intermittently reinforced and therefore take time to extinguish.

Despite the mechanistic sound of "schedules of reinforcement" and "controlling behavior," behavior

therapists have increasingly become aware that people not only act but also think and feel. This recognition has led to efforts to integrate stimulus–response behaviorism (Skinner, 1953) with cognitive theories (Mahoney, 1977). The central tenet of the cognitive approach is that our interpretation of other people's behavior affects the way we respond to them. Among the most troublesome of automatic thoughts are those based on *arbitrary inference,* distorted conclusions shaped by a person's **schemas,** or core beliefs about the world and how it functions. What makes these underlying beliefs problematic is that although they are generally not conscious, they bias how we respond to everything and everyone.

As behavior therapists shifted their attention from individuals to family relationships, they came to rely on Thibaut and Kelley's (1959) **theory of social exchange,** according to which people strive to maximize *rewards* and minimize *costs* in relationships. In a successful relationship, partners work to maximize mutual rewards. By contrast, in unsuccessful relationships, the partners are too busy trying to protect themselves from getting hurt to consider ways to make each other happy. According to Thibaut and Kelley, behavior exchanges follow a norm of reciprocity over time, so that aversive or positive stimulation from one person tends to produce reciprocal behavior from the other. Kindness begets kindness, and the opposite is also true.

Normal Family Development

According to **behavior exchange theory** (Thibaut & Kelley, 1959), a good relationship is one in which giving and getting are balanced—or in the theory's terms, there is a high ratio of benefits to costs. Put as generally as this, little is added to commonsense notions of family satisfaction. But behaviorists have begun to spell out the details of what makes for relationship satisfaction.

For example, Weiss and Isaac (1978) found that affection, communication, and child care are the most important elements in marital satisfaction. Earlier, Wills, Weiss, and Patterson (1974) found that unpleasant behavior reduced marital satisfaction more than pleasant behavior increased it. A good relationship, then, is one in which there is an exchange of positive responses and, even more important, minimal unpleasantness. Another way of putting this is that good relationships are under *positive reinforcement control.*

Having good communication skills—being able to talk, especially about problems—is considered by behaviorists to be the most important feature of good relationships (Gottman, Markman, & Notarius, 1977; Jacobson, Waldron, & Moore, 1980). (It's also the most easily observed feature of relationships.)

In time, all couples run into conflict, and therefore, a critical skill in maintaining family harmony is conflict resolution (Gottman & Krokoff, 1989). Healthy families aren't problem free, but they have the ability to cope with problems when they arise.

In a good relationship, partners are able to address conflicts. They focus on issues and keep them in perspective, and they discuss specific behaviors of concern to them. They describe their own feelings and request changes in the behavior of others, rather than just criticizing and complaining. "I've been feeling lonely and I wish you and I could go out more often" is more likely to get a positive response than "You never care what I want! All you care about is yourself!"

Some people assume that good relationships will evolve naturally if people love each other. Behaviorists emphasize the need to develop relationship skills. Good marriages, they believe, aren't made in heaven but are a product of learning effective coping behavior. The late Neil Jacobson (1981) described a good relationship as one in which the partners maintain a high rate of rewards.

> Successful couples . . . expand their reinforcement power by frequently acquiring new domains for positive exchange. Spouses who depend on a limited quantity and variety of reinforcers are bound to suffer the ill effects of satiation. As a result, over time their interaction becomes depleted of its prior reinforcement value. Successful couples cope with this inevitable reinforcement erosion by varying their shared activities, developing new common interests, expanding their sexual repertoires, and developing

their communication to the point where they continue to interest one another (p. 561).

Development of Behavior Disorders

Behaviorists view symptoms as learned responses. They don't look for underlying motives, nor do they posit marital conflict as leading to children's problems. Instead they concentrate on the symptoms themselves and look for responses that reinforce problem behavior.

At first glance it would seem puzzling that family members reinforce undesirable behavior. Why would parents reward temper tantrums? Why would a wife reinforce her husband's distance? The answer lies not in some kind of convoluted motive for suffering but in the simple fact that people often inadvertently reinforce precisely those responses that cause them the most distress.

Parents usually respond to misbehavior in their children by scolding and lecturing. These reactions may seem like punishment, but they may in fact be reinforcing because attention—even from a critical parent—is a powerful *social reinforcer* (Skinner, 1953). The truth of this is reflected in the sound advice to "Ignore it, and it will go away."

The problem is, most parents have trouble ignoring misbehavior. Notice, for example, how quickly children learn that certain words get a big reaction. Moreover, even when parents do resolve to ignore misbehavior, they usually don't do so consistently. This can make things even worse because as noted earlier, intermittent reinforcement is the most resistant to extinction (Ferster, 1963). This is why compulsive gambling is so difficult to extinguish.

In addition to behavior problems unwittingly maintained by parental attention, others persist because parents don't know how to make effective use of punishment. They make threats they don't follow through on; they punish too long after the fact; they use punishments so mild as to have no effect; and they use punishments so severe as to generate more anxiety than learning.

Learning, moreover, is not just a one-way street. Consider the behavior of a mother and daughter in the supermarket.

The little girl asks her mother for a candy bar. The mother says, "No." The child begins crying and complaining. The mother says, "If you think I'm going to buy you candy when you make such a fuss, you have another thing coming, young lady!" But the child escalates her tantrum, getting louder and louder. Finally, exasperated and embarrassed, the mother gives in: "All right, if you'll quiet down, I'll buy you some cookies."

Obviously, the child has been reinforced for throwing a temper tantrum. Not so obviously but also true, the mother has been reinforced for giving in—by the child's calming down. Thus, a spiral of undesirable behavior is maintained by *reciprocal reinforcement*.

The use of **aversive control**—nagging, crying, withdrawing—is often cited as a major determinant of marital unhappiness (Stuart, 1975). Spouses typically reciprocate their partners' use of aversive behavior, and a vicious cycle develops (Patterson & Reid, 1970).

People in distressed relationships also show poor problem-solving skills (Vincent, Weiss, & Birchler, 1975; Weiss, Hops, & Patterson, 1973). When discussing a problem, they frequently change the subject; they phrase wishes and complaints in vague and critical ways; and they respond to complaints with countercomplaints. The following exchange demonstrates sidetracking, cross-complaining, and name-calling, all typical of distressed marriages:

> "I'd like to talk about all the sweets you've been giving the kids lately."
> "What sweets! Talk about *me!* You're always stuffing your face. And what do you ever do for the kids? You just come home and complain. Why don't you just stay at the office! The kids and I get along better without you."

Most behavioral analyses point to a lack of reinforcement for positive behavior in distressed families. The old adage "The squeaky wheel gets the grease" seems to apply. Depression, headaches, and temper tantrums tend to elicit concern and therefore more attention than pleasant behavior. Because this process is unwitting, family members are often mystified about their role in reinforcing annoying behavior.

According to cognitive-behaviorists, the schemas that plague relationships are learned in the process of growing up. Some of these dysfunctional beliefs are assumptions about specific family roles, whereas others are about family life in general. These schemas are the underlying basis of the "shoulds," self-fulfilling prophesies, mind reading, jealousy, and bad faith that poison relationships by distorting family members' responses to each other's actual behavior.

How Therapy Works

The basic premise of behavior therapy is that behavior will change when the contingencies of reinforcement are altered. Behavioral family therapy aims to resolve targeted family problems through identifying behavioral goals, learning theory techniques for achieving these goals, and using social reinforcers to facilitate this process.

The hallmarks of behavioral family therapy are (1) careful and detailed assessment to determine the baseline frequency of problem behavior, to guide therapy, and to provide feedback about the success of treatment and (2) strategies designed to modify the contingencies of reinforcement in each unique client family.

Although behavior change remains the primary focus, more and more therapists are recognizing the role of cognitive factors in resolving relationship problems. The cognitive approach first gained attention as a supplement to behavioral couples therapy (Margolin, Christensen, & Weiss, 1975). Interest in cognitive-behavioral approaches to couples eventually led to the recognition that cognition plays a significant role in all family interactions (Alexander & Parsons, 1982).

$\mathcal{T}$HERAPY

Behavioral Parent Training

Most family therapists begin with the assumption that the family, not the individual, is the problem, so

Behavior therapists teach parents to use positive reinforcement rather than aversive control.

that the whole family is convened to solve it. Behavior therapists, on the other hand, accept the parents' view that the child is the problem and generally meet with one parent (guess which one) and the child, although some behaviorists (Gordon & Davidson, 1981) recommend that both parents and even siblings be included.

The most commonly used approach is operant conditioning, in which the reinforcers used may be tangible or social. In fact, praise and attention have been found to be as effective as money or candy (Bandura, 1969). Operant techniques may be further divided into shaping, token economies, contingency contracting, contingency management, and time-out.

Shaping (Schwitzgebel & Kolb, 1964) consists of reinforcing change in small steps. **Token economies** (Baer & Sherman, 1969) use points or stars to reward children for good behavior. **Contingency contracting** (Stuart, 1971), mentioned earlier, involves agreements by parents to make certain changes following changes made by their children. **Contingency management**

(Schwitzgebel, 1967) consists of giving and taking away rewards based on the children's behavior. **Time-out** (Rimm & Masters, 1974) is a punishment whereby children are made to sit in the corner or are sent to their rooms.

Assessment.   In common with other forms of behavior therapy, parent training begins with a thorough assessment. Although the procedure varies from clinic to clinic, most assessments are based upon Kanfer and Phillips's (1970) *SORKC* model of behavior: *S* for stimulus, *O* for the state of the organism, *R* for the target response, and *KC* for the nature and contingency of consequences. The following example illustrates how this model is applied.

In the case of parents who complain that their son pesters them for cookies between meals and throws tantrums if they don't give him any, the tantrums would be considered the target behavior, *R. O,* the state of the organism, might turn out to be hunger or more likely boredom. The stimulus, *S*, might be the sight of cookies in the cookie jar, and the contingency of consequences, *KC*, might be that the parents give in by feeding the boy cookies occasionally, especially if he makes enough of a fuss.

In simple cases such as this, applying the SORKC model is straightforward, but it quickly becomes more complex with families, in which there are long chains of interrelated behavior. Consider the following.

Mr. and Mrs. J. complain that their two small children whine and fuss at the dinner table. A home observation reveals that when Mr. J. yells at the children for misbehaving, they start to whine and stand by their mother's chair.

Given this sequence, it's not difficult to apply the SORKC model. Imagine, however, that the preceding sequence is only part of a more complex picture.

In the morning, Mr. J. makes a sexual overture to his wife, but she, tired from taking care of the children, rolls over and goes back to sleep. Mr. J. is hurt and leaves for work after making some unkind remarks to his wife. Feeling rejected by her husband, she spends the entire day playing with the children for solace.

By the time she has to cook dinner, Mrs. J. is exasperated with the children. Mr. J. comes home after a hard day at the office and tries to make up with his wife by hugging her. She responds but only perfunctorily because she's busy trying to cook. While she's at the stove, the children and Mr. J. vie for her attention, each wanting to tell her something. Finally, she blows up—at her husband—"Can't you see I'm busy!" He goes into the den and sulks until dinner is ready.

Just as his wife finds it difficult to express anger at the children and takes it out on him, Mr. J. has trouble directing anger at his wife and so tends to divert it onto the children. At the dinner table, he yells at them for the slightest infraction, at which point they whine and turn to their mother. She lets one sit on her lap while she strokes the other's hair.

In this longer but not atypical sequence, what is the stimulus and what is the response? Obviously, these definitions become circular, and their application depends on the perspective of the observer.

Assessment in behavioral parent training entails observing and recording the frequency of the behavior to be changed, as well as the events that precede it and those that follow. Interviews, usually with the mother, are designed to provide a definition of the problem and a list of potential reinforcers. Observations may be conducted behind a one-way mirror or during a home visit. Baseline data may be recorded by therapists or family members. Typically, parents are trained to pinpoint problem behavior, record its occurrence, and note actions that might serve as stimuli and reinforcers. Checklists and questionnaires provide information that may have been overlooked in interviews. The final product of this stage of the assessment is the selection of target behaviors for modification.

The measurement and functional analysis stage consists of observing and recording the target behavior as well as its antecedents and consequences. This may be done by the parents at home or by therapists in the clinic—and, now, more and more, by therapists in the natural setting (Arrington, Sullaway, & Christensen, 1988).

Therapeutic Techniques. Once the assessment is complete, the therapist decides which behaviors should be increased and which decreased. To accelerate behavior, the **Premack principle** (Premack, 1965) is applied; that is, high-probability behavior (particularly pleasant activities) is chosen to reinforce behavior with a low probability of occurrence.

Where once it was thought that reinforcers must satisfy some basic drive, such as hunger or thirst, it's now known that any behavior chosen more frequently (given a wide variety of choices) can serve as a reinforcer for those chosen less frequently.

Mrs. G. complained that she couldn't get her five-year-old son Adam to clean up his room in the morning. She went on to say that she tried rewarding him with candy, money, and toys, but "Nothing works!" A functional analysis of Adam's behavior revealed that, given his choice of things to do, the most probable behaviors were watching television, riding his bicycle, and playing in the mud behind his house. Once these activities were made contingent on tidying his room, he quickly learned to do so.

Various material and social reinforcers have been used to accelerate desired behaviors, but as the Premack principle demonstrates, to be effective, reinforcers must be popular with the child. Although money and candy seem like powerful rewards, they may not be as effective for some children as a chance to play in the mud.

Once effective rewards are chosen, parents are taught to *shape* behavior by reinforcing successive approximation to the final goal. They are taught to raise the criteria for reinforcement gradually and to present reinforcement immediately contingent on the desired behavior. Once the child is regularly performing the desired response, reinforcement becomes intermittent to increase the durability of the new behavior.

The most common technique for decelerating behavior is time-out. This means isolating the child immediately after he or she misbehaves. Studies have shown that about five minutes is most effective (Pendergrass, 1971). Children are first warned to give them a chance to control their own behavior before they are put into time-out.

Other techniques used to decelerate behavior include verbal reprimand and ignoring. Simply repeating commands to children has been shown to be the most ineffective way to change their behavior (Forehand et al., 1976). The importance of immediate proximity is what makes time-out such an effective punishment and grounding second only to lecturing as an ineffective one.

[handwritten margin note: Natural Consequences]

Because of the inconvenience of reinforcing behavior immediately after it occurs, token systems have been popular with parent trainers. Points are earned for desirable behavior and lost for undesirable behavior (Christophersen, Arnold, Hill, & Quilitch, 1972).

Case Study

Mrs. F. is a mother of two small children; she came to the clinic complaining of headaches and crying spells. The intake interviewer found her to be mildly depressed and concluded that the depression was a reaction to difficulty coping with the children. Suzie, age five, was a shy child who had frequent temper tantrums. Robert, who was eight, was more sociable but did poorly in school. The children were a handful, and Mrs. F. felt helpless in dealing with them.

A functional analysis of behavior revealed that Suzie's shyness resulted in extra attention from her anxious mother. Whenever Suzie declined an invitation to play with other children, her mother spent time doing things to make her feel better. The therapist selected social behavior (not shyness) as the first target response and instructed Mrs. F. to reinforce all efforts at socializing and to ignore Suzie when she avoided social contact. Thereafter, whenever Suzie made any attempt to socialize with other children, Mrs. F. would immediately reinforce her with attention and praise. When Suzie chose to stay home rather than play with other children, her mother ignored her, instead busying herself with her own activities. In three weeks, Mrs. F. reported that Suzie "seemed to be getting over her shyness."

Following this initial success the therapist felt it was time to help Mrs. F. tackle the more difficult problem of Suzie's tantrums. Because the tantrums were unlikely to occur while the family was at the clinic, the therapist instructed Mrs. F. to make observational notes for a week. These notes revealed that Suzie generally had tantrums when her parents denied her requests for a treat or some special indulgence, such as staying up to watch television. Tantrums were especially likely to occur at the end of the day when Suzie (and her parents) were tired. As to how the parents responded to these maddening outbursts, Mrs. F. reported, "We've tried everything. Sometimes we try to ignore her, but that's impossible; she just screams and shrieks until we can't stand it anymore. Then sometimes we spank her—or give her what she wants, just to shut her up. Sometimes after we spank her she cries so much that we let her watch television until she calms down. That usually works."

After listening to this description, the therapist explained how Mr. and Mrs. F. had inadvertently been reinforcing the tantrums and told them what they would have to do to stop them. For the next week, the F.s were instructed to ignore fits of temper whenever they occurred. If they occurred at bedtime, Suzie was to be put in bed; if she continued to cry and fuss, she was to be left alone until she stopped. Only when she stopped were her parents to talk with her about what was on her mind.

The following week Mrs. F. reported that the tantrums had indeed decreased, except for one night when they took on a new and more troubling form. When Suzie was told that she wouldn't be able to stay up late to watch television, she began to yell and cry as usual. Instead of relenting, Mrs. F. put Suzie in her room and told her to get ready for bed. However, realizing that her parents were going to ignore her, as they had earlier in the week, Suzie began to scream and smash things in her room. "She was completely out of control. She even smashed the little dog-shaped lamp I bought her. We didn't know what to do, so just that once we let her stay up." Again the therapist described the consequences of such behavior and explained to Mrs. F. how both parents should hold her until the tantrum subsided should Suzie again become destructive.

At the next session, Mrs. F. described how Suzie did "get out of control again." This time, however, instead of giving in, the parents held her as they had been told. Mrs. F. was amazed at the fury of the resulting tantrum. "But we remembered what you said—there was no way we were going to give in!" It took twenty minutes, but Suzie finally calmed

down. This, it turned out, was the last time Suzie ever became violent during a temper tantrum.

Nevertheless, she did continue to have occasional flare-ups during the next few weeks. According to Mrs. F., the few tantrums that did occur seemed to take place in different settings or under different conditions than the usual episodes at home (which Suzie had now learned would not be reinforced). For example, one episode took place in the supermarket, when Suzie was told she couldn't have a candy bar. By this time, however, Mrs. F. was thoroughly convinced of the necessity of not reinforcing the tantrums, and so she didn't. Because she was embarrassed at all the noise her daughter was making in public, she did find it necessary to take her out of the store. But she made Suzie sit in the car and took pains not to let it be a pleasant experience. Very few tantrums followed this one.

Next the therapist turned her attention to Robert's poor school performance. A careful assessment revealed that Robert usually denied that he had any homework. After checking with Robert's teacher, the therapist discovered that the children generally did have homework and that they were expected to work between thirty minutes and an hour a night. Mrs. F. selected a high-probability behavior, watching television, and made it contingent on Robert's having completed his homework.

For the first two weeks of this regimen, Mrs. F. found it necessary to call the teacher every night to verify the assignments. But soon this was no longer necessary. Doing homework fairly quickly became a habit for Robert, and his grades increased from Ds and Cs to Bs and As. At this point, everyone was happier, and Mrs. F. felt the family no longer needed help.

A follow-up session in the fall found things continuing to go well. Suzie was now much more sociable and hadn't had any temper tantrums in months. Robert was doing well in school, although he had begun to neglect some of his more difficult assignments. To address this, the therapist explained to Mrs. F. how to institute a token system, and she was able to use it with excellent results.

The preceding case illustrates a form of behavioral parent training in which the therapist meets with the mother and instructs her in the use of operant conditioning principles. Another format is to observe parent and child interacting behind a one-way mirror in the clinic. In this way, the therapist gets a first-hand look at what actually transpires. With this approach, parents can be taught how to play with their children as well as how to discipline and negotiate with them. Sometimes the observing therapist may communicate to the parents through a remote microphone, or "bug in the ear."

The techniques that have been described are particularly effective with young children. With teenagers, the use of contingency contracting (Alexander & Parsons, 1973; Rinn, 1978) is more widely used. Contracting is introduced as a way for everybody in the family to get something by compromising. Parents and teenagers are asked to specify what behavior they'd like each other to change. These requests form the nucleus of the initial contract. To help family members arrive at contracts, the therapist encourages (1) clear communication of content and feelings, (2) clear presentation of requests, leading to (3) negotiation, with each person receiving something in exchange for some concession.

Alexander and Parsons (1973) recommend starting with easy issues while the family is learning the principles of contingency contracting. Success in dealing with minor issues increases a family's willingness to tackle more difficult problems. Some parents are reluctant to negotiate with their children to do things "that they should do anyway, without being bribed." In fact, these parents have a legitimate point, and they should be helped to understand the difference between *rules* (which are nonnegotiable) and *privileges* (which can be negotiated).

Behavioral parent training is also conducted in packaged training programs designed for preventive education. The content of these programs varies from general principles of operant behavior to specific techniques for dealing with particular problems. Many of these programs include instruction in charting the target behavior. Parents are also taught how to state and enforce rules and the importance of consistency. Training in the use of positive reinforcement includes helping parents increase the frequency and variety of reinforcers they apply. In addition to increasing behavior that their children are already engaging in, parents are taught to develop new behaviors through shaping, modeling, instruction, and prompting.

Behavioral Couples Therapy

Assessment.   As with parent training, behavioral couples therapy begins with an elaborate structured assessment. This process usually includes clinical interviews, ratings of specific target behaviors, and marital questionnaires. The most widely used is the Locke-Wallace Marital Adjustment Scale (Locke & Wallace, 1959), a twenty-three-item questionnaire covering various aspects of marital satisfaction, including communication, sex, affection, social activities, and values.

Assessments are designed to reveal strengths and weaknesses in a couple's relationship and the manner in which rewards and punishments are exchanged. Interviews are used to specify and elaborate target behaviors. Some attempt is also made during interviews to understand the etiology of the problems couples describe as well as to observe problems other than those noted by the spouses themselves. In general, however, behavior therapists deemphasize interviews (Jacobson & Margolin, 1979) in favor of written questionnaires and direct observation of couples' interactions. Jacobson (1981) offers an outline for pretreatment assessment (Table 10.1).

Therapeutic Techniques.   After completing an assessment, the behavioral clinician presents the couple with an analysis of their relationship in social learning terms. In doing so, therapists take pains to accentuate the positive, striving to maintain optimistic expectancies and a collaborative set (Jacobson, 1981). Married partners often state their goals negatively: "I want less arguing from him" or "She nags too much." Most have difficulty describing behavior that they want their mates to accelerate. To help them do so, some therapists (Azrin, Naster, & Jones, 1973) ask couples to make a list of pleasing things their partners do during the week. Reviewing these lists in the following session provides an opportunity to emphasize the importance of positive feedback.

Table 10.1 Jacobson's Pretreatment Assessment for Marital Therapy

A. Strengths and skills of the relationship

What are the major strengths of this relationship?
What behaviors on the part of each spouse are highly valued by the other?
What shared activities do the couple currently engage in?
What common interests do they share?

B. Presenting problems

What are the major complaints, and how do these complaints translate into explicit behavioral terms?
What reinforcers are maintaining these behaviors?
What behaviors occur at less than the desired frequency or fail to occur at appropriate times from
    the standpoint of each spouse?
What are the current consequences of these behaviors when they occur?
How did the current problems develop over time?
What kinds of decisions are made collectively as opposed to unilaterally?

C. Sex and affection

Is either currently dissatisfied with the rate, quality, or diversity of sex life together?
If sex is currently a problem, was there a time when it was mutually satisfying?
What sexual behaviors seem to be associated with current dissatisfaction?
Are either or both partners dissatisfied with the amount or quality of nonsexual physical affection?
What is the couple's history regarding extramarital affairs?

D. Future prospects

Are the partners seeking therapy to improve their relationship, to separate, or to decide whether the
    relationship is worth working on?
What are each spouse's reasons for continuing the relationship despite current problems?

E. Assessment of social environment

What are each person's alternatives to the present relationship?
How attractive are these alternatives to him or her?
Is the environment (parents, relatives, friends, work associates, children) supportive of either
    continuance or dissolution of the present relationship?

F. Individual functioning of each spouse

Does either spouse exhibit emotional or behavioral problems?
Does either spouse present a psychiatric history of his or her own? Specify.
Have they been in therapy before, either alone or together? What kind of therapy? Outcome?
What is each spouse's past experience with intimate relationships?
How is the present relationship different?

Source: Adapted from Jacobson, N. S. 1981. Behavioral marital therapy. In *Handbook of Family Therapy*, A. S. Gurman and
D. P. Kniskern, eds. (pp. 565–566). New York: Brunner/Mazel.

Stuart (1975) lists five strategies that summarize the behavioral approach to troubled marriages:

1. Couples are taught to express themselves in clear, behavioral descriptions rather than in vague complaints.
2. Couples are taught new behavior exchange procedures, emphasizing positive in place of aversive control.
3. Couples are helped to improve their communication.
4. Couples are encouraged to establish clear and effective means of sharing power and making decisions.
5. Couples are taught strategies for solving future problems as a means to maintain and extend gains initiated in therapy.

Behavior exchange procedures are taught to increase the frequency of desired behavior. Couples are advised to express their wishes and complaints specifically and behaviorally. A typical device is to ask each partner to list three things he or she would like the other to do more often. While explicitly exchanging "strokes" in this way, couples are implicitly learning ways of influencing each other through positive reinforcement. An alternative tactic is to ask each partner to think of things the other might want, do them, and see what happens. Weiss and his associates direct couples to have "love days," where one partner doubles his or her pleasing behavior toward the other (Weiss & Birchler, 1978). Stuart (1976) has couples alternate "caring days," where one partner demonstrates caring in as many ways as possible.

The following vignette, taken from a video workshop series, illustrates how Richard Stuart concentrates on helping couples learn to make each other happy rather than trying to solve the problems that bring them to therapy.

Case Study

Wesley and Adele are a middle-aged, working-class couple. This is her third marriage and his fourth. Wesley feels rejected because Adele frequently works late; at the same time, she feels that he isn't affectionate with her and that he pulls away whenever she makes a sexual overture. Dr. Stuart begins with a brief family history of each spouse and then explores the history of their relationship. In the second half of the interview, Dr. Stuart offers suggestions for improving the couple's relationship by making an effort to act as if things were good and they cared for each other.

When Dr. Stuart tells the couple that they can *choose* to make their marriage work by acting in loving ways toward each other, they seem a little skeptical. When Adele reveals that she doesn't know if Wesley is committed to staying in the relationship, Dr. Stuart suggests that she needs to feel safe in his commitment and, using the example of his own marriage, tells them again that they can accentuate the positive by making a point of expressing their caring for each other.

Later Stuart suggests that Wesley start acting as if he felt close to Adele and reassures him that if he acts affectionately, she will respond in kind. Again Stuart uses his own marriage as an example of how two people can make themselves happy by making a point of acting lovingly toward each other. In fact, he guarantees Wesley that if he acts affectionately, Adele will respond, and Stuart asks Wesley to agree to try doing so as an experiment. Though they still seem a little skeptical, both Wesley and Adele agree to try the idea of acting positively toward each other.

In a carefully designed longitudinal study, Gottman and Krokoff (1989) found that disagreement and angry exchanges, which have often been considered destructive to relationships, may not be so harmful in the long run. These patterns were correlated with immediate dissatisfaction but were predictive of improved satisfaction after three years. Defensiveness, stubbornness, and withdrawal from conflict, on the other hand, *did* lead to long-term deterioration in marriages. Passive compliance may create a façade of harmony, but it doesn't work in the long run—as many dominating partners with compliant mates discover when their partners, who "used to be so agreeable," suddenly become "so unreasonable."

Conflict often makes couples uneasy, but it may be an essential prelude to facing and solving problems. The anger that accompanies direct expression of dissatisfaction may be painful, but it may also be healthy. Gottman and Krokoff (1989) conclude: "If the wife must introduce and elaborate disagreements in marriages, our data suggest that, for the sake of long-term improvement in marital satisfaction, she may need to do this by getting her husband to confront areas of disagreement and to openly vent disagreement and anger" (p. 51). In other words, confrontation is effective only if it doesn't make the partner defensive. It isn't just honesty that counts but honesty expressed in a way the partner can tolerate.

Training in communications skills may be done in a group format (Hickman & Baldwin, 1971; Pierce, 1973) or with individual couples. The training includes instruction, modeling, role-playing, structured exercises, behavior rehearsal, and feedback (Jacobson, 1977; Stuart, 1976). Couples are taught to be specific, phrase requests in positive terms, respond directly to criticism instead of cross-complaining, talk about the present and future rather than the past, listen without interruption, minimize punitive statements, and eliminate questions that sound like declarations.

Once a couple has been taught to communicate in ways that are conducive to problem solving, they are introduced to the principles of contingency contracting—agreeing to make changes contingent on the partner's making changes. In a **quid pro quo** contract (Knox, 1971), one partner agrees to make a change after a prior change by the other. Each partner specifies desired behavior changes, and with the therapist's help, they negotiate agreements. At the end of the session a written list is made and both partners sign it. Such a contract might take the following form:

Date_____

This week I agree to:

(1) Come home from work by 6 p.m.

(2) Play with the children for half an hour after supper.

_____

Husband's signature

Contingent on the above changes, I agree to:

(1) Go bowling once a week with my husband.

(2) Not serve leftovers for supper on weeknights.

_____

Wife's signature

An alternative form of contracting is the *good faith* contract, in which both partners agree to make changes that aren't contingent on what the other does (Weiss, Hops, & Patterson, 1973). Each partner's independent changes are independently reinforced. In the example above, the husband who comes home each night by 6:00 p.m. and plays with the children after supper might reward himself by buying a new shirt at the end of the week or be rewarded by his wife with a back rub.

Problem-solving training is used in situations that are too complicated for simple exchange agreements. Negotiations are preceded by a careful definition of problems. Discussions are limited to one problem at a time. Each partner begins by paraphrasing what the other has said, and the couple are taught to avoid inferences about motivation—especially inferences of malevolent intent. They're also encouraged to avoid aversive responses. When defining a problem, it's most effective to begin with a positive statement. Instead of saying, "You never . . . ," partners are taught to say "I appreciate the way you . . . and in addition I wish. . . ."

The following guidelines for problem-solving communication are adapted from *The Lost Art of Listening* (Nichols, 2009).

1. Speak for yourself and express your ideas as your own thoughts and feelings, not as absolute truths.
2. Ask for what you want in the form of specific requests, not general complaints.
3. Speak calmly and don't go on and on. Give your partner a chance to respond.
4. Knock to enter: Don't try to talk when your partner is doing something else.
5. Invite your partner to express his thoughts and feelings.

6. Listen with the intent to understand, rather than just waiting to respond.
7. Try to understand what the other person is feeling, rather than just reacting to the words.
8. Let your partner know that you understand by acknowledging what he or she has said—and invite him or her to elaborate or correct your impression.
9. When there is major conflict or misunderstanding, devote one entire conversation to drawing out and acknowledging your partner's point of view. Wait until you've demonstrated that you understand him or her before trying to express your side, perhaps in a subsequent conversation.
10. When it comes to discussing solutions, invite your partner's ideas first. Listen to and acknowledge those ideas.
11. When suggesting your own solutions, make sure they address both of your needs.
12. Find a solution that's agreeable to both of you, but plan to implement it on a trial basis, and review the solution at the end of the trial period.

In these early years of the twenty-first century, the most significant advance in behavioral treatment is the increasing use of cognitive-behavior methods (Dattilio, 1998; Epstein, Schlesinger, & Dryden, 1988). The *cognitive mediation model* (Beck, 1976) posits that emotions and actions are mediated by specific cognitions. Understanding these cognitions (beliefs, attributions, and expectancies) makes it possible to identify factors that trigger and maintain dysfunctional emotional and behavioral patterns. In practice, this boils down to uncovering assumptions that keep people stuck.

The Cognitive-Behavior Approach to Family Therapy

Cognitive family therapy followed the same progression as cognitive couples therapy—first as a supplement to the behavioral approach and then as a more comprehensive system of intervention. Munson (1993) noted at least eighteen different types of cognitive therapies used by various practitioners, but the focus of this discussion is limited to those approaches proposed by the rational-emotive (Ellis, 1962) and cognitive-behavior theories (Beck, 1988; Teichman, 1984).

The rational-emotive therapist helps family members see how illogical beliefs serve as the foundation for their emotional distress. The *A-B-C theory* is introduced, according to which family members blame their problems (*C*) on certain events in the family (*A*) and are taught to look for irrational beliefs (*B*), which are then challenged. The goal is to modify beliefs and expectations by putting them on a more rational basis (Ellis, 1978). The therapist's role is to teach the family that emotional problems are caused by unrealistic beliefs and that by revising these self-defeating ideas they may improve the quality of family life.

With rational-emotive therapy, it's hard to separate the approach from its creator. Ellis didn't merely challenge people's assumptions; he punctured them with fierce and gleeful sarcasm. It isn't necessary to imitate Ellis's acerbic style to take advantage of his insights. It seems fair to say, however, that rational-emotive therapists generally content themselves with lecturing people about generic assumptions rather than probing for more personal and closely held beliefs.

The cognitive-behavior method, which balances the emphasis on cognition and behavior, takes a more expansive and inclusive approach by focusing in greater depth on patterns of family interaction (Epstein, Schlesinger, & Dryden, 1988; Leslie, 1988). Cognitions, emotions, and behavior are viewed as exerting mutual influence on one another, so that a cognitive inference can evoke emotion and behavior, and emotion and behavior can influence cognition.

The cognitive-behavior approach is compatible with systems theory and includes the premise that members of a family simultaneously influence and are influenced by each other. The behavior of one family member triggers behavior, cognitions, and emotions in other members, which in turn elicit reactive cognitions, behavior, and emotions in the original member. As this process plays out, the volatility of family dynamics escalates, rendering the family vulnerable to negative spirals of conflict. Epstein and Schlesinger (1996) cite four means by which family members' cognitions, behaviors, and emotions may interact and build to a volatile climax:

1. The individual's own cognitions, behavior, and emotion regarding family interaction (e.g., the person who notices himself or herself withdrawing from the rest of the family)
2. The actions of individual family members toward him or her
3. The combined (and not always consistent) reactions several family members have toward him or her
4. The characteristics of the relationships among other family members (e.g., noticing that two other family members usually are supportive of each other's opinions)

As the number of family members involved increases, so does the complexity of the dynamics, adding momentum to the escalation process.

Cognitive therapy, as set forth by Aaron Beck (1976), emphasizes *schemas*, or "core beliefs" (DeRubeis & Beck, 1988). Therapeutic intervention is aimed at the assumptions whereby family members interpret and evaluate one another.

Just as individuals maintain core beliefs about themselves, they also maintain core beliefs about their families. Frank Dattilio (2005) suggests that individuals maintain two sets of schemas about family life: (1) a family schema related to the parents' experiences growing up in their own families, and (2) schemas related to families in general, or personal theories of family life. Both types of schemas influence how individuals react in the family setting.

For example, a woman raised with the belief that family members should do everything together will likely feel threatened if her husband wants to do certain things on his own. Conflict may be especially pronounced if the husband was brought up to believe that married partners should have their own independent interests.

Beliefs, conscious and unconscious, passed down from the family of origin contribute to jointly held opinions that lead to the development of the current family schema. This set of attitudes is conveyed to the children and, when combined with their own individual perceptions of their environment and life experiences, contributes to the further development of the family schema. Here's a case example taken from Dattilio and Epstein (2005).

Case Study

The family entered treatment because of conflict over the mother's rigid attitudes. Based on her experience with her own fragile and demanding parents, the mother tended to overreact to any sign of problems in her husband or children. Her anxiety made her intolerant of crying and complaining. The family felt they needed to "walk on eggshells" to avoid making her worry. Thus, the father and children became aligned against the mother, whom they came to regard as a "nut case."

The father's own mother was controlling and overbearing, which led to his developing a schema that women were bossy and unreasonable. His failure to challenge his wife about what he saw as her unreasonableness was thus partly a carryover from his experience with his mother. Instead of confronting his wife, he formed a coalition with his children against her, just as he and his father had joined forces to cope with his own domineering mother.

The therapist used the cognitive technique of *downward arrow* to identify the mother's core beliefs (see Figure 10.1). This technique was implemented by asking a series of questions to uncover the basic schemas underlying each person's assumptions: "So if that were to occur, what would it mean?"

The children were afraid to be themselves around their mother. They saw her as unreasonable and attributed her unyielding views to having grown up with a mother who had attempted suicide and blamed her daughter for not being attentive to her concerns. When the therapist attempted to uncover the children's core beliefs about the situation, one daughter said, "I think my mother is probably on the edge with all of the stress she's been under her

"There's no room for weakness in life."

↓

"If my family members are weak, they'll give in to the overwhelming forces of life."

↓

"That's when people break down, become immobilized,
and become a burden to others and a risk to themselves."

↓

"This outcome could easily result in death or suicide."

↓

"If I'm weak, I'll die."

↓

"Hence, we must avoid any signs of weakness."

Figure 10.1 **Downward arrow technique**

entire life. Therefore, we must go along with her or something bad might happen to her, and we don't need that—although we often resent having to live this way—all because of my stupid grandmother's problems." The schema adopted by this child was "Children must be cautious with their parents when they have problems."

In addressing the schemas in this family, the therapist followed a series of eight steps to uncover and reexamine them:

1. *Identify family schemas and highlight those areas of conflict that are fueled by them* (e.g., "We have to walk on eggshells with Mom. If we show any signs of weakness, she flips out"). Schemas are uncovered by probing automatic thoughts, using techniques such as the downward arrow. Once schemas have been identified, verification should be made by obtaining agreement from other family members.

2. *Trace the origin of family schemas and how they evolved to become an ingrained mechanism in the family process.* This is done by exploring the parents' backgrounds. Similarities and differences between the parents' upbringings should be

highlighted to help them understand areas of agreement and conflict. In this case the father was brought up to believe that it's okay to show vulnerability to those you love, while the mother was taught that it was dangerous to show any sign of weakness.

3. *Point out the need for change, indicating how the restructuring of schemas may facilitate more adaptive and harmonious family interaction.* The therapist stressed to the mother how she was overburdened by her belief that she was always responsible for everyone else in the family. The therapist emphasized how much her perceptions had been distorted by her experience with her mother and how she was unintentionally placing a similar burden on her own husband and children.

4. *Elicit acknowledgment for a need to change or modify existing dysfunctional schemas.* This step paves the way for collaborative efforts to change. When family members have different goals, the therapist's job is to help them find common ground.

5. *Assess the family's ability to make changes, and plan strategies for facilitating them.* In this case the mother was asked what evidence supported her idea that signs of weakness were always a problem.

She was helped to consider that this might be a distortion based on her own childhood experience. As an experiment she was asked to see if an occasional display of emotion really was dangerous by allowing herself to cry once in a while in front of her family. The fact that her husband and children seemed relieved to see her show her feelings helped her to think that maybe it's not so terrible to show unhappy emotions at times. "In fact, it felt kind of good," she noted. In a similar process the husband discovered that if he avoided interfering to protect his wife when she seemed upset, the children were able to be supportive and "nothing terrible happened." The children found out that when they expressed the wish to avoid being put in the middle of their parents' conflicts, they were free to be themselves without always worrying about negative consequences.

6. *Implement change*. The therapist encouraged family members to consider modifying some of their beliefs in a collaborative process of brainstorming ideas and weighing their implications. This family considered how they would act with each other if they decided to adopt the belief that "It is important to be tactful in expressing negative feelings to other family members, but family members should have the freedom to share such feelings with each other."

7. *Enact new behaviors*. This step involves trying out changes and seeing how they work. Family members were each asked to select an alternative behavior consistent with the modified schema and see how acting on it affected the family. Once the children began to see their mother's behavior as her way of expressing love for them in order to protect them from what she went through as a child, they became less defensive and more supportive of her—which in turn softened her anxious vigilance.

8. *Solidify changes*. This step involves establishing the new schema and its associated behavior as a permanent pattern in the family. Family members were urged to remain flexible about the possible need for future reevaluations. Although the mother might be seen as the identified patient in this family, the therapist felt it was important for the father

and children to discover their own roles in perpetuating the status quo. They began this process by expressing how they felt instead of just avoiding the mother. Then, in an effort to challenge their automatic thoughts about the family and see how their own beliefs might be part of the problem, all of the family members were asked to weigh alternative explanations and their implications. Dattilio notes that this process is similar to reframing but with an important difference: In cognitive-behavior therapy, family members are asked to gather data and weigh the evidence in favor of changing their thinking, rather than merely accept the therapist's alternative explanations.

The late 1980s and early 1990s saw the cognitive-behavior approach applied more widely in family therapy. Edited books by Epstein, Schlessinger, and Dryden (1988) and a short text produced by Huber and Baruth (1989) were among the first works to address the cognitive-behavior approach to family therapy. This was elaborated in subsequent articles by Schwebel and Fine (1992), Dattilio (1993, 1997), and Teichman (1992).

More recently, Dattilio (1998) has produced a major casebook that discusses the integration of cognitive-behavior strategies with various modalities of couples and family therapy. This important work discusses the compatibility of cognitive-behavior therapy with a wide array of modalities. The application of cognitive-behavior therapy to couples and families was also featured in the recent addition of *The Family Therapy Handbook* (Dattilio & Epstein, 2004).

Treatment of Sexual Dysfunction

Wolpe's (1958) introduction of *systematic desensitization* led to major advances in the treatment of sexual dysfunction. According to Wolpe, most sexual problems are the result of conditioned anxiety. His therapy consists of instructing couples to engage in a series of progressively intimate encounters while avoiding thoughts about erection or orgasm. Another approach that often proved useful was *assertiveness training* (Lazarus, 1965), in which socially and sexually inhibited persons are encouraged to accept and express their needs and feelings.

Although these behavioral remedies were often helpful, the real breakthrough came with the publication of Masters and Johnson's (1970) approach. This was followed by others who applied and extended Masters and Johnson's basic procedure (Kaplan, 1974, 1979; Lobitz & LoPiccolo, 1972).

Although the details vary, most sex therapists follow a general approach. As with other behavioral methods, the first step is a thorough assessment, including a complete medical examination and extensive interviews to determine the nature of the dysfunction and establish goals for treatment. In the absence of medical problems, cases involving lack of information, poor technique, and poor communication are most amenable to sexual therapy.

Therapists following Masters and Johnson tended to lump sexual problems into one category—anxiety that interferes with couples' ability to relax into passion. Kaplan (1979) pointed out that there are three stages of the sexual response and hence three types of problems: disorders of desire, arousal disorders, and orgasm disorders.

Disorders of desire range from low sex drive to sexual aversion. Treatment focuses on (1) deconditioning anxiety and (2) helping clients resist negative thoughts.

Arousal disorders include decreased emotional arousal and difficulty achieving and maintaining an erection or dilating and lubricating. These problems are often helped with a combination of relaxation and teaching couples to focus on the physical sensations of touching and caressing, rather than worrying about what comes next.

Orgasm disorders include the timing of orgasm (premature or delayed), the quality of the orgasm, and the requirements for orgasm (e.g., some people only have orgasm during masturbation). Premature ejaculation usually responds well to sex therapy; lack of orgasm in women may respond to sex therapy, usually involving teaching the woman to practice on her own and learning to fantasize (Weeks & Gambescia, 2000, 2002).

Although sex therapy must be tailored to specific problems, most treatments are initiated with *sensate focus,* in which couples are taught how to relax and enjoy touching and being touched. They're told to find a time when they're both reasonably relaxed and free from distraction and get in bed together naked. Then they take turns gently caressing each other. The person being touched is told to relax and concentrate on the feeling of being touched. Later the one being touched will let the partner know which touch is most pleasing and which is less so. At first couples are told not to touch each other in the breast or genital areas in order to avoid undue anxiety.

After they learn to relax and exchange gentle, pleasant caressing, couples are encouraged to gradually become more intimate—but to slow down if either should feel anxious. Thus, sensate focus is a form of *in vivo desensitization.* Couples who are highly anxious and fearful of having sex (which some people reduce to a hectic few minutes of poking and panting) learn to overcome their fears through a gentle experience of mutual caressing. As anxiety decreases and desire mounts, they're encouraged to engage in more intimate exchanges. In the process, couples are taught to communicate what they like and don't like. So, for example, instead of enduring something unpleasant until she finally gets so upset that she snaps at her partner or avoids sex altogether, a woman might be taught how to gently show him "No, not like that, like this."

Once sensate focus exercises have gone smoothly, the therapist introduces techniques to deal with specific problems. Among women the most common sexual dysfunctions are difficulties with orgasm (Kaplan, 1979). Frequently, these problems are rooted in lack of information. The woman and her partner may be expecting her to have orgasms reliably during intercourse without additional clitoral stimulation. In men, the most common problem is premature ejaculation, for which part of the treatment is the *squeeze technique* (Semans, 1956), in which the woman stimulates the man's penis until he feels the urge to ejaculate. At that point, she squeezes the frenulum (at the base of the head) firmly between her thumb and first two fingers until the urge to ejaculate subsides.

Stimulation begins again until another squeeze is necessary.

Techniques to deal with erectile failure are designed to reduce performance anxiety and increase sexual arousal. These include desensitization of the man's anxiety; discussions in which the partners describe their expectations; increasing the variety and duration of foreplay; the *teasing technique* (Masters & Johnson, 1970), in which the woman alternately starts and stops stimulating the man; and beginning intercourse with the woman guiding the man's flaccid penis into her vagina.

Successful sex therapy usually ends with the couple's sex life much improved but not as fantastic as frustrated expectations had led them to imagine— expectations that were part of the problem in the first place. As in any form of directive therapy, it's important for sex therapists to gradually fade out their involvement and control. Therapeutic gains are consolidated and extended by reviewing the changes that have occurred, by anticipating future trouble spots, and by planning in advance to deal with problems according to principles learned in treatment.

CURRENT STATUS OF THE MODEL

The distinctive methods of behavioral family therapy are derived from classical and operant conditioning and, increasingly, cognitive theory. Target behavior is precisely specified in operational terms; operant conditioning, classical conditioning, social learning theory, and cognitive strategies are then used to produce change. As behavior therapists have gained experience with family problems, they have begun to address such traditionally nonbehavioral concerns as the therapeutic alliance, the need for empathy, and the problem of resistance, as well as communication and problem-solving skills. However, even when dealing with such mainstream issues, behaviorists are distinguished by their methodical approach. More than by any technique, behavior therapy is characterized by careful assessment and evaluation.

Behavior therapy was born and bred in a tradition of research, and so it's not surprising that it is the most carefully studied form of family treatment. Two trends emerge from this substantial body of evidence.

The first is that both behavioral parent training and behavioral couples therapy have repeatedly been demonstrated to be effective. Among the most well-supported versions of these approaches are Gerald Patterson's parent training therapy (e.g., Patterson, Dishion, & Chamberlain, 1993; Patterson & Forgatch, 1995) and Neil Jacobson's behavioral couples therapy (e.g., Crits-Christoph, Frank, Chambless, Brody, & Karp, 1995).

The second trend in research on behavioral family therapy is that the leading exponents of these approaches have begun to see the need to extend their approaches beyond the basic contingency contracting and operant learning procedures of traditional behavior therapy. As already noted, one form this has taken has been the incorporation of cognitive techniques into more traditional stimulus-response behaviorism (e.g., Baucom & Epstein, 1990; Dattilio & Padesky, 1990).

Cognitive-behavior therapy still begins with behavior change. There are two general categories of intervention: substituting positive for aversive control and skills training. An example of the former would be the institution of "love days" or "caring days," on which partners are encouraged to increase positive things they do for each other. For example, to counteract the selective attention to negativity that characterizes many distressed couples, a cognitive-behavior therapist might ask each partner to write down one positive thing that the other person did each day, to compliment or express appreciation to that individual for these actions, and to bring the list to therapy for further discussion (Baucom, Epstein, & LaTaillade, 2002).

The cognitive component of cognitive-behavior therapy usually comes into play when the clients' attitudes and assumptions seem to get in the way of positive behavior changes—when, for example, family members notice only negative things about each other. The cognitive-behavior therapist helps clients explore their assumptions in a process of Socratic questioning. Thus, cognitive-behavior therapy still focuses on behavior. Therapists are still active and directive, but there is more attention paid to unhappy emotions and the assumptions underlying them.

The late Neil Jacobson, in partnership with Andrew Christensen, went even further in modifying traditional behavioral couples therapy along the lines of more traditional family therapy approaches. Jacobson and Christensen retained the behavioral change techniques and developed novel strategies to bring about increased emotional acceptance in clients. In other words, before they start working with couples to produce changes in the partners' behavior, they endeavor to help them learn to be more accepting of each other. So different, in fact, is the resulting approach that we will consider it more extensively in our chapter on integrative approaches (Chapter 14).

Summary

1. Although behavior therapists have been applying their techniques to family problems for more than thirty years, they have done so for the most part within a linear frame of reference. Family symptoms are treated as learned responses, involuntarily acquired and reinforced. Treatment is generally time limited and symptom focused.

2. Initially, the behavioral approach to families was based on social learning theory, according to which behavior is learned and maintained by its consequences, and can be modified by altering those consequences. This focus has been broadened considerably by the introduction of cognitive interventions to address unhelpful assumptions and distorted perceptions. An essential adjunct to social learning theory is Thibaut and Kelley's theory of social exchange, according to which people strive to maximize interpersonal rewards while minimizing costs. Hence, the general goals of behavioral family therapy are to increase the rate of rewarding exchanges, decrease aversive exchanges, and teach communication and problem-solving skills.

3. More contemporary approaches to cognitive-behavior therapy have expanded this approach to include the examination and restructuring of thoughts and perceptions. So while specific techniques are applied to target behaviors, families are also taught general principles of behavior management along with methods for reevaluating automatic thoughts with an attempt to identify distortions and address misconceptions.

4. The behaviorists' focus on modifying the consequences of problem behavior accounts for the strengths and weaknesses of this approach. By concentrating on presenting problems, behaviorists have been able to develop an impressive array of effective techniques. Even such relatively intractable problems as delinquent behavior in children and severe sexual dysfunctions have yielded to behavioral technology. Contemporary cognitive-behavior therapists take the posture, however, that behavior is only part of the human condition, and the problem person is only part of the family. You can't simply teach people to change if unresolved conflict is keeping them stuck.

5. Unhappiness may center around a behavioral complaint, but resolution of the behavior may not resolve the unhappiness. Treatment may succeed with the symptom but fail the family. Attitudes and feelings *may* change along with changes in behavior but not necessarily. And teaching communication skills may not be sufficient to resolve real conflict. Behavior change alone may not be enough for family members whose ultimate goal is to feel better. "Yes, he's doing his chores now" a parent may agree. "But I don't think he feels like helping out. He still isn't really part of our family." Behavior isn't all that family members in distress are concerned about, and to be responsive to all their needs, therapists need to deal with cognitive and affective issues as well.

6. Behaviorists rarely treat whole families. Instead they see only those subsystems they consider central to the targeted behavior. Unfortunately, failure to include—or at least consider—the entire family in therapy may doom treatment to failure. A therapeutic program to reduce a son's aggressiveness toward

his mother can hardly succeed if the father wants an aggressive son or if the father's anger toward his wife isn't addressed. Moreover, if the whole family isn't involved in change, new behavior may not be reinforced and maintained.

7. Despite these shortcomings, cognitive-behavior therapy offers impressive techniques for treating problems with children and troubled marriages. Furthermore, its weaknesses can be corrected by broadening the focus of conceptualization and the scope of treatment to include families as systems. Perhaps the greatest strength of behavior therapy is its insistence on observing what happens and then measuring change. Cognitive-behaviorists have developed a wealth of reliable assessment methods and applied them to evaluation, treatment planning, and monitoring progress and outcome. A second important advance has been the gradual movement from eliminating or reinforcing discrete marker behaviors to the teaching of general problem-solving, cognitive, and communicational skills. A third major advance in current behavioral family therapy is modular treatment interventions organized to meet the specific and changing needs of the individual and the family. Finally, the shift to address distorted cognitions that may underlie problematic family interactions has added a powerful new dimension to the behavioral approach.

Questions to Consider

1. What are some instances in which a systemic family therapist might usefully incorporate behavioral techniques?
2. What are some examples of the use of behavioral or cognitive-behavior techniques that might undermine the practice of systemic family therapy?
3. Can you think of examples of instances where a clinician has described a clichéd generalization (e.g., "You always expect the worst") as opposed to uncovering a specific cognitive schema that is actually held by the person in question?
4. Try keeping track for a day or so of the number of times you positively reinforce other people's behavior that you want to encourage.
5. Try keeping track for a day or so of the number of times you inadvertently (positively or negatively) reinforce other people's behavior that you *don't* want to encourage.

Key Concepts

aversive control   Using punishment and criticism to eliminate undesirable responses; commonly used in dysfunctional families.

behavior exchange theory   An explanation of behavior in relationships as maintained by a ratio of costs to benefits.

classical conditioning   A form of respondent learning in which an unconditioned stimulus (UCS), such as food, which leads to an unconditioned response (UCR), such as salivation, is paired with a conditioned stimulus (CS), such as a bell, the result of which is that the CS begins to evoke the same response; used in the behavioral treatment of anxiety disorders.

cognitive-behavior therapy   Treatment that emphasizes attitude change as well as reinforcement of behavior.

contingencies of reinforcement   The specific pattern of reinforcing (or punishing) consequences of a behavioral sequence.

contingency contracting   Agreements made between family members to exchange rewards for desired behavior.

contingency management Giving rewards and punishments based on children's behavior.

extinction Eliminating behavior by not reinforcing it.

functional analysis of behavior In operant behavior therapy, a study of a particular behavior, what elicits it, and what reinforces it.

modeling Observational learning.

operant conditioning A form of learning in which a person or animal is rewarded for performing certain behaviors; the major approach in behavior therapy.

Premack principle Using high-probability behavior (preferred activities) to reinforce low-probability behavior (nonpreferred activities).

quid pro quo Literally, "something for something"; an equal exchange or substitution.

reinforcement An event, behavior, or object that increases the rate of a particular response. A *positive reinforcer* is an event whose contingent presentation increases the rate of responding; a *negative reinforcer* is an event whose contingent withdrawal increases the rate of responding. *Intermittent,* or *irregular, reinforcement* is the most resistant to extinction.

reinforcement reciprocity Exchanging rewarding behaviors between family members.

role rehearsal Role-playing desired ways of behaving, especially in couples therapy.

schemas Cognitive constructions, or core beliefs, through which people filter their perceptions and structure their experience.

shaping Reinforcing change in small steps.

social learning theory Understanding and treating behavior using principles from social and developmental psychology as well as from learning theory.

systematic desensitization Gradual exposure to feared situations paired with relaxation.

theory of social exchange Thibaut and Kelley's theory according to which people strive to maximize rewards and minimize costs in relationships.

time-out A technique for extinguishing undesirable behavior by removing the reinforcing consequences of that behavior; typically, making a child sit in a corner or go to his or her room.

token economy A system of rewards using points that can be accumulated and exchanged for reinforcing items or behaviors.

Recommended Readings

Baucom, D. H., Epstein, N., and LaTaillade, J. 2002. Cognitive-behavioral couple therapy. In *Clinical handbook of couple therapy,* 3rd ed., A. S. Gurman and N. S. Jacobson, eds., New York: Guilford Press.

Dattilio, F. M. 1998. *Case studies in couple and family therapy: Systemic and cognitive perspectives.* New York: Guilford Press.

Dattilio, F. M., and Reinecke, M. 1996. *Casebook of cognitive-behavior therapy with children and adolescents.* New York: Guilford Press.

Epstein, N., Schlesinger, S. E., and Dryden, W. 1988. *Cognitive-behavioral therapy with families.* New York: Brunner/Mazel.

Falloon, I. R. H. 1988. *Handbook of behavioral family therapy.* New York: Guilford Press.

Gordon, S. B., and Davidson, N. 1981. Behavioral parent training. In *Handbook of family therapy,* A. S. Gurman and D. P. Kniskern, eds. New York: Brunner/Mazel.

Jacobson, N. S., and Margolin, G. 1979. *Marital therapy: Strategies based on social learning and behavior exchange principles.* New York: Brunner/Mazel.

Kaplan, H. S. 1979. *The new sex therapy: Active treatment of sexual dysfunctions.* New York: Brunner/Mazel.

Patterson, G. R. 1971. *Families: Application of social learning theory to family life.* Champaign, IL: Research Press.

References

Alexander, J. F., and Parsons, B. V. 1973. Short-term behavioral intervention with delinquent families: Impact on family process and recidivism. *Journal of Abnormal Psychology. 51:* 219–225.

Alexander, J. F., and Parsons, B. V. 1982. *Functional family therapy.* Pacific Grove, CA: Brooks/Cole.

Arrington, A., Sullaway, M., and Christensen, A. 1988. Behavioral family assessment. In *Handbook of behavioral family therapy,* I. R. H. Falloon, ed. New York: Guilford Press.

Azrin, N. H., Naster, J. B., and Jones, R. 1973. Reciprocity counseling: A rapid learning-based procedure for marital counseling. *Behavior Research and Therapy. 11:* 365–383.

Baer, D. M., and Sherman, J. A. 1969. Reinforcement control of generalized imitation in young children. *Journal of Experimental Child Psychology. 1:* 37–49.

Bandura, A. 1969. *Principles of behavior modification.* New York: Holt, Rinehart & Winston.

Bandura, A., and Walters, R. 1963. *Social learning and personality development.* New York: Holt, Rinehart & Winston.

Baucom, D. H., and Epstein, N. 1990. *Cognitive-behavioral marital therapy.* New York: Brunner/Mazel.

Baucom, D. H., Epstein, N., and LaTaillade, J. 2002. Cognitive-behavioral couple therapy. In *Clinical handbook of couple therapy,* 3rd ed., A. S. Gurman and N. S. Jacobson, eds., New York: Guilford Press.

Beck, A. T. 1976. *Cognitive therapy and the emotional disorders.* New York: International Universities Press.

Beck, A. T. 1988. *Love is never enough.* New York: Harper & Row.

Boardman, W. K. 1962. Rusty: A brief behavior disorder. *Journal of Consulting Psychology. 26:* 293–297.

Christophersen, E. R., Arnold, C. M., Hill, D. W., and Quilitch, H. R. 1972. The home point system: Token reinforcement procedures for application by parents of children with behavioral problems. *Journal of Applied Behavioral Analysis. 5:* 485–497.

Crits-Christoph, P., Frank, E., Chambless, D. L., Brody, C., and Karp, J. F. 1995. Training in empirically validated treatments: What are clinical psychology students learning? *Professional Psychology: Research and Practice. 26:* 514–522.

Dattilio, F. M. 1993. Cognitive techniques with couples and families. *The Family Journal. 1:* 51–65.

Dattilio, F. M. 1997. Family therapy. In *Casebook of cognitive therapy,* R. Leahy, ed. Northvale, NJ: Jason Aronson.

Dattilio, F. M. 1998. *Case studies in couple and family therapy: Systemic and cognitive perspectives.* New York: Guilford Press.

Dattilio, F. M. 2005. The restructuring of family schemas: A cognitive–behavioral perspective. *Journal of Family and Marital Therapy, 31:* 15–30.

Dattilio, F. M., and Epstein, N. B. 2004. Cognitive-behavioral couple and family therapy. In *The family therapy handbook,* G. Weekes and T. Sexton, eds. New York: Routledge.

Dattilio, F. M., and Epstein, N. B. 2005. Introduction to the special section: The role of cognitive and behavioral interventions in couple and family therapy. *Journal of Marital and Family Therapy. 31:* 7–13.

Dattilio, F. M., and Padesky, C. A. 1990. *Cognitive therapy with couples.* Sarasota, FL: Professional Resource Exchange.

DeRubeis, R. J., and Beck, A. T. 1988. Cognitive therapy. In *Handbook of cognitive-behavioral therapies,* K. S. Dobson, ed. New York: Guilford Press.

Ellis, A. 1962. *Reason and emotion in psychotherapy.* New York: Lyle Stuart.

Ellis, A. 1978. Family therapy: A phenomenological and active-directive approach. *Journal of Marriage and Family Counseling. 4:* 43–50.

Epstein, N., and Schlesinger, S. E. 1996. Cognitive-behavioral treatment of family problems. In *Casebook of cognitive-behavior therapy with children and adolescents,* M. Reinecke, F. M. Dattilio, and A. Freeman, eds. New York: Guilford Press.

Epstein, N., Schlesinger, S. E., and Dryden, W., eds. 1988. *Cognitive-behavioral therapy with families.* New York: Brunner/Mazel.

Falloon, I. R. H. 1991. Behavioral family therapy. In *Handbook of family therapy,* Vol. II, A. S. Gurman and D. P. Kniskern, eds. New York: Brunner/Mazel.

Ferster, C. B. 1963. Essentials of a science of behavior. In *An introduction to the science of human behavior,* J. I. Nurnberger, C. B. Ferster, and J. P. Brady, eds. New York: Appleton-Century-Crofts.

Forehand, R., Roberts, M. W., Doleys, D. M., Hobbs, S. A., and Resnick, P. A. 1976. An examination of disciplinary procedures with children. *Journal of Experimental Child Psychology. 21:* 109–120.

Gordon, S. B., and Davidson, N. 1981. Behavioral parent training. In *Handbook of family therapy,* A. S. Gurman and D. P. Kniskern, eds. New York: Brunner/Mazel.

Gottman, J., and Krokoff, L. 1989. Marital interaction and satisfaction: A longitudinal view. *Journal of Consulting and Clinical Psychology. 57:* 47–52.

Gottman, J., Markman, H., and Notarius, C. 1977. The topography of marital conflict: A sequential analysis of verbal and nonverbal behavior. *Journal of Marriage and the Family. 39:* 461–477.

Hickman, M. E., and Baldwin, B. A. 1971. Use of programmed instruction to improve communication in marriage. *The Family Coordinator. 20:* 121–125.

Huber, C. H., and Baruth, L. G. 1989. *Rational-emotive family therapy: A systems perspective.* New York: Springer.

Jacobson, N. S. 1977. Problem solving and contingency contracting in the treatment of marital discord. *Journal of Consulting and Clinical Psychology. 45:* 92–100.

Jacobson, N. S. 1981. Behavioral marital therapy. In *Handbook of family therapy,* A. S. Gurman and D. P. Kniskern, eds. New York: Brunner/Mazel.

Jacobson, N. S., and Margolin, G. 1979. *Marital therapy: Strategies based on social learning and behavior exchange principles.* New York: Brunner/Mazel.

Jacobson, N. S., Waldron, H., and Moore, D. 1980. Toward a behavioral profile of marital distress. *Journal of Consulting and Clinical Psychology. 48:* 696–703.

Jones, M. C. 1924. A laboratory study of fear: The case of Peter. *Journal of Geriatric Psychology. 31:* 308–315.

Kanfer, F. H., and Phillips, J. S. 1970. *Learning foundations of behavior therapy.* New York: Wiley.

Kaplan, H. S. 1974. *The new sex therapy: Active treatment of sexual dysfunctions.* New York: Brunner/Mazel.

Kaplan, H. S. 1979. *Disorders of sexual desire and other new concepts and techniques in sex therapy.* New York: Brunner/Mazel.

Knox, D. 1971. *Marriage happiness: A behavioral approach to counseling.* Champaign, IL: Research Press.

Lazarus, A. A. 1965. The treatment of a sexually inadequate male. In *Case studies in behavior modification,* L. P. Ullmann and L. Krasner, eds. New York: Holt, Rinehart & Winston.

Leslie, L. A. 1988. Cognitive-behavioral and systems models of family therapy: How compatible are they? In *Cognitive-behavioral therapy with families,* N. Epstein, S. E. Schlesinger, and W. Dryden, eds. New York: Brunner/Mazel.

Lobitz, N. C., and LoPiccolo, J. 1972. New methods in the behavioral treatment of sexual dysfunction. *Journal of Behavior Therapy and Experimental Psychiatry. 3:* 265–271.

Locke, H. J., and Wallace, K. M. 1959. Short-term marital adjustment and prediction tests: Their reliability and validity. *Journal of Marriage and Family Living. 21:* 251–255.

Lovibond, S. H. 1963. The mechanism of conditioning treatment of enuresis. *Behavior Research and Therapy. 1:* 17–21.

Mahoney, M. J. 1977. Reflections on the cognitive learning trend in psychotherapy. *American Psychologist. 32:* 5–13.

Margolin, G., Christensen, A., and Weiss, R. L. 1975. Contracts, cognition and change: A behavioral approach to marriage therapy. *Counseling Psychologist. 5:* 15–25.

Masters, W. H., and Johnson, V. E. 1970. *Human sexual inadequacy.* Boston: Little, Brown.

Munson, C. E. 1993. Cognitive family therapy. In *Cognitive and behavioral treatment: Methods and applications,* D. K. Granvold, ed. Pacific Grove, CA: Brooks/Cole.

Nichols, M. P. 2009. *The lost art of listening,* 2nd ed. New York: Guilford Press.

Patterson, G. R. 1971. *Families: Application of social learning theory to family life.* Champaign, IL: Research Press.

Patterson, G. R., Dishion, T. J., and Chamberlain, P. 1993. Outcomes and methodological issues relating to treatment of anti-social children. In *Effective psychotherapy: A handbook of comparative research,* T. R. Giles, ed. New York: Plenum Press.

Patterson, G. R., and Forgatch, M. S. 1995. Predicting future clinical adjustment from treatment outcomes and process variables. *Psychological Assessment. 7:* 275–285.

Patterson, G. R., and Reid, J. 1970. Reciprocity and coercion; two facets of social systems. In *Behavior modification in clinical psychology,* C. Neuringer and J. Michael, eds. New York: Appleton-Century-Crofts.

Pavlov, I. P. 1932. Neuroses in man and animals. *Journal of the American Medical Association. 99:* 1012–1013.

Pendergrass, V. E. 1971. Effects of length of timeout from positive reinforcement and schedule of application in suppression of aggressive behavior. *Psychological Record. 21:* 75–80.

Pierce, R. M. 1973. Training in interpersonal communication skills with the partners of deteriorated marriages. *The Family Coordinator. 22:* 223–227.

Premack, D. 1965. Reinforcement theory. In *Nebraska symposium on motivation,* D. Levine, ed. Lincoln, NB: University of Nebraska Press.

Rimm, D. C., and Masters, J. C. 1974. *Behavior therapy: Techniques and empirical findings.* New York: Wiley.

Rinn, R. C. 1978. Children with behavior disorders. In *Behavior therapy in the psychiatric setting,* M. Hersen and A. S. Bellack, eds. Baltimore: Williams & Wilkins.

Risley, T. R., and Wolf, M. M. 1967. Experimental manipulation of autistic behaviors and generalization into the home. In *Child development: Readings in experimental analysis,* S. W. Bijou and D. M. Baer, eds. New York: Appleton.

Schwebel, A. I., and Fine, M. A. 1992. Cognitive-behavioral family therapy. *Journal of Family Psychotherapy. 3:* 73–91.

Schwitzgebel, R. 1967. Short-term operant conditioning of adolescent offenders on socially relevant variables. *Journal of Abnormal Psychology. 72:* 134–142.

Schwitzgebel, R., and Kolb, D. A. 1964. Inducing behavior change in adolescent delinquents. *Behaviour Research and Therapy. 9:* 233–238.

Semans, J. H. 1956. Premature ejaculation: A new approach. *Southern Medical Journal. 49:* 353–357.

Skinner, B. F. 1953. *Science and human behavior.* New York: Macmillan.

Stuart, R. B. 1969. An operant-interpersonal treatment for marital discord. *Journal of Consulting and Clinical Psychology. 33:* 675–682.

Stuart, R. B. 1971. Behavioral contracting within the families of delinquents. *Journal of Behavior Therapy and Experimental Psychiatry. 2:* 1–11.

Stuart, R. B. 1975. Behavioral remedies for marital ills: A guide to the use of operant-interpersonal techniques. In *International symposium on behavior modification,* T. Thompson and W. Docken, eds. New York: Appleton.

Stuart, R. B. 1976. An operant interpersonal program for couples. In *Treating relationships,* D. H. Olson, ed. Lake Mills, IA: Graphic Publishing.

Teichman, Y. 1984. Cognitive family therapy. *British Journal of Cognitive Psychotherapy. 2:* 1–10.

Teichman, Y. 1992. Family treatment with an acting-out adolescent. In *Comprehensive casebook of cognitive therapy,* A. Freeman and F. M. Dattilio, eds. New York: Plenum.

Thibaut, J., and Kelley, H. H. 1959. *The social psychology of groups.* New York: Wiley.

Vincent, J. P., Weiss, R. L., and Birchler, G. R. 1975. A behavioral analysis of problem solving in distressed and nondistressed married and stranger dyads. *Behavior Therapy. 6:* 475–487.

Watson, J. B., and Raynor, R. 1920. Conditioned emotional reactions. *Journal of Experimental Psychology. 3:* 1–14.

Weeks, G. R., and Gambescia, N. 2000. *Erectile dysfunction: Integrating couple therapy, sex therapy and medical treatment.* New York: Norton.

Weeks, G. R., and Gambescia, N. 2002. *Hypoactive sexual desire: Integrating sex and couple therapy.* New York: Norton.

Weiss, R. L., and Birchler, G. R. 1978. Adults with marital dysfunction. In *Behavior therapy in the psychiatric setting,* M. Hersen and A. S. Bellack, eds. Baltimore: Williams & Wilkins.

Weiss, R. L., Hops, H., and Patterson, G. R. 1973. A framework for conceptualizing marital conflict, a technology for altering it, some data for evaluating it. In *Behavior change: Methodology, concepts and practice,* L. A. Hamerlynch, L. C. Handy, and E. J. Marsh, eds. Champaign, IL: Research Press.

Weiss, R. L., and Isaac, J. 1978. Behavior vs. cognitive measures as predictors of marital satisfaction. Paper presented at the Western Psychological Association meeting, Los Angeles.

Wills, T. A., Weiss, R. L., and Patterson, G. R. 1974. A behavioral analysis of the determinants of marital satisfaction. *Journal of Consulting and Clinical Psychology. 42:* 802–811.

Wolpe, J. 1948. An approach to the problem of neurosis based on the conditioned response. Unpublished M. D. thesis. University of Witwatersrand, Johannesburg, South Africa.

Wolpe, J. 1958. *Psychotherapy by reciprocal inhibition.* Stanford, CA: Stanford University Press.

11

Family Therapy in the Twenty-First Century

From a radical new experiment in the 1960s, family therapy grew into an established force, complete with its own literature, organizations, and legions of practitioners. Unlike approaches organized around a single model (psychoanalysis and behavior therapy), family therapy was always a diverse enterprise with competing schools and multiple theories. What they shared was a belief that problems run in families. Beyond that, however, each school was a distinct enterprise, with its own leaders, texts, and ways of doing therapy.

Today all of that has changed. The field is no longer neatly divided into separate schools, and practitioners no longer share a universal adherence to systems theory. As family therapists have always been fond of metaphors, we might say that the field has grown up. No longer cliquish or cocksure, the family therapy movement has been shaken and transformed by a series of challenges—to the idea that any one approach has all the answers, about the nature of men and women, about the shape of the American family, indeed about the possibility of knowing anything with certainty. In this chapter, we'll examine those challenges and see what family therapy looks like in the twenty-first century.

*E*ROSION OF BOUNDARIES

The boundaries between schools of family therapy have gradually blurred to the point where now fewer and fewer therapists would characterize themselves as purely Bowenian or structural or what have you. One reason for this decline in sectarianism was that as they gained experience, practitioners found no reason not to borrow from each other's arsenal of techniques. Suppose, for example, that a card-carrying structural therapist were to read White and Epston's (1990) little gem of a book *Narrative Means to Therapeutic Ends* and started spending more time exploring the stories clients tell about their lives. Would this therapist still be a structuralist? A narrative therapist? Or perhaps a little of both?

Suppose our hypothetical therapist were to hear Jim Keim at a conference describing his strategic approach to families with oppositional children and start using it in her own practice. What would we call this therapist now? Structural-narrative-strategic? Eclectic? Or maybe just a family therapist?

In response to this blurring of boundaries, Blow, Sprenkle, and Davis (2007) urged therapists to learn about theories of change rather than concentrate on learning a particular model of therapy. They suggest that therapists become familiar with several models of therapy so that they can apply them judiciously to the needs of particular clients. This may be good advice. However, we do not agree with those who say that what therapists actually do in therapy is similar across models (e.g., Davis & Piercy, 2007). While there are common elements to most therapies—empathy, encouragment, questioning unproductive assumptions—there are also sharp differences. While Bowenians reason with family members one at a time, structuralists push family members to talk to each other; while most schools carefully explore the presenting complaint, solution-focused therapists believe that this only reinforces problem-centered thinking. So, while it's clear that family therapists now borrow from each other, there are still distinct conceptual models, each with its own implications for doing therapy. While borrowing techniques can surely be useful, operating without a coherent theoretical model probably isn't.

Another reason for the erosion of orthodoxy was the growing recognition of the need for individualized techniques to deal with specific problems and populations. Once family therapists cherished their models. If a particular family didn't quite fit the paradigm, maybe they just weren't "an appropriate treatment case." Today, one-size-fits-all therapies are no longer seen as viable.

$\mathcal{P}$OSTMODERNISM

Advances in science at the beginning of the twentieth century gave us a sense that the truth of things could be uncovered through objective observation and measurement. The universe was conceived as a mechanism whose laws of operation awaited discovery. Once those laws were known, we could control our environment.

This modernist perspective was also the way family therapy's pioneers approached their clients—as cybernetic systems to be decoded and reprogrammed. The therapist was the expert. Structural and strategic blueprints were used to search for flaws that needed repair, regardless of whether families saw things that way themselves.

Postmodernism was a reaction to this kind of hubris. Not only were we losing faith in the validity of scientific, political, and religious truths, but we were also coming to doubt whether absolute truth can ever be known. As Walter Truett Anderson (1990) wrote in *Reality Isn't What It Used to Be,* "Most of the conflicts that tore the now-ending modern era were between different belief systems, each of which professed to have the truth: this faith against that one, capitalism against communism, science against religion. On all sides the assumption was that somebody possessed the real item, a truth fixed and beyond mere human conjecture" (p. 2). In family therapy it was structural truth versus psychodynamics, Bowen versus Satir.

Einstein's relativity undermined our faith in certainties. Marx challenged the right of one class to dominate another. In the 1960s we lost trust in the establishment. The feminist movement challenged assumptions about gender that had been considered laws of nature. As the world shrank and we were increasingly exposed to different cultures, we had to reexamine our assumptions about other people's "peculiar" beliefs.

This mounting skepticism became a major force in the 1980s and shook the pillars of every human endeavor. In literature, education, religion, political science, and psychology, accepted practices were **deconstructed**—that is, shown to be social conventions developed by people with their own agendas. Social philosopher Michel Foucault interpreted the accepted principles in many fields as stories perpetuated to protect power structures and silence alternative voices. The first and perhaps most influential of those voices to be raised in family therapy was the feminist critique.

$\mathcal{T}$HE FEMINIST CRITIQUE

Feminism prompted family therapy's rudest awakening. In an eye-opening critique heralded by an article by Rachel Hare-Mustin (1978), feminist family therapists not only exposed the gender bias inherent in existing models but also advocated a style of therapy that called into question systems theory itself.

Cybernetics encouraged us to view a family system as a flawed machine. Judith Myers Avis (1988) described this family machine as one that

> functions according to special systemic rules and is divorced from its historical, social, economic, and political contexts. By viewing the family out of context, family therapists locate family dysfunction entirely within interpersonal relationships in the family, ignore broader patterns of dysfunction occurring across families, and fail to notice the relationship between social context and family dysfunction (p. 17).

The Batesonian version of cybernetics had claimed that personal control in systems was impossible because all elements are continually influencing one another in circular feedback loops. If all parts of a system are equally involved in its problems, no one is to blame.

To feminists, however, the notion of equal responsibility for problems looked suspiciously like a sophisticated version of "blaming the victim and rationalizing the status quo" (Goldner, 1985, p. 33). This criticism was particularly germane in crimes against women, such as battering, incest, and rape, for which psychological theories have long been used to imply that women provoke their own abuse (James & MacKinnon, 1990).

The problematic family constellation most commonly cited by family therapists was the peripheral father, overinvolved mother, and symptomatic child. For years psychoanalysts had blamed mothers for their children's symptoms. Family therapy's contribution was to show how a father's lack of involvement contributed to a mother's overinvolvement, and so therapists tried to pry the mother loose by inserting the father in her place. This wasn't the boon for women that it might have seemed, because in too many cases mothers were viewed no less negatively. They were still "enmeshed," but now a new solution appeared—bringing in good old Dad to the rescue.

What feminists contended that therapists failed to see was that "the archetypal 'family case' of the

Peggy Papp, Olga Silverstein, Marianne Walters, and Betty Carter were founding members of the Women's Project in Family Therapy.

overinvolved mother and peripheral father is best understood not as a clinical problem, but as the product of an historical process two hundred years in the making" (Goldner, 1985, p. 31). Mothers were overinvolved and insecure not because of some personal flaw but because they were in emotionally isolated, economically dependent, overresponsible positions in families, positions that were crazy making.

Gender-sensitive therapists sought to help families reorganize so that no one, man or woman, remained stuck in such positions. Thus, instead of undermining a mother by replacing her with a peripheral father (who was likely to have been critical of her parenting all along), a feminist family therapist might help the family reexamine the roles that kept mothers down and fathers out. Fathers might be encouraged to become more involved with parenting—not because mothers are incompetent, but because it's a father's responsibility (Goodrich, Rampage, Ellman, & Halstead, 1988; Walters, Carter, Papp, & Silverstein, 1988).

Only when we become more gender sensitive will we stop blaming mothers and looking to them to do all of the changing. Only then will we be able to fully counter the unconscious bias toward seeing women as responsible for childrearing and housekeeping; as needing to support their husbands' careers by neglecting their own; as needing to be married or at least to have a man in their lives (Anderson, 1995). Only then can we stop relying on traditional male traits, such as independence and competitiveness, as the standards of health and stop denigrating or ignoring traits traditionally encouraged in women, like emotionality, nurturance, and relationship focus.

In the following section we'll see how these principles are translated into action.

*F*EMINIST FAMILY THERAPY

Traditional family therapists focused on interactions within the family but ignored the social, economic, and material realities that mold those interactions. Feminist therapists extend the level of analysis beyond the family to the social and cultural context and are committed to changing values that trap women and men in narrow and unequal roles.

Thus, feminist therapy is deliberately political. The aim is to replace patriarchy with a feminist consciousness. This involves helping clients realize that how they define themselves and relate to others is often distorted by gender-role expectations. But having a political agenda imposes a challenge for therapists. There is a fine line between *clinical neutrality,* not taking a position, and *indoctrination,* imposing one's position on clients.

Deborah Luepnitz (1988), whose book *The Family Interpreted* is one of the landmark texts of feminist family therapy, says that the ability to challenge patriarchy in a clinical context has to do with having a feminist *sensibility,* rather than a feminist *agenda.* Therapy is different from indoctrination. It has to do with creating space for people to examine their assumptions about what it means to live as women and men and to explore greater flexibility in their lives.

Luepnitz's own work exemplifies the feminist sensibility without veering into indoctrination, as illustrated by the following vignette, adapted from *The Family Interpreted* (Luepnitz, personal communication, September 25, 2006).

Case Study

LeRoy Johnson was an African American adolescent who had been in trouble since kindergarten. At fifteen, he was expelled from a school for delinquents and well on the road to jail. During the assessment for a thirty-day inpatient stay, his mother would hardly look at the consultant as she explained the one-way mirror.

The family had had nine bouts of therapy with as many therapists. Dr. Luepnitz had read their reports. They described Ms. Johnson as "ineffectual," "depressed," "narcissistic," "dependent," "disengaged," and "overinvolved." Attending to the countertransference and realizing that the hopelessness Ms. Johnson felt might be something she needed the therapist to experience and contain, Luepnitz tried, as a feminist therapist, to intervene constructively.

> *Luepnitz:* Ms. Johnson, I want to tell you something very important, something I don't think anyone has told you before.
> *Ms. Johnson:* Go ahead.
> *Luepnitz:* LeRoy's problems are not your fault.
> *Ms. Johnson:* (After a long pause) Well, that *is* news.

For ten years, schools, guidance counselors, judges, and relatives had let Ms. Johnson know that she had ruined her child's life and that if he was on his way to prison, that, too, was her doing. She sat, looking thoughtful.

> *Ms. Johnson:* I have done a lot of things wrong.
> *Luepnitz:* How about the things you've done right?
> *Ms. Johnson:* Such as?
> *Luepnitz:* Who has fed and clothed this child all his life? Who has talked to teachers and therapists and worked two or three jobs?
> *Ms. Johnson:* Any mother does those things if she has to.
> *Luepnitz:* Mothers need help. Who helped you?
> *Ms. Johnson:* I'm self-sufficient.
> *Luepnitz:* Self-sufficient people need loving friends. Who has loved you?
> *Ms. Johnson:* Nobody.

Following this interchange, Ms. Johnson formed a therapeutic alliance with the consultant, something she had never had with the more problem-solving, patriarchal clinicians she'd seen previously. From this base, the Johnson family was able to work hard and undergo a major transformation. LeRoy was allowed to return home. He went to college and was never in trouble with the law again.

Feminist therapists have also helped women rethink their relationship with their bodies (e.g., Orbach, 1997). By examining the effects of social expectations communicated by the media, women can assign less importance to appearance and focus more on being themselves.

To illustrate the difference between *advocacy* and *indoctrination*, consider how a therapist might raise the issue of cultural conditioning with a young woman struggling with an eating disorder. What are the implications of saying "Our society is obsessed with thinness" versus asking "Do you know where you got the idea that it was important for a woman to be thin?" The first comment suggests that the therapist knows why the client feels pressured to eat the way she does and invites her to join the therapist in seeing her problem as something imposed on her. The second comment invites the client to join in a mutual search for understanding her problem and empowers her to take an active role in that process.

When it comes to the politics of the family, feminists make a point of exploring the income and work potential of husbands and wives and the implications for the balance of power in their relationship. Feminists help couples clarify the rules by which roles are chosen and rewarded in the family. Useful questions include the following:

Who handles the finances?
Who handles emotional matters?
Who makes social arrangements?
Who decides where the couple is going to live and when they will move?
Who buys and wraps the birthday presents?
Who cleans the toilets?
What do the couples believe about appropriate gender roles for a wife and husband?
What gender roles were modeled by their own parents—both positive and negative?

One of the core elements of feminist therapy is *empowerment*. Women are typically brought up to empower others—to respond to the feelings and opinions of others and to foster other people's growth and well-being. If the greatest shame for a man is weakness, then the greatest shame for a woman is selfishness. Underlying the specific conflicts between men and women in families is the cultural programming for men to seek success and for women to nurture and support them, even at the expense of their own development. Feminist therapists aim to redress this imbalance by empowering women to feel competent. Thus, empowerment is in the service of *power to,* not *power over. Power to* means being able to perform and produce and having the freedom and resources to do so. *Power over* refers to domination and control.

Some men have trouble understanding how women are disempowered, because they don't feel powerful in their relationships with their wives and mothers. But the fact that a man may feel powerless in individual circumstances doesn't cancel his membership in the dominant class or eliminate the privileges that attend that membership (Goodrich, 1991).

Empowerment need not be a zero-sum game. Both people in a relationship can learn to interact in ways that increase their connection and enhance their own personal power (Miller, 1986; Surrey, 1991). Mutual empowerment means helping women (and men) differentiate between what they have been taught is socially acceptable and what is actually in their best interest.

In recent years the standard model of marriage has shifted from *complementary* to *symmetrical.* In an egalitarian marriage, mutuality and reciprocity replace hierarchy and control. But the reproduction of patriarchy still appears in the family—from who gets the kids ready for school to who drives the car, from who pleads for conversation to who has the last word, from minor acts of deference to major decisions. Here's an example of one couple's struggle to achieve mutual empowerment.

Case Study

Raised in a generation that takes gender equality for granted, Olivia and Noah found that actually implementing that ideal was easier said than done. Both of them believed that Noah should be as responsible for housework as Olivia, but he had trouble assuming that responsibility, and she had trouble letting go of it. Olivia expected to be in charge of looking after things, as her mother had been, and she tended to criticize Noah's efforts when he did make them.

Even when a man expresses willingness to assume more responsibility, both he and his partner need to make concessions. Noah insisted on doing the laundry his own way—even if it meant that stains would set and colors would bleed. He wanted to do the grocery shopping when he got around to it, even though that meant that occasionally there would be nothing to pack for school lunches.

A man who wants to share in the responsibility of being part of a family, rather than just offer to "help out," must submit to suggestions. In addition, his partner must let go some. Asking a husband to explain why it's so hard to accept advice from his wife may help clear away some of his resentment. Taking advice does involve a loss of freedom. One person can't just do things his or her own way if doing so will cause significant problems for the other person.

Family therapists are so used to having women as customers and men as reluctant presences that they tend to ask very little of men. This attitude begins with accepting that Dad can't attend sessions "because he has to work." A therapist who wants to be part of the solution to sexist family arrangements has to stop accepting men's nonparticipation and start insisting that both partners be actively involved in therapy.

Therapists who would challenge men to become more involved with their families must be sensitive to the price a man may have to pay for putting more priority on his family and less on his job. Both partners must be convinced that the therapist is equally committed to their well-being. But the feminist perspective isn't just about sacrificing male prerogatives. It's also about helping men learn to increase their capacity for intimacy, become more involved in the lives of their children, express their emotions, balance achievement and relationship needs, accept their vulnerabilities, and create collaborative relationships at work and with significant others that are not based on a power-over model of relating.

The political agenda in feminist therapy has evolved to include greater equality not only in the institution of the family but also in the world outside the home. For career-oriented women, the challenge has shifted from access to flexibility. Twenty years ago the gender debate centered on breaking the glass ceiling that kept women out of top management and professional jobs. Today, concerns often revolve around reshaping the climate of the work world to *keep* women involved, including compensating managers for achieving diversity goals and reaching out to women employees with families. Businesses and institutions are beginning to realize that women's needs are often different from those of men, and they are making efforts to accommodate the needs of women with families. For their part, women are becoming more aggressive about demanding fulfilling careers and family lives, and many are willing to walk away from organizations that fail to meet those needs.

For poor and working-class women, the challenge is not so much finding a rewarding career as finding someone to watch their kids so they can keep the minimum-wage job they so desperately need. Helping these women out of poverty takes more than talk therapy. What's needed are flexible schedules, affordable child care, and greater availability of part-time work.

ＳOCIAL CONSTRUCTIONISM AND THE NARRATIVE REVOLUTION

Constructivism was the lever that pried family therapy away from its claim to objectivity. Human experience is fundamentally ambiguous; fragments of experience are understood only through a process that organizes it and assigns meaning.

Instead of focusing on patterns of interaction, constructivism shifted the emphasis to exploring the perspectives that people have about their problems. Meaning itself became the primary target.

In the 1980s and 1990s Harlene Anderson and Harry Goolishian translated constructivism into an approach that democratized the therapist–client relationship. Along with Lynn Hoffman and others, these **collaborative** therapists were united in their opposition to the cybernetic model and its mechanistic implications. They sought to move the therapist out of the position of expert into a more egalitarian partnership with clients.

Perhaps the most striking example of this democratization was introduced by Norwegian psychiatrist Tom Andersen, who leveled the playing field by hiding nothing from his clients. He and his team openly discuss their reactions to what a family says. This **reflecting team** (Andersen, 1991) has become a widely used device in the collaborative model's therapy by consensus. Observers come out from behind the one-way mirror to discuss their impressions with the therapist and family. This process creates an open environment in which the family feels part of a team and the team feels more empathy for the family.

What these collaborative therapists shared was the conviction that too often clients aren't heard because therapists are doing therapy *to* them rather than *with* them. To redress this authoritarian attitude, Harlene Anderson (1993) recommended that therapists adopt a position of **not-knowing,** which leads to genuine conversations with clients in which "both the therapist's and the client's expertise are engaged to dissolve the problem" (p. 325).

This new perspective was in the tradition of an approach to knowledge that emerged from biblical studies called **hermeneutics,** from the Greek word for "interpretation." Before it surfaced in family therapy, hermeneutics had already shaken up psychoanalysis. In the 1980s Donald Spence, Roy Schafer, and Paul Ricoeur challenged the Freudian notion that there was one correct interpretation of a patient's symptoms, dreams, and fantasies. The analytic method isn't, they argued, archaeological or reconstructive; it's constructive and synthetic, organizing whatever is there into patterns it imposes (Mitchell, 1993).

From a hermeneutic perspective, what a therapist knows is not simply discovered through a process of free association and analysis—or enactment and circular questioning. Rather, it's organized, constructed, and fitted together by the therapist alone or collaboratively with the patient or family. Although there's nothing inherently democratic about hermeneutic exegesis, its challenge to essentialism went hand in hand with the challenge to authoritarianism.

It's hard to give up certainty. A lot is asked of a listener who, in order to be genuinely open to the speaker's story, must put aside his or her own beliefs and enter the other's world, at least temporarily. In so doing, the listener may find those beliefs challenged. This is more than some therapists are willing to risk.

Constructivism focused on how individuals create their own realities, but family therapy has always emphasized the power of interaction. As a result, another postmodern psychology called **social constructionism** now influences family therapy.

Social psychologist Kenneth Gergen (1985) emphasized the power of social interaction in generating meaning for people. Gergen challenged the notion that we are autonomous individuals holding independent beliefs and argued instead that our beliefs are fluid and fluctuate with changes in our social context. Gergen (1991) asks "Are not all the fragments of identity the residues of relationships, and aren't we undergoing continuous transformation as we move from one relationship to another?" (p. 28).

This view has several implications. The first is that no one has a corner on the truth; all truths are social constructions. This idea invites therapists to help clients explore the origins of their beliefs, even those they assumed were laws of nature. The second implication is that therapy is a linguistic exercise; if therapists can lead clients to new constructions about their problems, the problems may open up. Third, therapy should be collaborative. Because neither therapist nor client brings truth to the table, new realities emerge through conversations in which both sides share their opinions and respect each other's perspective.

Social constructionism was welcomed with open arms by those who were trying to shift the focus of therapy from action to cognition, and it became the basis for an approach that took family therapy by storm in the 1990s, *narrative therapy* (Chapter 13). The narrative metaphor focuses on how experience creates expectations and how expectations shape experience through the creation of organizing stories.

The question for the narrative therapist isn't one of truth but of which points of view are useful and lead to preferred outcomes. Problems aren't in persons (as psychoanalysis had it) or in relationships (as systems theory had it); rather, problems are embedded in points of view about individuals and their situations. Narrative therapy helps people reexamine these points of view.

*F*AMILY VIOLENCE

In the early 1990s family therapy took a look at the dark side of family life. For the first time, books and articles on wife battering and sexual abuse began appearing in the mainstream family therapy literature (e.g., Trepper & Barrett, 1989; Goldner, Penn, Sheinberg, & Walker, 1990; Sheinberg, 1992). The field was shaken out of its collective denial regarding the extent of male-to-female abuse in families.

Judith Myers Avis (1992) delivered a barrage of shocking statistics about the number of women who experience sexual abuse before the age of eighteen (37 percent), the percent of abusers who are men (95 percent), the number of women abused each year by the men they live with (one in six), the percent of male college students who had coerced sex from an unwilling partner (25 percent), and those who said they would commit rape if guaranteed immunity from punishment (20 percent). After reiterating the indictment of theories that call for therapist neutrality and that treat the abused as partially responsible for their abuse, Avis concluded the following:

> As long as we train therapists in systemic theories without balancing that training with an understanding of the non-neutrality of power dynamics, we will continue producing family therapists who collude in the maintenance of male power and are dangerous to the women and children with whom they work (p. 231).

The systemic view, now under attack, was that family violence was the outcome of cycles of mutual provocation, an escalation, albeit unacceptable, of the emotionally destructive behavior that characterizes many marriages. Advocates for women rejected this point of view. From their perspective, violent men don't lose control; they *take* control—and will stop only when they are held accountable.

Although the claim made by some women's advocates that couples therapy has no place in the treatment of violent marriages was controversial, their warnings provided a wake-up call. Domestic violence—let's call it what it is, wife battering and child beating—is a major public health problem, right up there with alcoholism and depression.

*M*ULTICULTURALISM

Family therapy has always billed itself as a treatment of people in context. In the postwar America of family therapy's birth, this principle was translated into a pragmatic look at the influence of family relationships. As we've become a more diverse country enriched by an influx of immigrants from Asia, Central and South America, Africa, and Eastern Europe, family therapy as a profession has shown its willingness to embrace the positiveness of others. Not only are we learning to respect that families from other cultures have their own valid ways of doing things, but also our journals and professional organizations are making an effort to become more diverse and inclusive.

Monica McGoldrick and her colleagues (McGoldrick, Pearce, & Giordano, 1982) dealt the first blow to our ethnocentricity with a book describing the characteristic values and structure of a host of different ethnic groups. Following this and a spate of related works (e.g., Boyd-Franklin, 1989; Falicov, 1983, 1998; Ingoldsby & Smith, 1995; McGoldrick, 1998; Mirkin, 1990; Okun, 1996; Saba, Karrer, & Hardy, 1989), we are now more sensitive to the need to know something about the ethnic background of our client families, so we don't assume they're sick just because they're different.

Multiculturalism is certainly an advance over ethnocentrism. Yet in highlighting differences, there is a danger of emphasizing identity politics. Segregation, even in the name of ethnic pride, isolates people and breeds prejudice. Perhaps *pluralism* is a better term than *multiculturalism* because it implies a balance between ethnic identity and connection to the larger group.

As we suggested in Chapter 4, ethnic sensitivity does not require becoming an expert—or thinking you're an expert—on every culture you might work with. If you don't know how a rural Latino family feels about their children leaving home or what Korean immigrant parents think about their teenage daughter dating American boys, you can always ask.

*R*ACE

In the early days of family therapy, African American families received some attention (e.g., Minuchin et al., 1967), but for many years it seemed that the field, like the rest of the country, tried to ignore this population and the racism they live with every day. Finally, however, African American family therapists such as Nancy Boyd-Franklin (1993) and Ken Hardy (1993) brought race out of the shadows and forced it on the field's consciousness.

White therapists still have the option to walk away from these issues. People of color don't have that luxury (Hardy, 1993):

> To avoid being seen by whites as troublemakers, we suppress the part of ourselves that feels hurt and outraged by the racism around us, instead developing an "institutional self"—an accommodating façade of calm professionalism calculated to be nonthreatening to whites. . . . Familiar only with our institutional selves, white people don't appreciate the sense of immediate connection and unspoken loyalty that binds black people together (pp. 52–53).

Laura Markowitz (1993) quotes an African American woman's therapy experience:

> I remember being in therapy years ago with a nice white woman who kept focusing me on why I was such an angry person and on my parents as inadequate individuals. . . . We never looked at my father as a poor black man, my mother as a poor black woman and the context in which they survived and raised us. . . . Years later, I saw a therapist of color and the first thing out of her mouth was, "Let's look at what was going on for your parents." It was a joyous

Nancy Boyd-Franklin's *Black Families in Therapy* was one of the first—and best—books on treating ethnic minority families.

moment to be able to see my dad not as a terrible person who hated us but as a survivor living under amazingly difficult conditions (p. 29).

It's hard for whites to realize how many doors were open to them based on their skin color and to understand how burdened by racism nonwhites are. African American families not only have to overcome barriers to opportunity and achievement but also the frustration and despair that such obstacles create.

The task of therapists working with nonwhite families is to understand their reluctance to engage in treatment (particularly if the therapist is white) in the context of a history of negative interaction with white people, including the many social service agents they encounter. In addition, the therapist must recognize the family's strengths and draw from their networks or (if the family is isolated) help them create networks of support.

Finally, therapists must look inside and face their own attitudes about race, class, and poverty. Toward this end, several authors recommend curricula that go beyond lectures to personal encounters—that is, confronting our own demons of racism (Boyd-Franklin, 1989; Green, 1998; Pinderhughes, 1989).

POVERTY AND SOCIAL CLASS

Money and social class are not subjects that most people like to discuss. The shame of economic disadvantage is related to the ethic of self-reliance—people are responsible for their own success. If you're poor, it must be your own fault.

Despite decreasing fees due to managed care, most therapists are able to maintain a reasonably comfortable lifestyle. They have little appreciation of the obstacles their poor clients face and of the psychological impact of those conditions. When poor clients don't show up for appointments or don't comply with directives, some therapists see them as apathetic or irresponsible. This is often the way poor people come to see themselves—and that negative self-image can be an enormous obstacle.

How can we counter this tendency to think that poor people just can't cut it? First, therapists need to educate themselves to the social and political realities of being poor in the United States. Journalist Barbara Ehrenreich (1999) spent a year trying to live like a welfare recipient coming into the workforce. Living in a trailer park and working as a waitress left her with almost nothing after expenses.

> How former welfare recipients and single mothers will (and do) survive in the low-wage workforce, I cannot imagine. Maybe they will figure out how to condense their lives—including child-raising, laundry, romance and meals—into the couple of hours between full-time jobs. Maybe they will take up residence in their vehicles [as she found several fellow workers had done], if they have one. All I know is that I couldn't hold two jobs and I couldn't make enough money to live on with one. And I had advantages unthinkable to many of the long-term poor—health, stamina, a working car, and no children to care for or support. . . . The thinking behind welfare reform was that even the humblest jobs are morally uplifting and psychologically buoying. In reality these are likely to be fraught with insult and stress (p. 52).

The fact is, this isn't the land of equal opportunity. The economy has built-in disparities that make it extremely difficult for anyone to climb out of poverty and that keep nearly one in four children living in poverty (Walsh, 1998).

These days, it isn't just families of poverty who live with financial insecurity. As mortgages, energy costs, and college tuitions mount up and corporations lay off employees suddenly and ruthlessly, family life at all but the wealthiest levels is increasingly dominated by economic anxiety. Median family income has declined in the past three decades to the point where young families can't hope to do as well as their parents, even with the two incomes needed to support a very modest standard of living.

Therapists can't pay their clients' rent, but they can help them appreciate that the burdens they live with are not all of their own making. Even when clients don't bring it up, a sensitive therapist should be aware of the role financial pressures play in their lives. Asking about how they manage to get by not only puts this issue on the table but also can lead to a greater appreciation of the effort and ingenuity it takes to make ends meet these days.

*G*AY AND LESBIAN RIGHTS

Family therapy's consciousness was raised about gay and lesbian rights in the same way it was about race. After a long period of neglect and denial, family therapy in the late 1980s began to face the discrimination that a sizable percentage of the population lives with (Carl, 1990; Krestan, 1988; Laird, 1993; Roth & Murphy, 1986; Sanders, 1993). The release in 1996 of a major clinical handbook (Laird & Green, 1996) and the magazine *In the Family* (edited by Laura Markowitz) meant that gay and lesbian issues were finally out of family therapy's closet.

Despite gains in tolerance in some segments of our society, however, gays and lesbians continue to face humiliation, discrimination, and violence because of their sexuality. After a childhood of shame and confusion, many gays and lesbians are rejected by their families when they come out. Because of the lack of social support, the bonds in gay and lesbian relationships can be strained, generating stress, jealousy, and the pressures of isolation.

Parents often feel guilty, in part because they blame themselves for their children's sexual orientation. Parental reactions range from denial, self-reproach, and fear for their child's future to hostility, violence, and disowning (LaSala, 1997). Therapists should remember that a gay or lesbian child may have struggled for years to come to grips with his or her identity, and that child's parents may need time to catch up after the initial shock.

When working with gay, lesbian, bisexual, or transgendered clients, we recommend that therapists get as much information as they can about the unique identity formation and relationship issues that these individuals face. Therapists who aren't well informed about gay and lesbian experience should seek supervision from someone who is or refer these clients to a clinician with more experience. It simply isn't true that individuals and families, regardless of their cultural context, all struggle with the same issues.

We hope the day will come when gay and lesbian families, bisexual and transgendered persons, African Americans, and other marginalized groups are studied by family therapists to learn not only about the problems they face but also about how they survive and thrive against such great odds. For example, gays and lesbians often create "families of choice" out of their friendship networks (Johnson & Keren, 1998). As Joan Laird (1993) suggested, these families have much to teach us "about gender relationships, about parenting, about adaptation to tensions in this society, and especially about strength and resilience" (p. 284). The question is whether we are ready to learn.

*A*DVANCES IN NEUROSCIENCE

Scientists have come a long way from looking at bumps on the skull for clues to brain functioning. Now, instead of phrenology, we have *fMRI*—functional magnetic resonance imaging, which measures increases in blood flow to the most active regions of the brain; *PET scan*—positron emission tomography, which provides a sectional view of the brain and its activity; *ERP*—event-related potentials, which measure brain activity via electrical signals; and *TMS*—transcranial magnetic stimulation—magnetic fields administered to the cortex to induce a virtual lesion if done repeatedly or to preactivate or interfere with a neural system using single pulses.

These technological advances have produced a growing body of evidence suggesting that people keep doing things they know they shouldn't, and fail to do things they know they should, because their brains are programmed to make decisions for them. Studies of the amygdala, hippocampus, and prefrontal cortex show that the brain becomes conditioned to respond automatically to certain cues by activating neural response circuits that propel people into programmed patterns of thinking and acting (LeDoux, 1996; Siegel, 1999).

These conditioned patterns of responding are similar to what cognitive-behavior therapists refer to as *schemata* (see Chapter 10)—cognitive constructions by which we interpret present experiences on the basis of past experience; but the difference is that many of these schemata are encoded in *implicit memory* and are therefore not subject to conscious recall or rational reevaluation.[1]

The evidence from neuroscience is that emotion, not cognition, is the primary organizer of human experience. Thinking counts, but not as much as we have assumed.

There is a good deal of evidence suggesting that the brain gets wired for specific kinds of neural activations at a very young age, and that once these activations are set, they tend to persist throughout a person's life. The discovery of the brain's neural operating systems helps explain why people often persist in self-defeating interactions, even when they know that it would be in their best interests to change. "Emotional responses are, for the most part, generated unconsciously" (LeDoux, 1996, p. 17). It turns out that Freud was right when he described consciousness as the tip of the iceberg.

Emotions do not, as we once thought, emanate strictly from the part of the brain called the limbic system (hypothalamus, hippocampus, and amygdala). Emotion is not limited to some specifically designed circuits of the brain, but rather the subcortical structures of the limbic system appear to have wide-ranging effects on most aspects of brain functioning and mental processes (Watt, 1998).

The amygdala acts like an emotional watchdog, constantly alert for signs of threat. If an experience registers as potentially dangerous, the amygdala broadcasts a distress signal to the entire brain, which sets off a surge of physiological responses, from the release of adrenaline and noradrenaline to speeded-up heart rate to rising blood pressure and muscles mobilized for fight or flight. We may explode with rage or freeze in fear well before our conscious minds can assess what's happening, much less persuade us to pause long enough to think about what to do.

When the amygdala tries to assess whether a situation is dangerous, it compares the situation with past emotionally charged events. If any of the key elements of the situation—the tone of voice, a facial expression—are similar, the amygdala sounds its warning siren and sets off an accompanying emotional reaction.

The role of this hair-trigger brain mechanism in creating marital misery has been documented by John Gottman's research at the University of Washington. What Gottman found was that the brain's atavistic emotional reactions were highly correlated with criticism, contempt, and stonewalling. The emerging portrait of the emotional brain offers an illuminating window on why many clients find it so difficult to contain their reactivity in intimate relationships. It turns out that the trajectory of divorce often originates with frequent, nasty arguments that eventually cause partners to develop a kind of bio-emotional hypersensitivity to each other.

For those who wish people could just learn to get along, the point to remember is that the amygdala often sets off its emotional fireworks before the neocortex ever gets into the act. That's why a clinician can spend hours getting a couple to communicate better only to see the whole thing go up in smoke

---

[1] Implicit memory is a form of memory based on emotional, behavioral, and perceptual priming, rather than conscious awareness.

when one partner says something that feels to the other like an arrow to the heart—or, to put it in the present context, activates a primitive neural circuit.

Exciting as some of these neuroscientific discoveries are, they can lead to unfortunate conclusions. When we describe an individual's actions in human terms— "She flies off the handle," "He doesn't listen," and so on—we tend hold people responsible. And we believe that therapy can help. But shifting to a biological explanation may seem to rob people of free will. How can you reason with a neural response circuit? Thus, the current vogue of biological determinism suggests that people do things *because of* what happens in their brain. But this is false.

Biological events don't cause human actions; they occur on a different level of analysis. Understanding that the primitive responses of the amygdala can overwhelm the logical deliberations of the prefrontal cortex sheds light on why it's difficult to avoid reacting emotionally in certain situations; but we can still hold people accountable for their actions.

If a man punches his wife during an argument, the fact that his amygdala triggered the emotional circuits of his brain doesn't excuse his behavior. It may explain what happened in biological terms, but we still expect the man to learn to resist his aggressive impulses—regardless of the level, biological or behavioral, on which we describe that process. In terms of human action, we might say that the man can learn to resist the impulse to hit his wife even when he gets very upset. In biological terms, affective neuroscientists, such as Richard Davidson (2001, 2003), have found that the prefrontal cortex can moderate emotional reactivity—and that people can learn to activate their prefrontal cortexes and restrain their emotional reactions.

It may be that cognitive intervention works only when clients are calm (Atkinson, 2005)—that is, before their amygdalas have short-circuited their prefrontal cortexes. But isn't this what Murray Bowen taught us fifty years ago: that family members can't reason together until the therapist has helped them reduce the level of their anxiety?

Neural circuits control the creation of meaning, the regulation of bodily states, the modulation of emotion, the organization of memory, and the capacity for interpersonal communication. But since these same functions are also influenced by relationship experiences, we can see that interpersonal experience and the structure of the brain interact in a circular fashion. In other words, the brain shapes experience and experience shapes the structure and function of the brain.

$\mathcal{S}$PIRITUALITY

Throughout the twentieth century, psychotherapists avoided bringing religion into the consulting room. They also tried to stay out of the moralizing business, striving to remain neutral so that clients could make up their own minds about their lives.

In the 1990s, as increasing numbers of people found modern life isolating and empty, spirituality and religion emerged as antidotes to a widespread feeling of alienation—both in the popular press (making the covers of both *Time* and *Newsweek*) and in the family therapy literature (Brothers, 1992; Burton, 1992; Doherty, 1996; Prest & Keller, 1993; Walsh, 1999).

Some of a family's most powerful influences have to do with how they find meaning in their lives and with their ideas about a higher power, yet most therapists never ask about such matters. Is it possible to explore a family's spiritual beliefs without proselytizing or scoffing? More and more therapists believe that it's not only possible but crucial. They believe that people's answers to those larger questions are intimately related to their well-being.

$\mathcal{T}$AILORING TREATMENT TO POPULATIONS AND PROBLEMS

When family therapists came down from the ivory towers of their institutes to grapple with the messy problems of the real world, they found it increasingly necessary to fit their approaches to the needs of their clients, rather than the other way around. The maturing of family therapy is reflected in its literature. Once most of the writing was about one of the classic models and how they applied to families in general (e.g., Haley, 1976; Minuchin & Fishman, 1981). In the 1980s books no longer tied to any one school began to focus on how to do family therapy with a host of specific problems and family constellations.

Books are now available on working with families of people who abuse drugs (Barth, Pietrzak, & Ramier, 1993), alcohol (Elkin, 1990), food (Root, Fallon, & Friedrich, 1986), and each other (Friedrich, 1990).

There are books about treating single-parent families (Morawetz & Walker, 1984), stepfamilies (Visher & Visher, 1988), divorcing families (Emery, 1994), and families in transition (Pittman, 1987).

There are also books on treating families with young children (Combrinck-Graham, 1989; Wachtel, 1994); with troubled adolescents (Micucci, 1998; Nichols, 2004; Price, 1996; Sells, 1998); with young adults (Haley, 1980); and with problems among siblings (Kahn & Lewis, 1988). There are even books on normal families (Walsh, 1993) and successful families (Beavers & Hampson, 1990).

There are books for working with schizophrenic families (Anderson, Reiss, & Hogarty, 1986); families with bipolar disorder (Miklowitz & Goldstein, 1997); families with AIDS (Walker, 1991); families who have suffered trauma (Figley, 1985), chronic illness, or disability (McDaniel, Hepworth, & Doherty, 1992; Rolland, 1994); families who are grieving a death (Walsh & McGoldrick, 1991), have a child with a disability (Seligman & Darling, 1996), or have an adopted child (Reitz & Watson, 1992); poor families (Minuchin, Colapinto, & Minuchin, 1998); and families of different ethnicities (Boyd-Franklin, 1989; Falicov, 1998; Lee, 1997; McGoldrick, Pierce, & Giordano, 2005; Okun, 1996). There are also books about treating gay and lesbian families (Greenan & Tunnel, 2003).

In addition to these specialized books, the field extended systems thinking beyond the family to include the impact of larger systems like other helping agents and social agencies and schools (Elizur & Minuchin, 1989; Imber-Black, 1988; Schwartzman,

1985), the importance of family rituals and their use in therapy (Imber-Black, Roberts, & Whiting, 1988), and the sociopolitical context in which families exist (McGoldrick, 1998; Mirkin, 1990).

There are practical guides to family therapy not connected to any one school (Patterson et al., 1998; Taibbi, 1996) and edited books that include contributions from all of the schools (Dattilio, 1998; Donovan, 1999). Thus, as opposed to the earlier days of family therapy, when followers of a particular model read little outside what came from that school, the trend toward specialization by content rather than by model has made the field more pluralistic in this postmodern age.

Among the most frequently encountered family constellations with unique challenges are single-parent families, African American families, and gay and lesbian families. The following recommendations are offered as introductions to some of the issues encountered in treating these groups.

Single-Parent Families

The most common structural problem in single-parent families is the same as in most two-parent families: an overburdened mother enmeshed with her children and disengaged from adult relationships. From this perspective, the goal of therapy is to strengthen the mother's hierarchical position in relation to her children and help her become more fulfilled in her own life. However, it's important to keep in mind that single parents rarely have the resources to manage much of a social life on top of working all day and then coming home to take care of the kids, cook dinner, wash dishes, and do three loads of laundry.

In working with single-parent families, therapists should keep in mind that supporting the parent's care of her children and helping her find more satisfaction in her own life are reciprocal achievements. A therapist should enter the system by addressing the presenting complaint, but whether that problem is, say, a mother's depression or a child's school performance, it's important both to help the parent take more effective charge of her children and increase her sources of support.

Effective therapy with a single parent begins with an actively supportive relationship. An empathic therapeutic alliance helps shore up a single parent's confidence to make positive changes and serves as a bridge to help her connect with other people in her environment. To begin with, it's well to recognize that single parents are often angry and disappointed over the loss of a relationship, financial hardship, and trying to cope with the demands of work and children.

Poverty may be the most overwhelming burden on single parents and their children (Duncan & Brooks-Gunn, 1997). Therapists should not underestimate the impact of poverty on a mother's depression, self-esteem, and independence and the decisions she makes about putting up with soul-draining jobs and abusive relationships. Many single-parent families live on the edge of crisis, managing most of the time but always aware that any unexpected emergency can push them over the edge. A supportive therapist recognizes the burdens of financial hardship, makes accommodations to the parent's work schedule, and in some cases helps the single parent consider options like going back to school that might help her to become more financially stable.

Often one of the most readily available sources of support for the single parent is her own family. Here, the therapeutic task is twofold: facilitating supportive connections and reducing conflicts. Sometimes it's easier to develop dormant sources of support than to resolve contentious ones. The sister who lives twenty miles away may be more willing to look after her nieces and nephews from time to time than a depressed single mother thinks. A single parent's family can provide financial support, a place to stay, and help with the children. However, since most parents have trouble getting over treating their grown children as children—especially when they ask for help—a therapist may have to meet with the grandparents, develop an alliance, and then help them and their adult children negotiate effective working relationships.

Pointing out these potential sources of assistance for single parents should not be taken to suggest that a family therapist's only or even primary function should be supportive counseling. Most families, single-parent or otherwise, seek clinical services because they are stuck in conflict—psychological, interpersonal, or both. In working with single parents, a therapist's most important job is to identify and help resolve the impediments holding clients back from taking advantage of their own personal and interpersonal resources.

Sometimes the most significant conflict for single-mother households isn't visible: It's the potential involvement of the children's father, who is not infrequently described as "out of the picture." He may be out of the picture, but in most cases he shouldn't be.

Many families of young mothers find it particularly difficult to support the involvement of the baby's father (Johnson, 2001). They may even consider him an enemy. If their understandable feelings are treated with respect, they can often be helped to support the father's involvement.

Facilitating the continued involvement of teen fathers deserves special attention because it's so challenging (Lehr & MacMillan, 2001). Since it's relatively easy for teen fathers to abandon their children, it's important to reach out to them, to establish rapport, and to encourage them in becoming responsible parents.

Even invisible fathers may well desire more contact and be willing to take on more responsibility for the sake of their children. The therapist should consider contacting the noncustodial father to assess his potential contribution to his children's emotional and financial support.

Here, too, triangles can complicate the picture. In an effort to be sympathetic to their mates (and sometimes from unconscious jealousy), new partners often fan the flames of conflict with the noncustodial parent, which only reinforces the cutoff.

Case Study

Elana Santos contacted the clinic because her ten-year-old son, Tony, was depressed. "He's having trouble getting over my divorce," she said. "I think he misses his father." After two sessions, the therapist determined that Tony was not depressed, and although he did miss his father, it was his mother who hadn't gotten over the divorce. Tony *had* stopped hanging out with his friends after school; however, it was worrying about his mother, who'd become bitter and withdrawn, rather than depression that was keeping him in the house.

The therapist's formulation was that Mrs. Santos was enmeshed with her son and both were disengaged from contacts outside the family. The therapist told Mrs. Santos that her son was sad because he worried about her. "Do you need Tony to be your protector?" the therapist asked.

"No," Mrs. Santos said.

"Then I think you need to fire him. Can you convince Tony that he doesn't need to take care of you, that he can spend time with friends and that you'll be all right?"

Mrs. Santos did "fire" her son from the job of being her guardian angel. The therapist then talked about getting Tony more involved in after school activities during which he could make friends. "Who knows," the therapist said, "maybe if Tony starts making friends, you'll have some time to do the same thing."

The only person Mrs. Santos could think of to help look after Tony was the boy's father, and he was "completely unavailable." Rather than accept this statement at face value, the therapist expressed surprise "that a father would care nothing about his son." When Mrs. Santos insisted that her ex wouldn't be willing to spend any time with Tony, the therapist asked permission to call him herself.

When the therapist told Mr. Santos that she was worried about his son and thought the boy needed his father's involvement in his life, Mr. Santos seemed responsive. But then the therapist heard someone talking in the background, and Mr. Santos started to back off.

What had begun as a problem firmly embedded in one person's head—"It's my son, he's depressed"—turned out to involve not just the interaction between the boy and his mother but also a triangular complication in which the father's girlfriend objected to his involvement because she didn't want "that bitch of an ex-wife taking advantage of him." What followed were a series of meetings— with the father and his girlfriend, the father and mother, the father and son, and finally all four of them together—in which the therapist concentrated on helping them clear the air by voicing feelings of resentment that stood in the way of their working cooperatively together.

The father's girlfriend had made the same mistake that a lot of us make when someone we love complains about how someone else is treating him or her. In response to his complaints about his ex-wife's angry phone calls, she had urged him to have nothing to do with her. In response to these feelings and to Mrs. Santos's own anger and resentment, the therapist helped them to understand an important distinction between two subsystems in a divorce. The first (the couple) was dead and needed to be buried; the second (the parents) still needed to find a way to cooperate in the best interests of their child. "Burying" the divorced couple's relationship in this case was facilitated by Mrs. Santos's having an opportunity to ventilate her bitterness and anger at having been abandoned by the man she loved, although most of these discussions took place in individual sessions with the therapist.

Reducing a single parent's disengagement from adult relationships enhances her ability to strengthen the generational boundary between herself and her children. This involves delegating age-appropriate responsibilities to older children, enforcing discipline, and helping the children get involved in activities of their own. The primary structural goal for the single parent is to assume power as the chief executive in the family system. This may be difficult for a parent who is demoralized by loss or depression. Therefore, some structural goals may not be practical. Setting up charts and token economies to rein in out-of-control children, for example, may require an unrealistic amount of monitoring for an overburdened single parent. When feeling overwhelmed, single parents often lose the ability to set effective limits. Some parents may permit more misbehavior than they think they should to make up for the loss their children have suffered from divorce or lack of father involvement. Chores should be delegated, not abdicated—Mother is still in charge—and a boy is not "the man of the house" (which implies that he has taken his father's place).

Live-in partners provide additional sources of support and conflict. Many compete with the children for the mother's attention. Some undermine the mother's authority, while others try to enforce their own rules, setting up a triangle in which the mother is forced to side either with her boyfriend or her children. Live-in partners' attempts to enforce discipline are frequently rebuffed, especially by adolescents. Their job isn't that of a parent but of a backup for the mother as the primary authority over her children.

Children may benefit from increased social contacts to help balance the intensity of the single-parent-and-child connection. Resources to consider include teachers, coaches, Big Brothers and Big Sisters, activity group leaders, community groups ("Parents Without Partners," "Mother's Day Out"), religious congregations, craft classes, and workplace contacts.

Families take many forms; the single-parent family is one of them. Families don't get broken or destroyed, but they do change shapes. Unfortunately, the transition from being together to being apart is a road without maps. No wonder there is so much pain and confusion.

African American Families

Therapists working with African American families should be prepared to expand the definition of family to include an *extended kinship system.* The kinship network remains one of the keys to coping with the pressures of oppression (Billingsley, 1992; Staples, 1994). There may be a number of aunts, uncles, "big mamas," boyfriends, older brothers and sisters, cousins, deacons, preachers, and others who operate in and out of the African American home (White, 1972, p. 45). However, many families who come to the attention of mental health workers have become isolated from their traditional support network. Part of a therapist's task is to search for persons in the family or kin network who represent islands of strength and enlist their support in

helping the family. Asking "Who can you depend on when you need help?" is one way to locate such individuals.

A structural assessment should consider not only those people who are involved with the family but also those who might be called on for support. In the African American community, these potential connections include an extensive kinship network, made up of both family and friends (Billingsley, 1968; McAdoo, 2002).

These extended connections, real and potential, mean that family boundaries and lines of authority can become blurred, as the following example illustrates.

Case Study

When Juanita Williams entered a residential drug treatment program, she was lucky to have her friend, Nancy, willing to take in her three children. Six months later Juanita was ready to leave rehab and return home. By that time, the Williams children had grown accustomed to living with "Aunt Nancy" and her two teenagers.

When the children's case worker arranged a meeting with Juanita and her children and "Aunt Nancy," Nancy praised Juanita for completing the rehab program and preparing to resume the responsibility for her children. "You know I love them, almost like they were my own," she said to Juanita, who nodded. "But now it's time for them to move back with their rightful mother." However, it appeared to the social worker that Nancy had effectively taken over the family and that Juanita had lost her authority. Nancy did most of the talking while Juanita sat quietly, looking down. Martin (fourteen), Jesse (twelve), and Coretta (eleven) said nothing.

The social worker concluded that Nancy and the Williams children were enmeshed while Juanita was disengaged, and the worker saw her job as helping Juanita and her children reconnect while Nancy stepped back into a supportive but less central role. Toward this end she said that Juanita was lucky to have such a good friend to act as foster mother to her children, but now it was time for her to reclaim her role as head of the family. She then set up an enactment in which she asked Juanita to talk with her children about her plans for the immediate future.

When Juanita began by telling the children how much she missed them, Nancy spoke up to say that the children missed her, too. Nancy's intentions were good, but her interruption was a sign of her overly central role. The therapist complimented Nancy for being helpful but said that it was time to show her support by letting Juanita speak for herself. Juanita resumed talking to her children, saying, "I know that I can't promise anything, but every day I will try my hardest to be the right kind of mother to you and not to give in to my disease. And," she went on with tears in her eyes, "I know that with God's help we can be the family that we used to be."

Martin looked down; Jesse and Coretta had tears in their eyes. Then Martin turned to the therapist and said, "Can I speak?" "Of course, Martin, you can say whatever you want."

"I love you, Mommy," he said. "And I hope to God that you don't go back to the drugs. But I will never—*never*—live in a house where I have to watch my mother going into the streets again. When I don't know whether we're going to have any supper that night because you're out getting high. You will never put me through that again."

"Martin—" Once again Nancy started to interrupt, and once again the social worker blocked her.

Martin went on talking for fifteen minutes about the pain and rage of growing up with a mother who was a drug addict. He held nothing back. Juanita was crying hard. When Martin finished, there was a long, heavy silence.

Then Juanita spoke up. "I know what I put you through, Martin. What I put all my children through. And I know that I can never, ever make up for that. But as God is my witness, I will do everything in my power never, ever again to let you down or make you ashamed of me. All I want is another chance."

It was a gut-wrenching exchange. Martin had spoken straight from the heart, and he and his mother had gotten through to each other—with no interference from well-meaning friends or helpful professionals anxious to put a good face on things.

The prominence of religion and spirituality in African American family life (Hines & Boyd-Franklin, 1982) provides both a real and potential resource. Many African American families have gained strength from church membership and connection to their church community (Billingsley, 1994; Walsh, 1999). Therapists who work with black families can profit from developing a relationship with ministers in the community who can often help mobilize support for an isolated single mother, an adolescent who is abusing drugs, or a mentally ill adult who is cut off from support following the death of a caregiver (Boyd-Franklin, 2003).

One reason father-absent households are so common among African Americans is that there are far fewer men than women in the African American community. Among the reasons for the absence of African American men are substance abuse, death related to hazardous jobs and delays in seeking vital health care, military service, homicide, and, of course, the astonishingly high percentage of African American men in prison (U.S. Bureau of the Census, 2003). There are not only fewer African American men, but also their participation in family life is often undermined by limited job opportunities and a tendency on the part of mental health professionals to overlook men in the extended family system, including a father's kinship network and a mother's male friends, who may be involved in the children's lives.

Too many therapists resign themselves to the non-participation of fathers in family therapy. A father who is regarded as unavailable may agree to attend if contacted directly by the therapist. Even if the father has trouble getting away from work, he may agree to come to one or two sessions if he's convinced that he's really needed. Therapists can also use phone calls and letters to keep a father involved in his family's treatment. Respecting a father's family role decreases the likelihood of his sabotaging treatment (Hines & Boyd-Franklin, 1996), and even limited participation may lead to a structural shift in the family.

Partly as a consequence of absent fathers, many families in the African American community are three-generational systems, made up of a mother, her children, and a grandmother. Sometimes grandmothers are asked to take over the job of raising a second set of children. At other times, single mothers or fathers and their children move back in with the grandparents. In some cases, teenage mothers will turn their children over to their mothers but later want to take back the responsibility of raising their own children. While none of these family structures is inherently dysfunctional, they all create complications.

Grandmothers who take over may have trouble letting go. They see their young adult children behaving irresponsibly, and they treat them accordingly. Unfortunately, this perpetuates the classic control-and-rebel cycle that so many young people get caught up in with their parents. Therapists can't always remain neutral in this kind of impasse. It may be useful to support the young mother or father in the role of parent while respecting the grandmother's contribution and availability for advice and support (Minuchin, Nichols, & Lee, 2007).

Even the healthiest families have trouble functioning effectively under the crushing weight of financial hardship. When survival issues—like food, housing, and utilities—are involved, these take precedence over family conflicts. Therapists can usefully act as resources to encourage family members to work with available community and social agents in dealing with housing, job training, employment, and child care (Rojano, 2004).

The combination of discrimination and oppression, aggravated by racism and poverty, has produced a "fierce anger" in many African Americans (Cose, 1993). Service providers must realize that some of this anger may be directed against them. It's important not to get defensive. Nancy Boyd-Franklin (1989) recommends that mental health providers expect a certain amount of distrust and join with their African American clients to build trust at the outset of treatment. Communicating respect is key to successfully engaging families.

In working with inner-city African American families, therapists must take into account that they may be enmeshed with a variety of agencies such as schools, hospitals, police courts, juvenile justice systems, welfare, child protective services, and mental health services (Henggeler & Borduin, 1990). Empowering families in this context can be accomplished by (1) setting up meetings with various organization involved with the family, (2) writing letters in support of the family, and (3) setting up conferences with the supervisors of resistant workers (Boyd-Franklin, 2003). The point is to empower families by encouraging them to take charge of these issues themselves. Therapists can help but shouldn't take over.

Gay and Lesbian Families

Gay and lesbian partners struggle with the same sorrows of confusion and longing as any intimate partners. Every couple must find a way to balance time together with independent interests, choose whether and when to have children, and decide whose family to spend the holidays with. But same-sex couples also face unique challenges, including homophobia; resolving relational ambiguities in the areas of commitment, boundaries, and gender-linked behavior; handling differences about being "out" professionally or socially; and developing networks of social support (Green & Mitchell, 2002). To work effectively with gay and lesbian clients, it's important for therapists neither to ignore nor exaggerate the unique nature of same-sex pairings.

While it may be reassuring for heterosexual therapists to dissociate themselves from the overt homophobia in our culture, it's a little more difficult to deal with internalized homophobia—in themselves and in their clients. Therapists who aren't comfortable with love and sex between two men or two women may have trouble talking frankly with gay couples or may behave with patronizing deference. A therapist who is overly anxious to convey his or her progressive attitude may find it difficult to push for change or to ask the tough questions that may be necessary with couples who aren't getting along.

Case Study

Stephen and David sought therapy during a crisis induced by Stephen's wanting to open up their relationship to other partners and David's refusing to even discuss this possibility. Their therapist, who was anxious to distance himself from the stereotype that gay men are promiscuous, got caught up in trying to solve the problem of Stephen's inability to commit, rather than exploring the broader problem of the couple's difficulty communicating and making decisions. Had the couple been a man and a wife disagreeing over whether to buy a house or rent an apartment, it's unlikely that the therapist would have so quickly taken sides and reduced therapy to an exercise in problem solving.

Homophobia may also manifest itself in subtle and not so subtle ways in lesbian and gay people themselves (Brown, 1994; Meyer & Dean, 1998). Anyone who grows up in a society in which homosexuality is considered deviant will find it impossible not to absorb at least some of this attitude.

In working with same-sex couples, it's important to probe for subtle manifestations of negative images of homosexuality and same-sex relationships. One stereotype that can be particularly destructive is the cultural expectation that same-sex pairings are inherently unstable. Many people, gay as well as straight, believe that enduring relationships between same-sex partners (especially gay men) are impossible to achieve.

As with many biases, it's probably more useful for therapists to examine their own assumptions than to imagine themselves to be without bias. Identifying your assumptions makes it easier to hold them in check; pretending that you don't have assumptions allows them to act on you unsuspectingly.

Working with gay and lesbian couples requires sensitivity to the internalization of traditional gender norms. Heterosexual partners have typically been socialized for complementary roles. Women and men may no longer expect to be "Leave-It-to-Beaver" parents, but like it or not, women are still taught to be

more caring and to have a less distanced sense of self (Jordan et al., 1991), while men are brought up to be in control, to be territorial, to tolerate distance, and to thrive on competition. So what happens when same-sex partners get together? Who picks up the towels from the bathroom floor? Who initiates sex?

Many gay and lesbian couples struggle as much as heterosexual couples over whether and when to have children. But unlike their heterosexual counterparts, gays and lesbians have to resolve the issue of who (if either) will be the biological parent.

Case Study

Rachel and Jan had been together for ten years and were considering having a child. Both agreed that they would like to have a biological child. However, both women wanted to be the sperm recipient.

Seeing that Rachel and Jan were at an impasse, the therapist suggested that they consider adopting. Worn out and frustrated by their inability to decide which of them would give up the wish to carry their baby, the women jumped at this suggestion. However, their relief turned to anger when they discovered that the state they lived in (which starts with the letter V) did not allow gay and lesbian couples to adopt children. Their experience made them lose confidence in their therapist and they dropped out of treatment.

One of the issues in therapy with same-sex couples is likely to be the need to negotiate clear agreements about commitments and boundaries and roles. Among the questions a therapist might usefully ask are these:

What are the rules in your relationship about monogamy?
What are your agreements about finances, pooling of resources, and joint ownership of property?
Who does which tasks in the household, and how is this decided?

Some of the usual expectations that heterosexuals bring to marriage don't apply to same-sex couples unless they are discussed and agreed to (Green & Mitchell, 2002). Among these expectations are monogamy, pooled finances, caring for each other through serious illness, moving together for each other's career advancement, caring for each other's families in old age, and mutual inheritance, to name just a few. Because there are no familiar models for being a same-sex couple, partners may have discrepant visions about how these issues will be handled. We suggest that therapists be aware of these issues and prepared to help clients discuss them but not introduce issues that clients don't yet seem ready to deal with.

Some therapists might be surprised to learn that many gay men maintain stable relationships that allow outside sexual activity (Bringle, 1995; Bryant & Demian, 1994). In studying this phenomenon, Michael LaSala (2004a) found no differences on the Dyadic Adjustment Scale between strictly monogamous and openly nonmonogamous gay male couples. However, couples who'd agreed to be monogamous but in which one or both partners engaged in extrarelational sex were less well adjusted. Thus, for some gay men, sexual monogamy may not be a necessary component of a satisfactory committed relationship. LaSala (2004b) found that men in successful open relationships establish guidelines that safeguard their health and affirm couple primacy. Obviously, therapists need to respect their clients' preferences and help them decide what type of relationship works best for them. But only by being aware of the various options available to male couples can a therapist be expected to help them discover what suits their specific needs.

Heterosexual therapists may underestimate the complexities involved in coming out to family and friends (LaSala, 1997). Here it may be well to remember that therapy isn't about pushing people to go where they're afraid to go but is about helping them recognize and resolve the fears that hold them back.

Another difficulty that heterosexual therapists may overlook in same-sex relationships is the prevalence of jealousy on the part of one of the partners (Green & Mitchell, 2002). This jealously is based on the belief that others are a threat because of lack of respect for the couple's commitment to each other. After all, how can a relationship be real if the partners aren't married?

Case Study

Jim enjoyed the club scene as a way to socialize with his friends in the gay community. His partner, Kyle, preferred to avoid bars and clubs. According to Kyle, his objections weren't so much to Jim's having a good time but that he believed other men in the clubs had little respect for the fact that Jim was part of a couple. "They don't care about us if they think they can get in your pants." Kyle was also concerned about the prevalence of drugs like ecstasy, cocaine, crystal meth, and special K that were part of the club atmosphere. Jim insisted that he wasn't interested in other men and didn't do drugs. He just wanted to hang out with his friends.

Although some therapists might see Jim's insistence on going to bars as a failure to accept that he was no longer single, the therapist in this case was aware that, in fact, *not* going to bars and clubs can result in a significant disconnect from much of the gay community. And so, rather than accept the options the couple presented—either Jim gave in and stayed home, or Kyle gave in and Jim continued to go clubbing—the therapist wondered out loud if there were alternative ways for the couple to socialize within the gay community.

Maybe the best advice for therapists working with gay and lesbian couples is to ask themselves "What messages am I communicating to this couple about the value of same-sex relationships?" It isn't just negative messages that therapists should be alert to but also the danger of glorifying same-sex relationships. Denigration and idealization have an equal potential for harm.

Sex and the Internet

Few things have transformed the landscape of the twenty-first century like electronic technology: e-mail, cell phones, pagers, instant messaging, electronic games, and, of course, the Internet. The Internet facilitates research and communication: It informs, it helps people connect, and it helps them disconnect—to escape from active participation in relationships into a private reverie of solitary pursuits.

Contemporary technologies bring many advantages, but it is important for anyone practicing marriage and family therapy to be aware of at least one area where technology can create problems in family relationships. That area is cybersex.

A recent survey found that the majority of marriage and family therapists see clients presenting with cybersex problems, and the number of such cases is increasing (Goldberg, Peterson, Rosen, & Sara, 2008). Therapists who see families with adolescents may be called on to deal with issues related to pornography and the dangers of inappropriate sexual contact. And therapists who work with couples will almost certainly encounter problems associated with compulsive consumption of pornography as well as more active forms of infidelity.

Complicating the clinician's task is the fact that although problems with cybersex are widespread, they are still shameful and therefore not easily talked about. Consequently, it's important to know what to look for and what kinds of questions to ask.

Although there are many areas of the Internet, the World Wide Web is usually the first place teens experiment with online sexual behavior or become victims of sexual harassment or offense. Social networking sites (MySpace, Facebook, Bebo), video and photo-sharing technologies (MySpace, Google, Video, Photobucket), and online gaming (Gunz, Runescape, World of Warcraft) all present opportunities for inappropriate sexual activities. These include posting sexually provocative photos and videos, as well as sexual communications via chat rooms, e-mail, or other postings (Gillispie & Gackenbach, 2007).

In addition to understanding the various online venues where teenagers may engage in problematic sexual behavior, it's important to have a grasp of the lingo used online. Two resources that can help educate parents and therapists about online slang are

Netlingo (www.netlingo.com) and Noslang (www.noslang.com). Here are some examples:

Cybering—Engaging in sexual activity with someone online
POS—Parent over shoulder
IWSN—I want sex now
Q2C—Quick to cum
Lurking—Nonparticipation in a chat room; chat observer
RUH—Are you horny?
LMIRL—Let's meet in real life
TDTM—Talk dirty to me.
P911—Parent alert
{ }—Hugs.

When discussing technology with families, it's important to inquire about all forms of Internet access, because cell phones, BlackBerries, gaming systems, and iPods all provide access to the Internet and its temptations. It can be hard for parents to supervise their children's computer use because in most families, it is the youngest members who are the most computer savvy. Moreover, the invention of removable storage media (jump drives, USB drives, portable hard drives) allows users to store information from the Internet and other sources onto small devices that can easily be hidden.

Various software programs are designed to screen out sexual content and conversations on a child's computer. But while these programs may be effective with younger children, such programs are easily circumvented by older teens. Although parents may appreciate recommendations about software to prevent problems, these programs should not give a false sense of security about adolescents' Internet use.

Even with the use of blocking software, most teens will be exposed to pornographic pictures, videos, stories, or sexual conversations on the Internet. In fact, 70 percent of all children from ten to seventeen admit that they have been exposed to some form of pornography on the Internet. The following are some indicators that online behavior problems may be occurring (Delmonico & Griffin, 2008).

- Sacrificing previously enjoyed activities to spend more time on the computer
- Maintaining secrecy about the frequency or types of online activities
- Signs of depression or anxiety, especially noticeable after Internet use or during times when Internet access is unavailable
- Taking increased risks with online activity—using computers for pornography at school, meeting people from the Internet without precautions
- Jeopardizing important activities because of Internet use—missing school or coming late, losing relationships, and so on

The dangers to which the Internet exposes children include not only pornography but also cyberbullying and cyberharassment and, more ominously, inappropriate sexual contact with people in the real world.

The friend a teenager meets online in a chat room may turn out to be adult predator. As many as 19 percent of American teenagers have been the target of unwanted sexual solicitation. Girls, older teens, troubled youth, frequent Internet users, chat room participants, and those who communicate online with strangers are at greatest risk. (Mitchell, Finkelhor, & Wolak, 2001). Therapists should be prepared to educate young people about these dangers, including urging them to report such encounters to their parents or other responsible adults.

Here are some suggestions for protecting children from cybersex predators (Weiss & Schneider, 2006).

- Limit computer privacy by placing any computer with Internet access where it can be easily monitored.
- Monitor the child's Internet use by checking the computer's bookmarks, history of Web sites accessed, and caches. Consider computer software such as Disk Tracy (www.disktracy.com) that provides a list of every online site accessed by the computer on which it is installed.
- Install blocking software such as CyberPatrol (www.cyberpatrol.com), which will deny access to sexually inappropriate sites, including instant messaging.

- Consider using a "family-oriented" Internet service provider that blocks sexually inappropriate material from ever reaching your computer.
- Teach children never to reveal to anyone their real name, address, or phone number or to provide any information (such as the name of their school) that will make it easy to locate them.
- Let children know that it is never acceptable to meet in person someone whom they have met online without parental supervision.
- Talk with children about their Internet activities. Encourage them to discuss any online experiences that make them feel guilty or uncomfortable.
- If you believe a child is being sexually exploited or that someone is attempting to exploit him or her, consider this a sex crime and report it to the FBI.

Finally, although technology may facilitate problematic sexual behavior, it would be a mistake to think that solving such problems is simply a matter of technology. Although parents may want to install protective software on their children's computers, it's probably more important for therapists to encourage dialogue between parents and teenagers regarding Internet use and sexuality. Moreover, therapists may need to help parents understand that when it comes to protecting teenagers from unhealthy sexual experiences, adult supervision and control isn't the only answer. Once children reach a certain age, parental control—especially if it's seen as unfair—may produce as much rebellion as compliance. If the issue is curfews or chores, the rebellion may be obvious and take the form of arguments. But when the issue is something as shame sensitive as sexuality, rebellion may take the form of "silent arguing" (Nichols, 2009)—that is, apparent compliance but with surreptitious acting out. Thus, it's wise to involve teenagers in discussions about limiting computer use, because they are far more likely to accept decisions to which they have had a chance to contribute.

• • •

When it comes to adults, it can be argued that pornography and other forms of sexual experience are harmless private activities and that they can even enhance the passion in a couple's relationship. But pornography, online relationships, and sexual behavior can become compulsions and are often characterized by secrecy that's detrimental to the trust and intimacy of relationships (Cooper, 2002). As a result, therapists have been seeing more and more cases involving compulsive viewing of pornography and Internet infidelity (Gonyea, 2004). Among the sexually oriented activities that can become problematic are:

- Viewing pornography and masturbating
- Reading and writing sexually oriented stories and letters
- Using e-mail to set up meetings
- Placing ads to meet sexual partners
- Visiting sexually oriented chat rooms
- Interactive affairs (including sharing nudity and sexual behavior via webcams)

With the advent of digital video streaming and the relatively modest cost of webcams, images can be captured and sent, and messages returned, all in real time. As the technology of the Internet has advanced, the experience of cybersex has gone beyond photos and recorded videos to live-action images and on-demand sexual responses, or virtual sex. These developments make the experience more compelling and the sense of betrayal in the partner more profound. Given the growing number of cases presenting with cybersex-related issues, therapists should be sufficiently well versed in the ways of technology to know what questions to ask and how to pose them.

The following questions adapted from Weiss and Schneider (2006) are designed to explore the nature and extent of a client's online sexual activities.

1. Do you find yourself spending increasing amounts of time online looking at porn or engaged in sexual or romantic intrigue?
2. Have you been involved in romantic or sexual affairs online?
3. Does pornography or online sexual activity violate your marital commitments?
4. Have you been unable to cut back on the frequency of your online sexual activity despite thinking that you should?
5. Have you been unable to stay away from sexual material, sites, or interactions that have made you feel guilty or ashamed of yourself?
6. Does your pornography use interfere with home life, work, or school (including making you tired or late for obligations)?
7. Does pornography use intrude on relationships that are important to you?
8. Do you collect pornography?
9. Do you engage in fantasy acts online or view porn depicting illegal or violent sexual acts, such as rape, bestiality, or child porn?
10. Has the time you spend with friends, family, and loved ones decreased because of your porn use or fantasy involvement?
11. Do you lie or keep secrets about the amount of time you spend viewing porn, the type of porn you choose, or the types of activities you engage in online?
12. Do you have sex—either in fantasy online or in person—with someone other than your spouse or partner?
13. Are you hearing complaints from family or friends about the amount of time you spend online using porn or the type of porn you use?
14. Do you get irritable or angry when asked to give up or reduce porn involvement?
15. Has the primary focus of your sexual or romantic life become increasingly related to images found in magazines, videos, or Internet activity?

Three or more positive answers are grounds for concern.

As with the old-fashioned kind of infidelity, it isn't fair to say that Internet infidelity is caused by problems in relationships. However, from the circular perspective of systems theory, it doesn't matter whether problems in a relationship caused problems with sex on the Internet or the other way around. They feed each other. Instead of worrying about which came first, a clinician can address both fronts simultaneously: encouraging an end to compulsive sexual activity and looking at problems in the relationship that may fuel this activity. For example, anger at one's partner—especially unexpressed or at least unresolved anger—lead some people to feel that they are entitled to seek soothing and excitement outside the relationship.

Like drug and alcohol addiction, sexual obsession affects both men and women. Approximately 25 percent of people in sex addiction recovery programs are women (Cooper, 2002). While men are more likely to download pornography, women typically prefer chat rooms and personal ads where there is more of a chance to actually get to know the objects of their interest.

Without outside intervention, most compulsive behavior escalates over time. This is especially true with highly reinforcing activities like drug taking and sexual behavior. Only when the consequences are severe enough do most people caught up in compulsive self-gratification seek help. When it comes to compulsive sexual behavior, these consequences may include relationship problems, job loss, public shaming, sexually transmitted diseases, arrest, and even imprisonment.

While there are obviously many different approaches to therapy and not all therapists see compulsive sexual behavior as a *sex addiction* or adhere to a twelve-step treatment model, it's important to remember that therapists should not attempt to treat problems outside the range of their expertise. If a therapist doesn't understand pornography abuse and compulsive sexual behavior or have training and experience in treating these problems, he or she should refer the case to someone who does. The Society for the Advancement of Sexual Health maintains a Web site (www.sash.net) that includes a list of professionals knowledgeable about compulsive sexual behavior organized by country and state.

The problems in couples' relationships that are related—as cause and effect—to outside sexual activity involve communication, boundaries, and commitment. In addressing problems in a couple's

communication, a therapist should encourage the partners to talk about their needs and how to meet them. The obvious boundary problem with extramarital affairs that originate with Internet pornography is an inadequate boundary that fails to protect the relationship from one or both partners straying. However, like all boundaries, this one is reciprocal. The complement of a diffuse boundary around a relationship is a rigid boundary (and disengagement) between the partners. And the thing to remember about disengagement is that it exists for a reason. If a couple is disengaged, one or both partners are probably harboring a great deal of unresolved resentment.

If one of the partners goes outside of a relationship to find sexual excitement and intimacy—or just plain attention—there is obviously a problem with commitment. The question for a therapist to explore is why.

HOME-BASED SERVICES

Like traditional family therapy, home-based services target the family as the primary recipient of mental health care (Friesen & Koroloff, 1990). Unlike conventional models, however, the home-based approach focuses more on enhancing family resources than on repairing family dysfunction (Henggeler & Borduin, 1990). While home-based services recognize and address problems in the family system, the primary emphasis is on building relationships between the family and various community resources.

Home-based services generally include four elements: family support services, therapeutic intervention, case management, and crisis intervention (Lindblad-Goldberg, Dore, & Stern, 1998). *Family support services* include respite care as well as assistance with food, clothing, and shelter. *Therapeutic intervention* may include individual, family, or couples treatment. The overriding therapeutic goal is strengthening and stabilizing the family unit. Families are empowered by helping them utilize their own strengths and resources for solving problems rather than relying on out-of-home placement of the child. *Case management* involves developing links to community resources, including medical care, welfare, education, job training, and legal services. *Crisis intervention* means making available twenty-four-hour emergency services, either with the home-based agency or by contracting with an outside mental health emergency service.

Visiting a family at home gives a therapist an opportunity to show interest in the things that define their identity—children, pets, religious artifacts, mementos, awards, and so on. Looking through photo albums can be a valuable method in joining with a family and learning about their history and their hopes and dreams.

Once a positive relationship has been established—but not before—the therapist can ask the family to reduce such distractions as smoking, loud television playing, and barking dogs. (Barking cats are less often a problem.) Roles and boundaries that are implicit in an office setting may need to be spelled out. Clarifying roles while in the home begins with defining what the process of treatment entails, the ground rules for sessions, and what the therapist's and family members' roles will be. The following comments illustrate the process of clarifying roles (adapted from Lindblad-Goldberg, Dore, & Stern, 1998):

"Before we start, I want to say that I have no intention of coming here and telling you how to run your lives. My job is to help you figure out how you want to deal with your children. I can't solve your problems. Only you can do that.

In our meetings, it's important for you to say whatever you think and feel. We need to be honest. Tell me what you expect of me, and I'll tell you what I expect of you. I won't act like I have all the answers, because I don't.

"Will Grandmother be coming tonight? If not, that's okay, but I would like her to attend future sessions, because I'm sure she has valuable ideas to contribute. Tonight, I'd like to get to know each of you a little bit. After that, I'd like to hear what concerns each of you has about your family life and what you'd like to change."

While family therapists tend to speak glibly about their "ecosystemic" orientation, home-based workers really must coordinate their efforts with other service systems. Rather than being critical of school personnel or juvenile justice workers who don't seem to support the family and child, home-based workers must learn to appreciate that these other agencies are equally concerned about the needs of their clients, even though their approaches may differ. A family served by multiple agencies who don't see eye to eye is no different from a child caught in a triangle between parents who can't function as a team.

While in-home therapy offers a unique opportunity to influence families in their natural environment, seeing people in their living rooms also increases the pressures of induction into a family's problematic patterns. Working with a cotherapist may help minimize the tendency to be drawn unwittingly into a family's unproductive way of seeing things. Home-based therapists who don't work with cotherapists must make special efforts to maintain professional boundaries and avoid being inducted into playing missing roles in the family. For example, if a child needs comforting, it's better to support the parents in providing it than to take over their function.

One of the most unfortunate things that happens in psychotherapy is that clients often recreate with their therapists the same unsatisfying kinds of relationships they have with most people. Perhaps the most important thing a therapist can do is to avoid being drawn in to the usual pattern. The most dangerous pattern for home-based workers to repeat is moving in too close and then pushing clients to go where they are afraid to go. Rather than start pushing for change right away, it's often more effective to begin by recognizing the obstacles to change.

Beleaguered families fear abandonment; insecure therapists fear not being helpful. The worker who feels pulled to do everything for a client may subsequently feel overwhelmed by the family's needs and back away by setting rigid limits and withholding support. The "rescuer" then becomes another "abandoner." This process reactivates the clients' anxiety and inevitably pushes them away. The lessons for the family are clear: Nothing will ever change—and don't trust anyone.

PSYCHOEDUCATION AND MEDICAL FAMILY THERAPY

Over the past fifteen years a new conception of family therapy has emerged. Rather than solving problems, the goal of this approach is to help families cope with disabilities. This represents a shift from the idea that families cause problems to the idea that problems, like natural disasters, sometimes befall families.

Psychoeducation and Schizophrenia

The search for a cure for schizophrenia launched the field of family therapy in the 1950s. Ironically, while we now know that schizophrenia is a biological illness, family therapy, or at least the psychoeducational model, is once again considered part of the most effective treatment for this baffling disorder.

The psychoeducational model was born of dissatisfaction with both traditional family therapy and psychiatric approaches to schizophrenia. As Carol Anderson, Douglas Reiss, and Gerald Hogarty (1986) lamented,

> We have blamed each other, the patients themselves, their parents and grandparents, public authorities, and society for the cause and for the too often terrible course of these disorders. When hope and money become exhausted, we frequently tear schizophrenic patients from their families, consigning them to the existential terror of human warehouses, single room occupancy hotels, and more recently to the streets and alleys of American cities (p. vii).

In their attempts to get at the function of the schizophrenic's symptoms, family therapists urged family members to express bottled-up feelings and thus created sessions of highly charged emotion, which often did little more than stir up tension. After noticing the frequent decline in functioning of patients and increased anxiety in their families after such sessions, Anderson and her colleagues (1986) "began to wonder if most 'real' family therapy was in fact antitherapeutic" (p. 2).

Meanwhile, studies began to show that the patients who fared best after hospitalization were those who returned to the least stressful households. A British group, including George Brown, John Wing, Julian Leff, and Christine Vaughn, focused on what they called *expressed emotion (EE)* in the families of schizophrenics—particularly criticism, hostility, and emotional overinvolvement—and found that patients returning to high EE households had higher rates of relapse (Brown, Birley, & Wing, 1972; Vaughn & Leff, 1976; Vaughn et al., 1984).

Research on expressed emotion suggests that schizophrenia is a thought disorder that renders individuals particularly sensitive to criticism and hostility. Intense emotional input makes it difficult for patients to cope with the welter of chaotic thoughts that plague them. When recovering patients return to stressful family settings, in which EE is high, intrusive overconcern and critical comments lead to increased emotional arousal, and it is this affective overload that triggers relapse.

Expressed emotion is now the most well-documented factor in the relapse of schizophrenia (Milkowitz, 1995):

> The family, then, is seen as a risk or protective factor that may augment or diminish the likelihood that underlying genetic and/or biological vulnerabilities in a family member will be expressed as symptoms of mental disorder (p. 194).

The benefits of reducing EE in helping families cope with schizophrenia has been repeatedly demonstrated (Atkinson & Coia, 1995). Lowering EE has also been shown to contribute to reduced relapse rates for major depression and bipolar disorder (Muesser & Glynn, 1995).

With this in mind, three different groups in the late 1970s began experimenting with ways to reduce stress in the most common environments for schizophrenic patients: their parents' homes. Michael Goldstein led a group at UCLA (Goldstein et al., 1978) who designed a brief, structured model focused on anticipating the stresses a family was likely to face and reducing conflict around the patient. Following the Goldstein study, groups headed by Ian Falloon at the

University of Southern California (whose model is primarily behavioral) and Carol Anderson at the Western Psychiatric Institute in Pittsburgh experimented with psychoeducational models.

Psychoeducators seek to establish a collaborative partnership, in which family members feel supported and empowered to deal with the patient. To achieve this kind of partnership, Anderson and her colleagues find that they must reeducate professionals to give up ideas that the family is somehow responsible for schizophrenia, reinforce family strengths, and share information with the family about this disease. It is this information sharing that constitutes the educational element of psycho*education.* Information about the nature and course of schizophrenia helps family members develop a sense of mastery—a way to understand and anticipate the often chaotic and apparently uncontrollable process.

One of psychoeducation's key interventions is to lower expectations—to reduce pressure on the patient to perform normally. For example, the goals for the first year following an acute episode are primarily the avoidance of a relapse and the gradual taking on of some responsibilities in the home. Family members are to view the patient as someone who's had a serious illness and needs to recuperate. Patients may need a great deal of sleep, solitude, and limited activity for some time following an episode; they may also seem restless and have trouble concentrating. By predicting these developments, psychoeducators try to prevent conflict between the patient and the family.

Anderson's psychoeducational approach looks very much like structural family therapy except that the family's organizational flaws are construed as the *result* rather than the *cause* of the presenting problem. Much of the therapy follows familiar themes: reinforcing generational boundaries, opening up the family to the outside world and developing support networks, urging parents to reinvest in their marriage, and getting family members not to speak or do for the patient.

Anderson and her colleagues begin with a daylong survival skills workshop in which they teach family members about the prevalence and course of schizophrenia, its biological etiology, current modes of pharmacologic and psychosocial treatment, common medications, and prognosis. The patient's needs and the family's needs are discussed, and family coping skills are introduced. Research findings on expressed emotion are presented and guidelines are offered for keeping EE in check. Families are encouraged not to pressure recovering patients or to urge them to hurry back to normal functioning. Families are also advised to respect boundaries and to allow the recovering family member to withdraw whenever necessary.

The goal for the patient is for symptoms to be reduced rather than cured. Families are encouraged to provide a quiet, stable milieu in which the recovering patient doesn't feel criticized or blamed and not to expect too much of him or her during recuperation. The goal for the family is to learn coping techniques for the difficult and long-term task of living with a schizophrenic person and preventing or delaying his or her relapse and rehospitalization. Table 11.1 presents a set of typical psychoeducational guidelines for managing rehabilitation following a schizophrenic episode.

Is the psychoeducational model effective? Yes. Consider these findings from the study by Anderson and colleagues (1986):

> Among treatment takers (*n* = 90), 19% of those receiving family therapy alone experienced a psychotic relapse in the year following hospital discharge. Of those receiving the individual behavioral therapy, 20% relapsed, but *no* patient in the treatment cell that received both family therapy and social skills training experienced a relapse. These relapse rates constitute significant effects for both treatments when contrasted to a 41% relapse rate for those receiving only chemotherapy and support (p. 24).

Other studies have shown equally impressive results (Falloon et al., 1982; Leff et al., 1982). There seems to be little question that psychoeducation can delay relapse and readmission to a hospital better than other approaches to schizophrenia.

Medical Family Therapy

If one considers schizophrenia a chronic disease, then psychoeducational family therapy can be seen as a

Table 11.1   Psychoeducational Guidelines for Families and Friends of Schizophrenics

Here is a list of things everyone can do to make things run more smoothly:

1. *Go slow.* Recovery takes time. Rest is important. Things will get better in their own time.
2. *Keep it cool.* Enthusiasm is normal. Tone it down. Disagreement is normal. Tone it down too.
3. *Give 'em space.* Time out is important for everyone. It's okay to offer. It's okay to refuse.
4. *Set limits.* Everyone needs to know what the rules are. A few good rules keep things calmer.
5. *Ignore what you can't change.* Let some things slide. Don't ignore violence or use of street drugs.
6. *Keep it simple.* Say what you have to say clearly, calmly, and positively.
7. *Follow doctor's orders.* Take medications as they are prescribed. Take only medications that are prescribed.
8. *Carry on business as usual.* Reestablish family routines as quickly as possible. Stay in touch with family and friends.
9. *No street drugs or alcohol.* They make symptoms worse.
10. *Pick up on early signs.* Note changes. Consult with your family physician.
11. *Solve problems step by step.* Make changes gradually. Work on one thing at a time.
12. *Lower expectations, temporarily.* Use a personal yardstick. Compare this month with last month rather than with last year or next year.

Source: Adapted from McFarlane, 1991, p. 375.

specialized form of medical family therapy. Medical family therapists work with families struggling with illness or disability in much the same way as described previously for families of schizophrenics.

Chronic illness has a devastating impact. It can take over a family's life, ravaging health, hope, and peace of mind. As Peter Steinglass says, it can be like a robber "who has appeared on the doorstep, barged inside the home and demanded everything the family has" (quoted in McDaniel, Hepworth, & Doherty, 1992, p. 21).

These demands of the illness interact with qualities of the family, such as the family's life-cycle stage and the role the stricken family member plays; the family's leadership resources and degree of isolation; and their beliefs about illness and who should help, derived from their ethnicity and history with illness. With an awareness of these factors, therapists can help families prepare to deal with an illness or, if the illness has been with them for years, gain perspective on their resulting polarizations and enmeshments.

In medical family therapy, the system isn't just the sick person's family; it's the family and the physicians and nurses involved in the sick person's care. The goal

therefore is to foster communication and support not only within the family but also between the family and medical personnel. Illness leaves people feeling helpless and confused. Medical family therapy is designed to combat such feelings by fostering communication and a sense of agency.

Medical family therapists work in collaboration with pediatricians, family practitioners, rehabilitation specialists, and nurses. They advocate that near the time of diagnosis, families should receive a routine consultation to explore their resources relative to the demands of the illness or disability. Therapists cite the growing body of research suggesting a strong relationship between family dynamics and the clinical course of medical conditions (Campbell, 1986) and more recent research showing that family therapy has a positive effect on physical health and health care use (Law, Crane, & Russell, 2000).

In conclusion, psychoeducational and medical family therapy share many elements with the other models in this chapter that together represent a significant trend: a move toward a collaborative partnership with families. Therapists are now encouraged to look for a family's strengths rather than deficits and to find ways to lift families out of the guilt and blame that often accompany their problems.

Relationship Enrichment Programs

The psychoeducational method has also been applied to couples and families who wish to acquire skills for coping with everyday relationship problems. Some therapists are skeptical that self-help courses can substitute for the individual attention of a professionally trained therapist, yet these programs are enormously popular, not least because participants in *marital enrichment programs* feel little of the stigma that attaches to "being in therapy."

One of the best known of these programs is the Relationship Enhancement system developed by Bernard Guerney Jr. (1977). Facilitators teach participants to clarify their conflicts and to express what they are feeling, accept each other's feelings, negotiate and work through problems, and learn to achieve satisfaction by becoming emotional partners (Ginsberg, 2000). Both lectures and experiential training take place in each session, and homework assignments are given to practice and extend skills in participants' everyday lives.

Relationship Enhancement programs provide couples with training in three sets of core skills (Ginsberg, 2000):

1. The *Expressive (Owning)* Skill—gaining awareness of one's own feelings and taking responsibility for them without projecting them onto others
2. The *Empathic Responding (Receptive)* Skill—learning to listen to the other person's feelings
3. The *Conversive (Discussion-Negotiation/Engagement)* Skill—learning to acknowledge the meaning of what was heard; partners may switch positions between listener and speaker

To help couples assess their preparation for marriage, David Olson and his colleagues developed the Premarital Personal and Relationship Inventory (PREPARE). This 165-item questionnaire (Olson, 1996) is designed to help couples understand and discuss their backgrounds, expectations, and areas where they might encounter difficulties. Attitudes and expectations are explored in eleven areas, including marriage expectations, communication, sexual relationship, personality differences, financial management, conflict resolution, child rearing, leisure, family and friends, marital roles, and spiritual beliefs. PREPARE has proved useful for identifying potential conflicts and promoting discussions that may head off problems in the future (Stahmann & Hiebert, 1997).

By far the most popular of the relationship enhancement programs is the *marriage encounter weekend,* first introduced in Barcelona by a Jesuit priest, Father Gabriel Calvo (Chartier, 1986). These weekend retreats, which provide support and enrichment for Catholic couples, were imported into the United States in the late 1960s and have since been widely adopted by a variety of church groups (Stahmann & Hiebert, 1997). Thousands of couples have taken advantage of these weekend enrichment programs to work on their communication, problem-solving skills, sexual intimacy, and spiritual issues. Some denominations even require couples to participate in such a program before they can be married in the church.

A more carefully researched relationship enrichment program is the Prevention and Relationship Enhancement Program (PREP) developed by Floyd, Markham, Kelly, Blumberg, and Stanley (1995) at the University of Denver. This social learning approach, developed in the 1980s, teaches communication and conflict resolution skills and explores attitudes and expectations about marriage. The primary goal is to help couples learn to face and resolve conflicts and thus avoid incorporating unhealthy defensive patterns in their relationship.

PREP sessions come in two formats: weekly meetings over several weeks and marathon sessions held in a hotel over one weekend. Both versions include lectures and experiential exercises focusing on conflict management, communication, and forgiveness, as well as religious practices, recreation, and friendship. Couples learn such things as how and when to bring up conflictual subjects, how to identify hidden issues behind chronic arguments, a structured approach to problem solving, and making time for fun.

Short-term gains in relationship satisfaction include improvement in communication, sexual satisfaction, and lower problem intensity. Long-term gains (at follow-up to four years) generally show sustained benefits, especially in communication (Silliman, Stanley, Coffin, Markman, & Jordan, 2002).

Table 11.2 offers some guidelines for making relationships work.

Table 11.2   **Critical Skills for Effective Functioning as a Couple**

A.   Structure

1. Accommodation
Learn to accept and adjust to each other's preferences and expectations, compromising on some issues, but not always giving in, so as not to build up resentment.
   She learned to accept his wish to eat supper early, while he agreed to join her for weekly religious services. But she didn't agree to put her career on a part-time basis, and he continued to take his yearly fishing trip with his brothers despite her hating to be left behind.
2. Boundary making
Create a protective boundary around your relationship that reduces but doesn't eliminate contact with outsiders.
   He stopped going out three nights a week with his buddies; she started asking him if it was okay before agreeing to let her parents come for the weekend.
Demonstrating your commitment to your partner builds a secure base of attachment as well as confidence in the permanence of your relationship. Make sure your partner knows that you care and that you are committed.
   He stopped defending himself by saying "If you don't like it, why don't you find someone else," because it only made her insecure and angry. She made a point of telling him who she had lunch with, because she knew his jealousy made him worry.

B.   Communication

1. Listen to and acknowledge your partner's point of view.
   She discovered that making a sincere effort to say things like "So you like that one better because . . ." before countering with her own opinion made him feel that she respected his point of view. When it came to the most contentious issues, he discovered that asking first how she felt and then listening at length was essential. In some cases it was a good idea not even to express his side of the matter until a later time.
2. Short-circuit escalation in arguments by learning to back off before negative spirals get nasty. Call a time-out and agree to talk at a specific time later.
   "I'm getting upset; let's stop and talk about this tonight after supper, okay?"
3. Avoid invalidation and criticism.
   "You're so irresponsible" may be an obvious criticism, but equally invalidating is "I think you're overreacting." Don't criticize your partner's personality or deny what he or she is feeling.

C.   Problem Solving

1. Make positive requests, such as "Would you be willing . . . ?" rather than criticisms, such as "You never . . . !"
2. If you ask for something, be prepared to give something in return.
   It was easier to get him to do things with her and the children if she also made a point of suggesting times when he could do some of the things he liked to do by himself. He learned that occasionally

Table 11.2 (*Continued*)

volunteering to do the shopping or cook dinner made her feel more like doing things for him—and that volunteering worked better than trying to make deals.

3. Wait until you're not angry before bringing up a problem to be solved. Raise concerns directly but gently.

   She was furious that he took her father's side against her in an argument. But she decided not to say anything until she calmed down. The following night after supper, she began by saying "Honey, I want to talk about something I'm feeling but I'm afraid to because it might make you mad." Emphasizing that it was her feelings and saying that she was concerned about how he might react helped put him in a receptive mood.

4. Think of the two of you as a team working against the problem.

   Instead of battling over his "coldness" and her "dependency," they started talking about how they could adjust for their "different comfort levels." As a result they planned their next vacation so they could play golf and tennis together and she could visit friends while he took one day off for fishing.

5. Be sure you understand your partner's concerns before trying to work on a solution.

   He was upset that she wanted to make only a minimal down payment on their new house, because it would result in large mortgage payments. To him it made more sense to put down as much as they could in order to make the monthly payments as low as possible. But instead of continuing to argue, he asked her what she was worried about. Her concern turned out to be that without a cushion of savings, they might be wiped out by some unforeseen emergency. Now at least he understood how she felt.

D. Consideration

1. Do pleasing things for your partner and the relationship.

   Spontaneous gestures—like compliments, hugs, little presents, calling in the middle of the day to say "I love you"—reassure your partner that you care and help to maintain a positive feeling about the relationship.

E. Fun

1. Make the effort to spend enjoyable time together, and don't use fun activities as a time to discuss difficult issues or conflicts.

   He got in the habit of inviting her to join him for a movie, a walk in the park, or a visit to the museum and then supper out on Saturdays. She learned that bringing up problems on these trips tended to spoil the mood.

Source: Adapted from Nichols, M. P., 2009.

Summary

1. Family therapists taught us to see past individual personalities to the patterns that make them a family—an organization of interconnected lives governed by strict but unspoken rules. But in the process, they created a mechanistic entity—the family system—and then set about doing battle with it. Most of the challenges that have rocked and reshaped family therapy have been in reaction to this mechanism. But if the systemic revolution went too far in one direction, the same may be true of some of its critics.

2. The feminist critique was the first and perhaps most influential of the challenges to family therapy's traditions. In taking a stand against mother bashing, feminists challenged the essence of systems thinking by pointing out that concepts such as complementarity and circular causality can imply that subjugated women were as much to blame as their oppressors.

3. Family therapy's bridge to the twenty-first century was social constructionism. Much as was the case when the pioneers shifted their focus from individuals to families, this recent shift from behavior to cognition and from challenging to collaborating is opening up a new world of possibilities. We'll see just how exciting some of those possibilities are in the next few chapters.

4. The headline story of family therapy's evolution from first- to second-order cybernetics, from MRI to solution-focused therapy, from Milan systemic to Hoffman and Goolishian, and from constructivism to social constructionism and now narrative is what's been in the forefront of intellectual discussion. While these front-page developments were taking place, family therapists practicing less trendy approaches (behavioral, psychoanalytic, structural, Bowenian, and experiential) have continued their work. So it can be a mistake to think that what's new and gets attention is the only or even major thing going on in the field.

5. The collaborative movement has raised new questions about the therapist's style of leadership. When Harlene Anderson and Harry Goolishian advocated a *collaborative approach,* what was being rejected was the medical model—an authoritarian role model in which the clinician plays the expert to whom the patient looks for answers. But being an expert doesn't mean being an ogre. Here the advance is challenging the medical model, which ironically was perpetuated in such avant garde models of family therapy as the strategic and Milan systemic approaches. No longer do we see the therapist as a technocrat of change. But that doesn't mean therapists shouldn't be experts—leaders in the process of change.

6. Just as family therapy hasn't stood still in recent years, neither has the family. Today's family is evolving and stressed. We've gone from the complementary model of the family in the 1950s to a symmetrical version—although we haven't come to terms with the new model yet. Perhaps it's time to ask this question: As the modern family struggles through this stressful time of transition, what concepts does family therapy offer to help us understand and deal with the protean family forms of the twenty-first century?

Questions to Consider

1. How would you respond to the statement that "family therapy is dead"? In what way is this true? In what way is it false?

2. Can you think of any advantages to entering the field of family therapy at a time when the excitement and enthusiasm for it as a revolutionary new approach have worn off?

3. How might you plan your education and training to maximize your potential to be a successful managed care provider?

4. Make a list of situations in which it might be difficult for a therapist to feel confident in challenging clients from other racial or ethnic groups or sexual orientations.

5. What are some advantages and disadvantages of offering to treat families in their own homes?

6. Should feminist family therapy be considered a school of family therapy (i.e., a distinct and coherent approach) or merely a sensitivity that can be applied by therapists of any particular model?

7. What distinguishes raising issues in therapy from indoctrination? Give examples.

Key Concepts

collaborative model An egalitarian view of the therapist's role; advocated by critics of authoritarianism in traditional approaches to family therapy.

constructivism A relativistic point of view that emphasizes the subjective construction of reality. Implies that what we see in families may be based as much on our preconceptions as to what's actually going on.

deconstruction A postmodern approach to exploring meaning by examining taken-for-granted assumptions, making possible newer and sounder constructions of meaning.

hermeneutics The art of analyzing literary texts or human experience by interpreting levels of meaning.

not-knowing Anderson and Goolishian's term for approaching families with as few preconceptions as possible.

postmodernism Contemporary antipositivism, according to which knowledge is relative and context dependent; questions assumptions of objectivity that characterize modern science.

reflecting team Tom Andersen's technique of having the observing team share their reactions with the family at the end of a session.

social constructionism Knowledge and meaning are shaped by culturally shared assumptions.

Recommended Readings

Anderson, C. M., Reiss, D., and Hogarty, B. 1986. *Schizophrenia and the family: A practitioner's guide to psychoeducation and management.* New York: Guilford Press.

Fowers, B., and Richardson, F. 1996. Why is multiculturalism good? *American Psychologist. 51:* 609–621.

Goldner, V. 1985. Feminism and family therapy. *Family Process. 24:* 31–47.

Goodrich, T. J., ed. 1991. *Women and power: Perspectives for family therapy.* New York: Norton.

Greenan, D. E., and Tunnell, G. 2003. *Couple therapy with gay men.* New York: Guilford Press.

Held, B. S. 1995. *Back to reality: A critique of post modern theory in psychotherapy.* New York: Norton.

Kellner, D. 1991. *Postmodern theory.* New York: Guilford Press.

Laird, J., and Green, R. J. 1996. *Lesbians and gays in couples and families: A handbook for therapists.* San Francisco: Jossey-Bass.

Luepnitz, D. 1988. *The family interpreted: Feminist theory in clinical practice.* New York: Basic Books.

McDaniel, S., Hepworth, J., and Doherty, W. 1992. *Medical family therapy.* New York: Basic Books.

McGoldrick, M., Pierce, J, and Giordano, J. 2005. *Ethnicity and family therapy,* 3rd ed. New York: Guilford Press.

Rolland, J. 1994. *Helping families with chronic and life-threatening disorders.* New York: Basic Books.

References

Andersen, T. 1991. *The reflecting team.* New York: Norton.

Anderson, C. M. 1995. *Flying solo.* New York: Norton.

Anderson, C. M., Reiss, D., and Hogarty, G. E. 1986. *Schizophrenia and the family: A practitioner's guide to psychoeducation and management.* New York: Guilford Press.

Anderson, H. 1993. On a roller coaster: A collaborative language systems approach to therapy. In *The new language of change,* S. Friedman, ed. New York: Guilford Press.

Anderson, W. T. 1990. *Reality isn't what it used to be.* San Francisco: Harper & Row.

Atkinson, B. J. 2005. *Emotional intelligence in couples therapy: Advances from neurobiology and the science of intimate relationships.* New York: Norton.

Atkinson, J. M., and Coia, D. A. 1995. *Families coping with schizophrenia: A practitioner's guide to family groups.* New York: Wiley.

Avis, J. M. 1988. Deepening awareness: A private study guide to feminism and family therapy. In *Women, feminism, and family therapy,* L. Braverman, ed. New York: Haworth Press.

Avis, J. M. 1992. Where are all the family therapists? Abuse and violence within families and family therapy's response. *Journal of Marital and Family Therapy. 18:* 223–230.

Barth, R., Pietrzak, J., and Ramier, M. 1993. *Families living with drugs and HIV.* New York: Guilford Press.

Beavers, W., and Hampson, R. 1990. *Successful families: Assessment and intervention.* New York: Norton.

Billingsley, A. 1968. *Black families in white America.* Englewood Cliffs, NJ: Prentice-Hall.

Billingsley, A. 1992. *Climbing Jacob's ladder: The enduring legacy of African-American families.* New York: Simon & Schuster.

Billingsley, A., ed. 1994. The Black church. *National Journal of Sociology. 8:* (1–2) (double edition).

Blow, A. J., Sprenkle, D. H., and Davis, S. D. 2007. Is who delivers the treatment more important than the treatment itself? The role of the therapist in common factors. *Journal of Marital and Family Therapy. 33:* 298–317.

Boyd-Franklin, N. 1989. *Black families in therapy: A multisystems approach.* New York: Guilford Press.

Boyd-Franklin, N. 1993. Race, class, and poverty. In *Normal family processes,* F. Walsh, ed. New York: Guilford Press.

Boyd-Franklin, N. 2003. Race, class and poverty. In *Normal family processes: Growing diversity and complexity,* 3rd ed., F. Walsh, ed. New York: Guilford Press.

Bringle, R. 1995. Sexual jealousy in the relationships of homosexual and heterosexual men: 1980 and 1994. *Personal Relationships, 2:* 313–325.

Brothers, B. J., ed. 1992. *Spirituality and couples: Heart and soul in the therapy process.* New York: Haworth Press.

Brown, L. S. 1994. *Subversive dialogues: Theory in feminist therapy.* New York: Basic Books.

Brown, G. W., Birley, J. L. T., and Wing, J. K. 1972. The influence of family life on the course of schizophrenic disorders: A replication. *British Journal of Psychology. 121:* 241–258.

Bryant, A.S., and Demian, S. 1994. Relationship characteristics of American gays and lesbians: Findings from a national survey. *Journal of Gay & Lesbian Social Services, 1:* 101–117.

Burton, L. A., ed. 1992. *Religion and the family.* New York: Haworth Press.

Campbell, T. 1986. Family's impact on health: A critical review and annotated bibliography. *Family Systems Medicine. 4:* 135–148.

Carl, D. 1990. *Counseling same-sex couples.* New York: Norton.

Chartier, M. R. 1986. Marriage enrichment. In *Psychoeducational approaches to family therapy and counseling,* R. F. Levant, ed. New York: Springer.

Combrinck-Graham, L. 1989. *Children in family contexts.* New York: Guilford Press.

Cooper, A. 2002. *Sex and the Internet: A guide for clinicians.* New York: Brunner-Routledge.

Cose, E. 1993. *The rage of the privileged class.* New York: HarperCollins.

Dattilio, F., ed. 1998. *Case studies in couple and family therapy.* New York: Guilford Press.

Davidson, R. J. 2001. The neural circuitry of emotion and affective style: Prefrontal cortex and amygdala contributions. *Social Science Information, 40* (1): 11–37.

Davidson, R. J. 2003. Seven sins in the study of emotion: Correctives from affective neuroscience. *Brain and Cognition, 52:* 129–132.

Davis, S. D., and Piercy, F.P. 2007. What clients of couple therapy model developers and their former students say about change, Part II: Model-independent common factors and an integrative framework. *Journal of Marital and Family Therapy. 33:* 344–363.

Delmonico, D. and Griffin, E. 2008. Cybersex and the e-teen: What marriage and family therapists should know. *Journal of Marital and Family Therapy. 34:*431–444.

Doherty, W. 1996. *The intentional family.* Reading, MA: Addison-Wesley.

Donovan, J. M., ed. 1999. *Short-term couple therapy.* New York: Guilford Press.

Duncan, G. J., and Brooks-Gunn, J. 1997. *Consequences of growing up poor.* New York: Russell Sage Foundation.

Ehrenreich, B. 1999. Nickel-and-dimed: On (not) getting by in America. *Harper's.* January: 37–52.

Elizur, J., and Minuchin, S. 1989. *Institutionalizing madness: Families, therapy and society.* New York: Basic Books.

Elkin, M. 1990. *Families under the influence.* New York: Norton.

Emery, R. 1994. *Renegotiating family relationships: Divorce, child custody, and mediation.* New York: Guilford Press.

Falicov, C. 1983. *Cultural perspectives in family therapy.* Rockville, MD: Aspen Systems.

Falicov, C. 1998. *Latino families in therapy.* New York: Guilford Press.

Falloon, I. J. R., Boyd, J. L., McGill, C. W., Razani, J., Moss, H. B., and Gilderman, A. M. 1982. Family management in the prevention of exacerbations of schizophrenia. *New England Journal of Medicine. 306:* 1437–1440.

Figley, C. 1985. *Trauma and its wake: The study and treatment of post-traumatic stress disorder.* New York: Brunner/Mazel.

Floyd, F. J., Markham, H., Kelly, S., Blumberg, S. L., and Stanley, S. M. 1995. Preventive intervention and relationship enhancement. In *Clinical handbook of couples therapy,* N. S. Jacobson and A. S. Gurman, eds. New York: Guilford Press.

Friedrich, W. 1990. *Psychotherapy of sexually abused children and their families.* New York: Norton.

Friesen, B. J., and Kroloff, N. M. 1990. Family-centered services: Implications for mental health administration and research. *Journal of Mental Health Administration. 17*(1): 13–25.

Gergen, K. 1985. The social constructionist movement in modern psychology. *American Psychologist. 40:* 266–275.

Gergen, K. 1991b. The saturated family. *Family Therapy Networker. 15:* 26–35.

Gillispie, J. and Gackenbach, J. 2007. *Cyber rules: What you really need to know about the Internet.* New York: Norton.

Ginsberg, B. G. 2000. Relationship enhancement couples therapy. In *Comparative treatments of relationship disorders,* F. M. Dattilio and L. J. Bevilacqua, eds. New York: Springer.

Goldner, V. 1985. Feminism and family therapy. *Family Process. 24:* 31–47.

Goldner, V., Penn, P., Sheinberg, M., and Walker, G. 1990. Love and violence: Gender paradoxes in volatile attachments. *Family Process. 29:* 343–364.

Goldstein, M. J., Rodnick, E. H., Evans, J. R., May, P. R., and Steinberg, M. 1978. Drug and family therapy in the aftercare treatment of acute schizophrenia. *Archives of General Psychiatry. 35:* 1169–1177.

Goldberg, P., Peterson, B., Rosen, K., and Sara, M. (2008) Cybersex: The impact of a contemporary problem on the practices of marriage and family therapists. *Journal of Marital and Family Therapy. 34:*469–480.

Goodrich, T. J. 1991. In *Women and power: Perspectives for family therapy,* T. J. Goodrich, ed. New York: Norton.

Goodrich, T. J., Rampage, C., Ellman B., and Halstead K., 1988. *Feminist family therapy: A casebook.* New York: Norton.

Green, R. J. 1998. Training programs: Guidelines for multicultural transformations. In *Re-visioning family therapy,* M. McGoldrick, ed. New York: Guilford Press.

Green, R. J., and Mitchell, V. 2002. Gay and lesbian couples in therapy: Homophobia, relational ambiguity, and social support. In *Clinical handbook of couple therapy,* 3rd ed., A. S. Gurman and N. S. Jacobson, eds. New York: Guilford Press.

Greenan, D., and Tunnell, G. 2003. *Couple therapy with gay men.* New York: Guilford Press.

Guerney, B. G., Jr., ed. 1977. *Relationship enhancement: Skills training for therapy problem prevention and enrichment.* San Francisco: Jossey-Bass.

Haley, J. 1976. *Problem-solving therapy.* San Francisco: Jossey-Bass.

Haley, J. 1980. *Leaving home.* New York: McGraw-Hill.

Hardy, K. 1993. War of the worlds. *Family Therapy Networker. 17:* 50–57.

Hare-Mustin, R. T. 1978. A feminist approach to family therapy. *Family Process. 17:* 181–194.

Henggeler, S. W., and Borduin, C. M., ed. 1990. *Family therapy and beyond: A multisystemic approach to treating the behavior problems of children and adolescents.* Pacific Grove, CA: Brooks/Cole.

Hines, P. M., and Boyd-Franklin, N. 1982. Black families. In *Ethnicity and family therapy,* M. McGoldrick, J. K. Pierce, and J. Giordano, eds. New York: Guilford Press.

Hines, P. M., and Boyd-Franklin, N. 1996. African American families. In *Ethnicity and family therapy,* 2nd ed., M. McGoldrick, J. K. Pierce, and J. Giordano, eds. New York: Guilford Press.

Imber-Black, E. 1988. *Families and larger systems: A family therapist's guide through the labyrinth.* New York: Guilford Press.

Imber-Black, E., Roberts, J., and Whiting, R. 1988. *Rituals in families and family therapy.* New York: Norton.

Ingoldsby, B., and Smith, S. 1995. *Families in multicultural perspective.* New York: Guilford Press.

Isay, R. A. 1989. *Being homosexual: Gay men and their development.* New York: Farrar Straus Giroux.

James, K., and MacKinnon, L. 1990. The "incestuous family" revisited: A critical analysis of family therapy myths. *Journal of Marital and Family Therapy. 16:* 71–88.

Johnson, W. E. 2001. Paternal involvement among unwed fathers. *Children and Youth Services Review. 23:* 513–536.

Johnson, T., and Keren, M. 1998. The families of lesbian women and gay men. In *Re-visioning family therapy,* M. McGoldrick, ed. New York: Guilford Press.

Jordan, J., Kaplan, A., Miller, J., Stiver, I., and Surrey J., eds. 1991. *Women's growth in connection: Writings from the Stone Center.* New York: Guilford Press.

Kahn, M., and Lewis, K. G. 1988. *Siblings in therapy.* New York: Norton.

Krestan, J. 1988. Lesbian daughters and lesbian mothers: The crisis of disclosure from a family systems perspective. *Journal of Psychotherapy and the Family. 3:* 113–130.

Laird, J. 1993. Lesbian and gay families. In *Normal family processes,* 2nd ed., F. Walsh, ed. New York: Guilford Press.

Laird, J., and Green, R. J. 1996. *Lesbians and gays in couples and families: A handbook for therapists.* San Francisco: Jossey-Bass.

LaSala, M. 1997. The need for thick skin: Coupled gay men and their relationships with their parents and in-laws. *Dissertation Abstracts International. 58:* 4444-A.

LaSala, M. 2004a. Extradyadic sex and gay male couples: Comparing monogamous and nonmonogamus relationships. *Families in Society: The Journal of Contemporary Social Services. 85* (3): 405-411.

LaSala, M. 2004b. Monogamy of the heart: Extrdyadic sex and gay male couples. *Journal of Gay & Lesbian Social Services, 17* (3).

Law, D. D., Crane, D. R., and Russell, D. 2000. The influence of marital and family therapy on utilization of healthcare in a health maintenance organization. *Journal of Marital and Family Therapy. 26:* 281–291.

LeDoux, J. 1996. *The emotional brain.* New York: Simon & Schuster.

Lee, E. 1997. *Working with Asian Americans.* New York: Guilford Press.

Leff, J., Kuipers, L., Berkowitz, R., Eberlein-Vries, R., and Sturgeon, D. 1982. A controlled trial of social intervention in the families of schizophrenic patients. *British Journal of Psychiatry. 141:* 121–134.

Lehr, R., and MacMillan, P. 2001. The psychological and emotional impact of divorce: The noncustodial fathers' perspective. *Families in Society. 82:* 373–382.

Lindblad-Goldberg, M., Dore, M. M., and Stern, L. 1998. *Creating competence from chaos.* New York: Norton.

Luepnitz, D. 1988. *The family interpreted: Feminist theory in clinical practice.* New York: Basic Books.

Markowitz, L. 1993. Walking the walk. *Family Therapy Networker. 17:* 18–24, 27–31.

McAdoo, H., ed. 2002. *Black children: Social, educational and parental environments,* 2nd ed. Thousand Oaks, CA: Sage.

McDaniel, S., Hepworth, J., and Doherty, W. 1992. *Medical family therapy.* New York: Basic Books.

McGoldrick, M., ed. 1998. *Re-visioning family therapy.* New York: Guilford Press.

McGoldrick, M., Pearce, J., and Giordano, J. 1982. *Ethnicity and family therapy.* New York: Guilford Press.

McGoldrick, M., Pearce, J., and Giordano, J. 2005. *Ethnicity and family therapy,* 3rd ed. New York: Guilford Press.

Meyer, I. H., and Dean, L. 1998. Internalized homophobia, intimacy, and sexual behavior among gay and bisexual men. In *Stigma and sexual orientation: Understanding prejudice against lesbians, gay men, and bisexuals,* G. M. Herek, ed. Thousand Oaks, CA: Sage.

Micucci, J. 1998. *The adolescent in family therapy.* New York: Guilford Press.

Milkowitz, D. J. 1995. The evolution of family-based psychopathology. In *Integrating family therapy: Handbook of family psychology and systems theory,* R. H. Mikesell, D-D. Lusterman, and S. H. McDaniels, eds. Washington, DC: American Psychological Association.

Miklowitz, D., and Goldstein, M. 1997. *Bipolar disorder: A family-focused treatment approach.* New York: Guilford Press.

Miller, J. B. 1986. *Toward a new psychology of women,* 2nd ed. Boston: Beacon.

Minuchin, P., Colapinto, J., and Minuchin, S. 1998. *Working with families of the poor.* New York: Guilford Press.

Minuchin, S., and Fishman, H. C. 1981. *Techniques of family therapy.* Cambridge, MA: Harvard University Press.

Minuchin, S., Montalvo, B., Guerney, B., Rosman, B., and Schumer, F. 1967. *Families of the slums.* New York: Basic Books.

Minuchin, S., Nichols, M. P., and Lee, W.-Y. 2007. *Assessing families and couples: From symptom to system.* Boston: Allyn & Bacon.

Mirkin, M. P. 1990. *The social and political contexts of family therapy.* Boston: Allyn & Bacon.

Mitchell, K., Finkelhor, D. and Wolak, J. 2001. Risk factors for and impact of online sexual solicitation of youth. *Journal of American Medical Association. 285:* 3011–3014.

Mitchell, S. 1993. *Hope and dread in psychoanalysis.* New York: Basic Books.

Morawetz, A., and Walker, G. 1984. *Brief therapy with single-parent families.* New York: Brunner/ Mazel.

Muesser, K. T., and Glynn, S. M. 1995. *Behavioral family therapy for psychiatric disorders.* Boston: Allyn & Bacon.

Nichols, M. P. 2004. *Stop arguing with your kids.* New York: Guilford Press.

Nichols, M. P. 2009. *The lost art of listening,* 2nd ed. New York: Guilford Press.

Okun, B. 1996. *Understanding diverse families.* New York: Guilford Press.

Olson, D. H. 1996. *PREPARE/ENRICH counselor's manual.* Minneapolis, MN: Life Innovations.

Orbach, S. 1997. *Fat is a feminist issue.* Edison, NJ: BBS.

Patterson, J., Williams, L., Graul-Grounds, C., and Chamow, L. 1998. *Essential skills in family therapy.* New York: Guilford Press.

Pinderhughes, E. 1989. *Understanding race, ethnicity and power: The key to efficacy in clinical practice.* New York: Free Press.

Pittman, F. 1987. *Turning points: Treating families in transition and crisis.* New York: Norton.

Prest, L., and Keller, J. 1993. Spirituality in family therapy. *Journal of Marital and Family Therapy. 19:* 137–148.

Price, J. 1996. *Power and compassion: Working with difficult adolescents and abused parents.* New York: Guilford Press.

Reitz, M., and Watson, K. 1992. *Adoption and the family system.* New York: Guilford Press.

Rojano, R. 2004. The practice of community family therapy. *Family Process. 43:* 59–77.

Rolland, J. 1994. *Helping families with chronic and life-threatening disorders.* New York: Basic Books.

Root, M., Fallon, P., and Friedrich, W. 1986. *Bulimia: A systems approach to treatment.* New York: Norton.

Roth, S., and Murphy, B. 1986. Therapeutic work with lesbian clients: A systemic therapy view. In *Women and family therapy,* M. Ault-Riche and J. Hansen, eds. Rockville, MD: Aspen Systems.

Saba, G., Karrer, B., and Hardy, K. 1989. *Minorities and family therapy.* New York: Haworth.

Sanders, G. 1993. The love that dares not speak its name: From secrecy to openness in gay and lesbian affiliations. In *Secrets in families and family therapy,* E. Imber-Black, ed. New York: Norton.

Schwartzman, J. 1985. *Families and other systems: The macrosystemic context of family therapy.* New York: Guilford Press.

Seigel, D. J. 1999. *The developing mind: How relationships and the brain interact to shape who we are.* New York: Guilford Press.

Seligman, M., and Darling, R. B. 1996. *Ordinary families, special children: A systems approach to childhood disability,* 2nd ed. New York: Guilford Press.

Sells, S. 1998. *Treating the tough adolescent.* New York: Guilford Press.

Sheinberg, M. 1992. Navigating treatment impasses at the disclosure of incest: Combining ideas from feminism and social constructionism. *Family Process. 31:* 201–216.

Silliman, B., Stanley, S. M., Coffin, W., Markman, H. J., and Jordan, P. L. 2002. Preventive intervention for couples. In *Family psychology: Science-based interventions,* H. A. Liddle, D. A. Santisban, R. F. Levant, and J. H. Bray, eds. Washington, DC: American Psychological Association.

Stahlmann, R. F., and Hiebert, W. J. 1997. *Premarital and remarital counseling.* San Francisco: Jossey-Bass.

Staples, R. 1994. *Black family: Essays and studies,* 5th ed. New York: Van Nostrand Reinhold.

Surrey, J. L. 1991. The "self-in-relation": A new theory of women's development. In *Women's growth in connection,* J. V. Jordan, A. G. Kaplan, J. B. Miller, I. P. Stiver, and J. L. Surrey, eds. New York: Guilford Press.

Taibbi, R. 1996. *Doing family therapy.* New York: Guilford Press.

Trepper, T. S., and Barrett, M. J. 1989. *Systemic treatment of incest: A therapeutic handbook.* New York: Brunner/ Mazel.

U.S. Bureau of the Census. 2003. *Statistical abstract of the United States,* 123rd ed. Washington, DC: U.S. Government Printing Office.

Vaughn, C., and Leff, J. 1976. The measurement of expressed emotion in the families of psychiatric patients. *British Journal of Psychology. 15:* 157–165.

Vaughn, C. E., Snyder, K. S., Jones, S., Freeman, W. B., and Falloon, I. R. H. 1984. Family factors in schizophrenic relapse: Replication in California of British research on expressed emotion. *Archives of General Psychiatry. 41:* 1169–1177.

Visher, E., and Visher, J. 1988. *Old loyalties, new ties: Therapeutic strategies with stepfamilies.* New York: Brunner/Mazel.

Wachtel, E. 1994. *Treating troubled children and their families.* New York: Guilford Press.

Walker, G. 1991. *In the midst of winter: Systemic therapy with families, couples, and individuals with AIDS infection.* New York: Norton.

Walsh, F. 1993. *Normal family processes,* 2nd ed. New York: Guilford Press.

Walsh, F. 1998. *Strengthening family resistance.* New York: Guilford Press.

Walsh, F., ed. 1999. *Spirituality in families and family therapy.* New York: Guilford Press.

Walsh, F., and McGoldrick, M., eds. 1991. *Living beyond loss: Death in the family.* New York: Norton.

Walters, M., Carter, B., Papp, P., and Silverstein, O. 1988. *The invisible web: Gender patterns in family relationships.* New York: Guilford Press.

Watt, D. E. 1998. Affect and the limbic system: Some hard problems. *Journal of Neuropsychiatry and Clinical Neurosciences, 10*: 113–116.

Weiss, R., and Schneider, J. 2006. *Untangling the web: Sex, porn, and fantasy obsession in the Internet age.* New York: Alyson Books.

White, J. 1972. Towards a black psychology. In *Black psychology,* R. Jones, ed. New York: Harper & Row.

White, M., and Epston, D. 1990. *Narrative means to therapeutic ends.* New York: Norton.

12

Solution-Focused Therapy

$\mathcal{S}$olution-focused practitioners assume that people who come to therapy are capable of behaving effectively but that their effectiveness has been blunted by a negative mind-set. Drawing their attention to forgotten capabilities helps release them from preoccupation with their failures and restore them to their more capable selves. Problems are seen as overwhelming because clients see them as *always* happening. Times when problems aren't happening aren't noticed or dismissed as trivial. The art of solution-focused therapy becomes a matter of helping clients see that their problems have **exceptions**—times when they don't occur—and that these exceptions are solutions they already have in their repertoires.

$\mathcal{A}$CCENTUATING THE POSITIVE

Solution-focused therapy takes the elegance of the MRI model and turns it on its head. Both of these pragmatic approaches focus on the presenting complaint and aim to resolve it as parsimoniously as possible. But while the MRI model does so by looking for failed attempts to solve problems, the solution-focused approach focuses on exceptions—times when the problem wasn't a problem.

$\mathcal{E}$VOLUTION OF THE MODEL

Solution-focused therapy grew out of the work of Steve de Shazer, Insoo Berg, and their colleagues at the Brief Family Therapy Center (BFTC) in Milwaukee. This private training institute was started in 1979 when some of the staff at a community agency who were drawn to the MRI model became dissatisfied with the agency's constraints and set off on their own. The initial group included married partners Steve de Shazer and Insoo Berg, along with Jim Derks, Elaine Nunnally, Marilyn La Court, and Eve Lipchik. Their students included John Walter, Jane Peller, and Michele Weiner-Davis.

The late Steve de Shazer was the primary architect of solution-focused therapy, and his writings are among the most inventive in this approach (e.g., de Shazer, 1988, 1991). A scholar as well as a clinician, de Shazer was intrigued by Bateson's theories of communication and Milton Erickson's pragmatic ideas about how to influence change. Early in his career de Shazer worked in Palo Alto and was strongly influenced by the MRI approach. De Shazer died on September 11, 2005, in Vienna.

Insoo Kim Berg was, along with de Shazer, one of the primary architects of the solution-focused approach. She trained therapists all over the world and

Steve de Shazer, founder of solution-focused therapy.

authored a host of books and articles applying the model to a variety of problems and service settings, including alcoholism (Berg & Miller, 1992), marital therapy (Berg, 1994a), and family-based services to the poor (Berg, 1994b). She died in 2007.

After training with de Shazer, Michele Weiner-Davis converted an agency program in Woodstock, Illinois, to the solution-focused model. Weiner-Davis (1992) applied the model to marital problems in her popular book *Divorce-Busting*.

Insoo Kim Berg, a leading practitioner of the solution focused model.

Although Bill O'Hanlon never formally studied at the BFTC, he was trained in brief problem-solving therapy by Milton Erickson, which made taking the step toward solution-focused therapy an easy one. O'Hanlon collaborated with Weiner-Davis to write one of the early books on solution-focused therapy (O'Hanlon & Weiner-Davis, 1989) and was thereafter prominently associated with the approach. He is a popular workshop presenter and has written a number of books and articles on his pragmatic approach, which he calls *possibility therapy* (O'Hanlon, 1998).

As a student of Berg and de Shazer since the mid-1980s, Yvonne Dolan has applied the solution-focused model to the treatment of trauma and abuse (Dolan, 1991) and co-authored an influential volume of case studies (Berg & Dolan, 2001). She has also written about the model's application in agency settings (Pichot & Dolan, 2003) and most recently the state of the art of solution-focused therapy (de Shazer, Dolan, Korman, Trepper, Berg, & McCollum, 2007). Dolan conducts training in solution-focused therapy around the world and is president of the Solution-Focused Brief Therapy Association.

Other prominent solution-focused therapists include Eve Lipchik, Scott Miller, John Walter, and Jane Peller. Lipchik, who worked at the BFTC for eight years until she left in 1988, pioneered the application of the solution-focused model to wife battering (Lipchik & Kubicki, 1996) and recently published one of the most useful books about how to do solution-focused therapy (Lipchik, 2002). Miller worked at the BFTC for three years, directing the alcohol and drug treatment services, and has written widely about the model. Walter and Peller practice together in Chicago. They trained at the BFTC and, after writing a book laying out the steps of the approach (Walter & Peller, 1992), have become popular presenters on the workshop circuit.

THE BASIC MODEL

Like the MRI group, solution-focused therapists believe that people are constrained by narrow views of their problems into perpetuating rigid patterns of false solutions. As O'Hanlon and Weiner-Davis (1989) put it:

> So, the meanings people attribute to behavior limit the range of alternatives they will use to deal with a situation. If the methods used do not produce a satisfactory outcome, the original assumption about the meaning of the behavior is generally not questioned. If it were, new meanings might be considered, which in turn might prompt a different, perhaps more effective, approach. Instead, people often redouble their efforts to solve the problem in an ineffective way, thinking that by doing it more, harder or better (e.g., more punishments, more heart-to-heart talks, and so on), they will finally solve it (p. 48).

The MRI model was inspired by Milton Erickson's view of people as containing untapped, and often unconscious, resources. According to this view, people may need only a slight shift of perspective to release their potential. Part of that shift involves changing the way people talk about their problems.

The language of problems tends to be different from the language of solutions. As Ludwig Wittgenstein put it (1958), "The world of the happy is quite another than that of the unhappy." Usually, problem talk is negative, focuses on the past, and implies the permanence of problems. The language of solutions is more positive, hopeful, and future oriented. Part of the therapist's job is to steer clients from problem talk to solution talk. In the solution-focused model, the future is negotiable.

Normal Family Development

In the solution-focused model, clients are assumed to be the experts on their own lives. Just as they know what's troubling them, so, too, they know what they need. This philosophy is exemplified by the practice of routinely asking clients "Is there anything else I should have asked you or that you need to tell me?" As described by De Jong and Berg (2002), "If as a practitioner, you wish to put clients into the position of being experts on their own lives, you will have to know how to set aside your own frame of reference as much as possible and explore those of your clients" (p. 20).

Solution-focused therapists assume that people are resilient and resourceful. The problems they have are not seen as evidence of failure to achieve some adaptive standard but rather as normal life-cycle complications. This optimistic perspective needn't be dismissed as Pollyannaish. Rather it can be seen as a commitment to the belief that families have the ability to construct solutions that can enhance their lives.

Implicit in this model is an asymptomatic perspective on family normality—that is, a normal family is simply one that has been freed of its presenting problems and returned to its own unique functional way of living.

> Solution-oriented therapists don't believe that there is any single "correct" or "valid" way to live one's life. We have come to understand that what is unacceptable behavior in one family or for one person is desirable behavior in another. Therefore, clients, not therapists, identify the goals to be accomplished in treatment (O'Hanlon & Weiner-Davis, 1989, p. 44).

Development of Behavior Disorders

In the solution-focused world, this subject is closed. The very act of categorizing people suggests that they are a certain way all the time. For example, when we say a couple is "disengaged," does this mean there are never times when they are not disengaged? Unfortunately, the act of labeling draws attention from those other times.

Just as solution-focused therapists steer clients away from speculating about problem formation, they also avoid such conjecture themselves. Their conviction is that solutions are often unrelated to the way problems developed and that exploring etiology is engaging in problem talk—exactly what they seek to avoid. They believe that problem-focused thinking keeps people from recognizing effective solutions they've already used or could come up with. Problems persist in the way people define situations and in the misdirected actions they persist in taking.

How Therapy Works

Solution-focused therapists assume that people already have the skills to solve their problems but have lost sight of these abilities because their problems loom so large that their strengths are crowded out of the picture. Sometimes a simple shift in focus from what's not going well to what's already working can remind clients of these resources. Other times people may have to search for abilities they aren't currently using and bring those dormant skills to bear on their problems.

Because solution-focused therapists aren't out to reorganize personalities or family structures, they're willing to settle for modest goals. A homeless woman may simply need to find a place to live; a single man may just need the courage to ask someone for a date. If a client's goal is vague—"I'd like to feel happier"—or utopian—"I never want to be sad again"—therapists ask questions designed to make the goal clear and specific. Helping clients set concrete and reachable goals is a major intervention in itself, and the process of thinking about the future and what one wants to be different is a large part of what solution-focused therapists do (Walter & Peller, 1996).

Solution-focused therapy works by helping clients amplify exceptions to their problems—effective solutions already in their repertoire. From Berg and de Shazer's (1993) point of view, what's needed for change is a shift in the way the problem is "languaged":

> Rather than looking behind and beneath the language that clients and therapists use, we think that the language they use is all that we have to go on. . . . What we talk about and how we talk about it makes a difference, and it is these differences that can be used to make a difference [to the client]. . . . We have come to see that the meanings arrived at in a therapeutic conversation are developed through a process more like negotiation than the development of understanding or an uncovering of what it is that is "really" going on (p. 7).

Thus, changing the way people talk about their problems is all that needs to be accomplished, because "as the client and therapist talk more and more about the solution they want to construct together, they come to believe in the truth or reality of what they are talking about. This is the way language works, naturally" (Berg & de Shazer, 1993, p. 9). This is why solution-focused therapy can be so brief: It's a lot easier to get people to talk differently about their problems than it is to get them to change their behavior. The assumption is, of course, that getting clients to talk positively will help them think positively—and ultimately to act positively to solve their problems.

$\mathcal{T}$HERAPY

Assessment

After getting a brief description of the presenting complaint, the therapist moves directly to asking clients how things will be different in their lives when their problems are solved. Then instead of formulating some kind of intervention plan, the therapist asks about times in the clients' lives when their problems do not happen or are less severe. The following questions (adapted from Lipchik, 2002) suggest the proactive nature of a solution-focused assessment:

> "What do you think the problem is now?"
> "How will you know when the problem is solved?"
> "How will you know you don't have to come here anymore? What will the signs be?"
> "What will have to be different for that to happen in terms of your behavior, thoughts, and feelings?"
> "What will you notice that is different about others involved in the situation?"
> "What is your wildest fantasy about what you want to have happen?"

Because they aren't interested in assessing family dynamics, solution-focused practitioners don't feel the need to convene any particular group of people. Instead they say that anyone who is concerned about the problem should attend sessions. They also need little intake information because they want to hear clients' constructions of their problems firsthand. Solution-focused therapists ask more about perceptions than about feelings. And they affirm the clients' position. All clients want some indication that their therapist has understood the point of view that guides their actions.

The process of assessment in this model differs radically from problem-solving approaches. The solution-focused therapist doesn't function as an expert in determining what's wrong (enmeshment, triangulation) and planning how to correct it. In this therapy, clients are the experts in what they want to change (Walter & Peller, 1992). Although solution-focused therapists don't play the role of an authority figure who will help clients solve their problems, they do take an active position in moving clients away from worrying about their predicament and toward steps to solution.

The following sorts of questions are asked to lay the groundwork for therapeutic goal development:

"What needs to happen as a result of coming here, so that afterward you will look back and be honestly able to say that it was a good idea?"

"What needs to happen so that this will not have been a waste of your time?"

"Often in our experience, we have found that in between scheduling an appointment and coming in, something happens that contributes to making a problem better. Did anything happen to improve the problem for which you decided to come here today?"

Based on the answers to these questions, the therapist and clients begin to construct a more detailed description of the therapeutic goal. Once this description of the goal has been developed, the therapist asks the clients to assess their current level of progress toward that goal by imaging a scale of 1 to 10, where 1 represents the problem at its worst and 10 is the point at which the problem is gone or the clients are coping with it so well that it's no longer problematic.

The clients' rating makes it possible to assess how far they are from their goal. Later the same scale can be used to determine what specific actions will allow the clients to move toward the goal and to evaluate progress. If the clients identify new problems,

then the therapist makes a new scale to depict desired outcomes and to assess progress toward new solutions.

In an approach as direct as solution-focused therapy, it's important to assess clients' motivation for change. Following de Shazer (1988), practitioners distinguish among *visitors, complainants,* and *customers.*

A **visitor** is someone who's not really in the market for therapy. Visitors are there at someone else's insistence—a judge, their mother, the school principal—but they don't really have a complaint and they don't want to be there. Therapists should not offer these clients any suggestions or seek to convince them that they really need therapy.

With visitors it's important to pay attention to how they were referred and to consider who the real client is—that is, the person who wants services to be provided. If the people in your office are present only because someone pressured them to be there, a useful strategy is to ask them what they need to do to satisfy the authority that compelled them to seek therapy:

"So, what has to happen to get your mother off your back?"

"What's the minimum we need to accomplish so that you won't have to keep coming for more sessions?"

Complainants do have clear complaints, but they're usually about someone else. Parents often seek therapy because their children are having problems. But while parents of young children may see the need for themselves to be involved in the solution, parents of older children often think that it's only the child who has the problem—drugs, depression, shyness—and may not see themselves as part of the solution. Wives seek couples therapy because their "husbands don't communicate," while husbands often show up only to placate their wives.

With complainants, it may be useful to suggest noticing exceptions in the problem behavior of the other family member. The solution-focused therapist accepts their views, gives them compliments, and may suggest observing exceptions to the complaint pattern, as the following example illustrates.

1———————————10

Problem at Its Worst   Therapeutic Goal

Therapist: How can I help you?

Client: It's my daughter. All she does is hang out with her friends. She never does her homework, and she never helps out around the house.

Therapist: So how can I be of help to you?

Client: Nothing I've ever done seems to make a difference. She just doesn't want to grow up and take responsibility for herself.

With such a client, a solution-focused therapist tries to shift the conversation from problem talk to solution talk.

Therapist: What do you think needs to happen so that your daughter will be a little easier to live with?

Client: She has to start doing her homework. I keep telling her that she won't get anywhere unless she finishes high school.

Therapist: That seems like a big change. But suppose that did happen—suppose she did start doing her homework. What would your daughter be saying about how you are different with her then?

Client: She hates it when I nag her. So she'd probably say that I wasn't nagging as much anymore.

Notice how the therapist at no point challenges the client's notion that the problem is her daughter. Nevertheless, by talking about solutions, the conversation comes around to how the mother might behave differently as part of the solution. This opens the door to her seeing that nagging less might be part of a more productive approach to her daughter.

Some clients who fit the description of a complainant are less flexible than the mother in this example. We've all seen people who steadfastly maintain that everything is someone else's fault. With such clients you can always ask "How were you hoping I might be useful to you?" and then strategize with them about how they can act differently to influence those recalcitrant others.

Customers have clear complaints and are ready to take action. Therapists can be more direct in guiding such clients toward solutions. With a customer, you can move directly to establish goals and then look for solutions. It's much easier to work with people who are ready to make changes.

The point de Shazer makes is that these distinctions—visitor, complainant, and customer—aren't qualities of character but qualities of the therapeutic relationship, and are therefore fluid. With an apparently unmotivated complainer, the therapist's job is to engage in a solution-focused conversation, compliment the client, and possibly give an assignment to observe exceptions to the problem. By not pushing for change but shifting attention away from problems and toward solutions, the therapist may mold the relationship into one in which the client becomes a customer for change.

Therapeutic Techniques

Solution-focused techniques are organized around two fundamental strategies. The first is developing well-focused goals within the clients' frame of reference, and the second is generating solutions based on exceptions (De Jong & Berg, 2002). Therapy is usually brief (three to five sessions on average), and appointments are made one at a time, on the assumption that one more may be enough.

Problem Description. Therapy begins with a description of the clients' problem: "How were you hoping I could help you?" Solution-focused therapists take pains to work within the clients' frame of reference. They ask for the clients' perceptions and are careful to acknowledge them, using the clients' own language as much as possible.

Therapist: So you were saying that you want to do something about being so disorganized?

Client: Yes, I can't keep track of half the things I'm supposed to be doing, and I end up scrambling to turn assignments in at the last minute. I hate myself for that! Sometimes I think maybe I just don't want to be doing this job.

Therapist: So you think that maybe being disorganized has something to do with not really liking the work you're doing and that you've been feeling discouraged and down on yourself. Is that right?

It's a good idea to ask clients what they've already tried to resolve their difficulties. People usually attempt various strategies to deal with their problems, and these efforts may have been more or less successful. Either way these previous attempts at solutions now play an important part in the clients' perception of what works and doesn't work for them.

Goal Setting. After hearing and acknowledging the clients' description of their problems and what they've tried to do about them, the next step is to establish clear and concrete goals. Solution-focused therapists help translate vague or amorphous goals into concrete, behavioral terms by asking questions like these:

"Specifically how will you be doing this?"

"How will the two of you know when you have solved your problems? How will things be different?"

"What specifically will tell you that you've solved your problem (or reached your goal)?"

"What will be the first sign (or smallest step) that will tell you that you're moving in the right direction? What else?"

The clearer the goal, the easier it is to measure progress. If, for example, a woman says that she would like to get along better with her husband, a solution-focused therapist might ask "Can you tell me more specifically what will be happening when you two are getting along better? What will you be doing differently? What specifically will your husband notice that will tell him you are getting along as opposed to not getting along?"

Notice in this example how the therapist asks the woman who wants to have a better relationship "What will you be doing differently?" Part of the process of solution-focused therapy is helping clients think about constructive actions *they* can take, rather than how they can get others to change. Useful goals are specific and include positive actions. They are also modest enough to be achievable.

A recently divorced woman who was anxious to get her life back in order wanted to quit smoking, get a job, lose twenty pounds, and start dating. The therapist suggested that she concentrate first on finding a job and postpone trying to lose weight and quit smoking until she had a little less stress in her life.

Once when Insoo Berg was interviewing a woman whose life seemed out of control, she asked the client what needed to happen in order for things to be better. The woman replied that she wasn't sure—she had so many problems. "Maybe only a miracle will help, but I suppose that's too much to expect." Picking up on the client's words, Berg asked, "OK, suppose a miracle happened, and the problem that brought you here is solved. What would be different about your life?" (De Jong & Berg, 2002, p. 85).

To Berg's surprise, this woman, who had seemed so overwhelmed and helpless, began to describe a clear and realistic picture of a well-functioning family. Thus was born one of the mainstays of solution-focused therapy: the **miracle question**. Here's how de Shazer (1988) phrases it:

Now, I want to ask you a strange question. *Suppose* that while you are sleeping tonight and the entire house is quiet, a *miracle* happens. The miracle is that *the problem which brought you here is solved.* However, because you are sleeping, you don't know that the miracle has happened. So, when you wake up tomorrow morning, *what will be different* that will tell you that a miracle has happened and the problem which brought you here is solved? (p. 5)

The miracle question invites clients to envision an unlimited range of possibilities and begins to activate a problem-solving mind-set by giving them a mental picture of their goals—perhaps in the same way that visualizing the perfect serve helps a tennis player.

The miracle question also helps clients look beyond the problem to see that what they really want may not be to eliminate the problem per se but to be able to do the things the problem has been obstructing. If the therapist can encourage the clients to begin doing these things despite the problem, suddenly the problem may not loom as large.

For example, Mary says that if she weren't bulimic, she'd get closer to people and have more fun. If, with her therapist's encouragement, Mary begins to take interpersonal risks and has more fun, then her bulimia may become less of a problem and less of an obstacle in her life.

Exploring Exceptions. Probing for exceptions—times when clients don't have the problem—invites them to recognize that some potential solutions may already be in their grasp. Such probing involves asking *exception questions* like these:

> "When in the recent past might the problem have happened but didn't (or was less intense or more manageable)?"
> "What's different about those times when the problem doesn't happen?"
> "How have you let your partner know when he or she does something that makes a positive difference to you?"

Finding exceptions in the recent past is most useful because clients can remember them in greater detail. Also, since these exceptions just happened, it's more plausible that they could happen again. By exploring these times and what was different about them, clients find clues to what they can do to expand these exceptions. In addition, when clients recognize that they were able to avoid or overcome the problem before, their outlook toward it may change. It may seem less insurmountable.

For example, Mary may remember times during the previous week when she had the urge to binge and

purge but didn't. She may discover that at those times she was away from her parents and so didn't feel like she was disappointing them. She may decide that it's time to become more independent.

Exploring exceptions allows the therapist and client to build on past successes. Failing that, the therapist can ask why things aren't worse—"How did you manage that?"—and then build on that accomplishment. *Coping questions* can help clients recognize that they are more resourceful than they realize simply for enduring:

> "What keeps you going under such difficult circumstances?"
> "How come things aren't worse?"
> "What have you done to keep them from getting worse?"

If the client provides answers, the therapist can build on them with questions about how that endurance can be maintained and how more of that effort can be brought to bear.

A solution-focused therapist spends most of the session listening for evidence of previous solutions, exceptions, and goals. When such evidence comes out, the therapist punctuates it with enthusiasm and support. The therapist then works to keep solution talk in the forefront. This requires different skills from those used in traditional problem-focused therapies. Whereas the problem-focused therapist is concerned about missing clues to what caused or is maintaining a problem, the solution-focused therapist is concerned about missing clues to progress and solution. Yvonne Dolan (personal communication) demonstrates this process in the following case study.

Case Study

Mother: She comes home and then just ignores me, acts like I'm not there. Comes home from school, just runs into her room. Who knows what she's doing in there, but I have a feeling it's not good.

Daughter: You say we fight all the time, so I just go in my room so we don't fight.

Mother: See? She admits she just tries to avoid me. I don't know why she can't just come home and talk to me a little about school or something, like she used to.

Therapist: Wait a second, when did she "used to"? Cheryl, when did you used to come home and tell your mom about school?

Daughter: I did that a lot. Last semesterI I did.

Therapist: Can you give me an example of the last time you did that?

Mother: I can tell you. It was last week, actually. She was all excited about her science project getting chosen.

Therapist: Tell me more, what day was that?

Mother: I think last Wednesday.

Therapist: And she came home . . . ?

Mother: She came home all excited.

Therapist: What were you doing?

Mother: I think I was getting dinner ready. And she came in all excited, and I asked her what was up, and she told me her science project was chosen for the display at school.

Therapist: Wow, that's quite an honor!

Mother: It is.

Therapist: So then what happened?

Mother: Well, we talked about it. She told me all about it.

Therapist: Cheryl, do you remember this?

Daughter: Sure, it was only last week. I was pretty happy.

Therapist: And would you say that this was a nice talk, a nice talk between you two?

Daughter: Sure. That's what I mean. I don't always go in my room.

Therapist: Was there anything different about that time, last week, that made it easier to talk to each other?

Mother: Well, she was excited.

Daughter: My mom listened. She wasn't doing anything else.

Therapist: Wow, this is a great example! Thank you. Let me ask this: If it were like that more often, where Cheryl talked to you about things

that were interesting and important to her, and where Mom, you listened to her completely without doing other things, is that what you two mean by "better communication"?

Daughter: Yeah, exactly.

Mother: Yes.

In this example the therapist used a variety of solution-focused interventions. First, she listened carefully for an exception to the problem, a time when the problem could have happened but didn't. Second, she punctuated that exception by getting more details about it and congratulating the clients on it. Third, she connected the exception to their goal by asking how their goal would be reached if this exception were to occur more often.

Scaling Questions. **Scaling questions** were introduced to help therapists and clients talk about vague topics such as depression and communication, for which it's difficult to identify concrete behavioral changes and goals. Berg and de Shazer (1993) describe this question type:

> The therapist asks the depressed client, for example, "On a scale of one to ten, with one being how depressed you felt when you called me and ten being how you feel the day after the miracle, how do you feel right now?"
>
> The client might say two and the therapist might say, "So you feel a little better than when you called. How did you achieve this improvement?" Or the therapist might ask, "What do you think you need to do to achieve a three?" In this way, the therapist and client can recognize and nurture small changes toward the goal rather than being stuck in the "I'm either depressed or I'm not" kind of thinking that typifies such problems.

Scaling questions are also used to get clients to quantify their confidence that they can maintain their resolve: "On a scale of 1 to 10, how confident are you that you will be able to avoid losing your temper this week?" In practice, this device has a kind of "prove it" implication. The response is followed up by asking clients what they might do to increase the odds of success: "What do you have to do to stick to your guns this time?" Asking scaling questions is a useful way of anticipating and disarming resistance and backsliding and of encouraging commitment to change.

Here's an example of the use of scaling questions from the case of a couple who wanted to improve their communication.

Case Study

Therapist: What I want to do now is scale the problem and the goal. Let's say 1 is as bad as the problem ever could be—you never talk, only fight or avoid all the time. And let's say 10 is where you talk all the time with perfect communication—never have a fight ever.

Susan: That's pretty unrealistic.

Therapist: That would be the ideal. So where would you two say it was for you at its worst? Maybe right before you came in to see me?

Susan: It was pretty bad . . . I don't know . . . I'd say a 2 or a 3.

Jim: Yeah, I'd say a 2.

Therapist: Okay (writing) . . . a 2 or 3 for you, and a 2 for you. Now tell me what you would be satisfied with when therapy is over and successful?

Jim: I'd be happy with an 8.

Susan: Well, of course I'd like a 10, but that's unrealistic. Yeah, I'd agree. An 8 would be good.

Therapist: What would you say it is right now?

Susan: I would say it's a little better, because he's coming here with me, and I see that he's trying. I'd say maybe a 4?

Jim: Well, that's nice to hear. I wouldn't have thought she'd put it that high. I would say it's a 5.

Therapist: Okay, a 4 for you and a 5 for you. And you both want it to be an 8 for therapy to be successful, right?

This intervention has two major characteristics. First, it's a solution-focused assessment device. That is, if it's used each session, the therapist and clients have an ongoing measure of their progress. Second, it's a powerful intervention in and of itself because it allows the therapist to focus on previous solutions and exceptions, and to punctuate new changes as they occur. Like the changes made before the first session, any of three things can happen between each session: Things can get better; things can stay the same; or things can get worse.

If the scale goes up and things get better from one session to the next, the therapist compliments the clients and then gets details about how they were able to make such changes. This not only supports and solidifies the changes but also leads to the obvious nudge to do more of the same. If things stay the same, the clients can be complimented on maintaining their changes or for not letting things get worse: "How did you keep it from going down?" It's interesting how often that question will lead to a description of changes clients have made, in which case the therapist can again compliment and support and encourage more of that change.

Case Study

Therapist: Susan, last week you were a 4 on the scale of good communication. I'm wondering where you are this week?

Susan: [Pause] I'd say a 5.

Therapist: A 5! Wow! Really, in just one week?

Susan: Yes, I think we communicated better this week.

Therapist: How did you communicate?

Susan: Well, I think it was Jim. He seemed to try to listen to me more.

Therapist: That's great. Can you give me an example of when he listened to you more?

Susan: Well, yes, yesterday for example. He usually calls me once a day at work, and—

Therapist: Sorry to interrupt, but did you say he calls you *once a day?*

Susan: Yes.

Therapist: I'm just a little surprised, because not all husbands call their wives every day.

Susan: He's always done that.

Therapist: Is that something you like? That you wouldn't want him to change?

Susan: Yes, for sure.

Therapist: Sorry, go on. You were telling me about yesterday when he called.

Susan: Well, usually it's kind of a quick call. But I told him about some problems I was having, and he listened for a long time, seemed to care, gave me some good ideas. That was nice.

Therapist: So that was an example of how you would like it to be—where you can talk about something, a problem, and he listens and gives good ideas? Support?

Susan: Yes.

Therapist: Jim, did you know that Susan liked your telephoning her at work and listening to her?

Jim: Yeah, I guess so. I've really been trying this week.

Therapist: That's great. What else have you done to try to make the communication better this week?

This example shows how going over the scale with the couple served as a vehicle for tracking their progress. The therapist gathered more and more information about the small changes the clients had made on their own that led to an improvement on the scale. This would naturally lead to suggesting that the couple continue to do the things that are working.

Compliments. Compliments are conveyed with questions that take the form of "How did you do that?" or, to be more accurate, "Wow! How did you do *that?*" Notice that this phrasing calls attention to the fact that the clients have already accomplished something. Rather than ask questions like "Have you ever had a job before?" ask "What kinds of jobs have you had before?" Doing so invites clients to describe their successes and thus helps foster their self-confidence.

To be effective, compliments should point toward what to do more, not what to eliminate. Most clients know what's wrong but have run out of ideas about how to avoid repeating the same old ineffective solutions. Compliments can be used to highlight successful strategies and keep clients focused on the ones that work.

Taking a Break and Giving Feedback. Solution-focused therapy is often practiced in a team approach, with a therapist in the session and colleagues observing behind the mirror. Whether working with a team or alone, the interviewing therapist usually takes a ten-minute break near the end of the session. During this time the therapist (with the team or alone) composes a summary message to the clients.

Building on the solution-focused idea that it is the clients who do the real work, Sharry, Madden, Darmody, and Miller (2001) describe how the session break can be used to promote a collaborative mind-set:

> We're nearing the end of the session and I'd like to take a ten-minute break. This is to give you time to think and reflect about what we have discussed; to pick out any important ideas that came up, or to make decisions or plans. You might also like to think about whether this session has been useful and how you would like us to be further involved, if that would be helpful. While you're thinking, I will consult with my team for their thoughts. We will think together about what you said. When we get back together, I'll be interested to hear what stood out for you today. I'll also share the team's thoughts with you. Together, then, we can put something together that will be helpful. (pp. 71–72).

The summary message begins with a recap of what the therapist heard the clients say during the interview, including the problem, its background, the clients' goals, and presession progress and strengths: "What I heard you tell me today, Mr. and Mrs. X, is that . . ."; "Did I hear all of you correctly?"; "Is there anything of importance that I omitted or that you want to add?"

This recap is followed by a statement reflecting the therapist's reaction, including an expression of empathy ("I'm not surprised you're depressed!"), a reflection of the emotional impact on the client ("My sense is that you must really be hurting"), compliments on presession changes or strengths ("I was impressed by how many times you've tried to make things better"), and some comment on the clients' shared goals.

The therapist then makes suggestions about building on positives: "I suggest that you notice what Patrick is doing at school that you want him to continue doing." "Patrick, I would suggest that you try to notice what's happening at school with the kids and your teacher that you like and want to continue to have happen."

Among the suggestions used commonly in solution-focused therapy are the following:

1. *The formula first-session task* (de Shazer, 1985). "Between now and next time we meet, I would like you to observe what happens in your family that you want to continue to have happen."

2. *Do more of what works.* "Since you said that you usually can talk together when you go for a walk, maybe you should try that once or twice and see what happens."

3. *Do something different.* "You mentioned that when you rely on Janine to be responsible for her own homework, she often fails to do it. Maybe you should try something different?" The suggestion to do something different can be given as an experiment. This was illustrated by Insoo Berg's example of parents who were exasperated by their son's encopresis. When given the suggestion to try something different, they started filling the boy's potty seat with water and a toy boat and told him that his job was to sink the boat (Berg & Dolan, 2001). It worked!

4. *Go slow.* This suggestion is designed to help clients overcome fear of change by asking about possible negative consequences and warning against trying to change too rapidly. "I have what may seem like a strange question: Could there possibly be any advantages to things staying the way they are?"

5. *Do the opposite.* This suggestion is based on the notion that many problems are maintained by attempted solutions. Suggesting that clients try the opposite of what they've been doing is especially useful for problems that exist between just two people (one member of a couple or a parent who's having trouble with a child). If scolding a child for being bad isn't working, parents can be encouraged to start praising him or her for being good. If a husband's attempt to avoid conversations with his wife about the relationship isn't working, he could try initiating them when he's in the mood.

6. *The prediction task* (de Shazer, 1988). "Before you go to bed tonight, predict whether the problem will be better or the same tomorrow. Tomorrow night, rate the day and compare it with your prediction. Think about what may have accounted for the right or wrong prediction. Repeat this every night until we meet again."

As you can see, the compliments and suggestions of the summation message continue the basic thrust of the solution-focused approach, drawing attention to the family's resources and encouraging them to capitalize on their strengths in order to focus on solutions rather than problems.

Later Sessions.   Later sessions are devoted to finding, amplifying, and measuring progress. When a family returns for a subsequent session, the solution-focused therapist endeavors to create a cooperative mind-set and then inquires about progress, seeking detailed descriptions of any movement toward the family's goal and the clients' role in attaining it. Then the therapist assists the clients in looking forward to how they will plan their next prosolution steps.

"What's better?" *or* "What happened that you liked?"

"Tell me more. Walk me through how the two of you did that."

"Wow! That sounds great. What part did you especially enjoy?"

"And what else is better? So what do you think the next step might be? On a scale of 1 to 10, you say your progress is now at a 5. What would a 6 look like?"

If there was no discernible progress, coping questions can be asked:

"How did you keep things from getting worse?"
"What's your idea about what might be helpful?"
"What do you think the next step should be?"

"Sure, If You Tell Them We Did Most of the Work." To illustrate the process of solution-focused therapy with couples, we will summarize a case reported by Michael Hoyt (2002).

Case Study

Frank, age twenty-nine, and Regina, thirty, had been living together for seven months. For the last three months, since Regina had become pregnant, all they seemed to do was argue.

The therapist began by saying "Welcome. The purpose of our meeting is briefly to work together to find a solution to whatever brings you here today. What's up?"

Regina said she was tired of all their arguing. Lately it seemed as if all she and Frank did was fight.

Frank responded to Regina's complaints by saying "Everything's all my fault, huh?"

After a few more minutes of bickering, the therapist broke in to say "Wait a minute! You came here because you wanted things to be better, don't you?" They nodded. "That's why you're here. You used to get along, so you know *how* to—it seems you came here because you want some help figuring out how to get back to being happy, right?"

They agreed but without much enthusiasm.

The therapist then asked each of them to rate where their relationship was now on a scale from 1 (horrible) to 10 (great). They both gave it a 2.

"Okay," said the therapist. "That gives us some room to work." Then he asked what each of them would have to do to move their level of satisfaction up to a 3 or a 4.

Neither of them had any ideas. So he asked the miracle question: "Suppose tonight, while you're sleeping, a miracle happens . . . and the problems that brought you here are solved! Tomorrow when

you wake up, what would be some of the things you'd notice that would tell you that 'Hey, things are better'?"

They both laughed.

Then Regina said, "We'd be getting along, not hassling."

"Yeah," Frank said, "we'd talk, and she wouldn't get so mad at me."

The therapist moved quickly to concretize this goal. "You'd be getting along. What would you be saying and doing?"

In the discussion that followed, the couple described their meeting and courtship, an enjoyable vacation they'd taken, and their hopes for raising a happy child together. When they slipped back into arguing, the therapist redirected them toward their positive experiences. With prompting—"When was the last time you got along okay, even for a few minutes?"—the couple identified some recent moments when things were briefly good between them. The therapist asked numerous questions to expand on these exceptions, and the conversation gradually took on a more optimistic quality.

As the session drew toward a close, the therapist asked whether the meeting had been helpful and, if so, how. The couple agreed that it was helpful to talk without arguing and to be reminded about how they had gotten along well. The therapist complimented them for coming in, describing it as an indication of their caring for each other and their desire to make a happy home for their baby. He then asked if they'd like to make another appointment. They did. He offered them a homework assignment to observe what they each do to make things better. "It may not be perfect, but try to keep track of whatever positives you or your partner do or attempt to do."

In the second session, Frank and Regina said that they'd had a couple of really good days. The therapist complimented them and asked, "How did you do that?" But then they described an argument that had taken place one evening when Frank came home late from work. The therapist interrupted and said that he had made a mistake. He went on to say that while some therapists try to figure out what people are doing wrong, his approach was to help them figure out what they're doing right and then help them do more of it.

Frank then said that the day after their fight, Regina had called him at work and apologized. "I know I was wrong for being late, but it really hurt my feelings the way she yelled at me."

"She called and apologized?"

"Yeah. I really appreciated it, too."

"You called?"

Thus, even though Frank and Regina were still upset about their argument, the therapist was able to help them focus on how they'd made a constructive effort to get past it. Having helped them recover more positive feelings about each other, he went on to ask them what they appreciated about each other and how they showed it.

Frank acknowledged that when his feelings got hurt, he withdrew, which served only to make Regina angrier. Here he was moving from a complainant to a customer.

The therapist then asked the couple for their ideas about how to handle tense situations better, and they discussed these and role-played a couple of examples.

At the end of the session, the therapist complimented them again for their efforts and suggested that they keep track of the things that happen that they wanted to continue to happen. When asked when they would like to return, they said three weeks, which would give them time to practice.

The couple began the third session by describing a series of positive things each of them had been doing. Regina appreciated Frank's increased help around the house, and he beamed at this praise. They each rated the relationship now as between a 5 and a 6.

The couple did, however, have one significant argument when they were buying things for the new baby's room. Regina was annoyed that Frank wasn't more enthusiastic, and he in turn felt that she didn't appreciate all the compromises and adjustments he was making. Rather than pursue the feelings behind these complaints, the therapist asked for examples of times when the couple had

compromised successfully: "What did you do differently during those times you coped constructively with your frustration?" This redirection helped them to think more about how they were able to work together when they didn't let their hurt and anger get the best of them.

The homework assignment this time was to keep track of whatever either of them did that showed they were working together. The therapist also suggested that they each pick a fun outing to do together.

The fourth session occurred three weeks later. The couple said it had been the best three weeks since Regina got pregnant. The therapist offered compliments ("Wow!") and asked for details to help them focus on the constructive things they'd done. At this point Regina rated the relationship a 9 and Frank said 10. The therapist congratulated them on their teamwork, and they scheduled a follow up session three weeks later.

In the fifth session, Regina complained about feeling tired. Frank was also feeling tired from working overtime, but he was able to express sympathy and support for Regina. They agreed that they had continued doing well and had even thought of canceling the session. But they decided to come in to review their progress and talk about how to keep it going. As the couple talked about what they had accomplished, the therapist offered compliments about all the constructive things they reported.

The therapist then asked how they would remember to work as a team if their problems once again got them down in the future. They replied that they knew they'd have problems in the future but that they'd learned that they can solve their problems. "Now when we start to have an argument, we stop and remember . . . what we've talked about in here. How to use what you called 'solution talk,' how we used to fight, and how we know how to treat each other respectfully, and how to take time out if we need it, and how to listen to each other, and stuff like that."

When the therapist asked whether they wanted to make another appointment, they said not now but that they would call if they needed one.

"I wished them well and asked whether it would be okay for me to write up their story and put it in a book chapter. 'Sure,' they said, 'but only if you promise to tell people that we did most of the work.'"

CURRENT STATUS OF THE MODEL

What is it (besides its remarkably appealing name) that has made solution-focused therapy so popular? It is brief and pragmatic, but so are many other approaches to family therapy. Perhaps the two most powerful ingredients in solution-focused therapy are building on what works and helping people identify what they want rather than what they don't want.

Searching for exceptions turns out to be a simple but powerful intervention. The clients who come to us for help often think of the times when their problems don't occur as unimportant because these occasions seem accidental or inconsistent. Calling attention to past successes helps people rediscover their own best coping strategies.

The miracle question, which can sound like just another gimmick when you first read about it, is also a powerful tool, tapping as it does that wonderful human capacity not just to see things as they are but also to imagine things as they might be. One of the great things about the imagination is that with a little encouragement, people can see themselves as succeeding rather than fumbling and failing (Singer, 1981). What makes this kind of positive thinking more than empty optimism is that in the solution-focused therapist, clients have a coach and guide to help them work toward this brighter future.

To critics, solution-focused therapy is simplistic, and its emphasis on solution talk is seen as manipulative. Like any approach in the early stages of evolution, solution-focused therapy has sometimes been presented in a cookbook style that has led some to imagine that treatment can be reduced to a set of formulaic techniques. Is it true that all you have to do in solution-focused therapy is ask the miracle question and then talk about times when the problem wasn't a problem? No, of course not. With any new model of therapy, there is a tendency to emphasize what is distinctive—in this case, the miracle question, the search for exceptions, scaling questions, and compliments. The unique features of solution-focused therapy are deceptively easy to describe, but like all therapies, it takes great skill to implement effectively.

A second major criticism of solution-focused therapy is that its insistence on solution talk may cut clients off from empathy and understanding. People want to tell their stories. When they come to therapy, they want someone to understand their problems and be willing to help solve them. Reassuring someone who's worried that there's nothing to worry about isn't very reassuring. It can make you believe that your feelings aren't valid because you wouldn't have them if you would only look at the bright side of things. Most people aren't very eager to be changed by someone they feel doesn't understand them.

The issue of whether solution-focused therapy is genuinely collaborative has been raised frequently (Efran & Schenker, 1993; Efron & Veendendaal, 1993; Miller, 1994; Nylund & Corsiglia, 1994; O'Hanlon, 1996; Storm, 1991; Wylie, 1990). This approach has even been called "solution-forced therapy" by some because of the perceived tendency for therapists to pressure clients into discussing only positives. As Efran and Schenker (1993) ask, "What assurance is there that clients of solution-focused therapists haven't simply learned to keep their complaints to themselves in the presence of the therapist?"

More recently, solution-focused therapists have stressed the importance of the therapeutic relationship. Eve Lipchik, for example, said, "The speed and success of solution construction depend on the therapist's ability to stay connected with the clients' reality throughout the course of therapy. This is the underpinning for the whole collaborative process, the grease that keeps the axles turning" (Lipchik, 2002, p. 329). Like any other therapy, the solution-focused approach isn't likely to be very effective if therapists, in a rush to get to their own agenda, fail to listen to clients and make them feel understood.

Considering the popularity of solution-focused therapy, it's unfortunate that more research hasn't been done to test its effectiveness. Thus far, most of the research has been conducted by solution-focused practitioners themselves. Initial followup studies conducted by de Shazer and his colleagues at the Brief Family Therapy Center in Milwaukee involved surveying clients about their progress and found good success rates (e.g., De Jong & Hopwood, 1996; de Shazer, 1985; de Shazer et al., 1986). More recently, de Shazer and Isebaert (2003) published a followup report on male alcoholics who received solution-focused therapy in a hospital setting in Belgium. Of 118 patients contacted by phone four years post-discharge, 84 percent were judged to be improved.

When possible, contacts with family members were used to confirm the patients' reports.

In a systematic review of outcome research on solution-focused therapy, Gingerich and Eisengart (2000) reviewed fifteen controlled outcome studies and judged five of them to be well controlled. Four of the studies found solution-focused therapy better than no treatment controls or treatment as usual, and the fifth found solution-focused therapy equally effective with interpersonal psychotherapy for depression. The less well controlled studies also generally supported solution-focused therapy. Gingerich and Eisengart concluded by saying that the studies they reviewed provide preliminary support for solution-focused therapy.

Summary

1. Solution-focused therapy takes the essence of the MRI model but reverses its emphasis: While the one helps clients do less of what doesn't work, the other promotes more of what does. Both of these pragmatic approaches focus on the presenting complaint and aim to resolve it as quickly as possible. The MRI model does so by looking for failed solutions to eliminate; the solution-focused approach searches for forgotten solutions to rediscover.

2. An additional difference between these schools is that the solution-focused model emphasizes cognition as well as behavior. MRI therapists urge clients to *do* things differently; solution-focused therapists urge them to *view* things differently (Shoham, Rohrbaugh, & Patterson, 1995). Problems are seen as persisting in the way people define situations and in the misdirected actions they persist in taking. The idea is that people often get stuck in their problems because by trying to get to the bottom of them, they overlook solutions that are right under their noses.

3. This notion has led to the development of a set of techniques for changing *problem talk* into *solution talk*. These techniques include: *exception questions* ("Can you think of a time when you didn't have the problem? What were you doing then?"); the *miracle question* ("Suppose you went to sleep and a miracle happened such that when you awoke, your problem was solved. What would be different?"); *scaling questions* ("On a scale from 1 to 10, how do you feel now compared to when you called?"); *coping questions* ("Given how bad that was, how were you able to cope?"); the *formula first-session task* ("After you leave today, observe what happens that you want to continue during the next week."); and giving *compliments* ("Wow, you're smart to have thought of that!"). These techniques are put into practice as soon as possible to keep the work brief and to discourage clients from dwelling on the negative side of their experience.

4. More recently, therapists have questioned the emphasis on technique and speculated that qualities of the therapist–client relationship may be at the heart of the model's effectiveness. This has led to a call for greater collaboration with clients so that their feelings are acknowledged and validated before solution-focused techniques are introduced.

5. Solution-focused therapy continues to have enormous appeal in the world of psychotherapy. Some of its popularity can be attributed to therapists' struggle to find ways to be effective while living with managed care's limited number of sessions. In addition, the techniques of this therapy are relatively easy to learn (the basics can be picked up in a few workshops), and its upbeat nature makes it more enjoyable for many therapists. Yet its easy-to-learn formula has led some therapists to dismiss it as superficial.

6. Critics question whether therapists are really having respectful conversations with clients when they only praise, search for exceptions, and coax optimism. Do such insistently upbeat dialogues have the effect of silencing people's doubts and pain? Can solution-focused therapists find ways to honor client perceptions that don't fit the formula? Can clients trust the feedback of therapists who never challenge or question them? Can clients be honest regarding the outcome of their therapy with therapists who seem to want so much for them to feel better about things?

7. Other questions highlight the model's strengths. For example, isn't it important for therapists to have clear, concrete guidelines so therapy doesn't become vague and directionless? Isn't it more empowering to help people envision their future goals and focus on their strengths rather than their problems and deficits? If people's experience of pain is tied to the way they think or talk about it, then isn't it better to use language that will lead people out of pain rather than dwell on it?

Questions to Consider

1. When might it be important to understand *why* problems develop? When might this not be important?
2. When a friend tells you about a problem, try to inquire about exceptions. What does this experiment teach you?
3. What are some practical differences between accepting a negative goal (to get rid of something undesirable) and trying to come up with a positive goal (to make something good happen or happen more often)?

Key Concepts

complainant   A client who describes a complaint but is at present unwilling to work on solving it.

customer   A client who describes a problem and is motivated to work on solving it.

exceptions   Times when a client is temporarily free of his or her problem. Solution-focused therapists focus on exceptions to help clients build on successful problem-solving skills.

formula first-session task   Asking clients at the end of the first session to think about what they *do not* want to change about their lives as a result of therapy. This focuses them on strengths in their lives and begins the solution-generating process.

miracle question   Asking clients to imagine how things would be different if they woke up tomorrow and their problem was solved. Used to help clients identify goals and potential solutions.

scaling questions   Using a scale of 1 to 10, clients rate how much they want to resolve their problems, how bad the problem is, how much better it is than it was at the time of the last session, and so on. If the problem is rated a 4, the therapist can ask why it isn't a 1 or how the client can move it to a 5.

visitor   A client who doesn't wish to be part of therapy, doesn't have a complaint, and doesn't wish to work on anything.

Recommended Readings

de Shazer, S. 1988. *Clues: Investigating solutions in brief therapy.* New York: Norton.

de Shazer, S. 1991. *Putting difference to work.* New York: Norton.

de Shazer, S., Dolan, Y., Korman, H., Trepper, T., Berg, L. K., and McCollum, E. 2007. *More than miracles: The state of the art of solution-focused brief therapy.* Binghamton, NY: Haworth Press.

Dolan, Y. 1991. *Resolving sexual abuse: Solution-focused therapy and Ericksonian hypnosis for adult survivors.* New York: Norton.

Lipchik, E. 2002. *Beyond technique in solution-focused therapy.* New York: Guilford Press.

Miller, S., Hubble, M., and Duncan, B. 1996. *Handbook of solution-focused brief therapy.* San Francisco: Jossey-Bass.

Walter, J., and Peller, J. 1992. *Becoming solution-focused in brief therapy.* New York: Brunner/Mazel.

References

Berg, I. K. 1994a. *Irreconcilable differences: A solution-focused approach to marital therapy* [Videotape]. New York: Norton.

Berg, I. K. 1994b. *Family-based services: A solution-focused approach.* New York: Norton.

Berg, I. K., and de Shazer, S. 1993. Making numbers talk: Language in therapy. In *The new language of change,* S. Friedman, ed. New York: Guilford Press.

Berg, I. K., and Dolan, Y. 2001. *Tales of solutions: A collection of hope-inspiring stories.* New York: Norton.

Berg, I. K., and Miller, S. 1992. *Working with the problem drinker: A solution-focused approach.* New York: Norton.

De Jong, P., and Berg, I. K. 2002. *Interviewing for solutions,* 2nd ed. Pacific Grove, CA: Brooks/Cole.

De Jong, P., and Hopwood, L. E. 1996. Outcome research on treatment conducted at the Brief Family Therapy Center. In *Handbook of solution-focused brief therapy,* S. D. Miller, M. A. Hubble, and B. L. Duncan, eds. San Francisco: Jossey-Bass.

de Shazer, S. 1985. *Keys to solutions in brief therapy.* New York: Norton.

de Shazer, S. 1986. An indirect approach to brief therapy. In *Indirect approaches in therapy,* S. de Shazer and R. Kral, eds. Rockville, MD: Aspen Systems.

de Shazer, S. 1988. *Clues: Investigating solutions in brief therapy.* New York: Norton.

de Shazer, S. 1991b. *Putting difference to work.* New York: Norton.

de Shazer, S. 1993. Creative misunderstanding: There is no escape from language. In *Therapeutic conversations,* S. Gilligan and R. Price, eds. New York: Norton.

de Shazer, S., Dolan, Y., Korman, H., Trepper, T., Berg, I. K., and McCollum, E. 2007. *More than miracles: The state of the art of solution-focused brief therapy.* Binghamton, NY: Haworth Press.

de Shazer, S., and Isebaert, L. 2003. The Bruges Model: A solution-focused approach to problem drinking. *Journal of Family Psychotherapy. 14:* 43–52.

Dolan, Y. 1991. *Resolving sexual abuse: Solution-focused therapy and Ericksonian hypnosis for survivors.* New York: Norton.

Efran, J., and Schenker, M. 1993. A potpourri of solutions: How new and different is solution-focused therapy? *Family Therapy Networker. 17*(3): 71–74.

Efron, D., and Veenendaal, K. 1993. Suppose a miracle doesn't happen: The non-miracle option. *Journal of Systemic Therapies. 12:* 11–18.

Gingerich, W. J., and Eisengart, S. 2000. Solution-focused brief therapy: A review of the outcome research. *Family Process. 39:* 477–498.

Hoyt, M. F. 2002. Solution-focused couple therapy. In *Clinical handbook of couple therapy,* 3rd ed., A. S. Gurman and N. S. Jacobson, eds. New York: Guilford Press.

Lipchik, E. 2002. *Beyond technique in solution-focused therapy.* New York: Guilford Press.

Lipchik, E., and Kubicki, A. 1996. Solution-focused domestic violence views: Bridges toward a new reality in couples therapy. In *Handbook of solution-focused brief therapy,* S. Miller, M. Hubble, and B. Duncan, eds. San Francisco: Jossey-Bass.

Miller, S. 1994. The solution-conspiracy: A mystery in three installments. *Journal of Systemic Therapies. 13:* 18–37.

Nylund, D., and Corsiglia, V. 1994. Becoming solution-focused in brief therapy: Remembering something important we already knew. *Journal of Systemic Therapies. 13:* 5–12.

O'Hanlon, W. 1996. Case commentary. *Family Therapy Networker.* January/February: 84–85.

O'Hanlon, W. 1998. Possibility therapy: An inclusive, collaborative, solution-based model of psychotherapy. In *The handbook of constructive therapies,* M. H. Hoyt, ed. San Francisco: Jossey-Bass.

O'Hanlon, W. H., and Weiner-Davis, M. 1989. *In search of solutions: A new direction in psycho therapy.* New York: Norton.

Pichot, T., and Dolan, Y. 2003. *Solution-focused brief therapy: Its effective use in agency settings.* New York: Haworth Press.

Sharry, J., Madden, B., Darmody, M., and Miller, S. D. 2001. Giving our clients the break: Applications of client-directed, outcome-informed clinical work. *Journal of Systemic Therapies. 20:* 68–76.

Shoham, V., Rohrbaugh, M., and Patterson, J. 1995. Problem- and solution-focused couple therapies: The MRI and Milwaukee models. In *Clinical handbook of couple therapy,* N. S. Jacobson and A. S. Gurman, eds. New York: Guilford Press.

Singer, J. L. 1981. *Daydreaming and fantasy.* Oxford: Oxford University Press.

Storm, C. 1991. The remaining thread: Matching change and stability signals. *Journal of Strategic and Systemic Therapies. 10:* 114–117.

Walter, J., and Peller, J. 1992. *Becoming solution-focused in brief therapy.* New York: Brunner/Mazel.

Walter, J., and Peller, J. 1996. Rethinking our assumptions: Assuming anew in a postmodern world. In *Handbook of solution-focused brief therapy,* S. Miller, M. Hubble, and B. Duncan, eds. San Francisco: Jossey-Bass.

Weiner-Davis, M. 1992. *Divorce-busting.* New York: Summit Books.

Weiner-Davis, M. 1993. Pro-constructed realities. In *Therapeutic conversations,* S. Gilligan and R. Price, eds. New York: Norton.

Wittgenstein, L. 1958. *The blue and brown books.* New York: Harper & Row.

Wylie, M. S. 1990. Brief therapy on the couch. *Family Therapy Networker. 14:* 26–34, 66.

13

Narrative Therapy

The narrative approach is a perfect expression of the postmodern revolution. When all knowledge is regarded as constructed rather than discovered, it's fitting that a leading approach to family therapy is concerned with the ways people construct meaning rather than the ways they behave.

The underlying premise is that personal experience is fundamentally ambiguous. This doesn't mean that experience isn't real or that it's necessarily mysterious or opaque. Rather, it means that understanding human experience, including our own, is never simply a matter of observing it. The elements of experience are understood only through a process that organizes those elements, puts them together, assigns meaning, and prioritizes them. To say that experience is fundamentally ambiguous is to say that its meaning isn't fixed but instead lends itself to multiple interpretations.

Consider the difference between calling the heart-racing tension most people feel before speaking in public "stage fright" or "excitement." The first description makes this agitation a problem, something to overcome. The second suggests that it's a natural response to standing up in front of people whose approval you hope to win.

Whether people experience anxiety or excitement depends on how they interpret their arousal. Strategic therapists give clients *reframes,* or new interpretations, for their experience: "The next time you're speaking, think of yourself as excited rather than frightened." Narrative therapists believe that such interpretations won't take unless they fit people's stories. A man who thinks he's boring will have trouble seeing his trembling hands as due to excitement, no matter how hard someone tries to convince him. If the same man were helped to construct a new, more positive view of himself, the reframe becomes unnecessary. Once he starts to think well of himself, he will expect people to appreciate what he has to say.

Unlike the cybernetic metaphor, which focused on self-defeating patterns of *behavior,* the narrative metaphor focuses on self-defeating *cognitions*—the stories people tell themselves about their problems. With the cybernetic metaphor, therapy meant blocking maladaptive interactions. The narrative metaphor, on the other hand, focuses on expanding clients' thinking to allow them to consider alternative ways of looking at themselves and their problems.

EVOLUTION OF THE MODEL

Michael White, founder of the narrative movement, lived in Adelaide, Australia. He and Cheryl White were based at the Dulwich Centre, which provides training, clinical work, and publications related to

White's approach. In the late 1970s, White was drawn to the work of Gregory Bateson but found himself more interested in what Bateson said about how people construe the world than in the behavioral patterns of systems-based models. Under the influence of Bateson and Michel Foucault, who criticized the dehumanizing aspects of institutions, White developed his novel ideas about how problems affect people—regarding them as something operating on persons rather than as something people are doing. Sadly, Michael White died in 2008.

David Epston, a family therapist from Auckland, New Zealand, is the second most influential leader of the narrative movement. Through his interest in anthropology, Epston encountered the narrative metaphor and convinced White that it was more useful than cybernetics. He'd long had an interest in literature and for years was known as a storyteller, writing the "Story Corner" for the *Australian and New Zealand Journal of Family Therapy.*

Epston has contributed to most aspects of narrative theory and practice but in particular has emphasized that for clients to maintain their new narratives, they need supportive communities. He fostered the development of self-help leagues—groups of clients battling similar problems, such as the Anti-Anorexia/ Anti-Bulimia League of New Zealand. He also advocates writing letters to clients, pointing out that long after the influence of the therapist's presence has faded, clients can reread letters that bolster their new stories and resolve.

Jill Freedman and Gene Combs codirect Evanston Family Therapy Center in Evanston, Illinois. Before becoming narrative therapists, they were strategic therapists and social activists, drawn to White's approach in large part by its political emphasis. This combination—strategic therapy and political activism—characterizes the backgrounds of many prominent narrative therapists. Freedman and Combs have applied narrative ideas in consultation and community work, as well as in therapy.

Their book *Narrative Therapy* (1996) is an excellent guide to narrative therapy, and their *Narrative Therapy with Couples . . . and a Whole Lot More!*(2002) was the first book on using narrative ideas with couples.

Jeffrey Zimmerman and Vicki Dickerson codirected of the Bay Area Family Therapy Training Associates and together with John Neal taught narrative therapy at the Mental Research Institute in Palo Alto. These two creative therapists pioneered the use of narrative therapy with difficult adolescents and couples (Dickerson & Zimmerman, 1992; Zimmerman & Dickerson, 1993).

Stephan Madigan (1994; Madigan & Epston, 1995) in Vancouver, Canada, has also contributed to narrative theory and is the founder of the Vancouver Anti-Anorexia/Anti-Bulimia League, a grass-roots organization that provides support and encouragement to resist media images that promote "body guilt." Other prominent narrative therapists include Kaethe Weingarten, Sallyann Roth, and Bill Madsen in Cambridge, Massachusetts, and Janet Adams-Wescott in Tulsa, Oklahoma.

Michael White

Michael White began his professional life as a mechanical draftsman but soon realized that he preferred people to machines. Following an initial attraction to the cybernetic thinking of Gregory Bateson, White became more interested in the ways people construct meaning in their lives than in the ways they behave.

White's innovative thinking helped shape the basic tenets of narrative therapy, which considers the broader historical, cultural, and political framework of the family. In the narrative approach, therapists try to understand how clients' personal beliefs and perceptions, or narratives, shape their self-concept and personal relationships.

Harlene Anderson and the late Harry Goolishian, who developed a collaborative, conversational approach to family therapy (described in Chapter 11), were forerunners of the narrative model. Their work was based on the premise that problems are maintained in language and are subsequently dissolved through conversation. By adopting a "not-knowing" stance, Goolishian and Anderson subsumed their own expertise to allow clients to become the experts on their own lives. The link between this work and the narrative school was the belief that conversation generates meaning and that therapy should be a collaborative enterprise.

𝒯HE BASIC MODEL

The narrative approach first found its way into psychotherapy in the **hermeneutic** tradition of psychoanalysis. Following Freud, classical analysts believed there was one correct way to interpret experience. Patients might not understand their dreams or symptoms because their motives were unconscious, but an analyst possessed of the truth of psychoanalytic theory could discover unconscious meaning much as an archaeologist uncovers the buried remains of the past.

Then in the 1980s, revisionists such as Donald Spence, Roy Schafer, and Paul Ricoeur began to argue against this positivistic conception of psychoanalytic reality. The truth of experience, they said, isn't discovered; it's created. The goal of therapy shifted from historical truth to narrative intelligibility. The challenge was to construct truths in the service of self-coherence—not a true picture of the past. The therapist became more of a novelist than an archaeologist.

Family therapists found this narrative metaphor extremely useful. As they began to ask clients about their lives, therapists came to recognize how much narrative accounts affected people's perceptions. Life stories function as filters that screen out experiences that don't fit the plot line or, if they can't be screened out, distort events until they somehow do fit.

𝒞ase 𝒮tudy

According to Tim, Kayla was never satisfied. All she did was complain. Their apartment, their furniture, her clothes—nothing was ever good enough. No matter what they had, she wanted more.

Kayla had no idea what Tim was talking about. She was, in fact, perfectly content. Well, except maybe for one thing. Every time she'd see a picture in a magazine of a beautiful sofa or a pretty dress, she'd point it out to Tim. "Wow, look at that," she'd say. "Maybe we should get one of those." She was just dreaming out loud. But to Tim, who was brought up never to ask for anything, Kayla's fantasies felt like complaints. In fact, it wasn't so much what Kayla said that hurt Tim but how he interpreted it.

Looking deeper, it turned out that Tim was never satisfied with his own accomplishments. Growing up with a mother who wasn't given to praise, Tim dreamed of someday doing great things. Unfortunately, his real achievements never lived up to his own expectations. Sure, other people praised him, but he still secretly dreamed the grand and glorious dreams of childhood.

Until Tim could begin to accept himself, it was hard for him to believe that anyone else could truly appreciate him. Trying to get such a man to change his behavior without addressing his controlling life story would be futile, because no matter how many successes had, he'd still find ways to dismiss them and continue to dwell on his failures—and his partner's (presumed) dissatisfaction.

Narrative therapists oppose the functionalist elements in family systems and psychoanalytic models, which imply that problems are inherent in individuals (as psychoanalysis would have it) or families (as family systems would have it). Instead, narrative therapists believe that problems arise because people are indoctrinated into narrow and self-defeating views of themselves (White, 2007).

To counter the way society convinces people that they are their problems, narrative therapists **externalize** problems. Instead of *having* a problem or *being* a

Family arguments are fueled by negative story lines about other family members.

problem, clients are encouraged to think of themselves as *struggling against* their problems. Neither the patient nor the family is the problem; the *problem is the problem.* Accordingly, narrative therapists aren't interested in problem-maintaining interactions or structural flaws. They aren't interested in the family's impact on the problem but rather in the problem's impact on the family.

As narrative therapists shifted their attention away from families as the source of problems and toward cultural beliefs and practices, they turned to the writings of Michel Foucault (1965, 1980), a French social philosopher who devoted his life to exposing how various social discourses objectified and dehumanized marginalized groups. Foucault believed not only that those constructing the dominant narratives in a society (those deemed to have expert knowledge) have the power to subjugate but also that the narratives themselves become internalized truths, such that people come to judge their bodies, achievements, and personalities on the basis of standards set by society's judges (doctors, educators, clergy, psychotherapists, politicians, celebrities). Thus, Foucault influenced White to take the **social constructionist** axiom that there are no absolute truths in a political direction, toward deconstructing (reexamining) established truths that oppress people's lives.

Normal Family Development

Narrative therapists not only avoid judgments about what is normal but also reject the very idea of categorizing people. Recall how Foucault criticized the way theories of normality were used to perpetuate patterns of privilege and oppression. Too often in human history, the judgments made by people in power regarding normality and abnormality have been used to subjugate those with no voice in the matter.

While it's easy to see the dangers of reducing people to DSM-IV diagnoses, family therapists may have trouble seeing their own concepts—such as *rigid boundaries, cross-generational coalitions,* and *enmeshment*—as dehumanizing. But becoming a postmodern narrative therapist means giving up all such categories. Narrative therapists avoid pigeonholing people by diagnosis or normality and abnormality and reject general principles about what causes problems or resolves them. They try not to stand over people in judgment—in any way—but instead strive to help them make sense of their own experience.

In the spirit of collaboration, narrative therapists endeavor to *situate* themselves with clients—that is, to disclose the beliefs that inform their therapy so that clients know what they're getting into. Clients are also encouraged to educate therapists regarding their cultural predicaments and to correct therapists when they make assumptions that don't fit the client's experience (Freedman & Combs, 1996).

Although narrative therapists try not to make judgments, it may be impossible not to have some assumptions about people and how they change. From the ideas described in the previous section, we can distill certain basic assumptions that narrative therapists make about normal families. People (1) have good intentions (they don't need or want problems), (2) are profoundly influenced by the discourses around them, (3) are not their problems, and (4) can develop alternative empowering stories once separated from their problems and the cultural myths they have internalized.

Development of Behavior Disorders

When the stories people take on lead them to construe their experience in unhelpful ways, they tend to get bogged down with problems. Such problems are likely to persist as long as these unhelpful stories remain fixed, obscuring other more preferred versions of events.

A single mother struggles to be everything she can be as a parent to her teenage daughter, believing that, as a single mother, she can never do enough. Thus, when her daughter violates her curfew, she tends to react furiously. The cultural narrative about being a perfect parent makes the mother notice all the times her daughter stays out late or leaves cigarette butts on the porch and not notice the times when she gets her homework done or volunteers to wash the dishes. Each of the daughter's transgressions confirms the mother's story line that she isn't doing a good job.

The daughter, in turn, dwells on how often her mother criticizes her friends or explodes over small mistakes but doesn't remember the times her mother showed respect for her opinions or praised her achievements. The daughter gradually develops a narrative around never being able to satisfy people and becomes increasingly controlled by "rebelliousness." This makes her not care what her mother thinks and instead prompts her to indulge in whatever makes her feel better, like partying late into the night.

In short, both sides remain stuck not simply in a pattern of control and rebellion but, more specifically, of noticing incidents only of control and rebellion.

This analysis may not sound all that different from one that other schools of family therapy might make of an escalating cycle of antagonism between a mother and daughter. The difference is that the narrative approach doesn't focus on behavior. Narrative therapists reject the cybernetic notion that the mother and daughter are stuck in a dysfunctional feedback loop—acting and reacting to each other in unhelpful ways. Instead, they concentrate on the way the mother and daughter narrate their exchange. It's their *stories* (needing to be the perfect mother, being picked on by a parent) that affect not only what they notice (lateness, scolding) but also how they interpret it.

Narrative therapists refer to these patterns of tunnel vision as **problem-saturated stories**, which, once they take hold, encourage people to respond to each other in ways that perpetuate the problem story. As long as parents focus on their children's misbehavior, they will concentrate on criticizing and controlling them. As long as children think of their parents as hassling them, they will remain reactive and rebellious. Their responses to each other become invitations to more of the same and lead to further hardening of problem stories.

Such closed and rigid narratives make people vulnerable to being overtaken by destructive emotional states that narrative therapists portray as alien invaders. These therapists don't really see problematic feelings or beliefs as external entities, but they do believe that such emotional responses *are* external in the sense that they are socially constructed. Externalizing problems cuts down on guilt and blame. The daughter isn't the problem, "rebelliousness" is. The mother isn't the problem; "oversensitivity" is. Mother and daughter can unite to combat rebelliousness and oversensitivity rather than each other.

How Therapy Works

Narrative therapists aren't problem solvers. Instead, they help people separate themselves from problem-saturated stories (and destructive cultural assumptions) to open space for new and more constructive views of themselves. Narrative therapy transforms identities from flawed to preferred, not by getting family members to confront their conflicts but by separating persons from problems and then uniting the family to fight a common enemy. This is facilitated by combing the family's history for **unique outcomes**, or "sparkling events"—times when they resisted the problem or behaved in ways that contradicted the problem story.

If Alice sees herself as codependent because of the way she relates to men, a narrative therapist wouldn't explore the reasons for this condition, nor would he or she give Alice suggestions for altering this pattern. Instead, the therapist would ask questions about what codependency means to Alice and come up with a name for the negative effects these ideas have on her.

If, for example, Alice says that her codependency gets her to blame herself, the therapist might ask about the effect of *Self-blame* on her life, ask family members to help her defeat *Self-blame*, and highlight times in Alice's life when she related

to men in ways she prefers. The therapist might also invite Alice to explore how society's view of women contributed to *Self-blame*'s grip on her life.

Thus, narrative therapists see their work as a political enterprise—freeing people from oppressive cultural assumptions and empowering them to become active authors of their own lives. Once liberated from problem-saturated stories, family members can unite with one another and with communities of support to deal with their problems with more optimism and persistence.

Narrative therapists help clients *deconstruct* unproductive stories in order to *reconstruct* new and more productive ones. **Deconstruction**, a term borrowed from literary criticism, involves questioning assumptions.

Reconstruction involves creating new and more optimistic accounts of experience. Narrative therapists use externalizing conversations to help separate persons from problems. This is one way to deconstruct disempowering assumptions. Rather than talk of "Sally's laziness," for example, they'll inquire about times when "*Procrastination* takes hold of her." Once a problem has been externalized and redefined in more experience-near terms, a person can begin to resist it. By viewing the problem as an external entity, narrative therapists free families to challenge its influence on their lives.

In externalizing conversations, therapists ask *effects questions*—for instance, How does the problem affect you? Your attitudes? Your ideas about yourself? Your relationships? Through this process, the problem's field of influence is broadened so that clients can begin to recognize areas of their lives where the problem has been less powerful. It is in these areas that clients can notice *unique outcomes*—experiences that would not be predicted by a telling of the problem story, times when they resisted the problem's influence. Identifying unique outcomes creates room for counterplots, new and more empowering ways of construing events. A man who identifies himself as depressed sees life through a glass darkly.

Depression becomes a career, a lifestyle. But if the man begins to think of, say, "*Self-doubt* getting the best of him," he may then be able to remember times when he didn't let *Self-doubt* get him down. These newly recognized times of effectiveness provide openings around which to weave a new and more optimistic story.

Just as narrative therapists use externalizing conversations to shift clients' perceptions of themselves, they also try to shift family members' perceptions of each other from *totalizing views*, which reduce them to one set of frustrating responses. Such views lead to antagonism and polarization. Thus, parents who see their teenagers as "irresponsible," as though that were the sum total of their being, are likely to be seen in return as "unfair." Likewise, parents who totalize their children as "lazy" may be seen as "bossy" or "demanding." As long as both sides remain fixed in such polarized perspectives, they may be too busy to think about their own preferences. In unhappy families, people are often so busy *not* being what others expect that they have no time to figure out what they want for themselves.

$\mathcal{T}$HERAPY

Assessment

A narrative assessment begins with getting the family's story—including not only their experience with their problems but also their presuppositions about those problems. Getting the family's story isn't just information gathering; it's also a deconstructive inquiry designed to move clients from passivity and defeatism toward realizing that they already have some power over the problems that plague them.

Once problems have been personified as alien entities, the narrative therapist *maps the influence of the problem* on the family and then *maps the influence of the family* on the problem. In mapping the influence of the problem on the family, the therapist explores the distressing impact of the problem on their lives. Clients' responses to this line of inquiry usually highlight their own sense of inadequacy.

Case Study

Alesha Jackson, a single mother of four with a live-in boyfriend, sought therapy because her four-year-old was getting into trouble at preschool. Two or three times a week, Jermaine got into arguments that resulted in his hitting and biting other children. Jermaine was also a problem at home. Although he got along reasonably well with his brothers and sisters, he frequently threw tantrums when his mother tried to make him do something. Alesha sheepishly admitted that she was probably too easy on Jermaine, but she had gotten to the point where she felt helpless.

"I don't know what to do," she said. "I've tried everything. Nothing I do makes any difference. Luke, that's my boyfriend, he can make Jermaine behave, but he can get mean about it. He thinks I spoil Jermaine. Lately, Luke's been getting mad and going out after supper by himself, which leaves me all alone with the kids."

The therapist listens not just to get Alesha's story of the problem (what Jerome Bruner [1991] called "the landscape of action") but also to explore the conclusions ("the landscape of consciousness") she has drawn from her experience. The therapist asks "What conclusions about yourself as a mother have you drawn because of your problems with Jermaine?" and "What conclusions have you drawn about your relationship with Luke because of this problem?" (Note that it is the problem affecting the relationship rather than the relationship causing the problem.)

This line of questioning allows Alesha to tell her unhappy story but also tries to make her aware that the problem is burdening her. She begins to realize that it's not that she and her family are somehow dysfunctional; rather, they're struggling against an enemy.

In mapping family members' influence on the problem, the therapist explores the extent to which they have been able to stand up to the problem's oppression. To supply this information, family members are encouraged to recognize their own competence. Questions of the following sort are useful:

"How have you been able to avoid making mistakes that most people with similar problems usually make?"

"Were there times in the recent past when this problem may have tried to get the better of you, and you didn't let it?"

"How did you do that?"

This mapping process not only creates a sense of empathy and understanding between the therapist and the family but also is an empowering experience for the family.

Case Study

Although Alesha continued to disparage her abilities as a mother, she was able to describe times when she had been firm with Jermaine and insisted that he do what he was told—"even though that boy pitched one heck of a fit!"

In this phase of the assessment, the therapist did not try to coax Alesha to be more optimistic. Rather, the therapist confined herself to helping her client remember incidents of effectiveness that didn't fit her idea of herself as being at the mercy of her problems.

We tend to think of memory as a recorder or a camera, where the past is filed and can be called up at will. But memory is neither of these things. Memory is a storyteller. It creates shape and meaning by emphasizing some things and leaving out others. The narrative therapist's assessment explores two sides of the clients' memory—beginning with the problem narrative, a story of affliction (not pathology). These problem stories are understood not as personal failings but as stories of domination, alienation, and frustration. Then the therapist helps clients search their memories for the other side of the story—the side that honors their courage and persistence, the side that offers hope.

Therapeutic Techniques

Narrative interventions take the form of questions. These therapists almost never assert anything or make interpretations. They just ask question after question, following the clients' lead, often repeating the answers and writing them down.

In the first session, the therapist begins by finding out how clients spend their time. This gives the therapist a chance to appreciate how clients see themselves without getting into a lengthy history and the attributions of blame that so frequently accompany such histories. The therapist pays special attention to clients' talents and competencies. As a further means of establishing a collaborative atmosphere, Zimmerman and Dickerson (1996) encourage clients to ask any questions they might have about the therapist: "Okay. Is there anything you would like to know about me, either professionally or as a person?" The therapist can also invite clients to read his or her notes if they wish. Therapists often take notes as each person talks; doing so helps them retain important points and gives clients the sense that their points of view are being respected.

Externalizing Conversations. Narrative therapists begin by asking clients to tell their problem-saturated story and listen long enough to convey their appreciation for what the family has been going through. By using externalizing language, the therapist separates the client from the problem, making its destructive effects apparent and establishing a sense of trust with the client.

Each person is asked for his or her own perspective on the problem. The therapist asks about the problem's effects rather than its causes (causative questions usually lead to attributions of blame), mapping the influence of the problem. Questions might include "How does *Guilt* affect you?" "What other effects does it have?" "What does *Guilt* 'tell' you?"

The therapist's questions about the identified problem imply that it isn't possessed by the clients but instead is trying to possess them. For example, in a case where the parents describe the problem as a lack of trust in their daughter because of her sneakiness, the therapist doesn't reflect back "So your daughter's sneakiness bothers you." Instead the therapist might say "So *Sneakiness* made your daughter act in ways that caused a rift between you. Is that right?"

Sometimes patterns of interaction are externalized. For example, in the case in which a teenager's parents were responding to her sneakiness with increasing control, Vicki Dickerson chose to highlight the rift that was encouraging this pattern, because one thing all could agree on was that they didn't like the breach that was splitting the family apart. Thus, instead of identifying the daughter's sneakiness or the parents' distrust as the problem, the *Rift* became the enemy: The *Rift* told the parents that their daughter couldn't be trusted; the *Rift* made the daughter more secretive and told her to pull away from her parents. The *Rift* was something they could join forces against (Zimmerman & Dickerson, 1996).

Problems are almost always personified—portrayed as unwelcome invaders that try to dominate people's lives. For example, while discussing her eating problems, a woman is asked how *Anorexia* convinces her to starve herself. A phobic child is asked how often *Fear* is able to make him do what it wants and how often he is able to stand up to it. A guilt-ridden mother is asked how *Self-hate* is making her feel bad about her parenting.

This line of questioning can be disconcerting, unaccustomed as most people are to talking about imaginary entities in their households. Therapists who treat externalization as a gimmick may lack the conviction necessary to overcome the initial awkwardness of talking this way. On the other hand, therapists will find that externalizing questions flow naturally if they actually learn to think of problems as enemies that feed on polarizations and misunderstandings. One way to get more comfortable with this way of thinking is to start using externalization as a way to think about problems in your own life. (It isn't just our clients who could benefit from a little more compassion.)

While externalization may initially be a difficult concept to embrace, it can be profoundly helpful in minimizing self-blame. For example, a woman who thinks of herself as *being insecure* or *having insecurity*

has internalized the problem and come to see it as who she is. Over time, people become identified with their problems. They believe that the problem's existence is proof of their flawed character.

This way of thinking poisons confidence. When the problem is externalized, it's as if the person can peek out from behind it, and family members can see the healthier person that the problem has been hiding from them. Helping an "insecure woman" shift to seeing herself as *struggling with* Self-Criticism frees her from identifying with this problem and encourages her to discover that she can do something about it.

Externalizing helps clinicians develop a more sympathetic view of clients who engage in "inappropriate behavior." For example, thinking of a woman as being captured by emotions such as fear of abandonment or rage, rather than as being histrionic or ill-tempered or a borderline personality, makes it easier to empathize with her. You can dislike the emotional reaction rather than the client. From there you can look for times when the woman was able to avoid being captured by those emotions or was able to respond differently despite the emotions' pressure.

Case Study

William Madsen (2007) describes how a young woman who came to therapy complaining of depression began to talk about Self-Doubt. As she examined her experience with Self-Doubt, "Marie" described her fear of not living up to expectations. "I'm not thin enough, I'm not attractive enough, I'm not making enough money to suit my middle-class parents, and I'm not sexually satisfying to my boyfriend."

Madsen's inquiring about the *Expectations* that encouraged Self-Doubt helped Marie consider the pernicious effects of gender stereotypes. When asked where her life would be headed if *Expectations* were to set the direction, Marie said that *Expectations* would encourage her to "starve myself, get plastic surgery, get a job I hated to satisfy my parents, and become a sexual slave to my boyfriend." From there, she began to consider what direction she would prefer to set for her own life.

Placing *Expectations* in a larger cultural context helped Marie not only to escape the burden of self-loathing but also to develop a more sympathetic view of her parents and boyfriend as also falling under the influence of *Expectations*. As Marie put it, "They're just caught up in that middle-class success thing, and he's just worried that he's not gonna be a real man without some Barbie Doll on his arm."

Sallyann Roth and David Epston (1996) developed an exercise to help therapists grasp what it's like to think of problems as external. They have a group of trainees take turns being a problem—such as *Self-hatred*—while others interview him or her. The interviewers might ask the person playing *Self-hatred* such questions as "Under what circumstances do you manage to get into X's world?" and "How are you intervening in the lives of X's family and friends?"

Who's in Charge: The Person or the Problem? Over many sessions therapists ask a multitude of questions to explore how the problem has managed to disrupt or dominate the family versus how much they have been able to control it. These are called **relative influence questions**. By including all family members in the discussion, it usually becomes clear that the problem has succeeded in disturbing their relationships with each other, dividing and conquering them. The therapist can ask questions like these:

"How much has the *Bulimia* that's taken over Jenny kept you from being the way you want to be with her?"

"When *Depression* gets the better of Dad, how does that affect family life?"

"When *Tantrums* convince Joey to yell and scream, do you think your response gives *Tantrums* more or less fuel?"

Reading Between the Lines of the Problem Story. While asking relative influence questions, the therapist listens for sparkling events or unique outcomes—times clients were able to avoid the problem's effects—and then asks for elaboration on how those times came about:

"Can you remember a time when *Anger* tried to take you over, but you didn't let it? How did you do that?"

"Have there been times when your daughter didn't believe the lies *Anorexia* tells her about her body?"

"When Jenny has withstood the tremendous pressure she feels from *Alcoholism*, have you appreciated the magnitude of that accomplishment?"

These unique outcomes become the building blocks of new, more preferred stories.

Case Study

In *Collaborative Therapy with Multistressed Families,* Bill Madsen (2007) describes his work with a secretary referred by her employee assistance plan after a run-in with her boss in which she became distraught and angry. "Fran" described herself as depressed, disorganized, and intimidated by her boss. She had trouble sleeping and couldn't focus at work.

In the first session, Fran said that she felt worthless and unlikable, an accusation supported by an abusive father and a painful history of being teased at school. Depression's hold on Fran was strong, and she quickly dismissed the few exceptions to its influence she had noticed as inconsequential.

In the second session, Fran came in looking tired after attending a science fiction movie marathon. She was an avid fan who read voraciously and was familiar with almost every science fiction movie made. Even though she was exhausted, there was a sparkle in her eyes, which contrasted sharply with how she looked in the first session. In that session, when Fran described coping with the teasing she experienced as a child by watching endless hours of science fiction movies on TV, Madsen had viewed this as her escape from painful reality. Now he began to wonder what science fiction might be an entry into rather than an escape from.

When Fran spoke enthusiastically about an upcoming science fiction conference, Madsen asked her to describe the Fran one would see at this conference. "A big kid," she replied, "a nut who has fun, wears outrageous costumes, and enjoys herself; a girl who is confident and not afraid of people; someone who is friendly and open." They agreed that the conference was like a depression-free zone, and the following conversation ensued:

Fran: You know, it's like I live in a Sea of Depression and there are these Islands of Sanctuary where it can't get me. Some, like the conference, are bigger islands, and some are very small. Some aren't even islands. They're like coral reefs where I can just keep my head above water.

Bill: What is it that you like about the islands?

Fran: I'll drown out in the sea. The sea will kill me. The islands sustain me.

They talked further about Fran's struggle with teasing and taunting in grade school and then eventually returned to her metaphor of islands and coral reefs.

Bill: You talked about wanting to get more solid places to stand, like islands. What do you think would need to happen to build some of those coral reefs into islands?

Fran: I need to do what always happens to coral reefs—add sediment. The sediment is the people around me who will help me remember who I am and not get washed away by depression.

In the sessions that followed, Fran and her therapist fleshed out what she felt was the solid foundation in her life and the people who made her happy and brought out the best in her. In looking back on this successful treatment, Madsen observed:

All too often in our work as therapists, we focus on the sea of problems, rather than the islands of client abilities, skills, and know-how. It is an ironic and tragic paradox that our attempts to help often result in therapists and clients learning more about problems' influence and less about clients' resistance and coping. Again, it is important to not ignore the influence of problems but to juxtapose the dominant tragic story of the problem's influence with a heroic counterstory of client agency.

Reauthoring. Evidence of competence relative to the problem, gathered from sifting through the clients' history, can serve as the start of new narratives regarding what kind of people they are. To make this connection, the therapist begins by asking what past victories over the problem say about the client: "What does it say about you as a person that you were able to defeat *Depression* on those occasions?" or "What qualities of character must your son possess to be able to do that?" The therapist can also expand the historical purview beyond episodes relating to the problem to find more evidence to bolster the new self-narrative: "What else can you tell me about your past that will help me understand how you were able to handle *Anger* so well?" or "Who knew you as a child who wouldn't be surprised that you have been able to stand up to *Fear* on these occasions?"

As the new self-narrative begins to take shape, the therapist can shift the focus to the future, inviting the client or family to envision upcoming changes that will fit the new story: "Now that you've discovered these things about yourself, how do you think these discoveries will affect your relationship with *Self-hate?*" The self-story now has a past, present, and future. It's a complete narrative.

Reinforcing the New Story. Because narrative therapists believe that the self is constituted in social interaction, they make a point of helping clients find audiences to support their progress in constructing new stories for themselves. Clients might be asked to contact people from their past who can authenticate their new story—who can confirm and add to examples of their acting capably. Clients are also encouraged to recruit people who can serve as supportive witnesses, or "allies" (Dickerson, 2004), to their new story. Sometimes "leagues" are formed, support groups of people with similar problems who can reinforce one another's efforts to resist the problem. For example, the Vancouver Anti-Anorexia/ Anti-Bulimia League (Madigan, 1994) has a newsletter and monitors the media, writing letters to company presidents, newspapers, and magazines that portray an emaciated ideal for women and encourage them to diet.

David Epston (1994) has pioneered the use of letter writing to extend the therapeutic conversation beyond the session. These letters often convey a deep appreciation of what the client endured, the outline of a new story, and the therapist's confidence in the client's ability to continue to progress. The advantage of this technique is that the words in a letter don't vanish the way words do after a conversation. Clients have reported to Epston that they reread letters he sent them years earlier to remind themselves what they went through and how far they have come (Epston, 1994).

All of these efforts—recruiting authenticators and audiences, forming teams and leagues, writing letters—are in keeping with the social constructionist emphasis on interaction in creating and maintaining change. For people to solidify a new identity, they need communities that confirm and reinforce revisioned narratives and that counter cultural and familial messages to the contrary. What happens in a session is just the beginning. The goal isn't just to solve a problem; it's to change the whole way of performing one's life.

At the end of each session, the narrative therapist summarizes what happened, being sure to use externalizing language and emphasizing any unique outcomes that were mentioned. Information from these summaries is what Epston often puts into his letters to clients. The effect of these reviews is to convey to clients that the therapist is with them and celebrates their blossoming new identity. This sense of being cheered on by the therapist can be extremely encouraging.

Deconstructing Destructive Cultural Assumptions.
At times, narrative therapists make the connection to cultural narratives more explicit. For example, an anorexic woman might be asked how she was recruited into the belief that her worth depended on her appearance. This would lead to other questions regarding the position of women in society. Similarly, a violent man might be asked how he came to believe that men should never be weak or tender, and a deconstructing of the messages men receive would ensue.

Case Study

To clarify what this deconstructing of cultural attitudes might look like, we will present one of White's cases, as described by Mary Sikes Wylie (1994):

> John . . . came to see White because, says White, "he was a man who never cried"—he had never been able to express his emotions— and he felt isolated and cut off from his own family. As a child, John had been taught, both at home and at his Australian grammar school, that any show of gentleness or "softness" was unmanly and would be met with harsh punishment and brutal public humiliation. White asks John a series of questions that are at once political and personal, eliciting information about the man's "private" psychological suffering and linking it to the "public" cultural practices, rigidly sexist and aggressively macho, that dominated his youth. "How were you recruited into these thoughts and habits [of feeling inadequate, not sufficiently masculine, etc.]? What was the training ground for these feelings? Do you think the rituals of humiliation [public caning by school authorities, ridicule by teachers and students for not being good at sports or sufficiently hard and tough] alienated you from your own life? Were they disqualifications of you? Did these practices help or hinder you in recognizing a different way of being a male?" (p. 43)

After deconstructing the masculine image in this way, White helped John to remember times when he resisted it and to recognize the nobility of his efforts to remain gentle and loving in spite of his socialization.

A Case of Sneaky Poo.   White's therapy comes to life in his case descriptions, as in the following excerpt from his description of a family with an encopretic child (White, 1989).

Case Study

When mapping the influence of family members in the life of what we came to call "Sneaky Poo," we discovered the following:

1. Although Sneaky Poo always tried to trick Nick into being his playmate, Nick could recall a number of occasions during which he had not allowed Sneaky Poo to "outsmart" him. These were occasions during which Nick could have cooperated by "smearing," "streaking," or "plastering," but he declined to do so. He had not allowed himself to be tricked into this.

2. There was a recent occasion during which Sneaky Poo could have driven Sue into a heightened sense of misery, but she resisted and turned on the stereo instead. Also, on this occasion, she refused to question her competence as a parent and as a person.

3. Ron could not recall an occasion when he had not allowed the embarrassment caused by Sneaky Poo to isolate him from others. However, after Sneaky Poo's requirements of him were identified, he did seem interested in the idea of defying these requirements. . . .

4. It was established that there was an aspect to Sue's relationship with Nick that she thought she could still enjoy, that Ron was still making some attempts to persevere in his relationship with Nick, and that Nick had an idea that

Sneaky Poo had not destroyed all of the love in his relationship with his parents.

After identifying Nick's, Sue's, and Ron's influence in the life of Sneaky Poo, I introduced questions that encouraged them to perform meaning in relation to these examples, so that they might "reauthor" their lives and relationships.

How had they managed to be effective against the problem in this way? How did this reflect on them as people and on their relationships? . . . Did this success give them any ideas about further steps that they might take to reclaim their lives from the problem? . . . In response to these questions, Nick thought that he was ready to stop Sneaky Poo from outsmarting him so much, and decided that he would not be tricked into being its playmate anymore (pp. 10–11).

Two weeks later, White found that Nick had fought Sneaky Poo valiantly, having only one minor episode, and he seemed happier and stronger. Sue and Ron had also done their parts in the battle. In her effort not to cooperate with Sneaky Poo's requirements for her to feel guilty, Sue had begun to treat herself when Sneaky Poo was getting her down. Similarly, Ron had fought Sneaky Poo's attempts to keep him isolated by talking to friends about the problem. White noted:

> I encouraged the family to reflect on and to speculate about what this success said about the qualities that they possessed as people and about the attributes of their relationships. I also encouraged them to review what these facts suggested about their current relationship with Sneaky Poo. In this discussion, family members identified further measures that they could take to decline Sneaky Poo's invitations to them to support it (p. 11).

White also reported that the family expanded these efforts in the interim, and by the third session they felt confident that Sneaky Poo had been defeated. At a six-month follow-up, they were still doing well.

CURRENT STATUS OF THE MODEL

By externalizing problems, deconstructing pessimistic life stories, and conveying unswerving confidence in their clients, narrative therapists have constructed a powerful recipe for change. Packaging interventions in the form of questions makes their input less like advice to be resisted and fosters a sense of partnership with clients.

The two most powerful ingredients in narrative therapy are the narrative metaphor itself and the technique of externalizing problems. Both the strength and the weakness of this approach is its cognitive focus. In rejecting the cybernetic model (families stuck in dysfunctional feedback loops) narrative therapists repudiated the idea that families with problems have something wrong with them. Unfortunately, at least early on, narrative therapists also turned their backs on the three defining innovations of family therapy: (1) recognizing that psychological symptoms are often related to family conflict, (2) thinking about human problems as interactional, which means thinking in terms of twos (complementarity, reciprocity) and threes (triangles), and (3) treating the family as a unit.

Viewing problems as stories to be deconstructed overlooks the fact that some families have real conflicts that don't disappear because they join together temporarily to fight an externalized problem. For example, parents whose lives are empty may have trouble letting their children grow up. Does that emptiness evaporate after they help their children battle *Rebelliousness*?

In the process of helping people restory their experience, narrative therapists often view unhappy emotions—anger, fear, anxiety, depression—as annoyances to avoid rather than explore. They ask how anger or fear "defeats" clients but rarely why clients are angry or what they are afraid of.

Early versions of family therapy *did* cast families in a bad light and blamed them for their problems. The narrative movement helped shift the field toward a more collaborative stance. In the process of rejecting the patronizing consciousness of that earlier age, however, narrative therapists have often neglected systems thinking (Phipps & Vorster, 2009), emphasizing its mechanistic elements while ignoring its more humanistic elements.[1] One of family therapy's greatest contributions was to bring a contextual understanding of people and their problems into the consulting room. Nonsystemic therapists, influenced by the disease model, had encouraged people to fight problems (with medication, support groups, education) rather than explore the network of relationships in which their problems were embedded. Although opposed to the disease model, narrative therapists return to a similarly acontextual view of problems as things to be fought, and they eschew efforts to understand their interpersonal roots.

Most narrative therapists would agree with Vicki Dickerson's statement that narrative therapy is "primarily about situating problems in their cultural context" (Freedman, 1996). That is helping clients identify and challenge the ubiquitous but commonly unexamined prejudices that permeate society and make self-worth and harmonious relating difficult at best. But how does one do that without imposing one's own political biases?

Although some therapists still make a case for strict therapeutic neutrality, many now agree that it's sometimes necessary to question invidious cultural assumptions. It's true that popular culture promotes many unhelpful values. The question is, what is the best way for therapists to help people free themselves from those influences without imposing their own values? This is a complex problem, and narrative therapy answers it one way. We hope that example inspires all family therapists to grapple with this issue.

---

[1]What adherents of this approach maintain is that the narrative metaphor is applicable to either an intrapsychic or a systemic approach (Dickerson, 2007).

Summary

1. The narrative approach is built around two organizing metaphors: personal narrative and social construction. When memory speaks, it tells a narrative truth, which comes to have more influence than historical truth. The "facts" presented to a therapist are partly historical and partly constructed. The constructions that make up the shared reality of a family represent mutual understandings and shared prejudices—some of which are useful, some of which are not.

2. Narrative therapists seek to break the grip of unhelpful stories by *externalizing* problems. By challenging pessimistic versions of events, therapists make room for hope. Uncovering *unique outcomes* provides an opening for new and more optimistic stories. Finally, therapists help clients create audiences of support to encourage their progress in restorying their lives along preferred lines.

3. The strategies of narrative therapy are applied in three stages: (1) recasting the problem as an affliction (externalizing) by focusing on its effects rather than its causes, (2) finding exceptions, or partial triumphs over the problem and instances of effective action, and (3) recruiting support. Encouraging some kind of public ritual to reinforce new and preferred interpretations moves cognitive constructions past private insight into socially supported action.

4. Putting these strategies into practice involves an elaborate series of questions:

- *Deconstruction questions*—To externalize the problem. "What does Depression whisper in your ear?" "What conclusions about your relationship have you drawn because of this problem?"

- *Opening space questions*—To uncover unique outcomes. "Has there ever been a time when Arguing could have taken control of your relationship but didn't?"

- *Preference questions*—To make sure unique outcomes represent preferred experiences. "Was this way of handling things better or worse?" "Was that a positive or a negative development?"

- *Story development questions*—To develop a new story from the seeds of (preferred) unique outcomes. "How is this different from what you would have done before?" "Who played a part in this way of doing things?" "Who will be the first to notice these positive changes in you?"

- *Meaning questions*—To challenge negative images of self and to emphasize positive agency. "What does it say about you that you were able to do that?"

- *Questions to extend the story into the future*—To support changes and reinforce positive developments. "What do you predict for the coming year?"

5. The social constructionist foundation of narrative therapy gives the approach its political cast and deemphasizes family dynamics and conflict. Instead of looking within families for dysfunctional interactions, narrative therapists look outside for the destructive influences of cultural values and institutions. These therapists invite family members to pull together to oppose these values and practices. Instead of neutrality, narrative therapists offer advocacy.

Questions to Consider

1. Reread the cases in this chapter to see when you think narrative therapists do too much leading and not enough following of the client's narrative.

2. How relevant are social and political concerns to the practice of therapy?

3. How might it be possible to incorporate systems thinking into the practice of narrative therapy?

4. How might externalizing problems detract from a client's personal responsibility? How can therapists prevent this from happening?

5. In what ways, if any, do the actual interventions of narrative therapy differ from those of other cognitive approaches?

Key Concepts

deconstruction   Exploring meaning by examining taken-for-granted categories and assumptions, making possible newer and more sound constructions.

externalization   Personifying problems as external to persons.

hermeneutics   Analysis of literary texts or human experience, understood as fundamentally ambiguous, by interpreting levels of meaning.

problem-saturated stories   The usual pessimistic accounts clients bring to therapy, which may help keep them stuck.

reconstruction   The creation of new and more optimistic accounts of experience.

relative influence questions   Questions that explore how the problem has dominated the client versus how much he or she has been able to control it.

social constructionism   Knowledge and meaning are shaped by culturally shared assumptions.

unique outcomes   Times when clients acted free of their problems, even if they were unaware of doing so. Narrative therapists identify unique outcomes as a way to help clients challenge negative views of themselves.

Recommended Readings

Diamond, J. 2002. *Narrative means to sober ends: Treating addiction and its aftermath.* New York: Guilford Press.

Dickerson, V. C., and Zimmerman, J. 1992. Families with adolescents: Escaping problem lifestyles. *Family Process. 31:* 341–353.

Freedman, J. H., and Combs, G. 1996. *Narrative therapy: The social construction of preferred realities.* New York: Norton.

Gilligan, S., and Price, R. 1993. *Therapeutic conversations.* New York: Norton.

White, M. 1989. *Selected papers.* Adelaide, Australia: Dulwich Centre Publications.

White, M. 1995. *Re-authoring lives: Interviews and essays.* Adelaide, South Australia: Dulwich Centre Publications.

White, M., and Epston, D. 1990. *Narrative means to therapeutic ends.* New York: Norton.

Zimmerman, J., and Dickerson, V. 1996. *If problems talked: Adventures in narrative therapy.* New York: Guilford Press.

References

Bruner, J. S. 1991. The narrative construction of reality. *Critical Inquiry. 18:* 1–21.

Dickerson, V. 2004. Allies against self-doubt. *Journal of Brief Therapy* (special edition): 83–95.

Dickerson, V. 2007. Remembering the future: Situating oneself in a constantly evolving field. *Journal of Systemic Therapy.*

Dickerson, V., and Zimmerman, J. 1992. Families with adolescents: Escaping problem lifestyles. *Family Process. 31:* 341–353.

Epston, D. 1994. Extending the conversation. *Family Therapy Networker. 18:* 30–37, 62.

Foucault, M. 1965. *Madness and civilization: A history of insanity in the age of reason.* New York: Random House.

Foucault, M. 1980. *Power/knowledge: Selected interviews and other writings.* New York: Pantheon.

Freedman, J. H. 1996. AFTA voices on the annual meeting. *AFTA Newsletter.* Fall: 30–32.

Freedman, J. H., and Combs, G. 1996. *Narrative therapy: The social construction of preferred realities.* New York: Norton.

Madigan, S. 1994. Body politics. *Family Therapy Networker. 18:* 27.

Madigan, S., and Epston, D. 1995. From "spy-chiatric gaze" to communities of concern: From professional monologue to dialogue. In *The reflecting team in action,* S. Friedman, ed. New York: Guilford Press.

Madsen, W. C. 2007. *Collaborative therapy with multi-stressed families,* 2nd ed. New York: Guilford Press.

Phipps, W. D., and Vorster, C. 2009. Narrative therapy: A return to the intrapsychic perspective? *South African Journal of Psychology, 39*: 32-45.

Roth, S. A., and Epston, D. 1996. Developing externalizing conversations: An introductory exercise. *Journal of Systemic Therapies. 15:* 5–12.

White, M. 1989. *Selected papers.* Adelaide, Australia: Dulwich Centre Publications.

White, M. 2007. *Maps of narrative practice.* New York: Norton.

Wylie, M. S. 1994. Panning for gold. *Family Therapy Networker. 18:* 40–48.

Zimmerman, J., and Dickerson, V. 1993. Bringing forth the restraining influence of pattern in couples therapy. In *Therapeutic conversations,* S. Gilligan and R. Price, eds. New York: Norton.

14

Integrative Models

In breaking with the dominant paradigm of the time, the first family therapists defined themselves in opposition to all things psychoanalytic. Did psychoanalysis maintain that behavior was an artifact of unconscious forces? Then family therapists would insist that an individual's behavior was dictated by the structure of the family and that insight was unnecessary for problem solving.

Similarly, as they worked out the implications of their own insights, the various schools of family therapy emphasized not only their own strengths but also their differences. Bowen sought to reason with family members one at a time; Minuchin insisted that the way to get at relationships was to have people talk to each other. The new schools aren't immune from this us-against-them mentality; on the contrary, solution-focused and narrative therapists have made a point of rejecting many of the defining features of the traditional schools. They are antimechanistic, and decidedly not behavioral, and they pretty much ignore conflict as a source of family problems. Just as it took systems therapists years to get over their denigration of psychodynamics, it will probably take time for these postmodernists to bring back what we learned about family dynamics to their work.

In any field of endeavor, it seems that integration is possible only after a period of differentiation. It's no surprise then that in the early years of family therapy,

when the emerging schools were trying to differentiate themselves, the idea of *integration* had a negative connotation. It was seen as a watering down, rather than an enrichment, of the classic models.

During the past decade, however, there has been a growing awareness that no single approach has a monopoly on the truth. The time of competitive schools of family therapy has passed. As family therapy moves ahead in the twenty-first century, the dominant trend is integration.

When it's described as respect for the multiplicity of truth, integration seems like an unassailably good idea. The obvious argument for incorporating elements from different approaches is that human beings are complicated creatures—thinking, feeling, and acting—who exist in a complex system of biological, psychological, and social influences. No therapy can succeed without affecting all of these dimensions. There is, however, an equally valid argument that eclecticism can rob therapy of the intensity made possible by focusing on particular elements of experience. There may be many ways to skin a cat, but it might not be advisable to try all of them at once.

As we see in this chapter, *integration* refers to three very different kinds of approaches. First there is **eclecticism**, which draws from a variety of models and methods. Second is **selective borrowing**, in which relative purists use a few techniques from other approaches. Third are **specially designed integrative models**.

ℰCLECTICISM

What do you do in the first session? Try to make sure that everyone attends, greet each of them, and try to make them comfortable. Ask about the presenting problem, of course. But then what?

Suppose a mother says that her fourteen-year-old has become rude and disrespectful. Do you focus on her feelings? Set up an enactment with her teenager? Ask about exceptions? Any of these options might be useful. But trying to do all of them may lead to a lack of focus.

In creating a workable integration, there are two things to avoid. The first is sampling techniques from diverse approaches without conceptual focus. The problem here isn't so much inelegance as inconsistency.

A student who was being supervised in a psychodynamic approach asked to present at a case conference when, after some initial progress, the therapy bogged down. Most of the people at the case conference weren't familiar with the psychodynamic model, and they were impressed by what the student had accomplished. But when it came time for discussion, several of those present suggested that the way to get things moving again might be to try a different approach—cognitive-behavioral, structural, or what have you, depending on who was doing the suggesting.

The second thing to avoid is switching horses in midstream. Almost every treatment runs into difficulty at some point. When this happens, beginners may be tempted to shift to a different model. If a structural approach isn't working, maybe a narrative one will. The problem here is that almost any strategy

will work for a while—and then stall. Getting stuck isn't a reason to change models; rather, it may mean that you and your clients are getting to the heart of their problems. This is the time to sharpen your tools, not discard them.

𝒮ELECTIVE BORROWING

To borrow selectively, you need a solid foundation in one paradigm. Which one you choose will depend in part on what is available in your training program. It's a good idea to take advantage of what's offered by learning as much as you can from whoever happens to supervise you. However, the approach you eventually specialize in should also make sense to you. At some point you will be free to seek out training and supervision, and the approach you choose should be consistent with how you think about people and how you prefer to interact with them. If narrative therapy inspires you, seek out training in this approach. In graduate school you may not have a lot of choice about what your instructors offer. But after that it can be a mistake to settle for a particular kind of training merely because it's convenient.

Therapists who eventually manage to combine approaches or successfully master more than one don't try to learn them all at once. Using techniques from here and there without conceptual focus produces a muddled form of eclecticism. Effective borrowing doesn't mean a hodgepodge of techniques, and it doesn't mean switching from one approach to another whenever therapy reaches a temporary impasse. Borrowing techniques from other approaches is more likely to be effective if you do so in a way that fits into the basic paradigm within which you are operating.

Consider, for example, a structural therapist treating a mother and daughter who are locked in a battle in which the mother constantly criticizes the daughter for being irresponsible and the daughter constantly acts irresponsibly. If the mother would back off and stop criticizing, the girl might feel less browbeaten and begin to take more responsibility for herself—or if the daughter would start to take more responsibility, maybe the mother would back off. But as long as each of them remains preoccupied with the other one and the awful things she's doing, neither is likely to break this cycle.

Suppose the therapist were to try the narrative technique of externalizing the problem. Instead of "nagging" and "irresponsibility" polarizing the mother and daughter, perhaps they could be convinced to start thinking in terms of a "breach" that's come between them. This shift might open space for them to recapture a more cooperative way of relating. But if the mother and daughter's quarreling is a product of enmeshment, attempting to bring them together in a more harmonious way might not solve the problem.

In fact, the case we've just described isn't hypothetical. Here's how the therapist actually did introduce the technique of externalizing in this situation.

Case Study

Because he saw the mother and daughter's quarreling as a result of their enmeshment, the therapist concentrated first on helping the mother address with her husband some of the conflicts that were keeping them apart. As they started to get closer, the mother began to spend less time worrying about what her daughter was or wasn't doing.

Then in separate sessions with the daughter, the therapist found a useful way to introduce the externalizing technique. As a result of her mother's nagging, the daughter had gotten into the habit of shirking responsibility, and as a result, her school performance had plummeted. It was as though when she had a homework assignment, she felt the same kind of oppression she felt from her mother's nagging.

The therapist pointed this out but found that the girl had begun to internalize her mother's harsh characterizations. "I guess I'm just lazy," she'd say in what was becoming a self-fulfilling prophecy. The

therapist responded by asking her about times when *Procrastination* got the better of her and times when It didn't. This device proved effective in helping the girl separate herself from the negative introject she'd adopted, and, thus energized, she was able to start getting back on track with her schoolwork.

$\mathcal{S}$PECIALLY DESIGNED INTEGRATIVE MODELS

Although most practitioners eventually become selective borrowers, grafting ideas and practices onto their basic model, some therapists create a new synthesis out of complementary aspects of existing models. Some of these integrative efforts are comprehensive systems that include a whole range of approaches under one umbrella, whereas others simply combine elements of one approach with another, forming a hybrid model.

Comprehensive, Theoretically Inclusive Models

The advantage of these comprehensive approaches is that they bring a wider range of human experience into focus. They also offer more options for intervention. For example, rather than simply trying to pry apart an enmeshed mother and child, a therapist whose purview includes cultural issues might help the mother examine the assumptions keeping her from getting more satisfaction out of her own life.

Here we will present two examples of models designed to increase comprehensiveness. The first, *metaframeworks*, selects key ideas that run through the different schools of family therapy and connects them with superordinate principles. The second, *integrative problem-centered therapy*, links several approaches in sequence and provides a decision tree for shifting from one to another when therapists get stuck.

The Metaframeworks Model. This approach offers a unifying theoretical framework operationalized with six core domains of human functioning, or metaframeworks: intrapsychic process, family organization, sequences of family interaction, development, culture, and gender (Breunlin, Schwartz, & Mac Kune-Karrer, 1992). The application of metaframeworks is conceived in terms of releasing the constraints keeping a family from solving its problems.

For example, a depressed woman might be constrained on many fronts simultaneously. At the level of internal process, she may be burdened by guilt over wanting a little time for herself or because her children complain that they have no friends. (If children are unhappy, it must be their mother's fault, right?) At the level of family organization, she may be stuck in a stale second marriage to a man obsessed with his career while she's left to run the house and raise the kids. In addition, she may be preoccupied with her hyperactive son and polarized with her own mother over how to deal with him. This pattern may be part of a sequence in which her son's behavior gets worse after monthly visits with her ex-husband. Finally, the woman's situation may be part of a transgenerational pattern maintained by the family and cultural belief that women should be devoted to their families and never be "selfish."

As the therapist considers the network of constraints impeding this woman and her family, one framework often emerges as a point of departure, but the therapist is always aware of the others and can shift when necessary. Thus, therapy may start in the gender metaframework by reexamining the woman's beliefs about selfishness and her husband's unbalanced expectations about the proper roles of men and women. The focus might shift to the internal framework when the therapist asks about the parts of each partner that hold these beliefs and what they are related to from their pasts. This exploration might make the woman want to reorganize the family responsibilities, and the shift is to the organizational metaframework. At another point the couple might discuss their son's oscillation between acting younger and older than his age, and they're in the developmental framework, and so on.

The metaframeworks model isn't simple. In an age when therapists often fall back on formulaic techniques, it challenges clinicians to consider a range of possibilities. Yet for therapists who've felt boxed in by the narrow scope of the original models of family therapy, the metaframeworks model offers a broader range of options.

Integrative Problem-Centered Therapy. Whereas metaframeworks distills elements from different theories into a new synthesis, integrative problem-centered therapy incorporates a variety of family and individual approaches in sequence without trying to combine them.

Like many therapists, William Pinsof began his career convinced that the model he was trained in (strategic family therapy) could be effective with any sort of problem. Unlike selective borrowers, however, he didn't just add new techniques when he ran up against his theory's limitations; he added whole new approaches. For example, if his strategic model didn't seem to be working, he might help family members explore their emotions à la Virginia Satir. If problems persisted, he might recommend a psychopharmacological assessment. With continued failure, he might bring in grandparents or even offer individual therapy to some family members.

This sequencing made sense because some problems are deep-seated whereas others are not. Some families respond to behavioral interventions while others may need more of an in-depth focus. Why not consider the whole spectrum of psychotherapies if necessary?

To illustrate Pinsof's approach, consider a couple in their sixties who have been caught up in picky but intense fights for the past year. They relate the fighting to the husband's increasing impotence. In exploring the meaning each attaches to these events, the therapist finds that the wife sees her husband's lack of sexual response as a reflection of her diminished attractiveness, whereas he considers it a sign of waning virility. These conclusions are painful to each of them, and so they avoid discussing, much less having, sex.

The therapist forms an alliance with each of them so they feel safe enough to disclose their private pain and clear up their misconceptions about each other's feelings. If at that point they respond well—fewer fights and more satisfactory sex—therapy can stop. If not, the therapist will explore possible physiological causes of the impotence—fatigue, depression, incipient diabetes. If improvements don't follow exploration at that level, the therapist might discuss with each partner unexamined assumptions about the aging process. If the problem still remains unsolved, the focus will shift to intrapsychic blocks, and either or both of them might be engaged in individual therapy.

Pinsof doesn't expect therapists to be competent in all of these approaches. Integrative therapy often involves teamwork among a number of therapists, particularly when key family members are vulnerable and need their own therapists. Although separate therapists with differing orientations can be a nightmare, the integrative framework provides common ground for collaboration.

The metaframeworks and integrative approaches represent two reactions to the realization that all models have their limitations. One solution (metaframeworks) is alchemical—taking pieces from here and there to forge a new synthesis. The other (integrative) is additive—linking whole models together without trying to revise them or connect them theoretically.

Models That Combine Two Distinct Approaches

Some theorists who found one approach too limiting were satisfied to improve their model by combining it with just one other, believing that two heads were better than one—and probably also better than five or six.

The Narrative Solutions Approach. Among the reasons strategic therapy fell into disfavor were its mechanistic assumptions and manipulative techniques. The way some strategists applied the cybernetic model, families were seen as stubborn and not to be reasoned with. You can't talk sense to a machine. Family histories were irrelevant. Therapy was ideological and therefore often impersonal. The meretriciousness of this kind of thinking, however, wasn't essential to the insight that families often get stuck applying solutions that don't work. Joseph Eron and Thomas Lund (1993) resuscitated that insight and incorporated it into a blend of strategic and narrative therapy.

Eron and Lund began collaborating in the early 1980s as brief strategic therapists. Although they were attracted to the narrative model, they didn't want to give up the strategic approach. So they put the two together. The resulting narrative solutions approach revolves around the concept of the **preferred view**. Eron and Lund (1996) assume that people have strong preferences for how they like to see themselves and to be seen by others:

- Preferred views include the qualities people would like to possess and have noticed by others—for example, "determined," "caring," "responsible."
- Preferred views shape the attributions one makes about behavior. "I did that (got into that fight) because I am strong, cool, able to manage my own affairs."
- Preferred views also include people's hopes, dreams, and intentions for living their lives. "I want to be different from my mother, who was a self-sacrificing martyr."
- Preferred views may or may not have anything to do with one's actual behavior. "I may not be doing well in school, but I can be hard-working and self-disciplined. I expect to succeed in graduate school, even though, given how I'm doing now, it isn't likely."

Eron and Lund believe that problems arise when people aren't living according to their preferred views. To address this discrepancy, they use a combination of reframing from the MRI model and restorying from the narrative approach. They assume that people begin to think and act in problematic ways when they experience a discrepancy between their preferred view of themselves and their perception of their actions or their impression of how others regard them.

The following questions may be asked to help clients get in touch with their preferred views:

- When are you at your best—at home, work, school, with friends?
- Who notices—family, colleagues, teachers, friends?
- What do they notice about you at these times?
- Who are your favorite relatives, friends, teachers, other adults?
- What do they like about you?
- When you think back on your life, are there other times when you felt at your best?
- When you look into the future and you are the person you would like to be, what do you envision?

In *Narrative Solutions in Brief Therapy*, Eron and Lund (1996) offer the example of "Al," who became depressed in the wake of retirement and the onset of emphysema. Al preferred to think of himself as productive and useful. Yet he worried that he might not be able to remain as active as in the past and that his family would no longer view him as someone to rely on. The disjunction between Al's preferences and his perceptions led to his feeling sad and listless. The more depressed Al seemed, the more family members began to do for him, finishing projects he started and trying to cheer him up, which only deepened his despondency.

The negative frame through which Al viewed his current circumstances affected the stories he recalled from the past. For example, he pictured himself following in the footsteps of his own father, who deteriorated rapidly after retiring. According to Eron and Lund, negative frames of the present shape the stories people recall from the past, which in turn influence their perspectives on the future.

Eron and Lund (1996) offer the following guidelines to therapists for managing helpful conversations:

1. Maintain an interest in clients' preferences and hopes, paying attention to stories that reflect how they prefer to see themselves.
2. Explore how the problem keeps people from acting in line with their preferences.
3. Find past and present stories that are in line with their preferences and contradict problem-maintaining views.
4. Discuss what the future will look like when the problem is resolved.
5. Ask **mystery questions**—for example, how did a person with X preferred attributes (hard working, productive) wind up in Y situation (acting listless and feeling depressed)?
6. Coauthor with clients alternative explanations for the evolution of the problem that fit with how they prefer to be seen and inspire new actions.
7. Encourage clients to talk to significant others about their preferences, hopes, and intentions.

As the therapist follows these guidelines, clients become aware that he or she is seeing them in their preferred ways and they begin to notice their own strengths. They begin seeing the problem as a mystery to be explained rather than as truth that speaks to who they really are. They begin to restory how the problem evolved (a narrative practice) and to reframe (a strategic technique) their immediate situation.

For example, Al felt empowered to talk to his doctor about his illness after he was able to recall preferred experiences indicating that he was a take-charge kind of guy. He also began reframing the motives of family members away from the belief that they saw him as useless to viewing them as bewildered, not knowing how to help him. Al's depression lifted after he met with his family and told them what was and wasn't helpful.

Integrative Couples Therapy. Neil Jacobson of the University of Washington, one of the preeminent behavioral family therapists, teamed with Andrew Christensen of UCLA to figure out how to improve the limited success rates they were finding with traditional couples therapy. They discovered that their results improved when they added a humanistic element to the standard behavioral mix of communication training, conflict resolution, and problem solving. The approach they developed is called *integrative couple therapy* (Jacobson & Christensen, 1996).

Traditional behavioral couples therapy is based on the behavior exchange model. After a *functional analysis* shows how partners in a relationship influence one another, they're taught to reinforce changes they wish to bring about in each other.

Anyone who's been married for a long time can tell you what's missing from this formula. Therapy may be about change, but a successful relationship involves a certain amount of acceptance of differences. Some things in an unhappy marriage may need to change, but some things are part of the package, and couples who survive the break-in period learn to accept these things. It's this element, *acceptance,* that Jacobson and Christensen added in their new approach.

In contrast to the teaching and preaching of traditional behavioral therapy, integrative couples therapy emphasizes support and empathy, the same qualities that therapists want couples to show each other. They begin with a phase called the *formulation,* which is aimed at helping couples let go of blaming and open themselves to acceptance and personal change. The formulation consists of three components: a *theme* that defines the primary conflict; a *polarization process* that describes their destructive pattern of interaction; and the *mutual trap,* which is the impasse that prevents the couple from breaking the polarization cycle once it's triggered.

Common themes in couples' problems include conflicts around closeness and distance, a desire for control but unwillingness to take responsibility, and disagreements about sex. Whereas partners view these differences as problems to be solved, Jacobson and Christensen encourage couples to see that some differences are inevitable. This kind of acceptance can break

the cycles that build up when partners are constantly trying to change each other. Also, as the formulation phase continues, the couples begin to see that they aren't victims of each other but of the pattern in which they've been trapped. As with Michael White's externalizing, the couple can unite to fight a mutual enemy, the pattern. Here's what happened when Jacobson asked one couple to describe their pattern:

> The husband replied, "We fight over whether or not to be close. When she is not as close to me as she wants to be, she pressures me into being close, and I withdraw, which leads to more pressure. Of course, sometimes I withdraw before she has a chance to pressure me. In fact, that's how it usually starts." (Jacobson & Christensen, 1996, p. 100)

Notice how the formulation process helps this couple describe their fight as a pattern to which they both contribute, rather than in the accusatory language typical of distressed couples.

Strategies to produce change include the two basic ingredients of behavioral couples therapy: behavior exchange and communication skills training. Behavior exchange interventions involve "quid pro quo" and "good faith" contracts by which couples learn to trade favors or to initiate pleasing behavior in the hope of getting the same in return. For example, each partner might be asked to generate a list of things he or she could do that would lead to greater satisfaction for the other. (Ask not what your partner can do for you; ask what you can do for your partner.) After compiling their lists, they're instructed to start doing some of the things they think will please their partner—and observe the effect of this benevolence on the relationship.

The second ingredient—communication training—involves teaching couples to listen and to express themselves in direct but nonblaming ways. Learning to use *active listening* and to make *I-statements* is taught by assigned reading, instruction, and practice. As couples learn to communicate less defensively, they not only are better able to resolve conflicts but also are more accepting of each other.

In emphasizing acceptance and compassion, integrative couples therapy joins other family therapies of the twenty-first century—from solution-focused to strategic to narrative—in recognizing the importance of nurturing relationships. Carl Rogers would be proud.

Other Integrative Models. Although we've singled out some of the most innovative examples, there are in fact so many integrative approaches that it's impossible to list them all. While many of these models are new, some of them have been around so long they don't always get the attention they deserve.

Carol Anderson and Susan Stewart wrote one of the most useful integrative guides to family therapy back in 1983. Two other integrative approaches that have been around for a while are those designed by Larry Feldman (1990) and William Nichols (1996). The tradition of offering practical advice that transcends schools of family therapy is upheld in a splendid book by Robert Taibbi (1996) called *Doing Family Therapy*. Others have attempted to integrate structural and strategic therapies (Liddle, 1984; Stanton, 1981), strategic and behavioral (Alexander & Parsons, 1982), psychodynamic and systems theory (Kirschner & Kirschner, 1986; M. P. Nichols, 1987; Sander, 1979; Scharff, 1989; Slipp, 1988), and experiential and systems theory (Duhl & Duhl, 1981; Greenberg & Johnson, 1988).

One particularly elegant model that's been around for a while (first described in 1981) is Alan Gurman's *brief integrative marital therapy,* which combines social learning theory and psychodynamics. As in behavior therapy, marital problems are seen as due to poor communication and problem solving, but as in object relations theory, these deficits are understood as having roots in unconscious conflicts. What might seem like simply a lack—poor relationship skills—may turn out to serve a protective function of limiting intimacy to a level that a couple can tolerate without undue anxiety. Gurman's assessment begins with problematic themes in a couple's relationship.

Case Study

In a recent chapter on brief integrative marital therapy, Gurman (2002) describes a case in which Sue is angry and critical of Karl's emotional unavailability.

This familiar demand-and-withdraw pattern is assumed to reflect not only the couple's interaction but also intrapsychic conflicts that motivate this interaction.

Like an analyst, Gurman sees Sue's attacking as serving the defensive function of avoiding dealing with her own fears of abandonment. Meanwhile, Karl's distance helps him avoid his conflicts about intimacy. The partners' complaints about each other ("nagging," "withdrawing") allow them to maintain a consistent and tolerable sense of themselves, even if it limits the satisfaction they share in their relationship.

Like a behaviorist, Gurman also looks at the consequences of the couple's problematic interaction, noting what (positive and negative) reinforcements or punishments may be maintaining these patterns. Karl negatively reinforced Sue's criticism by apologizing and coming closer to her after her complaints reached the shouting stage. Sue inadvertently punished Karl's closeness by venting her anger and frustration whenever the couple did spend time together—thus violating the First Law of Social Learning Theory.[1]

In order to explore the impact of one or both partners' personal conflicts on the couple's relationship, Gurman may talk at some length to each partner individually while the other just listens. Talking separately to the partners (à la Murray Bowen) helps minimize anxiety and thus makes therapy a safer "holding environment."

Gurman's blocking of Sue's criticism allowed Karl to explore how he felt about trying to balance his commitments to career and family. As Karl opened up about his fears of failure, Sue softened enough to empathize with his struggles—and to share her own fears of being alone.

In addition to addressing couples' problematic interactions and the conflicts underlying them, Gurman's brief integrative marital therapy also includes practical problem-solving discussions, advice, teaching of self-control techniques, exploration of the past,

---

[1] You catch more flies with honey than with vinegar.

modeling, coaching, bibliotherapy—in short, the wide and flexible variety of interventions that characterize the best kind of integration.

• • •

Other integrative approaches haven't received as much attention in mainstream family therapy as they have by federal funding agencies. These include Scott Henggeler's *multisystemic model* (Henggeler & Borduin, 1990) and Howard Liddle's *multidimensional family therapy* (Liddle, Dakoff, & Diamond, 1991). These approaches evolved out of research projects with difficult adolescents, a population that challenges theorists to expand their views beyond the limits of one school of therapy or one level of system.

Liddle developed his integrative approach while working with drug-abusing inner-city adolescents. His multidimensional family therapy brings together the risk factor models of drug and problem behavior, developmental psychopathology, family systems theory, social support theory, peer cluster theory, and social learning theory. In practice, the model applies a combination of structural family therapy, parent training, skills training for adolescents, and cognitive-behavioral techniques.

One of the most useful aspects of Liddle's approach is the way he integrates individual and systems interventions. Although he makes liberal use of the structural technique of enactment, he frequently meets with individual family members to coach and prepare them to participate more effectively in these family dialogues. Liddle also uses individual sessions to focus on teenagers' experiences outside the home. Here, sensitive subjects like drug use and sexual behavior can be explored more safely in private. The need to meet with teenagers to focus on their lives outside the family reflects a growing recognition of the limited influence families have in comparison with peers and culture.

Scott Henggeler of the University of South Carolina and a number of research-oriented colleagues who work with difficult-to-treat children tried to improve on their systems-oriented family therapy by (1) more actively considering and intervening in the extrafamilial systems in which families are embedded, in particular their school and peer contexts, (2) including individual developmental issues in assessments,

and (3) incorporating cognitive-behavioral interventions (Henggeler & Borduin, 1990). This multisystemic model has shown promising results in several well-designed outcome studies of juvenile offenders and families referred for abuse or neglect (Henggeler et al., 1997, 1999). For that reason, it is highly regarded among governmental funding agencies, and Henggeler has received a number of large grants.

mODELS DESIGNED FOR SPECIFIC CLINICAL PROBLEMS

One sign that family therapy was maturing was when therapists began focusing on specific clinical problems rather than generic families. Some groups applied preexisting models to the problems they were wrestling with; for example, structural family therapy was used with anorexia nervosa and brittle diabetes (Minuchin, Rosman, & Baker, 1978). Other groups had to be more creative because they decided to tackle problems that weren't typically seen in the practice of family therapy. Such problems often require more than any single approach offers.

Working with Family Violence

One of the most impressive integrative efforts is the approach to treating spousal abuse developed by Virginia Goldner, Peggy Penn, Marcia Sheinberg, and Gillian Walker at the Ackerman Institute in New York (Goldner, 1998; Goldner, Penn, Sheinberg, & Walker, 1990; Walker & Goldner, 1995). When Goldner and Walker began studying violence in couples, the standard approach involved separating partners and treating the man in a group with other offenders and the abused woman in a support group. This treatment was informed by the feminist critique of systems-based therapies that implied that both partners were responsible for the violence and consequently could be treated together like any other couple.

Goldner and Walker share the feminist conviction that regardless of the woman's role, the man is responsible for his violent behavior, no matter what provocation he might feel. But they also believe that there is value to treating the couple together and to attending to the woman's part in these couples' dangerous dramas. Instead of taking sides in the systems theory versus feminism debate, they bridged the polarized thinking that pervaded the field of family violence.

Is it possible to take both positions simultaneously? Yes, the man is responsible for controlling his violence, but both partners participate in a process of interaction that must change. As Goldner says, "A battered woman is not equally responsible for her broken nose, even if she acknowledges having been angry or 'provocative'; just as the victim of sexual abuse is not equally responsible for what happened in the middle of the night, even if she felt aroused" (Goldner, 1998, p. 266). With this more nuanced position, it became possible to examine both partners' roles in their escalations of conflict without blaming the victim.

Rather than see each partner individually and insist that they separate, Goldner and Walker work with the couple together but insist that the violence must cease immediately and the man must take responsibility for that. Here they combine the feminist emphasis on safety and responsibility with a systemic interest in the way the couple interacts. Goldner points out that separating violent couples rarely promotes safety because they are often so symbiotically attached that

they quickly reunite, and those women who do leave are the most likely to be attacked. On the other hand, if they are together in treatment, the victim can explain to the abuser how damaging his aggression is in the presence of a therapist who can emphasize the moral imperative to stop.

Goldner and Walker use the language of "parts" to help partners detach from global labels like *abuser* and *victim* and to bring intrapsychic insights into the conversation. He can talk about the angry part of himself and she the part that needs to protect him rather than look after herself. As they inquire into the origin of these parts, Goldner and Walker find themselves listening to painful stories from each partner's past. "Here we typically find ourselves back in a time when the man was a boy, subject to sadistic acts of violence, power and control" (Goldner, 1998, p. 275). This compassionate witnessing helps reduce the partners' antagonism toward each other.

Goldner and Walker also incorporate an active listening format so that not only are past traumas witnessed but also the man listens to the woman describe the pain and terror she suffered from his attacks. Here again there's a both/and message to the man: Yes, you suffered as a boy, and that's related to your violent behavior. But you are still choosing to be violent, and that's unacceptable. Similarly, regardless of how passive the woman has been in the past, she can choose to protect herself without feeling disloyal.

This nondichotomous position is an advance over the either/or positions of both the feminist and psychoanalytic models. Feminist therapists believe that exploring a man's troubled childhood implies excusing his violence, whereas psychoanalysts too often see violence as a symptom of an underlying pathologic condition for which they don't hold anyone accountable. Goldner writes, "From a both/and perspective, violence is best conceptualized as simultaneously willful and impulse-ridden, as both instrumental and dissociative" (Goldner, 1998, p. 279).

Although Goldner and Walker's approach was designed for violent couples, it offers important lessons for the integration of therapy models in general. It illustrates the value of stepping out of the dichotomies that dominate clinical work (especially around volatile issues like domestic violence) to see that more than one

Virginia Goldner's work with violent couples combines a highly sophisticated clinical approach with a passionate feminist sensitivity.

perspective has validity and can coexist with others. Too often, "Ideas that could mutually enrich one another have instead been set up as oppositional positions, creating a polarizing context of forced choices between adequate alternatives" (Goldner, 1998, p. 264). The depolarizing effect is a major virtue of integration.

Community Family Therapy

Many family therapists start out working in agencies with poor families, but as they realize how powerless therapy is to deal with many of the problems impoverished families face, they get discouraged and opt for private practice with middle-class clients. This recognition of family therapy's limits had the opposite effect on Ramon Rojano.

According to Rojano, the greatest obstacle poor people face is a sense of powerlessness that comes with being controlled by a multitude of dehumanizing bureaucracies and the futility of having no hope of achieving the dream of a decent job and a comfortable home. Rojano uses his knowledge of and personal connections with the helping systems to make clients feel reconnected to their communities and empowered to advocate for what they need. Not only does he help families find the resources to survive— child care, jobs, food stamps, housing—which is the essence of traditional casework, but also he begins encouraging aspirations beyond mere survival.

Laura Markowitz (1997) describes Rojano's work this way:

> Ramon Rojano is a professional nudge. Let's say you're a single mother on welfare who goes to him because your teenage son is skipping school and on the verge of being expelled. Leaning forward in his chair, the stocky, energetic Rojano will start prodding and poking with his questions in his Spanish accent, zeroing in on your son like he's herding a stray lamb back into the fold. After some minutes of this interrogation, you actually hear your boy admit what's going on with him and promise in a small, sincere voice you haven't heard come out of him in a long time, that he will go to school regularly if he can graduate. As your mouth opens in surprise, Rojano won't even pause. Now he'll urge the 15-year-old boy to apply for an after-school job he just heard about from someone who runs a program. . . . Rojano will write the phone number down and put it directly into the boy's hand, look him in the eye and use his name a few times to make sure he knows Rojano actually cares whether or not this kid ends up on the streets or in a gang. . . . You think the session is over, right? Not quite. He has plans for you too. Be prepared—he might ask you something outrageous, like whether you've thought about owning your own house. You may be a single mother barely getting by, but as he leans toward you it's like the force of his confidence in you pulls you in, and now he's pressing a piece of paper into your hand with the number of a woman he knows who runs a program that helps people with no money buy a home of their own. (Markowitz, 1997, pp. 25–26)

Rojano asks clients about things that they, in their state of hopelessness and disconnection, never considered—running for the school board, going to college, starting a business or an advocacy program— in such a way that these things seem possible. This is partly because Rojano can see strengths that disheartened clients have forgotten and partly because he has the connections to get the ball rolling.

Rojano also recognizes that community empowerment is not enough. Without ongoing family therapy, it wouldn't be long before the single parent in the scenario above might start being late for work because of renewed conflicts with her son, and that dream of a house would evaporate.

So this is the integration: family therapy with community psychology and social work. Rojano has taken a version of structural family therapy and bolstered it with hands-on advocacy. Structural family therapy was developed in the Wiltwyck agency in Harlem in the late 1950s. But in retrospect, Braulio Montalvo, one of its developers, said, "We couldn't get the resources around the family to uphold the changes they were able to make in family therapy" (quoted in Markowitz, 1997, p. 28). Forty years later, someone has taken the next step by incorporating those resources.

Once again we see that integration requires a new way of thinking. Rojano had to step out of the mind-set that said therapy takes place in an office, even though clients are often constrained by forces untouched in the office. Why not take it to the street so the whole system is addressed? It seems like an obvious question— but maybe not so obvious when you're trapped in your circumstances.

Summary

1. In the founding decades of family therapy, a number of models were developed, and most family therapists became disciples of one of these approaches. Each of the major schools concentrated on a particular aspect of family life. Experientialists opened people up to feeling, behaviorists helped them reinforce more functional behavior, and Bowenians taught them to think for themselves. By concentrating their attention this way, practitioners of the classic models focused their power for change. If in the process they got a little parochial and competitive, what was the harm?

2. The harm was that by ignoring the insights of other approaches, disciples of the various schools limited their impact and applicability. But maybe this parochialism should be understood from a developmental perspective—as a necessary stage in the consolidation of the original insights of the founding models. Perhaps it was useful for the schools to pursue the truth as they knew it in order to mine the full potential of their ideas. If so, that time has passed.

3. Most of the schools of family therapy have been around long enough to have solidified their approach and proven their worth. That's why the time is ripe for integration.

4. Valuable as integrative efforts are, however, there remains a serious pitfall in mixing ingredients from different approaches. You don't want to end up with what happens when you blend too many colors from a set of poster paints. The trick is to find a unifying conceptual thread. A successful integration draws on existing therapies in such a way that they can be practiced coherently within a consistent framework. Adding techniques willy-nilly from here and there just doesn't work.

5. A successful synthesizing effort must strike a balance between breadth and focus. Breadth may be particularly important when it comes to conceptualization. Contemporary family therapists are wisely adopting a broad, biopsychosocial perspective in which biological, psychological, relational, community, and even societal processes are viewed as relevant to understanding people's problems. When it comes to techniques, on the other hand, the most effective approaches don't overload therapists with scores of interventions.

6. Finally, an effective integration must have clear direction. The trouble with being too flexible is that families have a way of inducting therapists into their habits of avoidance. Good family therapy creates an environment where conversations that should happen at home, but don't, can take place. These dialogues won't happen, however, if therapists abruptly shift from one type of intervention to another in the face of resistance.

7. Family therapy is ultimately a clinical enterprise, its worth measured in results. The real reason to combine elements from various approaches is to maximize their usefulness, not merely their theoretical inclusiveness. To contradict Billy Crystal, it's better to be effective than to look marvelous.

Questions to Consider

1. What are the advantages of *not* integrating models of therapy?
2. List several pairs of family therapy models that might effectively be combined and say how. List models that probably should not be combined and say why.
3. In one column list several attributes of your preferred view of yourself. In a second column

list a few important people in your life and how you think they view you in terms of these attributes. In a third column make guesses as to why these people see you in ways that you do or do not prefer to be seen.

4. Make a list of problems for which it's probably a good idea to develop specific treatment approaches (rather than simply applying one of the generic approaches).

Key Concepts

eclecticism   A form of integration in which a large number of elements from different approaches are combined.

mystery questions   Questions designed to help clients begin to wonder how their problems got the best of them, which in turn helps to externalize the problems.

preferred view   Eron and Lund's term for the way people would like to think of themselves and be seen by others.

selective borrowing   A form of integration in which one follows a consistent model but makes occasional use of techniques from other approaches.

Recommended Readings

Anderson, C., and Stewart, S. 1983. *Mastering resistance: A practical guide to family therapy.* New York: Guilford Press.

Eron, J., and Lund, T. 1996. *Narrative solutions in brief therapy.* New York: Guilford Press.

Goldner, V. 1998. The treatment of violence and victimization in intimate relationships. *Family Process. 37:* 263–286.

Gurman, A. S. 2002. Brief integrative marital therapy: A depth-behavioral approach. In *Clinical handbook of couples therapy,* 3rd ed. A. S. Gurman and N. S. Jacobson, eds. New York: Guilford Press.

Jacobson, N. S., and Christensen, A. 1996. *Integrative couple therapy.* New York: Norton.

Taibbi, R. 1996. *Doing family therapy.* New York: Guilford Press.

References

Alexander, J., and Parsons, B. 1982. *Functional family therapy.* Pacific Grove, CA: Brooks/Cole.

Anderson, C., and Stewart, S. 1983. *Mastering resistance: A practical guide to family therapy.* New York: Guilford Press.

Breunlin, D., Schwartz, R., and Mac Kune-Karrer, B. 1992. *Metaframeworks: Transcending the models of family therapy.* San Francisco: Jossey-Bass.

Duhl, B. S., and Duhl, F. J. 1981. Integrative family therapy. In *Handbook of family therapy,* A. S. Gurman and O. P. Kniskern, eds. New York: Brunner/Mazel.

Eron, J., and Lund, T. 1993. An approach to how problems evolve and dissolve: Integrating narrative and strategic concepts. *Family Process. 32:* 291–309.

Eron, J., and Lund, T. 1996. *Narrative solutions in brief therapy.* New York: Guilford Press.

Feldman, L. 1990. *Multi-dimensional family therapy.* New York: Guilford Press.

Goldner, V. 1998. The treatment of violence and victimization in intimate relationships. *Family Process. 37:* 263–286.

Goldner, V., Penn, P., Sheinberg, M., and Walker, G. 1990. Love and violence: Gender paradoxes in volatile attachments. *Family Process. 29:* 343–364.

Greenberg, L. S., and Johnson, S. M. 1988. *Emotionally focused therapy for couples.* New York: Guilford Press.

Gurman, A. S. 2002. Brief integrative marital therapy: A depth-behavioral approach. In *Clinical handbook of couples therapy,* 3rd ed. A. S. Gurman and N. S. Jacobson, eds. New York: Guilford Press.

Henggeler, S., and Borduin, C. 1990. *Family therapy and beyond: A multisystemic approach to treating the behavior problems of children and adolescents.* Pacific Grove, CA: Brooks/Cole.

Henggeler, S. W., Melton, G. B., Brondino, M. J., Scherer, D. G., & Hanley, J. H. (1997). Multisystemic therapy with violent and chronic juvenile offenders and their families. *Journal of Consulting and Clinical Psychology. 65:* 821–833.

Henggeler, S. W., Pickrel, S. G., & Brondino, M. J. (1999). Multisystemic treatment of substance abusing and dependent delinquents. *Mental Health Services Research. 1:* 171–184.

Jacobson, N., and Christensen, A. 1996. *Integrative couple therapy.* New York: Norton.

Kirschner, D., and Kirschner, S. 1986. *Comprehensive family therapy.* New York: Brunner/Mazel.

Liddle, H. A. 1984. Toward a dialectical-contextual-coevolutionary translation of structural-strategic family therapy. *Journal of Strategic and Systemic Therapies. 3:* 66–79.

Liddle, H. A., Dakoff, G. A., and Diamond, G. 1991. Adolescent substance abuse: Multidimensional family therapy in action. In *Family therapy with drug and alcohol abuse,* 2nd ed. E. Kaufman and P. Kaufman, eds. Boston: Allyn & Bacon.

Markowitz, L. 1997. Ramon Rojano won't take no for an answer. *Family Therapy Networker. 21:* 24–35.

Minuchin, S., Rosman, B., and Baker, L. 1978. *Psychosomatic families: Anorexia in context.* Cambridge, MA: Harvard University Press.

Nichols, M. P. 1987. *The self in the system.* New York: Brunner/Mazel.

Nichols, W. C. 1996. *Treating people in families: An integrative framework.* New York: Guilford Press.

Pinsof, W. 1995. *Integrative problem-centered therapy.* New York: Basic Books.

Sander, F. M. 1979. *Individual and family therapy: Toward an integration.* New York: Jason Aronson.

Scharff, J., ed. 1989. *The foundations of object relations family therapy.* New York: Jason Aronson.

Slipp, S. 1988. *Technique and practice of object relations family therapy.* New York: Jason Aronson.

Stanton, M. D. 1981. An integrated structural/strategic approach to marital and family therapy. *Journal of Marital and Family Therapy. 7:* 427–440.

Taibbi, R. 1996. *Doing family therapy.* New York: Guilford Press.

Walker, G., and Goldner, V. 1995. The wounded prince and the women who love him. In *Gender and power in relationships,* C. Burcke and B. Speed, eds. London: Routledge, Chapman and Hall.

15

Comparative Analysis

$\mathcal{T}$he exponential growth of family therapy crowded the field with competing models and produced a rich and varied literature, bearing witness to the vitality of the profession, while at the same time creating a confusing array of concepts and techniques. See Table 15.1 for a summary of these models. In this chapter we offer a comparative analysis of the various approaches.

$\mathcal{T}$HEORETICAL FORMULATIONS

Theories bring order out of chaos. They organize our observations and help us make sense of what families are doing. Instead of seeing a "blooming, buzzing confusion," we begin to see patterns of pursuit and distance, enmeshment and disengagement, and problem-saturated stories. Once you begin to see ineffectual attempts to settle arguments between children as enmeshment, your goal shifts from intervening more effectively to backing off and letting the children settle their own disputes. Here we evaluate theories in terms of their pragmatic function: understanding families in order to better help them.

Families as Systems

Communications therapists introduced the idea that families are systems. More than the sum of their parts, **systems** are the parts *plus* the way they function together.

Once not accepting systems theory was like not believing in apple pie and motherhood. Now the postmodern movement has challenged systems thinking as just another modernist framework, a metaphor taken too literally, and has shifted emphasis from action to meaning and from the organization of the family to the thinking of its members.

It's easy to say that a good therapist takes into account both the self *and* the system. In practice, however, deciding when to delve into individual experience or focus on interactional patterns presents a host of hard choices.

Stability and Change

Communications theorists described families as rule-governed systems with a tendency toward stability or homeostasis (Jackson, 1965). But in order to adjust to changing circumstances, families must also be capable of revising their rules and modifying their structure.

Table 15.1   **Models of Family Therapy**

	Bowenian	Strategic	Structural
Founder(s)	Murray Bowen	Don Jackson Jay Haley	Salvador Minuchin
Key Theoretical Constructs	Differentiation of self	Homeostasis Feedback loops	Subsystems Boundaries
Core Problem Dynamic	Triangles Emotional reactivity	More-of-the-same solutions	Enmeshment/ Disengagement
Key Techniques	Genogram Process questions	Reframing Directives	Enactments Boundary making

	Experiential	Psychodynamic	Cognitive-Behavioral
Founder(s)	Virginia Satir Carl Whitaker	Nathan Ackerman Henry Dicks Ivan Boszormenyi-Nagy	Gerald Patterson Robert Liberman Richard Stuart
Key Theoretical Constructs	Authenticity Self-actualization	Drives Selfobjects Internal objects	Reinforcement Extinction Schemas
Core Problem Dynamic	Emotional suppression Mystification	Conflict Projective identification Fixation and regression	Inadvertent reinforcement Aversive control
Key Techniques	Confrontation Structured exercises	Silence Interpretation	Functional analysis Teaching positive control

	Solution-Focused	Narrative
Founder(s)	Steve de Shazer Insoo Kim Berg	Michael White David Epston
Key Theoretical Constructs	Language creates reality	Narrative theory Social constructionism
Core Problem Dynamic	Problem talk	Problem-saturated stories
Key Techniques	Focusing on solutions Identifying exceptions	Externalization Identifying unique outcomes Creating audiences of support

The dual nature of families—*homeostatic* and *changing*—is best appreciated by the communications, structural, and strategic schools. They don't presume that symptomatic families are inherently dysfunctional but rather that they have failed to adapt to changing circumstances.

Anyone who ignores this developmental principle runs the risk of placing undue emphasis on pathology.

A therapist who sees a family having trouble but fails to consider that they may be stuck at a transitional impasse is apt to think they need an overhaul when a tuneup might do. Therapies that emphasize long-range goals are all susceptible to this therapeutic overkill. Psychoanalytic, experiential, and extended family practitioners are inclined to assume that families need fundamental reorganization. Because they have the equipment for major surgery—long-term therapy—they tend to see their clients as needing it.

The pioneers of family therapy (with the notable exception of Virginia Satir) overestimated homeostatic forces in families and underestimated their flexibility and resourcefulness. This perspective encouraged therapists to act as provokers, controllers, and strategizers. The corollary of the family trapped by systemic forces they can't understand was the clever therapist who would do the understanding for them.

Many of the newer approaches are designed to elicit families' resources rather than battle with their resistance. These models encourage therapists to collaborate with families to work out solutions rather than assume that they won't change unless provoked. But when some of these "collaborative" approaches—like solution-focused therapy, for example—presume that change is easy, that seems as much naive as optimistic.

Process/Content

Most schools of family therapy emphasize the **process** of family interaction. Psychoanalysts and experientialists try to reduce defensiveness and foster open expression of thoughts and feelings; communications therapists increase the flow of interactions and help family members reduce the incongruence between levels of communication; Bowenians block triangulation and encourage I-statements; strategic therapists counter problem-maintaining interactions; behaviorists teach parents to use positive control and couples to eliminate coercive communication; structural therapists realign boundaries and strengthen parental authority.

Despite their commitment to process, however, therapists often get caught up in **content** issues. Psychoanalysts lose sight of interactional processes when they concentrate on individual family members and their memories of the past. Experientialists often become overly central while working with individual family members to help them overcome emotional defensiveness. The danger is that by so doing, the therapist will neglect personal processes that affect individual expression.

Behavior therapists neglect process in favor of content when they isolate behavior and ignore the relationship patterns surrounding it. They often interfere with the process of family interaction by assuming a directive, teaching role. (As long as a teacher stands in front of the class lecturing, there's little opportunity to find out what the students can do on their own.)

Process concepts are so central to Bowen systems therapy that there's little danger of forgetting them. Only naive misunderstanding of Bowen's theory would lead someone to think merely of reestablishing family ties without also being aware of processes of triangulation, fusion, and differentiation. The same is true of structural family therapy and communications therapy; process issues are always at center stage.

The newer models, with their deemphasis on systems thinking, have moved away from process. Narrative constructivists are less interested in interactional patterns than in the ways family members understand their problems. They're less interested in changing behavior than in expanding stories. Similarly, because solution-focused therapists have no interest in how problems got started, they ignore the family processes that surround them. The only processes they do attend to are interactions that constitute "exceptions"—times when the problem wasn't a problem.

Monadic, Dyadic, or Triadic Model

Some therapists (e.g., psychoeducational) continue to think of the individual as the patient and include the rest of the family as an adjunct to that person's treatment. Keep in mind that psychoeducational therapists work primarily with serious mental illness (schizophrenia, bipolar disorder) where the family's influence is almost certainly less than in the majority of cases treated by family therapists.

The same cannot be said for narrative therapists, whose focus on cognition leads them to concentrate on individuals and largely ignore the defining characteristics of family therapy: (1) understanding that psychological symptoms are often the result of family conflict; (2) thinking about human problems as interactional, which means thinking in twos and threes (complementarity, triangles); and (3) treating the family as a unit. Although narrative therapists disregard family conflict in their formulations, their efforts to redefine problems as alien invaders have the effect of uniting families to overcome the problem's influence. It would be interesting to speculate on whether ignoring family conflict but rallying family members to unite in concern would be more effective in cases like anorexia, where problems take on a life of their own, than in others, like school refusal or misbehavior, where the problem is more likely to be a result of family conflicts.

Psychoanalysts tend to think about personality dynamics, whether they meet with individuals or families. They see family life as a product of internalized relationships from the past, and they're often more concerned with these mental ghosts than with the flesh-and-blood family of the present. Behavior therapists use a **monadic model** when they accept a family's definition of a symptomatic child as the problem and set about teaching parents to modify the child's behavior. Experiential therapists focus on individuals to help them uncover and express their feelings.

Actually, no living thing can adequately be understood with a monadic model. A bird's egg may be the closest thing in nature to a self-contained unit. The fetus is locked away inside its shell with all the nutrients it needs to survive. Even this view is incomplete, however, for there is an exchange of heat between the egg and the surrounding environment. Without its mother's warmth, a baby bird will die.

Dyadic concepts are necessary to explain the fact that people act in relation to one another. Even the psychoanalytic patient, free-associating on the couch, filters memories and dreams through reactions to the analyst. Most of the time family therapists operate with dyadic concepts. Even with a large family in treatment,

the focus is usually on various pairs or units of the family.

Helping two people learn to relate better doesn't always mean that the therapist thinks in dyadic terms. Behavior therapists work with couples but treat them as individuals, each deficient in the art of communicating. A true **dyadic model** is based on the recognition that two people in a relationship aren't independent entities interacting with each other; each defines the other. Using this model, a wife's agoraphobia would be understood as a reaction to her husband and as a means of influencing him. Likewise, his decision to send her for behavior modification reflects his reluctance to accept his role in her life.

Family therapists of all schools use dyadic concepts: unconscious need complementarity, expressive/instrumental, projective identification, symbiosis, intimacy, quid pro quo, double bind, symmetrical/complementary, pursuer–distancer, and behavioral contract. Some terms are based on dyadic thinking even though they may involve more than two people: compliant (referring to a family's relationship to a therapist) or defiant. Some seem to involve only one: countertransference, dominant, and supercompetent. Still other concepts are capable of encompassing units of three or more but are often used to refer to units of two: boundary, coalition, fusion, and disengagement.

Too often family therapists neglect triadic complications. Murray Bowen did more than anyone to point out that human behavior is always a function of triangles. Structural therapists have consistently emphasized that enmeshment or disengagement between two people is a function of reciprocal relationships with third parties. Communications therapists wrote about triadic relationships but tended to think in units of two. The same is true of most strategic therapists, although Haley, Selvini Palazzoli, and Lynn Hoffman are consistently aware of triangles.

The advantage of the **triadic model** is that it permits a more complete understanding of behavior in context. If a child misbehaves when his mother doesn't use firm discipline, teaching her to be stricter won't work if her behavior reflects her relationship with her husband. Perhaps she allows her child to misbehave as a way of undermining her husband's authority, or she and her husband may have worked out a relationship in which her ineffectiveness reassures him that he's the strong one.

The fact that triadic thinking permits a more complete understanding doesn't mean that family therapists must always include all parties in treatment. The issue isn't how many people are in the consulting room but whether the therapist considers problems in their full context.

The Nuclear Family in Context

Just as most family therapists endorse the idea of systems theory, most also describe families as **open systems**. The family is open in that its members interact not only with each other but also with extrafamilial systems. Indeed, a major emphasis in contemporary family therapy has been to expand the focus of attention to include how families are affected by race, gender, ethnicity, class, and sexual orientation. For today's therapist, talking about the social context of families is no longer an idle abstraction.

It is impossible to understand relationships without taking into account the social and cultural forces impinging on the partners.

Members of the Palo Alto group introduced the concept of open systems but treated families as self-contained units. They paid little attention to stressors outside the family and rarely considered the impact of the community or extended family. The first to take the extrafamilial into account were Murray Bowen and Ross Speck. Bowen stressed the role of extended family relationships, and Speck mobilized networks of friends and neighbors to aid in treatment.

Bowen systems therapists and network therapists almost always include people outside the nuclear family in treatment; psychoanalytic, solution-focused, behavioral, and narrative therapists rarely do. Among experientialists, Whitaker routinely invited members of the extended family for one or two sessions.

Including extended family members or friends in treatment is often useful, sometimes essential. It is not, however, the same as thinking of the family as an open system. An open system isn't a larger system; it's a system that interacts with its environment.

Nowhere is the idea of families as open systems better articulated than in Minuchin's (1974) *Families and Family Therapy*. Writing about "Man in His Context," Minuchin contrasts family therapy with psychodynamic theory. The latter, he says, draws on the concept of man as a hero, remaining himself despite the circumstances.[1] On the other hand, "The theory of family therapy is predicated on the fact that man is not an isolate. He is an acting and reacting member of social groups" (p. 2). Minuchin credits Gregory Bateson with erasing the boundary between inner and outer space and goes on to say that just as the boundary separating the individual from the family is artificial, so is the boundary separating the family from the social environment.

One of the things that anyone who works with agency families quickly learns is that attempts to help them often get caught in a sticky web of competing influences from courts, probation departments, child

---

[1]Although we recognize that it was until recently the rule, use of the masculine pronoun here may be particularly apt. The model of the hero is of a man who keeps his moral integrity hard and intact. He is an isolate, stoic and enduring, cut off from family, community, and faith—that is, the trivial, suffocating world of women.

protective agencies, family services, housing programs, group homes, domestic violence agencies, and so on. Middle-class families can be treated as organizationally closed units but that's impossible with poor families. Poor families live in homes without walls.

As services proliferate, fiefdoms multiply. The most obvious problem is lack of coordination.

Take, for example, a recent case involving a fifteen-year-old boy who had sexually abused his two adolescent sisters and a younger brother. There were agencies working with the female victims, one with the older girl and another with the younger one. One agency worked with the younger boy, one worked with the perpetrator, and one worked with the mother of the victims. There was an art therapist in the public school working with the sexually abused children, and the fifteen-year-old was in a residential school where he had individual and group therapy. Is it any wonder that these helpers were pulling in different directions?

A second, more invidious, problem is that most agencies are mandated to serve individuals—victims or victimizers, adults or children. By addressing themselves to the rights of persons in need of protection or correction, these agencies support individuals, not the family unit.

The usual reaction of therapists who run into these networks of unorganized altruism is to make an effort to coordinate the various inputs. Then when they discover their lack of leverage with all of these agencies and helpers, they give up and do the best they can with the family in the office. Among those who aren't willing to give up, Evan Imber-Black (1988) and Richard Kagan and Shirley Schlosberg (1989) have written practical books about working with families in perpetual crisis. Patricia Minuchin, Jorge Colapinto, and Salvador Minuchin (2007) published an inspiring account of their efforts to bring a

family focus to agency social work with families of the poor.

Under the influence of social constructionism, the newer models of family therapy have become acutely aware of the social context of the families they treat. This awareness is, however, less likely to take the form of including people outside the family in treatment than of being sensitive to social and political influences on the modern family.

Boundaries

The most useful concepts of interpersonal boundaries are found in the works of Murray Bowen and Salvador Minuchin. Bowen is best at describing the boundary between the self and the family; Minuchin is best at identifying boundaries among various subsystems. In Bowen's terms, individuals vary on a continuum from **fusion** to **differentiation**, whereas Minuchin describes boundaries as ranging from diffuse to rigid, with resultant **enmeshment** or **disengagement**.

Bowen's thinking reflects the psychoanalytic emphasis on *separation* and *individuation* (Mahler, Pine, & Bergman, 1975), with special attention to the resolution of oedipal attachments and leaving home. In this model, we become ourselves by learning to stand alone. Bowen paid less attention to the emotional isolation stemming from rigid boundaries, treating this as an artifact—a defense against a lack of psychological separateness. Bowen used a variety of terms—*togetherness, fusion, undifferentiation, emotional reactivity*—all referring to the danger of people losing themselves in relationships.

Minuchin offers a more balanced view, describing problems that result when **boundaries** are either too weak or too strong. *Diffuse boundaries* allow too much interference into the functioning of a subsystem; *rigid boundaries* allow too little support. Bowen described only one boundary problem—fusion—and only one goal—differentiation. Fusion is like a disease—you can have a bad case or a mild one. Minuchin speaks of two possibilities—enmeshment or disengagement— and his therapy is designed to fit the specific case.

Bowen's fusion and Minuchin's enmeshment both deal with blurred boundaries, but they aren't synonymous. *Fusion* is a psychological quality of individuals, the opposite of individuation. The dynamics of fusion have an impact on relationships (especially in the form of reactivity and triangulation), but fusion is *within* the person. Enmeshment is *between* people.

These conceptual differences also lead to differences in treatment. Bowenian therapists encourage relationships but emphasize autonomy. Success is measured by differentiation of self. Structuralists encourage authenticity but strive to restructure family relationships by strengthening or weakening boundaries. Success is measured by the harmonious functioning of the whole family.

*N*ORMAL FAMILY DEVELOPMENT

As a rule, family therapists have had little to say about developmental issues. One of the distinguishing characteristics of family therapy is its focus on here-and-now interactions. Normal family development, which involves the past and what's healthy, has therefore been underemphasized.

Most therapists, however, have assumptions about what's normal, and these ideas influence their work. The problem is that as long as these implicit models remain unarticulated, they may reflect personal bias as much as anything else. When it comes to setting goals for family treatment, the choice isn't between having or not having a model of what's healthy but between using a model that's been spelled out and examined or operating on the basis of ill-defined, personal standards.

Family therapists concerned with the past, especially members of Bowenian and psychoanalytic schools, have had the most to say about normal development. Although most schools of family therapy aren't concerned with how families get started, Bowenians and psychoanalysts have a great deal to say about marital choice. Bowen talked about *differentiation, fusion,* and *triangles,* while psychoanalytic writers speak of *unconscious need complementarity,*

projective identification, and *idealization;* however, they seem to be using different terms to describe similar phenomena. Psychoanalysts speak of marital choice as an object of *transference* from the family of origin and of people choosing partners to match their own level of maturity; Bowen said that people pick partners who replicate familiar patterns of family interaction and select mates at similar levels of differentiation.

These are descriptions of ways in which people marry their own alter egos. Both schools also discuss how people choose mates who appear to be different, at least on the surface, in ways that are exciting and seem to make up for deficiencies in themselves. Obsessive individuals tend to marry hysterical individuals, and according to Bowen, togetherness-oriented people often marry distancers.

This brings up another way in which the Bowenian and psychodynamic schools are similar to each other and different from others. Both recognize that personalities have layers. Both think that the success of a relationship depends not only on shared interests and values but also on the nature of the partners' internal object images.

Even if they don't emphasize the past, most of the other schools of family therapy have concepts for describing normal family development. For example, communications therapists speak of the *quid pro quo*s (Jackson, 1965) exchanged in normal marriages, while behaviorists describe the same phenomenon in terms of **social exchange theory** (Thibaut & Kelley, 1959).

Virginia Satir described normal families as those in which communication is direct and honest, where differences are faced rather than hidden, and where emotions are openly expressed. Under these conditions, she believed, people develop healthy *self-esteem* that enables them to take the risks necessary for authentic relationships.

According to Minuchin (1974), clinicians should have some appreciation of the facts of ordinary family life to become effective therapists. Therapists need to distinguish functional from dysfunctional structures, as well as pathological structures from structures that are simply transitional.

Because structural therapy begins by assessing the adequacy of a family's organization, it sometimes appears to impose a standard. In fact, however, normality is defined in terms of functionality, and structural therapists recognize that diverse patterns may be equally functional. The clarity of subsystem boundaries is more important than the composition of the subsystem. For example, a parental subsystem made up of a single parent and oldest child can function effectively if the lines of authority are clearly drawn. Patterns of enmeshment and disengagement are viewed as preferred styles, not necessarily as indications of abnormality.

Most therapists don't think in terms of remaking families and therefore believe they have little need for models of what a family should be like. Instead, they intervene around specific problems— problem-maintaining interactions, problem-saturated stories, forgotten solutions—conceptualized in terms of function, not structure. The patterns they observe are dysfunctional; therefore, by implication, what's functional must be just the opposite.

While it may not be necessary to understand a family's past in order to help them, it is useful to have a way of understanding the family's organization in the present, using a model of normal behavior to set goals for treatment. Such a model should include a design for the present and for change over time. Among the ideas presented in this book, the most useful for a basic model of normal family functioning include *structural hierarchy, effective communication,* and *family life-cycle development.*

*D*EVELOPMENT OF BEHAVIOR DISORDERS

In the early days of family therapy, patients were seen as victims—"scapegoats"—whose symptoms maintained family stability. Much of the literature was about dysfunctional ways of keeping the peace: for example *scapegoating, pseudomutuality, family projection process, double bind, mystification.* These malignant mechanisms may have driven young people crazy, but they helped keep families together.

It was a simple and satisfying tale of malevolence. No one exactly blamed the parents—their coercions weren't really deliberate—but these explanations rested on parental faults and failings and as such had mythic force. The idea that schizophrenia was a sacrifice children made for their families was absolutely riveting—and absolutely untrue.

Today family therapists think less about what causes problems than about how families unwittingly perpetuate them.

Inflexible Systems

Early observers of schizophrenic families emphasized their inflexibility. Wynne coined the term *rubber fence* to dramatize how psychotic families resist outside influence and *pseudomutuality* to describe their façade of harmony. R. D. Laing showed how parents, unable to tolerate their children's individuality, used **mystification** to deny their experience. Communication theorists said that schizophrenic families lacked mechanisms for changing their rules. They were programmed for negative feedback, treating novelty and change as deviations to be resisted.

This tradition of viewing families of mentally ill patients as rigidly homeostatic was taken into the 1980s by Selvini Palazzoli in the form of her concept of "dirty games." Carol Anderson and Michael White countered this negative perspective by suggesting that rigidity might be the result of living with serious problems—and being blamed for them by mental health professionals.

Explaining family problems in terms of homeostatic inflexibility was a cornerstone of the strategic school. Dysfunctional families respond to problems with a limited range of solutions. Even when the solutions don't work, these families stubbornly keep trying. Behaviorists use a similar idea when they explain symptoms as resulting from faulty efforts to control behavior. Often when parents think they're punishing misbehavior, they're actually reinforcing it with attention.

According to psychoanalytic and experiential theories, intrapsychic rigidities, in the forms of *conflict, developmental arrest,* and *emotional suppression,* are the individual's contribution to family inflexibility. Psychoanalysts see unhealthy families as **closed systems** that resist change. When stressed, inflexible families regress to earlier levels of development where unresolved conflicts left them fixated.

Experientialists describe dysfunctional families as emotionally stagnant. If it's true that you sometimes have to try something different just to know you're alive, families afraid of rocking the boat become timid and lifeless. The symptom bearer is a victim of the family's opposition to the life force.

Structural therapists locate the inflexibility of families in the boundaries between subsystems. But structural problems aren't necessarily the result of some flaw in the family. Normal families may develop problems if they are unable to modify a previously functional structure to cope with a crisis. Family therapists should be clear on this point: Symptomatic families are often basically sound; they may simply need help adjusting to changed circumstances.

Solution-focused and narrative therapists avoid implicating family members in the development of their problems. Both camps prefer to focus on the strengths of individuals in the family and on times when they used their resources to triumph over their troubles. What these models identify as problematic are rigid habits of thought that lead people to consider themselves defeated. Solution-focused therapists leave it at that; they don't speculate about the origins of defeatist thinking. Narrative therapists point to what they consider toxic beliefs in the culture that are internalized by family members. It's society, not the family, that's inflexible.

Pathologic Triangles

Pathologic triangles are at the heart of several family therapy explanations of behavior disorder. Among these, Bowen's theory is the most elegant. Bowen explained how when two people are in conflict, the one who experiences more anxiety will triangle in a third person. This model not only provides an explanation of systems pathology but also serves as a warning: As long as a therapist remains tied to one party in an emotional conflict, he or she is part of the problem.

In psychoanalytic theory, oedipal conflicts are seen as the root of neurosis. Here the triangle is triggered by family interactions but lodged in the individual psyche. Mother's tenderness may be seductive and Father's jealousy threatening, but the wish to do away with the father and possess the mother is a product of fantasy. Pathological fixation of this conflict may be caused by developments in the outer space of the family, but the conflict is harbored in the inner space of the child's mind.

Structural family theory is based on triangular configurations in which a dysfunctional boundary between two subsystems is the reciprocal of a boundary with a third. Father and Son's enmeshment reflects Father and Mother's disengagement. A single mother's disengagement from her children is the counterpart of her overinvolvement outside the family. Structural theory also uses the concept of pathologic triangles to explain *conflict-detouring triads* in which parents divert their conflicts onto a child. Minuchin, Rosman, and Baker (1978) have even demonstrated that physiological changes occur when parents in conflict transmit their stress to a psychosomatic child.

Strategic therapists typically work with a dyadic model in which one person's symptoms are maintained by others' efforts to resolve them. Haley and Selvini Palazzoli, however, used a triangular model in the form of **cross-generational coalitions**. These "perverse triangles," as Haley (1977) called them, occur when a parent and child collude to form a bastion of covert opposition to the other parent.

Triangular functioning is less central to the newer models because they're not concerned with *how* families develop problems. It might even be argued that ignoring family dynamics is one of the strengths of narrative and solution-focused approaches, if doing so helps these therapists zero in on the constricting habits of thought they're interested in. It might also be said, however, that ignoring family dynamics is one of the weaknesses of these approaches, especially in cases in which conflict in a family isn't just going to disappear because family members work together to solve a common problem.

• • •

When things go wrong, it's tempting to look for someone to blame. Your partner never talks about his feelings? He must be from Mars. Families drop out after the first couple of sessions? They must be resistant.

Before we get too judgmental, let's recognize that it's perfectly natural to attribute our problems to other people's influence. Because we look at life from inside our own skins, we're most aware of other people's contributions to our problems. But therapists, we'd hope, aren't handicapped by this egocentric bias. No, they're handicapped by another bias.

Whenever you hear one side of an unhappy story, it's natural to sympathize with the person doing the telling. If a friend tells you her boss is a jerk, your sympathy puts you automatically on her side. Experience suggests that most stories have two sides. But when your impulse is to show solidarity with someone who's telling you his or her troubles, the temptation is to look abroad for villains. Among professional helpers, this temptation is too often not resisted.

One reason for blaming family problems on easily vilified influences—men, racism, mothers—is that it's hard to see past individual personalities to the patterns of interaction that make them a family, unless you see the whole group and see them in action. That's why family therapy was invented in the first place.

$\mathcal{T}$HERAPY

Assessment

Each school of family therapy has a theory about families that determines where they look for problems and what they see. Some consider the whole family (Milan, structural, Bowenian); some concentrate on individuals (psychoanalytic, experiential); some focus on sequences that maintain symptoms (strategic, behavioral); and some pay very little attention to what causes problems, preferring instead to mobilize people to work against them (solution-focused, narrative).

Behaviorists place the greatest emphasis on assessment and use the most formal procedures. Assessment is the first order of business. The advantage of the behavioral emphasis on assessment is that it provides baseline data, definite goals, and a reliable way to determine whether therapy succeeds. The disadvantage is that by using standardized interviews and questionnaires, you don't see families in action. By looking at only part of the family (mother and child or marital couple), you miss the total context; by relying on questionnaires, you learn only what a family reports.

Structural therapists also emphasize assessment, but their evaluations are based on observation. Enactments give the therapist a chance to observe enmeshment and disengagement. The strengths of this school's assessment procedure are that it uses the family's patterns of interaction among themselves, it includes the entire family, and it's organized in terms that point directly to desired changes.

The Bowenian school also does an excellent job of considering the whole family. Unlike structuralists, however, Bowenians rely on what they're told, and they're interested in the past as well as the present.

The breadth of psychoanalytic theory enables practitioners to speculate well ahead of their data; a little information suggests a great deal. The advantage is that the theory provides inroads to hidden meanings. The danger is that the theory may distort the data, leading clinicians to see only what they expect to see. Experientialists have neither these advantages nor disadvantages. Their evaluations are guided by a simple notion about feelings and how they are suppressed; they may not uncover much that's hidden, but they also tend not to see things that aren't there.

Two of the newer schools, narrative and solution-focused, eschew any form of assessment. Solution-focused therapists believe that dwelling on problems undermines the positive thinking they hope to generate. They also believe that solutions aren't necessarily related to the ways problems come about. Narrative therapists believe that looking within families for problems perpetuates the therapist-as-expert stance they want to avoid. By personifying problems and talking about their effects rather than their causes, they circumvent the fingerpointing that often accompanies discussions of how problems got started.

The danger is that by disregarding how problems arise, they may overlook real conflicts. And conflict, as you may have noticed, doesn't necessarily go away simply because you ignore it.

Decisive Interventions

Family therapists use a wide variety of techniques—some dictated by their model, others by the therapist's personality and experience. Even if we limited our attention to the techniques specific to each of the schools, the list would be long and confusing. Some techniques are used by virtually everyone—asking questions, reflecting feelings, clarifying communication—and this list has been growing as the field has become more integrated. Each school, however, relies on one or two techniques that are unique and decisive.

In psychoanalytic therapy there are two definitive techniques. The first of these, *interpretation,* is well known but not well understood. Properly used, interpretation refers to elucidating unconscious meaning. It does not mean statements of opinion—"You need to express your feelings before you can really be close"; advice—"As long as you continue writing to him, the affair isn't over"; theory—"Some of the reasons you were attracted to him were based on unconscious needs"; or confrontation—"You said you didn't care, but you were really angry." Interpretations are statements about unconscious meaning: "You've been complaining about your son's arguing with you all the time. Based on what you've said previously, I think that some of your anger is deflected from your husband. He does the same thing, but you're afraid to tell him so, and that's why you get so mad at your son."

By refraining from asking questions and giving advice, psychoanalytic practitioners maintain a stance of listening and fostering understanding. By limiting interventions to interpretations, the therapist makes it clear that treatment is designed for learning; whether families take advantage of this atmosphere and change their behavior as a result of what they learn is up to them.

The second decisive technique in analytic treatment is *silence.* A therapist's silence permits him or her to discover what's on a patient's mind and to test a family's resources; it also lends force to eventual interpretations. When a therapist is silent, family members talk, following their own thoughts rather than responding to the therapist's. When they learn that the therapist won't interrupt, they respond to each other. This produces a wealth of information that might not otherwise emerge. If a father begins by saying "The problem is my depression," and the therapist immediately asks "How long have you been depressed?" he or she may not discover what thoughts are associated in the man's mind with his depression or how the man's wife responds to his complaint.

The decisive technique in experiential therapy is *confrontation.* Confrontations are designed to provoke emotional reactions and are often blunt. It isn't unusual for experiential therapists to tell clients to shut up or to mock them for being insincere. Confrontations are often combined with *personal disclosure,* the second signature technique of this school. Experientialists use themselves as emotionally expressive models. Finally, most experiential therapists also use *structured exercises.* These include role-playing, psychodrama, sculpting, and family drawings. The rationale for these techniques is that they stimulate emotional experiencing; their drawback is that they're artificial. Family members may get something off their chests in a structured exercise but may not transfer this to their interactions at home.

Most people associate reinforcement with behavior therapy, but reinforcement isn't a technique used in cognitive-behavioral family therapy; *observation* and *teaching* are the vehicles of this approach. Behavioralists begin by observing contingencies of reinforcement. Their aim is to discover the antecedents and consequences of problem behavior. Once they've completed a *functional analysis of behavior,* they become instructors, teaching families how they inadvertently reinforce undesirable behavior. As teachers, their most useful lesson is the use of *positive control.* They tell parents that it's more effective to reward good behavior than to punish bad behavior; they teach married couples to substitute being nice to each other for their usual bickering.

Positive control—that is, rewarding desirable behavior—is one of the most useful principles in psychotherapy. It's a valuable lesson for families and for therapists. Therapists, like parents, tend to chide their charges for mistakes; unfortunately, if you're told that you're suppressing your feelings, spoiling your children, or using coercive control, you're apt to feel picked on and put down. Although it may be necessary to point out people's mistakes, it's more effective to concentrate on praising the positive aspects of their behavior. Among practicing family therapists, this point seems best understood by structuralists, who speak of working with the family's strengths; by strategists and Milan therapists, who use reframing and positive connotation to support efforts to do the right thing; and of course by solution-focused and narrative therapists, who have raised the power of positive thinking to an art form.

Bowen systems therapists are also teachers, but they follow a different curriculum. They *teach people to be responsible for themselves* and how by doing so they can transform their entire families. Being responsible for yourself means getting clear about what you think and feel—not what your mother says or what you read in *The New York Times* but what you really believe—and then being true to your beliefs in dealings with other people. You don't take responsibility by changing others or wishing they were different; you do so by speaking for yourself and maintaining your own values. The power of this position is tremendous. If a client can accept who he or she is and that other people are different from himself or herself, then he or she no longer has to approach relationships with the idea that someone has to change. This enables the client to be in contact with people without becoming unduly upset or emotionally reactive.

In addition to teaching differentiation, Bowenian therapists promote two corollary lessons: *avoiding triangulation* and *reopening cut-off family relationships*. Taken together, these three lessons enable one person to transform his or her whole family system. Even if her spouse nags, if his children are disobedient, if her mother never comes to visit, the *client* can create a change. Other schools of therapy gain leverage by including the entire family in treatment; Bowenians teach individuals to be themselves, to make contact with others, and to deal directly with the people with whom they have conflicts. This gives clients a tool for change that's portable and lasting.

Communications family clinicians contributed so much to the theoretical base of family therapy that it's difficult to single out their interventions. Perhaps their greatest achievement was pointing out that communication is multilayered and that often the most important things being said are said covertly. Therapy was designed to make the covert overt. Initially this was done by *clarifying communication* and pointing out hidden messages. When this direct approach met with resistance, therapists began using directives to make the rules of family functioning explicit and to provoke changes in the rules.

Strategic therapy is an offshoot of communications theory, and the techniques used by strategists are refinements of those used by communicationists. Principal among these are *reframing, directives,* and *positive connotation.* Strategic practitioners begin by getting concrete descriptions of problems and attempts to solve them. In the process, they pay particular attention to the family's language and expectations. They try to grasp the family's point of view and acknowledge it—in a positive connotation; then they use reframing to shift the family's point of view and directives to interrupt problem-maintaining behavior.

Directives are designed to interrupt homeostatic patterns, they are assigned to be carried out when the family is at home, and they are often paradoxical. Although strategic therapists emphasize fitting the treatment to the patient, they often assume that indirect interventions are necessary to outwit resistance. This is sometimes but not always true. It's not so much that some families are resistant and others aren't. Rather, it's that resistance isn't a property in families; it's a product of the interaction between therapist and family. A therapist who proceeds on the assumption that families are unable and unwilling to follow advice is likely to encounter the expected resistance.

Structural family therapy is also a therapy of action, but in this approach the action occurs in the session.

The decisive techniques are *enactments* and *boundary making*. Rigid boundaries are softened when the therapist gets people to talk with each other and blocks attempts to interrupt them. Diffuse boundaries are strengthened when the therapist works to support the autonomy of individuals and subsystems.

Several promising techniques emerged in the 1980s around which whole models of therapy were built. Steve de Shazer and his colleagues expanded the technique of focusing on successful *solutions* that family members had tried but abandoned. The result was solution-focused therapy. Michael White did the same with the technique of *externalization*—personifying problems and attributing oppressive intentions to them, which is a powerful device for getting family members to unite against a common enemy.

Actually, externalization is a concept, not a technique. The decisive technique of narrative therapy is a persistent and forceful series of *questions*—whereby the therapist begins by trying to understand the clients' experiences of suffering but then switches from understanding to prodding clients to think about their problems as malevolent agents. Narrative therapists use a relentless series of questions to challenge negative images and convince clients that they have reason to be proud of themselves and that their fates are in their own hands.

In reaction to the sectarian techniquism that reached a peak in the early 1980s, family therapists today borrow freely from other approaches and deemphasize technique in favor of a less hierarchical and more respectful quality of therapist–family relationship. Both trends are healthy, but we would like to end this section with two questions: When is cross-fertilization enriching, and when does eclecticism rob approaches of their muscle by watering down their distinctive elements? How best can family therapists get away from a formulaic emphasis on technique without losing leverage altogether by practicing a more congenial but less effective form of treatment?

Summary

1. The theme of the early years in the development of family therapy was the proliferation of competing schools, each advertised as unique and uniquely effective. Today, the theme is integration. So many talented therapists have been working for so long that the field has accumulated a number of useful ways of looking at and treating families. In what follows, we offer some very subjective comments about a few of the concepts and methods that have proved themselves classics of family therapy.

2. Theories of family functioning have both a scientific and a practical purpose. The most useful theories treat families as systems; have concepts to describe forces of stability and change; notice the process underlying the content of family discussions; recognize the triadic nature of human relationships; remember to consider the context of the nuclear family rather than viewing it as a closed system; and appreciate the function of boundaries in protecting the cohesiveness of individuals, subgroups, and families.

3. Although clinicians are more concerned with pathology and change than with normality, it's useful to have some ideas about normal family functioning, both to mold treatment goals and to distinguish what's problematic and needs changing from what's normal and doesn't. Some of the most useful concepts of normal family functioning include the structural model of families as open systems in transformation; the communications model of direct, clear, and honest communication, with rules firm enough to ensure stability and flexible enough to allow change; the behavioral model of equitable exchange of interpersonal costs and benefits, the use of positive control instead of coercion, and mutual reinforcement between partners; the strategic model of systemic flexibility, which allows adjustment to changing circumstances and the ability to find new solutions when old ones don't work; and the Bowenian model, which explains how differentiation of self enables people to be independent at times, intimate at others.

4. Most family therapy concepts of behavior disorder focus on systems and interactions, but the psychoanalytic, Bowenian, narrative, and experiential models add depth to the interactional view, bridging the gap between inner experience and outward behavior. The fact that many divorced people repeat the mistakes of their first marriages supports the idea that some of what goes on in families is a product of individual character. Some of the most valuable concepts of personal dysfunction in families are Bowen's concept of fusion; the experiential concepts of repressed affect and fear of taking risks; and the psychoanalytic concepts of developmental arrest, internal object relations, instinctual conflict, and hunger for appreciation.

5. These concepts of individual dynamics are useful adjuncts, but the major ideas in the field explain behavior disorder in terms of systems theory. The most influential of these are about inflexible systems, too rigid to accommodate individual strivings or to adjust to changing circumstances; symptomatic family members promoting cohesion by stabilizing the nuclear and extended families; inadequate hierarchical structure; families too tightly or too loosely structured; and pathologic triangles.

6. Some of the goals of family therapy are universal—clarifying communication, solving problems, promoting autonomy—and some are unique. Some of the schools take presenting problems at face value; whereas others treat them as metaphors. In either case, goals shouldn't be so broad as to neglect symptom resolution or too narrow to ensure the stability of symptom resolution. Incidentally, values are seldom discussed in the family therapy literature, the notable exception being Boszormenyi-Nagy. Too little consideration has been given to therapists' ethical

responsibilities, including the possibility of conflicting responsibilities to individuals, families, and the larger community.

7. If narrative therapists have tended to ignore family dynamics in order to emphasize the ills of the culture, perhaps this will turn out to be one of those swings of the pendulum that eventually correct themselves. There's surely no need to neglect systems theory to introduce an ethical dimension to working with people in context.

8. Some of the major differences among family therapists about how behavior is changed are focused on the following issues: action or insight; change in the session or change at home; duration of treatment; resistance; family–therapist relationship; paradox; and the extent to which it's important to work with the whole family system, part of it, or just motivated individuals. Even though consensus exists about some issues—for example, most family therapists once believed that action was primary and insight was secondary—there have always been divergent opinions on every one of these points. Strategic therapists, for example, flatly deny that insight is useful.

9. We've looked at some of the major methodological issues and tried to separate the decisive techniques of the different schools. As is always the case when a number of factors are involved in a final result, it's not easy to know how much each variable contributes to that result or how important each one is. Furthermore, the more we talk about techniques, the greater the danger of seeing family therapy as a purely technological enterprise. Studying families is like solving a riddle; the art of treating them is to relieve suffering and anguish. The job of the theoretician is to decode and decipher, which requires theory and ingenuity. The job of the therapist is healing, which requires theory but also conviction, perseverance, and caring. Treating families isn't only a matter of theory and technique; it's also an act of love.

Questions to Consider

1. Can you think of examples of when a problem was understood in monadic or dyadic terms that ignored triangular complications to the detriment of solving the problem?
2. Can you think of unfortunate examples of ignoring the context of a nuclear family?
3. When might it be more useful to use Bowen's concept of *fusion?* When might it be more useful to use Minuchin's concept of *enmeshment?*
4. What therapeutic changes are more likely to happen at home? Which are more likely to happen in the consulting room? Which should a therapist focus on?
5. What are some useful consequences of the concept of *resistance?*
6. How important is it that you choose to practice an approach to therapy that fits your personality? Which approaches seem to fit your personality, and why?
7. In which models are interventions delivered primarily in the form of questions?

Key Concepts

boundaries   Emotional and physical barriers that protect and enhance the integrity of individuals, subsystems, and families.

closed system   A group of elements regarded as forming a collective entity that doesn't interact with the environment.

content   See **process/content**.

cross-generational coalition   An inappropriate alliance between a parent and child that sides against a third member of the family.

differentiation   Psychological separation of intellect and emotions and independence of self from others; opposite of fusion.

disengagement   Psychological isolation that results from overly rigid boundaries.

dyadic model   Explanations based on the interactions between two people: Johnny shoplifts to get his mother's attention.

enmeshment   Loss of autonomy due to a blurring of psychological boundaries.

fusion   A blurring of psychological boundaries between self and others and a contamination of emotional and intellectual functioning; opposite of differentiation.

monadic model   Explanations based on properties of a single person: Johnny shoplifts because he's rebellious.

mystification   R. D. Laing's concept that many families distort their children's experience by denying or relabeling it.

open system   A group of elements that exchange information, energy, and material with the environment.

process/content   The distinction between how members of a family or group relate (process) and what they talk about (content).

social exchange theory   An explanation of behavior in relationships as maintained by a ratio of costs to benefits.

system   An organized group of parts plus the way they function together.

triadic model   An explanation based on the interactions among three people or objects: Johnny shoplifts because his father covertly encourages him to defy his mother.

Recommended Readings

Dattilio, F. M. 1998. *Case studies in couple and family therapy: Systemic and cognitive perspectives.* New York: Guilford Press.

Donovan, J. M., ed. 1999. *Short-term couple therapy.* New York: Guilford Press.

Piercy, F. P., Sprenkle, D. H., and Wetchler, J. L. 1996. *Family therapy sourcebook,* 2nd ed. New York: Guilford Press.

Simon, G. M. 2003. *Beyond technique in family therapy: Finding your therapeutic voice.* Boston: Allyn & Bacon.

Sluzki, C. E. 1983. Process, structure and world views: Toward an integrated view of systemic models in family therapy. *Family Process. 22:* 469–476.

References

Haley, J. 1977. Toward a theory of pathological systems. In *The interactional view,* P. Watzlawick and J. Weakland, eds. New York: Norton.

Imber-Black, E. 1988. *Families and larger system: A family therapist's guide through the labyrinth.* New York: Guilford Press.

Jackson, D. D. 1965. Family rules: The marital quid pro quo. *Archives of General Psychiatry. 12:* 589–594.

Kagan, R., and Schlosberg, S. 1989. *Families in perpetual crisis.* New York: Norton.

Mahler, M. S., Pine, F., and Bergman, A. 1975. *The psychological birth of the human infant.* New York: Basic Books.

Minuchin, P., Colapinto, J., and Minuchin, S. 2007. *Working with families of the poor,* 2nd ed. New York: Guilford Press.

Minuchin, S. 1974. *Families and family therapy.* Cambridge, MA: Harvard University Press.

Minuchin, S., Rosman, B., and Baker, L. 1978. *Psychosomatic families: Anorexia in context.* Cambridge, MA: Harvard University Press.

Thibaut, J. W., and Kelley, H. H. 1959. *The social psychology of groups.* New York: Wiley.

16

Research on Family Intervention

Family Treatment and Prevention Programs

George W. Howe and Colleen M. Varga
George Washington University

*T*HE EVOLUTION OF FAMILY-FOCUSED INTERVENTIONS

As family therapy has matured in the twenty-first century, so too have attempts to study when and how it is effective. In this chapter we describe how scientific methods have been used to test effectiveness. We use the somewhat cumbersome term *family-focused interventions* to encompass the wide range of methods developed to work with families. Some of these interventions involve traditional family therapy, while others work with families to prevent problems in the future; some focus on helping families adapt to new life challenges, and some are designed to enrich family life rather than to treat problems.

Family Therapy for Patients with Diagnosable Psychopathology

Some of the earliest family therapists worked with the families of individuals with severe psychopathology such as schizophrenia, bipolar disorder, major depression, and substance abuse. Because severe psychopathology is typically treated pharmacologically, the emphasis for families has shifted to

psychoeducational programs to provide guidance in managing these conditions. Most of the research on program effectiveness has been conducted on such psychoeducational programs, which integrate education about psychopathology, practical problem solving during rehabilitation, and occasional family sessions to reduce hostile family interactions. Given strong evidence that depression is associated with relationship distress, family interventions for adult depression have developed a focus on the couple's relationship.

Children with Behavior and Conduct Problems

Aggressive, oppositional, and delinquent behaviors are among the primary reasons children are referred for treatment, and early family therapists began to see parents and children together in an effort to change such behavior. More recent programs have integrated family sessions with a broader ecological focus that attends to other aspects of the child's life, including school functioning and peer relationships. Other clinicians developed parent training programs to help parents learn new ways to respond to such behavior, working with parents individually and in groups.

More recently, parent-focused programs have been designed to prevent problem behavior and have been used with parents who have physically abused their children. These include prevention programs designed for high-risk families such as single-parent families, low-income families, families of children with subclinical problem behavior, and families going through major life changes or other stressful challenges.

Troubled Marriages

The development of behavioral marital therapy and more recent emotion-focused techniques have been accompanied by substantial research on their effectiveness. This work has also expanded into the field of prevention, as clinicians have developed programs for premarital couples, building on intervention techniques from therapy and integrating them with education about how marriages develop and change over time.

Families Facing Stressful Transitions

Both clinical experience and a growing body of research have found that exposure to major stressful events increases the likelihood of emotional and behavioral disorders. This is particularly true of transitions involving major disruptions in relationships, such as separation and divorce. Family-oriented clinicians have developed a number of programs to support families during such challenging times. These include family life education programs, first developed over twenty years ago, as well as more recent programs designed to help families weather specific transitions, such as the birth of a child, divorce, or remarriage.

Characterizing Family-Focused Interventions

This brief sample of family interventions illustrates the burgeoning of intervention methods focusing on family relationships. Such programs have become increasingly common for a wide range of goals across a number of service delivery systems, both public and private. We provide a summary of this diversity in Table 16.1.

Such programs can be characterized in terms of their emphasis on prevention, treatment, or care for chronic conditions. Some models work only with individual family members. These include parent training programs and programs for reducing the burden of those who care for disabled or infirm family members. Other programs work with dyads, including couples or parents and children, or larger groups of family members. Lastly, programs can be characterized by the outcomes they are designed to achieve. These include programs to treat or prevent emotional or behavioral problems, treat or prevent relationship distress, and assist families in adapting to major life challenges.

THE EMERGENCE OF SCIENTIFIC METHODS FOR STUDYING PROGRAM EFFECTIVENESS

Over the past few decades, clinical medicine has come to rely on **randomized clinical trials** for testing the effectiveness of medical treatments, and psychiatrists began to apply this method to study the effects of drug therapies for emotional and behavioral disorders. Around the same time that clinical psychologists began to apply methods from experimental psychology to study the effects of behavioral treatments, researchers began to use these methods to study interventions that targeted family relationships. This period also saw the emergence of *program evaluation research,* developed to study the effectiveness of government-sponsored social programs, such as Head Start.

Finally, this period saw the growth of medical insurance, including reimbursement for treatment of psychiatric disorders. As insurance costs grew, insurers began to search for ways to contain costs by identifying the most efficient practices. This stimulated interest in scientific evidence to support the use of specific treatment methods. Terms such as *evidence-based practice* and *empirically supported therapy* reflect this emphasis on the use of scientific methods to test intervention effectiveness.

To adequately test a particular family intervention, researchers need to be certain that all intervention

Table 16.1   Program Focuses and Outcomes

Target of Intervention	Focus of Intervention Program			Specific Intervention Targets Found to Change
	Individual	Dyad	Triad or Greater	
Interventions for Individual Disorders				
Child or adolescent depression			X	Family conflict; Parent-child relationship problems; Suicidality; Functional impairment; Depressive symptoms
Child or adolescent anxiety			X	Decrease in parental psychological control of the adolescent; Depressive symptoms; Anxiety
Child or adolescent conduct disorder		X	X	Decreased externalizing behavior; Decreased school suspensions and arrests; Improved familial communication
Child or adolescent ADHD	X	X	X	Decreased ADHD-related symptoms; Decreased parental ratings of negative child behavior; Decreased observed negative parent-child interactions; Decreased child internalizing symptoms; Decreased school-related problems
Adolescent substance abuse	X	X	X	Decreased drug use; Improved family functioning; Reduced family conflict; Increased GPA; Prevention of substance abuse problems in younger siblings
Adult depression		X		Decreased depression for maritally distressed couples; Increased marital satisfaction
Adult substance abuse	X	X		Increased initiation of treatment among substance-abusing partners whose spouses participated in unilateral treatment; Decreased spousal enabling behavior; Increased sobriety
Adult schizophrenia	X	X		Decreased patient relapse and psychiatric symptoms; Improved family member well-being; Increased patient participation in vocational rehabilitation; Improved patient social functioning

(Continued)

Table 16.1 (**Continued**)

Target of Intervention	Focus of Intervention Program			Specific Intervention Targets Found to Change
	Individual	**Dyad**	**Triad or Greater**	
Interventions for Relational Disorders				
Attachment disorders	X	X		Maternal sensitivity; Security of attachment
Child maltreatment	X	X	X	Reduce risk of physical maltreatment; Develop more child-friendly attitudes and beliefs; Change beliefs about corporal punishment
Marital conflict		X		Decrease marital distress
Domestic violence	X			Small decrease in recidivism
Interventions for Transition or Adversity				
Transition to marriage		X		Couples communication; Couples conflict management; Satisfaction with relationship
Transition to parenthood	X	X		Couples communication; General satisfaction with relationship; Satisfaction with sexual relationship
Transition to school		X		Child school functioning; Child emotional functioning; Child problem behavior; Positive parenting
Divorce and postdivorce parenting	X	X		Positive parenting; Diagnosable psychopathology in children; Maternal depression; Child externalizing
Remarriage and stepparenting	X		X	Parenting; Child problem behavior
Later life burden of care	X			Caretaker feelings of burden; Caretaker depression; Caretaking skills; Symptoms of care recipient
Palliative and end-of-life care	X			Family member depression
Loss and bereavement	X	X		Child internalizing and externalizing symptoms

activities are carried out in similar ways for all families. For example, it would be difficult to claim that a program of family communication training was responsible for reduced conflict if some of the families in the study didn't actually receive training in most of the communication exercises. Researchers have developed two methods for insuring that interventions are delivered as planned: **program manuals** provide specific guidelines for how the intervention should be carried out, and *fidelity checks* are used to observe how well these guidelines are followed.

No single study can provide incontrovertible evidence that an intervention program is effective. The more studies we have that show evidence of effectiveness, the more confidence we can have in the intervention. This is because each study likely conducts the intervention in a slightly different way with different therapists and different types of families. If intervention effects are robust across these variations, we can be more confident that the effects are powerful, and clinicians can have greater confidence in their usefulness.

The *box score review* provides a simple count of how many studies report significant effects. A **meta-analytic review** uses more sophisticated statistical methods for combining results across studies. Meta-analysis has two important advantages. First, it creates a common metric for determining the size of the effect attributable to treatment, regardless of the specific measures employed. This allows investigators to combine findings from studies using different measurement methods. Second, meta-analysis uses statistical methods that combine treatment effects from all studies to form an overall estimate of *treatment effect size,* with each study contributing to this effect size in proportion to the number of participants in that study. This allows the investigator to test for treatment effects using a much larger combined sample, leading to more stable estimates of effect size than are possible for any single study and increasing the ability to detect effects that might not reach significance for single studies with smaller samples. Meta-analyses can also be applied to more complex questions, such as whether there is evidence of different effects for different treatment

components and whether evidence concerning mediators is found with consistency.

RESEARCH FINDINGS ON THE EFFECTIVENESS OF FAMILY-FOCUSED INTERVENTION

We covered three broad areas of outcome: individual clinical outcomes, relationships, and adaptation to stressful transitions. We also include in-depth descriptions of three exemplary trials. These exemplary trials represent the state of the art in terms of family therapy research.

FAMILY INTERVENTIONS FOR INDIVIDUAL DISORDERS

Child and Adolescent Disorders

Child and adolescent problems are often described in terms of externalizing or internalizing disorders. **Externalizing disorders** involve oppositional, defiant, or aggressive behavior, as well as problems with attention and hyperactivity. They also include conduct problems involving rule breaking, as well as delinquency and substance abuse. **Internalizing disorders** involve anxiety and depression.

Externalizing Disorders.   Chamberlain and Rosicky (1995) summarized the results of eighteen trials in a meta-analysis of programs for child conduct disorders. They concluded that family interventions were significantly more effective than comparison treatments. Five of these studies found that family interventions, including structural family therapy (see Chapter 7), were effective in reducing aggression and other conduct problems. A more recent review by Kazdin and Weisz (1998) reinforced this conclusion, finding that family therapy led to significant improvements in both parent and teacher reports of child externalizing behavior, as well as in independent indicators based on records of school suspensions and police reports.

Behavioral parent training (see Chapter 10) has garnered substantial support for reducing children's externalizing problems. Parent training helps parents develop skills for increasing children's prosocial behavior and decreasing conduct-disordered behavior (Patterson, 1976). A significant research base exists for the effectiveness of such studies (Carr, 2009). For example, in a recent meta-analysis of thirty behavioral parenting training studies and forty-one individual therapy studies, behavioral parent training was found to be significantly more effective than individual therapy in reducing childhood problem behavior (McCart, Priester, Davies, & Azen, 2006).

The literature frequently differentiates between childhood externalizing behaviors and those more commonly diagnosed in adolescence, such as conduct disorder. A number of meta-analyses of the effects of family therapy for adolescent conduct disorder have been conducted, with increased attention in the last decade. In a meta-analysis of eight studies, Woolfenden, Williams, and Peat (2002) found that functional family therapy (FFT) and multi-systemic therapy (MST) were more effective than usual care in reducing jail time and recidivism. Another review of four studies investigated the effectiveness of family therapy with low-socioeconomic-status delinquent adolescents and found that treatment involving eight to thirty-six sessions of behavioral or functional family therapy led to improved family communication, decreased externalizing behavior, and lower recidivism rates (Brosnan & Carr, 2000). Curtis, Ronan, and Borduin (2004) conducted a meta-analysis of eleven studies of MST and found that in comparison to those receiving usual care, adolescents receiving MST maintained lower levels of negative outcomes for up to four years after treatment had been concluded.

Because of concerns that family therapy is more expensive than individual intervention, the results of a study by Crane, Hillin, and Jakubowski (2005) were particularly noteworthy. This study found that family therapy treatment was more effective than individual therapy treatment and reduced costs for care by 32 percent over the next thirty months. As a result, it seems that any additional resources required to manage the logistics of including family members

in treatment for adolescent conduct disorders may be offset by decreased need for follow-up care.

Attention-deficit hyperactivity disorder (ADHD) is another externalizing problem often treated with family intervention. Nevertheless, pharmacotherapy remains the most frequent treatment for ADHD, as up to 85 percent of diagnosed children take stimulant medication (Barkley, 2005). However, because ADHD has been associated with problematic family relationships (Johnston & Mash, 2001), family therapy has been viewed as a promising intervention that can alter maladaptive relationship patterns associated with this condition. A large-scale randomized controlled trial recently found that during the first two years of treatment, a combination of medication management and multimodal behavioral therapy (parent, school, and child components, with therapist involvement gradually reduced over time) was more effective than either component alone or usual community care (Jensen et al., 2007). However, this difference was not found at thirty-six months, suggesting that the research on medication and multi-modal treatment for ADHD is still inconclusive.

A recent review of twenty-eight studies concluded that manualized family treatments for children with ADHD led to a decrease in parental rating of negative child behavior and a decrease of negative parent–child interactions (Chronis, Chacko, Fabiano, & Pelham 2004). Results of a meta-analysis of programs involving parents in ADHD treatment indicated that parent training and family therapy were in the low-to-moderate effectiveness range in decreasing ADHD-related behavior and had a moderate effect on decreasing child internalizing symptoms and school-related problems (Corcoran & Dattalo, 2006). Several factors were found to moderate the effectiveness of treatment. Older children received greater benefit from parent training than younger children. Children in single-parent families did not improve as much as children in two-parent families. In sum, research indicates that parental involvement in child ADHD treatment can be effective in treating both core symptoms and comorbid difficulties.

Finally, results of recent research have shown that family therapy can serve as an effective treatment for adolescent substance abuse. The family system appears to play an important role in adolescent substance abuse problems, due to both heritability and negative relationship patterns (Muck, Zempolich, Titus, Fishman, Godly, & Schwebel, 2001). Williams and Chang (2000) reviewed fifty-three studies and concluded that family therapy was more effective than individual therapy, therapeutic communities, outward-bound programs, and twelve-step programs. Armed with the knowledge of its efficacy, researchers are currently exploring the utility of family-oriented treatment for preventing adolescent substance use. A randomized controlled study of Hispanic youth found that a parent-centered prevention program focused on improved family functioning and increased HIV awareness reduced smoking and unsafe sexual behavior as well as illicit drug use by strengthening the family system (Prado et al., 2007). Such results were found above and beyond those achieved by an HIV awareness intervention alone or in combination with an intervention targeting specific health behavior, substantiating claims that improving family functioning is an important path for treating adolescent substance abuse.

Two recent meta-analyses indicate that family-based treatments should now be considered well-established interventions for substance abuse (Becker & Curry, 2008; Waldron & Turner, 2008). Functional family therapy (FFT), brief strategic family therapy (BSFT), and multidimensional family therapy (MDFT) are all manualized treatments whose effects have been replicated by independent investigators across multiple sites, and Becker and Curry (2008) indicate that the quality of evidence for MDFT is particularly strong for its effects on both substance abuse and conduct problems.

One randomized controlled trial of MDFT compared with two other treatment approaches (one involving groups of families and one consisting of group treatment of adolescents) found that those adolescents treated with MDFT showed the greatest improvement at the end of treatment, as well as significant changes in academic performance and family functioning at one-year follow-up (Liddle et al., 2001). We have included a detailed description of this trial as one of our exemplary trials of family intervention.

Exemplary Trial
Multidimensional Family Therapy (MDFT) for Adolescent Drug Abuse

Based on research suggesting that adolescent drug abuse is influenced by a variety of social contexts, Howard Liddle and his colleagues developed multidimensional family therapy as a means of treating adolescents who are abusing drugs (Liddle et al., 2001). MDFT targets several aspects of an adolescent's life, including individual, emotional, and cognitive functioning, family and peer relationships, and social behavior in general. Moreover, MDFT works with parents to help them develop more positive relationships with their children. MDFT consists of three phases in which adolescents and parents receive both individual therapy and sessions as a family. The first phase seeks to build alliances among the adolescent, family members, and other individuals who play a role in the adolescent's life. The therapist personalizes the therapeutic program by helping the adolescent and family identify specific goals while also integrating more general goals, such as reducing drug use and becoming involved with healthier activities.

The second phase of MDFT helps adolescents build concrete skills, such as effective communication of thoughts, feelings, and experiences, and healthy ways of handling stress. The therapist helps parents reflect on their relationship with their children and enacts scenarios in which they practice parenting techniques. The third phase of the treatment helps families apply newly learned skills to the outside world.

Liddle and his colleagues (2001) used a randomized trial to test the effectiveness of the MDFT program, comparing it to two other treatment approaches. The first, a multifamily educational intervention (MEI), differs from MDFT in that it is conducted as a group treatment. A group of three to four families met weekly to receive lectures and homework assignments, participate in structured group discussions and skill-building exercises, and confer with the other families in family problem solving. In general, the treatment emphasized stress reduction, risk and protective factors for individuals and families, family organization and rules, and family communication and problem solving. The therapist encouraged families to support each other and act as a supportive community. MEI has a more psychoeducational focus than MDFT.

The second comparison condition involved adolescent group therapy (AGT). AGT focuses on building individual social skills including communication, self-control, self-acceptance, problem solving, and solidarity among members of the group. This intervention had four phases. Phase 1 involved two family sessions and one individual session with the adolescent and focused on information gathering, promoting family support, and motivating participants. Phases 2 and 3 were conducted with groups of six to eight adolescents and paired activities designed to encourage self-disclosure and increase group cohesiveness with skill-building exercises and homework focusing on how to refuse offers of drugs, conflict resolution, anger management, development of healthy activities, and communication skills. The last phase emphasized maintenance and application of newly acquired skills.

This trial used referrals from juvenile justice services, schools, and other health and mental health agencies to identify 182 youth aged thirteen to eighteen who were currently using illegal substances other than alcohol. They and their families were randomly assigned to either MDFT or one of the two **comparison groups**. The investigators developed detailed treatment manuals for training and supervising clinicians in all three interventions to maintain program fidelity. They collected data on drug use through adolescent and parent reports, as well as through urinalysis. They also videotaped families during discussion tasks and trained raters to assess family interactions. These measures were taken before the intervention began, immediately after it ended, and again twelve months later.

All three treatments resulted in improvement for participants, but MDFT showed the greatest gains in terms of improved academic performance, healthier family functioning, and reduced problem behavior and drug use. These improvements remained stable over a twelve-month period. The investigators concluded that MDFT's focus on the specific issues faced by individual families and adolescents led to its increased effectiveness compared to the group approaches of AGT and MEI.

Internalizing Disorders. Internalizing problems such as anxiety and depression often co-exist with externalizing problems, and as noted earlier, some interventions for externalizing also have a positive effect on these problems. The results of several randomized trials provide mixed support for the effectiveness of family interventions for childhood internalizing disorders. Birmaher and his colleagues (Birmaher et al., 2000) compared individual cognitive–behavioral therapy (CBT), systematic behavioral family therapy (SBFT), and non-directive supportive therapy for adolescent depression. No significant differences were found in long-term reduction of depressive symptoms. More recently, Trowell and colleagues (Trowell et al., 2007) found integrative family therapy as effective as psychodynamic therapy in reducing depressive symptoms. Integrative family therapy utilizes techniques from several family therapy models, focusing on the links between the child's depression, problematic family scripts, and insecure family attachment patterns (Byng-Hall, 1995). Both family therapy and psychodynamic therapy led to a significant reduction in double depression (major depression and dysthymia) and rates of other co-morbid disorders, but family therapy achieved these effects in less than one-third the number of sessions required by psychodynamic therapy (Trowell et al., 2007). Overall, a recent review by Carr (2009) suggests that family-focused interventions for depression are as effective as individual cognitive–behavioral interventions.

Siqueland, Rynn, and Diamond (2005) reported mixed success with a family-focused intervention for adolescent anxiety disorders. This program combined individual CBT sessions for the adolescent with family-focused sessions designed to coach parents to provide appropriate support for their children and to help them overcome feelings of anxiety. In addition, restructuring techniques were used to alter family interaction patterns, encourage parents to be open to and respectful of their adolescents' wishes, and increase the children's level of freedom in expressing their emotions and seeking age-appropriate autonomy. Families were randomly assigned to this sixteen-session program or to a sixteen-session program of individual CBT for the adolescent.

Results indicated no differences between the two treatments in reducing adolescent anxiety or increasing adolescent-reported acceptance by parents (Siqueland, Rynn, and Diamond, 2005). However, adolescents in the family intervention rated their parents as less psychologically and emotionally restrictive and more tolerant of their autonomy. One recent meta-analysis which reviewed nine studies of individual CBT versus CBT accompanied by varying amounts of parent involvement suggests that although family-focused programs may be more effective in improving the quality of family functioning, the evidence for the superiority of either model in decreasing anxiety symptoms is lacking at the present time (Barmish & Kendall, 2005). Overall, these findings suggest that family interventions may lead to changes in family interactions that perpetuate adolescent anxiety disorders, but to date no conclusive evidence exists that such interventions increase effectiveness in treating anxiety.

Summary. Support for the effectiveness of family therapy for a host of child and adolescent externalizing disorders is robust. For some disorders, including substance abuse and conduct disorder, family treatment is more effective than other approaches, suggesting that family approaches are the treatment of choice for these diagnoses. For other areas, including ADHD, more research is needed to determine how child and family factors (e.g., child age and two-parent versus one-parent family) influence the effectiveness of family treatments in order to best identify the subset of children and adolescents with ADHD who would most benefit from family intervention.

Evidence for the utility of family interventions for internalizing disorders of childhood and adolescence is less strong, particularly in regard to anxiety. There is only weak evidence that family-focused anxiety interventions add to the effectiveness of individual cognitive-behavioral forms of intervention. However, there is growing evidence for the effectiveness of family therapy in the treatment of childhood depression (Carr, 2008).

Adult Disorders

Clinical trials of family interventions to treat emotional and behavioral disorders of adulthood have focused on three areas: depression, substance abuse, and severe mental illness.

Depression. Substantial research has documented associations between marital conflict and depression. As a result, a number of clinicians have developed couples treatments for depression. A recent meta-analysis of eight controlled trials involving over 500 subjects compared couples therapy to individual psychotherapy, drug therapy, or a wait list condition (Barbato & D'Avanzo, 2008). Therapies included emotionally focused couples therapy, behavioral marital therapy, cognitive marital therapy, interpersonal marital therapy, and systemic marital therapy. The results indicate that couples therapy is as effective as individual treatment in reducing depressive symptoms. Couples therapy was found to be significantly more effective than no treatment, and the results concurred with previous literature suggesting that couples treatment is more effective in reducing relationship distress, a common risk factor for adult depression (Barbato & D'Avanzo, 2008; Gilliam & Cottone, 2005).

However, the effects of couples therapy may depend on whether the depression occurs in the presence of marital distress. For example, Jacobson and colleagues (Jacobson et al., 1991) conducted a randomized controlled trial of BMT (See Chapter 10), individual cognitive therapy (CT), and combined therapy (including elements of both). Each group received twenty sessions of treatment. BMT focused on behavioral exchange, communication, and problem-solving training, and included such techniques as behavior rehearsal and contingency management supplemented with cognitive techniques such as reframing. CT focused on the re-assessment of maladaptive cognitions and behavioral aspects of depressive symptoms. The combined therapy included at least eight sessions of BMT and six sessions of individual CT. Results indicated that BMT was as effective as CT for individuals who reported marital distress but was less effective for individuals who did not report marital distress. This suggests that marital therapy for depression may be most effective in treating depressed individuals who also report marital distress.

Substance Abuse.   Research indicates that involving family members in the treatment of adult substance abusers plays a key role in influencing the course of chronic alcoholism. In a review of thirty-eight controlled studies of marital and family therapy (MFT) O'Farrell and Fals-Stewart (2003) concluded that several MFT approaches are effective in encouraging alcoholics to enter treatment and in helping family members cope if the alcoholic does not enter treatment. Effective approaches include Barber and Crisp's (1995) pressure to change approach (PCA), the community reinforcement and family change (CRAFT) approach, and the twelve-step family disease approach with Al-Anon participation. O'Farrell and Fals-Stewart (2003) also concluded that in the acute treatment phase, MFT is clearly more effective than individual treatment at increasing rates of abstinence and improving family functioning, particularly in the case of behavioral couples therapy (BCT).

Results are less promising in the aftercare phase of treatment, with no treatment demonstrating effectiveness in the long term (two or more years following primary treatment). Thus, while many programs have proved effective in short-term decreases of substance abuse, a high proportion of substance abusers relapse regardless of the use of these family-focused treatments (Edwards & Steinglass, 1995).

Research on the cost-effectiveness of MFT has yielded inconclusive results. Two studies found that the reduction in jail and hospital stays after behavioral

couples therapy saved over five times the cost of delivering BCT (O'Farrell et al., 1996a, 1996b). For drug-abuse patients, BCT was equally cost-effective when compared with individual treatment (Fals-Stewart et al., 1997). In summary, MFT demonstrates a clear advantage over individual treatment in active treatment focused on abstinence and in improving family functioning during treatment. However, more research is needed on the cost-effectiveness of marital and family therapy, as well as on the comparative effectiveness of MFT in getting alcoholics to enter treatment.

Major Mental Illness.   Some of the earliest applications of family therapy were designed to treat schizophrenia (see Chapter 1). As research on schizophrenia and bipolar disorder progressed, attention turned to biological factors, with an emerging consensus that vulnerability for major mental illness is influenced by genetics and neurobiology. This paralleled the development of pharmacotherapies that helped to reduce many of the more extreme symptoms of schizophrenia. However, these drug therapies had less impact on certain symptoms of schizophrenia, and research on the emotional climate of families with schizophrenic members found that *expressed emotion* (reflecting a critical, hostile, and overinvolved family climate) had a profound impact on relapse and on the general functioning of the family member with schizophrenia (Miklowitz, 2004). This led to the development of psychoeducational family programs for schizophrenia and their adaptation for families with members who have bipolar disorder (See Chapter 11).

These programs are designed to reduce symptom relapse and to facilitate return to independent functioning. Family psychoeducation has two main goals: (1) to obtain the best possible treatment and outcome for the individual with mental illness, and (2) to support family members in their efforts to aid in that individual's recovery. This often includes an explicit focus on how family climate can trigger symptoms and how families can reduce expressed emotion to prevent this. The term "psychoeducation" can be misleading, as it includes many elements of cognitive, behavioral, and supportive therapeutic models.

Pfammatter, Junghan, and Brenner (2006) recently conducted a meta-analysis of the thirty-one most methodologically sound randomized controlled trials of family psychoeducation, while simultaneously providing a review of the three prior meta-analyses of psychoeducational family therapy (Pharaoh et al., 2006; Pilling et al., 2002; and Pitschel-Walz et al., 2001). All four meta-analyses found that compared to medication alone, family psychoeducation in combination with anti-psychotic medication consistently led to fewer relapses, fewer hospitalizations, and increased adherence to medication regimes. Long-term family interventions were found to be more effective than short-term relatives' groups. Pfammetter's new meta-analysis further found that compared with medication alone, family psychoeducation increased knowledge of the disorder among family members, reduced expressed emotion, improved patients' social adjustment, and resulted in lower rates of symptoms up to two years post-intervention. In sum, the evidence is robust for the effectiveness of family therapy for patients with schizophrenia, particularly when offered within a multi-modal program including anti-psychotic medication.

Summary.   Family-focused interventions for adult disorders appear to be most useful when they target specific aspects of family functioning associated with onset or maintenance of the disorder or when they help family members support independent functioning of the person experiencing the disorder. For depression, data suggest that marital therapy is a strong treatment option when clients report high levels of relationship distress. In treating substance abuse, spouse involvement is related to gains in treatment engagement and decreases in substance use in the short term, but no treatment has been shown to maintain these gains in the long term. Finally, involving family members of patients with major mental illness in psychoeducation programs can provide those family members the resources to provide long-term care to the client, while maximizing the possibility that family members will feel adequately supported in that task.

𝓕AMILY INTERVENTIONS FOR RELATIONSHIP DISORDERS

The programs we reviewed earlier all assumed that individual disorders are influenced by family relationships. However, it is also possible to view some relationship patterns as problematic in their own right. The *DSM-IV-TR* (American Psychiatric Association, 2000) includes V codes that address this issue, and there have been suggestions that relational disorders should be included more completely in revisions of this diagnostic system (Beach, Wamboldt, Kaslow, Heyman, & Reiss, 2006).

We were able to identify empirical studies of family interventions for three types of relational problems: disorders of attachment, child maltreatment, and marital conflict.

Disorders of Attachment

Attachment theory, supported by substantial research (see Chapter 4), indicates that the majority of children form secure attachments with one or more adults, seeking proximity and comfort when under stress (Bowlby, 1977; Zilberstein, 2006). However, some children develop anxious-avoidant or resistant attachment styles and are less able to use a parent as a source of comfort and safety. The most disturbed form of attachment involves *disorganized attachment,* often occurring in response to physical abuse or a caretaker who is frightening or unpredictable (Main & Solomon, 1990). While all insecure attachments are risk factors for later emotional problems, a disorganized attachment style places a child at highest risk for a variety of negative developmental outcomes (AACAP, 2005).

Severe problems of attachment have also been incorporated into *DSM-IV-TR. Reactive attachment disorder* is defined as resulting from pathogenic care and is associated with abnormal social interactions across multiple contexts (*DSM-IV-TR,* 2000). There are two types of reactive attachment disorders: inhibited and disinhibited. The *inhibited* type involves social withdrawal and emotional constriction. A child diagnosed with the *disinhibited* type doesn't discriminate among attachment figures, which signifies that the child has poor boundaries that can put him or her at risk for being taken advantage of. Reactive attachment disorder is a relatively recent addition to the diagnostic system, and little research is available on treatment effectiveness (Hanson & Spratt, 2000; AACAP, 2005; Chaffin et al., 2006).

A number of programs have been developed to treat children with insecure attachment. These programs work directly with parents, and many involve dyadic work with the child and the primary caretaker. A few programs have included both mothers and fathers. Some attachment therapies have been proposed that use coercive strategies, such as holding and rebirthing. These interventions are controversial, and a number of professional organizations warn against using them, based on reports that children have died as a result of their application (AACAP, 2005; Chaffin et al., 2006).

Two recent meta-analyses have examined the effectiveness of various interventions for insecure attachment. Bakersman-Kranenburg, van Ijzendoorn, and Juffer (2003) reviewed seventy studies testing the impact of early preventive interventions on the child's attachment security and maternal sensitivity to the child, with the majority of programs attempting to influence child attachment through changing maternal sensitivity. The authors concluded that these interventions were generally effective in improving both maternal sensitivity and child attachment and that interventions focusing on increasing parental sensitivity led to the most improvement in attachment. These programs taught mothers to carry infants close to their chests for extended periods of time and to recognize and respond to infants' signals of distress.

These programs were also effective with multiproblem families. Although shorter inventions were more effective overall, adding long-term and broadly focused support to the targeted intervention appeared better able to help multiproblem families

cope with the multitude of stressors they face. Although only a few programs included fathers, doing so was associated with increased effectiveness. Recently, Van Zeijl et al. (2006) developed a home-based intervention program that focuses not only on promoting sensitive parenting but also on parental discipline. A randomized, controlled trial found this program effective on multiple levels, improving maternal sensitivity and sensitive discipline as well as reducing externalizing behaviors in children (Van Zeijl, et al., 2006).

In a more recent meta-analysis, Bakersman-Kranenburg, van Ijzendoorn, and Juffer (2005) examined fifteen studies that included disorganized attachment as an outcome measure. The results indicate that the most effective interventions began after children were more than six months old. Interventions that focused on parental sensitivity were more effective than interventions that focused on support or parents' mental representations of their children. Interventions that focused on at-risk children were more effective than interventions that focused on at-risk parents.

Child Maltreatment

Over 3.2 million cases of child maltreatment were reported in the United States in 2007, with over 794,000 confirmed incidences of abuse (U.S. Department of Health and Human Services, Administration on Children, Youth and Families, 2007). *Child maltreatment* is the umbrella term used to describe neglect as well as physical, emotional, or sexual abuse (Cicchetti & Toth, 2005). Exposure to abuse is strongly associated with emotional problems in both childhood and adulthood. Furthermore, a recent meta-analysis demonstrated that maltreated infants were significantly more likely to have insecure or disorganized attachment, suggesting a strong link between maltreatment and attachment disorders (Baer & Martinez, 2006).

Child maltreatment raises a host of difficulties for treatment (Cicchetti & Toth, 2005). The various definitions of child maltreatment represent legal definitions and do not describe specific parenting practices.

There are no clear standards of acceptable discipline and parenting, and to further complicate matters, different cultures have different ideas about child-rearing and what is considered appropriate.

A number of recent reviews concur that for child maltreatment, effective therapy is family-based, structured and extended over at least six months. Effective programs address multiple aspects of child maltreatment, including children's post-traumatic adjustment problems, parenting skills, and the supportiveness of the family environment (Lundahl, Nimer & Parsons, 2006; MacLeod & Nelson, 2000). In a meta-analysis of twenty-one studies of child maltreatment therapies, Skowron and Reinemann (2005) found that all types of treatment, including family, individual parent, individual child, and parent training programs including both parent and child, led to approximately equal improvements compared to placebo, wait list, or community case management control groups.

Other controlled studies have focused on physical abuse. One study of both conjoint and concurrent cognitive-behavioral family therapy found that these treatments were more effective than standard care in reducing the risk of further physical abuse (Kolko & Swenson, 2002). Multi-systemic therapy (MST), discussed earlier as a treatment for adolescent externalizing disorders, has also been found effective for child abuse and neglect. Brunk, Henggeler, and Whelan (1987) found that both MST and parent training were effective in decreasing parental psychiatric symptomology, reducing family stress and the severity of problems. MST was more effective than parent training at restructuring parent-child relations, while parent training was more effective than MST at reducing social problems.

Lundahl, Nimer, and Parsons (2006) recently conducted a meta-analysis to examine the effects of twenty-three parent training programs. The results indicate that parent training was effective in reducing the risk of further physical or emotional abuse, although it did not influence the risk for sexual abuse. Through parent training, parents developed more child-friendly beliefs and attitudes and changed their attitudes about corporal punishment. Behavioral

programs resulted in better parenting, while nonbehavioral programs were more effective in changing attitudes. Greater attitude change occurred with a greater number of sessions and when the format included both group and individual work (Lundahl et al., 2006).

Treatment for sexual abuse has received increasing attention. A recent meta-analysis of seven studies found that in comparison to child-only treatment, treatment involving the non-offending parent is more effective at reducing internalizing behaviors, externalizing behaviors, sexualized behaviors, and post-traumatic stress symptoms in children (Corcoran & Pillai, 2008).

A number of family-focused programs have been developed to *prevent* child maltreatment in at-risk families. Geerart, Van den Noortgate, Grietens and Onghena (2004) conducted a meta-analysis of early family prevention programs which found that these programs are highly effective in decreasing abusive and neglectful acts as well as improving child functioning, parent-child interaction, and overall family functioning. MacLeod and Nelson (2000) conducted a meta-analysis of fifty-six programs designed to promote family wellness and prevent child maltreatment. Proactive interventions showed increasing effectiveness over time.

Programs using home visits to work with parents on preventing child maltreatment have also shown positive effects (Geerart et al., 2004; MacLeod & Nelson, 2000). These programs were more effective if they included more than twelve visits and lasted six months or longer. Programs that included a strengths-based approach, social support components, and had a high participation rate were more effective than programs that did not.

Other reviews have examined the effectiveness of existing programs. Abuse-focused cognitive–behavioral therapy and parent–child interaction therapy both include a family component and were identified as "best practices" (Herschell & McNeil, 2005). In addition, because child maltreatment often creates an insecure attachment, treatments that are effective in treating attachment disorders also work well for child maltreatment (Hanson & Spratt, 2000).

Because many cases of maltreatment go unreported, Peterson, Tremblay, Ewigman, and Saldana (2003) have suggested that programs designed to prevent child maltreatment are likely to be more cost effective and may have wider impact. Recently, Prinz and colleagues (Prinz et al., 2009) implemented a randomized trial of the "Triple P" Positive Parenting Program in 18 counties with over 600 service providers. The program resulted in large effect sizes indicating fewer substantiated child maltreatment reports, child out-of-home placements, and child maltreatment injuries. The results of this study point to the feasibility and cost benefits of implementing a large-scale parenting intervention to prevent child maltreatment.

Exemplary Trial
Parent–Child Therapy with Physically Abusive Parents

Mark Chaffin and his colleagues developed parent–child interaction therapy (PCIT) as a means of reducing instances of child abuse in families where parents had been reported for such behavior (Chaffin et al., 2006). PCIT is a two-part program. The first six sessions focus on orientation of the participants and seek to motivate participants to actively involve themselves in the program and homework assignments. The second component, lasting between twelve and fourteen sessions, entails instruction on healthy parent–child interactions and live coaching as parents interact with their children. Instructors focus on helping parents practice basic parenting skills, such as praising good behavior, eliminating sarcasm and criticism, and ignoring minor misbehavior.

Chaffin and colleagues (Chaffin et al., 2006) conducted a randomized trial to investigate the effectiveness of PCIT, guided by several questions. First, does PCIT reduce future abuse more effectively than standard group parent training? Second, does PCIT improve interaction between parents and children and decrease parental behaviors that characterize the coercive cycle of abuse? More exactly, does PCIT treat these behaviors specifically and not

other untargeted factors, such as parent distress, attitudes, and perceptions of children's behavior that might show changes with more standard interventions? Finally, can PCIT alone reduce future abuse without supplemental treatments for parents, and will supplemental treatments augment the effectiveness of PCIT?

To investigate these questions, 112 parent–child pairs, consisting of an abusive parent and his or her physically abused child, were recruited from the child welfare system. The children ranged in age from four to twelve. Sixty-four percent of the families fell below the poverty line, 65 percent received public assistance, and 48 percent were of ethnic minority status.

The researchers randomly assigned each parent–child pair to one of three groups: PCIT, PCIT with supplemental services (enhanced PCIT or EPCIT), or a standard community group. The PCIT group completed the standard program and also participated in four added sessions, during which participants had the opportunity to discuss issues of concern. This was added so that the PCIT program would last as long as the six-month standard community parenting group intervention.

The participants in EPCIT received the same basic regimen of PCIT but with the addition of home visits to help with application of PCIT skills in the home, cognitive therapy and antidepressant medication for parental depression, and psychotherapy for family, marital, and domestic violence issues. Participants received supplemental services depending on the individual issues identified as problem areas.

The standard community group provided a three-part intervention that focused on improving parenting practices. The first six sessions served as an orientation during which parents learned about the agency's services as well as basic information on listening skills, the influence of parenting practices on child development, and the influence of parents' own upbringing on their discipline and parenting. The second twelve sessions emphasized child development, appropriate praise and discipline, behavior management, communication skills, stress management, and how the problems of parents can affect children. Finally, the third twelve sessions focused on anger management, self-awareness, self-control, and the cultivation of compassion and empathy. The main difference between PCIT and this intervention entailed the emphasis that PCIT placed on detailed, live coaching of positive parenting practices as the parents interacted with their children.

The results of this study indicated that PCIT alone effectively reduced future abuse among abusive parents. Compared to the standard group intervention, PCIT was significantly more effective. Only 19 percent of PCIT participants had additional reports of abuse after 850 days, whereas 49 percent of participants in the standard community group had additional reports of abuse. The study also showed that PCIT specifically targets parent behaviors that lead to abuse, rather than untargeted factors such as parent distress, attitudes, and perceptions of children's behavior. Although these factors may be related to abuse, the researchers concluded that more standard interventions can treat these issues, while PCIT offers a particularly effective means of preventing parental abuse. Additionally, the researchers found that therapists implementing PCIT need not have high levels of expertise in PCIT but only a basic level of competence. This suggests that therapists with brief training in PCIT can achieve positive results. Finally, supplemental services (EPCIT) did not increase the effectiveness of PCIT.

Couples Conflict

Research on couples therapy has a longer history than other areas of family therapy research, and more reviews have compared the efficacy of different treatments. Early reviews comparing the various methods found evidence of the "dodo bird effect," whereby all treatments were effective and none were found to be superior (Luborsky, Singer, & Luborsky, 1975).[1] Three more recent reviews and meta-analyses provide a more nuanced picture.

Behavioral approaches to couples therapy have received the most attention to date. Behavioral couples therapy (see Chapter 10) focuses on helping partners develop communication and problem-solving skills to negotiate a more equitable relationship. Shadish and Baldwin (2005) conducted a meta-analysis of thirty randomized controlled trials of behavioral marital therapy (BMT). Consistent with earlier reviews, they concluded that BMT is more effective than no treatment. However, they also found that the overall level of effectiveness was lower than had been reported in earlier reviews. The authors suggested that this finding could be due in part to publication bias, which is the tendency for studies to be published only if they have significant findings.

Trials of other approaches to couples therapy are becoming more frequent. This is particularly true of emotionally focused couples therapy (EFT), which uses attachment theory to focus on developing ways of adjusting emotional responses to meet each other's attachment needs and build attachment security within the relationship (see Chapter 8). Wood, Cran, Schaalje, and Law (2005) used a meta-analysis to compare the effectiveness of EFT and BMT based on results of twenty-three studies. For couples experiencing mild levels of distress, both of these approaches were equally effective. Moderately distressed couples appeared to experience more improvement with EFT. The authors could find only one trial of BMT for couples who were seriously distressed, and this approach was found to be highly effective for that group. The authors concluded that EFT was significantly more effective than treatments using isolated components of BMT. Overall, using a full treatment model provided more consistent results than using isolated components of a treatment.

Byrne, Carr, and Clark (2004) also conducted a review of trials to compare the efficacy of different forms of marital therapy. Consistent with Wood et al. (2005), they found that BMT leads to both short- and long-term gains for moderate to severely distressed couples and that EFT leads to both short- and long-term gains for mild to moderately distressed couples. Adding a cognitive component didn't increase the effectiveness of either BMT or EFT. The authors also

---

[1] In Lewis Carroll's *Alice in Wonderland*, it was the dodo bird who declared, "Everyone has won, and all must have prizes!"

reviewed a sample of trials of integrated systemic therapy and insight-oriented therapy for couples. There were indications that these approaches were effective, as well as indications that integrated systemic therapy may lead to more rapid and sustained improvement in couples who stay together (Christensen et al., 2006).

Couples-based sex therapy has been found effective for sexual problems including hypoactive sexual desire, female orgasmic disorder, female sexual pain disorders, and premature ejaculation (see Chapter 10). While there have been no meta-analyses conducted on couples-based treatments for these disorders, a number of narrative reviews have found that couples-based cognitive–behavioral therapy is effective in challenging attitudes and expectations that interfere with sexual desire and psychological intimacy (Duterte et al., 2007; Meston, 2006; Meston & Bradford, 2007). However, there is also some evidence that these improvements are not always well sustained, particularly in regard to treatment for hypoactive sexual desire and premature ejaculation (Duterte et al., 2007). Overall, Carr (2009) suggests that services for couples with psychosexual difficulties should be multi-modal, including both couples sex therapy and medication. Further, sexual problems are often accompanied by relationship distress, highlighting the importance of the couples therapy component of treatment.

The research on treatment for domestic violence is still sparse, with little evidence concerning empirically supported treatments (O'Leary & Vega, 2005). Research on the treatment of male perpetrators suggests that some interventions may be effective, but the evidence isn't strong (Edleson & Tolman, 1992; Rosenfield, 1992). A meta-analysis by Babcock, Green, and Robie (2004) found a small effect of treatment, but the studies included in the analysis weren't all rigorous. Some research exists on the use of couples therapy to treat domestic violence, although Stith and Rosen (2003) suggest that this research has been hampered by a prejudice against doing therapeutic relationship work with couples when violence has occurred (see chapters 3 and 11). In a narrative review of six studies, Stith and Rosen (2003) found that

careful and appropriately delivered couples therapy can be as effective as individual treatment if couples are committed to staying together and the violent partner agrees to a no-harm contract. Stith, Rosen, McCollum and Thomsen (2004) found in one randomized trial that group couples therapy may be more effective than single-couple therapy. Multi-couple therapy was found to reduce male violence, decrease marital aggression, and increase marital satisfaction. Single-couple therapy didn't demonstrate the same results. However, this sample of couples was small, and researchers in this area continue to call for a greater focus on family and couples treatments for domestic violence (Murray, 2006; Sartin, Hansen, & Huss, 2006).

INTERVENTIONS TO HELP FAMILIES WEATHER NORMATIVE CHANGE, ADVERSITY, AND HIGH-RISK TRANSITIONS

Times of change and adversity pose significant risks for families. This is true for changes that are unforeseen as well as those that are expected. There is substantial evidence that stressful events, such as losing a job, going through a separation or divorce, or being a victim of violent crime, increases the risk for depression (Kendler et al., 2003). Exposure to more enduring adversity also contributes to emotional distress (Brown & Harris, 1978). In addition, exposure to severe stressors or ongoing adversity can disrupt family life, in part through increasing conflict and reducing support among family members (Howe, Levy, & Caplan, 2004). Such events and adversities can also disrupt parenting and interfere with the support and socialization of children (Conger & Elder, 1994).

Predictable events and life transitions also pose threats to the emotional functioning of individuals and to the quality of family relationships. Normative life transitions, such as marriage or the birth of a child, place new demands on families. Many families successfully adapt, but others fail to make these transitions without distress.

Family therapists have paid close attention to both expected and unexpected transitions and life challenges, because they increase the risk for emotional, behavioral, and interpersonal problems and because they can usher in periods of pain and discomfort worthy of intervention in their own right. Many programs have been developed to help families make transitions more smoothly or to cope with stressful life challenges. Some of these programs were designed as educational interventions, including family life education workshops developed almost fifty years ago. A number of training programs for family life educators still thrive, and the National Council on Family Relations has an active certification program.

There have also been many efforts to develop programs that work with individuals and families to address the interpersonal patterns that increase support and decrease conflict within the family during such times and to develop new ways to adapt to and resolve the challenges attendant on such transitions or stressful events (see Chapter 11). These programs usually include education around the transition or stressful context but integrate that component with family therapy techniques, such as communications training and structural realignment.

Programs to Help Families Make Normative Developmental Transitions

Our search of the empirical literature identified studies on three sets of programs designed to help families make normative transitions. These include programs for couples planning to marry, programs for new parents, and programs for couples with a child about to begin school or with a teenager about to begin high school.

Preparation for Marriage or Long-Term Commitment. Carroll and Doherty (2003) were able to identify thirteen studies testing the effects of programs working to help couples develop and maintain more satisfying and less conflictual relationships as they moved toward marriage. These studies, conducted between 1970 and 2001, involved slightly over 1,000 couples who were mostly young, middle class, and of European descent. All programs used a couples group format and often included practice in communication skills. The theoretical orientations guiding these programs were predominantly family development theory, social learning theory, and communications theory. Groups met for three to eight sessions, across a total of twelve to twenty-four hours.

Using a meta-analysis to assess the effectiveness of these programs, Carroll and Doherty concluded that as a group, the programs were effective in improving how couples communicated, how they managed conflict, and how they felt about the overall quality of their relationship. There was also evidence that these gains lasted for at least six months to three years. A study of the premarital enrichment program (PREP: Markman et al., 1993) followed couples for longer periods of time and found somewhat reduced rates of divorce, though not at a level that reached statistical significance.

Maintaining Relationship Quality. A substantial number of trials have been conducted to test the effects of marriage and relationship education (MRE) programs for couples. Recent meta-analyses (Blanchard, Hawkins, Baldwin, & Fawcett, 2009; Hawkins, Blanchard, Baldwin, & Fawcett, 2008) identified 117 studies, with 41 using randomized trial designs. Most of the programs in these studies involved couples group psychoeducational programs ranging from 9 to 20 hours in length. The meta-analyses found moderate effects on both relationship quality and communication skills lasting for at least six months.

Birth of a Child. The birth of a child increases stress for many couples and can be associated with growing dissatisfaction with the relationship if a couple doesn't adapt well to the transition to parenthood (Glade, Bean, & Vira, 2005). Glade and colleagues were able to find only three trials of programs designed to help couples make this adaptation.

The best documented trial to date involves an experimental test of Cowan and Cowan's (1992)

Becoming a Parent program. This program employed a couples support group that met for three months before and three months after the birth. Although the content of group discussion was structured around concrete topics related to how couples make this transition, group leaders allowed group members to discuss any issues emerging over this period. A two-year follow-up indicated that participating couples reported higher continuing satisfaction and better communication, and were more likely to stay together than control couples.

Kermeen (1995) tested a less intensive program that integrated relationship enhancement strategies with prenatal childbirth classes, finding increased satisfaction with sexual aspects of the relationship postpartum but no differences in overall marital satisfaction. Glade et al. (2005) noted that several trials of such programs are currently underway, including a recently completed trial by Feinberg and Kan (2008), who tested a couples group intervention for first-time parents that focused on coparenting. Posttest data collected when infants were six months old found significant positive effects on coparenting support, the parent-child relationship, and infant self regulation, as well as reductions in maternal depression. Overall, these studies suggest that programs helping couples with the transition to parenthood hold promise but need further testing.

Transition to School. Families can face significant challenges in helping children make a successful transition into school or when moving from middle school to high school. Although school readiness has become an important topic of study, there are as yet few reports of trials testing programs to help families deal with these transitions.

Cowan, Cowan, and Heming (2005) provide a comprehensive report of their test of a couples-based program. Using a family development and family systems framework, they designed and compared two types of sixteen-week couples group interventions, one targeting relationship issues and one targeting parenting skills, for couples with a young child soon to begin school. Using a randomized trial design, they found that both programs had a positive impact on

child school and emotional functioning during and after the transition, although each affected somewhat different aspects of child adjustment. In addition, the relationship-based intervention had a positive impact on parenting, but the parenting intervention had no impact on the quality of the couples' relationship.

Australian researchers have recently tested the efficacy of applying a parent training program named Triple P (Positive Parenting Program) as part of an intervention available to all parents of young children beginning school (McTaggart & Sanders, 2003). This behaviorally oriented program involved four parenting group sessions with video presentations on positive parenting and homework, as well as weekly follow-up calls to each family by a program facilitator. Teachers were asked to rate children's problem behavior, and their reports indicated the program was successful both in improving child behavior and in maintaining that improvement over six months.

Children's transition to high school can also be a challenging time for families, and direct parent involvement is associated with better adolescent adjustment (Falbo, Lein, & Amador, 2001). However, we were able to identify only one preliminary report of a program to help families during this time (Ralph & Sanders, 2003). This program, an extension of the Triple P program for families of adolescents, showed initial evidence of positive effects on parent behavior, attitudes, and experience of stress in an uncontrolled study of Australian families.

Effectiveness of Programs Helping Families Cope with Stress

We have identified five sets of programs designed to help families cope with stressful events or ongoing adversity that have been subjected to empirical tests of efficacy. These include programs for families facing divorce and postdivorce parenting, remarriage and stepparenting, providing later-life care for impaired family members, palliative and end-of-life care, and loss and bereavement.

Divorce. Divorce is a risk factor for adult depression (Kendler et al., 2003) and reduced well-being

(Amato & Keith, 1991). Parental divorce also increases the risk for problems in children's academic achievement, conduct, psychological adjustment, self-concept, and social relations (Amato, 2001).

Family therapists have developed interventions for helping families weather the stress and conflicts that arise as couples go through breakup and divorce (Kaslow, 1995), but we were unable to identify any rigorous tests of such interventions, with the exception of divorce mediation programs. Divorce mediation programs have been developed largely within family court systems for the purpose of reducing conflict and supporting the establishment of custody and visitation rules to benefit children and reduce litigation. Although earlier research on the efficacy of these programs suggested that they were effective in helping divorcing couples in conflict (Benjamin & Irving, 1995), recent reviews have suggested a more complex picture (Beck & Sales, 2001; Beck, Sales, & Emery, 2004).

In one of the few randomized trials, Emery and Wyer (1987) found that families assigned to mediation reported greater satisfaction with dispute settlement and with its effects on the family when compared to couples who used traditional legal services. However, there is little evidence that mediation has an impact on the emotional functioning of the divorcing adults in terms of reducing depression, frustration, worry, or anger.

A subset of programs involving private fee-for-service mediation did show increases in positive couples interaction. Such programs are quite different from most court-mandated mediation in that they offer many sessions, address a wide range of issues, and include referral for therapy when necessary. Even with this level of intervention, the effects disappeared after two years, although Emery and colleagues (Emery et al., 2001) found that nonresidential parents who had gone through mediation remained more involved with their children twelve years later. Cost-comparison research in general failed to find that mediation leads to reduced court costs, and in some cases it actually increased those costs (Beck et al., 2004). However, little work has been done to study overall cost–benefit patterns of mediation.

Postdivorce Parenting. Substantial evidence shows that the postdivorce adjustment of children is strongly influenced by the quality of their relationships with their parents in the first year or two after divorce and by how much they are exposed to continuing conflict between the divorced parents (Whiteside & Becker, 2000). A number of programs have been developed to help children during this period. Most programs subjected to rigorous evaluation have focused only on the children (Stathakos & Roehrle, 2003), but a handful have tested more family-focused interventions.

We were able to locate three randomized trials of programs that work with families facing divorce. The New Beginnings Program (Wolchik, West, Westover, & Sandler, 1993), which integrated both parent and child group sessions, has received one of the most rigorous long-term evaluations, and we describe it in detail as an exemplary trial. Notably, this trial included a six-year follow-up that demonstrated reductions in psychopathology for children whose families were involved in the intervention (Wolchik et al., 2002).

Exemplary Trial
The New Beginnings Program

The New Beginnings Program, developed by Sharlene Wolchik, Irwin Sandler, and their colleagues at Arizona State University, was designed to reduce the negative impact of parental divorce on children (Wolchik et al., 2002). The program consists of two components.

The first is a structured program for mothers, involving eleven ninety-minute group sessions and two individual sessions. Group sessions, conducted by two group leaders, involve structured activities, including review of videotape models and role-playing practice, as well as regular homework assignments. The groups focus on four aspects of family relationships associated with positive adjustment following divorce: the use of effective discipline, ways of maintaining a positive and supportive relationship with the child, ways of supporting the child's relationship with the father, and methods for handling conflict between parents.

The second program component involves eleven ninety-minute child groups. These groups also focus on factors associated with positive adjustment to divorce, including the use of active as opposed to avoidant coping, ways of appraising divorce-related stressors, and positive communication with the child's mother. The groups teach such skills as recognizing and labeling feelings, deep-breathing relaxation, and problem-solving approaches. The group leaders use videotape models and model skills directly, and the children practice applying the skills to divorce-related situations. This component also includes a conjoint session where children practice communication skills with their mothers. Program activities were documented in a detailed manual, and group leaders were trained to carry out the program following this manual.

The research team employed a number of methods to test the efficacy of this program. To engage a broad range of divorced families, they used computerized court records and media advertisements to identify potential families and were able to enroll 240 families from a wide range of economic backgrounds in their study. Families were randomly assigned to experimental or comparison conditions. To test whether the child component was important, some families participated only in the mother program, while another group of families participated in both the mother and the child programs. The remaining families were given a set of readings about adjustment to divorce to use as a self-study guide. The investigators also used several methods to be sure the programs were conducted with fidelity. Sessions were videotaped and viewed by raters who assessed whether each intervention segment was completed. Attendance data were kept to gauge levels of participation. Mothers were asked to keep diaries about homework to assess completion of homework assignments.

The primary goals of the program were to reduce emotional and behavioral problems in children who had experienced divorce and to prevent such problems in the future. The investigators measured both

externalizing and internalizing symptoms before and after the program. They also collected data on more proximal targets that they felt would influence child symptoms, including quality of parent–child relationships, mothers' use of effective discipline, conflict between parents, and children's contact with fathers. They recontacted families six months and again six years after the end of the program to study whether changes had been maintained and whether the program had a long-term protective effect.

These results demonstrated that the mother program had positive effects on mother–child relationship quality, mothers' use of effective discipline, mothers' attitudes toward father–child contact, and on child externalizing problems, particularly for those children who were showing higher levels of such problems before the program started. The six-year follow-up indicated that the program had a strong preventive effect. Children whose families participated in the program were only half as likely as those in the comparison group to have diagnosed mental disorders at that time. In addition, those children who had higher levels of problems before the program were even less likely to be using alcohol or drugs at the six-year follow-up.

The Parenting Through Change Program, developed at the Oregon Social Learning Center (see Chapter 10), has also been subjected to rigorous evaluation in a study of single mothers with sons between the ages of six and ten (Forgatch & DeGarmo, 1999). This program included both weekly parenting groups and weekly telephone support of homework assignments over fourteen weeks. Follow-ups over the next three years found a moderately positive effect on parenting that waned somewhat but still remained significant after thirty months. The program also demonstrated "sleeper effects," leading to reductions in maternal depression and child externalizing that appeared at the end of the follow-up period (Bullock & Forgatch, 2005).

Research has also pointed to the importance of postdivorce relationships with fathers as a factor in children's adjustment, but we were only able to identify one program that has been tested for efficacy, the Dads for Life program (Braver et al., 2005). This program developed dramatic videotape material used in eight group sessions and included two individual sessions with fathers. Preliminary results indicated that the program reduced child internalizing problems for those children who were initially more troubled and reduced interparental conflict for families that were initially more highly conflicted.

Remarriage and Stepparenting.   Remarriage and adaptation to stepfamily life have also been the target of family interventions (Bray, 1995), but we were only able to identify two randomized trials of programs for stepfamilies.

Nicholson and Sanders (1999) compared therapist-directed and self-directed behavioral family interventions to a control condition and found no differences between the two methods; both methods reduced child behavior problems and couples' conflict regarding parenting at the end of the intervention. Forgatch, DeGarmo, and Beldav (2005) extended the Parenting Through Change Program described earlier to stepfamilies, finding evidence for strong benefits to effective parenting practices and resultant decreases in child noncompliance in both home and school behavior.

Later-Life Burden of Care.   Increasing life expectancy has greatly increased the number of families faced with caring for elderly members with physical ailments and dementia. Sorensen, Pinquart, and Duberstein (2002) recently conducted a meta-analysis of seventy-eight studies testing the effects of programs to help caregivers of elderly family members. These programs focused on the caregiver and employed psychoeducational programs, support groups, skills training, respite care, and psychotherapy.

None of the programs appeared to include multiple caregivers within the immediate or extended family. Findings suggested that these programs had an immediate positive impact on the caretaker's feelings of burden, depression, and well-being, as well as on caretaking skills and symptoms of the care recipients.

Effects on the caretaker were maintained at follow-ups from six to twelve months, but effects on care recipient symptoms were not. However, these effects varied across caretakers and situations and were stronger for adult children than for spouse caretakers, for younger caretakers, and for caretakers of family members who did not have dementia. Shorter programs of seven to nine sessions appear adequate for increasing caretaking skills, but more extended programs appear necessary to reduce caretaker depression.

Palliative and End-of-Life Care.   Families are also faced with the emotional and practical burdens of caring for dying family members. Although a number of palliative care team programs have been studied, few have focused on the family as a unit.

Higginson and colleagues (Higginson et al., 2003) reported a meta-analytic review of twenty-six programs with palliative care teams, finding modest positive effects on patient quality of life, particularly when care was provided in the home. However, there was little evidence of positive effects on family caregivers (although very few studies tested for such effects). Higginson et al. also suggested that measures of quality of life may not as yet adequately assess the deeper personal meanings around death and dying that could be affected by such programs.

Although a number of family therapists have developed approaches to working with families with dying members, a study by Kissane and colleagues (Kissane et al., 2006) appears to be the only randomized trial to date of a family-focused grief therapy. Families having a member dying of cancer received standard palliative care, including counseling and medication as necessary. In addition, half of these families were randomly assigned to brief family-focused grief therapy. Family therapy was associated with modest reductions in depression for all family members and had the strongest effects for family members reporting the highest level of depression before the intervention. The program did not, however, appear to be beneficial for families with high levels of hostility.

Loss and Bereavement.   Families must also deal with the grief and readjustment that follows the death of a family member. Particular effort has focused on developing programs for children who have lost a parent (Tremblay & Israel, 1998). However, only a handful of these programs have been evaluated for effectiveness.

The Family Bereavement Program (Sandler et al., 2003), developed to work with children and surviving parents, is one of the only programs to be studied using a randomized trial. Results indicated that the program led to improved parenting, coping, and caregiver mental health. One year later, children in the program had fewer problems, but this was true only for girls and those who had more problems at the beginning of the program.

A recent meta-analysis of interventions for bereavement, mostly involving individuals or peer groups, may have important implications for future work on family interventions. Currier, Neimeier, and Berman (2008) found that such interventions had small and vanishing effects on adjustment for those experiencing a normal course of bereavement, but could be very effective when targeting grievers showing marked difficulties in adapting to loss.

Summary. Programs designed to help families weather a wide range of transitions and adversities have demonstrated some success in strengthening and stabilizing family relationships as well as reducing emotional difficulties. However, not all of these efforts have proved successful, and in many instances, the effects have dissipated over time.

Most of the programs subjected to empirical testing have tried to integrate relationship skills training with education around transitions or ways of coping with adversity and have been based on a combination of family development and social learning frameworks. Few attempts have been made to focus on broader systemic characterizations of family process (with the work of Cowan and Cowan being an important exception). As a result, many of these programs have worked only with individual family members, even when the goal was to change patterns of family interaction. In addition, long-term follow-ups are uncommon but clearly needed to study whether program effects are lasting. This is particularly important for programs designed to prevent future problems.

Finally, very little work has been done to test whether family and individual characteristics might influence the effectiveness of these programs. Studies in several different areas suggest that such programs may be most helpful for people who are experiencing stronger emotional reactions to these challenges. However, it also seems that the most challenging situations, such as those involving separation, divorce, or death of a family member, may require longer and more intensive interventions.

*P*ROCESS RESEARCH

The clinical trials described thus far have been concerned with the *outcome* of family interventions, but they've said little about the mechanisms responsible for therapeutic effects. Family researchers have also developed a variety of techniques for studying the *process* of family intervention to understand which interventions are most effective.

Process Research Methods

Process researchers often employ direct observation or recording of family therapy sessions to describe therapists' activities and their effects. For example, Michael Robbins and his colleagues studied the effects of therapist *reframing,* or noncritical statements that frame adolescent behavior as normal, by recording and rating each statement by the therapist and by family members during initial sessions of functional family therapy with families of delinquent adolescents (Robbins, Alexander, Newell, & Turner, 1996). Robbins and colleagues found that adolescents were less likely to respond negatively to reframing than to any other type of therapist statement.

Observational systems have been developed to capture a variety of family therapy processes, including specific strategies such as enactment (Allen-Eckert et al., 2001) and general therapist styles such as supportiveness and defensiveness (Waldron et al., 1997). Methods of discourse analysis have been imported from linguistics to study meaning formation and change during family therapy sessions (Burck, Frosh, Lisa, & Morgan, 1998). More recently, researchers have begun studying the degree to which therapists adhere to specific manualized therapies for family interventions. For example, Hogue and colleagues (Hogue et al., 2008) developed the Therapist Behavior Rating Scale-Competence (TBRS-C) to assess how closely therapists adhere to evidence-based practices for adolescent substance abuse treatment.

Process researchers have typically employed correlational designs to study the associations between various aspects of the intervention process and later outcomes. Such designs need to be interpreted with caution. For example, characteristics of a family and the therapist—such as problem severity, family rigidity, and the personality style of the therapist—can shape both the processes observed in therapy and the functioning of the family at the end of treatment. Statistical and sampling methods for reducing or eliminating plausible confounds can be used to increase confidence in study findings. Randomized experiments are a more powerful means of eliminating such confounds, although they have been used infrequently.

Butler and Wampler (1999) used a randomized design to study the effects of couples therapist strategies described as "couples-responsible," including enactment and use of accommodation, when compared to strategies labeled "therapist-responsible," such as therapist–couple interaction, therapist interpretation, and direct instruction. Couples therapists were randomly assigned to use one of the two methods in therapy sessions. Couples ratings indicated that perceived responsibility was higher and conflict lower when therapists employed couple-responsible strategies. These types of studies help family intervention researchers understand not only *if* certain types and aspects of therapy are effective, but *how* and *by what means* these therapies create change.

The Therapeutic Alliance

Process research has been applied most frequently to the study of *therapeutic alliance*. A positive alliance,

defined in terms of a client's willingness to talk openly and freely with a therapist and to work jointly with the therapist to address the client's problems (Robbins et al., 2006), is considered essential in keeping clients engaged in therapeutic activity and reducing the likelihood of premature termination. Process research in this area asks the question, "What makes for good alliances with couples and families?" (Alexander, Robbins & Sexton, 2000). In a review of the past forty years of family research, Friedlander, Escudero, and Heatherington (2006) conclude that a large body of studies supports the importance of the therapeutic alliance in leading to both therapy continuation and positive outcomes. Another recent review of 19 studies of therapeutic alliance concluded that the therapeutic alliance is an integral aspect of family counseling (Mahaffey & Granello, 2007). However, this review also noted that many studies lacked diversity in participant demographics and treatment sources, and none of the studies reviewed addressed the role of therapist experience and setting as they affect the formation of alliances.

In an attempt to address these criticisms, a number of researchers have developed methods for tracking the formation and outcome of therapeutic alliances across diverse family groups, while others have focused on analyzing the mechanisms by which a positive alliance leads to positive outcomes. Process researchers have studied the effects of specific therapist strategies on improving alliance in family therapy. Diamond, Liddle, Hogue, and Dakoff (1999) found that significant gains in working alliance were more evident when the therapist attended to an adolescent's experience, formulated personally meaningful goals, and acted as the adolescent's ally. Lack of improvement or deterioration in alliance was associated with the therapist spending too much time explaining the nature of therapy and waiting too long to discuss how the therapy could be personally meaningful for the teenager.

The alliance between therapist and client can also be affected by cultural and demographic concerns. Jackson-Gilfort, Liddle, Tejeda, and Dakof (2001) found that the discussion of culturally specific themes enhanced treatment engagement of African American male substance-abusing youth. Exploration of particular themes in one session, including anger and rage, alienation, and the meaning of the journey from boyhood to manhood as an African American man, were associated with both increased participation and decreased negativity by adolescents.

The therapeutic alliance is more complicated in family therapy because of the need to form multiple alliances. For example, working with family psychoeducation interventions for relatives of individuals with schizophrenia, Smerud and Rosenfarb (2008) found that a positive alliance with the therapist was correlated with fewer signs of relapse and lower likelihood of rehospitalization for the patient. Further, relatives who developed a positive alliance with the therapist were less rejecting and less likely to feel burdened.

Garfield's (2004) review of research on alliance in couples therapy corroborated the findings of previous reviews, noting that the alliance is predictive of treatment outcomes across a variety of individual therapeutic approaches. Further, Garfield provided a number of helpful recommendations for working with couples with a variety of problems. He identified three dimensions affecting the therapeutic alliance—the loyalty dimension, the impact of couples' early family-of-origin experiences, and the impact of couples' gender concerns—and presented empirical rationales and clinical considerations related to each dimension.

However, conceptualizing the alliance as an aspect of the relationship between clients and therapists overlooks crucial aspects of clients' experience of the alliance. Recent research on integrative psychotherapy alliance models (see Chapter 14) highlights the importance of considering and measuring the systemic alliances within couples and families (Pinsof, Zinbarg, & Knobloch-Fedders, 2008). In other words, the alliances, coalitions, and splits that can form within families have a significant effect on treatment outcome. In many cases, these outcomes are negative, as when angry adolescents refuse to cooperate with therapists because they see the therapist as on their parents' side. However, Friedlander, Escudero, and Heatherington (2006) note that the multiple alliances of family therapy can also be beneficial, as when

strong therapist-parent alliances lead to improvements in parenting skills.

Recently, Escudero, Friedlander, Varela, and Abascal (2008) found that families' sense of having a Shared Sense of Purpose (one aspect of Friedlander et al.'s 2006 System for Observing Family Therapy Alliances, or SOFTA) was consistently associated with perceptions of progress in therapy. In another study utilizing SOFTA, Friedlander, Lambert, and de la Pena (2008) found in a sample of low-income, multiproblem families that feeling safe in the therapeutic environment with other family members led to productive family collaboration, which in turn resulted in symptom improvement and perceived progress in therapy.

An examination of the alliance-building process in MDFT found that adolescents were more likely to complete treatment when therapists had stronger relationships with their parents. Additionally, stronger therapeutic relationships with adolescents were associated with greater decreases in their drug use but only when the therapeutic alliance with the parent was also strong (Shelef, Diamond, Diamond, & Liddle, 2005).

These and other studies of the alliance in family therapy have yielded clinically important findings. Currently, researchers are attempting to use observational tools to examine the links between the therapeutic relationship and outcomes in family therapy, but much more work needs to be done in this area of family intervention.

Critical Events and Change Points

Process research has also focused on focal events during therapy that appear to usher in significant changes in family interaction. *Change event analysis* (Woolley, Butler, & Wampler, 2000) requires researchers to identify likely critical events and determine whether these events do, in fact, lead to important changes in interaction or problem resolution.

Friedlander, Heatherington, Johnson, and Skowron (1994) identified structural family therapy cases in which families had been able to move successfully from disengagement to engagement (for a review of structural family therapy, see Chapter 7). Using an inductive approach, they identified events where engagement was successfully sustained during the sessions. Although no consistent pattern characterized the resolution of each family's impasse, periods of sustained engagement generally involved active solicitation by the therapist of each family member's thoughts and feelings about the impasse and the benefits of reengagement and therapist strategies aimed at helping family members hear each other's point of view. Similarly, Greenberg, Ford, Alden, and Johnson (1993) compared peak to poor session events during emotion-focused couples therapy. Peak events were more frequently characterized by affiliative, self-disclosing statements and accepting statements by partners. Therapist facilitation of self-disclosure in one partner led to increased likelihood that the other partner would respond with an affiliative statement.

Michael Nichols and his students have studied highly trained and experienced family therapists (Nichols & Fellenberg, 2000), focusing on the use of enactments. Their findings indicate that breaking through family conflict and helping families shift their relational stance is a complex process that requires active, directive facilitation by the therapist. Essential ingredients of successful enactments include preparing the family prior to the enactment, specifying an agenda and explaining the need for dialogue, giving directions about how the discussion should go, avoiding unnecessary interruption, pushing family members to work harder during the enactment, and closing by providing clients with clear direction on how to communicate with each other.

Additional studies by this group have demonstrated that the most effective sessions of family therapy appear to be those in which therapists establish a clear and focused systemic goal (e.g., helping to overcome parental disengagement, rather than just working on parenting techniques) while intensely pushing for change to occur within the session (Favero, 2002; Fellenberg, 2003; Miles, 2004). However, Hammond and Nichols (2008) found that an empathic therapeutic alliance was a prerequisite to making these focused and forceful interventions effective. That is, focused and forceful intervening seems to be important in producing change in family therapy, but family members appear more willing to accept such

forceful challenges when the therapist has established an empathic bond with them.

Diamond and Liddle (1996, 1999) used task analysis of MDFT sessions to identify interventions likely to resolve in-session impasses involving negative exchange, emotional disengagement, and poor problem solving. Successful interventions included actively blocking or addressing and working through negative affect and evoking thoughts and feelings that promote constructive dialogue. A kind of "shuttle diplomacy" also proved fruitful, where therapists created emotional treaties among family members by working in alternate sessions with parents alone and adolescents alone. In cases with a successful resolution of the impasse, the therapist was able to transform the nature and tone of the interaction, shifting the parent from blaming to feelings of regret and loss and eliciting the adolescent's thoughts and feelings about relationship roadblocks with parents and others.

Summary.   Process studies have clarified a number of therapeutic strategies that contribute to effective family therapy. Approaches that emphasize building of alliances through understanding and supporting the goals of family members are likely to increase engagement and reduce dropout. The alliance between therapists and clients is an important contributor to positive outcomes, but recent research has also highlighted the importance of focusing on the alliances among members of a family. Lastly, the results of critical event studies suggest that change events are facilitated when the therapist moves family members to a more vulnerable, self-disclosing level and helps other family members to listen and respond.

CONCLUSIONS AND FUTURE DIRECTIONS

Our review of family-focused interventions strongly supports the basic underlying principle of family therapy: that family relationships are important targets for clinical interventions designed to treat a range of emotional and behavioral problems. The application of this principle has evolved over the past few decades, as therapists and program developers have attempted to apply it in a growing number of contexts. The parallel growth of scientific methods for testing the effects of interventions and studying intervention processes has led to a large and growing body of research on the effectiveness of these efforts.

Some areas of intervention have been studied longer and in greater detail, allowing more confidence in findings and more attention to how and when particular forms of intervention are likely to be most effective. These areas include family and parent therapy and family-focused prevention programs for childhood externalizing problems, family psychoeducational programs for major mental illness, parent-focused programs for insecure attachment and reduction of child maltreatment, behavioral marital therapy and emotion-focused marital therapy for marital conflict, and communication training programs in preparation for marriage or long-term commitment.

Research supports the effectiveness of family-focused interventions in each of these areas but also raises important concerns about the limits of current interventions. For example, some family-focused interventions for child maltreatment may be more successful at changing parental attitudes than in changing parental behavior, and reactive interventions had initial effects that tended to fade over time. Fading effectiveness may also be a concern with couples therapy. These findings are limited by the absence of long-term follow-ups in the majority of studies and point to the importance of such follow-ups in future work.

Empirical tests of other areas of family-focused intervention are less advanced, but the findings are often promising. These include couples therapy for depression in individuals who are also experiencing marital distress, family engagement in treatment of alcohol abuse, and programs to help families weather adversity and high-risk transitions such as divorce, remarriage, and late-life palliative care. Findings from these programs suggest that family-focused interventions hold particular promise for supporting emotional development and preventing the destructive effects of major life stressors on emotional functioning, including severe emotional disorders.

However, insufficient rigorous trials have been conducted to provide full confidence in these programs' effectiveness and to clarify which families are most likely to benefit.

Research has also advanced in studying the specific strategies and techniques that lead to effective intervention, although this work is still at a relatively early stage and no meta-analytic reviews were found in this area. Alliance building through sensitivity to the goals of family members and facilitation of change during family sessions have received the most attention. Heatherington, Friedlander, and Greenberg (2005) note that this area would benefit from more integration with theories of family change process.

We end by noting two issues that will be important in the next stage of this work. First, it is becoming clear that our understanding of emotional and behavioral problems must be placed in developmental perspective. The emergence of developmental psychopathology as a framework for understanding how disorders develop, are maintained, and are resolved or recur over the lifespan has become a guiding framework for those interested in preventing or treating them (Howe, Reiss, & Yuh, 2004). Families play a central role in both normal and problematic development. Family-focused interventions informed by developmental research and theory are an increasingly critical part of our intervention tool kit and already guide many of the programs reviewed here.

Second, many of the family-focused interventions we reviewed here have attempted to influence family relationships through working with individual family members or with dyads. This approach has been effective but leaves open the questions of when and how we need to work with larger groupings, including family households and extended family groups, to effect change. A few trials have given hints that systemic and multisystemic approaches may be essential to bring about long-term change, but other trials have failed to find much added value in more intensive interventions. It's clear that many families benefit from more limited problem-focused interventions with individuals or dyads, but we suspect that other families will require more in-depth systemic approaches to bring about lasting benefit.

Questions to Consider

1. What are some of the concepts and techniques you've read about in this book that you think are most in need of empirical evaluation?
2. What are some of the practical difficulties of evaluating the effectiveness of experienced family therapists practicing sophisticated clinical work—as opposed to therapists in training, following manualized approaches?
3. What are some of the dangers inherent in being guided by evidence-based practices?
4. What are the relative merits of outcome studies versus process studies, and which are likely to have more impact on insurance companies? On practicing therapists?

Key Concepts

comparison groups   Alternative treatment approaches or no-treatment control groups.

cost-benefit analysis   Evaluation of the relative expense of treatment versus the consequences of no treatment.

externalizing disorders   Disorders that are expressed in outward, often aggressive, behavior.

internalizing disorders   Disorders that are expressed in subjective symptoms, such as anxiety or depression.

mediating variables   Extraneous factors that can influence the impact of treatments under study.

meta-analysis   Using statistical analysis to combine the results from a number of studies and to estimate an overall treatment effect size.

outcome research   Studies designed to test how well treatments lead to desired outcomes, such as symptomatic improvement and prevention of relapse.

process research   Studies designed to explore which therapeutic activities lead to in-session consequence, such as improving the therapeutic alliance or leading to more productive in-session enactments.

program manuals   Carefully spelled out guidelines used to ensure uniform application of treatments under study.

randomized clinical trials   Testing new treatments by randomly assigning patients to experimental or control conditions.

Recommended Readings

Barbato, A., and D'Avanzo, B. 2008. Efficacy of couples therapy as a treatment for depression: A meta-analysis. *Psychiatric Quarterly, 79*(2): 121–132.

Blanchard, V. L., Hawkins, A. J., Baldwin, S. A., & Fawcett, E. B. 2009. Investigating the effects of marriage and relationship education on couples' communication skills: A meta-analytic study. *Journal of Family Psychology, 23*(2): 203–214.

Carr, A. 2009. The effectiveness of family therapy and systemic interventions for child-focused problems. *Journal of Family Therapy, 31*: 3–45.

Carr, A. 2009. The effectiveness of family therapy and systemic interventions for adult-focused problems. *Journal of Family Therapy, 31*: 46–74.

The Cochrane Collaboration: Cochrane Reviews. http://www.cochrane.org/index.htm.

Friedlander, M.L., Escudero, V., and Heatherington, L. 2006. *Therapeutic alliances in couple and family therapy: An empirically informed guide to practice.* Washington, DC: American Psychological Association.

Pinsof, W. M., and Lebow, J. L. (Eds.). 2005. *Family psychology: The art of the science.* New York: Oxford University Press.

Stith, S., and Rosen, K. 2003. Effectiveness of couples treatment for spouse abuse. *Journal of Marital and Family Therapy,* 29(3): 407–426.

References

AACAP. 2005. Practice parameters for the assessment and treatment of children and adolescents with reactive attachment disorder of infancy and early childhood. *Journal of the American Academy of Child and Adolescent Psychiatry.* 44(11): 1206–1219.

Alexander, J. F., Robbins, M. S., and Sexton, T. L. 2000. Family-based interventions with older, at-risk youth: From promise to proof to practice. *The Journal of Primary Prevention. 21:* 185–205.

Allen-Eckert, H., Fong, E., Nichols, M. P., Watson, N., and Liddle, H. A. 2001. Development of the Family Therapy Enactment Scale. *Family Process. 40*(4): 469–478.

Amato, P. R. 2001. Children of divorce in the 1990s: An update of the Amato and Keith (1991) meta-analysis. *Journal of Family Psychology. 15*(3): 355–370.

Amato, P. R., and Keith, B. 1991. Parental divorce and adult well-being: A meta-analysis. *Journal of Marriage & the Family. 53*(1): 43–58.

American Psychiatric Association. 2000. *Diagnostic and statistical manual of mental disorders* (text revision). Washington, DC: Author.

Babcock, J. C., Green, C. E., and Robie, C. 2004. Does batterers' treatment work? A meta-analytic review of domestic violence treatment. *Clinical Psychology Review.* 23(8): 1023.

Baer, J. C., and Martinez, C. D. 2006. Child maltreatment and insecure attachment: A meta-analysis. *Journal of Reproductive and Infant Psychology, 24*(3): 187–197.

Barbato, A., and D'Avanzo, B. 2008. Efficacy of couples therapy as a treatment for depression: A meta-analysis. *Psychiatric Quarterly, 79*(2): 121–132.

Barkley, R. 2005. *Attention deficit hyperactivity disorder: A handbook for diagnosis and treatment* (3rd ed.).New York: Guilford Press.

Barmish, A., and Kendall, P. 2005. Should parents be co-clients in cognitive-behavioral therapy for anxious youth? *Journal of Clinical Child and Adolescent Psychology, 34:* 569–581.

Beach, S. R. H., Wamboldt, M. Z., Kaslow, N. J., Heyman, R. R., and Reiss, D. 2006. Describing relationship problems in DSM-V: Toward better guidance for research and clinical practice. *Journal of Family Psychology. 20:* 353–355.

Beck, C. J., and Sales, B. D. 2001. Future mediation theory. In *Family mediation: Facts, myths, and future prospects* (pp. 181–204). Washington, DC: American Psychological Association.

Beck, C. J., Sales, B. D., and Emery, R. E. 2004. Research on the impact of family mediation. In *Divorce and family mediation: Models, techniques, and applications* (pp. 447–482), J. Folberg, A. L. Milne, and P. Salem, eds. New York: Guilford Press.

Becker, S. J., and Curry, J. F. 2008. Outpatient interventions for adolescent substance abuse: A quality of evidence review. *Journal of Consulting and Clinical Psychology, 76*(4): 531–543.

Benjamin, M., and Irving, H. H. 1995. Research in family mediation: Review and implications. *Mediation Quarterly. 13*(1): 53–82.

Birmaher, B., Brent, D., Kolko, D., Baugher, M., Bridge, J., Holder, D., Iyengar, S., and Ulloa, R. 2000. Clinical outcome after short-term psychotherapy for adolescents with Major Depressive Disorder. *Archives of General Psychiatry, 57*(1): 29–36.

Blanchard, V. L., Hawkins, A. J., Baldwin, S. A., and Fawcett, E. B. 2009. Investigating the effects of marriage and relationship education on couples' communication skills: A meta-analytic study. *Journal of Family Psychology, 23*(2): 203–214.

Bowlby, J. 1977. The making and breaking of affectional bonds: I. Aetiology and psychopathology in the light of attachment theory. *British Journal of Psychiatry. 130:* 201–210.

Braver, S. L., Griffin, W. A., Cookston, J. T., Sandler, I. N., Williams, J., Wolchik, S. A., Winslow, E., and Smith-Daniels, V. 2005. Programs for promoting parenting of residential parents: Moving from efficacy to effectiveness. In *Family psychology: The art of the science* (pp. 295–324). New York: Oxford University Press.

Bray, J. H. 1995. Systems-oriented therapy with stepfamilies. In *Integrating family therapy: Handbook of family psychology and systems theory* (pp. 125–140), R. H. Mikesell, D.-D. Lusterman, and S. H. McDaniel, eds. Washington, DC: American Psychological Association.

Brosnan, R., and Carr, A. 2000. Adolescent conduct problems. In *What works with children and adolescents?: A critical review of psychological interventions with children, adolescents, and their families* (pp. 131–154), A. Carr, ed. Florence, KY: Taylor & Francis/Routledge.

Brown, G. W., and Harris, T. O. (Eds.). 1978. *Social origins of depression: A study of psychiatric disorder in women.* London: Tavistock.

Brunk, M., Hengeller, S., and Whelan, J. 1987. Comparison of multi-systemic therapy and parent training in the brief treatment of child abuse and neglect. *Journal of Consulting and Clinical Psychology, 55*(2): 171–178.

Bullock, B. M., and Forgatch, M. S. 2005. Mothers in transition: Model-based strategies for effective parenting, *Family psychology: The art of the science* (pp. 349–371). New York: Oxford University Press.

Burck, C., Frosh, S., Lisa, S.-C., and Morgan, K. 1998. The process of enabling change: A study of therapist interventions in family therapy. *Journal of Family Therapy. 20*(3): 253–267.

Butler, M. H., and Wampler, K. S. 1999. Couple-responsible therapy process: Positive proximal outcomes. *Family Process. 38*(1): 27–54.

Byng-Hall, J. 1995. Rewriting family scripts. Improvisation and change. New York: Guilford.

Byrne, M., Carr, A., and Clark, M. 2004. The efficacy of behavioral couples therapy and emotionally focused therapy for couple distress. *Contemporary Family Therapy: An International Journal. 26*(4): 361–387.

Carr, A. 2009. The effectiveness of family therapy and systemic interventions for child-focused problems. *Journal of Family Therapy, 31*: 3–45.

Carr, A. 2009. The effectiveness of family therapy and systemic interventions for adult-focused problems. *Journal of Family Therapy, 31*: 46–74.

Carroll, J. S., and Doherty, W. J. 2003. Evaluating the effectiveness of premarital prevention programs: A meta-analytic review of outcome research. *Family Relations: Interdisciplinary Journal of Applied Family Studies. 52*(2): 105–118.

Chaffin, M., Hanson, R., Saunders, B. E., Nichols, T., Barnett, D., Zeanah, C., Berliner, L., Egeland, B.,

Newman, E., Lyon, T., LeTourneau, E., and Miller-Perrin, C. 2006. Report of the APSAC Task Force on attachment therapy, Reactive Attachment Disorder, and attachment problems. *Child Maltreatment. 11*(1): 76–89.

Chamberlain, P., and Rosicky, J. G. 1995. The effectiveness of family therapy in the treatment of adolescents with conduct disorders and delinquency. *Journal of Marital and Family Therapy. 21*(4): 441–459.

Christensen, A., Atkins, D., Yi, J., Baucom, D., and George, W. 2006. Couple and individual adjustment for 2 years following a randomized clinical trial comparing traditional versus integrative behavioral couple therapy. *Journal of Consulting and Clinical Psychology, 74*(4): 1180–1191.

Chronis, A. M., Jones, H. A., and Raggi, V. L. 2006. Evidence-based psychosocial treatments for children and adolescents with attention-deficit/hyperactivity disorder. *Clinical Psychology Review. 26*(4): 486–502.

Cicchetti, D., and Toth, S. L. 2005. Child maltreatment. *Annual Review of Clinical Psychology. 1*(1): 409–438.

Conger, R. D., and Elder, G. H. 1994. *Families in troubled times: adapting to change in rural America.* New York: Aldine de Gruyter.

Corcoran, J., and Dattalo, P. 2006. Parent involvement in treatment for ADHD: A meta-analysis of the published studies. *Research on Social Work Practice. 16*(6): 561–570.

Corcoran, J., and Pillai, V. 2008. A meta-analysis for parent-involved treatment for child sexual abuse. *Research on Social Work Practice, 18*(5): 453–464.

Cowan, C. P., and Cowan, P. A. 1992. *When partners become parents: The big life change for couples.* New York: Basic Books.

Cowan, C. P., Cowan, P. A., and Heming, G. 2005. Two variations of a preventive intervention for couples: Effects on parents and children during the transition to school. In *The family context of parenting in children's adaptation to elementary school* (pp. 277–312), P. A. Cowan, C. P. Cowan, J. C. Ablow, V. K. Johnson, and J. R. Measelle, eds. Mahwah, NJ: Erlbaum.

Crane, D., Hillin, H., and Jakubowski, S. 2005. Costs of treating conduct disordered Medicaid youth with and without family therapy. *American Journal of Family Therapy. 33*(5): 403–413.

Currier, J. M., Neimeyer, R. A., and Berman, J. S. 2008. The effectiveness of psychotherapeutic interventions for bereaved persons: A comprehensive quantitative review. *Psychological Bulletin, 134*(5): 648–661.

Curtis, N., Ronan, K., and Borduin, C. 2004. Multisystemic treatment: a meta-analysis of outcome studies. *Journal of Family Psychology, 18*(3): 411–419.

Diamond, G., and Liddle, H. A. 1996. Resolving a therapeutic impasse between parents and adolescents in multidimensional family therapy. *Journal of Consulting and Clinical Psychology.* 64(3): 481–488.

Diamond, G., and Liddle, H. A. 1999. Transforming negative parent–adolescent interactions: From impasse to dialogue. *Family Process.* 38(1): 5–26.

Diamond, G., Liddle, H. A., Hogue, A., and Dakof, G. A. 1999. Alliance-building interventions with adolescents in family therapy: A process study. *Psychotherapy: Theory, Research, Practice, Training.* 36(4): 355–368.

Edleson, J. L., and Tolman, R. M. 1992. *Intervention for men who batter: An ecological approach.* Thousand Oaks, CA: Sage.

Edwards, M. E., and Steinglass, P. 1995. Family therapy treatment outcomes for alcoholism. *Journal of Marital and Family Therapy.* 21(4): 475–509.

Emery, R. E., Laumann-Billings, L., Waldron, M. C., Sbarra, D. A., and Dillon, P. 2001. Child custody mediation and litigation: Custody, contact, and coparenting 12 years after initial dispute resolution. *Journal of Consulting and Clinical Psychology.* 69(2): 323–332.

Emery, R. E., and Wyer, M. M. 1987. Child custody mediation and litigation: An experimental evaluation of the experience of parents. *Journal of Consulting and Clinical Psychology.* 55: 179–186.

Escudero, V., Friedlander, M.L., Varela, N., and Abascal, A. 2008. Observing the therapeutic alliance in family therapy: Associations with participants' perceptions and therapeutic outcomes. *Journal of Family Therapy.* 30(2): 194–214.

Falbo, T., Lein, L., and Amador, N. A. 2001. Parental involvement during the transition to high school. *Journal of Adolescent Research.* 16(5): 511–529.

Fals-Stewart, W., O'Farrell, T.J., and Birchler, G.R. 1997. Behavioral couples therapy for male substance abusing patients: A cost outcomes analysis. *Journal of Consulting and Clinical Psychology,* 65: 789–802.

Fals-Stewart, W., Yates, B. T., and Klostermann, K. 2005. Assessing the costs, benefits, cost-benefit ratio, and cost-effectiveness of marital and family treatments: Why we should and how we can. *Journal of Family Psychology.* 19(1): 28–39.

Favero, D. 2002. Structural enactments as methods of change in family therapy. Unpublished doctoral dissertation, Virginia Consortium Program in Clinical Psychology, Virginia Beach.

Feinberg, M. E. and Kan, M. L. 2008. Establishing family foundations: Intervention effects on coparenting, parent/infant well-being, and parent-child relations. *Journal of Family Psychology,* 22(2): 253–263.

Fellenberg, S. 2003. The contribution of enactments to structural family therapy: A process study. Unpublished doctoral dissertation, Virginia Consortium Program in Clinical Psychology, Virginia Beach.

Forgatch, M. S., and DeGarmo, D. S. 1999. Parenting through change: An effective prevention program for single mothers. *Journal of Consulting & Clinical Psychology.* 67(5): 711–724.

Forgatch, M. S., DeGarmo, D. S., and Beldavs, Z. G. 2005. An efficacious theory-based intervention for stepfamilies. *Behavior Therapy.* 36(4): 357–365.

Friedlander, M. L., Escudero, V., and Heatherington, L. 2006. Therapeutic alliances in couple and family therapy: An empirically informed guide to practice. Washington, DC: American Psychological Association.

Friedlander, M. L., Heatherington, L., Johnson, B., and Skowron, E. A. 1994. Sustaining engagement: A change event in family therapy. *Journal of Counseling Psychology.* 41(4): 438–448.

Friedlander, M. L., Lambert, J. E., and de la Pena, C.M. 2008. A step toward disentangling the alliance/improvement cycle in family therapy. *Journal of Counseling Psychology.* 55(1): 118–124.

Garfield, R. 2004. The therapeutic alliance in couples therapy: Clinical considerations. *Family Process.* 43(4): 457–465.

Geerart, L., Van den Noortgate, W., Grietens, H., and Onghena, P. 2004. The effects of early prevention programs for families with young children at risk for physical child abuse and neglect: A meta-analysis. *Child Maltreatment,* 9(3): 277–291.

Gilliam, C., and Cottone, R. 2005. Couple or individual therapy for the treatment of depression?: An update of the empirical literature. *American Journal of Family Therapy.* 33(3): 265–272.

Glade, A. C., Bean, R. A., and Vira, R. 2005. A prime time for marital/relational intervention: A review of the transition to parenthood literature with treatment recommendations. *American Journal of Family Therapy.* 33(4): 319–336.

Greenberg, L. S., Ford, C. L., Alden, L. S., and Johnson, S. M. 1993. In-session change in emotionally focused therapy. *Journal of Consulting and Clinical Psychology.* 61(1): 78–84.

Hammond, R., and Nichols, M. P. 2008. How collaborative is structural family therapy? *The Family Journal: Counseling and Therapy for Couples and Family.* 16(2): 118–124.

Hanson, R. F., and Spratt, E. G. 2000. Reactive attachment disorder: What we know about the disorder and implications for treatment. *Child Maltreatment.* 5(2): 137–145.

Hawkins, A. J., Blanchard, V. L., Baldwin, S. A., Fawcett, E. B. 2008. Does marriage and relationship education work? A meta-analytic study. *Journal of Consulting and Clinical Psychology,* 76(5): 723–734.

Heatherington, L., Friedlander, M. L., and Greenberg, L. 2005. Change process research in couple and family therapy: Methodological challenges and opportunities. *Journal of Family Psychology.* 19(1): 18–27.

Herschell, A. D., and McNeil, C. B. 2005. Theoretical and empirical underpinnings of parent–child interaction therapy with child physical abuse populations. *Education and Treatment of Children.* 28(2): 142–162.

Higginson, I. J., Finlay, I. G., Goodwin, D. M., Hood, K., Edwards, A. G., Cook, A., Douglas, H.-R., and Normand, C. E. 2003. Is there evidence that palliative care teams alter end-of-life experiences of patients and their caregivers? *Journal of Pain and Symptom Management.* 25(2): 150–168.

Hogue, A., Dauber, S., Chinchilla, P., Fried, A., Henderson, C., Inclan, J., et al. 2008. Assessing fidelity in individual and family therapy for adolescent substance abuse. *Journal of Substance Abuse Treatment.* 35(2): 137–147.

Howe, G. W., Levy, M. L., and Caplan, R. D. 2004. Job loss and depressive symptoms in couples: Common stressors, stress transmission, or relationship disruption? *Journal of Family Psychology.* 18: 639–650.

Howe, G. W., Reiss, D., and Yuh, J. 2004. Can prevention trials test theories of etiology? *Development & Psychopathology.* 14(4): 673–694.

Jackson-Gilfort, A., Liddle, H. A., Tejeda, M. J., and Dakof, G. A. 2001. Facilitating engagement of African American male adolescents in family therapy: A cultural theme process study. *Journal of Black Psychology.* 27(3): 321–340.

Jacobson, N. S., Dobson, K., Fruzzetti, A. E., Schmailing, K. B., and Salusky, S. 1991. Marital therapy as a treatment for depression. *Journal of Consulting & Clinical Psychology.* 59(4): 547.

Jensen, P., Arnold, L., Swanson, J., Vitiello, B., Abikoff, H., and Greenhill, L., 2007. 3-year follow-up of the NIMH MTA study. *Journal of the American Academy of Child and Adolescent Psychiatry,* 46: 989–1002.

Johnston, C., and Mash, E. J. 2001. Families of children with Attention-Deficit/Hyperactivity Disorder: Review and recommendations for future research. *Clinical Child and Family Psychology Review.* 4(3): 183–207.

Kaslow, F. 1995. The dynamics of divorce therapy. In *Integrating family therapy. Handbook of family psychology and systems theory* (pp. 271–284), R. H. Mikesell, D.-D. Lusterman, and S. H. McDaniel, eds. Washington, DC: American Psychological Association.

Kazdin, A. E., and Weisz, J. R. 1998. Identifying and developing empirically supported child and adolescent treatments. *Journal of Consulting & Clinical Psychology.* 66(1): 19.

Kendler, K. S., Hettema, J. M., Butera, F., Gardner, C. O., and Prescott, C. A. 2003. Life event dimensions of loss, humiliation, entrapment, and danger in the prediction of onsets of major depression and generalized anxiety. *Archives of General Psychiatry.* 60(8): 789–796.

Kermeen, P. 1995. Improving postpartum marital relationships. *Psychological Reports.* 76(3, Pt. 1): 831–834.

Kissane, D. W., McKenzie, M., Block, S., Moskowitz, C., McKenzie, D. P., and O'Neill, I. 2006. Family focused grief therapy: A randomized, controlled trial in palliative care and bereavement. *American Journal of Psychiatry.* 163(7): 1208–1218.

Liddle, H. A., Dakof, G. A., Parker, K., Diamond, G. S., Barrett, K., and Tejeda, M. 2001. Multidimensional family therapy for adolescent drug abuse: Results of a randomized clinical trial. *American Journal of Drug and Alcohol Abuse.* 27(4): 651.

Luborsky, L., Singer, B., and Luborsky, L. 1975. Comparative studies of psychotherapies: Is it true that "Everyone has won and all must have prizes? *Clinical Psychology: Science and Practice.* 2: 106–109.

Lundahl, B. W., Nimer, J., and Parsons, B. 2006. Preventing child abuse: A meta-analysis of parent training programs. *Research on Social Work Practice.* 16(3): 251–262.

Macleod, J., and Nelson, G. 2000. Programs for the promotion of family wellness and the prevention of child maltreatment: A meta-analytic review. *Child Abuse and Neglect.* 24(9): 1127–1149.

Mahaffey, B.A., and Granello, P.F. 2007. Therapeutic alliance: A review of sampling strategies reported in marital and family therapy studies. *The Family Journal.* 15(3): 207–216.

Main, M., and Solomon, J. 1990. Procedures for identifying infants as disorganized/disoriented during the Ainsworth Strange Situation. In *Attachment in the preschool years: Theory, research, and intervention* (pp. 121–160), M. T. Greenberg, D. Cicchetti, and M. E. Cummings, eds. Chicago: University of Chicago Press.

Markman, H. J., Renick, M. J., Floyd, F. J., Stanley, S. M., and Clements, M. 1993. Preventing marital distress through communication and conflict management training: A 4- and 5-year follow-up. *Journal of Consulting and Clinical Psychology. 61*(1): 70–77.

McCart, M., Priester, P., Davies, W., and Azen, R. 2006. Differential effectiveness of cognitive-behavioral therapy and behavioral parent-training for antisocial youth: A meta-analysis. *Journal of Abnormal Child Psychology, 34:* 527–543.

McTaggart, P., and Sanders, M. R. 2003. The Transition to School Project: Results from the classroom. *AeJAMH (Australian e-Journal for the Advancement of Mental Health). 2*(3): n.p.

Meston, C. 2006. Female orgasmic disorder: treatment strategies and outcome results. In *Women's Sexual Function and Dysfunction: Study, Diagnosis, & Treatment*. I. Goldstein, C. Meston, S. Davis, and A. Traish (Eds.), pp. 449–461. London: Taylor & Francis.

Meston, C., and Bradford, A. 2007. Sexual dysfunctions in women. *Annual Review of Clinical Psychology. 3,* 233–256.

Miklowitz, D. J. 2004. The role of family systems in severe and recurrent psychiatric disorders: A developmental psychopathology view. *Development and Psychopathology. 16*(3): 667–688.

Miles, D. 2004. The effectiveness of therapist interventions in structural family therapy: A process study. Unpublished doctoral dissertation, Virginia Consortium Program in Clinical Psychology, Virginia Beach.

Muck, R., Zempolich, K. A., Titus, J. C., Fishman, M., Godley, M. D., and Schwebel, R. 2001. An overview of the effectiveness of adolescent substance abuse treatment models. *Youth and Society. 33:* 143–168.

Murray, C. E. 2006. Controversy, constraints, and context: Understanding family violence through family systems theory. *Family Journal: Counseling and Therapy for Couples and Families. 14*(3): 234–239.

Nichols, M. P., and Fellenberg, S. (2000). The effective use of enactments in family therapy: A discovery- oriented process study. *Journal of Marital & Family Therapy. 26*(2): 143–152.

Nicholson, J. M., and Sanders, M. R. 1999. Randomized controlled trial of behavioral family intervention for the treatment of child behavior problems in stepfamilies. *Journal of Divorce & Remarriage. 30*(3–4): 1–23.

O'Farrell, T. J., Choquette, K. A., Cutter, H. S. G., Brown, E. D., Bayog, R., McCourt, W., et al. 1996a. Cost-benefit and cost-effectiveness analyses of behavioral marital therapy with and without relapse prevention sessions for alcoholics and their spouses. *Behavior Therapy. 27:* 7–24.

O'Farrell, T. J., Choquette, K. A., Cutter, H. S. G., Floyd, F. J., Bayog, R. D., Brown, E. D., et al. 1996b. Cost-benefit and cost-effectiveness analyses of behavioral marital therapy as an addition to outpatient alcoholism treatment. *Journal of Substance Abuse. 8:* 145–166.

O'Farrell, T. J., and Fals-Stewart, W. 2003. Alcohol abuse. *Journal of Marital and Family Therapy. 29*(1): 121–146.

O'Leary, K., and Vega, E. M. 2005. Can partner aggression be stopped with psychosocial interventions? In *Family psychology: The art of the science.* (vol. 18, pp. 243–263), W. M. Pinsof and J. L. Lebow, eds., New York: Oxford University Press.

Patterson, G. 1976. *Living with Children.* Champaign, Il: Research Press.

Peterson, L., Tremblay, G., Ewigman, B., and Saldana, L. 2003. Multilevel selected primary prevention of child maltreatment. *Journal of Consulting and Clinical Psychology. 71:*601–612.

Pfammatter, M., Junghan, U., and Brenner, H. 2006. Efficacy of psychological therapy in schizophrenia: conclusions from meta-analyses. *Schizophrenia Bulletin. 32*(Suppl. 1): S64–S80.

Pilling, S., Bebbington, P., Kuipers, E., Farety, P., Geddes, J., Orbach, G., and Morgan, C. 2002. Psychological treatments in schizophrenia: I. Meta-analysis of family intervention and cognitive behavior therapy. *Psychological Medicine. 32:* 763–782.

Pinsof, W. M., Zinbarg, R., and Knobloch-Fedders, L. M. 2008. Factorial and construct validity of the revised short form Integrative Psychotherapy Alliance Scales for family, couple, and individual therapy. *Family Process. 47*(3): 281–301.

Pitschel-Walz, G., Leucht, S., Bäuml, J., Kissling, W., and Engel, R. 2001. The effect of family interventions on relapse and rehospitalization in schizophrenia - a meta-analysis. *Schizophrenia Bulletin. 27:* 73–92.

Prado, G., Pantin, H., Briones, E., Schwartz, S. J., Feaster, D., Huang, S., Sullivan, S., Tapia, M.I., Sabillon, E., Lopez, B., and Szapocsnik, J. 2007. A randomized controlled trial of a parent-centered intervention in preventing substance use and HIV risk behaviors in Hispanic adolescents. *Journal of Consulting and Clinical Psychology. 75:* 914–926.

Prinz, R. J., Sanders, M. R., Shapiro, C. J., Whitaker, D. J., and Lutzker, J. R. 2009. Population-based prevention of child maltreatment: The U.S. Triple P system population trial. *Prevention Science.* 10, 1–12.

Ralph, A., and Sanders, M. R. 2003. Preliminary evaluation of the Group Teen Triple P program for parents of teenagers making the transition to high school. *Australian e-Journal for the Advancement of Mental Health. 2*(3): 1–10.

Robbins, M. S., Alexander, J. F., Newell, R. M., and Turner, C. W. 1996. The immediate effect of reframing on client attitude in family therapy. *Journal of Family Psychology. 10*(1): 28–34.

Robbins, M. S., Liddle, H. A., Turner, C. W., Dakof, G. A., Alexander, J. F., and Kogan, S. M. 2006. Adolescent and parent therapeutic alliances as predictors of dropout in Multidimensional Family Therapy. *Journal of Family Psychology. 20*(1): 108–116.

Rosenfield, B. D. (1992). Court-ordered treatment of spouse abuse. *Clinical Psychology Review. 12:*205–226.

Sandler, I. N., Ayers, T. S., Wolchik, S. A., Tein, J.-Y., Kwok, O.-M., Haine, R. A., Twohey-Jacobs, J., Suter, J., Lin, K., Padgett-Jones, S., Weyer, J. L., Cole, E., Kriege, G., and Griffin, W. A. 2003. The Family Bereavement Program: Efficacy evaluation of a theory-based prevention program for parentally bereaved children and adolescents. *Journal of Consulting and Clinical Psychology. 71*(3): 587–600.

Sartin, R. M., Hansen, D. J., and Huss, M. T. 2006. Domestic violence treatment response and recidivism: A review and implications for the study of family violence. *Aggression and Violent Behavior. 11*(5):425–440.

Shadish, W. R., and Baldwin, S. A. 2005. Effects of behavioral marital therapy: A meta-analysis of randomized controlled trials. *Journal of Consulting and Clinical Psychology. 73*(1): 6–14.

Shelef, K., Diamond, G. M., Diamond, G. S., and Liddle, H. A. 2005. Adolescent and parent alliance and treatment outcome in Multidimensional Family Therapy. *Journal of Consulting and Clinical Psychology. 73*(4): 689–698.

Siqueland, L., Rynn, M., and Diamond, G. S. 2005. Cognitive behavioral and attachment based family therapy for anxious adolescents: Phase I and II studies. *Journal of Anxiety Disorders. 19*(4): 361–381.

Skowron, E., and Reinemann, D. 2005. Effectiveness of psychological interventions for child maltreatment: a meta-analysis. *Psychotherapy: Theory, Research, Practice, Training. 42*(1): 52–71.

Smerud, P. E., and Rosenfarb, I. S. 2008. The therapeutic alliance and family psychoeducation in the treatment of schizophrenia: An exploratory prospective change study.

Journal of Consulting and Clinical Psychology. 76(3): 505–510.

Sorensen, S., Pinquart, M., and Duberstein, P. 2002. How effective are interventions with caregivers? An updated meta-analysis. *Gerontologist. 42*(3): 356–372.

Stathakos, P., and Roehrle, B. 2003. The effectiveness of intervention programmes for children of divorce— A meta-analysis. *International Journal of Mental Health Promotion. 5*(1):31–37.

Stith, S., and Rosen, K. 2003. Effectiveness of couples treatment for spouse abuse. *Journal of Marital and Family Therapy. 29*(3): 407–426.

Stith, S., Rosen, K., McCollum, E., and Thomsen, C. 2004. Treating intimate partner violence within intact couple relationships: Outcomes of multi-couple versus individual couple therapy. *Journal of Marital and Family Therapy. 30*(3): 305–318.

Tremblay, G. C., and Israel, A. C. 1998. Children's adjustment to parental death. *Clinical Psychology: Science and Practice. 5*(4):424–438.

Trowell, R., Joffe, I., Campbell, J., Clemente, C., Almqvist, F., Soininen M., Koskenranta-Aalto, U., Weintraub, S., Kolaitis, G., Tomaras, G., et al. 2007. Childhood depression: A place for psychotherapy. An outcome study comparing individual psychodynamic psychotherapy and family therapy. *European and Adolescent Psychiatry. 16*(3):157–167.

U.S. Department of Health and Human Services, Administration on Children, Youth, and Families. 2007. *Child maltreatment.* Washington, DC: Author.

Van Zeijl, J., Mesman, J., Marinus, H., van Ijzendoorn, M., Bakermans-Kranenburg, F. J., Stolk, M. N., et al. 2006. Attachment-based intervention for enhancing sensitive discipline in mothers of 1- to 3-year-old children at risk for externalizing behavior problems: A randomized controlled trial. *Journal of Consulting and Clinical Psychology. 74*(6): 994–1005.

Waldron, H. B., Turner, C. W., Barton, C., Alexander, J. F., and Cline, V. B. 1997. Therapist defensiveness and marital therapy process and outcome. *American Journal of Family Therapy. 25*(3): 233–243.

Waldron, H.B., and Turner, C.W. 2008. Evidence-based psychosocial treatments for adolescent substance abuse. *Journal of Clinical Child and Adolescent Psychology. 37*(1): 238–261.

Whiteside, M. F., and Becker, B. J. 2000. Parental factors and the young child's postdivorce adjustment: A meta-analysis with implications for parenting arrangements. *Journal of Family Psychology. 14*(1): 5–26.

Williams, R., and Chang, S. 2000. A comprehensive and comparative review of adolescent substance abuse treatment outcome. *Clinical Psychology: Science and Practice. 7:* 138–166.

Wolchik, S. A., Sandler, I. N., Millsap, R. E., Plummer, B. A., Greene, S. M., Anderson, E. R., Dawson-McClure, S. R., Hipke, K., and Haine, R. A. 2002. Six-year follow-up of preventive interventions for children of divorce. A randomized controlled trial. *JAMA: Journal of the American Medical Association. 288*(15): 1874–1881.

Wolchik, S. A., West, S. G., Westover, S., and Sandler, I. N. 1993. The children of divorce parenting intervention: Outcome evaluation of an empirically based program. *American Journal of Community Psychology. 21*(3): 293–331.

Wood, N. D., Crane, D., Schaalje, G., and Law, D. D. 2005. What works for whom: A meta-analytic review of marital and couples therapy in reference to marital distress. *American Journal of Family Therapy. 33*(4): 273–287.

Woolfenden, S., Williams, K., and Peat, J. 2002. Family and parenting interventions for conduct disorder and delinquency a meta-analysis of randomized controlled trials. *Archives of Diseases in Childhood. 86*(4): 251–256.

Woolley, S. R., Butler, M. H., and Wampler, K. S. 2000. Unraveling change in therapy: Three different process research methodologies. *American Journal of Family Therapy. 28*(4): 311–327.

Zilberstein, K. 2006. Clarifying core characteristics of attachment disorders: A review of current research and theory. *American Journal of Orthopsychiatry. 76*(1): 55–64.

General Principles of Family Systems

Carter, B., and McGoldrick, M. 1999. *The expanded family life cycle: A framework for family therapy,* 3rd ed. Boston: Allyn & Bacon.

Guerin, P. J., Fogarty, T. F., Fay, L. F., and Kautto, J. G. 1996. *Working with relationship triangles: The one-two-three of psychotherapy.* New York: Guilford Press.

Kerr, M. E., and Bowen, M. 1988. *Family evaluation.* New York: Norton.

Minuchin, S. 1974. *Families and family therapy.* Cambridge, MA: Harvard University Press.

Nichols, M. P. 2009. *Inside family therapy,* 2nd ed. Boston: Allyn & Bacon.

Culture and Family Therapy

Boyd-Franklin, N. 1989. *Black families in therapy: A multisystems approach.* New York: Guilford Press.

Davis, L., and Proctor, E. 1989. *Race, gender, and class: Guidelines for practice with individuals, families and groups.* Englewood Cliffs, NJ: Prentice-Hall.

Fontes, L. A. 2008. *Interviewing clients across cultures.* New York: Guilford Press.

Sue, D. W., and Sue, D. 1990. *Counseling the culturally different: Theory and practice,* 2nd ed. New York: Wiley.

Marriage

Dicks, H. V. 1967. *Marital tensions.* New York: Basic Books.

Guerin, P. J., Fay, L., Burden, S., and Kautto, J. 1987. *The evaluation and treatment of marital conflict: A four-stage approach.* New York: Basic Books.

Lederer, W., and Jackson, D. 1968. *The mirages of marriage.* New York: Norton.

Scarf, M. 1987. *Intimate partners: Patterns in love and marriage.* New York: Random House.

Solot, D., and Miller, M. 2002. *Unmarried to each other.* New York: Marlowe & Company.

Families with Babies and Small Children

Brazelton, T. B. 1983. *Infants and mothers: Differences in development,* rev. ed. New York: Dell.

Combrinck-Graham, L., ed. 1988. *Children in family contexts: Perspectives on treatment.* New York: Guilford Press.

Faber, A., and Mazlish, E. 1974. *Liberated parents, liberated children.* New York: Grosset & Dunlap.

Ginott, H. 1969. *Between parent and child.* New York: Macmillan.

Nichols, M. P. 2004. *Stop arguing with your kids.* New York: Guilford Press.

Families with Older Children

Blos, P. 1979. *The adolescent passage: Developmental issues.* New York: International Universities Press.

Faber, A., and Mazlish, E. 1987. *Siblings without rivalry.* New York: Norton.

Micucci, J. 1998. *The adolescent in family therapy.* New York: Guilford Press.

Sells, S. 1998. *Treating the tough adolescent.* New York: Guilford Press.

Divorce, Remarriage, and Stepparenting

Ahrons, C., and Rodgers, R. 1987. *Divorced families: A multidisciplinary developmental view.* New York: Norton.

Isaacs, M. B., Montalvo, B., and Abelsohn, D. 1986. *The difficult divorce.* New York: Basic Books.

Vaughan, D. 1986. *Uncoupling: Turning points in intimate relationships.* New York: Oxford University Press.

Visher, E., and Visher, J. 1988. *Old loyalties, new ties: Therapeutic strategies with stepfamilies.* New York: Brunner/Mazel.

Family Therapy Technique

Anderson, C., and Stewart, S. 1983. *Mastering resistance: A practical guide to family therapy.* New York: Guilford Press.

Dattilio, F., ed. 1998. *Case studies in couple and family therapy: Systemic and cognitive perspectives.* New York: Guilford Press.

Donovan, J. M. 1999. *Short-term couple therapy.* New York: Guilford Press.

Fisch, R., Weakland, J., and Segal, L., 1982. *The tactics of change.* San Francisco: Jossey-Bass.

Gerson, M-J. 1996. *The embedded self: A psychoanalytic guide to family therapy.* New York: Analytic Press.

Guerin, P. J., Fay, L., Burden, S., and Kautto, J. 1987. *The evaluation and treatment of marital conflict: A four-stage approach.* New York: Basic Books.

Minuchin, S., and Fishman, H. C. 1981. *Family therapy techniques.* Cambridge, MA: Harvard University Press.

Minuchin, S., Nichols, M. P., and Lee, W-Y. 2006. *Assessing families and couples: From symptom to system.* Boston: Allyn & Bacon.

Taibbi, R. 2007. *Doing family therapy: Craft and creativity in clinical practice,* 2nd ed. New York: Guilford Press.

White, M., and Epston, D. 1990. *Narrative means to therapeutic ends.* New York: Norton.

Becoming a Family Therapist

There are many paths to becoming a family therapist. Not all involve going through an academic program in marital and family therapy, although that's the most direct path. Many people who have a state marital and family therapy (MFT) license or certificate graduated with a more traditional degree—a master's or Ph.D. in clinical psychology, an MSW from a social work program, or a master's in counseling or nursing. Depending on their state's requirements, these therapists, after completing their non-MFT degree, have to take some additional MFT coursework and receive extensive supervision in order to be able to call themselves marital and family therapists.

Which path you choose should depend on what you want to do in your career. For example, if you hope to teach or do research, you would do well to go through a Ph.D. program. If you primarily want to do clinical practice, you may not need a Ph.D. and could go to one of the many master's programs in MFT. (For a list of approved MFT academic programs, contact the American Association for Marriage and Family Therapy, described later.)

If you're interested in studying an aspect of mental health not thoroughly covered in MFT programs, for example, psychological testing, social policy, individual psychotherapy, or psychopharmacology, you could get a non-MFT degree and then pick up the required courses and supervision from one of the many nonacademic family therapy institutes described later in this appendix.

Professional Organizations

The *American Association for Marriage and Family Therapy* (AAMFT), located in Alexandria, Virginia, was organized in 1942 by Lester Dearborn and Ernest Graves to set standards for marriage counselors. In 1970 it was expanded to include family therapists and has become the major credentialing body for the field. Through its requirements for membership, standards have been set for becoming a family therapist that are used by the various states that regulate the profession. AAMFT also lobbies state and federal governments for the interests of family therapists, such as state licensing.

AAMFT's membership has more than doubled since 1982 and now includes more than 24,000 marriage and family therapists. This has made AAMFT a powerful player in mental health politics and has aided in public and governmental recognition of family therapy as a distinct field.

AAMFT has a code of ethics that covers the following issues: responsibility to clients; confidentiality; professional competence and integrity; responsibility to students, employees, supervisees, and research subjects; financial arrangements; and advertising. AAMFT is located at 112 South Alfred Street, Alexandria, VA 22314; telephone: 703-838-9808; Web site: www.aamft.org.

Although the AAMFT has a presence in California, the dominant organization for MFTs there is the California Association of Marriage and Family Therapists (CAMFT). With twenty-nine regional chapters and 29,000 members, CAMFT's size has given it a strong voice in the state legislature. CAMFT sponsors an annual conference and publishes *The Therapist.* For further information, contact CAMFT, 7901 Raytheon Road, San Diego, CA 92111; telephone: 858-292-2638; Web site: www.camft.org.

The *American Family Therapy Academy* (AFTA) was organized in 1977 to serve the field's senior researchers, clinicians, and trainers who wanted a more intimate context for sharing ideas and developing common interests. Despite high standards for membership regarding years of teaching and clinical experience, AFTA's membership has doubled since 1983, from 500 to over 1,000. AFTA is a high-level think tank focused around its annual conference and its newsletter. For more information, contact AFTA, 1608 20th Street, NW, 4th Floor, Washington,

DC 20009; telephone: 202-483-8001; Web site: www.afta.org.

The *International Family Therapy Association* (IFTA) was begun in 1987 as a way for family therapists around the globe to connect. Each year IFTA sponsors the World Family Therapy Congress in a different country. So far the countries that have hosted the congress include Finland, Greece, Holland, Ireland, Israel, Hungary, Mexico, Poland, Germany, the United States, Norway, Brazil, and Slovenia. In addition, IFTA biannually publishes *The International Connection.* The official journal of IFTA is the *Journal of Family Psychotherapy.* IFTA can be reached through William Hiebert, General Secretary, IFTA, Marriage and Family Counseling Services, 1800 3rd Avenue, Suite 512, Rock Island, IL 61201, 309-786-4491; Web site: www.ifta-family therapy.org.

Conferences

Besides the multitude of workshops or conferences privately sponsored and presented by local chapters of AAMFT, there are four main national meetings. The largest is AAMFT's annual conference each October. With over 200 presentations on various family therapy topics to select from, there is usually something for everyone.

The second largest (over 3,600) is the Psychotherapy Network Symposium held each March in Washington, D.C. Sponsored by the *Psychotherapy Networker* magazine (described later), all presenters are invited so that quality throughout the eighty workshops is ensured. Each year the symposium has a theme, and invited plenary speakers are often famous for work done outside the field of family therapy. For information, telephone: 202-537-8950.

AFTA's annual meeting deliberately has a flavor different from that of other conferences. Because of its small size (usually around 300—it's not open to nonmembers), it's the one place where leaders in the field can gather in a relatively informal setting to discuss ideas. Rather than conduct workshops, the meeting is organized around interest groups and brief presentations designed to promote dialogue and debate.

The other conference where many family therapists can be found isn't devoted exclusively to family therapy. The American Orthopsychiatric Association is a multidisciplinary organization whose annual conference usually contains a sizable percentage of presentations devoted to family therapy and issues of interest to systems-oriented clinicians.

Publications

The first book devoted entirely to the diagnosis and treatment of families was Nathan Ackerman's *Psychodynamics of Family Life,* published in 1958. The field's first journal, *Family Process,* was founded in 1961. Since then the family therapy literature has proliferated to the point where it is virtually impossible to keep up with it. We count over twenty journals or newsletters devoted to family therapy published in the United States, with many other countries publishing their own journals. The number of books is equally overwhelming. (See Appendix A, Recommended Readings, for a selective guide to some of the most useful books and articles in the field.) Some of the major periodicals include these:

Family Process continues to exert a powerful influence on the field. Many of the debates and developments described in earlier chapters of this book appeared first in its pages. Founded in 1961 by Don Jackson and Nathan Ackerman, its editors have included Jay Haley, Don Bloch, Carlos Sluzki, Peter Steinglass, and Carol Anderson. The *Journal of Marital and Family Therapy* is also quite influential and, as the official journal of AAMFT, has a large readership. Under the editorship of Alan Gurman during the 1980s and Douglas Sprenkle and Froma Walsh in the 1990s, it increased its focus on research and improved its standards. Current editor Ronald J. Chenail is balancing the research and clinical foci.

The *Psychotherapy Networker,* a magazine devoted to issues related to family therapy and psychotherapy in general, also has a strong influence. Its large readership (over 70,000) has been won through tackling provocative issues with high-quality writing. Rich Simon turned what began as a small newsletter into the most widely read publication on psychotherapy and, in so doing, introduced many of family therapy's ideas to therapists throughout the country.

There are a number of other well-established journals that, like *Family Process* and *Journal of Marital and Family Therapy,* are devoted to general issues in the field. These include the *American Journal of Family Therapy, Journal of Family Psychotherapy, International Journal of Family Therapy, Contemporary Family Therapy,* and *Family Therapy Collections.* In addition, a number of specialized journals have emerged. For example, the *Journal of Systemic Therapies* (formerly the *Journal of Strategic and Systemic Therapies*) is widely read by therapists who use those adjectives to describe themselves, while Bowen systems therapists read *Family Systems* and those interested in Michael White's work subscribe to the *Dulwich Centre Review* and *Family Therapy Case Studies.*

The cross-fertilization of family therapy with other fields is represented by *Families, Systems, and Health,* a journal devoted to the collaboration between medicine and family therapy; by the *Journal of Family Psychology,* published by a division of the American Psychological Association; and by *Feminism and Family Therapy,* which reflects the growing influence of feminist thought on the field.

News within the field and digests of important developments are conveyed through AAMFT's newsletter, *Family Therapy News,* and through the *Brown University Family Therapy Newsletter.* Those interested in the branch of sociology called family studies have much in common with family therapists and read *Family Relations* and the *Journal of Marriage and the Family.*

Licensing

Forty-eight states currently regulate MFTs; many states are also currently considering licensing bills. Most state requirements for licensure are comparable to the standards for Clinical Membership in AAMFT. Common requirements include graduation from an accredited marital and family therapy program, two years of postdegree supervised clinical experience, and passing the state exam or the national

exam for MFTs, which is conducted by the Association of Marital and Family Therapy Regulatory Board.

Training Centers

As discussed earlier, family therapy developed primarily outside academia. There are, however, a handful of doctoral programs and a larger number of master's degree programs specializing in marital and family therapy in universities around the country. The American Association for Marriage and Family Therapy accredits 105 graduate and postgraduate programs. Because we are aware of no comparable list of the major nonacademic training centers, we will describe some of the best-known centers in the United States here. Although other major centers exist throughout the world, our space is too limited to list them.

The *Family-Centered Services Project* in the Boston area was founded by William Madsen in 2000 as an attempt to move from simply training family therapists to developing family-centered agencies. This organizational change project offers a mix of clinical and organizational training and consultation as well as ongoing coaching and support. For more information, contact William Madsen, Director, or Philip Decter, Associate Director, The Family-Centered Services Project, 51 Kondazian Street, Watertown, MA 02472, (617) 868-9044.

The *Family Solutions Institute,* originally the *Kantor Institute,* was founded by David Kantor and then reestablished as Family Solutions by Rob Guise and Jackie Gagliardi and Michael Vickers in 1993. The institute is informed by David Kantor's structural/analytic model of therapy, as well as by psychodynamic and other family therapy influences. This institute offers a sequence of three 1-year training programs that build on each other but can be taken independently. They also offer a specialized program in couples treatment and in organizational consultation, as well as a variety of apprenticeships, internships, and courses. For more information, contact Rob Guise, 19 Peter Parley Road, Jamaica Plain, MA 02130.

The *Minuchin Center for the Family* is a nonprofit training and consultation institute in New York City, founded in 1981 by Salvador Minuchin. The faculty also includes Amy Bagel, Ema Genijovich, David Greenan, Richard Holm, Wai-Yung Lee, and George Simon. Special programs are designed for onsite training and consultation with agencies that work with poor families, foster care, substance abuse, the homeless, and children in psychiatric facilities. The extern training program is at three levels: beginning family therapists, more experienced therapists, and supervision for supervisors. The orientation emphasizes structural family therapy but has been influenced by feminism and multiculturalism. A summer intensive and one-day workshops offer clinicians with limited time opportunities to study at the center. Inquiries may be directed to Patricia Dowds, Executive Director, 303 Fifth Avenue, Suite 603, New York, NY 10016, or to the Web site: www.minuchincenter.org.

The *Ackerman Institute for the Family* in New York City was founded as the Family Institute by Nathan Ackerman in 1960. Following Ackerman's death in 1971, the center was renamed in his honor, and the directorship was assumed by Donald Bloch, who was followed by Peter Steinglass and now Lois Braverman. The institute's faculty includes noted family therapists Peggy Papp, Jorge Colapinto, Marcia Sheinberg, Peter Fraenkel, Constance Scarf, Marcia Stern, and Evan Imber-Black. The institute offers training in systemic family therapy. It offers a two-year clinical externship program for more experienced family therapists and weekend workshops throughout the year. For further information, contact Marcia Sheinberg, Director of Training and Clinical Services, 149 East 78th Street, New York, NY 10021.

The *Family Institute of Westchester* in Harrison, New York, is directed by Elliott Rosen. The institute teaches the multicontextual approach, which includes aspects of structural and strategic techniques, and is based on the Bowenian model. The institute has been in operation since 1977 and is primarily known for its training program, which usually takes three years to complete. There is also a two-year advanced program that meets weekly. Specialized training programs are offered in multicultural family therapy and therapy with gay and lesbian couples and families. Additional information is available from Pat Colucci-Coritt, Director of Training, Family Institute of Westchester, 600 Mamaroneck Ave., Suite 303, Harrison, NY 10528.

The *Center for Family Learning* in Rye Brook, New York, was founded in 1973 by Philip Guerin, who was trained by Murray Bowen. The center has maintained a threefold mission for thirty years: the development of family systems models of clinical intervention; postgraduate education in these models; and community education through the mechanism of public meetings and cable television. Postgraduate training is tailored to the specific educational needs of individuals, groups, or organizations. For additional information, contact Patricia Schmolling, Administrator, at 14 Rye Ridge Plaza, Suite 228, Rye Brook, NY 10573. Telephone: 914-253-9190. E-mail: PJGuerinM.D.@aol.com.

The *Family Therapy Training Program at the University of Rochester* was established in 1983 by Judith Landau-Stanton and M. Duncan Stanton. This program teaches the Rochester model, an integration of structural, strategic, transgenerational, experiential, and ecosystemic approaches in a series of externships and seminars. Special areas of interest are cultural transition and medical family therapy. Cases are provided for trainees. The faculty includes Lyman Wynne, Susan McDaniel, David Seaburn, and the founders. For more information, contact Pieter le Roux, Director, Family Therapy Training Program, Department of Psychiatry, University of Rochester, 300 Crittenden Boulevard, Rochester, NY 14642-8409.

The *Multicultural Family Institute* was founded in 1991 by its directors, Monica McGoldrick and Nydia Garcia Preto. The institute is committed to training, research, and service in support of cultural diversity and the empowerment of those voices our society silences. In addition to a two-year certificate program and an annual cultural conference, the institute offers a variety of workshops, lectures to the community, and consultation to schools and other organizations. Minority scholarships are available. Other notable therapists participating on the faculty include Eliana Gil, Paulette Moore Hines, Ken Hardy, Joanne Krestan, and CharlesEtta Sutton. For further information contact Monica McGoldrick, 328 Denison St., Highland Park, NJ 08904; Telephone: 732-565-9010; Web site: www.Multicultural Family.org.

The *International Institute of Object Relations Therapy* is led by codirectors David and Jill Scharff and is located in the suburbs of Washington, D.C. Formerly at the Washington School of Psychiatry, the Scharffs are the leading exponents of object relations family therapy. The institute has a variety of training programs, speakers, and workshops, including two-year courses in object relations theory and couple, child, and family therapy. Both programs consist of weekly seminars and two-week summer institutes. In addition to the Scharffs, the faculty includes many distinguished clinicians from throughout the world (notably from the Tavistock Center). In addition to its headquarters in Washington, D.C., the institute has satellite programs in Burlington, Vt.; Charlottesville, Va.; Long Island, N.Y.; Manhattan, N.Y.; New Orleans, La.; Omaha, Neb.; Philadelphia, Pa.; Salt Lake City, Utah; San Diego, Calif.; and Panama City, the Republic of Panama. For more information, Telephone: 301-215-7377; E-mail: iiort @mindspring.com; Web site: www.iiort.org; or write David Scharff, M.D., and Jill Savege Scharff, M.D., Codirectors, International Institute of Object Relations Therapy, 6612 Kennedy Drive, Chevy Chase, MD 20815-6504.

The *Bowen Center for the Study of the Family* (formerly *Georgetown Family Center*), founded by Murray Bowen and located in Washington, D.C., exists to refine, test, and extend Bowen systems theory. Michael Kerr, Daniel V. Papero, and Ruth Sagar comprise the current board of directors. Training programs include a biweekly postgraduate program and a special program for out-of-towners that meets for three consecutive days, four times a year. Other learning opportunities include the monthly clinical conference, the main symposium in the fall, and the annual spring conference, usually in April. Descriptions of these programs can be found on the center's Web site: www.thebowencenter.org.

The *Family Therapy Practice Center of Washington, D.C.,* was founded in 1980 by Marianne Walters after she left the Philadelphia Child Guidance Clinic. The center has a structural family therapy base and offers a postgraduate externship. In addition, the center develops programs for dealing with at-risk populations and changing family structures, such as its adolescent foster care project, family violence assistance project, and runaway youth/multiple family group project. For more information, contact Director of Training, 2153 Newport Place NW, Washington, DC 20037.

The *Philadelphia Child and Family Training Center, Inc.,* was created in the late 1990s to continue the training programs previously conducted at the famous Philadelphia Child Guidance Center. Most of the center's faculty taught at the former institution and worked there with Salvador Minuchin as he developed structural family therapy. The faculty include notable structural therapists: Marion Lindblad-Goldberg, Edward A. Igle, Ann Itzkowitz, C. Wayne Jones, and Steve Simms. The center runs a two-year, COAMFTE-accredited postgraduate program, a three-week summer practicum, AAMFT-approved correspondence courses, and an AAMFT-approved supervision mentoring course. Traveling faculty conduct training in agencies and institutions nationally and abroad. The center is known for its development of an updated clinical model, ecosystemic structural family therapy, and its use in mental health home-based services and training. For more information, contact Marion Lindblad-Goldberg, Director, Philadelphia Child and Family Therapy Training Center, Inc., P.O. Box 4092, Philadelphia, PA 19118-8092; Web site: www.philafamily.com.

The *Brief Family Therapy Center* (BFTC) of Milwaukee is known for its specialization in the research, training, and clinical practice of brief, solution-focused therapy. BFTC provides short- and long-term training in solution-focused therapy that attracts practitioners from across North America, Europe, and Asia. The leading figure is Insoo Kim Berg, who has presented workshops and seminars in more than thirty countries and written extensively on solution-focused therapy. For further information, contact Brief Family Therapy Center, P. O. Box 13736, Milwaukee, WI 53213.

The *Family Institute at Northwestern University* (formerly of Chicago) was founded in 1968 by Charles Kramer to provide training, research, and clinical services. William Pinsof is the president of the institute, which probably has the largest full-time faculty in the country, including notable family therapists Douglas Breunlin, Cheryl Rampage, and Jay Lebow. The Institute offers a variety of training programs grounded in a multilevel, integrative approach. Elements of the approach include integrative problem-centered therapy, the metaframeworks perspective, feminism, and multiculturalism. It offers a two-year certificate program that is accredited by AAMFT, a master's program in family therapy in affiliation with Northwestern University, a one-year clinical training practicum, a psychology internship, a postgraduate fellowship, and a variety of courses, consultation, continuing education workshops, and conferences. In 1994, the institute opened a spacious new facility in Evanston, Ill. For more information, contact the Family Institute, Bette D. Harris Center, 618 Library Place, Evanston, IL 60201; Telephone: 847-733-4300.

The *Chicago Center for Family Health (CCFH)* was begun in 1991 by codirectors John Rolland and Froma Walsh. Affiliated with the University of Chicago, the center's strengths-based family resilience orientation integrates systems theory with a multigenerational family life-cycle frame work. In addition to general training in family therapy, CCFH offers specialized training in couples therapy, school-based partnerships, divorce mediation, and family-oriented health care. Training programs include a two-year certificate program, workshops and courses, and consultation groups. Faculty also includes other notable family therapists such as Gene Combs, Jill Freedman, and Tom Todd. For more information, contact CCFH, Suite 1442, 20 North Wacker Drive, Chicago, IL 60606; Telephone: 312-372-4731.

The *Mental Research Institute* (MRI) in Palo Alto, Calif., was founded in 1959 by the late Don Jackson and is considered one of the birthplaces of family therapy. The MRI is best known for its brief therapy approach to families. It offers a wide variety of training programs, including workshops, continuing seminars, and programs in brief therapy and strategic therapy. For further information, contact MRI, 555 Middlefield Road, Palo Alto, CA 94301.

Name Index

Subject Index

Credits